Fodor's
Israel

SO-BXW-757

PRAISE FOR FODOR'S GUIDES

"Fodor's guides . . . are an admirable blend of the cultural and the practical."
—The Washington Post

"Researched by people chosen because they live or have lived in the country, well-written, and with good historical sections . . . Obligatory reading for millions of tourists."
—The Independent, *London*

"Usable, sophisticated restaurant coverage, with an emphasis on good value."
—Andy Birsh, Gourmet *restaurant columnist, quoted by Gannett News Service*

"Packed with dependable information."
—Atlanta Journal Constitution

"Fodor's always delivers high quality . . . thoughtfully presented . . . thorough."
—Houston Post

"Valuable because of their comprehensiveness."
—Minneapolis Star-Tribune

Fodor's Travel Publications, Inc.
New York • Toronto • London • Sydney • Auckland

Second Edition

ISBN 0–679–02727–0

Fodor's Israel

Editor: Caroline Haberfeld
Contributors: Steven Amsterdam, Hannah Borgeson, Echo Garrett, Judy Stacey Goldman, Amy Hunter, Laura M. Kidder, Bevin McLaughlin, Lisa Perlman, Mike Rogoff, Melanie Roth, Mary Ellen Schultz, Barbara Sofer, Nancy van Itallie, Karen Wolman
Creative Director: Fabrizio La Rocca
Cartographer: David Lindroth
Illustrator: Karl Tanner
Cover Photograph: Sarah Stone/Tony Stone Images

Design: Vignelli Associates

Special Sales

Contents

Maps

Contents

Foreword

We wish to express our gratitude to the following individuals and organizations who helped in the preparation of this guide: Delta Airlines; Arkia Israeli Airlines; Israel Ministry of Tourism; Tourism Department, Akko Municipality; Haifa Tourist Board; Negev Tourism Development Administration; the Israeli National Parks Authority; Idit Herzog, Society for the Protection of Nature in Israel (SPNI); Ya'acov Shkolnik, deputy editor of *Eretz* magazine; Roni Nir; Arie Kutz; and Jill Rogoff. Special thanks go to Amy Hunter.

While every care has been taken to ensure the accuracy of the information in this guide, the passage of time will always bring change, and, consequently, the publisher cannot accept responsibility for errors that may occur.

All prices and opening times quoted here are based on information supplied to us at press time. Hours and admission fees may change, however, and the prudent traveler will avoid inconvenience by calling ahead.

Fodor's wants to hear about your travel experiences, both pleasant and unpleasant. When a hotel or restaurant fails to live up to its billing, let us know, and we will investigate the complaint and revise our entries where the facts warrant it.

Send your letters to the editors of Fodor's Travel Publications, 201 East 50th Street, New York, NY 10022.

Highlights and Fodor's Choice

Highlights

Jerusalem At press time, the atmosphere in the politically volatile **Arab sector** of Jerusalem had become noticeably more relaxed. Nevertheless, it is still unwise to park your rented car on an East Jerusalem side street, and few tourists are seen in the area's hotels and restaurants. These necessary precautions, however, have made little difference in visitors' itineraries. In fact, Jerusalem continues to add to its attractions in almost every area. Of archaeological significance is the government's plan to clear the narrow 458-yard **water tunnel** under Armon Hanatziv (the Promenade). The tunnel was part of the extraordinary Lower Aqueduct, built some 2,000 years ago during the Roman period to bring water to Jerusalem from the south. The two ends of the now-dry tunnel can still be seen.

The end is at last in sight for the long-awaited and somewhat grandiose Mamilla project, outside the Old City's Jaffa Gate. The completed deluxe condominiums are soon to be joined by the Dan Pearl all-suite hotel, while construction continues apace on a shopping center, restaurants, entertainment facilities, and a much-needed underground parking lot.

With tourism to Israel on the upswing, the scarcity of hotel space in the capital is cited as one of the major obstacles to serious expansion of the industry. Current plans include an additional wing to the landmark Holiday Inn Crowne Plaza (formerly the Jerusalem Hilton), and, tentatively, some other new hotels in that district near the city's western entrance.

Around Jerusalem While Masada is easily climbed from the west by way of the Roman ramp, and with greater difficulty from the east up the Snake Path, most visitors ascend by cable car from the eastern (Dead Sea) side to within 85 steps of the summit. In high season this creates pressure on the system, and some significant waiting in line. There are plans to relieve the pressure by building a second cable-car system, still from the eastern base of the mountain, but terminating on the summit itself, somewhat south of the present entrance.

The vast complex of ancient man-made **caves and underground workshops** at Bet Guvrin has undergone general improvements, and the National Parks Authority is taking steps to open a labyrinth of several dozen chambers for the more intrepid spelunker. Also in progress is the excavation and partial restoration of an impressive 18th-century Roman-style **amphitheater.**

Tel Aviv Driving in the city is becoming more and more difficult, with the number of cars on the road ever increasing and not enough being done to widen streets and improve parking facilities. But if you can wait 20 years, you may be able to ride an **electric rail system** linking Tel Aviv with the surrounding suburbs. This quiet, nonpolluting system, still in the planning stages, would replace the buses now being used. Meanwhile, **intercity roads** are being improved: The Ayalon Highway (Route 1), for example, is currently being widened to ease congestion on Tel Aviv's access roads.

One of Tel Aviv's biggest problems for tourists is a shortage of reasonably priced accommodations. With any luck, this is going to change—slowly—over the coming years. In the next year or so, 5,000 additional hotel rooms are planned for the city, with that number likely to double by the year 2000. Many of these, city officials state, will be much more budget-price than the average today.

1995 will also see the introduction of four marked **walking tours**, all of which begin at the Government Tourist Office in Shalom Aleichem Street (between Hayarkon and Ben Yehuda streets). Two are inner city tours, one goes south to Jaffa, and the fourth heads north of the city beyond Hayarkon River. Maps are available at the Tourist Office.

Something is also being done to promote the city's **architectural history:** City Hall wants to make Tel Aviv "the world's largest open-air International Style museum." One thousand International-style buildings dating from the 1930s and '40s are slated for restoration. Although these buildings' characteristic straight lines and simple forms can still be seen, their whitewash is blackened, and plastic shutters and ugly air conditioners have become their dominant visual elements. Progress is slow because money for the massive project is hard to come by, but the city's change in attitude toward preservation and restoration is a step in the right direction.

Northern Coast and Western Galilee The big draw in this area, and indeed one of the country's most fascinating archaelogical sites, is **Caesarea.** Visitors have long enjoyed the remains of Herod the Great's port city, the looming Roman-Byzantine theater, and the medieval Crusader gatehouse and city walls, all with the sparkling blue Mediterranean as a backdrop. The latest discoveries include an ancient sports and games area with a stadium and a hippodrome, the home of a wealthy Byzantine merchant, and a lovely bathhouse from the same period.

The jewel in the crown of the city of **Haifa** is the landmark golden dome of the Baha'i Shrine. As part of the center's $200 million development program, the magnificent terraced gardens at the Shrine are being expanded down the hillside area.

Lower Galilee Excavations continue in more than a half dozen sites in the region, with some exciting results. It seems that **mosaic floors** were as common in the Byzantine period as linoleum is in our own, but those in **Zippori (Sepphoris),** west of Nazareth, are the finest ever found in Israel. The site was officially opened in 1992, and its dozen mosaic floors will in time be developed as a "Park of Mosaics." At press time only the fine Dionysian motifs of the Roman villa were on view (including the wonderous "Mona Lisa of the Galilee"), but the next few years should see the site reach its full potential.

The 16th-century **castle** built into the sheer cliffs of **Arbel** is soon to become accessible even to those without a diploma in cliff climbing. Plans call for a nature trail from the Arbel spring to the castle; the trail will offer sweeping views and a bit of history.

Upper Galilee The range of accommodations in this region is constantly expanding, with a recent emphasis on the Great Outdoors. Among the new entrants are **vegetarian inns** that offer health-and-beauty packages, and **sports-oriented vacations** centered around activities such as horseback riding and kayaking.

Eilat and the Negev Israelis are chafing at the bit to visit Jordan. Peace between the two neighbors means that **Petra,** which beckoned elusively for so many years, can finally be visited by simply stepping across the border at the official crossing near Eilat. Petra was the capital of the Nabatean kingdom, which some 2,000 years ago controlled a lucrative perfume and spice route. A link road between the Indo-Chinese markets and the Mediterranean world led from Transjordan through Israel's Negev desert and on to the coastal city of Gaza. One of the stops along the way was **Avdat,** which may be explored today (*see* Tour 1 *in* Chapter 8, Eilat and the Negev).

Tourists have always been able to enter Israel from Jordan, via the Allenby Bridge near Jericho, but travel in the opposite direction was prohibited. Now it is possible to make back-and-forth visits between the two countries. Eilat, on the Red Sea, is the jumping-off point in the south of the country, and tour companies are hard at work putting together one-day excursions.

Meanwhile, in the resort city of Eilat, the **new hotels** are taller, wider, and more extravagant. A new arrival on the scene is the plush Royal Beach, on the northern beach near the Jordanian border. Every one of the 370 rooms has a view of the Red Sea and the stunning sunsets. Hotel lobbies in Eilat have long been venues for nightly entertainment. The Royal Beach, however, has two separate lobbies: one for guests who prefer to relax in the quietude of the evening, while the other is set up for flamboyant stage shows. At the other end of town, close to the Egyptian border, the **Princess** reigns supreme, a gleaming white hotel with a spa that offers Dead Sea health and beauty treatments.

Fodor's Choice

No two people will agree on what makes a perfect vacation, but it can be fun and helpful to know what others think. We hope you'll have a chance to experience some of Fodor's Choices yourself while visiting Israel. For detailed information on individual entries, see the relevant sections of this guidebook.

Lodging

Jerusalem	American Colony (*$$$$*)
	Hyatt Regency (*$$$$*)
	Louise Waterman-Wise (*$*)
Tel Aviv	Sheraton Tel Aviv Hotel and Towers (*$$$$*)
N. Coast and Western Galilee	The Baron's Heights and Terraces, Zichron Ya'akov (*$$$*)
	Dan Panorama, Haifa (*$$$*)
	Akko Youth Hostel (*$*)
Lower Galilee	Galei Kinneret, Tiberias (*$$$$*)
	Ma'agan, Sea of Galilee (*$$*)
	Bet Berger, Tiberias (*$*)
Upper Galilee	Rimon Inn, Zfat (*$$$$*)
	Vered Hagalil, Korazim (*$$$*)
Eilat	Sport Hotel (*$$$$*)

Dining

Jerusalem	Cézanne (*$$$*)
	Mamma Mia (*$$*)
	Minaret (*$$*)
Tel Aviv	Le Relais Jaffa (*$$$$*)
	Shipudei Hatikva (*$*)
N. Coast and Western Galilee	The Pine Club Restaurant, Mt. Carmel (*$$$$*)
	Shuni Castle, Shuni (*$$$*)
	Abu Christo, Akko (*$$*)
Lower Galilee	Pagoda and the House, Tiberias (*$$–$$$*)
Upper Galilee	The Farmyard Restaurant, Hula Valley (*$$$$*)
Eilat	The Last Refuge (*$$$$*)

Biblical Highlights

Jerusalem	Calvary: Church of the Holy Sepulcher, Garden Tomb
	Jesus betrayed and arrested: Garden of Gethsemane
	Site of the First and Second Temples: Temple Mount
	Stations of the Cross: Via Dolorosa
Around Jerusalem	Birthplace of Jesus: Church of the Nativity, Bethlehem
	David killed Goliath: Elah Valley
	Enemy's walls fell before Joshua: Jericho
	Tomb of the Patriarchs: Cave of Machpelah, Hebron
Tel Aviv	Where Jonah set sail before being swallowed by the whale: Old Jaffa
N. Coast	Elijah and the priests of Ba'al: Carmelite Monastery, Muhraka
Lower Galilee	Base of Jesus's ministry: Capernaum, Sea of Galilee
	Mary visited by Gabriel: Church of the Annunciation, Nazareth
Upper Galilee	Joshua defeated the Canaanites: Tel Dan Nature Reserve
The Negev	Abraham's well: Tel Beer Sheba

Synagogues, Churches, Mosques, and Shrines

Jerusalem and Around Jerusalem	Church of All Nations, Mount of Olives
	Dome of the Rock, Old City
	Rachel's Tomb, near Bethlehem
	Western (Wailing) Wall, Old City
Tel Aviv	St. Peter's Monastery, Old Jaffa
N. Coast	Baha'i Shrine, Haifa
	El-Jazzar Mosque, Akko
Lower Galilee	Church of the Multiplication of the Loaves and Fishes, Tabgha
	Church of St. Gabriel, Nazareth
	Mount of Beatitudes, Sea of Galilee
	Tomb of Moses Maimonides, Tiberias
Upper Galilee	Abouhav Synagogue, Zfat
	Tomb of Rabbi Shimon Bar Yochai, Mt. Meron

Archaeological Gems

Jerusalem and Environs	Second Temple Period mansions at Herodian Quarter, Jewish Quarter, Old City
	Herod's palace/fortress of Masada, Judean Desert

N. Coast   Crusader City, Akko

Herodian port and Crusader city, Caesarea

Lower Galilee   4th-century AD synagogue at Hammat Tiberias, Sea of Galilee

Roman, later Byzantine, city of Scythopolis at Bet She'an, Jordan Valley

Upper Galilee   Crusader and Ottoman ruins, Nimrod's Fortress

9th-century BC plaza and gate, Tel Dan Nature Reserve

The Golan   Second millennium BC burial monuments at Gamla

The Negev   Nabatean ruins at Avdat

Nature Reserves and National Parks

Around Jerusalem   Nahal David and Nahal Arugot, Ein Gedi

Sorek Cave, Judean Hills

N. Coast   Carmel National Park, Mt. Carmel

Nahal Me'arot Nature Reserve

Upper Galilee   Hula Nature Reserve

Mt. Meron Nature Reserve

Eilat   Coral Beach Reserve

Timna Valley Park

The Negev   En Avdat National Park

Mitzpe Ramon Visitors Center

Great Views

Jerusalem   Morning panorama of Old City from the top of the Mount of Olives

Around Jerusalem   Gazing from the top of the minaret at Nebi Samwil, north of Jerusalem, at the biblical landscape of the West Bank

Looking out at the Dead Sea from Masada at sunrise or in the late afternoon

Tel Aviv   The Tel Aviv skyline from the top of Mifratz Shlomo Street in Old Jaffa

N. Coast   The sea grottoes of Rosh Hanikra viewed from the top of the cliff

Lower Galilee   Looking east at the Jordan Valley from the Crusader fortress of Belvoir

View of the Lower Galilee and Jezreel Valley from the summit of Mt. Tabor

View of the Sea of Galilee in the afternoon from the Mount of the Beatitudes

Upper Galilee	Gazing down toward the Hermon River (Banias) Nature Reserve from Nimrod's Fortress
	Looking at Lebanon from the Good Fence at Metulla
	Watching birds of prey from a lookout point at Gamla
Eilat	Sunset over the Red Sea
The Negev	The vastness of Makhtesh Ramon seen from the Mitzpe Ramon Visitors Center
	The Wilderness of Zin viewed from David Ben Gurion's grave site, Sde Boker

Quintessentially Israeli

Jerusalem	Bar mitzvah ceremonies and celebrations at the Western (Wailing) Wall on Monday and Thursday mornings
	Vendors competing for customers before Shabbat at the Machaneh Yehuda market
Tel Aviv	Hanging out at a café on the Nahalat Binyamin mall or Sheinkin Street on Friday afternoon
	Shopping for fruit and vegetables amid the throngs in the Carmel Market
N. Coast and Western Galilee	Bargaining at the Arab *souk* (outdoor market), Akko
	Saturday lunch overlooking the Mediterranean at the Crusader City, Caesarea
Lower Galilee	Floating and lakeside discos on a summer night at the Sea of Galilee
Upper Galilee	Wildflower-gazing in the nature reserves
Eilat	Gathering at the Dolphin Reef tent pub in Coral Beach for *Kabbalat Shabbat* (welcoming Shabbat) late Friday afternoon

Works of Art

Jerusalem	Billy Rose Sculpture Garden, Israel Museum
	Chagall stained-glass windows, Hadassah Hospital
	Judaica collection, Israel Museum
	Reliefs from Hisham's Palace, Rockefeller Museum of Archaeology
Tel Aviv	Miniature replicas of synagogues at Beth Hatefutsoth (Diaspora Museum)
N. Coast	Ancient-art collection at the Haifa Museum, Haifa
Lower Galilee	Ancient synagogue mosaics at Hammat Tiberias
	"Banners" in the Church of the Annunciation, Nazareth
Upper Galilee	Olivewood ark at the Ha'Ari Synagogue, Zfat (Safed)
The Negev	Outdoor sculpture park, Mitzpe Ramon

Israel

LEBANON

Kiryat Shmona

DISENGAGEMENT ZONE

GOLAN HEIGHTS

SYRIA

Ma'alot Tarshiha

Nahariya

Akko

85

Meron

Zfat

Katzrin

Haifa

Tirat Carmel

Tiberias

77

Sea of Galilee

Gamla

Ein Hod

Nazareth

Pardes Hanna-Kakur

Umm el Fahm

65

Afula

Degania

Caesarea

Bet She'an

Hadera

Baqa el Gharbiya

Jenin

Netanya

57

Kfar Sava

Tulkarm

Hod Ha'Sharon

Herzlia Pituach

Qalqilya

Shekhem

4

Ramat Gan

Rosh Ha'Ayin

Tel Aviv-Jaffa

Petah Tikva

WEST BANK

Rishon LeZiyyon

Lod

Amman

Rehovot

Ramla

Ramallah

Ashdod

Jerusalem

Jericho

Ashkelon

Kiryat Gat

Bethlehem

90

Gaza

4

40

Hebron

Dead Sea

GAZA STRIP

60

Beit Qama

Ein Gedi

Qfaqim

25

Masada

Beersheba

Arad

JORDAN

222

Ein Bokek

Mashabel

Dimona

Telalim

Mamshit

25

Sde Boker

Ein Hazeva

N E G E V

Ein Yahav

Mitzpe Ramon

A R A V A

90

40

Paran

EGYPT

N

Ketura

Eilat

Aqaba

Gulf of Eilat

Mediterranean Sea

Jordan River

0   30 miles

0   45 km

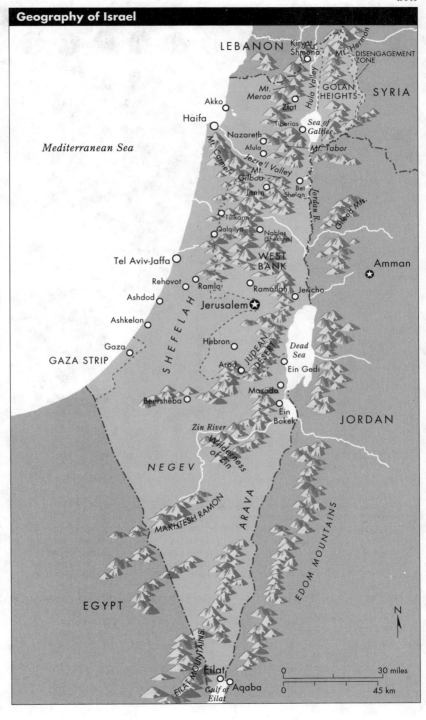

Geography of Israel

LEBANON

Kiryat Shmona

Mt. Hermon

DISENGAGEMENT ZONE

GOLAN HEIGHTS

SYRIA

Mt. Meron

Hula Valley

Akko

Zfat

Haifa

Tiberias

Sea of Galilee

Mediterranean Sea

Nazareth

Mt. Tabor

Mt. Carmel

Afula

Jezre'l Valley

Mt. Gilboa

Bet She'an

Jenin

Jordan R.

Gilead Mts.

Tulkarm

Qalqilya

Nablus (Shekhem)

Tel Aviv-Jaffa

WEST BANK

Amman

Rehovot

Ramla

Ramallah

Jericho

Ashdod

Jerusalem

SHEFELAH

Ashkelon

Gaza

GAZA STRIP

Hebron

JUDEAN DESERT

Dead Sea

Ein Gedi

Arad

Masada

Beersheba

Ein Bokek

JORDAN

Zin River

Wilderness of Zin

NEGEV

MAKHTESH RAMON

ARAVA

EDOM MOUNTAINS

EGYPT

N

EILAT MOUNTAINS

0   30 miles

0   45 km

Eilat

Aqaba

Gulf of Eilat

World Time Zones

MONDAY
SUNDAY

International Date Line

+12 +13

-9

-4

-3

25 0

+11

+12

1

-10

-11

-10

2

3

7

4

-7

5 -8 8

6

9

10

11

12

13

14 15

16

17

18

-6

-5 -4

-3:30

-4

19

22

20

-5

-4

-3

23

21

24

-3

+11   +12 -   -11   -10   -9   -8   -7   -6   -5   -4   -3   -2

Numbers below vertical bands relate each zone to Greenwich Mean Time (0 hrs.).
Local times frequently differ from these general indications,
as indicated by light-face numbers on map.

Algiers, **29**	Berlin, **34**	Delhi, **48**	Istanbul, **40**
Anchorage, **3**	Bogotá, **19**	Denver, **8**	Jerusalem, **42**
Athens, **41**	Budapest, **37**	Djakarta, **53**	Johannesburg, **44**
Auckland, **1**	Buenos Aires, **24**	Dublin, **26**	Lima, **20**
Baghdad, **46**	Caracas, **22**	Edmonton, **7**	Lisbon, **28**
Bangkok, **50**	Chicago, **9**	Hong Kong, **56**	London (Greenwich), **27**
Beijing, **54**	Copenhagen, **33**	Honolulu, **2**	Los Angeles, **6**
	Dallas, **10**		Madrid, **38**
			Manila, **57**

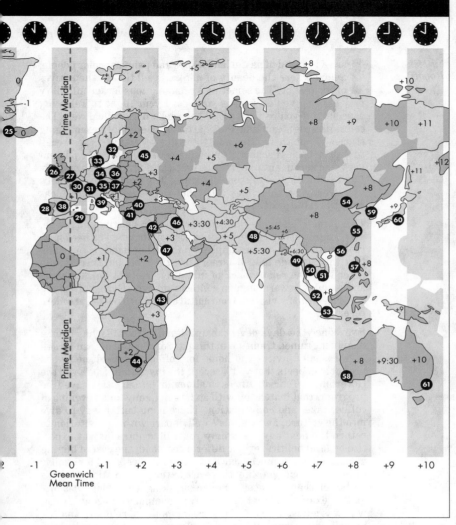

Mecca, **47**
Mexico City, **12**
Miami, **18**
Montréal, **15**
Moscow, **45**
Nairobi, **43**
New Orleans, **11**
New York City, **16**

Ottawa, **14**
Paris, **30**
Perth, **58**
Reykjavík, **25**
Rio de Janeiro, **23**
Rome, **39**
Saigon (Ho Chi Minh City), **51**

San Francisco, **5**
Santiago, **21**
Seoul, **59**
Shanghai, **55**
Singapore, **52**
Stockholm, **32**
Sydney, **61**
Tokyo, **60**

Toronto, **13**
Vancouver, **4**
Vienna, **35**
Warsaw, **36**
Washington, D.C., **17**
Yangon, **49**
Zürich, **31**

Introduction

by Mike Rogoff

Israel is a land of pastel landscapes and primary-color people; a land where the beauty of nature is subtle but the natives often are not. The sometimes rambunctious Israeli affability may envelop you as soon as you board your flight to Tel Aviv, especially if you're flying El Al, Israel's national carrier. The cries of recognition and the chatter of passengers exchanging stories about their trips and their duty-free purchases recall first days back at school after summer vacations. Some passengers, the sentimental tourists, greet El Al touchdowns on Holy Land soil with spontaneous applause. The red-blooded Israelis are already on their feet collecting their bags, despite pleas from the cabin staff.

This Israeli feistiness can come across as assertive, intrusive, even aggressive; the fighter-pilot style of driving you see on Israeli roads is the best example. On the other hand, many claim that this attitude helped Israel tame the land and successfully defend it. The related lack of inhibition leads to quickly made and genuinely warm human contacts that come as a refreshing surprise to many visitors from cultures in which people are more reserved.

Ever since the days of Abraham's tent, hospitality has been a deeply ingrained tradition in this part of the world; if an Israeli even casually invites you home for coffee or a meal, he or she probably expects that you'll accept the invitation. Do. Even the Government Tourist Offices in all major Israeli cities have free programs that match you with an Israeli family for an evening of coffee, cake, and conversation. There is no better way to dive into the culture, and you may well depart with an invitation to return the next day. Certainly you will acquire instant expertise on local politics, ethnic differences, food, the cost of buying a house, and how much your host earns. Be prepared for similar questions about *your* life; there are fewer conversational taboos in Israel than in most English-speaking countries. An oft-quoted example is that of the Israeli company rep sent abroad who was advised, to avoid discussing politics, religion, and sex in social situations. "What *else* is there to talk about?" asked the Israeli.

The key to understanding Israel is the fact that it was created as the modern reincarnation of an ancient Jewish state. Israel was the "Promised Land" of Abraham and Moses, the Israelite kingdom of David and Solomon, and home to Jesus of Nazareth and the Jewish Talmudic sages. Although the Jewish presence in the country has been unbroken for over 3,000 years, massive exiles—first by the Babylonians in 586 BC, and then by the Romans in AD 70—created a diaspora, a dispersion of the Jewish people throughout the world.

The Jewish attachment to the ancient homeland weaves through the entire fabric of Jewish history and religious tradition. For 2,000 years, wherever they lived, Jews daily turned their faces toward Jerusalem in prayer. The Jewish liturgy is saturated with prayers for the restoration of "Zion and Jerusalem." Over the centuries, many Jews trickled back to "Eretz Yisrael" (the Land of Israel); others looked forward to fulfilling their dream of return in some future messianic age. An 18th-century story tells of a certain Rabbi Yitzhak of Berdichev in Poland who sent out invitations to his daughter's wedding: "It will take place next Tuesday in the Holy City of Jerusalem. If, God forbid, the Messiah has not arrived by then, it will take place in the village square."

Not all were prepared to wait for divine assistance. During the late 19th century, Zionism was founded as a political movement to give a framework and an impetus to the idea of bringing the Jewish people back to Israel. Some early Zionist leaders believed, like founding father Theodore Herzl, that the urgent priority was a Jewish haven safe from persecution, wherever that might be. Argentina was suggested. Great Britain offered Uganda. In the light of their historical and emotional links to the land of Israel, however, most Jews rejected such suggestions as bizarre. Perplexed British statesman James Earl Balfour asked Zionist leader Chaim Weizmann to explain the Jewish refusal. "Mr. Balfour," Dr. Weizmann responded, "if I were to offer you Paris instead of London, would you accept it?" "Of course not," Balfour replied, "London is our capital." "Precisely," said Weizmann, "and Jerusalem was our capital when London was still a marsh!"

Not everyone greeted the establishment of the State of Israel with rejoicing. To the Arab world, it was anathema, an alien implant in a Muslim Middle East. To many ultra-Orthodox Jews, it was an arrogant pre-empting of God's divine plan; to make matters worse, the new state was blatantly secular, despite its concessions to religious interests. This internal battle over the character of the Jewish state, together with the implacable hostility of Israel's neighbors, which has resulted in a half-century of almost constant conflict, have been the main issues engaging the country since its birth.

Israel is no more than 460 kilometers (under 300 miles) long from Metulla on the northern Lebanese border to the southern resort city of Eilat on the Red Sea, and as little as 50 kilometers (30 miles) across the Galilee from west to east—merely the size of Wales, or just larger than Massachusetts. Yet despite its small size, it offers an astonishing diversity of climate and terrain. Drive east from Tel Aviv via Jerusalem to the Dead Sea, and in 1½ hours you pass by classic Mediterranean white beaches and orange groves and through olive-draped hills; you go up rugged pine-wooded mountains and then plunge almost 4,000 feet down the other side, through wild barren desert, to the subtropical oasis of Jericho (oldest city in the world) and the Dead Sea at the lowest point on the planet.

There are many large towns in Israel, but only three major cities. Jerusalem, the capital and spiritual center, lies 60 kilometers (38 miles) inland, at an elevation of 2,500 feet, and is a limestone blend of the ancient and the modern. Tel Aviv, on the Mediterranean coast, is unlovely but lively—the country's commercial and entertainment center, the city that never sleeps. Two out of every five Israelis live within its metropolitan area. Haifa, 100 kilometers (63 miles) north of Tel Aviv, sprawls up the slopes of Mt. Carmel, offering much greenery, sweeping views, and one of the country's two main ports and industrial areas. But wherever you are, the countryside is not far away.

Visitors so often think of Israel as mostly arid (read: boring). Half the country *is* desert, in fact, but don't think in terms of endless sand dunes. Awesome canyons slice through the Judean Desert to the Dead Sea, a few with sweet waterfalls and brilliant shocks of greenery. The Negev highlands, south of Beersheba, are punctuated by three huge erosion craters, the only such formations in the world. The sun-and-fun city of Eilat sits on the coral-reefed Red Sea against a backdrop of jagged granite peaks and desert moonscapes. And in the spring, after the meager winter rains, the deserts burst into often unexpected bloom, the hard landscapes softened by a fuzz of grass and multicolored wildflowers. For the even slightly adventurous visitor, a desert excursion—by foot, Jeep, or camel—is not quickly forgotten.

The northern and western part of the country is a complete antidote to the desert. True, it's also hot in the summer, and somewhat parched in the rainless season from May through October, but it's a land of good winter rains, some springs and streams, miles of Mediterranean beaches, extensive irrigated fields and orchards, mountainsides of evergreen forests, lush nature reserves, and the freshwater "Sea" of Galilee.

The American writer Mark Twain was astonished by the smallness of the Holy Land when he visited it in 1867. He had envisioned, he wrote, "a country as large as the United States . . . I suppose it was because I could not conceive of a small country having so large a history."

Mark Twain's astonishment is instructive: In Israel the past is more ever present than almost anywhere else on earth. There is something about the place that seeps into one's soul. For the Jewish visitor, it is a feeling of coming home, of getting back to one's roots. For the Christian pilgrim, it is the awe of retracing footsteps into a scriptural landscape, where the Bible takes on new meaning and will never be read the same way again.

Indeed, the country's biblical past has made names like Jerusalem, the Galilee, or the Jordan River household words for almost half the human race. Many a pilgrim has reached Israel expecting a Jerusalem preserved as an uncommercialized shrine, a Galilee of donkey traffic and tiny fishing boats, a River Jordan "deep and wide." The reality hits as you find the ancient names on the store billboards and the signposts of fast modern highways. And you discover that Jerusalem is a modern national capital of 600,000; Galilee is the name of the professional basketball team that finally toppled Maccabi Tel Aviv in 1994; and Jericho, Joshua's first target 33 centuries ago, is now a Palestinian autonomous zone.

The past is far from forgotten. Archaeology is almost a national sport (though less for today's video-game generation than for its ancestors), and an unusual find in any of the many ongoing excavations is sure to make the prime-time news. There are prehistoric settlement sites dating from over 1 million years ago! Jericho is almost 10,000 years old; Tel Dan has a gate through which Abraham might have passed (c. 18th century BC); King Solomon's walls lie exposed at Megiddo and Hazor; and a clay seal bearing the name of a royal scribe mentioned in Jeremiah was baked into permanence in the Babylonian fire that consumed Jerusalem in 586 BC. You can stand on the Temple Mount steps that Jesus almost certainly climbed, or marvel at a contemporary wooden boat by the Sea of Galilee. There is a lot of *old* stuff in the country, but here, it has to be more than, say, 1,500 years old to be called *ancient*.

About 83% of Israel's almost 5.5 million citizens are Jewish, some proudly tracing their family roots many generations in local soil, others first, second, or third generation *olim* (immigrants) from more than 100 countries.

The first modern pioneers arrived from Russia beginning in 1882, purchased land, and set about developing it with romantic zeal. A decade or two later, inspired by the socialist ideas then current in Eastern Europe, a much larger wave founded the first *kibbutzim*, collective villages or communes. In time, these fiercely idealistic farmers became something of a moral elite, having little financial power, but providing a greatly disproportionate percentage of the country's political leadership, military officer cadre, and intelligentsia. "We are workers," they liked to say, "but not working class!" The kibbutz movement today numbers some 280 settlements, 2.5% of the country's population. While their contribution to the economy is considerable, both in traditional agriculture and in more recently developed industry and tourism projects, they are no longer the dominant force they once were. And a more ambitious and materialistic younger generation has increasingly eschewed the communal lifestyle in favor of the attractions of the big city.

While most who immigrated before Israel's independence in 1948 were so-called Ashkenazi Jews whose background was Central or Eastern European, the big waves of immigration in the first decade of statehood were the Sephardim, who came from the Arab lands of North Africa and the Middle East. Israel's Jewish population—600,000 at Independence—doubled within 3½ years, and tripled within 10! The cities could not absorb the influx. The transit camps that were set up then (the memory of the difficult conditions in those *ma'abarot* still rankles some) eventually became the nuclei of often-remote development towns across the land. It has been wryly noted that the development towns are the part of the country that has developed least. With a few exceptions, these towns have not attracted significant industry or well-educated settlers, and they have the country's highest unemployment rates, with all the attendant economic and social problems.

For a long time, the visible differences between the haves and have-nots seemed to break down along the lines of the more established and better-educated Ashkenazim and the poorer unskilled Sephardim. Resentment may still simmer in some disadvantaged neighborhoods, and some stereotypes still survive, but, in general, both the distinction and the prejudices have subsided.

Israel was founded just three years after the end of World War II, in which the Nazis annihilated fully a third of the world's Jewish population. The new state's first order of business was to provide a haven for the scattered remnants of the shattered European communities, and the 1949 Law of Return recognized the right of any Jew to Israeli citizenship. Immigration and immigrant absorbtion became national priorities, warranting a full government ministry and the high-scale involvement of several nongovernmental agencies. Absorbtion centers were eventually established to give new immigrants an orientation period and teach them Hebrew in the renowned immersion method known as the *ulpan*.

While generally very successful, the system's resources and creativity have been sorely taxed in recent years. Between 1989 and 1992, Israel absorbed over half a million new immigrants from the former Soviet Union, increasing the national population by a full 10%! The initial urgent housing problem has been solved, but unemployment and underemployment linger, and only a minority of the often well-trained immigrants work in their own fields. After all, sigh the powers-that-be, how many doctors, engineers, computer programmers, and classical musicians can a small country accommodate? The 14,400 Ethiopian Jews airlifted to Israel in just one day in May 1991 posed a radically different problem: how to help them bridge a centuries-wide cultural and technological gap to cope with a modern society.

Currently, the vast majority of Israel's 1 million non-Jewish minority are Muslim Arabs, with about 60,000 Christian Arabs, 80,000 Druze, and a similar number of Bedouin (nominally Muslim Arabs, but a community apart). All are citizens, equal under the law, who vote for and may be voted into the Knesset, the Israeli parliament. (Excluded from this voting population are the almost 2 million *Palestinian* Arabs of the West Bank and autonomous Gaza Strip, currently under Israeli rule.)

The Muslims are mainstream Sunnis, regarded as both politically and religiously moderate by the standards of the region. The younger men of recent years are less so, both politically (in their identification with the Palestinian liberation movement) and religiously (in their sympathy with the Islamic fundamentalism sweeping the Middle East).

Of the Christian Arabs, most belong to the Greek Catholic, Greek Orthodox, or Roman Catholic churches; a handful of tiny eastern denominations and a few Protestant sects account for the rest. The western Christian community is miniscule, and with few exceptions consists of clergy and such temporary sojourners as diplomats.

The Druze, though Arabic-speaking, are a separate and secret religion that broke away from Islam about 1,000 years ago. Larger kindred communities exist in long-hostile Syria and Lebanon, but Israeli Druze have solidly identified with Israel, and the communities' young men are routinely drafted into the Israeli army. The Arab community is not liable for military service, in order to avoid the possibility of a battlefield confrontation with kinsmen from neighboring countries. They are entitled to volunteer, but, with the exception of the seminomadic Bedouin, few do.

There is no firm separation of religion and state in Israel; and matters of "personal status"—marriage, divorce, adoption, burial, inheritance—are the preserve of the religious authorities of the community concerned. For this reason there is no recognized civil marriage: If one partner does not convert to the faith of the other, the couple must marry abroad.

Within the Jewish community, such functions fall under the supervision of the rabbinate of Orthodox Judaism, much to the chagrin of members of the tiny but growing Conservative and Reform movements (mostly American expats) and of the hordes of nonobservant Jews.

The confrontation between the hard-line ultra-Orthodox and secular Israelis has escalated over the years, as the religious community tries to impose on an "apostate" citizenry its vision of how a "Jewish" state should behave. Hot issues include a *religious* definition of "Who is a Jew?" for the purpose of Israeli citizenship and public observance of the Sabbath and of dietary laws. For many nonreligious Israelis already irked by what they regard as religious coercion, the fact that most ultra-Orthodox men have successfully avoided military service on the grounds of continuing religious studies just rubs salt in the wound.

Israel prides itself on being the only democracy in the Middle East, and it sometimes seems bent on politically tearing itself apart in the process. This is how the system works (or doesn't): Once every four years, before national elections, every party publishes a list of its candidates for the 120-member Knesset. There are no constituencies or voting districts; each party that breaks the minimum threshhold of 1.5% of the *national* vote gets in, winning as many seats as its *proportion* of the votes cast nationwide entitles it to (hence "Proportional Representation").

Israel was saddled with this brand of democracy through a twist of historical circumstance. Born in the midst of a war for its own survival (1948), the fledgling state could ill afford a divisive election campaign, which, with so many citizens under arms, was technically impossible anyway. The first (provisional) Knesset was thus made up of delegates from the four main political blocs at the time—socialists, conservatives, liberals, and the religious—in proportion to their relative strength in the Jewish pre-State leadership bodies. The system became permanent. Any attempts to change it have been doomed to failure because the small parties that stand to lose if the system is changed are precisely those on whose support the *current* government depends. Catch 22.

The good news is that the system is intensely democratic. A relatively small grouping of like-minded voters *country-wide* (currently about 25,000–30,000) can elect an M.K. to represent its views. The largest party able to gain a parliamentary majority—that is, at least 61 seats—through a coalition with other parties becomes the government, and its chair the prime minister.

The bad news is that the system creates a proliferation of relatively small parties, whose support the government needs in order to rule. During the General Elections of 1981, 31 parties competed, and 19 of them made it into the Knesset. Since no party has ever won enough seats to rule alone, Israeli governments have always been based on compromise, with small parties exerting a degree of political influence quite out of proportion to their actual size. To reduce that influence, the prime minister will be elected directly in the 1996 elections, on a separate ballot from that of the Knesset. Time will tell whether this innovation will improve the system—or complicate it.

Time is different in Israel. The "western" Gregorian calendar—the solar year from January to December—is the basis of day-to-day life and commerce, of course, but there's more to it than that. The school year, for example, which runs from September through June, follows the *Hebrew* lunar calendar (supposedly counted from Creation). Thus 1995–1996 is the equivalent of the Hebrew 5756, reckoned from Rosh Hashanah, the Jewish New Year, which usually falls in September. Since the lunar year is 11 days shorter than the solar year, Jewish holidays are out of phase with the Gregorian calendar, and fall on quite different dates (though within the same season) from one year to the next. These Jewish religious festivals are observed as national public holidays, and businesses and some museums are closed.

The Muslim calendar is also lunar, but without the compensatory leap-year mechanism of the Hebrew one. Muslim holidays thus drift through the seasons and can fall at any time of the year.

Even the Christian calendar is not monolithic: Christmas in Bethlehem is celebrated by the Roman Catholic ("Latin") community on December 25, by the Greek Orthodox on January 6, and by the Armenians on January 19.

The "Day of Rest" in Israel is Saturday, the Sabbath of the Jewish majority, beginning at sundown Friday and ending at nightfall Saturday. Most Jewish-owned businesses close until Saturday night or Sunday morning. Devout Jews do not cook, travel, answer the telephone, or use money or writing materials during this time, a fact which explains the Sabbath ban on photography at Jewish holy sites like the Western Wall. Except for hotel restaurants, where some menu restrictions apply, kosher restaurants close on the Sabbath. In Jerusalem, where the religious influence is strong, this cuts down the choices considerably; in more open Tel Aviv, Haifa, and Eilat, the Sabbath is hardly felt.

In Arab areas, like East Jerusalem and Nazareth, the Muslims take time off for the week's most important devotions on Friday, while most Christian shopkeepers take Sunday off. Saturday is market day, and the towns buzz with activity.

All this means that in Israel, according to the old quip, Monday blues begin on Sunday, the regular first day of the work week. The country is moving rapidly toward a five-day week, however, with the weekend including *Friday*, already a half-day, and holy to the country's Muslim minority. The public sector and most corporations already work Sunday through Thursday only, and the schools may soon follow suit.

Despite its heritage and location—think of it as *Eastern Mediterranean* rather than *Middle Eastern*—Israel is as European as it is Levantine. Scientifically, the country is at the forefront of agriculture, electronics, lasers, medicine, and biotechnology. Seven universities, some of them world-renowned, set exceptional standards. Communications have improved dramatically in recent years, relagating to history the old jokes about the Israeli telephone system. Large-scale road-building has improved the already well-marked interurban highways, though urban congestion remains an urgent problem.

Violent crime is extremely low in Israel. Politically motivated violence is infrequent, typically having occurred in confrontation areas, like the West Bank, which are not recommended tourist destinations anyway. You *will* see automatic weapons on the street, obviously in the hands of uniformed security personnel, but also sometimes over the shoulder of a young off-duty soldier in "civvies." The Israeli Defense Force is a people's army: Almost everybody serves, and a national serviceman or woman, once issued a weapon, is *wedded* to it for the duration. The criminal misuse of army-issue firearms is very, very rare.

Although Israel's health system is groaning under the weight of financial deficits, and hospital conditions sometimes reflect this, the high medical standards do not seem to have been compromised. Most Israelis are covered by one or another of four public health funds (or is it *sick* funds?), but many doctors moonlight doing private work. Doctors on call for your hotel will speak English and likely be on par with physicians back home.

Culturally, classical music is the country's long suit, with several good orchestras—led by the famous Israel Philharmonic—and many smaller ensembles. Many recent Russian immigrants have made their mark here, and young homegrown virtuosi seem to be keeping up the tradition of Israeli superstars like Itzhak Perlman, Pinchas Zuckerman, Daniel Barenboim, and Shlomo Mintz, all of whom periodically reappear on Israeli stages. Opera's revival in Tel Aviv—new location, new company—recalls the days 25 years ago when a young tenor named Placido Domingo got his start there!

Jazz and blues are popular, and excellent summer festivals have developed, though they're somewhat dependent on foreign artists like Dizzy Gillespie and Keith Jarrett. The local pop scene tends to be of the softer type, but visiting stars like Sting and Dire Straits help heat it up. Middle Eastern sounds remain popular, but fusion variations that incorporate western musical elements have won adherents. Even folk music is alive and well, both the Israeli and the Anglo variety.

There is not a lot of English-language theater, but quite a few Hebrew productions provide simultaneous translation. Dance—particularly modern—can be very good. Watch out especially for Inbal, a modern troupe thats works are inspired by regional folklore traditions; and Kol Udemama ("sound and silence"), made up of both deaf and hearing dancers.

Israelis are very keen on sport—from the comfort of their TV chairs. Participant sports are not greatly promoted in schools, and even the keenly followed weekend soccer games draw very small crowds. Soccer has always been king, but basketball has had its successes, with the help of American players who couldn't make the NBA.

For the visitor, there are pools and gyms, tennis and squash courts, sailboats and Windsurfers, scuba equipment and Para-Sails, horses and canoes; water skis (on the Sea of Galilee) and snow skis (on Mt. Hermon). You can hike or go rock climbing, or just hang out in the sun, eat well, and check out the nightlife in what you're sure to find is one of the most intriguing travel destinations around.

1 Essential Information

Before You Go

Government Information Offices

By Barbara Sofer

Updated by Lisa Perlman

For information about traveling in Israel, contact the nearest branch of the **Israel Government Tourist Office** (IGTO). **In the United States:** 350 5th Ave., New York, NY 10118, tel. 212/560–0600, fax 212/629–4368; 5 S. Wabash Ave., Chicago, IL 60603, tel. 312/782–4306, fax 312/782–1243; 6380 Wilshire Blvd., Suite 1700, Los Angeles, CA 90048, tel. 213/658–7462, fax 213/658–6543; 25 S.E. 2nd Ave., Suite 745, Miami, FL 33131, tel. 305/539–1919 or 305/539–8222, fax 305/539–1311; 12700 Park Central Dr., Dallas, TX 75251, tel. 214/991–9097, fax 214/392–3521; c/o Consulate-General of Israel, 1100 Spring St. NW, Suite 440, Atlanta, GA 30309, tel. 404/875–9924, fax 404/875–9926.

The U.S. Department of State's **Overseas Citizens Emergency Center** (Room 4811, Washington, DC 20520; enclose S.A.S.E.) issues Consular Information Sheets, which cover crime, security, political climate, and health risks as well as embassy locations, entry requirements, currency regulations, and other routine matters. For the latest information, stop in at any U.S. passport office, consulate, or embassy; call the interactive hot line (tel. 202/647–5225; fax 202/647–3000); or, with your PC's modem, tap into the Bureau of Consular Affairs' computer bulletin board (tel. 202/647–9225).

In Canada: 180 Bloor St. W, Suite 700, Toronto, Ontario, M5S 2V6, tel. 416/964–3784, fax 416/961–3962.

In the United Kingdom: 18 Great Marlborough St., London W1V 2DX, tel. 0171/434–3651.

Tours and Packages

Before selecting a tour, be sure to find out exactly what expenses are included (particularly tips, taxes, service charges, side trips, additional meals, and entertainment), and expect only what is specified. In addition, check the ratings of all hotels on the itinerary and their facilities, cancellation policies for you and the tour operator, and, if you are traveling alone, the cost of a single supplement. Most tour operators request that bookings be made through a travel agent—there is no additional charge for doing so.

Fully Escorted Tours

U.S.-Based Operators

American Jewish Congress (15 E. 84th St., New York, NY 10028, tel. 212/879–4588 or 800/231–4694) offers combination tours to Israel and other countries, 12- and 15-day introduction tours to the major Israeli cities, family tours, and other special-interest tours (*see below*). **El Al** (120 W. 45th St., New York, NY 10036, tel. 212/768–9200 or 800/352–5786) offers four escorted tours to Israel ranging from 9 to 22 days. **Gate 1 Ltd.** (101 Limekiln Pike, Glenside, PA 19038, tel. 215/572–7676 or 800/682–3333) offers an almost limitless variety of escorted tours to Israel from 7 to 29 days. **Globus** (5301 S. Federal Cir., Littleton, CO 80123, tel. 303/797–2800 or 800/221–0090) and its more budget-minded sister company, **Cosmos Tourama,** spend 10 days touring Israel and 18 days touring Israel and Egypt. **Hadassah Tours** (50 W. 58th St., New York, NY 10019, tel. 212/355–7900 or 212/303–8031) has 11- and 15-day tours leaving every week to Israel. **International Tours** (Box 108, Naperville, IL 60566, tel. 708/369–4507 or 800/582–8380) takes nine days to tour Israel. A 16-day tour includes both Israel and Egypt. **Isram Tours** (630 3rd Ave., New

York, NY 10017, tel. 212/661–1193 or 800/223–7460) is a veritable supermarket of tours to Israel. **Maupintour** (1515 St. Andrews Dr., Lawrence, KS 66047, tel. 919/843–1211 or 800/255–6162) spends "Christmas in Israel" on a 10-day deluxe excursion, including five nights in Jerusalem, Christmas eve services in Bethlehem, and a Sea of Galilee cruise. **Tourlite** (1 E. 42nd St., New York, NY 10017, tel. 212/599–3355 or 800/272–7600) has a 10-day tour. **Travcoa** (Box 2630, Newport Beach, CA 92658-2630, tel. 714/476–2800 or 800/992–2004) offers a 12-day tour of Israel and a 28-day tour combining Israel and Egypt. **Unitours** (411 W. Putnam Ave., Greenwich, CT 06830, tel. 203/629–3900 or 800/777–7432) offers tours of Israel of 11 and 15 days. Also try **Classical Tours** (4401A Commonwealth NW, Suite 334, Washington, DC 20008, fax 202/363–0009), **Galilee Tours** (310 1st Ave., Needham, MA 02194, tel. 617/449–8996 or 800/874–4445), **Heavenly Tours** (6944 N. Port Washington Rd., Milwaukee, WI 53217, tel. 414/352–8622 or 800/322–8622), **Israel Connection, Inc.** (1276 E. Chicago Ave., Naperville, IL 60540, tel. 708/961–1684 or 800/848–9272), **Mosaic Tours & Travel** (420 Lincoln Rd., Suite 448, Miami Beach, FL 33139, tel. 305/672–0011 or 800/524–7726), **Smithsonian International Tours** (1100 Jefferson Dr. SW, Room 3045, Washington, DC 20560, tel. 202/357–4700), **Trafalgar Tours** (11 E. 26th St., Suite 1300, New York, NY 10010, tel. 212/689–8977 or 800/626–6603), **Travel Magic** (505 5th Ave., Suite 1200, New York, NY 10017, tel. 212/697–3600 or 800/883–6244), and **Tursem Tours** (420 Madison Ave., Suite 1003, New York, NY 10017, tel. 212/935–9210 or 800/223–9169).

U.K.–Based
Operators

Several Christian pilgrimage tours under the heading "Travels Round the Bible" are offered by **Orientours** (0171/613–4441), including a nine-day escorted trip from the Sermon on the Mount to the Way of the Cross. The **Israel Travel Service** (0161/839–1111) offers synagogue tours, kibbutzim fly-drives, unusual specialist vacations, like railway enthusiasts' tours, and can tailor a holiday of any length. **Superstar Holidays** (185 Regent St., London W1R 8EU, tel. 0171/437–9277), El Al's subsidiary, has a wide range of holidays and tours.

Special-
Interest Tours
Adventure
Tours

American Jewish Congress (15 E. 84th St., New York, NY 10028, tel. 212/879–4588) arranges an 18-day "Israel Adventure." **Far Horizons Incorporated** (2015 Spring Rd., Suite 235, Oakbrook, IL 60521, tel. 708/573–0062) runs deluxe outdoor tours. **Fox Travel** (271 Route 46W, No. D107, Fairfield, NJ 07006, tel. 201/575–4050), associated with Neot Hakikar, offers one- to six-day jeep and camel safaris in the Sinai. **Isratrek** (600 Central Ave., No. 295, Highland Park, IL 60035, tel. 708/831–6671 or 800/878–5344) specializes in customized adventure tours throughout the country. **Tracks** (10 Kaplan St., Tel Aviv 64734, Israel, tel. 03/695–2226) organizes weekend Jeep tours, hikes, rafting, and ranch stays.

Archaeological
Tours

The Israel Antiquities Authority (Coordinator of Volunteers, Box 586, Jerusalem 91911, Israel, tel. 02/292607, fax 02/292628) fields volunteers for long-term digs. **Heritage Excavations** (19 Hahaganah St., New Industrial Zone, Rishon LeZion 75706, Israel, tel. 03/9619171, fax 03/9618940) offers a "Dig for a Day" program. **Archaeological Seminars** (Box 14002, Jaffa Gate, Jerusalem 91400, Israel, tel. 02/273515) has six-day packages including active archaeology and kibbutz stays. **Archeological Tours** (271 Madison Ave., Suite 904, New York, NY 10016, tel. 212/986–3054) spends 15 days exploring the country's many layers of ancient and modern history. **Earthwatch** (680 Mount Auburn St., Watertown, MA 02272, tel. 617/926–8000) recruits volunteers to serve as short-term assistants to scientists on research expeditions. **Institute of Judaic-Christian Research, Inc.** (Box 120366, Arlington, VA 76012, tel. 817/792–3304), headed by Vendyl Jones (the inspiration for the Indiana Jones film character), runs yearly spring excavations in the Judean wilderness.

Biblical Tours Tour operators that offer tours of particular interest to Christians or Jews: **Ayelet Tours** (21 Aviation Rd., Albany, NY 12205, tel. 518/437–0695 or 800/237–1517) offers nine-day Christian tours, 10- to 15-day Jewish heritage tours, and special bar and bat mitzvah tours. **El Al Israel Airlines Ltd.** (120 W. 45th St., New York, NY 10036, tel. 212/852–0628) offers the nine-day "Holyland Experience Tour." **Insight International Tours** (745 Atlantic Ave., Boston, MA 02111, tel. 617/482–2000 or 800/582–8380), **INT** (13907 Ventura Blvd. 102, Sherman Oaks, CA 91423, tel. 818/789–3033 or 800/488–3679) has a nine-day Christian tour and special bar and bat mitzvah tours. **Israel Tour Connection** (134 Old Indian Rd., W. Orange, NJ 07052, tel. 201/736–8515 or 800/247–7235) includes special cantor-led bar and bat mitzvah tours. **IST/Cultural Hosts** (225 W. 34th St., Dept. TAI, New York, NY 10122, tel. 212/563–1327 or 800/833–2111) provides in-depth contact with political, cultural, and educational figures shaping the country today. **Journeys Unlimited** (150 W. 28th St., New York, NY 10001, tel. 212/366–6678 or 800/486–8359) sponsors Christian tours and a special Easter tour. **Shalom K Tours** (Centrepoint Mall, 6464 Yonge St., Suite S6, Willowdale, Ontario, Canada M2M 3X4, tel. 416/224–2080 or 800/465–1019; in the United States, 190 W. Palmetto Park Rd., Boca Raton, FL, 33432, tel. 407/750–4556 or 800/343–6505), offers Christian and Jewish escorted tours and individual travel packages. **Synagogue Travel, Inc.** (600 Hempstead Tpke., Suite 120, West Hempstead, NY 11552, tel. 516/489–6586 or 800/448–0399) offers 14-day tours to Jewish sites in Jerusalem, Tel Aviv, and Tiberias. **Tourlite International, Inc.** (551 5th Ave., New York, NY 10176, tel. 212/599–3355 or 800/272–7600) offers a nine-day tour for Christian and Jewish travelers.

Cruises Many cruise lines combine Israel with other stops around the eastern Mediterranean. Contact your travel agent for more information.

College Tours **Jerusalem Fellowships** (28 Park Ave., Monsey, NY 10954, tel. 914/425–8255, 212/643–8802, or 800/335–5097; in Canada, c/o Aish Hatorah, 296A Wilson Ave., Downsview, Ontario M3H 1S8, Canada, tel. 416/636–7530; in the United Kingdom, c/o Aish Hatorah, 8 Hendon House, Brent St., Hendon, London NW4 2QL, tel. 0181/203–1457) runs a six-week study tour with emphasis on politics, philosophy, history, and religion for less than the price of a regular plane ticket. **World Academic Holidays** (3901 Westerly Pl., No. 101, Newport Beach, CA 92660, tel. 714/757–4373) is another source for studious approaches to the country.

Diving Tropical Adventures Travel (111 2nd Ave. N, Seattle, WA 98109, tel. 206/247–3483 or 800/247–3483) offers a selection of dive packages to the Red Sea. **International Diving Expeditions** (11360 Matinicus Ct., Cypress, CA 90630, tel. 714/897–3770 or 800/544–3483) has packages to the Red Sea and other maritime delights in the south.

Ecology **Earthwatch** (680 Mount Auburn St., Watertown, MA 02272, tel. 617/926–8000) needs people to help scientists continue its 15-year study of flood behavior in the southern Negev desert.

Language-Learning Tours **Ulpan Akiva** (Box 6086, Netanya 42160, Israel, tel. 09/523123) offers Hebrew and Arabic study courses in combination with tours around the country.

Nature Tours The **Society for the Protection of Nature in Israel** (SPNI, 330 7th Ave., 21st Floor, New York, NY 10001, tel. 212/398-6750 or 800/524-7726) organizes tours that often take in archaeological sites. **Vered Travel & Tours** (Hairusim St., New Center, Nez Ziona 70400, Israel, tel. 08/400777, fax 08/404142) has 13-day agricultural study tours with seminars and visits to farming sites.

Photography Photo Adventure Tours (2035 Park St., Atlantic Beach, NY 11509, tel. 516/371-0067 or 800/821-1221) has 12- to 16-day prepackaged and customized visits that are a bit slower paced than general-interest tours.

Teen Tours Many Jewish organizations run specialized summer programs for teenagers, some of which contain serious study components. Most tours include some time working on a kibbutz. For a listing contact the **World Zionist Organization** (515 Park Ave., New York, NY 10022, tel. 212/752-0600).

Independent Packages

American Express Vacations (300 Pinnacle Way, Norcross, GA 30093, tel. 800/421-5785 in GA, or 800/241-1700) offers two independent tours of Israel with English-speaking guides, sightseeing tours, free time, and visits to Old Jerusalem, Haifa, Jericho, Tiberias, and more. Also available are "Go-Any-Day" packages to Haifa, Jerusalem, and/or Tel Aviv, with two-night minimum stays.

Arkia Israeli Airlines provides a number of tour packages, including desert tours, driving safaris, windsurfing and diving courses, and various fly/tour plans and fly/drive plans throughout the whole of Israel (in Israel: Sde Dov Airport, Tel Aviv, tel. 03/524-0220, 03/553-3255, or 03/699-2222; in New York: **Isram Wholesale Tours and Travel, Ltd.**, 630 3rd Ave, New York, NY 10117, tel. 212/661-1193; in California: **Uniworld Travel International, Inc.**, 9025 Wilshire Blvd., Beverly Hills, CA 90211, tel. 213/858-0600). Arkia's flight/hotel packages are offered in Eilat, Rosh Pina, and the Dead Sea.

Delta (Delta Dream Vacations Center, Box 1525, Ft. Lauderdale, FL 33301, tel. 800/872-7786) has a nine-day "The Holy Land" vacation, combining sightseeing tours led by your own guide and days in which to explore on your own. The **Delta Dream Vacations Affordable Hotels** program combines discounted rates at several top hotels in Tel Aviv with a Delta round-trip ticket. **El Al** (120 W. 45th St., New York, NY 10036, tel. 212/768-9200 or 800/352-5786) offers a supermarket of packages for independent travelers. **TWA Getaway Vacations** (10 East Tow Rd., Marlton, NJ 08053, tel. 800/438-2929) offers 11-, 12-, and 14-day options including "freestyle" independent packages and combination guided land and sea tours to Israel.

Cavalcade Tours (450 Harmon Meadow Blvd., Secaucus, NJ 07096, tel. 201/617-8922 or 800/356-2405) offers independent tours of Israel for eight or 14 days and a fly/drive package for seven nights. **Trafalgar Tours** (11 E. 26th St., Suite 1300, New York, NY 10010-1402, tel. 212/689-8977 or 800/854-0103) offers the "Best of Israel" in 11 days. **Abercrombie & Kent** (1520 Kensington Rd., Oak Brook, IL 60521, tel. 708/954-2944 or 800/323-7308) has an eight-day package combining Israel with Egypt. In the United Kingdom, **Classic Orientours** (Kent House, 87 Regent St., London W1R 8LS, tel. 0171/434-1551) covers all of Israel and can tailor an itinerary to special requirements. **WST Charters** (Priory House, 6 Wrights La., London W8 6TA, tel. 0171/938-4362) specializes in low-cost travel to and within Israel.

When to Go

There's no bad time to visit Israel. There are no rainy days at all from May through September, but some visitors prefer risking rain and coming in the cooler, less expensive season of November through March. In the winter months, snow falls occasionally in the northern and central hills. In the months of April, May, September, and October, the weather is generally sunny but not uncomfortably hot.

During school holidays, particularly in mid- to late August, Israelis themselves take vacations. Accommodations and attractions are crowded and surcharges are often added to hotel rates. Hotel prices jump during the Passover and Sukkoth holiday periods (early April and late September–early October, respectively), and services and commerce are sharply curtailed; many Israelis simply go away for Passover. Reservations should be booked at least four months in advance and plane reservations six months to a year in advance for this busy week. Many hotels require full board for the week of Passover.

Climate Temperatures along the Mediterranean coast are similar to those of Tel Aviv. Hill cities and towns have climates more like that of Jerusalem. Temperatures in the Negev desert and at the Dead Sea can get very high, but because of the mountainous terrain, they drop sharply at night. The following are average daily maximum and minimum temperatures for Tel Aviv, Jerusalem, and Eilat.

Eilat	**Jan.**	70F	21C	**May**	95F	35C	**Sept.**	97F	36C
		49	9		70	21		76	24
	Feb.	74F	23C	**June**	100F	38C	**Oct.**	92F	33C
		52	11		76	24		68	20
	Mar.	79F	26C	**July**	102F	39C	**Nov.**	81F	27C
		58	14		77	25		61	16
	Apr.	86F	30C	**Aug.**	102F	39C	**Dec.**	72F	22C
		65	18		77	25		52	11

Jerusalem	**Jan.**	52F	11C	**May**	77F	25C	**Sept.**	81F	27C
		45	7		59	15		65	18
	Feb.	58F	14C	**June**	81F	27C	**Oct.**	77F	25C
		45	7		65	18		61	16
	Mar.	61F	16C	**July**	83F	28C	**Nov.**	67F	19C
		49	9		67	19		54	12
	Apr.	68F	20C	**Aug.**	83F	28C	**Dec.**	56F	13C
		54	12		67	19		47	8

Tel Aviv	**Jan.**	63F	17C	**May**	70F	21C	**Sept.**	85F	29C
		49	9		61	16		70	21
	Feb.	65F	18C	**June**	81F	27C	**Oct.**	81F	27C
		50	10		68	20		65	18
	Mar.	68F	20C	**July**	85F	29C	**Nov.**	74F	23C
		52	11		72	22		58	14
	Apr.	74F	23C	**Aug.**	85F	29C	**Dec.**	67F	19C
		58	14		72	22		52	11

Information For current weather conditions and forecasts for cities in the United
Sources States and abroad, plus the local time and helpful travel tips, call the **Weather Channel Connection** (tel. 900/932–8437; 95¢ per minute) from a Touch-Tone phone.

National and Religious Holidays

Israelis take holidays seriously. Nearly every holiday is celebrated with traditional foods and festivities. Diaspora Jews follow a slightly different calendar from Israelis, often adding an additional day to holidays. Hotels cater to these needs by providing holiday meals and religious services, but public transport and shops have sharply curtailed hours. Below is a calendar of holidays as they are observed in Israel. **Remember that Jewish holidays begin at sundown and end one hour after sundown the following day.** The dates listed below for Jewish holidays in 1995 are the day *after* the sundown beginnings of the holidays.

Sabbath
Shabbat Shabbat—the Sabbath—takes on many forms in Israel, sometimes bamboozling a visitor. Friday is rapidly becoming a day off, and by the afternoon you can feel things winding down all over the country (except in Muslim areas, as they celebrate Sabbath on Friday). If you happen to visit both Tel Aviv and Jerusalem on a Saturday, you'll wonder if you're not in two different countries. Although quiet in some parts, coastal Tel Aviv is thronging with crowds (most of them from elsewhere in the country) the entire length of the city. Restaurants are all open (unless they are kosher, which is the minority in Tel Aviv, in contrast to Jerusalem) and although businesses are closed, there is a new trend for shops to reopen on Saturday evening, especially in the shopping centers. Jerusalem has a much more religious flavor to it, and since orthodox Jews do not drive, use the phone, or conduct even small transactions on Shabbat, many can be seen walking to synagogue, to visit friends, or just strolling on their day of rest. In a few parts of Jerusalem and Bnei Brak, certain streets are closed to cars.

Public transportation in the cities is minimal (taxis and sometimes minibuses), except in mostly Arab areas. There is no public intercity transportation, although the *sherut* taxis drive between the main cities. Shabbat is also the busiest day for the nature reserves and national parks—indeed, anywhere the city folk can get away for a day. Keep this in mind for long drives: the highways can be choked with weekend traffic on Saturday afternoon.

Tu B'Shvat **February 6:** Israelis eat fruit and plant trees on the New Year of Trees, when the white-blossom almond tree traditionally blooms.

Purim and **March 7** (most of Israel), **March 8** (Jerusalem and Zfat [Safed]): For
Shushan days before Purim, children dress up in costumes. In synagogues
Purim and on public television, pious Jews read the Scroll of Esther, the story of the valiant Jewish woman who prevented the massacre of her people in ancient Persia. Street festivals are held in many towns, and the Ode Lo Yadah parade is held in Tel Aviv.

Passover **April 6–13:** Passover is preceded by a month of vigorous household
Pesach cleaning to remove all traces of leavened bread. During the seven-day holiday, no bread is for sale in Jewish stores, and matzo replaces bread in most hotels. On the first evening of the holiday, Jews retell the story of the Exodus out of Egypt and eat a symbolic, festive meal called the *seder* (which means "order" in Hebrew). Hotels have communal seders, and the IGTO can sometimes arrange for tourists to join Israelis in their homes.

Holocaust **April 27:** Special services take place at the Yad Vashem Holocaust
Memorial Day Memorial in Jerusalem. Places of entertainment are closed, and at
Yom Hashoah 11 AM all stand silent as a siren is sounded in memory of the 6 million Jews who were killed.

Memorial Day **May 3:** This is a day of mourning for Israel's war dead. Com-
Yom Hazikaron memorative ceremonies are held around the country, places of entertainment are closed, and at 11 AM a siren is sounded in memory of
the fallen.

Independence **May 4:** This holiday (Yom Lag B'Omer) begins with hikes and picnics
Day and ends with street parties and fireworks.

Ha'atzmaut **May 18:** The 33rd day of counting between Passover and Shavuot
marks the end of a string of historic tragedies, and the com-
memoration of the death of Rabbi Shimon Bar Yochai. Observers
build bonfires and make trips to the rabbi's grave in Meron, near
Zfat.

Feast of **June 4:** This holiday, seven weeks after Passover, marks the harvest
Weeks of the first fruits. Observant Jews stay up all night studying the
Shavuot Torah.

The Ninth **August 6:** Both the First and Second Temple were destroyed on this
of Av day in antiquity; the Jews were expelled from Spain; and World War
Tisha B'Av I began. Naturally, Jews consider the Ninth of Av to be ill fated. Observant Jews fast, read Ecclesiastes, and refrain from entertainment; they also refrain from swimming and eating meat for the nine
days leading up to Tisha B'Av.

Jewish **September 25–26:** This two-day holiday traditionally begins a 10-day
New Year period of introspection and repentance. Observant Jews attend
Rosh rather long synagogue services and eat festive meals, which empha-
Hashanah size such sweet foods as apples and honey. Non-observant Jews of-
ten use this holiday break for picnics and for going to the beach.

The Day of **October 4:** This is the most solemn day of the Jewish year. Observant
Atonement Jews fast, wear white clothing, and avoid leather footwear. There
Yom Kippur are no radio and television broadcasts. In much of the country, espe-
cially Jerusalem, only emergency vehicles are in use.

Feast of **October 9–15:** Observant Jews build open-roof huts on porches and in
Tabernacles backyards, and spend a festive week of entertaining, making family
Sukkot trips, and hiking.

Right before the holiday, colorful street markets open in which special decorations and four kinds of trees—citron, palm, willow, and
myrtle—are sold. The first day of the holiday is observed like a Sabbath, except that food can be cooked. The intervening days are half-
holidays, and shopkeepers often take vacations. Nightly musical
programs are planned as part of the holiday's Water Drawing Festival, and an annual hike to Jerusalem takes place. Christians celebrate the tabernacle festival at this time as well.

Simhat Torah **October 16:** This holiday marks the receiving of the Torah on Mt.
Sinai. On the evening and morning of the holiday, observant Jews
gather in synagogues, dance, and pray. Additional dancing takes
place in public squares right after the holiday.

Hanukkah **December 18–25:** A Jewish rebellion in the 2nd century BC regained
Jewish rights in the Temple in Jerusalem. A single container of ritu-
ally acceptable oil lasted for eight days, hence the eight-day holiday.
Children have school vacations, and families often gather in the early evening to light the Hanukkah lights. Israelis eat potato pancakes
(*latkes* or *levivot*) and a local version of the jelly doughnut called
sufganiah. Shops, businesses, and services all remain open.

Christian Holidays

For up-to-date holiday information, contact the IGTO (tel. 02/ 754863) and the Christian Information Service (tel. 02/287647) in Jerusalem before the holiday.

Easter **April 16:** Most Christian groups celebrate Easter, which marks the resurrection of Jesus. **April 18:** Greek, Russian, and Armenian Orthodox have Easter services; celebrations are centered in Jerusalem churches.

Christmas Most Christians celebrate Christmas Eve **December 24;** the Greek Orthodox do so on **January 7,** and the Armenian Orthodox on **January 18.** Buses from the major cities bring tourists to services in Bethlehem. Information is available from the IGTO.

Muslim Holidays

Muslims observe Friday as their Sabbath.

The dates of Muslim holidays vary widely each year. Like the Jews, the Muslims follow a lunar calendar, but dates of holidays move around since it has no leap year.

Ramadan Observant Muslims fast all day and eat in the evening for a month following **February 2;** special festivities mark the end of the holiday.

Festivals and Seasonal Events

More festivals appear each year on the national calendar. The dates of some of these may change; check with the IGTO for details. Most festivals include events open to the public. Tickets for musical events can be purchased in advance at ticket agencies.

January The **Liturgical Festival of Choral Music** is organized by the Jerusalem Symphony Orchestra IBA. The **International marathon** takes place in Tiberias on January 11.

March The 12–17 sees the **International Book Fair** in Jerusalem, while the **Spring migration bird-watchers' festival** in Eilat happens on the 19–25.

April Look for **Rock at the Red Sea** in Eilat. During Passover, numerous activities and events will take place. Watch newspapers for details, or ask at your hotel.

May–June The **Israel Festival** international performing arts festival takes place May 18–June 10 in Jerusalem. Get tickets to major events well in advance. Haifa hosts a **Blues Festival.**

July The **International Folklore Festival** has dance groups from Israel and abroad. The **Israeli Folkdance Festival** in Karmiel has ethnic groups from around the world, plus community dancing. A **film festival** is held in Jerusalem. **Jacob's Ladder** folk festival takes place at Hurshat Tal (Upper Galilee), and there is a **hot-air balloon festival** in the Ayalon Valley (4–7).

August The **Klezmer Festival** in Safed showcases Jewish soul music. In Jerusalem, you can check out the **International Festival of Puppet Theater** and the **Khutzot Hayotzer Arts and Crafts Fair,** where handmade items are displayed, and there's nightly entertainment. The **Red Sea Jazz Festival** is held in Eilat. The **Wine Festival** in Binyamina has wine tasting and performances by singers and dance groups. The **Sea of Galilee Crossing** is a 4-kilometer (2.5-mile) swim from Kibbutz Haon to Tzemach.

October The **Israel Fringe Theater Festival** in Akko has original Israeli theater productions, street theater, children's shows, and musicals. Also look for the **Jewish Music Festival** in Merom Hagalil and the **European Sailing Championships** at Sdot Yam. The **Hiluliya Wine Festival** in Rishon LeZion has special exhibitions and nightly performances by Israeli singers and dance troupes. **Christian Celebration of the Feast of Tabernacles** takes place in Jerusalem, and the **Music in Tabgha** in Kefar Nahum features early Italian Baroque chamber-music concerts.

November The **International Guitar Festival** is held at various locations.

December At the **International Christmas Choir Assembly,** local and foreign choirs sing Christmas songs on Manger Square, Bethlehem, as well as in Jerusalem and Nazareth.

What to Pack

Clothing Israel is a casual country where comfort comes before fashion. Rarely will you need more than an afternoon dress or sports jacket to feel comfortable at any event. Very few restaurants require a jacket and tie. For touring, cool, easy-care clothing is a must in the summer months. If you are coming from May through September, you won't need a coat, but you will need a sun hat. Take one sweater for cool nights, particularly in the hilly areas. Women need modest dress for touring in religious neighborhoods. Bring long pants to protect your legs and a spare pair of walking shoes for adventure travel. A raincoat with a zip-out lining is ideal for October to April, when the weather can get cold enough for snow (or as likely be warm enough in the south for outdoor swimming). Rain boots may also be a useful accessory in winter; pack a bathing suit for all seasons.

Miscellaneous Bring an extra pair of eyeglasses or contact lenses in your carry-on luggage. If you have a health problem that requires a prescription drug, pack enough to last the duration of the trip or have your doctor write a prescription using the drug's generic name, because brand names vary from country to country (you'll need a prescription from a doctor in the country you're visiting to get the medication from a pharmacy there). Always carry prescription drugs in their original packaging to avoid problems with customs officials. Don't pack them in luggage that you plan to check in case your bags go astray. Pack a list of the offices that supply refunds for lost or stolen traveler's checks. Take plenty of sunscreen, insect repellent, a water canteen, sunglasses, and a sun hat that completely shades your face and neck.

Electricity The electrical current in Israel is 220 volts, 50 cycles alternating current (AC); the United States runs on 110-volt, 60-cycle AC current. Unlike wall outlets in the United States, which accept plugs with two flat prongs, outlets in Israel take Continental-type plugs, with two round prongs.

Adapters, To use U.S.-made electric appliances abroad, you'll need an adapter
Converters, plug. Unless the appliance is dual-voltage and made for travel, you'll
Transformers also need a converter. Hotels sometimes have 110-volt outlets for low-wattage appliances marked "For Shavers Only" near the sink; don't use them for a high-wattage appliance like a blow dryer. If you're traveling with an older laptop computer, carry a transformer. New laptop computers are auto-sensing, operating equally well on 110 and 220 volts, so you need only the appropriate adapter plug. For a copy of the free brochure "Foreign Electricity is No Deep Dark Secret," send a S.A.S.E. to adapter-converter manufacturer

Franzus Company (Customer Service, Dept. B50, Murtha Industrial Park, Box 142, Beacon Falls, CT 06403, tel. 203/723–6664).

Luggage Free airline baggage allowances depend on the airline, the route,
Regulations and the class of your ticket; ask in advance. In general, on domestic flights and on international flights between the United States and foreign destinations, you are entitled to check two bags—neither exceeding 62 inches, or 158 centimeters (length + width + height), or weighing more than 70 pounds (32 kilograms). A third piece may be brought aboard; its total dimensions are generally limited to less than 45 inches (114 centimeters), so it will fit easily under the seat in front of you or in the overhead compartment. In the United States, the Federal Aviation Administration (FAA) gives airlines broad latitude to limit carry-on allowances and tailor them to different aircraft and operational conditions. Charges for excess, oversize, or overweight pieces vary.

If you are flying between two foreign destinations, note that baggage allowances may be determined not by piece but by weight— generally 88 pounds (40 kilograms) of luggage in first class, 66 pounds (30 kilograms) in business class, and 44 pounds (20 kilograms) in economy. If your flight between two cities abroad *connects* with your transatlantic or transpacific flight, the piece method still applies.

Safeguarding Before leaving home, itemize your bags' contents and their worth in
Your Luggage case they go astray. To minimize that risk, tag them inside and out with your name, address, and phone number. (If you use your home address, cover it so that potential thieves can't see it.) Put a copy of your itinerary inside each bag, so that you can easily be tracked. At check-in, make sure that the tag attached by baggage handlers bears the correct three-letter code for your destination. If your bags do not arrive with you, or if you detect damage, file a written report with the airline before you leave the airport.

Taking Money Abroad

Traveler's Traveler's checks are preferable in metropolitan centers, although
Checks you'll need cash in rural areas and small towns. The most widely recognized are **American Express, Citicorp, Thomas Cook,** and **Visa,** which are sold by major commercial banks, usually for a fee of 1%–3% of the checks' face value. Both American Express and Thomas Cook issue checks that can be countersigned and used by you or your traveling companion, and they both provide checks, at no extra charge, denominated in six non-U.S. currencies. (Some foreign banks charge as much as 20% for cashing traveler's checks denominated in dollars.) Buy a few checks in small denominations to cash toward the end of your trip, so you won't be left with excess foreign currency. Record the numbers of the checks, cross them off as you spend them, and keep this list separate from the checks.

Currency Banks offer the most favorable exchange rates. If you use currency
Exchange exchange booths at airports, rail and bus stations, hotels, stores, and privately run exchange firms, you'll typically get less favorable rates, but you may find the hours more convenient.

You can avoid long lines at airport currency-exchange booths by getting a *small* amount of currency before you depart at **Thomas Cook Currency Services** (630 5th Ave., New York, NY 10111, tel. 212/757–6915 or 800/223–7373 for locations in major metropolitan areas throughout the United States) or **Ruesch International** (tel. 800/

424–2923 for locations). Check with your travel agent to be sure that the currency of the country you will be visiting can be imported.

Getting Money from Home

Cash Machines

Many automated-teller machines (ATMs) are tied to international networks such as **Cirrus** and **Plus.** You can use your bank card at ATMs to withdraw money from an account and get cash advances on a credit-card account if your card has been programmed with a personal identification number, or PIN. Check in advance on limits on withdrawals and cash advances within specified periods. Ask whether your bank-card or credit-card PIN will need to be reprogrammed for use in the area you'll be visiting. Four digits are commonly used overseas. Note that Discover is accepted only in the United States. On cash advances you are charged interest from the day you receive the money from ATMs as well as from tellers. Although transaction fees for ATM withdrawals abroad may be higher than fees for withdrawals at home, Cirrus and Plus exchange rates are excellent because they are based on wholesale rates only offered by major banks. They also may be referred to abroad as "a withdrawal from a credit account."

Wiring Money

You don't have to be a cardholder to send or receive funds through **MoneyGram℠ from American Express.** Just go to a MoneyGram℠ agent, located in American Express Travel Offices. Pay up to $1,000 with cash or a credit card, anything over that in cash. The money can be picked up within 10 minutes in the form of U.S. dollar travelers checks or local currency at the nearest MoneyGram℠ agent. Call 800/926–9400 for locations and more information, or, abroad, the nearest American Express Travel Office. There's no limit, and the recipient need only present photo identification. The cost, which includes a free long-distance phone call, runs from 3% to 10%, depending on the amount sent, the destination, and how you pay.

You can also use **Western Union.** To wire money, take either cash or a cashier's check to the nearest agent or call 800/325–6000 and use MasterCard or Visa. Money sent from the United States or Canada will be available for pickup at agent locations in 100 countries within minutes. Once the money is in the system it can be picked up at *any* one of 25,000 locations (call 800/325–6000 for the one nearest you; 800/321–2923 in Canada). Fees range from 4% to 10%, depending on the amount you send.

Currency

Israel's money is the shekel (NIS). There are 100 agorot to the shekel. A one-shekel coin is about the size of an American dime, but thicker. The half-shekel coin is larger, as is the 10-agorot coin. There is also a five-shekel coin, about the size of an American quarter. Paper money comes in 10-, 20-, 50-, 100-, and 200-shekel denominations.

Israeli currency fluctuates against the U.S. dollar, so exact rates vary daily. At press time (summer 1994), the exchange rate was about 3 shekels to the dollar. Because of the frequent fluctuations, prices quoted throughout the book are in shekels and in approximate U.S.-dollar prices. Because paying bills at hotels, car-rental firms, and special tourist shops in foreign currency eliminates the value-added tax (VAT), price charts in the dining and lodging sections of the book are in U.S. dollars.

What It Will Cost

Israel is a moderately priced country compared to Western Europe, but it is more expensive than many of its Mediterranean neighbors. Tourist costs, calculated in dollars, are little affected by inflation. Prices are much the same all over the country. To save money, try the excellent prepared food from supermarkets (buy local brands), take public transportation, eat your main meal at lunch, avoid ordering drinks (ask for water), eat falafel one meal a day, and stay at apartment-hotels and guest houses. Plane fares are lowest in winter.

Taxes   A value-added tax (which at press time was 17%) is charged on all purchases and transactions except tourists' hotel bills and car rentals paid in foreign currency (cash, traveler's checks, foreign credit cards). You are entitled to a refund of this tax on purchases made in foreign currency of more than $50 on one invoice, but keep in mind that not all stores are organized with VAT return forms. Stores so organized display TAXVAT signs and give 5% discounts. If you charge meals and other services to your room at a hotel, there is no VAT if you pay with foreign currency, but other restaurants charge VAT even so. Keep your receipts and ask for a cash refund at Ben Gurion airport or Haifa Port (there is a special Bank Leumi desk set up for this); if you leave from other departure points, the VAT refund will be sent to your home address. Allow time for this procedure when you plan your departure.

At press time, there was an airport exit tax of $12, payable in shekels or dollars, which may or may not have been included in your fare.

Sample Prices   Cup of coffee, $2; falafel, $1.80; beer at a bar, $3; canned soft drink, $1–$2; hamburger at a fast-food restaurant, $3; 2-kilometer (1-mile) taxi ride, about $3.50; movie $6.

Long-Distance Calling

The country code in Israel is 972. AT&T, MCI, and Sprint have international services that make calling home relatively affordable and convenient and let you avoid hotel surcharges. Before you go, call the company of your choice to learn the number you must dial in Israel to reach its network: **AT&T** USA Direct (tel. 800/874–4000), **MCI** Call USA (tel. 800/444–4444), or **Sprint** Express (tel. 800/793–1153). All three companies offer message delivery services to international travelers and have added debit cards so that you don't have to fiddle with change.

Passports and Visas

If your passport is lost or stolen abroad, report the loss immediately to the nearest embassy or consulate and to the local police. If you can provide the consular officer with the information contained in the passport, he or she will usually be able to issue you a new passport promptly. For this reason, keep a photocopy of the data page of your passport separate from your money and traveler's checks. Also leave a photocopy with a relative or friend at home.

U.S. Citizens   All U.S. citizens, even infants, need a valid passport to enter Israel. Three-month tourist visas are issued free of charge at the point of entry when a valid passport is presented. At press time Arab (and some non-Arab) countries refuse to admit travelers whose passports carry an Israeli visa entry stamp. If you are concerned about having an Israeli stamp or visa in your passport, (1) you can ask the customs officer at your point of entry to issue a tourist visa on a separate piece of paper to keep with your passport; or (2) apply for a second passport, including with the application a letter explaining that you need it to travel to Israel. Be advised that it is not unheard of for Israeli customs officers to stamp passports despite requests not to do so; if you plan to travel repeatedly between Israel and Arab states hostile to Israel, a second passport is advisable.

You can pick up new and renewal application forms at any of the 13 U.S. Passport Agency offices and at some post offices and courthouses. Although passports are usually mailed within four weeks of your application's receipt, allow five weeks or more from April through summer. Call the Department of State Office of Passport Services' information line (tel. 202/647–0518) for fees, documentation requirements, and other details.

Canadian Citizens Canadian citizens need a passport and a visa to enter Israel. Three-month tourist visas are issued free of charge at the point of entry. Application forms are available at 28 regional passport offices as well as at post offices and travel agencies. Whether for a first or a subsequent passport, you must apply in person. Children under 16 may be included on a parent's passport but must have their own to travel alone. Passports are valid for five years and are usually mailed within two to three weeks of an application's receipt. For fees, documentation requirements, and other information in English or French, call the passport office (tel. 819/994–3500 or 800/567-6868).

U.K. Citizens Citizens of the United Kingdom need a valid passport and visa to enter Israel. Three-month tourist visas are issued free of charge at the point of entry. Applications for new and renewal passports are available from main post offices as well as at the six passport offices, located in Belfast, Glasgow, Liverpool, London, Newport, and Peterborough. You may apply in person at all passport offices, or by mail to all except the London office. Children under 16 may travel on an accompanying parent's passport. All passports are valid for 10 years. Allow a month for processing.

Customs and Duties

On Arrival Those over 17 may import duty-free into Israel: 250 cigarettes or 250 grams of tobacco products; two liters of wine and one liter of spirits; ¼ liter of eau de cologne or perfume; and gifts totaling no more than $125 in value. Fresh meats may not be imported.

Nonresidents may bring any amount of foreign currency and shekels into Israel, but may not take out more foreign currency than they brought in. Save your bank receipts. You can reconvert up to $5,000 worth of shekels. In addition, up to $500 worth of shekels can be reconverted at the airport bank on departure (without receipts).

A large deposit is sometimes required at Israeli customs to bring expensive and/or professional-quality video and computer equipment into the country. This is to ensure that it is not being imported for sale. The deposit is refundable in the original currency on departure and can be paid in cash, in traveler's checks, or by Visa credit card.

If you are bringing any foreign-made equipment with you from home, such as cameras, it's wise to carry the original receipt or register it with Customs before you leave (U.S. Customs Form 4457). Otherwise, you may end up paying duty on your return.

Returning Home
U.S. Customs

If you've been out of the country for at least 48 hours and haven't already used the exemption, or any part of it, in the past 30 days, you may bring home $400 worth of foreign goods duty-free. So can each member of your family, regardless of age; and your exemptions may be pooled, so one of you can bring in more if another brings in less. A flat 10% duty applies to the next $1,000 worth of goods; above $1,400, the rate varies with the merchandise. (If the 48-hour or 30-day limits apply, your duty-free allowance drops to $25, which may not be pooled.) Please note that these are the *general* rules, applicable to most countries, including Israel.

Travelers 21 or older may bring back 1 liter of alcohol duty-free, provided the beverage laws of the state through which they reenter the United States allow it. In addition, 100 non-Cuban cigars and 200 cigarettes are allowed, regardless of your age. Antiques and works of art more than 100 years old are duty-free.

Gifts valued at less than $50 may be mailed to the United States duty-free, with a limit of one package per day per addressee, and do not count as part of your exemption (do not send alcohol or tobacco products or perfume valued at more than $5); mark the package "Unsolicited Gift" and write the nature of the gift and its retail value on the outside. Most reputable stores will handle the mailing for you.

For a copy of "Know Before You Go," a free brochure detailing what you may and may not bring back to the United States, rates of duty, and other pointers, contact the **U.S. Customs Service** (Box 7407, Washington, DC 20044, tel. 202/927–6724).

Canadian Customs

Once per calendar year, when you've been out of Canada for at least seven days, you may bring in C$300 worth of goods duty-free. If you've been away less than seven days but more than 48 hours, the duty-free exemption drops to C$100 but can be claimed any number of times (as can a C$20 duty-free exemption for absences of 24 hours or more). You cannot combine the yearly and 48-hour exemptions, use the $300 exemption only partially (to save the balance for a later trip), or pool exemptions with family members. Goods claimed under the C$300 exemption may follow you by mail; those claimed under the lesser exemptions must accompany you.

Alcohol and tobacco products may be included in the yearly and 48-hour exemptions but not in the 24-hour exemption. If you meet the age requirements of the province through which you reenter Canada, you may bring in, duty-free, 1.14 liters (40 imperial ounces) of wine or liquor *or* two dozen 12-ounce cans or bottles of beer or ale. If you are 16 or older, you may bring in, duty-free, 200 cigarettes, 50 cigars or cigarillos, and 400 tobacco sticks or 400 grams of manufactured tobacco. Alcohol and tobacco must accompany you on your return.

An unlimited number of gifts valued up to C$60 each may be mailed to Canada duty-free. These do not count as part of your exemption. Label the package "Unsolicited Gift—Value under $60." Alcohol and tobacco are excluded.

For more information, including details of duties on items that exceed your duty-free limit, ask the Revenue Canada Customs, Excise and Taxation (2265 St. Laurent Blvd. S, Ottawa, Ontario, K1G 4K3, tel. 613/957–0275) for a copy of the free brochure "I Declare/Je Déclare."

U.K. Customs

From countries outside the EU, such as Israel, you may import duty-free 200 cigarettes, 100 cigarillos, 50 cigars or 250 grams of tobacco; 1 liter of spirits or 2 liters of fortified or sparkling wine; 2 liters of still table wine; 60 milliliters of perfume; 250 milliliters of toilet water; plus £136 worth of other goods, including gifts and souvenirs.

For further information or a copy of "A Guide for Travellers," which details standard customs procedures as well as what you may bring into the United Kingdom from abroad, contact HM Customs and Excise (Dorset House, Stamford St., London SE1 9PY, tel. 0171/928–3344).

Traveling with Cameras, Camcorders, and Laptops

Film and Cameras If your camera is new or if you haven't used it for a while, shoot and develop a few test rolls of film before you leave. Store film in a cool, dry place—never in the car's glove compartment or on the shelf under the rear window.

Airport security X-rays generally aren't harmful to film with ISO below 400. To protect your film, carry it with you in a clear plastic bag and ask for a hand inspection. Such requests are honored at U.S. airports, usually not abroad. Don't depend on a lead-lined bag to protect film in checked luggage—the airline may increase the radiation to see what's inside. Call the Kodak Information Center (tel. 800/242–2424) for details.

Camcorders and Videotape Before your trip, put camcorders through their paces, invest in a skylight filter to protect the lens, and check all the batteries. Most newer camcorders are equipped with batteries that can be recharged with a universal or worldwide AC adapter charger (or multivoltage converter) usable whether the voltage is 110 or 220. All that's needed is the appropriate plug.

Videotape is not damaged by X-rays, but it may be harmed by the magnetic field of a walk-through metal detector, so ask for a hand-check. Airport security personnel may ask you to turn on the camcorder to prove that it's what it appears to be, so make sure the battery is charged. Note that rather than the National Television System Committee (NTSC) video standard used in the United States and Canada, Israel uses PAL technology. You will not be able to view your tapes through the local TV set or view movies bought there in your home VCR. Blank tapes bought in Israel can be used for NTSC camcorder taping, but they are pricey.

Laptops Security X-rays do not harm hard-disk or floppy-disk storage, but you may request a hand-check, at which point you may be asked to turn on the computer to prove that it is what it appears to be. (Check your battery before departure.) Most airlines allow you to use your laptop aloft except during takeoff and landing (so as not to interfere with navigation equipment). For international travel, register your foreign-made laptop with U.S. Customs as you leave the country. If your laptop is U.S.-made, call the consulate of the country you'll be visiting to find out whether or not it should be registered with customs upon arrival. Before departure, find out about repair facilities at your destination, and don't forget any transformer or adapter plug you may need (*see* Electricity, *above*).

Language

Hebrew has a unique curriculum vitae: The language of the Bible was long relegated to one of holy scriptures until a revival began a century ago gave it a whole new life. These days, it thrives—and thanks not only to the Academy of the Hebrew Language, which officially introduces new words, but also to a comedy trio, *Hagashash Hachiver*, which has made an art of street language. If Abraham, Isaac, and Jacob came back today they'd have to take *ulpan* classes just like new immigrants. English has also had an impact on Hebrew to the extent that you will hear not only official words like bank and telefon, but also slang such as *diskusti* (I discussed) *heppening* (happening, event), and *lefaxes* (to fax). Arabic is Israel's other official language, and it is spoken by Arabs as well as many Jews (especially those with origins in Arab states). In this country of immigrants, mistakes and a variety of accents are tolerated cheerfully. In fact, so many different languages are spoken by polyglot Israelis that you might be able to try out French, Spanish, Italian, or, particularly in recent years, Russian. All Israeli schoolchildren study English, and speak with a range of fluency.

Israelis use a lot of hand gestures when they talk. A common gesture that sometimes annoys foreigners is turning a palm and pressing the thumb and forefinger together to mean "wait a minute." Rest assured that this gesture has no negative connotations. Just as harmless in intention is the Israeli who says he "doesn't believe you" when he means something is unbelievably wonderful. Few Israelis differentiate between bus stop and bus station (because one Hebrew word covers both), so if you want the central bus station, make sure you ask for it. Different systems of transliteration have produced widely inconsistent spellings: So is it the Golan city Katzrin or Qazrin or Catsrin?

You can hear news in English on Kol Yisrael, the main radio station, at 7 AM, 1 PM, 5 PM, and 8 PM. There's an English news broadcast on the main television channel every evening. Nearly all movies are shown in their original languages with Hebrew subtitles. You can pick up a copy of *The Jerusalem Post*, Israel's daily English-language newspaper and the semimonthly news magazine, the *Jerusalem Report*, at most newsstands. *The International Herald Tribune* is sold at many newsstands, many hotels, and at airports. Stores carry a wide range of English titles.

Staying Healthy

It's safe in Israel to drink tap water and eat fresh produce after it has been washed, but take care when buying cooked products from outdoor food stands; in some cases, the food may have been sitting unrefrigerated for a long time.

A sun hat is a must, and carry a canteen or bottled water (available even in the most remote places) to guard against dehydration. Drink at every opportunity, whether you feel thirsty or not.

If you have a health problem for which you might need to buy medicine while in Israel, have your doctor write a prescription using the drug's generic name (proprietary names can vary widely). Get a local doctor to reissue the prescription. Nearly all pharmacists speak English.

Finding a Doctor **International Association for Medical Assistance to Travellers** (IAMAT, 417 Center St., Lewiston, NY 14092, tel. 716/754–4883; 40 Regal Rd., Guelph, Ontario, Canada N1K 1B5; 57 Voirets, 1212 Grand-Lancy, Geneva, Switzerland) publishes a worldwide directory of English-speaking physicians whose qualifications meet IAMAT standards and who have agreed to treat members for a set fee. Membership is free.

Assistance Companies Pretrip medical referrals, emergency evacuation or repatriation, 24-hour telephone hot lines for medical consultation, dispatch of medical personnel, relay of medical records, cash for emergencies, and other personal and legal assistance are among the services provided by several organizations specializing in medical assistance to travelers. Among them are **International SOS Assistance** (Box 11568, Philadelphia, PA 19116, tel. 215/244–1500 or 800/523–8930; Box 466, Pl. Bonaventure, Montréal, Québec, Canada H5A 1C1, tel. 514/874–7674 or 800/363–0263), **Medex Assistance Corporation** (Box 10623, Baltimore, MD 21285, tel. 410/296–2530 or 800/874–9125), **Near Services** (450 Prairie Ave., Suite 101, Calumet City, IL 60409, tel. 708/868–6700 or 800/654–6700), and **Travel Assistance International** (1133 15th St. NW, Suite 400, Washington, DC 20005, tel. 202/331–1609 or 800/821–2828). Because these companies will also sell you death-and-dismemberment, trip-cancellation, and other insurance coverage, there is some overlap with the travel-insurance policies discussed under Insurance, *below.*

Publications *The Safe Travel Book* by Peter Savage (Lexington Books, 132 E. 23rd St., New York, NY 10010, tel. 212/702–4771 or 800/257–5755, fax 800/562–1272; $13.95) is packed with handy lists and phone numbers to make your trip smooth. *Traveler's Medical Resource* by William W. Forgey (ICS Books, Inc., Box 10767, Merrillville, IN 45410, tel. 800/541–7323; $19.95) is also a good, authoritative guide to health care overseas.

Insurance

For U.S. Residents Most tour operators, travel agents, and insurance agents sell specialized health-and-accident, flight, trip-cancellation, and luggage insurance as well as comprehensive policies with some or all of these features. Before you make any purchase, review your existing health and homeowner policies to find out whether they cover expenses incurred while traveling.

Health and Accident Insurance Specific policy provisions of supplemental health-and-accident insurance for travelers include reimbursement for $1,000 to $150,000 worth of medical and/or dental expenses caused by an accident or illness during a trip. The personal-accident, or death-and-dismemberment, provision pays a lump sum to your beneficiaries if you die or to you if you lose one or both limbs or your eyesight; the lump sum awarded can range from $15,000 to $500,000. The medical-assistance provision may reimburse you for the cost of referrals, evacuation, or repatriation and other services, or it may automatically enroll you as a member of a particular medical-assistance company (*see* Assistance Companies, *above*).

Flight Insurance Often bought as a last-minute impulse at the airport, flight insurance pays a lump sum when a plane crashes either to a beneficiary if the insured dies or sometimes to a surviving passenger who loses eyesight or a limb. Like most impulse buys, flight insurance is expensive and basically unnecessary. It supplements the airlines' coverage described in the limits-of-liability paragraphs on your ticket. Charging an airline ticket to a major credit card often automatically entitles you to coverage and may also embrace travel by bus, train, and ship.

Baggage Insurance In the event of loss, damage, or theft on international flights, airlines' liability is $20 per kilogram for checked baggage (roughly about $640 per 70-pound bag) and $400 per passenger for unchecked baggage. On domestic flights, the ceiling is $2,000 per passenger. Excess-valuation insurance can be bought directly from the airline at check-in for about $10 per $1,000 worth of coverage. However, you cannot buy it at any price for the rather extensive list of excluded items shown on your airline ticket.

Trip Insurance Trip-cancellation-and-interruption insurance protects you in the event you are unable to undertake or finish your trip, especially if your airline ticket, cruise, or package tour does not allow changes or cancellations. The amount of coverage you purchase should equal the cost of your trip should you, a traveling companion, or a family member fall ill, forcing you to stay home, plus the nondiscounted one-way airline ticket you would need to buy if you had to return home early. Read the fine print carefully, especially sections defining "family member" and "preexisting medical conditions." **Default** or **bankruptcy insurance** protects you against a supplier's failure to deliver. Such policies often do not cover default by a travel agency, tour operator, airline, or cruise line if you bought your tour and the coverage directly from the firm in question. Tours packaged by one of the 33 members of the United States Tour Operators Association (USTOA, 211 E. 51st St., Suite 12B, New York, NY 10022; tel. 212/750-7371), which requires members to maintain $1 million each in an account to reimburse clients in case of default, are likely to present the fewest difficulties. Even better, pay for travel arrangements with a major credit card, so that you can refuse to pay the bill if services have not been rendered—and let the card company fight your battles.

Comprehensive Companies supplying comprehensive policies with some or all of the
Policies above features include **Access America, Inc.** (Box 90315, Richmond, VA 23286, tel. 800/284-8300); **Carefree Travel Insurance** (Box 9366, 100 Garden City Plaza, Garden City, NY 11530, tel. 516/294-0220 or 800/323-3149); **Near** (Box 1339, Calumet City, IL 60409, tel. 708/868-6700 or 800/654-6700; **Tele-Trip** (Mutual of Omaha Plaza, Box 31762, Omaha, NE 68131, tel. 800/228-9792); **Travel Insured International** (Box 280568, East Hartford, CT 06128, tel. 203/528-7663 or 800/243-3174); **Travel Guard International** (1145 Clark St., Stevens Point, WI 54481, tel. 715/345-0505 or 800/826-1300); and **Wallach and Company, Inc.** (107 W. Federal St., Box 480, Middleburg, VA 22117, tel. 703/687-3166 or 800/237-6615).

U.K. For advice, or a copy of the free booklet, "Holiday Insurance," which
Residents sets out what to expect from a holiday insurance policy and gives price guidelines, contact the **Association of British Insurers** (51 Gresham St., London BC2V 7HQ, tel. 0171/600-3333; 30 Gordon St., Glasgow G1 3PU, tel. 0141/226-3905; Scottish Provincial Bldg., Donegall Sq., W. Belfast BT1 6JE, tel. 01232/249-176).

Car Rentals

All major car-rental companies are represented in Israel, including **Alamo** (tel. 800/522-9696); **Avis** (tel. 800/331-1084, 800/879-2847 in Canada); **Budget** (tel. 800/527-0700); **Hertz** (tel. 800/654-3001, 800/263-0600 in Canada); and **National** (tel. 800/227-3876), known internationally as InterRent and Europcar. In cities, unlimited-mileage rates range from $45 per day for an economy car to $272 for a large car; weekly unlimited-mileage rates range from $140 to $707. There is no tax on car rentals in Israel.

Requirements Your own driver's license is acceptable. An International Driver's Permit, available from the American or Canadian Automobile Association, is a good idea.

Extra Charges Picking up the car in one city and leaving it in another may entail substantial drop-off charges or one-way service fees. The cost of a collision or loss-damage waiver (*see below*) can be high, also. Some rental agencies will charge you extra if you return the car *before* the time specified on your contract. Ask before making unscheduled drop-offs. Be sure the rental agent agrees *in writing* to any changes in drop-off location or other items of your rental contract. Fill the tank just before you turn in the vehicle to avoid being charged for refueling at what you'll swear is the most expensive pump in town. In Europe, manual transmissions are standard and air-conditioning is a rarity and often unnecessary. Asking for an automatic transmission or air-conditioning can significantly increase the cost of your rental. Find out what the standard rentals are in the country you'll be visiting and weigh that factor when making your reservation.

Cutting Costs Major international companies have programs that discount their standard rates by 15% to 30% if you make the reservation before departure (anywhere from 24 hours to 14 days), rent for a minimum number of days (typically three or four), and prepay the rental. More economical rentals may come as part of fly/drive or other packages, even bare-bones deals that only combine the rental and an airline ticket (*see* Tours and Packages, *above*).

Several companies operate as wholesalers—they do not own their own fleets but rent in bulk from those that do and offer advantageous rates to their customers. Rentals through such companies must be arranged and paid for before you leave the United States. Among them is the **Kemwel Group** (106 Calvert St., Harrison, NY 10528, tel. 914/835–5555 or 800/678–0678). You won't see these wholesalers' deals advertised; they're even better in summer, when business travel is down. Always ask whether the prices are guaranteed in U.S. dollars or foreign currency and if unlimited mileage is available. Find out about any required deposits, cancellation penalties, and drop-off charges, and confirm the cost of any required insurance coverage.

Insurance and Collision Damage Waiver Until recently, standard rental contracts included liability coverage (for damage to public property, injury to pedestrians, and so on) and coverage for the car against fire, theft, and collision damage with a deductible. Due to law changes in some states and rising liability costs, several car rental agencies have reduced the type of coverage they offer. Before you rent a car, find out exactly what coverage, if any, is provided by your personal auto insurer. Don't assume that you are covered. If you do want insurance from the rental company, secondary coverage may be the only type offered. You may already have secondary coverage if you charge the rental to a credit card. Only Diners Club (tel. 800/234–6377) provides primary coverage in the United States and worldwide.

In general if you have an accident, you are responsible for the automobile. Car rental companies may offer a collision damage waiver (CDW), which ranges in cost from $4 to $14 a day. You should decline the CDW only if you are certain you are covered through your personal insurer or credit card company.

Student and Youth Travel

The **Israel Student Travel Association,** or **ISSTA** (105 Ben Yehuda St., Tel Aviv, tel. 03/544–8151) has 12 branches, most of them on university campuses throughout Israel. Other main offices are in Tel Aviv (109 Ben Yehuda St., tel. 03/544–0111), Jerusalem (31 Haniviim St., tel. 02/240462), and Haifa (29 Nordau St., tel. 04/670222). ISSTA offers discounted tours, car rentals, hotels, and flights. Students from abroad often take advantage of ISSTA's international travel programs.

Council Travel Services (CTS), a subsidiary of the nonprofit Council on International Educational Exchange (CIEE), specializes in low-cost travel arrangements abroad for students and is the exclusive U.S. agent for several discount cards. Also newly available from CTS are domestic air passes for bargain travel within the United States. CIEE's twice-yearly *Student Travels* magazine is available at the CTS office at CIEE headquarters (205 E. 42nd St., 16th Floor, New York, NY 10017, tel. 212/661–1450) and in Boston (tel. 617/266–1926), Miami (tel. 305/670–9261), Los Angeles (tel. 310/ 208–3551) and at 43 branches in college towns nationwide (free in person, $1 by mail). **Campus Connections** (1100 E. Marlton Pike, Cherry Hill, NJ 08034, tel. 800/428–3235) specializes in discounted accommodations and airline fares for students. The **Educational Travel Centre** (438 N. Frances St., Madison, WI 53703, tel. 608/256– 5551) offers low-cost domestic and international airline tickets, mostly for flights departing from Chicago, and rail passes. Other travel agencies catering to students include **TMI Student Travel** (100 W. 33rd St., No. 813, New York, NY 10001, tel. 212/356–1515 or 800/ 245–3672), and **Travel Cuts** (187 College St., Toronto, Ontario, Canada M5T 1P7, tel. 416/979–2406).

Discount Cards For discounts on transportation and on museum and attractions admissions, buy the **International Student Identity Card** (ISIC) if you're a bona fide student or the **International Youth Card** (IYC) if you're under 26. In the United States the ISIC and IYC cards cost $16 each and include basic travel accident and illness coverage and a toll-free travel assistance hot line. Apply to **CIEE** (*see* address *above*, tel. 212/661–1414; the application is in *Student Travels*). In Canada the cards are available for $15 each from **Travel Cuts** (*see above*). In the United Kingdom they cost £5 and £4 respectively at student unions and student travel companies, including Council Travel's London office (28A Poland St., London W1V 3DB, tel. 0171/ 437–7767).

Hosteling A **Hostelling International** (HI) membership card is the key to more than 5,000 hostels in 70 countries; the sex-segregated, dormitory-style sleeping quarters, including some for families, go for $7–$20 a night per person. Membership is available in the United States through **Hostelling International-American Youth Hostels** (HI-AYH, 733 15th St. NW, Suite 840, Washington, DC 20005, tel. 202/783– 6161), the U.S. link in the worldwide chain, and costs $25 for adults 18–54, $10 for those under 18, $15 for those 55 and over, and $35 for families. HI membership is available in Canada through **Hostelling International-Canada** (205 Catherine St., Suite 400, Ottawa, Ontario K2P 1C3, tel. 613/748–5638) for $26.75, and in the United Kingdom through the **Youth Hostel Association of England and Wales** (Trevelyan House, 8 St. Stephen's Hill, St. Albans, Hertfordshire AL1 2DY, tel. 01727/855215) for £9.

Tour Operators **Contiki** (300 Plaza Alicante, No. 900, Garden Grove, CA 92640, tel. 714/740–0808 or 800/266–8454) specialize in package tours for travelers 18 to 35.

Traveling with Children

Israel welcomes young tourists, and baby supplies are easily available. Children travel half-price on domestic flights and on trains. Many tourist sites offer excellent programs that children will enjoy.

Check the local paper for child-centered activities in the big cities. Bring along a canteen for each child. Remember that children dehydrate faster than adults. Sunscreen and sun hats are also essential.

Publications **Family Travel Times,** published 10 times a year by **Travel With Your**
Newsletter **Children** (TWYCH, 45 W. 18th St., New York, NY 10011, tel. 212/ 206–0688; annual subscription $55), covers destinations, types of vacations, and modes of travel.

Books *Traveling with Children—And Enjoying It,* by Arlene K. Butler (Globe Pequot Press, Box 833, 6 Business Park Rd., Old Saybrook, CT 06475, tel. 800/243–0495, or 800/962–0973 in CT; $11.95 plus $3 shipping per book) helps plan your trip with children, from toddlers to teens. For basics with little ones, check *Take Your Baby and Go! A Guide for Traveling with Babies, Toddlers and Young Children,* by Sheri Andrews, Judy Bordeaux, and Vivian Vasquez (Bear Creek Publications, tel. 800/326–6566; $5.95). TWYCH (*see above*) also publishes *Cruising with Children ($22)* and *Skiing with Children* ($29). Family Travel Guides catalog (tel. 510/527–5849; $1) lists about 200 books and articles on family travel. *Kids Love Israel, Israel Loves Kids—A Travel Guide for Families,* by Barbara Sofer, offers a comprehensive, firsthand look at the many activities, facilities, and attractions for children in Israel (Kar-Ben Copies, Inc., 6800 Tildenwood La., Rockville, MD 20852, tel. 301/984–8733; $11.95).

Pen Pals Young tourists who would like to make contact with Israeli children before their visit should write to Etty Moskowitz, Pen Pals in Israel, ICCY, Box 8009, Jerusalem, 93107, Israel.

Getting There On international flights, the fare for infants under age two not occu-
Airfares pying a seat is generally either free or 10% of the accompanying adult's fare; children ages 2–11 usually pay half to two-thirds of the adult fare. On domestic flights, children under two not occupying a seat travel free, and older children currently travel on the lowest applicable adult fare.

Baggage In general, infants paying 10% of the adult fare are allowed one carry-on bag, not to exceed 70 pounds or 45 inches (length + width + height) and a collapsible stroller; check with the airline before departure, because you may be allowed less if the flight is full. The adult baggage allowance applies for children paying half or more of the adult fare.

Safety Seats The FAA recommends the use of safety seats aloft and details approved models in the free leaflet "Child/Infant Safety Seats Recommended for Use in Aircraft" (available from the FAA, APA–200, 800 Independence Ave. SW, Washington, DC 20591, tel. 202/267–3479; Information Hot Line, tel. 800/322–7873). Airline policies vary. U.S. carriers allow FAA-approved models bearing a sticker declaring their FAA approval. Because these seats are strapped into regular passenger seats, airlines may require that a ticket be bought for an infant who would otherwise ride free. Foreign carriers may not allow infant seats, may charge the child's rather than the infant's fare for their use, or may require you to hold your baby during take-off and landing, thus defeating the seat's purpose.

Facilities Aloft Some airlines provide other services for children, such as children's meals and freestanding bassinets (only to those with seats at the bulkhead, where there's enough legroom). Make your request when reserving. Biannually the February issue of *Family Travel Times* details children's services on three dozen airlines (*see above;* $12). "Kids and Teens in Flight," free from the U.S. Department of

Transportation's Office of Consumer Affairs (R-25, Washington, DC 20590, tel. 202/366-2220), offers tips for children flying alone.

Car Travel To get a copy of the American Academy of Pediatrics' "Family Shopping Guide to Car Seats" send a S.A.S.E. to Safe Ride Program, American Academy of Pediatrics, 141 Northwest Point Boulevard, Box 927, Elk Grove Village, IL 60009. Car crashes remain the leading cause of death for people ages 5–34, according to U.S. government statistics, and car seats are among the top items recalled by the Consumer Product Safety Commission. If you are renting a car, ask if a free car seat is available and request it when you reserve.

Lodging Hotel policy varies greatly on pricing for children. In most luxury hotels, children under 12 sharing a hotel room with adults either stay free or receive a discount rate. Children's discounts are often less generous at kibbutz guest houses. Many hotels especially in resorts such as Eilat, feature entertainment that appeals to children and activities such as arts and crafts or field trips. Most hotels and resorts have baby-sitters available through the concierge or front desk, at a charge of about $5 an hour.

The **Hilton** hotels (reservations tel. 800/445–8667; in Britain, tel. 0181/780–1155) in Jerusalem and Tel Aviv offer a family plan, an organized youth camp during the summer months and/or an all-day children's program. The **Dan** hotels (reservations tel. 212/752–6120, in Britain 0171/439–9893) offer a Family Advantage plan and usually recreation programs during vacations. **Ramada** hotels in Jerusalem and Tel Aviv offer a family plan, as do the **Moriah Plaza** hotels (tel. 800/221–0203) in Jerusalem, Tel Aviv, the Dead Sea, Eilat, and Tiberias, which also have children's programs during school vacations.

Hints for Travelers with Disabilities

Facilities for people with disabilities in Israel still lag behind those of many Western countries. Crowded, hilly streets and steps can make it difficult to get around without a companion, and adapted minibuses and rental cars are extremely hard to come by. However, new hotels are now required to provide adequate facilities for guests with disabilities, and improvements are being made at several tourist sights.

Organizations Several organizations provide travel information for people with disabilities, usually for a membership fee, and some publish newsletters and bulletins. Among them are the **Information Center for Individuals with Disabilities** (Fort Point Pl., 27–43 Wormwood St., Boston, MA 02210, tel. 617/727–5540 or 800/462–5015 in MA between 11 AM and 4 PM, or leave message; TTY 617/345–9743); **Mobility International USA** (Box 10767, Eugene, OR 97440, tel. and TTY 503/343–1284:; fax 503/343–6812), the U.S. branch of an international organization based in Britain that has affiliates in 30 countries; **MossRehab Hospital Travel Information Service** (tel. 215/456–9603, TTY 215/456–9602); the **Travel Industry and Disabled Exchange** (TIDE, 5435 Donna Ave., Tarzana, CA 91356, tel. 818/344–3640, fax 818/344–0078); and **Travelin' Talk** (Box 3534, Clarksville, TN 37043, tel. 615/552–6670, fax 615/552–1182).

In Israel The **Roof Association of Organizations of Persons with Disabilities** (97 Jaffa Rd., Jerusalem, tel. 02/228283, and 30 Ibn-Gvirol St., Tel Aviv, tel. 03/210780); **MILBAT—The Israeli Center for Technical Aids and Transportation** (52621 Tel Hashomer, Ramat Gan, Tel Aviv, tel. 03/711739); and **The Israeli Foundation for Handicapped**

Children (ILAN, 2 Buki Ben Yogli St., Tel Aviv, tel. 03/281217). To obtain a copy of *Access in Israel*, a guide to accessible sights and accommodations in Israel, contact **Pauline Hephaistos Survey Projects** (39 Bradley Gardens, West Ealing, London W13 8HE, England). The **Jerusalem Action Committee** (tel. 02/639839) offers advice on special problems.

Travelers who need assistance with guide dogs can contact **Orna and Noah Braun** (Kfar Yedidye, tel. 053/332544). In Jerusalem, the **ritual bath** (tel. 02/717597) in the Baka neighborhood has special facilities for visitors with disabilities.

In the United Important information sources include the **Royal Association for**
Kingdom **Disability and Rehabilitation** (12 City Forum, 250 City Rd., London EC14 8AF, tel. 0171/250–3222) offers advice and information for travelers with disabilities.

Travel Agency **Flying Wheels Travel** (143 W. Bridge St., Box 382, Owatonna, MN 55060, tel. 507/451–5005 or 800/535–6790) is a travel agency specializing in domestic and worldwide cruises, tours, and independent travel itineraries for people with mobility problems.

Publications Several free publications are available from the U.S. Consumer Information Center (Pueblo, CO 81009): "New Horizons for the Air Traveler with a Disability" (include Dept. 608Y in the address), a U.S. Department of Transportation booklet describing changes resulting from the 1986 Air Carrier Access Act and from the 1990 Americans with Disabilities Act, and the Airport Operators Council's *Access Travel: Airports* (Dept. 5804), which describes facilities and services for people with disabilities at more than 500 airports worldwide.

The 500-page *Travelin' Talk Directory* (*see* Organizations, *above;* $35 check or money order with a money-back guarantee) lists names and addresses of people and organizations who offer help for travelers with disabilities. Twin Peaks Press (Box 129, Vancouver, WA 98666, tel. 206/694–2462 or 800/637–2256) publishes the *Directory of Travel Agencies for the Disabled* ($19.95, plus $2 for shipping), which lists more than 370 agencies worldwide.

Hotels Accessible accommodations in Tel Aviv include the **Sheraton** hotel (tel. 800/325–3535) and the **Kfar Maccabiah** (tel. 03/671–5715); in Jerusalem, the **Hilton** hotel (tel. 800/445–8667) and the **Laromme** (tel. 02/697777); and in Haifa, the **Dan Panorama** (tel. 212/752–6120). The **Club Med** (tel. 800/258–2633) at Coral Beach, just south of Eilat, has wheelchair ramps. **Moriah Plaza** hotels (tel. 07/361111) at Ein Bokek, on the Dead Sea, have special elevators to help disabled persons reach the water.

Hints for Older Travelers

Organizations The **American Association of Retired Persons** (AARP, 601 E St. NW, Washington, DC 20049, tel. 202/434–2277) provides independent travelers who are members of the AARP (open to those age 50 or older; $8 per person or couple annually) with the Purchase Privilege Program, which offers discounts on lodging, car rentals, and sightseeing, and arranges group tours, cruises, and apartment living through AARP Travel Experience from American Express (400 Pinnacle Way, Suite 450, Norcross, GA 30071, tel. 800/927–0111 or 800/745–4567).

Two other organizations offer discounts on lodgings, car rentals, and other travel products, along with such nontravel perks as magazines and newsletters: the **National Council of Senior Citizens** (1331 F St. NW, Washington, DC 20004, tel. 202/347–8800; membership $12 annually) and **Mature Outlook** (6001 N. Clark St., Chicago, IL 60660, tel. 800/336–6330; $9.95 annually).

Note: For reduced rates, mention your senior-citizen identification card when booking hotel reservations, not when checking out. At restaurants, show your card before you're seated; discounts may be limited to certain menus, days, or hours. If you are renting a car, ask about promotional rates that might improve on your senior-citizen discount.

Discounts for the elderly are given on flights to Israel, at many tourist sites, and on public transportation. A passport is adequate proof of age if necessary. Usually your word will be enough.

Educational Travel   The nonprofit **Elderhostel** (75 Federal St., 3rd Floor, Boston, MA 02110, tel. 617/426–7788) has offered inexpensive study programs for people 60 and older since 1975. Held at more than 1,800 educational and cultural institutions, courses cover everything from marine science to Greek myths and cowboy poetry. Participants usually attend lectures in the morning and spend the afternoon sightseeing or on field trips; they live in dormitory-type lodgings. Fees for two- to three-week international trips—including room, board, and transportation from the United States—range from $1,800 to $4,500.

Publications   *The 50+ Traveler's Guidebook: Where to Go, Where to Stay, What to Do,* by Anita Williams and Merrimac Dillon (St. Martin's Press, 175 5th Ave., New York, NY 10010; $12.95) is available in bookstores and offers many useful tips. "The Mature Traveler" (Box 50820, Reno, NV 89513, tel. 702/786–7419; $29.95), a monthly newsletter, contains many travel deals.

Hints for Gay and Lesbian Travelers

Organizations   The **International Gay Travel Association** (Box 4974, Key West, FL 33041, tel. 800/448–8550), which has a membership of 800 travel-related businesses, will provide you with names of travel agents and tour operators who specialize in gay travel.

Tour Operators and Travel Agencies   Tour operator **Olympus Vacations** (8424 Santa Monica Blvd., No. 721, West Hollywood, CA 90069; tel. 310/657–2220) offers all-gay-and-lesbian resort holidays. **Skylink Women's Travel** (746 Ashland Ave., Santa Monica, CA 90405, tel. 310/452–0506 or 800/225-5759) handles individual travel for lesbians all over the world and conducts international and domestic group trips annually. **Toto Tours** (1326 West Albion 3W, Chicago, IL 60626, tel. 312/274–8686) specializes in gay and lesbian travel and offers guided trips to such destinations as Costa Rica, the British Virgin Islands, the Florida Keys, Tanzania, Yellowstone National Park, the Grand Canyon, France, Alaska, the Canadian Rockies and Munich, Germany.

Publications   The premier international travel magazine for gays and lesbians is *Our World* (1104 N. Nova Rd., Suite 251, Daytona Beach, FL 32117, tel. 904/441–5367; $35 for 10 issues). "Out & About" (tel. 203/789–8518 or 800/929–2268; $49 for 10 issues, full refund if you aren't satisfied) is a 16-page monthly newsletter with extensive information on resorts, hotels, and airlines that are gay-friendly.

Security

Security checks on airlines flying to Israel are stringent. Be prepared for what might sound like nosy questions about your itinerary, packing habits, and desire to travel to Israel. Remember that the men and women on duty have a difficult job and they are concerned with protecting you. Once you are in Israel, expect to have your handbags searched as a matter of course when you enter department stores, places of entertainment, museums, and public buildings. These checks are generally fast and courteous.

Traveling throughout most of Israel is safe and comfortable. You'll see Jews and Arabs peacefully coexisting in any of the major cities. Tourists should take a common-sense approach to driving or walking in isolated areas at night.

The term *intifada* refers to the violent and nonviolent protests by Palestinians beginning in 1987 in the occupied territories (the West Bank, Gaza, Golan, East Jerusalem, and Jerusalem's Old City). Visitors should be vigilant using public transportation or traveling by car in these areas. The single biggest problem has been the stoning of vehicles; nearly all public buses traveling in these areas have reinforced glass. If you do want to travel in the West Bank—and many tourists will want to visit Bethlehem and Jericho—go on an organized tour or with a guide who is familiar with the area. If you need to visit the most problematic security areas, such as Nablus and Gaza, arrangements should be made with a recognized Arab touring company. There are standard security road checks along the roads to the West Bank, but they are only closed off in periods of particular political upheaval.

Further Reading

History and Biography If you haven't opened the **Bible** in a while, this is a good time to review biblical narratives; better yet, bring it along on your trip. For a modern look at the Bible, try *Genesis and the Big Bang*, by Gerald Schroeder (Bantam). To better understand the leading players, try: *The Life of Moshe Dayan*, by Robert Slater (St. Martin's Press); *Ben-Gurion*, by Shabtai Teveth (Houghton Mifflin); *The Revolt*, by Menachem Begin (Steimatzky), the former prime minister's account of the fighting unit he headed; and *My Life*, by Golda Meir (Weidenfeld and Nicolson). *Heritage, Civilization and the Jews*, by Abba Eban (Steimatzky) is a pictorial survey illustrating 5,000 years of Jewish civilization. *O Jerusalem*, by Larry Collins and Dominique Lapierre (Simon and Schuster) is a dramatic account of the establishment of the Israeli state. *Understanding the Dead Sea Scrolls*, edited by Hershel Shanks (Random House) gives insight into that important discovery. *Jews, God and History*, by Max I. Dimont (Signet) is an old but very readable history of the region (and fairly portable for traveling). *The Source*, by James Michener (Fawcett), is the novelist's vivid look at Israel's early history. *The Book of Our Heritage*, by Eliayahv Kitov (Feldheim) is a superb guide to Jewish holidays and traditions. Last, but far from least, is Flavius Josephus's *The Jewish War*.

Fiction *Exodus*, a novel by Leon Uris (Doubleday), deals with the founding of the State of Israel. *Closing the Sea*, by Yehudit Katzir (Harcourt, Brace, Jovanovich) is a book of short stories set in Israel. *The Black Box*, by Amos Oz (Flamingo) is a modern love story. *Saturday Morning Murder*, by Batya Gur (Harper Collins) is a psychological mystery. Other contemporary Israeli writers worth looking out for are A. B. Yehoshua, Meir Shalev, David Grossman, and Irit Linor.

Modern Israel   *To Jerusalem and Back,* by Saul Bellow (Avon) conveys the flavor of modern Israeli life through the impressions of the Nobel prize-winning author. *In the Land of Israel,* by Amos Oz (Chatto and Windus) is a series of articles depicting various settlements and towns and conversations with local people. In *Arab and Jew,* (Times Books), David K. Shipler, a former *New York Times* correspondent, takes a contemporary look at the relationship. *Intifada,* by Zeev Schiff and Ehud Yaari (Touchstone) gives background and analysis of the current uprising. In *My Enemy, Myself* (Penguin), Yoram Binur, a journalist, imagines himself a Palestinian. Thomas Friedman looks at modern events and politics in the Middle East in *From Beirut to Jerusalem* (Farrar, Straus & Giroux). And try *Jerusalem, City of Mirrors,* by Amos Elon (Fontana) and *Safed, the Mystical City,* by David Rossoff (Feldheim Publishers).

Arriving and Departing

From North America by Plane

Flights are either nonstop, direct, or connecting. A **nonstop** flight requires no change of plane and makes no stops. A **direct** flight stops at least once and can involve a change of plane, although the flight number remains the same; if the first leg is late, the second waits. This is not the case with a **connecting** flight, which involves a different plane and a different flight number.

Airports and   Flights leave North America for Israel from New York, Miami, Los
Airlines   Angeles, Chicago, Baltimore/Washington, Dallas/Ft. Worth, Montréal, and Toronto. Below is a list of the major airlines that fly nonstop to Israel. Additional airlines offer connecting flights to Israel from North America. A nonstop flight from New York takes between 10 and 11 hours.

Israel's main international airport is **Ben Gurion International Airport,** about halfway between Jerusalem and Tel Aviv. Charter flights from the United States sometimes land at **Atarot Airport** in Jerusalem and at **Eilat Airport** in Eilat.

El Al Israel Airlines (tel. 212/768–9200 or 800/223–6700; in Canada tel. 514/875–8900 and 416/804–9779), the national airline, has the most nonstop flights to Israel. From New York there are 12 nonstop flights weekly; from Los Angeles and Miami three direct flights depart per week. El Al flights also leave from Boston, Dallas/Ft. Worth, Chicago, and Baltimore/Washington. In Canada there are flights from Montréal and Toronto. All meals are kosher, and there are special children's meals. There are no flights on the Sabbath.

Czechoslovak Airlines (tel. 212/765–6022) offers budget flights twice a week from New York to Tel Aviv. An overnight stay in Prague is required, but the airline pays for two meals and accommodations.

Delta Airlines (tel. 800/241–4141, TDD 800/831–4488) has daily direct flights from New York (Delta flights from its hubs in Cincinnati, Atlanta, and Orlando connect with this flight) to Tel Aviv, with a brief stop in Paris.

Tower Air (tel. 718/553–8500 or 800/221–2500) has three weekly nonstop flights from New York to Israel. The return flights make a refueling stop in Ireland. Kosher food is offered, and there are no flights on the Sabbath.

TWA (tel. 800/892–4141, TDD 800/421–8480) has three nonstop flights per week from New York to Israel, and direct flights via Paris almost daily.

Cutting Costs The Sunday travel section of most newspapers is a good source of deals. When booking, particularly through an unfamiliar company, call the Better Business Bureau and your local or state Consumer Protection Bureau to find out whether any complaints have been registered against the company, pay with a credit card if you can, and consider trip-cancellation and default insurance (*see* Insurance, *above*).

Promotional Less expensive fares, called promotional or discount fares, are
Airfares round-trip and involve restrictions, which vary according to the route and season. You must usually buy the ticket—commonly called an APEX (advance purchase excursion) when it's for international travel—in advance (7, 14, or 21 days is usual), although some of the major airlines have added no-frills, cheap flights to compete with new bargain airlines on certain routes.

With the major airlines, the cheaper fares generally require minimum and maximum stays (for instance, over a Saturday night or at least 7 and no more than 30 days). Airlines generally allow some return date changes for a $25 to $50 fee, but most low-fare tickets are nonrefundable. Only a death in the family would prompt the airline to return any of your money if you cancel a nonrefundable ticket. However, you can apply an unused nonrefundable ticket toward a new ticket, again with a small fee. The lowest fare is subject to availability, and only a small percentage of the plane's total seats will be sold at that price. Contact the U.S. Department of Transportation's Office of Consumer Affairs (I–25, Washington, DC 20590, tel. 202/366–2220) for a copy of "Fly-Rights: A Guide to Air Travel in the U.S."

Consolidators Consolidators or bulk-fare operators—"bucket shops"—buy blocks of seats on scheduled flights that airlines anticipate they won't be able to sell. They pay wholesale prices, add a markup, and resell the seats to travel agents or directly to the public at prices that still undercut the airline's promotional or discount fares (higher than a charter ticket but lower than an APEX ticket and usually without the advance-purchase restriction). Moreover, some consolidators sometimes give you your money back. Carefully read the fine print detailing penalties for changes and cancellations. If you doubt the reliability of a company, call the airline once you've made your booking and confirm that you do, indeed, have a reservation on the flight.

The biggest U.S. consolidator, C. L. Thomson Express, sells only to travel agents. Well-established consolidators selling to the public include **BET World Travel** (841 Blossom Hill Rd., Suite 212-C, San Jose, CA 95123, tel. 800/747–1476); **Council Charter** (205 E. 42nd St., New York, NY 10017, tel. 212/661–0311 or 800/800–8222); **Euram Tours** (1522 K St. NW, Suite 430, Washington, DC, 20005, tel. 800/848–6789); **TFI Tours International** (34 W. 32nd St., New York, NY 10001, tel. 800/745–8000); **Travac Tours and Charter** (2601 E. Jefferson, Orlando FL 32803, tel. 407/896–0014). UniTravel (Box 12485, St. Louis, MO 63132, tel. 314/569–0900 or 800/325–2222).

Discount Travel clubs offer members unsold space on airplanes, cruise ships,
Travel Clubs and package tours at as much as 50% below regular prices. Membership may include a regular bulletin or access to a toll-free hot line

giving details of available trips departing from three or four days to several months in the future. Most also offer 50% discounts off hotel rack rates, but double check with the hotel to make sure it isn't offering a better promotional rate independent of the club. Clubs include **Discount Travel International** (114 Forrest Ave., Suite 203, Narberth, PA 19072, tel. 215/668–7184; $45 annually, single or family), **Entertainment Travel Editions** (Box 1014, Trumbull, CT 06611, tel. 800/445–4137; price, depending on destination, $25–$48), **Great American Traveler** (Box 27965, Salt Lake City, UT 84127, tel. 800/548–2812; $49.95 annually), **Moment's Notice Discount Travel Club** (425 Madison Ave., New York, NY 10017, tel. 212/486–0503; $45 annually, single or family), **Privilege Card** (3391 Peachtree Rd. NE, Suite 110, Atlanta GA 30326, tel. 404/262–0222 or 800/236–9732; domestic annual membership $49.95, international, $74.95), **Travelers Advantage** (CUC Travel Service, 49 Music Sq. W, Nashville, TN 37203, tel. 800/548–1116; $49 annually, single or family), and **Worldwide Discount Travel Club** (1674 Meridian Ave., Miami Beach, FL 33139, tel. 305/534–2082; $50 annually for family, $40 single).

Publications Both "Consumer Reports Travel Letter" (Consumers Union, 101 Truman Ave., Yonkers, NY 10703, tel. 914/378–2562 or 800/234–1970; $39 a year) and the newsletter "Travel Smart" (40 Beechdale Rd., Dobbs Ferry, NY 10522, tel. 800/327–3633; $37 a year) have a wealth of travel deals and tips in each monthly issue. *The Official Frequent Flyer Guidebook*, by Randy Petersen (4715-C Town Center Dr., Colorado Springs, CO 80916, tel. 719/597–8899 or 800/487–8893; $14.99, plus $3 shipping and handling) yields valuable hints on getting the most for your air travel dollars, as does *Airfare Secrets Exposed*, by Sharon Tyler and Matthew Wonder (Universal Information Publishing, $16.95 in bookstores). Also new and helpful is *202 Tips Even the Best Business Travelers May Not Know* by Christopher McGinnis (Box 52927, Atlanta, GA 30355, tel. 404/659–2855; $10 in bookstores).

Enjoying the Flight Fly at night if you're able to sleep on a plane. Because the air aloft is dry, drink plenty of fluids while on board. Drinking alcohol contributes to jet lag, as do heavy meals. Bulkhead seats, in the front row of each cabin—usually reserved for people who have disabilities, are elderly, or are traveling with babies—offer more legroom, but trays attach awkwardly to seat armrests, and all possessions must be stowed overhead.

Smoking Since February 1990, smoking has been banned on all domestic flights of less than six hours' duration; the ban also applies to domestic segments of international flights aboard U.S. and foreign carriers. On U.S. carriers flying to Israel and other destinations abroad, a seat in a no-smoking section must be provided for every passenger who requests one, and the section must be enlarged to accommodate such passengers if necessary as long as they have complied with the airline's deadline for check-in and seat assignment. If smoking bothers you, request a seat far from the smoking section.

Foreign airlines are exempt from these rules but do provide no-smoking sections, and some nations, including Canada as of July 1, 1993, have gone as far as to ban smoking on all domestic flights; other countries may ban smoking on flights of less than a specified duration. The International Civil Aviation Organization has set July 1, 1996, as the date to ban smoking aboard airlines worldwide, but the body has no power to enforce its decisions.

From the United Kingdom by Plane

Airports and Airlines   **British Airways** (52 Grosvenor Gardens, London SW1, tel. 0181/897–4000) offers nonstop flights from Heathrow to Ben Gurion Airport.

El Al (185 Regent St., London W1, tel. 0171/437–9255) offers nonstop flights almost daily from Heathrow to Ben Gurion Airport, and twice a week from Manchester (tel. 0161/541–2005); there are no flights on the Sabbath.

Flying Time   Flying time from London to Tel Aviv is 4½ hours.

From the United Kingdom by Ship

Luxury liners sailing from Southampton sometimes dock in Haifa. Among them are the *Queen Elizabeth II*, Seabourn Cruises, and Intercruise Line, all run by **Cunard Lines** (South Western House, Canute Road, Southampton S09 IZA, tel. 01703/229933).

Staying in Israel

Getting Around

By Plane   **Arkia Israeli Airlines** has flights from Jerusalem and Tel Aviv (Sde Dov Airport) to Eilat and Rosh Pina, and from Tel Aviv to Haifa, Masada (Bar Yehuda), Mitzpe Ramon, Gush Katif, the Dead Sea (Ein Yahav) and Rosh Pina. There is also service from Haifa to Jerusalem, Eilat, and the Dead Sea. Children fly for half-price. Tour packages sometimes offer better deals on these flights. For reservations contact the Arkia reservations center (Sde Dov Airport, Box 39301, Tel Aviv 61392, tel. 03/690–2222, fax 03/699–1390). There are Arkia offices in Jerusalem (Clal Center, tel. 02/234855, fax 02/242686), Eilat (Shalom Center, tel. 07/376102/3/4/5, fax 07/373370), and Haifa (84 Ha'atzmaut Blvd., tel. 04/643371, fax 04/663097), among other cities. In the United States contact **Isram Wholesale Tours and Travel, Ltd.** (630 3rd Ave., New York, NY 10117, tel. 212/661–1193) or **Uniworld Travel International, Inc.** (9025 Wilshire Blvd., Beverly Hills, CA 90211, tel. 213/858–0600). In Jerusalem, **Kanfei Jerusalem** (tel. 02/831444) offers air tours. **Nesher Airlines** (tel. 09/505054) and **Avia Airlines** (tel. 09/506221) arrange plane tours and lease aircraft.

By Train   The train ride from Jerusalem to Tel Aviv's Southern Station is slow and scenic. It takes about 1½ hours and costs $2.50 (half-price for children). Trains leave twice a day in each direction.

In contrast, there's a frequent train service running almost hourly between Tel Aviv's Northern Station (also called Arlozoroff) and Haifa. Express trains take an hour to make the trip; local trains, about 1½ hours. Many of these trains travel as far north as Nahariya. Request an up-to-date schedule. A ticket from Tel Aviv to Nahariya costs about $4 (children half-price).

By Bus   You can get almost anywhere in Israel by bus, and the Central Bus Station is a fixture in most towns. Ask for the *"tahanah merkazit,"* and anyone will direct you. The **Egged** cooperative (tel. 03/537–5555) handles all the country's bus routes except those in metropolitan Tel Aviv, where the **Dan** company (tel. 03/561–4444) operates. Rates are relatively low, and timetables are accurate. You do not need exact change on city buses. If you get on a bus at a highway stop, you can pay the driver. Public transportation generally stops for Shabbat (late Friday afternoon to Saturday evening) although some lines run minibuses in Tel Aviv and Haifa, with a large Arab population, also provides some lines. It is advisable to reserve seats in advance on buses from the major cities to Eilat and the Dead Sea. For city bus information call Egged in Jerusalem (tel. 02/340704) or Haifa (tel. 04/549250). The Tel Aviv bus station number is 03/638–3939.

Egged offers a variety of bus passes. The *Israbus* pass, payable in shekels and available only at Egged Tours offices in Israel, allows tourists unlimited travel. A one-week pass costs NIS 185 ($61.70); two weeks, NIS 290 ($96.70); three weeks, NIS 360 ($120); four weeks, NIS 400 ($133.35). You must present your passport at the time of purchase. Within each city you can purchase multiride tickets, or *kartisiot* (20 rides) and monthly tickets (unlimited service within the month) at nearly any city bus station or on the bus. These are particularly good for children and senior citizens, who get large discounts.

By Car   The Hebrew word for a native-born Israeli is sabra, the prickly cactus with sweet fruit inside. You'll meet the sweet Israeli should you get lost or have automotive difficulties—helping hands are quick to arrive—but behind the wheel, Israelis are prickly and very aggressive, and honk their horns far more than their Western counterparts. Try not to take it personally.

Highways are basically good, except in some rural areas. Avoid entering and leaving the main cities at rush hours (7:30 AM–8:30 AM and 4 PM–6 PM), when roads are absolutely jammed. Roads are marked with international traffic symbols, and, because signs are often in Hebrew only, it's smart to write down the road numbers before setting out. Good maps in English are available at bookstores and through the IGTO.

It's a good idea to carry extra water, for your car and for yourself, while driving any time of year. Every winter there are several days of flash flooding in the desert; if it's raining, try to find a police officer or call the IGTO to ask about road and weather conditions.

Service stations are full-service, but attendants don't mind if you prefer to fill your own tank. Most rental cars still use leaded gas. At press time, a liter of high-test gasoline costs about 60¢ ($2.50 a gallon). Most city gas stations close at 7:30 PM, but those on highways stay open all night.

Israel is slowly assigning numbers to its roads and highways (north–south even, east–west odd), but most people still know them simply by the towns they connect, for example, the "Tiberias–Nazareth road." Intersections and turnoffs are referred to similarly: the "Eilat junction." The local representative of the AAA and British AA in Israel is **Memsi** (in Tel Aviv, tel. 03/564–1133 for tourist information; in Jerusalem, tel. 02/250661). Rental-car companies usually provide road service.

By Guide-Driven Limousine or Minibus   Modern, air-conditioned limousines or minibuses driven by expert guides are often available at prices lower than those of taxis. This is a good value for a family or group of five to seven passengers. At press time costs are NIS 690 ($230) a day (nine hours) for up to four passengers, NIS 780 ($260) for five to seven passengers, and NIS 930 ($310) for 9 to 11 passengers. Rates are based on 200 kilometers (124 miles) of travel a day and nine hours of touring. An additional NIS 165–210 ($55–$70) per night (depending on location) is charged for the driver's expenses if he or she sleeps away from home base. Half-day tours are also available. Companies specializing in guide/ driver services include **Eshkolot-Yehuda Tours** (36 Karen Hayesod St., Jerusalem, tel. 02/635555 or 02/665555, fax 02/632101); and **Twelve Tribes** (29 Hamered St., Tel Aviv, tel. 03/510–1911, fax 03/ 510–1943).

By Taxi Taxis are plentiful and relatively inexpensive and can be reached by phone. On the whole, drivers are cheerful. According to law, every driver must use the meter unless you hire him for the day or to make a special trip out of town. Gently remind your driver to use the meter if he offers you a ride for a set price. If he gives you a hard time, write down his cab number and report him to an IGTO office.

Certain shared taxis or minivans run fixed routes, such as from Tel Aviv to Haifa or from the airport to Jerusalem, leaving when they're full. These are called **sherut** (as opposed to *special*, the term used for a private cab). There are fixed rates for these routes, generally slightly more expensive than bus rates, and smoking is allowed. Some sheruts can be booked in advance; in Tel Aviv call 03/566–0222, in Jerusalem call 02/231231, and in Haifa call 04/672672.

Telephones

Local Calls The telephone company in Israel is called **Bezek**. Because Israel is changing over to a digital telephone system, many of the phone numbers have been changed in recent years. Double-check a number if you don't get an answer.

Toll-free numbers in Israel begin with 177. For local and out-of-town directory assistance dial 144 (which charges four phone units for the service). When calling an out-of-town number in Israel, be sure to dial the zero that begins every area code. Public telephones operate with either an *asimon* (token) that is good for one phone unit and costs about 14¢, or a telephone card (telecard), available in phone units of 10, 20, 50, 120, and 250. Both are sold at post offices, all Bezek offices, many newsstands, hotel reception desks, and some kiosks. On the public telephones using the telecard, which are swiftly replacing the phone tokens, the number you are dialing appears on a digital readout; to its right are the number of units remaining on your card.

International The country code for Israel is 972. You can make international calls
Calls using a telecard from a public phone. A call from Israel when discount rates are in effect costs about 13 units per minute. Large cities have Central Phone Agencies usually near or at main post offices where you make your phone call and pay upon completion. You can reach an international operator at 188. Remember that hotels often add a hefty surcharge on phone calls. The country code for Canada and the United States is 1, for Great Britain 44.

By dialing Israel's toll free number (177) and the number of your long-distance service, you can link up directly to an operator in your home country. For example: For AT&T's USA Direct, dial 177/100–2727; for MCI's USA Direct, call 177/150–2727; for Sprint Express, 177/102–2727.

Operators and Dial 144 for information. If the operator doesn't speak English or
Information can't find your number, you can ask for a *mifakahat* (supervisor) to help you with the number.

Mail

Israel's mail service has improved dramatically in recent years. The post office handles regular and express letters, sends and receives faxes, takes bill payments, sells phone tokens and telephone cards, and offers a quick delivery service. Nearly every neighborhood has a post office, identified by a flying deer, and English is almost always spoken. The main branches are usually open from 8 to 6 or 7, and small offices are usually open Sunday, Monday, Tuesday, and Thursday from 8 to 12:30 and 3:30 to 6, Wednesday from 8 to 1:30, and Friday from 8 to noon. In Muslim cities and in Gaza the post office is closed Friday, in Christian towns it's closed Sunday, and in Jericho it's closed Saturday. Identification is required to send packages.

Postal Rates A regular letter within Israel costs about 30¢. An air letter to the United States or Europe costs about 45¢. If you bring a letter to the post office before 10 AM, same-day delivery is guaranteed for about NIS 9 ($3) within the city, NIS 12 ($4) out of town. A letter of 20 grams or less to Europe costs about NIS 1.20 (40¢), and about NIS 1.65 (55¢) to the United States. An airmail postcard to the United States requires an NIS 1.05 (35¢) stamp. Mail abroad takes 5 to 10 days. The first page of a fax costs about NIS 7.50 ($2.50) within Israel, NIS 18 ($6) to the United States.

In most big cities, yellow mailboxes are for mail being sent within the same city, and red boxes are for all other mail.

Receiving Mail Tourists who want to receive mail at a local post office should have it addressed to Post Restante in the town. Mail is held for up to three months, and the service is free. **American Express** offices in the big cities also receive and hold mail free for card members; for a list of foreign American Express offices call 212/477–5700 in New York City or 800/525–4800.

Tipping

There are no hard and fast rules on tipping in Israel. Taxi drivers do not expect tips. If the service has not been included on a restaurant bill, add 10%—but don't if you feel the service was particularly bad. Hotel bellboys are tipped a lump sum of NIS 5–NIS 10 ($1.70–$3.35), not per bag. Even if a service charge is tacked on, tip the bellhop 10% of the bill for room service. Guides, tour bus drivers, and chauffeurs don't expect tips either, though they are grateful if someone in the group takes up a collection for them. (Private guides, however, should get tipped NIS 60–NIS 75/$20–$25 a day.) A small tip is expected by both the person who washes your hair and the beautician—except if one of them owns the salon. Leave NIS 1 for bathroom and coatroom attendants.

Etiquette for Visitors

Etiquette is not a word that ranks high on the Israeli vocabulary list. In this very informal society, there are many traditions but few rules. Having said that, certain sectors of Israeli society—Jewish and Arab—have their own sets of rules and etiquette that should be taken into account by a visitor. Ultra-orthodox quarters, such as Bnei Brak, near Tel Aviv, and the Jerusalem neighborhood of Mea Shearim, call for modest dress by visitors (women in particular). Local women keep their knees and elbows covered, and they do not wear pants; married women keep their heads covered as well (keep a scarf handy). Tourists wandering the streets will feel more comfortable if they keep this in mind, and it is essential for anyone wanting to enter a synagogue or other important institutions (again, women in particular, though head covering for men will also be appreciated). Very religious Jews, who wear black garb, do not shake hands or mingle socially with members of the opposite sex.

Guests in Muslim households insult their hosts if they will not accept a drink (usually strong coffee or a soft drink is offered). Muslims do not drink alcohol, so a gift of wine is inappropriate. Like religious Jews, Muslims do not eat pork. When entering mosques, remove your shoes. Women should cover their hair. Shaking hands or picking up food with the left hand is considered impolite.

Opening and Closing Times

Since the intifada began, Arab-owned stores have usually opened at 8 and closed at 1. As a rule, though, businesses are open by 8:30 in Israel; neighborhood grocery stores often open as early as 6 AM. Some businesses still close for siesta for two or three hours between 1 and 4 PM. Most stores do not close before 7 PM. Supermarkets are often open later, and in large cities, there are all-night supermarkets.

In Jerusalem, most stores in the western part of the city are closed Friday afternoon. In other parts of the country, tourist facilities are often open Saturday morning, and some supermarkets are open Saturday night. Museums don't have a fixed closing day, and, although hours are usually 10–6, you must call.

Although hours can differ among banks, almost all open by 8:30. Most close from 12:30 to 4 and reopen until 5:30, but some stay open longer, and in large cities there are branches open in the evening. Banks are closed on Saturday except in Muslim areas, where they're closed Friday. In Christian areas they're open Saturday morning and closed Sunday.

Shopping

The Ministry of Tourism publishes a guide to shopping in Israel, with frequent updates on special discounts for tourists. It is available at IGTO offices.

Jewelry, gems, and locally cut diamonds are considered to be good buys in Israel. The large cities have many reputable jewelry outlets. Ethnic items such as embroidered skullcaps (or yarmulke), tie-dyed scarves, spice boxes, Hanukkah lights, and the like are popular gifts.

Israeli clothing is not inexpensive, but the high fashion designs, particularly in bathing suits and leather goods, often appeal to visitors. Tel Aviv is the fashion center. Sandals are particularly well made.

Jerusalem is a good place to look for antiques and Judaica, Jewish religious items. The downtown area known as Arts and Crafts Lane, the Cardo in the Jewish Quarter of the Old City, and the neighborhood called Mea She'arim have a large selection. Christian objects are also plentiful in Jerusalem, especially in the Old City. If you are shopping in an outdoor market (except a food market), stall owners expect you to bargain.

Sports and the Outdoors

Boating   Tel Aviv and Eilat have marinas with sailboats and yachts that can
be chartered, glass-bottom and glass-side boats, and even a submarine. You can also spend a day on the Sea of Galilee, in anything from
a yacht to a pedal boat.

Camping   Most Israeli campsites offer water, bathrooms, showers, first aid,
telephones, cabins for rent, and often mobile homes set on blocks.
Some even have swimming pools or are located near beaches. They
are all guarded and lighted at night. Advance reservations are recommended for July, August, and Jewish holidays. Information is
available from the IGTO or the **Israel Camping Union** (Box 53,
Nahariya, 22100, tel. 04/925392).

Cliff   A favorite area for cliff rappelling, a popular sport in Israel, is at
Rappelling   Metzoke Dragot, between Jerusalem and the Dead Sea.

Golf   Israel's only golf course, the **Caesarea Golf Club** (Box 30660, Caesarea, tel. 06/366–1172/4) on the northern coast, is open seven days a
week. Tourists can get special memberships, and all equipment can
be rented.

Hiking   Israelis are avid hikers, and there are about 4,500 kilometers (2,800
miles) of hiking routes marked in Israel. Hikes are organized almost
daily by the **SPNI**, and the **Nature Reserves Authority** has marked
hiking trails. Passes to these nature reserves can be obtained from
any of the site offices. A recently opened 1,000-kilometer (620-mile)
route called the **Israel Trail** runs from the northern town of Dan,
near the Lebanese border, to Eilat.

Horseback   You can tour Israel by horse—or by donkey or camel—especially in
Riding   the Negev, Eilat, Galilee, and the northern coast.

Parachuting,   Parachuting, paragliding, hang gliding, and aeromodeling (ma-
Gliding,   nipulating model airplanes) can be arranged through the **Aero Club**
Aeromodeling   **of Israel** (67 Hayarkon St., Tel Aviv 63903, tel. 03/517–5038).

Skiing   Israel's only ski resort sits on **Mt. Hermon** (tel. 06/740121) and offers
gentle as well as steep slopes. There is a rental shop and a ski school
in season.

Tennis   Tennis centers are located throughout the country. There are nominal court fees, and you should reserve in advance. Ask for the **National Tennis Center** in your area (central office: Box 51, Ramat
Hasharon 47100, tel. 03/544–7222 or 03/544–7992).

Water Sports   Scuba diving and snorkeling are popular amidst the beautiful coral
reefs of Eilat and off the Mediterranean beaches of Ashkelon, Tel
Aviv, Hadera, Caesarea, Haifa, Akko, and Nahariya. Information is
available from the **Federation for Underwater Activities in Israel** (Box
8110, Tel Aviv, tel. 03/457432). Divers must present a two-star license or take a course. Windsurfing and waterskiing are offered at
various beaches, not at hotels.

White-Water   Kayaks, canoes, and inner-tubes are all for rent along the Jordan
Rafting   and its tributaries in the north and at beach sites on the Sea of Galilee.

Nature Reserves and Parks

For such a small, arid country, Israel has many parks and nature reserves. A full list of parks, including those with camping facilities,
can be obtained from the **Jewish National Fund**, or **JNF** (corner of
Keren Kayemet and Keren Hayesod Sts., Jerusalem, tel. 02/

707411). The JNF also runs summer camping programs for families (tel. 02/258210). For information on nature reserves, contact the **Nature Reserve Authority** (78 Yirmiyahu St., Jerusalem 94467, tel. 02/387471). For about NIS 36 ($12) for adults and NIS 18 ($6) for children over age five, you can purchase a pass valid for entry to all 13 reserves in Israel for one month.

The **Green Card,** priced at NIS 41–NIS 50 ($13.70–$16.70), allows unlimited entry for 14 days to any of the 40 parks and historical sites administered by the **National Parks Authority** (4 Makleff St., Hakirya, Tel Aviv 61070, tel. 03/695–2281). The ticket can be purchased from the National Parks Authority or at the following sites: Avdat, Beit She'an, Hazor, Herodion, Masada, Megiddo, and Qumran. The **Around Kinneret** ticket (NIS 15/$5 adults, NIS 8/$2.70 children), good for one week, admits you to three of the following sites: Belvoir, Bet She'an, Hammat Tiberias, Kursi, and Korazim.

Beaches

Israel's Mediterranean coastline has many public beaches, which usually offer changing facilities and bathrooms for a modest fee. It is advisable to swim only at the designated areas where lifeguards are on duty. A flag system indicates how dangerous the waves and undertow are: A black flag means that conditions are rough and swimming is not allowed; a red flag means moderate waves, swim with discretion; a white flag indicates a calm sea.

Women often sunbathe topless on the beaches in Eilat. At the other extreme, there are many beaches that offer sections for women and men who prefer to bathe separately for reasons of modesty. Some of the Mediterranean beaches, and most of the beaches on the Dead Sea and the Sea of Galilee, are stony. Be sure to wear rubber beach shoes, especially when swimming amidst the spiky coral reefs of the Red Sea.

Dining

Israel is not a "must-do" stop on a gastronomic world tour, and yet some of the best tastes and tantalizing aromas can be found here. This is, after all, the Middle East: Fresh grilled fish and a plate of hummus and warmed pita bread come to mind, but unlike just a few years ago, today you can also taste any nationality you desire—Italian, Indian, Chinese, Turkish, Indonesian, Hungarian—even American! And whereas previously, "kosher" meant unvaried, today kosher restaurants have to compete with a growing number of nonkosher restaurants (that serve seafood and milk and meat together), and thus the variety is becoming larger all the time. Moreover, with street stalls and ice cream stores all over the place, you can be sure you won't go hungry in Israel.

In the hotels, the day begins with a huge buffet-style breakfast that includes a variety of breads and rolls, eggs, oatmeal, excellent yogurt, cheeses, vegetable and fish salads, and Western-style breakfast foods like cornflakes and granola. Every city and small town has modestly priced soup-salad-and-grilled-meat restaurants that open in mid-morning. Many restaurants offer business-lunch specials or fixed-price menus, but à la carte menus are most common. A service charge (*sherut* in Hebrew) of 10%–15% is sometimes charged and should be noted separately on your bill.

Israelis like Western-style fast food such as hamburgers and pizza, but more traditional favorites are falafel served with salad and condiments in a pita pocket, *shwarma* (grilled meat), cheese, and *borekas* (phyllo-dough turnovers with spinach or potato filling). Many falafel stands have salad bars at which you can fill the pita yourself. Supermarkets, particularly in the large cities, have long, eclectic counters of take-out food—everything from fried eggplant to chocolate croissants.

Lodging

Nearly all hotel rooms in Israel have private bathrooms with a combined shower/tub. A buffet breakfast is almost always included in the room rate. You can expect a swimming pool, a health club, and tennis courts in the best hotels; with rare exceptions in the major cities, all hotels have parking facilities. Although the government star ratings of hotels have officially been abolished, people still talk of "five-star hotels" as the top category of hotel.

Suites In recent years, there have been several new trends in hotels. The first is toward suites, now common in Eilat as well as in some of the cities; these often provide fully equipped kitchens.

Bed-and-Breakfasts The second new trend is the opening of B&B accommodations at many of the country's kibbutzim. Typically, a tourist can rent a simple room and eat meals in the kibbutz dining room. Most kibbutzim have large lawns, swimming pools, and athletic facilities, and offer lectures and tours of the settlement. Private home owners are also increasingly opening their doors to guests.

Kibbutz Guest Houses Kibbutz guest houses, which have been a popular lodging in Israel for years, are similar to motels; guests are taken in as a source of extra income for the kibbutz and are not involved in its social life. Unlike motels, though, these offer rustic, quiet settings, and usually have swimming pools and athletic activities. For more information, contact **Kibbutz Hotels** (90 Ben Yehuda St., Box 3193, Tel Aviv 61031, Israel, tel. 03/524–6161; 60 E. 42nd St., Suite 620, New York, NY 10165, tel. 212/697–5116; Israel Hotel Reservation Center Inc., 20 S. Van Brunt St., Englewood, NJ 07631, tel. 201/816–0830 or 800/522–6401).

Holiday Villages Holiday villages can range from the near primitive to quite luxurious. Commonly they offer simple facilities, usually sleeping from four to six persons in a unit, with basic cooking facilities in each unit. Some villages have full kitchens and even televisions. Most holiday villages have a grocery store on the grounds. The rooms vary from huts and trailers to little houses. Such villages, often located near beaches or in resort areas, are relatively inexpensive.

Home Exchange You can find a house, apartment, or other vacation property to exchange for your own by becoming a member of a home-exchange organization, which then sends you its annual directories listing available exchanges and includes your own listing in at least one of them. Arrangements for the actual exchange are made by the two parties to it, not by the organization. For more information about the process contact the **International Home Exchange Association** (IHEA, 41 Sutter St., Suite 1090, San Francisco, CA 94104, tel. 415/673–0347 or 800/788–2489). Among the principal clearinghouses are **HomeLink International** (Box 650, Key West, FL 33041, tel. 305/294–3720 or 800/638–3841), with thousands of foreign and domestic listings, which has four annual directories plus updates (the $50 membership includes your listing in one book); **Intervac International** (Box 590504, San Francisco, CA 94159, tel. 415/435–3497), with three annual directories ($62 membership, or $72 to receive directories but remain unlisted); and **Loan-a-Home** (2 Park La., Apt. 6E, Mount Vernon, NY 10552, tel. 914/664–7640), which specializes in long-term exchanges (no charge to list your home, but directories cost $35 or $45 depending on the number you receive).

Apartment and Villa Rentals If you want a home base that's roomy enough for a family and comes with cooking facilities, a furnished rental may be the solution. It's generally cost-wise, too, although not always—some rentals are luxury properties (economical only when your party is large). Home-exchange directories do list rentals—often second homes owned by prospective house swappers—and some services search for a house or apartment for you (even a castle if that's your fancy) and handle the paperwork. Some send an illustrated catalogue and others send photographs of specific properties, sometimes at a charge; up-front registration fees may apply.

Among the companies are **Europa-Let** (92 N. Main St., Ashland, Oregon 97520, tel. 503/482–5806 or 800/462–4486) and **Property Rentals International** (1008 Mansfield Crossing Rd., Richmond, VA 23236, tel. 804/378–6054 or 800/220–3332).

Christian Hospices Christian hospices, located mainly in Jerusalem and the Galilee, provide lodging and sometimes meals. Some are real bargains, others merely reasonable, and their facilities range from spare to luxurious. Preference is given to pilgrimage groups, but when space is available, almost all will accept secular tourists. A full listing of hospices is available from the IGTO.

Youth Hostels Youth hostels in Israel have improved in recent years. Many of the 31 hostels in Israel provide family rooms with private baths. Some are air-conditioned, some have communal cooking facilities, and all provide meals. It is worthwhile to come equipped with a valid HI (Hostelling International, formerly the International Youth Hostel Association) membership card—otherwise, the attractive modern hostels charge guest house prices. The **Israel Youth Hostel Association** (3 Dorot Rishonim St., Jerusalem, tel. 02/252706, fax 02/250676; 36 Bnei Dan, Tel Aviv, tel. 03/546–0719 or 03/544–1748, fax 03/5441030) features several bargain travel packages.

Credit Cards

The following credit card abbreviations are used: AE, American Express; DC, Diners Club; D, Discover; MC, MasterCard; V, Visa.

Traveling in Egypt

Just across the border from Israel's southernmost town, Eilat, is the Sinai desert, which Moses and the Children of Israel crossed en route from Egypt to the Promised Land. The return trip today is considerably less arduous—the chosen means of travel being an airplane or sightseeing bus—and the Sinai Peninsula offers much to do and see: visits to Mt. Sinai and the Monastery of St. Catherine, which houses Byzantine art treasures; snorkeling in the Red Sea; jeep and hiking trips through canyons and wadis, a stark and majestic desert landscape. From the peninsula, if you have a week or more, you may wish to venture farther into Egypt to visit Cairo and environs, or travel 645 kilometers (400 miles) south to the Valley of the Kings (and Queens), or sail down the Nile on a *felucca* (riverboat). Costs are surprisingly low.

Essential Information

Important Addresses and Numbers

Tourist Information Headquarters of the **Egyptian Government Tourist Information Office** are in Cairo (Adly St., tel. 02/391–3454). Branches are in Cairo on Pyramids Road (tel. 02/385–0259) and at the airport (Terminal 1, tel. 02/667475), and in Alexandria at the Marine Passenger Station (tel. 03/492–5986) and on Saad Zaghloul Street (tel. 03/807985).

Consulates in Israel Egyptian consulates are in north Tel Aviv (54 Basle St., tel. 03/546–4151 or 03/546–4152) and Eilat (68 Avrony St., tel. 07/376882).

Embassies and Consulates in Egypt **Canada:** The embassy is in Cairo (6 Mohamed Fahmy-el-Sayed St., Garden City, tel. 02/354–3110 or 02/354–3119, fax 02/356–3548); or write Box 2646, Kafr-el-Doubara Post Office, Cairo.

United Kingdom: The embassy is in Cairo (7 Ahmed Ragheb St., Garden City, tel. 02/354–0850), and the Consulate General is in Alexandria (3 Mina St., Kafre Abdou, Roushdi, 21529, tel. 03/546–7001).

United States: The embassy is in Cairo (8 Salah-El-Din St., Garden City, tel. 02/355–7371), and the Consulate General is in Alexandria (110 El Hourri Ave., Unit 6490400, tel. 03/482–1911, fax 03/483–8830).

Passports and Visas Valid passports are required of both children and adults. If a child shares his or her parent's passport, the parent cannot enter Egypt without the child, even for a one-day visit. You need an Egyptian visa if you're staying in Sinai longer than 14 days or if you are going farther into Egypt for *any* length of time. Passports and passport-type photos are required, and visas can be issued on the spot by Egyptian consulates, or, more conveniently, for a fee of about $5, through tour operators (*see* Tours and Packages, *below*).

Border Crossings The two crossing points between Israel and Egypt are at **Taba,** just south of Eilat, and at **Rafiah,** near the Mediterranean coast. Crossing the border either way can take anywhere from five minutes to five hours—five minutes if you are crossing alone, the more usual two hours, or more, if you encounter traffic or delays.

At the Rafiah border you will pay a $25 exit tax to leave Israel and a $5 entrance tax to enter Egypt. At the Taba crossing the taxes are $15 to leave Israel and $8 to enter Egypt. You are exempt from the taxes if you are going only to the Taba Hilton, in Sinai.

Currency Travelers are asked to declare cash and traveler's checks at the border. The unit of currency in Egypt is the Egyptian pound (LE), which is divided into 100 piasters and can be written as LE 1 or LE 1.000 or 100 pt. (piasters). Foreign currency must be exchanged for Egyptian currency at an Egyptian bank (keep your receipts). At press time (fall 1994), the exchange rate was LE 3.35 to the U.S. dollar, LE 5.16 to the pound sterling, and LE 2.70 to the Canadian dollar. Israeli shekels are not valid currency in Egypt and cannot be exchanged there.

Getting There

If you rent a car in Israel, you won't be allowed to drive it into Egypt. Shared taxis are not very comfortable, safe, or affordable. The best way to Egypt from Israel is by plane or bus. Check and recheck departure times, and always arrive early.

By Plane The one-hour-and-20-minute flight between Tel Aviv and Cairo can be made by **El Al** (32 Ben Yehuda St., Tel Aviv, tel. 03/514–1222; 12

Hillel St., Jerusalem, tel. 02/256934 or 02/254330) or **Air Sinai** (Migdalor Bldg., 1 Ben Yehuda, 13th Floor, tel. 03/510–2481). Both charge $136 one-way, $272 round-trip, plus an $11 airport tax.

El Al service to Cairo is on Sunday, Tuesday, and Thursday—ostensibly at 8 PM, although flights may leave as much as an hour earlier or later. Air Sinai flies to Cairo on Sunday, Monday, and Wednesday at 10:15 AM and on Friday at 9:45 AM.

By Bus   Several old, established travel companies operate regular air-condi-
To Cairo   tioned bus service on the 12-hour route from Tel Aviv and Jerusalem to Cairo, stopping at points in between; purchase tickets in person the day before departure at their offices (less than $25 one-way, about $35 round-trip), and be ready to leave at least 45 minutes before scheduled departure. On these buses, English-speaking Israelis accompany you to the border to ensure a smooth crossing, and Egyptian escorts join you for the trip through Sinai to Cairo. During a half-hour stop about an hour out of Tel Aviv you can have a snack, buy provisions for the trip ahead, and visit the rest rooms. Later, after crossing the border, you travel in an Egyptian bus, with one security vehicle in front and one to the rear—a measure mandated by Egyptian authorities.

Operators include **Galilee Tours** (42 Ben Yehuda St., Tel Aviv, tel. 03/546–6333; 3 Hillel St., Jerusalem, tel. 02/258866 or 02/252806, fax 02/231303; Hotel Neptune, Eilat, tel. 07/335141, fax 07/376001), **Mazada Tours** (141 Ibn Gvirol St., Tel Aviv, tel. 03/544454; 24 Ben Sira St., Jerusalem, tel. 02/255453, fax 02/255454; Paulus VI St., Nazareth, tel. 06/565937; Sheraton Hotel, Cairo, tel. 2/348600), and **Nitza,** a subsidiary of the national bus company, Egged (15 Frishman St., Tel Aviv, tel. 03/523–1502 or 03/523–1723; Central Bus Station, 224 Jaffa Rd., Jerusalem, tel. 02/304880). Egged operates a somewhat speedier trip, with a guard on board, several days a week between Cairo and Tel Aviv (Bus 100). Egged offices can also book Nitza tours. In addition, **Johnny Desert Tours** (Shalom Center, near airport, tel. 07/376777 or 07/372608) operates a 5½-hour trip from Taba to Cairo from October through mid-May.

To Sinai   **Mazada Tours** (*see above*) has service from Tel Aviv to Sinai. From Eilat you can catch Egged Bus 15 every half-hour from the Central Bus Station; at Taba you will switch to an Egyptian bus, which leaves for Nuweiba, Dahab, and Sharm el-Sheikh at 6 AM, 10 AM, and 3 PM daily, Middle Eastern Time (that is, not always punctual).

Tours and Packages

Even if you have only one day, an organized tour is the quickest way to see the most sites. From Israel, trips to Egypt are available in every length and description, from daylong forays across the border to weeklong journeys to Cairo and longer explorations. You can book them on the spot. Prices vary widely, and breakfasts are usually included.

Operators include those listed above as well as **El Al Egypt Services** (44 Hayarkon St., Tel Aviv, tel. 03/662443, fax 03/660359; represented in Eilat by Tour Eilat, Khan Center, tel. 07/334706, fax 07/371057); **Neot Hakikar** (78 Ben Yehuda St., Tel Aviv, tel. 03/522–8161, fax 03/522–1020; 36 Keren Hayesod, Jerusalem, tel. 02/636494; Etzion Hotel, Eilat, tel. 07/371329, fax 07/375284); and an adventure-travel specialist, the **SPNI** (3 Hashfela St., Tel Aviv, tel. 03/537–4425 or 03/375063, fax 03/383940 or 03/377695; 13 Helene Hamalka St., Jerusalem, tel. 02/252357 or 02/244605).

Dive Trips At Coral Beach on the Eilat–Taba road, several diving clubs offer diving safaris to some of the world's most spectacular reefs, on the Red Sea coast and to Sharm el Sheikh. Try **Aqua Sport** (Box 300, Coral Beach 88102, tel. 07/334404, fax 07/333771), the **Dolphin Reef Diving Center** (Box 104, Southern Beach, tel. 07/375935, fax 07/375921), and the **Red Sea Sports Club** (Kings Wharf, the Lagoon, Eilat, tel. 07/379685 or 07/376569, fax 07/373702). *Fantasea II* (Box 234, Hofit 40295, tel. 053/663555, fax 053/663262) provides luxury diving and water-sports yacht cruises in the Red Sea.

Traveling to Other Arab Countries

The long-awaited peace treaty between Israel and Jordan was finally signed and autonomy was granted to the Palestinians of the Gaza Strip in 1994. Relations between Israel and the other Arab countries remain cordially difficult at best, however, but such advances in the peace process cannot but further the hope of amicable relations between Israel and its Arab neighbors.

Tourists can cross the Allenby Bridge (east of Jericho and north of Almog Junction, at the beginning of the Jordan Valley Road) into Jordan, and on to Syria or Lebanon from there. But first look into government travel advisories.

Customs officials of Arab countries other than Egypt may turn away a tourist who has a passport that indicates travel to Israel. If you plan to visit an Arab country, ask the Israeli official at the airport to stamp your entry on a separate card and not your passport (*see* Passports and Visas *in* Before You Go, *above*).

If you are entering Israel from Jordan via the Allenby Bridge, be prepared for prolonged questioning and detailed searches—though you may receive just a routine interrogation. It goes without saying that security is extremely tight. Everything from your toothpaste to your camera may be carefully scrutinized, and questionable items may be confiscated. You'll have to demonstrate that electric appliances actually work.

Great Itineraries

Highlights of the Holy Land

Jerusalem is a city in which history wraps its mantle around the present. Abraham brought Isaac to Mt. Moriah. King David made the city his capital, and his son, King Solomon, built the Holy Temple there. Conqueror after conqueror battled for this city, but Jerusalem transcends its martial past, and you'll be struck by its beauty and its spiritual quality.

As you wander on foot through some of the ethnic neighborhoods, notice how, even today, so many men and women of different beliefs cover their heads before God. In contrast, **Tel Aviv** is a new city, the fulfillment of modern pioneers who believed a metropolis could rise atop sand dunes. On Friday, Jerusalemites hurry in the streets to prepare for the Sabbath. But the city seems sleepy the rest of the time compared to fast-paced, modern Tel Aviv, home of fashion and industry. Tel Avivians boast that their city never sleeps.

Tiberias is a small city perched on the Sea of Galilee, a perfect base for seeing the Galilee and Golan.

By booking reservations in these three cities and relying on public transportation, you can see most of Israel in a short time and do a minimum of packing and unpacking.

Duration   Seven nights

Getting Around
By Car

Pick up a rental car at Ben Gurion Airport, and drive to Jerusalem. Leave Jerusalem from the main westbound exit, near the central bus station, and follow signs for Highway 1 into Tel Aviv. Leave Tel Aviv by the Ayalon Highway (Route 2), drive north along the coast, and turn east, just after Hadera (look for power station chimneys on your left), on Route 65, toward Afula to reach Tiberias.

By Bus

Buses leave the airport every half-hour for Jerusalem; buses from North Tel Aviv leave every 10 minutes or less. Buses also leave from many neighborhoods of the city early in the morning. There are frequent buses to Tiberias from the Central Bus Station in Tel Aviv.

The Main Route

Three nights: Old and New Jerusalem. Wear good walking shoes for Old City tours. Begin with a visit to the Tower of David Museum just inside Jaffa Gate in the Old City, which recounts the history of Jerusalem. Spend an evening at a folklore show. Have dinner at an ethnic restaurant. Local specialties are *kubeh* soup (a rich vegetable soup with semolina-stuffed meatballs inside), Jerusalem mixed grill, and hummus. Have coffee or onion soup on Ben Yehuda Street and enjoy the atmosphere of a street fair. For the fourth day, book a full-day tour to the Dead Sea and Masada with a tour company or a private guide. Return to Jerusalem for dinner.

Two nights: Tel Aviv. Frequent buses make the trip between Jerusalem and Tel Aviv in less than an hour. Improvised military vehicles from the War of Independence have been left as memorials to the days when the city was under siege. Further along, the bus passes through the Ayalon Valley, where, according to the biblical account, the sun stayed in the heavens for Joshua.

In Tel Aviv, make sure to window-shop on Dizengoff Street and visit the Diaspora Museum. Shop at the outdoor Carmel Market. Have dinner at a beachside restaurant, or eat authentic falafel. Catch local performers at a Jaffa nightclub or hear the Israel Philharmonic Orchestra at the Mann Auditorium.

Two nights: Tiberias. Around the Sea of Galilee on the first day, see the synagogue at Capernaum, the Hammat Gader hot springs in the remains of the Roman baths, Israel's oldest kibbutz and the Tabgha, said to be where Jesus multiplied the loaves and the fishes. Swim or go boating in the sea. Have dinner on the wharf; the local specialty is *tilapia*, also known as St. Peter's fish (*amnun* in Hebrew). On the second day, join a daylong excursion to Galilee and the Golan Heights to see the old Syrian bunkers, the Banias waterfall, ancient Gamla, the town of Katzrin, the Mt. Hermon ski resort and Nimrod's Castle. Return to Tiberias via Zfat, a city of mystics and artists, and take a nighttime cruise across the Sea of Galilee.

On the eighth and last day of the tour, return to the airport via Rosh Hanikra, the Good Fence, and Haifa. In Haifa, ride up to the top of Mt. Carmel for the view.

Information   *See* chapters 2, 4, and 6.

Action Tour

The weather is so good in Israel that outdoor adventure lovers can always find plenty to do. You can go diving in Eilat and skiing on Mt. Hermon in the same day (if you drive fast); the only limits are your energy and, sometimes, the heat. Drink a lot of fluids, and watch out for the sun. Israelis are great hikers. Trails are well marked, and you can add day hikes to any of the suggested activities below.

Duration 10 nights

Getting Around Pick up a rental car at Ben Gurion Airport and follow signs east to Jerusalem. You can park at one of the lots adjacent to the Old City.

Buses from the airport leave every half-hour; those from Tel Aviv to Jerusalem leave every 10 minutes.

The Main Route **Three nights: Jerusalem.** Park outside Jaffa Gate and walk along the walls of the Old City. Join a half-day walking tour through the archaeological tunnels under the Western Wall. Eat in an ethnic restaurant. Folk dance in Liberty Bell Park (Saturday night) or attend a folklore show. On a second day, visit key West Jerusalem sites including Yad Vashem, the Knesset, the Turgemon Post, the Chagall windows at Hadassah Hospital, the Biblical Zoo, and the Israel Museum. Return to the Old City for a moonlight tour.

On the third day, take a donkey ride or a vigorous walking tour through the Judean Hills. (Check with the SPNI for a schedule.) Visit a kibbutz (perhaps Kibbutz Tzora) and the Sorek Caves.

Two nights: Dead Sea area. Visit Masada (by way of the steep Snake Path if you're fit) and hike in the Ein Gedi Nature Reserve for the day, then stay overnight on the shore of the Dead Sea at a kibbutz guest house, a hotel at Ein Bokek, or at the SPNI field school at Ein Gedi. The next day, go cliff rappelling at Mitzukay Dragot, near Kibbutz Shalem. Soothe your skin in the local mud baths. Take a night jeep tour of the area.

Two nights: Eilat. Take a one-day camel tour into the breathtaking hills around Eilat; swim with the dolphins and snorkel at a superb coral beach. Take a self-driven jeep tour or go for a desert hike in the magnificent Red Canyon and in Ein Netifim.

One night: Tel Aviv. Rest up in Tel Aviv with a walk on the boardwalk. Rent a sailboat at the marina.

Two nights: Tiberias. You can hike and horseback ride in the Golan Heights, or, depending on the weather, ski on Mt. Hermon or take an inner-tube or kayak ride down the Jordan River. Try parasailing on the Sea of Galilee.

Information *See* chapters 2, 3, 4, 6, and 8.

Archaeology Tour

Israel is an archaeology lover's dream, with a wide variety of fascinating sites within a small geographical area. Visitors may want to consider joining a dig for part of the time. Most prehistoric sites are in the Lower Galilee and the northern coast, and Jerusalem is a treasure trove of ancient sites from all periods of history. Following the archaeologists' trails will take you around most of the country.

Duration Seven nights

Getting Around Except in Jerusalem, it's best to rent a car to reach most of the archaeological sites.

Buses will get you everywhere, but plan carefully to make sure you have return transportation.

The Main Route **Four nights: Jerusalem with day trips.** Plan on at least two days in the Old City and two days in museums. Some essential sites for archaeology buffs in Jerusalem are the City of David, the Southern Wall excavations, St. Anne's Church, the Pools of Bethesda, the Jewish Quarter, the Herodian Mansions, the Broad Wall, and the Cardo, which are all grouped together; also the Tower of David Museum, the Israel Museum (where the Dead Sea Scrolls are displayed, as well as countless other ancient artifacts), and the Bible Lands Museum. Be sure to have dinner at the Culinaria (Jewish Quarter, Old City, tel. 02/894155), a restaurant modeled after a dining establishment of 2,000 years ago and run by archaeologists.

Make a day trip to the Qumran caves, where the Dead Sea Scrolls were found; the Chalcolithic temple at Ein Gedi; and the great desert fortress at Masada (where the sound and light program makes a perfect evening). On remaining days, visit the Ein Yael Roman village outside Jerusalem, the Beit Guvrin Caves, and the Hazan Caves near Ashkelon.

Two nights: Tiberias. Travel along the Jordan Valley to Beit Shean via the Crusader castle Belvoir and Hammat Gader, with its excavated Roman baths, hot springs, and pools. Leave time to bathe in the hot pools and visit the site's alligator farm. Travel to the Golan Heights town of Katzrin to visit its small but fascinating museum.

One night: Nahariya. See the mosaics in the church at Givat Katznelson, the Crusader City in Akko, and the ancient city of Megiddo, described in James Michener's *The Source*. Stay either in the resort town of Nahariya or in a coastal kibbutz guest house.

On the final day, visit a cluster of sites in the Western Galilee and along the northern coast: Bet She'arim, with its Jewish catacombs dating from the AD 2nd–4th centuries; the healing center and baths at Shuni, near Zichron Yaakov; and the Roman city and port of Caesarea.

If you have two extra days, head south to the Negev to see the biblical city at Tel Beersheba and the ancient copper works of Timna Valley, north of Eilat.

Information *See* chapters 2, 3, 5, 6, and 8.

Israel at a Glance: A Chronology

By Mike Rogoff

As the only land bridge between Africa and Asia, Israel has been a thoroughfare and battlefield through the ages. Its position between the desert and the Mediterranean Sea has determined not only its climate and economy but contributed to its vulnerability.

The country was once called Canaan, then the Land of Israel (in Hebrew, Eretz Yisra'el), then Israel. Later, the name Israel came to represent just the Northern Israelite kingdom, including Samaria and Galilee, while the southern kingdom was called Judah. Judah became the Greek "Judea," first applying only to a small part of the country centered around Jerusalem and later to a much larger territory. After the Bar-Kochba Revolt (AD 2nd century), the Roman emperor Hadrian changed the name Judea to Palaestina (after the long-gone Philistines) in order to dissociate the country from its

Jewish identity. Palestine later became the name of this tiny district in the huge medieval Muslim empires. To Christians it was always the Holy Land; to Jews, Eretz Yisra'el. The use of the name Israel in the following chronology does not always imply any specific set of borders, past or present, but the country as a whole, the ancient Land of Israel.

c. 1.2 million years ago   Earliest known human habitation in Israel (Lower Paleolithic period), at Ubeidiya in Jordan Valley.

c. 7800   The establishment of Jericho (Neolithic Pre-Pottery Period), the oldest walled town ever found.

Canaanite Period (Bronze Age), c. 3200 BC–1250 BC

c. 3200–2150   Writing is developed in Mesopotamia; beginning of recorded history. Major cities are built: Jerusalem, Megiddo, and Hazor.

c. 2150–1550   Age of the Patriarchs: Abraham, Isaac, and Jacob.

c. 1550–1250   Time of Hebrews' enslavement in Egypt. Decline of Egyptian power. Moses leads Hebrews in exodus from Egypt.

c. 1290   The Hebrews—the "Children of Israel"—receive the Torah (the "Law") at Mt. Sinai. The nation of Israel is formed, the basis of its religion established, and its relationship with one god defined. Forty years of desert wandering separate the nation from its Promised Land.

First Temple—Old Testament Period (Iron Age), c. 1250 BC–568 BC

c. 1250   Moses dies within sight of the Promised Land. Joshua leads the nation across the Jordan River and embarks on the conquest of Canaan, beginning with Jericho.

c. 1200–1025   Period of the Judges (e.g., Deborah, Gideon, Samson), charismatic regional leaders.

c. 1150   The Philistines invade from the west and establish a league of five city-states. Israelites appeal to the prophet Samuel for a king.

1025   Saul, of humble origin, first King of Israel.

1006   Saul and three sons, including Jonathan, are killed fighting the Philistines. David rules Judah.

1000   David conquers Jerusalem, a Jebusite enclave, and makes it the national capital of unified Israel. Having brought the sacred ark of the covenant to Jerusalem, he establishes the city as the new religious center.

968   Solomon becomes king, consolidates David's kingdom, and, in 950, builds the First Temple to the Lord in Jerusalem.

928   Division of the monarchy after death of Solomon. The Northern Tribes under Jeroboam break away to form the Kingdom of Israel. The Southern Tribes, now known as the Kingdom of Judah, with its capital at Jerusalem, are ruled by Rehoboam, Solomon's weak son.

c. 865   Ahab rules as King of Israel (871–851) and Jehosophat as King of Judah (867–843). Peace between the sister kingdoms. Ahab's wife, Jezebel, introduces pagan idol-worship.

721   Kingdom of Israel destroyed by the Assyrians (now the region's superpower), and exile of its population (the "Ten Lost Tribes"). Kingdom of Judah comes under the Assyrian yoke.

701 Hezekiah, King of Judah, revolts against Assyria. Assyrians lay siege to Jerusalem. With new fortifications, a superb water system, and inspiration of the prophet Isaiah, the city withstands the siege.

609 Josiah, last great king of Judah (640–609) and important religious reformer, is killed trying to block Egyptian advance. Jeremiah prophesies national catastrophe.

586 Assyrians defeated by new power, the Babylonians, whose king, Nebuchadnezzar, conquers Judah and destroys Jerusalem and the First Temple. Of those that survive, large numbers are exiled to the "rivers of Babylon."

Second Temple Period, 538 BC–AD 70

Although the Babylonians are defeated during this period and the Temple in Jerusalem is rebuilt and the sacrificial rites restored, the Land of Israel must share its preeminence with important Jewish centers in Babylon, Egypt, and elsewhere. From the 3rd century BC on, deep divisions appear within the Jewish nation over theological issues and seductive Hellenistic culture, introduced to the region by Alexander the Great. The Sadducee party, which draws its strength from the upper classes, takes a literal, Bible-based view and is willing to accommodate elements of Hellenism. The Pharisees, a party of the common people, add "Oral Law" (rabbinic interpretation) to the authority of the Bible. They reject accommodation with the pagan world and give rise to spin-off groups like the ascetic Essenes and militant Zealots.

538 Cyrus, King of Persia, conquers Babylon and allows the Jewish exiles to return home. In Jerusalem, the returnees rebuild the Temple (completed ca. 516). In Babylon, the synagogue, a communal place of assembly with an emphasis on the reading of the Bible and (eventually) on prayer, develops.

445 Nehemiah, a Jewish nobleman, is sent by the Persian king with authority to rebuild Jerusalem's walls and rule the district.

333 Persian Empire is defeated by Alexander the Great, and all the Near East comes under Hellenistic sway.

323 Death of Alexander and struggle for control of his empire. Ptolemy rules in Egypt, Seleucus in Syria and Mesopotamia.

301 Ptolemy establishes control over Judea (as Judah is now called) and Samaria (an area once known as Israel) to the north of it. Egypt's now Greek-speaking Jewish population burgeons. The Bible is translated into Greek and called the *Septuagint*.

198 The Syrian Seleucids defeat the Egyptian Ptolemies at Banias, the headwaters of the Jordan, annex Judea, and establish good relations with the Jewish community.

167 The Seleucid king Antiochus IV outlaws all Jewish religious practices. Beginning of the Maccabean Revolt.

165 After four decisive victories over Hellenistic armies, Judah the Maccabee (Judas Maccabeus) enters the desecrated Temple in Jerusalem, purifying and rededicating it.

142 Simon achieves independence for Judea and establishes the Hasmonean dynasty.

63   Pompey, the Roman general, enters the country to settle a civil war between the last Hasmonean princes and annexes it as a Roman province.

48   The influential royal counselor Antipater, a Jewish convert, appoints his sons, among them Herod, to key administrative positions.

40   Mark Antony appoints Herod King of the Jews.

37   After fighting his way through the country, Herod claims his throne in Jerusalem. Hated by the Jews, he seeks to legitimize his reign by marrying a Hasmonean princess (whom he later murders).

31   Antony is defeated by Octavian, now the emperor Caesar Augustus. Herod pays homage to Augustus in Rome and is confirmed in his titles and territories, then rebuilds the Second Temple in Jerusalem on a grand scale, winning great esteem.

c. 5   Birth of Jesus in Bethlehem.

4   Death of Herod, called by history "the Great." His kingdom is divided among three sons: Archelaus rules in Jerusalem (and is exiled 10 years later, replaced by direct Roman rule of Judea by procurators based in Caesarea); Herod Antipas rules the Galilee and Perea, east of the Jordan River; and Philip controls Golan, Bashan, and the sources of the Jordan River.

AD c. 27   Beginning of Jesus's Galilean ministry. He calls the disciples, heals and performs miracles, teaches and preaches, mostly around the Sea of Galilee.

c. 29   Jesus and his disciples celebrate Passover in Jerusalem. Arrest, trial, and crucifixion of Jesus by the Romans on orders of the Roman governor, Pontius Pilate. For the Romans, the claim of Messiah ("the anointed one"), with its implication of kingship, is tantamount to high treason. The New Testament relates that Jesus' death and resurrection were divinely determined, an expiation for the sins of humanity. Identification with this event as the way to personal salvation becomes the basis for the community of faith that is Christianity.

66   Start of Great Revolt against Roman oppression. Jews briefly reassert their political independence.

67   Galilee falls to the Romans. The Jewish commander defects to the enemy. Romanizing his name to Josephus Flavius, he follows the Roman campaigns, eventually recording them in *The Jewish War*.

69   Before the fall of Jerusalem, the sage Yochanan Ben Zakkai leaves the city, settling with his disciples in the town of Yavneh in the coastal plain, by grant of Roman general and caesar-elect Vespasian.

70   Jerusalem, torn by internal factional fighting, falls to the Roman general Titus after long siege. The Second Temple is destroyed. Slaughter and slavery of the Jews follow. The revolt is officially at an end.

73   The last Jewish stronghold, at Masada, falls. Its defenders take their own lives rather than surrender. With the destruction of Jerusalem and the Temple, Yavneh becomes the seat of the Sanhedrin, the Jewish High Court. Its sages find religious responses to the new reality of Judaism without the Temple, and the spiritual and legal authority of Yavneh is established.

Late Roman and Byzantine Period, AD 73–AD 640

132 When the Roman emperor Hadrian threatens to rebuild Jerusalem as a pagan city, another Jewish revolt breaks out, led by Bar-Kochba and supported by Rabbi Akiva. Secret preparations and a strong unified command lead to spectacular initial successes.

135 Death of Bar Kochba. The revolt is brutally suppressed, but only after severe Roman losses. Hadrian plows over Jerusalem and builds Aelia Capitolina, a pagan city off limits to Jews, changes the name of the country to Palaestina, and outlaws Jewish religious practice. The Sanhedrin relocates to the Lower Galilee.

c. 200 At Bet She'arim, Judah the "Nasi" (Patriarch), spiritual and political head of the Jewish community, compiles the Mishnah, the summary of the "Oral Law," the basis of Jewish jurisprudence. Period of peace and prosperity under the tolerant Severan emperors.

313 Emperor Constantine the Great legalizes Christianity and eventually converts to the faith. His mother, Helena, comes to the Holy Land in 326 and initiates the building of major churches—the Holy Sepulcher in Jerusalem and the Nativity in Bethlehem.

330 Constantine transfers his capital from Rome to Byzantium, now renamed Constantinople. Beginning of the Byzantine Period. Judaism on the defensive.

351 Jewish revolt, primarily in the Galilee, against the Roman ruler Gallus, is brutally suppressed.

361 Emperor Julian the Apostate (r. 361–363) tries to reintroduce pagan cults.

c. 400 Final codification of the so-called Jerusalem Talmud, comprising 150 years of rabbinic elaboration of the Mishnah. (The Babylonian Talmud, codified a century later, is regarded as more authoritative.)

527–565 Reign of Emperor Justinian. Many important churches built or rebuilt, among them the present Church of the Nativity in Bethlehem. Vibrant Jewish community despite persecution.

614 Persian invasion, with destruction of churches and monasteries.

622 Mohammed's "flight" (*hejira*) from Mecca to Medina in Arabia; beginnings of Islam.

628 Persians defeated and Byzantine rule restored in Israel.

632 Death of Mohammed. His followers, ruled by a series of caliphs, burst out of Arabia and create a Muslim empire that within a century would extend from India to Spain.

636 Arab invasion of the country, and, in 638, fall of Byzantine Jerusalem to the Caliph Omar (ruled 634–644).

Medieval Period, AD 640–AD 1516

691 Caliph Abd al-Malik builds the Dome of the Rock in Jerusalem.

1099 Sworn to wrest Christian holy places from Muslim control, the European armies of the First Crusade reach the Holy Land. Jerusalem is taken and most of its population, Muslim and Jew alike, is massacred.

1100 Establishment of the Latin Kingdom of Jerusalem, with Baldwin I at its head. Chronic shortage of manpower puts the burden of defense on the monastic orders (Hospitallers, Templars, etc.), who build castles (among them Belvoir and the underground quarter in Akko).

1110   Most coastal cities in Crusader hands.

1187   Crusader armies decimated by the Arab ruler Saladin. Crusaders expelled from the country.

1191   The Third Crusade arrives, led by Richard the Lionheart of England and Philip II (Augustus) of France. The Latin Kingdom of Jerusalem never regains its former size and glory—or indeed the Holy City itself—and the Crusaders content themselves with the coast from Tyre to Jaffa and later with the Galilee. Akko becomes royal capital.

1228   Jerusalem is gained by treaty but lost again in 1244.

1250   The militant Mamluk class seizes power in Egypt. The Crusade of King Louis IX (St. Louis) against Egypt fails. He is captured, but later comes to Holy Land and remains.

1260   The Mamluks check the Mongol invasion at Ayn Jalout (Ein Harod) in the Jezreel Valley.

1265   Muslim reconquest of the land begins under the Mamluk sultan Baybars.

1291   Fall of Akko and end of Crusader kingdom. Commerce and trade decline with destruction of coastal cities. Beginning of period of outstanding architecture, especially in Jerusalem's Temple Mount (Haram esh-Sharif) and Muslim Quarter, and in the Cave of Machphelah in Hebron.

1492   Expulsion of the Jewish community from Spain. Many of these Sephardic Jews later immigrate to Israel.

The Modern Period, 1516–1948

1516   Mamluk armies defeated in Syria by the Ottoman Turks, who extend control over the land of Israel (Palestine) as well. Jewish community throughout the country grows. Safed (Zfat) center of Kabalah.

1520–1566   Suleiman the Magnificent reigns. His many projects include rebuilding Jerusalem's walls.

1700   Large numbers of Ashkenazi (Eastern European) Jews arrive.

1799   Invasion by Napoléon Bonaparte founders at Akko.

1832   Egyptian nationalists under Muhammed Ali and Ibrahim Pasha take control of Israel. They are expelled in 1840 with the help of European nations.

1853   The Crimean War breaks out in Europe against the background of conflict between Catholic France and Orthodox Russia over the custody of holy places in Israel.

1882   First Aliyah (wave of Jewish immigration), mostly idealistic Eastern Europeans. Baron Edmond de Rothschild establishes new villages and wineries in the coastal plain and the Galilee.

1897   First World Zionist Conference, organized by Theodore Herzl in Basel, Switzerland, gives great impetus to the idea of a "Jewish national home."

1906 The Second Aliyah of young Jewish idealists from Russia and Poland, including David Ben Gurion, later Israel's first prime minister.

1909 Tel Aviv founded. Degania, the first kibbutz, established on the southern shore of the Sea of Galilee.

1917 British government issues Balfour Declaration expressing support for a "Jewish national home" in Palestine. General Edmund Allenby captures Jerusalem.

1918 Ottoman Turkey, which had sided with Germany during World War I, abandons Palestine.

1920–1939 As Arab nationalism rises in the post-Ottoman Middle East, tension increases between Jews and Arabs in Palestine, peaking in the massacres of Jews in 1920, 1929, and 1936. Jewish militia form to counter the violence. Substantial immigration of European Jews with growing urgency, as Nazis take power in Germany.

1921 Transjordan is separated from Palestine.

1922 The newly formed League of Nations confirms the "Mandate" entrusting the rule of Palestine to Great Britain and incorporating the text of the Balfour Declaration.

1939 British Government issues White Paper restricting Jewish immigration to Israel and Jewish purchase of land there in an attempt to secure Arab good will in the coming war. In World War II, Jews enlist on Allied side. "We shall fight the war as if there were no White Paper," said Palestinian Jewish leader David Ben Gurion, "but we shall fight the White Paper as if there were no war."

1945 When British policy does not change, underground movements challenge British authority. Illegal immigrants, many of them Holocaust survivors, brought in on ships; many don't get through British blockade. Clashes with Arabs increase.

1947 United Nations special commission on Palestine recommends plan to partition the country into a Jewish and an Arab state (three disconnected territorial segments in each), and the internationalization of Jerusalem and Bethlehem. Jewish euphoria, Arab rejection. Beginning of Israel's War of Independence. Discovery of the first Dead Sea Scrolls at Qumran.

1948 May 14: Last British forces depart, ending British Mandate. David Ben Gurion declares Israel an independent state. The new state survives invasion by the armies of seven Arab countries.

1949 End of fighting in January. UN-supervised cease-fire agreements signed. Transjordan annexes the West Bank (of the Jordan River) and East Jerusalem, which it captured in the war. Egypt annexes the Gaza Strip along the southern Mediterranean coast. Palestinian Arabs who fled during the conflict are housed in refugee camps in neighboring countries; those who remain behind become citizens of Israel. First elections to the Knesset, Israel's parliament. David Ben Gurion is elected first prime minister; Dr. Chaim Weizmann, first president.

1949–1952 Israel absorbs great numbers of Jewish refugees, trebling its Jewish population by the end of the decade.

1950 The Knesset enacts the Law of Return, giving any Jew the right to Israeli citizenship.

1956 Sinai War, in which British, French, and Israeli forces oppose Egyptian nationalization of the Suez Canal. *Fedayeen* terrorist attacks from Egyptian-controlled Gaza Strip become less frequent, but sporadic Syrian shelling of Israeli villages below the Golan Heights is a major security issue into the 1960s.

1964 Formation of the Palestine Liberation Organization (PLO). Seeks independent state for Palestinians and refuses to recognize the legitimacy of the state of Israel.

1967 June: Outbreak of Six Day War. Egypt, Jordan, and Syria are routed; Israel occupies the Sinai peninsula, Gaza Strip, West Bank, East Jerusalem and the Golan Heights and finds itself in control of almost 1 million Palestinian Arabs. Some Jewish settlements are established in the West Bank and Golan Heights.

1973 Egypt and Syria attack Israel on the holiest Jewish holiday, the Day of Atonement (hence, the Yom Kippur War). Israel beats off the invasion, but is sobered.

1974–1975 Signing of Disengagement Agreement on the Golan with Syria, Interim Agreement with Egypt.

1976 Dramatic Israeli commando raid frees Air France passengers taken hostage in Entebbe, Uganda, by Palestinian hijackers.

1977 Menachem Begin's Likud party comes to power in May, ending almost four decades of Labor domination of Israeli politics. Egyptian President Anwar Sadat visits Israel.

1978 Camp David Accords give direction to Egypt-Israel peace talks and produce guidelines for a solution to the Palestinian problem.

1979 Israel–Egypt peace agreement signed.

1980 Israeli prime minister Menachem Begin and Egyptian president Anwar Sadat share the Nobel Peace Prize.

1982 Israeli forces cross into southern Lebanon in pursuit of Palestinians shelling civilian settlements in Israel. This escalates into the Lebanon War (1982–85), with unprecedented opposition at home.

1987 A road accident in the Gaza Strip triggers the beginning of the intifada, sustained Palestinian Arab street violence, demonstrations, strikes, and sporadic terrorist activity.

1989–1992 Israel absorbs over 500,000 Soviet Jewish immigrants.

1991 Persian Gulf War; Israel under constant attack but restrained from retaliating. June: 14,500 Ethiopian Jews airlifted to Israel. December: Peace talks in Madrid between Israel and Jordan, Syria, Lebanon, and the Palestinians.

1992 In June the Labor Party under Yitzhak Rabin, vowing to step up the peace process and halt Israeli "political" settlements in West Bank, is voted in after 15 years out of office.

1993–1994 Israel and PLO recognize each other and agree on Palestinian autonomy in the Gaza Strip and Jericho.

2 Jerusalem

By Mike
Rogoff

Mike Rogoff,
a professional
tour guide
and writer,
has been
exploring and
studying the
byways of
Israel since
he moved
there from
South Africa
in 1970. He
has
contributed to
Fodor's Israel
since the 1985
edition.

"Unique" is one of the most overworked words in the travel industry, but Jerusalem makes a strong claim to be just that. A mountainous walled city with a 5,000-year history of continuous habitation, Jerusalem is holy to more than one-third of the world's population.

For Jews, Jerusalem has always been the focal point of devotion and spiritual yearnings and the psychic center of their nationhood. "The world is like a human eye," wrote a Jewish sage in the 1st century AD: "The white is the ocean that girds the earth, the iris is the earth upon which we dwell, the pupil is Jerusalem, and the image therein is the Temple of the Lord."

Christians have venerated Jerusalem for two millennia as the place where the most momentous events of their faith took place—the death, burial, and resurrection of Jesus of Nazareth. A famous Renaissance map shows the continents of Asia, Africa, and Europe as the leaves of a clover meeting in the Holy City, a reality at once spiritual, historical, and (almost) geographical.

Islamic tradition identifies Jerusalem as the *masjad el aksa*, the "furthermost place" from which Mohammed ascended to Heaven for his portentous meeting with God, making the city third in holiness to Muslims, after Mecca and Medina. A Muslim tradition claims that the great rock of Jerusalem's Mt. Moriah, site of the onetime Jewish Second Temple and present Dome of the Rock, is made of the stones of the Garden of Eden, and that on the Day of Judgment, "the holy Kaaba stone of Mecca will come to Jerusalem to be joined with it."

The first known mention of Jerusalem is in Egyptian "hate texts" of the 20th century BC, although recent archaeological evidence gives the city a founding date at least 1,000 years earlier. Many scholars identify Jerusalem with the Salem of Abraham's time (18th century BC). Joshua defeated the Amorite king of Jerusalem in the mid-13th century BC, but the Israelites were unable to retain possession of the city, and it was only King David, in 1000 BC, who took it again, made it his capital, and thus propelled it onto the center stage of history. His son Solomon built the Temple of the Lord, known as the First Temple, in Jerusalem, giving the city a preeminence it enjoyed until its destruction by the Babylonians in 586 BC.

Returning exiles at the end of the 6th century BC rebuilt the Temple—known now as the Second Temple—and began the slow process of revival. By the 2nd century BC, Jerusalem was again a vibrant Jewish capital, albeit with a good dose of Hellenistic cultural influence. Herod the Great (reigned 37 BC–4 BC) renovated the Second Temple on a magnificent scale and expanded the city into a cosmopolis of world renown. This was the Jerusalem Jesus knew, a city of monumental architecture, teeming—especially during the Jewish pilgrim festivals—with tens of thousands of visitors from elsewhere in the country and abroad. It was here that the Romans crucified Jesus (circa AD 29), and here, too, that the Great Jewish Revolt against the Roman overlords erupted, to end, in AD 70, with the total destruction (once again) of the city and the Temple.

The Roman emperor Hadrian redesigned Jerusalem as the pagan *polis* of Aelia Capitolina (AD 135), an urban plan that became the basis for the Old City of today. The Byzantines made it a Christian center with a massive wave of church building (4th–6th centuries AD), until the Arab conquest of AD 638 brought the holy city under Muslim sway. Except during the golden age of the Ummayad dynasty in the late 7th and early 8th centuries, Jerusalem was no more than a provincial town under the Muslim regimes of the early Middle Ages, until the Crusaders stormed it in 1099 and made it the capital of their Latin Kingdom. With the reconquest of Jerusalem by the Muslims, the city lapsed again into a languid provincialism for seven centuries under the Mamluk and Ottoman empires. The British conquest in 1917 brought the Holy City back into the world limelight, as rising rival nationalisms vied to possess it.

Jerusalem was divided by war in 1948, with Jordan annexing the smaller eastern sector (including the Old City), while the much larger western sector became the capital of the State of Israel. The Six Day War of 1967 reunited the city under Israeli rule, but the concept of an Arab "East" and Jewish "West" Jerusalem still remains, even though new Jewish neighborhoods in the northeast and southeast have made the distinction somewhat oversimplified today.

The focal point of any visit to Jerusalem is the walled Old City, a square kilometer of exotic sights, sounds, and smells, its air as thick with chanting as with charcoal smoke, the *souk* (market) redolent with the tang of tamarind and alive with the tinkle of trinkets. Its 40,000 inhabitants—Jewish, Christian, and Muslim—jostling in the cobblestone lanes all carry an air of ownership, at best merely tolerating the "intruders" from other quarters. Devout Jews in black and white scurry from their neighborhoods north and west of the Old City, through the Damascus Gate and the Muslim Quarter, toward the Western ("Wailing") Wall, a holy relic of the Second Temple enclosure. Arab women with baskets of fresh produce on their heads flow across the Western Wall plaza to the Dung Gate and the village of Silwan beyond it. It is not unusual to stand at the Western Wall, surrounded by the burble of devotions, and hear the piercing call of the muezzin above you, with the more distant bells of the Christian Quarter providing a counterpoint.

Step outside the Old City, and you will discover a vibrant, modern city of a half-million inhabitants—not as cosmopolitan as Tel Aviv, to be sure, but possessing a variety of good restaurants, concert halls, markets, and high-quality stores, and quaint neighborhoods that embody an earlier simplicity.

No matter how oblivious they are to the burden of the city's past or to the various grand designs for its future, contemporary Jerusalemites are not untouched by the subtle spirit that infuses the place. Even the irreverent Mark Twain, who visited Jerusalem in 1867, was moved to write: "The thoughts Jerusalem suggests are full of poetry, sublimity, and, more than all, dignity." He may have been a bit carried away, but watch the limestone buildings glow golden in the sunset, and the mystical hold the city has had on people's minds and hearts for millennia becomes almost tangible.

Essential Information

Important Addresses and Numbers

Tourist Information The **Government Tourist Information Office**, or GTIO, is at 24 King George St., tel. 02/754863, 02/754888, 02/754910, or 02/754912. There is a smaller office at the Jaffa Gate in the Old City, tel. 02/282295 or 02/282296. Both offices are open Sunday–Thursday 8:30–5 and Friday 8:30–1. (The Jaffa Gate office is open until 2.)

The **Christian Information Center** at Jaffa Gate, in the Old City (tel. 02/272692) is open daily 8:30–1 (closed Sunday and Christian holidays).

Consulates **United States Consulate-General:** 18 Agron Street, West Jerusalem, tel. 02/253288; 27 Nablus Road, East Jerusalem, (consular services) tel. 02/895118. **British Consulate-General:** Tower House, next to Street Andrew's Church, West Jerusalem, tel. 02/717724; Sheikh Jarrah, East Jerusalem, tel. 02/828281 or 02/828482. This consulate also serves citizens of Australia and New Zealand.

Car Rental **Avis,** 22 King David Street, tel. 02/249001; **Budget,** 8 King David Street, tel. 02/248991 or 02/248992; **Eldan,** in the King David Hotel, 23 King David Street, tel. 02/252151; **Europcar,** 8 King David Street, tel. 02/248464; **Hertz,** 18 King David Street, tel. 02/231351, and in the Hyatt Regency Hotel, 32 Lehi Street, tel. 02/815069; **Reliable,** 14 King David Street, tel. 02/248204 or 02/248205.

Taxis Twenty-four-hour service: **Hapalmach,** tel. 02/792333; **Rehavia,** tel. 02/254444, 02/254445, or 02/254446.

Emergencies **Police:** tel. 100 or 02/391111; **ambulance:** Magen David Adom (the Israeli version of the Red Cross), tel. 101 or 02/523133.

Hospital Emergency rooms in major hospitals are on duty 24 hours a day in
Emergency rotation. The duty list is published in the daily press. In an emergen-
Rooms cy, call Magen David Adom (tel. 101) to find out which hospital is on 24-hour duty that day. Be sure to take your passport with you. A fee will be charged. The major hospitals in Jerusalem are **Bikur Holim,** Strauss Street, tel. 02/701111; **Hadassah,** Ein Kerem, tel. 02/ 427427, emergency room tel. 02/776555, children's emergency room tel. 02/777215; **Hadassah,** Mt. Scopus, tel. 02/818111; **Sha'arei Tzedek,** Bayit Vegan, tel. 02/555111, emergency room tel. 02/ 555508.

Doctors **Magen David Adom** (7 Hamag Street, Romema, tel. 02/523133) is an emergency ambulance service. In the same building is the privately run, 24-hour **Terem Emergency Care Center** (Magen David Adom Bldg., 7 Hamag Street, Romema, tel. 02/521748) for first-aid and other medical attention. **Yad Sarah** (43 Hanevi'im Street, tel. 02/ 244242) is a voluntary organization that lends paramedical equipment (wheelchairs, crutches, walking sticks, etc.) in emergencies. It is open Sunday–Thursday 9–7, and Friday 9–noon.

Dentists The **Jerusalem Emergency Dental Center,** 7 Eliash Street, Rejwan Square (the plaza is above 16 King George Street), tel. 02/254779, is open 364 days a year (closed on Yom Kippur) 8 AM–midnight.

Late-Night The daily press publishes the addresses of pharmacies on duty at
Pharmacies night, on Saturday, and on holidays. This information is also available from Magen David Adom (tel. 02/523133). **Super-Pharm** (tel. 02/ 784139), at 5 Burla Street, Nayot, is open Sunday–Thursday 8:30– midnight, Friday 8:30–3, and Saturday 9 PM–midnight. Its downtown location (3 Hahistadrut Street, tel. 02/246249) closes at 11 PM.

Travel **American Express,** 40 Jaffa Road, tel. 02/231710 or 02/231908; **ISSTA**
Agencies (for students and academics), 31 Hanevi'im Street, tel. 02/257257; **Ziontours,** 23 Hillel Street, tel. 02/254326 or 02/254327.

Arriving and Departing by Plane

International Most visitors entering Israel fly into Ben Gurion International Air-
Flights port outside of Tel Aviv, 50 kilometers (31 miles) from Jerusalem.

Between the **Egged** Buses 423, 428, 945, and 947 to Jerusalem's Central Bus Sta-
Airport and tion run reasonably frequently (it's seldom more than 30 minutes'
Center City wait) except in the evenings, and cost NIS 12.70 ($4.25). There is no

Jerusalem *(Boxes Refer to Detail Maps)*

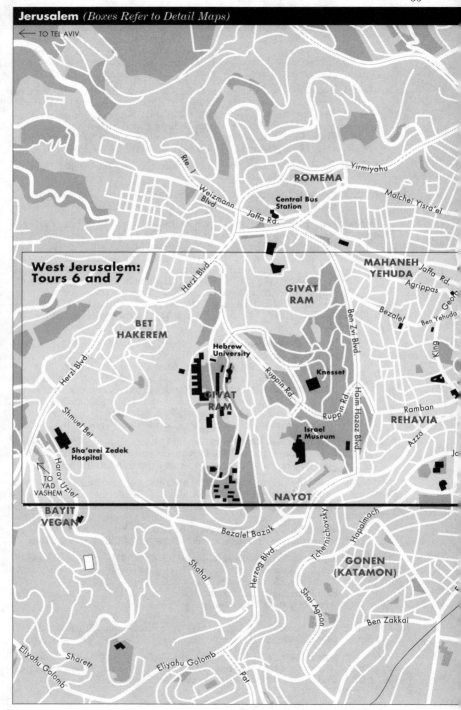

← TO TEL AVIV

Rte 1

Weizmann Blvd.

Jaffa Rd.

ROMEMA

Yirmiyahu

Malchei Yisra'el

Central Bus Station

West Jerusalem: Tours 6 and 7

Herzl Blvd.

GIVAT RAM

MAHANEH YEHUDA

Jaffa Rd.

Agrippas

Bezalel

Ben Yehuda

Ben Zvi Blvd.

BET HAKEREM

Hebrew University

Ruppin Rd.

Knesset

King Geor...

Herzl Blvd.

GIVAT RAM

Ruppin Rd.

Haim Hazaz Blvd.

Ramban

REHAVIA

Shmuel Bet

Israel Museum

Azza

Sha'arei Zedek Hospital

Jo...

Harav Uziel

TO YAD VASHEM

NAYOT

BAYIT VEGAN

Bezalel Bazak

Herzog Blvd.

Tchernichovsky

Hapalmach

GONEN (KATAMON)

Shahal

Shai Agnon

Ben Zakkai

Eliyahu Golomb

Sharett

Eliyahu Golomb

Pat

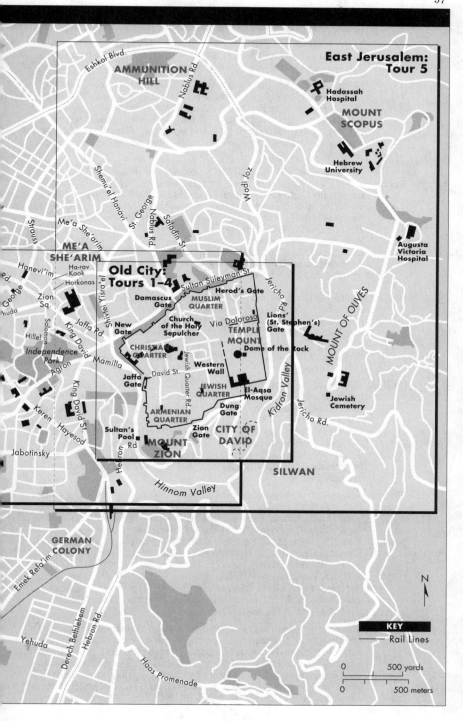

East Jerusalem: Tour 5

AMMUNITION HILL

Eshkol Blvd.

Nablus Rd.

Hadassah Hospital

MOUNT SCOPUS

Hebrew University

Shemu'el Hanavi St.

Me'a She'arim

St. George St.

Nablus Rd.

Saladin St.

Wadi Joz

Augusta Victoria Hospital

ME'A SHE'ARIM

Strauss

Hanevi'im

Ha-rav Kook

Horkonas

Zion Sq.

George

huda

Shivtei Yisra'el

Old City: Tours 1–4

Sultan Süleyman St.

Damascus Gate

MUSLIM QUARTER

Herod's Gate

Jericho Rd.

Lions' (St. Stephen's) Gate

MOUNT OF OLIVES

Jaffa Rd.

Hillel

King David Rd.

Mamilla

New Gate

Church of the Holy Sepulcher

Via Dolorosa

CHRISTIAN QUARTER

TEMPLE MOUNT

Dome of the Rock

Independence Park

Salomon

Agron

Jaffa Gate

David St.

Jewish Quarter Rd.

Western Wall

JEWISH QUARTER

El-Aqsa Mosque

Jewish Cemetery

Kidron Valley

Jericho Rd.

Keren

King David St.

Hayesod

ARMENIAN QUARTER

Dung Gate

CITY OF DAVID

Jabotinsky

Sultan's Pool Rd.

MOUNT ZION

Zion Gate

SILWAN

Hebron Rd.

Hinnom Valley

GERMAN COLONY

Emek Refa'im

Derech Bethlehem

Hebron Rd.

Yehuda

Haas Promenade

N

KEY

Rail Lines

0   500 yards

0   500 meters

bus service from Friday afternoon to Saturday night, or on religious holidays. For bus schedules call 03/537555.

The drive from the airport, on Route 1 east, takes about 35 minutes. A taxi should cost NIS 95 ($31.70), NIS 127 ($42.35) after 9 PM and on Saturday and holidays.

Seven-seat **sherut** taxis (limo-vans) depart when they fill up and drop passengers off at whatever address they request for NIS 26 ($8.70). To get from Ben Gurion Airport to Jerusalem by limousine, call **Nesher** (tel. 02/253233 or 02/231231) to book a place, preferably the day before. They will pick you up at any Jerusalem address. Nesher also makes the reverse trip; look for their stand outside the terminal.

Domestic Flights **Atarot Airport** (tel. 02/833440), 8 kilometers (5 miles) north of Jerusalem off the Ramallah road, services domestic flights only, specifically, daily flights to and from Eilat, Haifa, and Rosh Pina on Arkia, Israel's domestic carrier. Arkia runs a shuttle service geared to its flight schedule, costing NIS 7 ($2.35), between the airport and Arkia's downtown office (tel. 02/255888 or 02/255355) at the Clal Building, 97 Jaffa Road.

Arriving and Departing by Car, Bus, Sherut Taxi, and Train

By Car Route 1 is the chief route to the center of Jerusalem from both the west (Tel Aviv, Ben Gurion Airport, Mediterranean Coast) and the east (Galilee via Jordan Valley, Dead Sea area, Eilat). Route 1 becomes Jaffa Road, which runs into the city center. The road from Tel Aviv is a divided highway that presents no problems, except at morning rush hour (7:30–9), when traffic gets backed up at the entrance to the city.

By Bus The **Egged** National Bus Cooperative (tel. 02/304555) serves Jerusalem with comfortable air-conditioned buses from all major cities in Israel to the **Central Bus Station,** Jaffa Road. Egged buses in and out of Jerusalem stop service about a half-hour before sunset on Friday and religious holiday eves, and resume after dark on Saturday or at the end of religious holidays. The **East Jerusalem Bus Station,** on Sultan Suleiman Street, opposite Damascus Gate, is the terminus for private Arab-run lines serving West Bank towns such as Bethlehem and Hebron.

By Sherut Taxi Seven-seat taxis (stretch cabs or minivans) to share ply the same routes as the Egged buses to and from Tel Aviv, Haifa, and Beersheba and charge about the same fares (25% more on Saturday and holidays, when the buses do not run). **In Jerusalem: Habira** (1 Harav Kook St., near Zion Sq., tel. 02/232320) has routes to Tel Aviv; **Ha'ooma** (Ram Hotel, behind Central Bus Station, tel. 02/389999) goes to Tel Aviv; **Aviv/Kesher** (12 Shammai St., tel. 02/254034) goes to Haifa; **Yael Daroma** (12 Shammai St., tel. 02/256985) has routes to Beersheba and Eilat. Sheruts from Tel Aviv to Jerusalem congregate at the Tel Aviv Central Bus Station. Sheruts to Jerusalem from Haifa leave from the Hadar district.

By Train One rides the train between Tel Aviv and Jerusalem for the scenery and novelty of the experience, not for the convenience. There are only two trains a day in each direction, Sunday–Thursday at 8:45 AM and 3:05 PM, and Friday at 8:50 AM and 12:05 PM. The schedule is subject to change, so call ahead before setting out for the station. The trip takes twice as long as the bus, about 1¾ hours, and costs NIS 12 ($4) for adults, NIS 6 ($2) for children 4–10, NIS 8.50 ($2.85) for students

and senior citizens. The railway station in Jerusalem (David Remez
St., tel. 02/733764) is on several city bus routes (nos. 4, 7, and 8), and
you can normally hail a passing cab. The route ends at Tel Aviv Central
on Arlozorov Street, well served by taxis and numerous bus routes.

Getting Around

By Bus The **Egged** National Bus Cooperative enjoys a monopoly on bus lines
within Jerusalem. Routes within the city are extensive. Service
begins at 5:30 AM and ends around midnight (depending on the route).
There is no service from half an hour before sunset on Friday (or on the
eve of a religious holiday) until half an hour after sundown on Saturday.
The fare on all routes is NIS 2.80 (95¢); you do not need exact change.
There are no transfers. Buses do not automatically stop at every bus
stop; you should signal the driver to stop for you. Egged's local information service can be reached at tel. 02/304555. Bus maps are sometimes available at the Central Bus Station in West Jerusalem. Your
best bet is to get advice from your hotel or the locals.

The two small Arab-run bus stations in East Jerusalem primarily
serve routes to towns in the West Bank (*see* Essential Information *in*
Chapter 3, Around Jerusalem).

Egged's Bus 99 runs a loop that sets out from the small terminal on
Mamilla Road (off King David Street), and, in the opposite direction, from the Central Bus Station on Jaffa Road, and takes almost
two hours to complete. The route, which has 35 stops, includes a circuit of the Old City walls (including stops at Jaffa Gate, Damascus
Gate, and the Western Wall) and stops at Mt. Zion, the Israel Museum, the Knesset, Mt. Herzl, Yad Vashem, the Holyland Hotel (with
its model of Jerusalem during the Second Temple Period), the Promenade, Mt. Scopus, Mea She'arim, Ammunition Hill, Turjeman
Post, and several hotel districts. The route stops at sites that are
otherwise difficult to reach except by taxi, such as the Holyland Hotel. Buses leave Mamilla Road station Sunday–Thursday at 10,
noon, 2, and 4, and on Friday and holiday eves at 10 and noon only
and at the Central Bus Station at 11, 1, and 3. There is no service on
Saturday or religious holidays. The cost is NIS 8 ($2.70) for an unin-
terrupted journey, NIS 21 ($7) for a one-day ticket with unlimited
transfers on this route.

By Taxi Taxis can be flagged down on the street, ordered by phone, or picked
up at a taxi rank or at major hotels. There are usually taxis waiting
outside the Israel Museum and Yad Vashem. The law dictates that
taxi drivers must operate their meters; passengers can insist on it.
Negotiating the fare puts you at a disadvantage unless you are familiar with the distance involved. A 10- to 15-minute ride (day rates until 9 PM) should cost between NIS 10 and 18 ($3.35 and $6). The fare is
25% higher at night.

Guided Tours

Orientation The following tour operators offer half- and full-day tours of Old and
New Jerusalem, with different itineraries covered on different days
of the week: **Egged Tours**, 224 Jaffa Road, tel. 02/304422; **Galilee
Tours**, 3 Hillel Street, tel. 02/258866, 02/252866, or toll-free 177/022-
2525; **United Tours**, King David Hotel Annex, 23 King David Street,
tel. 02/252187, 02/252188, or 02/252189. A tour costs about NIS 60
($20) for a half day, NIS 114 ($38) for a full day (including pickup and
drop off at your hotel), and can be booked directly or through your
hotel concierge.

At press time the daily rate for a private guide with an air-conditioned car or limousine was NIS 230–NIS 260 ($77–$87); many guides will offer their services without a car for about $110–$130 ($37–$44). The customary rate for a half day is 60% of the full-day rate. For listings of private guides contact **Eshcolot Tours** (36 Keren Hayesod St., tel. 02/635555) or Fodor's writer and guide Mike Rogoff (tel. and fax 02/790410).

Special Interest **Society for the Protection of Nature in Israel,** or **SPNI** (13 Helene Hamalka St., tel. 02/252357 or 02/244605, fax 02/254953), emphasizes nature in its tours, often in off-the-beaten-track locations. Although most commentaries are in Hebrew, some are in English, and among those travelers for whom the experience matters more than the explanations, SPNI tours are highly regarded. Tours change throughout the year, so call for details.

Walking Tours **Archaeological Seminars** (tel. 02/273515) specializes in visiting sites of archaeological importance. A slide lecture precedes the tour, and the guides are generally excellent. Three three-hour itineraries (NIS 36/$13), are offered Sunday through Thursday several times a week. No reservations are required. Discounts are available for students, and are also offered when you take more than one tour. All tours depart from 34 Habad Street in the Jewish Quarter of the Old City.

David's City of David (tel. 02/522568 or 02/818758) operates tours with one full-day and two half-day itineraries. Some are offered several times a week. Prices range from NIS 21 to NIS 42 ($7 to $14) and include entrance fees. Discounts are available for students and senior citizens, and package deals are offered. Tours depart from the Citadel courtyard, outside Jaffa Gate.

Zion Walking Tours (office inside Jaffa Gate, opposite the police station, tel. 02/287866) covers seven itineraries Sunday through Friday, including one to the Mount of Olives area. Tours last about 3½ hours and cost NIS 21 to NIS 48 ($7 to $16) with student discounts available. Some tours are repeated during the week.

Exploring Jerusalem

Jerusalem is built on a series of hills, part of the Judea-Samaria range, and straddles the "watershed," the mountain divide that runs north–south through much of the country. The eastern edge of the city is marked by the high ridge of Mt. Scopus–Mount of Olives, beyond which the arid Judean Desert tumbles down to the Dead Sea. To the west are the Judean Hills, or the Mountains of Judah, many capped by modern farming villages and draped in the new pine forests that have transformed and softened the rugged landscape. North and south of the city—Samaria and Judea, respectively—is the so-called West Bank, since 1967 a contested area, administered by Israel, and part of the same highlands, geographically and historically, of which Jerusalem has always been a part.

The city has two centers of gravity: the downtown area of West Jerusalem, with its central triangle of Jaffa Road, King George Street, and Ben Yehuda Street; and the Old City farther east. Most restaurants and a good number of the hotels recommended below are in or near the downtown area. Almost all the rest are farther west, where the modern Jewish neighborhoods share the hills with the best of the city's museums. The squarish, walled Old City is divided into four major residential quarters—Jewish, Christian, Muslim, and

Armenian—and entered through seven gates, of which the Jaffa Gate is the one most used by tourists.

Since 1987 the nationalist unrest in the Arab community (one-quarter of the city's population) has made East Jerusalem a far less welcoming place than it once was. One should exercise some caution in the Arab neighborhoods north of the Damascus Gate, the Old City's Muslim Quarter, the City of David, and on the Mount of Olives.

When all is said and done, however, Jerusalem is a safe city, as Israeli cities are in general. Jerusalem is a fun city to see on foot, and most outlying sites are fairly accessible by public transportation. With the exception of Tour 6, driving a rental car on any of the tours discussed below is sometimes more a bother than a boon, and you can spend the money more productively on cabs.

Plan on spending *at least* three full days in Jerusalem. Tour 1, which takes you from the Western (Wailing) Wall to the Church of the Holy Sepulcher, plunges you in at the deep end, with a heady whirl of ancient ruins and the all-important sites of the three religions that call this city holy. Tour 2 explores the attractively restored Jewish Quarter and its intriguing potpourri of archaeological sites unearthed in the 1970s. Jaffa Gate and Mt. Zion (where David's Tomb and the site of Christ's Last Supper are located) are covered in Tour 3, which skirts the Old City walls, beginning with the Tower of David Museum. Tour 4 focuses on Old Testament Jerusalem and the City of David. Mainly Christian landmarks in East Jerusalem are explored in Tour 5, with the Mount of Olives and its spectacular view, the Garden of Gethsemane, and the Garden Tomb among its highlights. Also covered are the Rockefeller Museum, Damascus Gate, and a walk along the Old City ramparts. Tour 6 of West Jerusalem swings you across town to Yad Vashem, Israel's most prominent Holocaust memorial/museum complex, the famous Chagall stained-glass windows at the Hadassah Hospital, the village of Ein Kerem, and a large-scale model of Second Temple Period Jerusalem. Tour 7 keeps you on the west side of town, the highlight unquestionably being the Israel Museum, where the Dead Sea Scrolls (and much else) are displayed. You'll also visit the nearby Knesset, Israel's parliament, and the new Bible Lands Museum.

Highlights for First-Time Visitors

Church of the Holy Sepulcher (*see* Tour 1)
Garden of Gethsemane (*see* Tour 5)
Garden Tomb (*see* Tour 5)
Israel Museum (*see* Tour 7)
Jewish Quarter (*see* Tour 2)
Mount of Olives (*see* Tour 5)
Mt. Zion (*see* Tour 3)
Temple Mount (*see* Tour 1)
Tower of David Museum (*see* Tour 3)
Via Dolorosa (*see* Tour 1)
Western (Wailing) Wall (*see* Tour 1)
Yad Vashem (*see* Tour 6)

Tour 1: From the Western Wall to the Church of the Holy Sepulcher

Numbers in the margin correspond to points of interest on the Old City map.

All the holy sites on this tour demand modest dress: no shorts and no sleeveless shirts.

Begin the tour at the **Dung Gate,** literally "Refuse Gate" in Hebrew, because of the ancient practice of dumping garbage over the adjacent walls. Just inside is the **Ophel Archaeological Garden,** often known as the **Western and Southern Wall Excavations.** The extensive dig in the 1970s under archaeologist Benjamin Mazar unearthed a few remains of Old Testament Jerusalem, and far more substantial ones of the Herodian, Byzantine, and Arab periods. Have a look at an artist's reconstruction of the area on display at the entrance (you can buy your own copy from the attendant for NIS 10, or $3.35), and walk down to the very corner of the massive wall facing you. King Solomon's "First Temple" on Mt. Moriah was destroyed by the Babylonians in 586 BC. Fifty years later, Jews returning from the Babylonian Exile began building the "Second Temple" on the same site (where the golden Dome of the Rock now stands). In the 1st century BC, when King Herod the Great rebuilt that Second Temple, he expanded the enclosure around it by constructing a massive retaining wall on the slopes of Mt. Moriah, filling it with thousands of tons of rubble, thus producing the huge plaza still known today as the Temple Mount. The great stones near the corner—their well-cut borders characteristic of the Herodian period—are not held together with mortar; their sheer weight gives the structure its stability.

To the right of the corner, in an excavation trench, is the pavement of a Second Temple–period street. Two thousand years ago, the retaining wall would have been more than 50% higher above the street than today, and its foundations, plumbed by British army engineer Charles Warren in 1867, are as deep below you as the present height of the wall is above you. Left of the corner and way above your head is the protrusion known as **Robinson's Arch** (named for the 19th-century American explorer Edward Robinson), the beginning of a bridge to the Temple Mount, once reached by a staircase from the commercial area where you now stand.

On the wall a few yards north of the arch is an upbeat piece of biblical graffiti in Hebrew, written possibly in the 4th century AD by a Jewish pilgrim and filled with messianic dreams: "You shall see, and your heart shall rejoice, and your bones shall flourish like the grass" (Isaiah 66).

Return to the fork in the path and turn left. On your left you will pass a reconstructed labyrinth of Byzantine dwellings, mosaics and all, below present ground level. A small gate brings you outside the present city walls. The wide staircase to your left, a good part of it original, once brought hordes of pilgrims to the now-blocked gates of the southern wall of the Temple Mount and into the sacred Temple precincts. A prominent archaeologist was once heard to declare: "Ladies and gentlemen, these steps are the one place in the city I can guarantee you Jesus walked!" The rock-hewn *mikvaot* (plural of Mikeh), Jewish ritual baths, at the bottom of the steps, are a visual reminder of the rites of purification once demanded of Jews before entering the Temple Mount. *Dung Gate, tel. 02/254403. Admission: NIS 6 ($2) adults, NIS 3 ($1) children. Open Sun.–Thurs. 9–4, Fri. and holiday eves 9–2.*

Return to the entrance of the site and turn right. A short ascent brings you to the gate of the **Western (Wailing) Wall** plaza. The Western Wall can also be reached by descending from the Jewish Quarter, or from the Street of the Chain in the Arab souk. Bus 1 will deposit you inside the Dung Gate. From whichever direction you walk, expect a routine check of your bags by security personnel at the entrance to the plaza. The wall, the most important Jewish shrine, is not part of the Second Temple itself but of the surrounding retaining wall of the Temple Mount you saw in the nearby dig. After the Roman destruction of Jerusalem in AD 70, and especially after the dedication of its pagan successor in 135, the Holy City became off-limits to Jews for generations. Although the general location of the Temple was known (the vicinity of today's Dome of the Rock; *see below*), its precise location was lost. Even when access eventually became possible, Jews avoided ascending the Temple Mount for fear of unwittingly trespassing on the most sacred—and thus forbidden—areas of their ancient sanctuary. With time, the closest remnant of the period took on the aura of the Temple itself; the Wall, as it is simply known, is really a holy place "by proxy," and, in a sense, it is *through* the stones rather than *to* them that devout Jews pray. It is the tears of generations of such worshippers, grieving for the lost Temple, to which the gentile name for the wall—the Wailing Wall—refers.

The Western Wall functions under the authority of the rabbinic authorities, with all the trappings of an Orthodox synagogue: a dress code (modest dress; men are required to cover their heads), segregation of men and women in prayer (men on the left—a noticeably larger section of the wall), and prohibition of smoking and photography on the Sabbath and Jewish holidays. Go up to the Wall itself. The cracks between the stones are stuffed with slips of paper carrying petitions, and the swaying and praying of the devout leaves no doubt of the powerful hold the place still has on the minds and hearts of many Jews.

There is free access to the Wall 24 hours a day. Try to make a point of visiting on Monday or Thursday morning, when separate and often colorful family services celebrate the bar mitzvah, the coming of age, of a 13-year-old boy; and around sunset on Friday evening, when the young men of a nearby yeshiva (Jewish seminary) come dancing and singing down to the Wall to welcome in the "Sabbath bride." Many visitors, however, claim that it is only when the crowds have gone (the Wall is floodlit at night), and you share the warm, prayer-drenched stones with just a handful of bearded stalwarts, that the true spirituality of the Western Wall can be felt.

A long tunnel beyond the men's side (north of the plaza) was excavated in recent years, exposing ancient arches and chambers and several courses of the Western Wall along almost its entire length. Among the masonry were two stones estimated to weigh 400 and 540 tons, respectively. (The Tunnel is open to organized tour groups only. (Call Archaeological Seminars, tel. 02/273515, or W. W. Heritage, tel. 02/271333, for details.)

Between the Western Wall and the Ophel Archaeological Garden, a ramp ascends to the vast 40-acre plaza covering the summit of the biblical Mt. Moriah, called the **Temple Mount** by Jews and Christians, and **Haram esh-Sharif** (the Noble Enclosure) by Muslims. In the 1st century BC Herod expanded the Temple Mount—identified by some scholars as one of the greatest religious enclosures of the ancient world—and rebuilt the temple into a thing of splendor. That was the Temple Jesus knew. The Romans reduced it to ashes in the summer of AD 70.

The Temple Mount today is a Muslim preserve (modest dress is essential), administered by the Waqf, the Supreme Muslim Religious Council. Tall cypress trees create shady retreats from the glare of

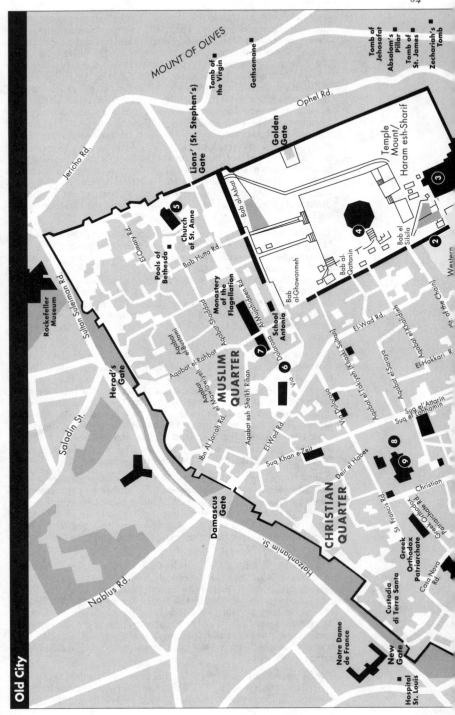

Old City

MOUNT OF OLIVES

Tomb of the Virgin

Gethsemane

Tomb of Jehosafat

Absalom's Pillar

Tomb of St. James

Zechariah's Tomb

Ophel Rd.

Jericho Rd.

Lions' (St. Stephen's) Gate

Golden Gate

El Omari Rd.

Church of St. Anne

Pools of Bethesda

Bab Hutta Rd.

Bab al-Asbat

Temple Mount/ Haram esh-Sharif

③

④

Bab el Sitsila

②

Rockefeller Museum

Sultan Suleiman Rd.

Monastery of the Flagellation

Aqabat Shaddad

Aqabat el Bustami

Aqabat el-Rahbat

Al Mujahideen Rd.

School Antonia

Via Dolorosa

Bab al-Ghawanmeh

Bab el-Qattanin

Bab al-Qattanin

Western

Herod's Gate

MUSLIM QUARTER

Ibn Al Larrah Rd.

Aqabat el Mawlawiyeh

Aqabat esh Sheikh Rihan

⑦

⑥

El Wad Rd.

Via Dolorosa

El Wad Rd.

Aqabat et-Takiyeh (Khalqi Sultan)

Aqabat el-Saraya

El-Hakkari Rd.

El Aqabat el-Khanqah

Saladin St.

Damascus Gate

Suq Khan e-Zeit

Deir el Habes

Suq el'Attarin

Suq el Tahhamin

⑧

⑨

Nablus Rd.

Hativat Hanilayim St.

CHRISTIAN QUARTER

St. Francis Rd.

Greek Orthodox Patriarchate

Greek Orthodox Patriarchate Rd.

Christian

Notre Dame de France

New Gate

Custodia di Terra Santa

Casa Nova Rd.

Hospital St. Louis

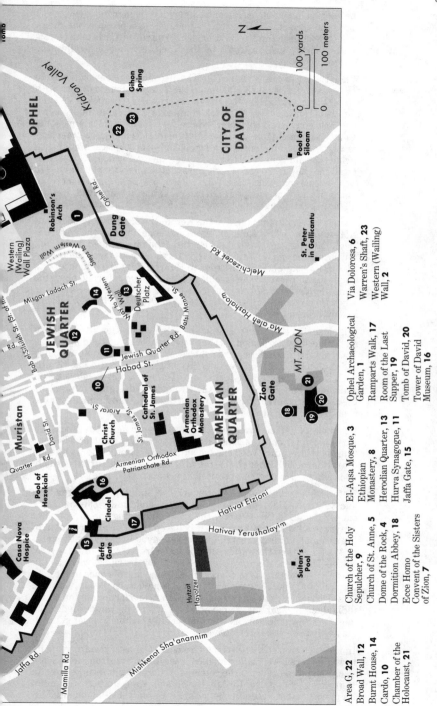

100 yards

100 meters

N

OPHEL

Kidron Valley

Gihon Spring

23

22

CITY OF DAVID

Pool of Siloam

Robinson's Arch 1

Dung Gate

Ophel Rd.

St. Peter in Gallicantu

Melchizedek Rd.

Western (Wailing) Wall Plaza

Western (Wailing) Wall

Steps to Western Wall

Misgav Ladach St.

Deutscher Platz

14 Western Wall

13

Batei Mahase St.

Ma'aleh Hashalom

JEWISH QUARTER

Bab el-Silsila St. (St. of the ...)

12

11

Jewish Quarter Rd.

Habad St.

10

MT. ZION

21

20

18

19

Muristan

Pool of Hezekiah

Quarter Rd.

David St.

Christ Church

St. James St.

Ararat St.

Cathedral of St. James

Armenian Orthodox Monastery

ARMENIAN QUARTER

Zion Gate

Armenian Orthodox Patriarchate Rd.

16

Citadel

17

Hativat Etzioni

Hativat Yerushalayim

Casa Nova Hospice

7

15

Jaffa Gate

Sultan's Pool

Hurvat Hovlzer

Mishkenot Sha'ananim

Jaffa Rd.

Mamilla Rd.

Area G, **22**
Broad Wall, **12**
Burnt House, **14**
Cardo, **10**
Chamber of the
Holocaust, **21**

Church of the Holy
Sepulcher, **9**
Church of St. Anne, **5**
Dome of the Rock, **4**
Dormition Abbey, **18**
Ecce Homo
Convent of the Sisters
of Zion, **7**

El-Aqsa Mosque, **3**
Ethiopian
Monastery, **8**
Herodian Quarter, **13**
Hurva Synagogue, **11**
Jaffa Gate, **15**

Ophel Archaeological
Garden, **1**
Ramparts Walk, **17**
Room of the Last
Supper, **19**
Tomb of David, **20**
Tower of David
Museum, **16**

Via Dolorosa, **6**
Warren's Shaft, **23**
Western (Wailing)
Wall, **2**

the whitish limestone pavements. Immediately in front of you as you enter the area is the large, black-dome **El-Aqsa Mosque,** the third-holiest mosque in the Muslim world. Two hundred yards to the left is the brilliantly golden **Dome of the Rock,** erroneously called the Mosque of Omar.

When the Arab caliph Omar Ibn-Khatib conquered Jerusalem from the Byzantines in AD 638, he found the Temple Mount covered with rubbish and had to clear the site to expose the great rock at its summit. It is related that Omar asked his aide Ka'ab al'Akhbar, a Jew who had converted to Islam, where he should build his mosque. Ka'ab recommended a spot north of the rock, hoping, the tale suggests, that the Muslims, praying south toward Mecca, would thus include the old Temple site in their obeisance. "You dog, Ka'ab," bellowed the caliph. "In your heart you are still a Jew, for you want us to include the rock in our *kibla* [direction of prayer]!" Omar's mosque, which finally was built south of the rock, has not survived, but the splendid gold-dome shrine completed in AD 691 still stands.

Jerusalem is not mentioned in the Koran, the Muslim holy book, but Mohammed's "Night Ride" is. Awakened one night by the angel Gabriel, Mohammed was taken on the fabulous winged horse, el-Burak, to the *masjad el-aqsa,* the "furthermost place" (hence the El-Aqsa Mosque). There he rose to Heaven, came face to face with God himself, received the teachings of Islam, and returned home the same night. The tradition evolved that the masjad el-aqsa was none other than Jerusalem, and the great rock the spot from which the Prophet ascended.

It is clear that the triumphant Arabs of the generation after Mohammed venerated Jerusalem as the city of biblical kings and prophets. Many modern scholars agree, however, that the feeling of being Johnnys-come-lately in the holy city of rival faiths did not sit well with the new masters of Jerusalem. The masjad el-aqsa tradition, and the magnificent Dome of the Rock, were designed to proclaim the ascendancy of the "true faith" and the new Arab Empire over the rival Byzantine Christians.

Buy tickets, which cover admission to the Dome of the Rock, El-Aqsa Mosque, and the Islamic Museum, to the right of El-Aqsa. Guards will require you to leave shoes, bags, and cameras outside (at your own risk, though theft is rare here. A small purse is usually allowed, but be sure your outfit has pockets just in case).

Enter El-Aqsa's cavernous interior. The building is 89 yards long and 60 yards wide. At the far (southern) end, under the landmark copper dome, is the *mihrab,* the niche indicating the direction of prayer toward Mecca. This wall is believed to be the only remnant of the original building created by the Ummayad dynasty in 8th century AD. Since then the mosque has been destroyed and rebuilt several times. The rows of square stone columns on the right (west) as you enter date from the 14th century; the round marble ones in the center and on the left are the products of renovations in the 1920s and '30s. Persian rugs are interspersed with modern runners, on which individual "prayer mats" have been patterned. Undoubtedly the mosque's finest feature is the wonderfully complex set of stained-glass windows under the dome.

In the 12th century, one of the Crusader monastic orders made its headquarters here, taking its name, the Templars, from the ancient site. The place has been the setting for more recent dramas, too. In 1951, King Abdullah of Jordan (the present King Hussein's grandfather) was assassinated in the mosque; and in 1969, a demented arsonist set fire to a priceless wooden *minbar*, or pulpit, in an attempt to destroy the building. To the right of the mosque is the **Islamic Museum,** displaying some fine stone relief work and carved wood from El-Aqsa's earlier incarnations.

Pick up your chattels, cross the plaza, and ascend a flight of steps toward the splendid **Dome of the Rock,** whose octagonal plan closely resembles that of the Byzantine church of San Vitale in Ravenna, Italy. Its exterior glazed ceramic tiles in shades of blue and its golden dome are the results of renovations made in the 1950s and '60s. The newly restored dome is copper, plated with 80 kilograms (176 pounds) of 24-carat gold.

The interior of the shrine is wondrous. Granite columns support arches, some bearing the original green and gold mosaics set in arabesque motifs. Although Christian Syrians created the mosaics, Islam forbade them to depict human figures, so the walls are covered with stylized plantlike forms. Although the mosaics in the dome were restored in 1027, it is believed that the original designs were retained. Some of the Arabic inscriptions in the mosaics are quotations from the Koran, others are dedications. One of the latter originally lauded Abd al-Malik, caliph of the Damascus-based Ummayad dynasty, who built the shrine. Some 140 years later, the caliph of a rival dynasty removed el-Malik's name and replaced it with his own, neglecting, however, to change the date! Notice the outstanding marble slabs that adorn the walls. Without benefit of power tools, medieval stonemasons were able to expose the natural grain of the marble, creating impressive symmetries.

The huge **rock** at the center of the building is considered by more than one tradition to be the center of the world. Jewish tradition identifies it as the place where Abraham bound and almost sacrificed his son Isaac (Genesis 22). With King David's conquest of Jerusalem in 1000 BC, however, the rock became part of (relatively) indisputable history. Against the warning of his counselors that it was arrogant to count the people of Israel (who were supposedly like "the sands of the sea and the stars of the sky"), the triumphant king undertook a national census, thus inviting divine retribution in the form of a plague (II Samuel 24). To stay the plague, David erected an altar and burned a repentance offering on "the threshing floor of Araunah [or Ornan] the Jebusite." In the absence of other suitable candidates, modern scholars identify the rock with that threshing floor.

One generation later, David's son Solomon built his Temple here. Did the rock become the innermost chamber, the Holy of Holies, of the Temple (with the sanctuary thus being where the Dome of the Rock stands today)? Or did it become the altar in the Court of the Israelites (with the sanctuary a bit to the west)? Judaism continues to grapple with these questions to this day. At the southwestern corner of the rock, a 10-foot-high ornamented canister is said to contain several hairs of the Prophet Mohammed's beard. The reliquary is opened for the Muslim faithful for one day a year, during the holy month of Ramadan. A small opening in the marble facade below it allows you to put your hand in and feel the indentation in the rock made, the faithful believe, by the Prophet's foot as he ascended to heaven. A few steps to the right bring you to a marble staircase leading down to a small grotto, perhaps once a water cistern or a grain store in the pre-Davidic days. Legend calls it the Well of Souls, the entrance to the nether world, and the place where the dead pray. An Islamic tradition relates that as Mohammed rose to heaven, the rock tried to follow him, and had already left a void (the cave) when the archangel Gabriel intervened to hold it down. *Tel. 02/283292 or 02/ 283313. Admission (combined ticket for El-Aqsa Mosque, Dome of the Rock, and Islamic Museum): NIS 30 ($10) adults, NIS 18 ($6) children. Open Sat.–Thurs. 8–11:30, 12:30–3. (Seasonal changes are made without notice to accommodate changing prayer times.)*

To the west of the Dome of the Rock is a large *sabil*, a public drinking fountain (now defunct) with an elaborate ornamented stone dome, built by the Egypt-based Mamluk rulers in the 14th or 15th century. A large number of the nearby buildings lining the western edge of the Temple Mount are from this period, distinguished by their impressive jigsaws of fitted red, white, and black stone.

You can leave the Temple Mount at the northwest corner. The long building to the right of the Bab al-Ghawanmeh gate that overlooks the plaza, today an elementary school, is built on the artificial scarp that once protected Herod's Antonia fortress. The probably authentic Christian tradition identifies the site with the *praetorium* where Jesus was tried. The gate leads to the **Via Dolorosa** (The Way of the Cross) at the **Ecce Homo Convent** (*see below*).

If you're not in a hurry, head for the northeast corner of the Temple Mount. In the eastern outer wall, facing the Mount of Olives, is the ornate, domed inner **Golden Gate,** or "Gate of Mercy," now blocked. The present masonry is Byzantine, though the gate—the "Eastern Gate" of Christian tradition, through which Jesus is believed to have entered the area on Palm Sunday—existed in the Second Temple period. Jewish tradition still awaits the Messiah's coming through the same gate.

As you exit the Temple Mount through the al-Asbat gate, the Lions' Gate, or St. Stephen's Gate, is on your right. Stay within the city walls and turn left. Twenty yards on, an unobtrusive dark wooden door on your right opens onto the courtyard of the **Church of St. Anne** and the **Pools of Bethesda.**

The transition is sudden and complete from the raucous cobbled streets and persistent vendors to the drooping pepper trees, flower patches, and birdsong of this serene Catholic cloister. The Romanesque Crusader church, built in 1140, was restored in the 19th century, and, with its austere and unadorned stone interior, is one of the finest examples of medieval architecture in the country. According to local tradition, Anne, the mother of the Virgin Mary, was born in the grotto above which the church is built. It is worth waiting for one of the frequent pilgrim groups who invariably test the church's extraordinarily reverberant acoustics with some hymn singing.

On the facade of the church, above the main door, is an unexpected five-line inscription in Arabic. After Saladin's defeat of the Crusaders in 1187, the church was turned into a *madrasa*, a Muslim house of study, and, despite the Christian restoration, the inscription—a dedication to Saladin—has survived.

In the same compound, and just a few steps from the church, are the excavated **Pools of Bethesda,** a large public double reservoir in use in the 1st century BC and 1st century AD. The New Testament (John 5) speaks of Jesus miraculously curing a lame man by "a pool, which is called in the Hebrew tongue Bethesda (the Place of Mercy)." The actual bathing pools used by the citizens were the small ones, east of the reservoir, but it was over the big pools that both the Byzantines and the Crusaders built churches, now destroyed, to commemorate the miracle. *Al-Miyahideen Rd., tel. 02/283285. Admission NIS 3 ($1). Open Mon.–Sat. 8–noon, 2–5 (summer till 6).*

Time Out Return to the street and turn right (your back will be to Lions' Gate). Some 150 yards up the road, on a corner to your left, is a small, no-name coffee shop that serves tea, Turkish coffee, and fresh orange juice. Public toilets are opposite. There are few alternatives in the area.

Continue walking for about 200 yards in the same direction. You will start to see souvenir shops. Look for a ramp on your left leading to the cream-color door of a school. On Friday afternoon at 3, the brown-robed Franciscans begin their **procession of the Via Dolorosa**—the Way of the Cross—in the school courtyard beyond the door. Its upper (southern) terrace gives you a commanding view of the Temple Mount through a barred opening. Herod's **Antonia Fortress** stood on the site of the school 20 centuries ago. (Sometimes the procession starts at 4; ask at the Christian Information Center; *see* Important Addresses and Numbers *in* Essential Information, *above*.)

❻ The route called **Via Dolorosa** is a 12th-century Crusader tradition drawing partly on older Byzantine beliefs. Its 14 "stations" (shown on the walls of all Roman Catholic churches) mark Jesus's last journey, from the place of his trial (Stations I and II) to that of his crucifixion and burial (stations X through XIV). Some of the incidents represented by the stations are scriptural, some (III, IV, VI, VII, and IX) are not. Most of the stations on the route, which winds through the Muslim and Christian quarters, are marked by tiny chapels opened only during the Franciscan ceremonies. The last five stations are contained within the Church of the Holy Sepulcher itself.

The school courtyard is **Station I,** the setting of the trial and condemnation of Christ. Across the road is the **Monastery of the Flagellation, Station II,** where Jesus was scourged and took up the cross. Its shaded cloister and cool greenery offer some relief from the noisy street, if not actual solitude. The Roman pavement within the two chapels dates from the century after Christ. *Admission free. Open Apr.–Sept., Mon.–Sat. 8–noon, 2–6; Oct.–Mar., Mon.–Sat. 8–noon, 1–5.*

Continue walking with your back to the Lions' Gate. Some 30 yards on, an arch crosses the road. In the 19th century the arch was thought to have been the spot where Pilate presented Jesus to the crowd with the words *Ecce homo,* "Behold, the man!" Recent scholarship, however, has established that the structure was a triumphal arch built by the Roman emperor Hadrian in the 2nd century AD. On the street corner on the right before the arch is the entrance to the **❼** **Ecce Homo Convent of the Sisters of Zion.** (The street on the left is the exit from the Temple Mount you would have taken had you opted to skip St. Anne's Church.)

The basement of the convent boasts two sites of interest. The first is an impressive arched reservoir with a barrel-vault roof, apparently built by Hadrian in the moat of Herod's older Antonia Fortress, and still filled with clear water. The second is the famous *lithostratos,* or stone pavement, etched with games played by bored Roman legionnaires. One such diversion—the notorious "Game of the King"—called for the execution of a mock king, a sequence tantalizingly reminiscent of the New Testament description of the treatment of Jesus by the Roman soldiers. Contrary to tradition, however, the pavement of large, foot-worn brown flagstones is not from Jesus' day, but was laid down a century later. *Via Dolorosa, tel. 02/277292. Admission: NIS 3 ($1). Open Mon.–Sat. 8:30–12:30, 2–5.*

Back on the street, pass under the arch. Twenty yards farther, steps on your right bring you into a small vestibule separated by a glass panel from the chapel of the convent. The altar of the chapel is under the northern span of the originally three-span triumphal arch.

The Via Dolorosa runs down into El-Wad Road, one of the Old City's important thoroughfares. To the right, the street climbs toward the Damascus Gate; to the left, it passes through the heart of the Muslim Quarter and reaches the Western Wall. It's a sensorial experience to sit at a café on a low rattan stool, sipping cardamom-flavor Turkish coffee, and watching the passing parade of buxom Arab matrons in bright embroidered dresses rubbing shoulders with black-hatted Hasidic Jews in beards and side curls. Local Muslim kids in the universal uniform of T-shirt, jeans, and sneakers dodge around groups of pious pilgrims almost oblivious to the cacophonous scene through which they waft.

As you turn left onto El-Wad Road, **Station III,** where Jesus fell for the first time, is immediately on your left. The chapel was built after World War II by soldiers of the Free Polish Forces. A few steps beyond it, also on the left, is **Station IV** (where Mary embraced her son), and on the next corner, **Station V** (where Simon of Cyrene picked up the cross). The Via Dolorosa turns right and begins its ascent toward Calvary. Halfway up the street, a brown wooden door on your left marks **Station VI.** It was here that a woman wiped the face of Jesus, whose image remained on the cloth. (Her name has come down to us as Veronica, apparently derived from the words *vera* and *icone,* meaning true image.)

At the top of the stepped street is a brown metal door: **Station VII,** where Jesus fell for the second time. The little chapel contains one of the columns of the Byzantine Cardo, the main street of 6th-century Jerusalem, which ran from the Damascus Gate (off to your right) through to today's Jewish Quarter, some 300 yards to your left. Step to the left, then walk 30 yards up the street facing you. You are now at **Station VIII** (where Jesus addressed the women), marked by nothing more than an inscribed stone. It's easy to miss: Ask the locals.

Return to the main street (Suq Khan e-Zeit) and turn right (left as you reach Station VII from VI). The street is almost impossibly crowded on Saturday, when Arab Jerusalem does its shopping. One hundred yards from Station VII, a ramp parallel to the street ascends to your right. Take the ramp and the small lane above it to its end. A column in the wall represents **Station IX,** where Jesus stumbled and fell a third time.

Step through the open door on your left into the courtyard of the **❽ Ethiopian Monastery,** also known as **Deir es-Sultan.** Above you is the medieval bulge of the Church of the Holy Sepulcher, revered by most of Christendom. Apart from the Ethiopian and neighboring Coptic monasteries, the skyline you see is broken by a Russian Orthodox gable, a Lutheran bell tower, and the crosses of the Greek Orthodox, Armenian, and Roman Catholic rivals who occupy the Holy Sepulcher.

The robed Ethiopian monks, tall and slender, gentle and shy, live in tiny cells on the monastery rooftop. Their small, dark church is adorned with modern paintings, one of which depicts the visit of the

Queen of Sheba to King Solomon. Ethiopian tradition has it that more passed between the two than is related in the Bible (I Kings 10), and that their supposed union produced an heir to the Ethiopian royal house. The unfamiliar script in the paintings is Gehz, the ecclesiastical language of the Ethiopian church. *Admission free. Open daylight hours.*

Down through the lower chapel and out a small wooden door, you find yourself in the court of the **Church of the Holy Sepulcher** (*see map below*).

Most Christians venerate this site as that of the death, burial, and resurrection of Christ, events that stand at the very core of their faith. (Many Protestants identify the Garden Tomb, north of the Damascus Gate, as the possible tomb of Jesus. *See* Tour 5, *below*.) The first, grand church was built circa AD 326 by Helena, mother of the Byzantine emperor Constantine the Great, and destroyed by Persian invaders in AD 614. It was rebuilt almost immediately, destroyed again by the Egyptian caliph El-Hakim in 1009, and once more restored, on a much reduced scale, apparently as a cluster of shrines not under one roof. In the 12th century the Crusaders unified the shrines in the present vast structure (which is only two-thirds the length of its Byzantine predecessor). The very antiquity of the tradition argues in favor of its authenticity, many claim, for the persecuted early Christian community, fiercely committed to the point of martyrdom, would likely have preserved the memory of the site where events on which their entire faith hinged had taken place. The church is outside the city walls *of Jesus's day*—an important point, for no executions or burials took place within Jerusalem's sacred precincts.

Note the fine stone carving above the Gothic entrance. Enter the church and turn right. Steep steps take you up to **Golgotha** (from Aramaic through Greek), or **Calvary** (through Latin), meaning "the place of the skull" (Mark 15). The chapel on the right is Roman Catholic and contains **Station X** (where Jesus was stripped of his garments) and **Station XI** (at the front—note the mosaic—where Jesus was nailed to the cross). On the right wall is a mosaic depicting the Old Testament story of Abraham's binding of Isaac—the sacrifice of the son by the father, in which some Christians perceive a symbolic parallel to the death of Jesus.

The central chapel, all candlelight, oil lamps, and icons, is Greek Orthodox. Under the altar, and capping the rocky hillock on which you stand, is a bronze disc with a hole, purportedly the place where the cross actually stood, and thus **Station XII,** where Jesus died on the cross. The Franciscans indicate the spot between XI and XII, at the icon of Mary, as **Station XIII,** where Jesus's body was taken down. Walk back down the steps to the floor just inside the church entrance. There you will see a rectangular pink slab called the **Stone of Unction,** where, it is said, the body of Jesus was cleansed and prepared for burial. Greek pilgrims can often be seen rubbing crosses and clothing on the stone to take home. The **tomb** itself (**Station XIV**) is in the cavernous, dimly lit rotunda to the left of the entrance, encased in a small pink marble edifice.

Some 50 feet above you is the great dome that is the landmark of the Christian Quarter. With scaffolding for its repair still in place—the work ground to a halt in the 1980s—the dome is a symbol (and victim) of the denominational rivalry that has beset the Holy Land sites in general, and the Holy Sepulcher in particular, for centuries. (Critical structural repairs did take place in the 1970s, however, and

Church of the Holy Sepulcher

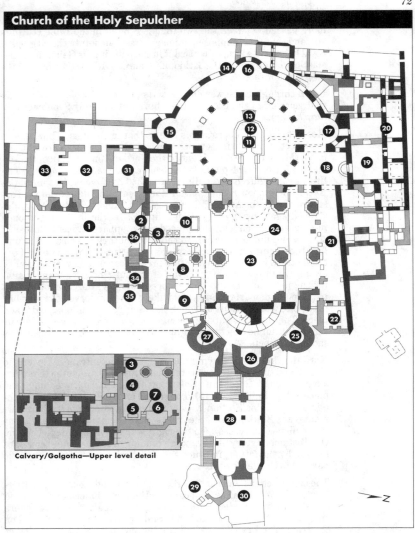

Calvary/Golgotha—Upper level detail

Entrance courtyard, **1**

Twelfth-century facade and entrance to church, **2**

Calvary/Golgotha steps, **3**

Station X, **4**

Station XI, **5**

Station XII, **6**

Station XIII, **7**

Chapel of Adam, **8**

Rock of Golgotha, **9**

Stone of Unction, **10**

Chapel of the Angel, **11**

Tomb of Christ (Station XIV), **12**

Coptic Chapel, **13**

Tomb of Joseph of Aramathea, **14**

Southern apse, 4th-century church, **15**

Western apse, 4th-century church, **16**

Northern apse, 4th-century church, **17**

Altar of Mary Magdalene, **18**

Chapel of the Apparition, **19**

Franciscan Convent, **20**

Arches of the Virgin, **21**

Prison of Christ, **22**

Crusader church, **23**

"Center of the World," **24**

Chapel of St. Longinus, **25**

Chapel of the Division of the Raiment, **26**

Chapel of the Mocking, **27**

Chapel of St. Helena, **28**

Chapel of the Holy Cross, **29**

Byzantine wall etching of ship, **30**

Chapel of 40 Martyrs, **31**

Chapel of St. John, **32**

Chapel of St. James, **33**

Chapel of the Franks, **34**

Chapel of St. Michael and exit from Ethiopian Monastery, **35**

Tomb of Philip d'Aubigny, **36**

the huge pink stone pillars surrounding the rotunda are the result.) The Status Quo Agreements, a list of possessions and privileges frozen in the 19th century, are in effect in the church and jealously guarded. In the late afternoon, for example, each of the church's "shareholders"—Greek Orthodox, Latins (Roman Catholics), Armenians, and Copts (Egyptians)—exercises its right to a procession from Calvary to the Tomb, with full-frocked chanting clergy, and censers streaming pungent smoke.

Enter the tomb between the sentinels of giant brass candle holders. The only hint left of what it must have been like two millennia ago is the ledge in the inner chamber (now covered with marble) on which the body would have been laid. On the Greek Orthodox Easter, the Holy Fire ceremony takes place here. The church is typically packed with candle-carrying pilgrims tense with excitement. The Patriarch enters the tomb, there is a flash of fire seen through its portholes, a messenger emerges with a flaming torch, and within moments the whole church is ablaze with thousands of candles.

Among the church's many chapels, the most interesting is the **Chapel of St. Helena.** From the corridor at the eastern end of the church, steps lead down to a crypt, adorned with a fine Armenian mosaic floor and an ancient wall "etching," probably Byzantine, of a ship. Tradition has it that here Helena found the True Cross of Christ circa AD 326. *Tel. 02/273314. Admission free. Open Apr.–Sept., daily 5 AM–8 PM; Oct.–Mar., daily 5 AM–7 PM.*

To get to the Jaffa Gate from the courtyard, ascend to the right, turn left at the main street, Christian Quarter Road, go as far as David Street, and make a right again. You can reach the Jewish Quarter (*see* Tour 2, *below*) by going left from the courtyard, taking an immediate right past the high white stone Lutheran Church of the Redeemer and continuing as far as David Street, then turning left, and making the first right.

Tour 2: Jewish Quarter

When the Crusaders reached Jerusalem in 1099, the Jewish community was concentrated in the northeastern quadrant of the city, today's Muslim Quarter of the Old City. The Crusaders' destruction of that quarter and its population was so complete that when the Spanish rabbi Nachmanides, known as "the Ramban," reached the city in 1267, he found there "only two Jews, brothers, dyers by trade." The men established themselves in the city's southern quadrant—perhaps on Mt. Zion—eventually occupying the medieval building in today's Jewish Quarter that still bears the Ramban's name. The community slowly revived, then mushroomed with the influx of Sephardic Jews expelled from Spain in 1492, and again with the flow of Ashkenazi Jews from Central and Eastern Europe in the 18th century. By 1865, more than half the population of Jerusalem was Jewish, most living in the Jewish Quarter in very difficult conditions, some in the Muslim Quarter, and a handful in the new neighborhoods developing beyond the city walls.

During Israel's War of Independence in 1948, the Jewish Quarter was severely damaged, forced to capitulate to Jordan's Arab Legion, evacuated, plundered, and abandoned for a generation. With the reunification of Jerusalem after the Six Day War of 1967, the restoration of the quarter began in earnest. With so many of the buildings little more than rubble, Israeli archaeologists were given a unique opportunity to explore the area systematically, and a decade of frantic excavation to keep ahead of construction schedules yielded a smorgasbord of sites of major archaeological importance. The simultaneous reconstruction of the quarter emphasized the restoration of the old as much as possible, as well as the design of new buildings to re-create the original architectural style. The result is an eye-pleasing harmony of limestone masonry, arched windows and buttresses, cobblestone alleyways, open archaeological sites, and splashes of greenery, and it has made the Jewish Quarter the Old City's most attractive neighborhood.

Begin the tour at the quarter's parking lot, reached by following Armenian Orthodox Patriarchate Road from the Jaffa Gate (500 yards), or by entering the Zion Gate and continuing right (100 yards). With your back to the bus stop, cross the lot and enter Jewish Quarter Road (there will be a small supermarket on your right). One hundred yards down the road, on your left, and some 15 feet below you are the excavated and partly restored remains of the **Cardo,** the colonnaded main street of 6th-century AD Byzantine Jerusalem.

The Roman emperor Hadrian built his town of **Aelia Capitolina** on the ruins of Jerusalem in AD 135, an urban plan that has essentially been preserved in the Old City of today. The *cardo maximus* (the main street) of his city, beginning at the Damascus Gate in the north, did not run this far south, but with the Christianization of the Roman Empire in the 4th century, access to Mt. Zion and its important Christian sites (*see* Tour 3, *below*) became a priority, and the main street was eventually extended. The original width—today we see only half—was 73 feet, about the width of a six-lane highway. Some 15 feet below modern ground level, one can walk among the flagstones and columns of Byzantine Jerusalem in its heyday.

Some 30 yards farther on, and on the right, is the entrance to the ruined **Hurva Synagogue.** In 1700 a large group of devout Eastern European Jews arrived in the Holy City, led by the venerable Rabbi Judah the Pious. The old man died days after their arrival, throwing his followers into despair and leaving them with a problem: With the death of the rabbi, the promised funds from the Old Country never materialized, and the money for building a synagogue had to be borrowed from their Muslim neighbors. By 1720, the loan was still outstanding, and the creditors burned down the synagogue, exiling Ashkenazi Jews from the city for more than a century. In 1862, a new and splendid synagogue was completed on the *hurva* (ruins) of the old, its high dome a Jewish Quarter landmark until its destruction after the quarter fell into Jordanian hands in 1948.

Time Out The Crusaders turned part of the Cardo into a market; their arched facades have become part of a small modern shopping arcade specializing in jewelry, crafts, and Judaica (*see* Shopping, *below*). For lunch, try the excellent **Culinaria,** billed as a Roman-style restaurant and actually adapting ancient recipes to modern tastes, using only ingredients native to the ancient Mediterranean world. *Tel. 02/894155. No dinner Fri. or lunch Sat.*

The second lane to the right beyond the Hurva Synagogue brings you to the **Broad Wall,** 23 feet thick and 2,700 years old. The wall was built in 701 BC by Hezekiah, King of Judah and a contemporary of the prophet Isaiah, to protect the city against an Assyrian invasion (II Chronicles 32). Seemingly attached to the Broad Wall are the scanty foundations of a dwelling, once in an unfortified outer neighborhood, possibly inhabited by refugees from the devastated northern Kingdom of Israel (721 BC). "And you [Hezekiah] counted the houses of Jerusalem, and you broke down the houses to fortify the wall" (Isaiah 22). The concept of eminent domain is not a modern in-novation: Hezekiah's city planners had expropriated private houses for the more urgently needed city wall.

Facing the Broad Wall, and with your back to the Cardo, bear right for 50 yards to **Hurva Square,** the center of the Jewish Quarter. On the eastern side of the square, take a few steps down the lane some 25 yards to the right of Tony's Deli. On your right is the **Wohl Ar-chaeological Museum,** better known as the **Herodian Quarter.** Exca-vations in the 1970s exposed the area's most visually arresting site: the remains of mansions from the luxurious Upper City of Second Temple–period Jerusalem. Preserved in the basement of the yeshi-va built later over the ruins, the geometrically patterned mosaic floors, colorful frescoes, and costly glassware, stone objects, and ce-ramics evoke life at the top in the days of Herod and Jesus.

In the first hall, several small stone cisterns have been identified as private mikvaot; holograms reconstruct their use. A small ascend-ing staircase ends abruptly, a reminder that nothing above ground level survived the Roman devastation of AD 70.

The quality, and even rarity, of some of the goods displayed in the second hall would have been the pride of any aristocratic household in those days: decorated ceramic plates, a ribbed green glass bowl, an imported mottled-alabaster vase. Large stone water jars are just like those described in the New Testament story of the marriage at Cana (John 2; *see* Exploring Lower Galilee *in* Chapter 6). Rare stone tables are the incarnation of the dining room furniture depicted in Roman stone reliefs found in Europe.

Ancient steps bring you down to the last level, a mansion with an estimated original area of more than 6,000 square feet. None of the upper stories has survived, of course, but the frescoes, half replaced by the later, more fashionable stucco, and the quality of the artifacts found here indicate a standard of living so exceptional that some scholars have suggested that this might have been the long-sought palace of the High Priest. At the southern end of the fine reception hall is a badly scorched mosaic floor with a charred ceiling beam ly-ing on it. The Upper City held out against the Roman army for a month after the destruction of the Second Temple, but in September of AD 70, "on the eighth day of [the Hebrew month of] Elul," wrote the Jewish historian Josephus in his contemporary account of Jerusalem's last hours, "the sun rose over a city in flames." Precise-ly 19 centuries later, the victims' compatriots uncovered evidence of destruction so vivid, wrote archaeologist Nahman Avigad, "that we could almost smell the burning, and feel the heat of the flames." *Hakara'im Rd., tel. 02/283448. Admission (combined ticket with Burnt House; see below): NIS 10 ($3.35) adults, NIS 9 ($3) chil-dren. Herodian Quarter only: NIS 8 ($2.70) adults, NIS 7.50 ($2.50) children. Open Sun.–Thurs. 9–5, Fri. 9–1.*

Once outside the site, you can descend a wide staircase to the West-ern Wall and the Dung Gate (*see* Tour 1, *above*). To return to Hurva Square, ascend the staircase. Just beyond the top of the steps, on your right, is **Burnt House,** once the basement industrial workshop, during the Second Temple period, of the priestly Bar Katros family (a fact gleaned from inscribed stone weights discovered here). The evidence of destruction by burning is strongest here, with charred cooking pots and debris giving a vivid sense of the devastation of 19 centuries ago. An audiovisual presentation illuminates the period, putting the artifacts in clear context. *Tiferet Israel St. Admission (combined ticket with Herodian Quarter): NIS 10 ($3.35) adults,*

*NIS 9 ($3) children. Burnt House only: NIS 4.50 ($1.50) adults,
NIS 4 ($1.35) children. Open Sun.–Thurs. 9–5, Fri. 9–1.*

Tour 3: Tower of David and Mt. Zion

⑮ Begin the tour at **Jaffa Gate,** which can be reached by city Buses 1, 2,
19, 20, 38, and 99. If you have your own car, look for parking in the
Mamilla area opposite the walls (undergoing renovation at press
time). Walk to the bottom of the road that leads up to Jaffa Gate, and
pause to look at the **Old City walls** above you. Built between 1536 and
1542 by the Ottoman sultan Suleiman the Magnificent, the walls incorporate clearly visible chunks of the so-called First Wall, some 21
centuries old. The older stones, distinguishable by the chiseled border characteristic of the Hasmonean period, in some places project
out of the line of the Turkish wall, tracing the foundations of ancient
defense towers. Above your head is the photogenic **Tower of David,** in
fact a Turkish tower and minaret, which has become one of
Jerusalem's landmarks.

The road enters the Jaffa Gate through the gap in the wall created
by the Ottoman Turks to accommodate the carriage of Kaiser Wilhelm II in 1898. On your left is the original 16th-century gate, which
you would enter if you come from the downtown area by way of Jaffa
Road. The gate got its name from its westerly orientation, toward
the once-important Mediterranean harbor of Jaffa, now part of Tel
Aviv. In Arabic, the gate is called Bab el-Halil, the Gate of the
Beloved (referring to Abraham, the "Beloved of God" in Muslim
tradition), for from here another road strikes south toward Hebron,
El-Halil in Arabic, where Abraham is buried.

On your left as you enter is the GTIO, offering maps and information. Next to it is a tiny recessed terrace fronted by a grille. Between the two tall cypress trees in the recess are two Muslim tombs,
said to be those of the architects of Suleiman the Magnificent's city
walls. One story is that Suleiman had them executed for rebuilding
the city walls without encompassing Mt. Zion and the venerated
Tomb of David. Another version has it that they met their fate because they were too good at their jobs: Suleiman made sure they
would never build anything grander for anyone else!

The road immediately bends to the right. Directly ahead is David
Street (not to be confused with King David Street, in West Jerusalem), one of the main streets of the souk. On your right is a huge
stone tower built of well-cut stones reminiscent of those in the Western Wall. This is the last survivor, once called Phatza'el, of the three
towers built by King Herod the Great in the 1st century BC. This,
too, has become known as the Tower of David, but has as little to do
with that biblical king as the Turkish tower you viewed from outside
Jaffa Gate. Apart from this tower, Herod's fortress here is gone, but
Crusaders and Muslims continued to fortify this vulnerable spot in
the city's defenses, creating **The Citadel,** as it is still known locally
today.

Follow the vehicular road (Armenian Orthodox Patriarchate Road).
On your left, 30 yards after the bend, is the entrance to the Anglican
Christ Church, a neo-Gothic structure built in the 1840s and the oldest Protestant church in the Middle East. On your right is the platform from which British general Edmund Allenby officially
reviewed his victorious troops on December 11, 1917.

⑯ Ascend the ramp, cross a moat, and enter the **Tower of David Museum,** one of Jerusalem's highlights. This relatively new museum, still

popularly known as the Citadel, tells the 5,000-year-old story of Jerusalem, not with original artifacts but through a variety of state-of-the-art visual and audiovisual aids, including models, maps, holograms, videos, computers, and animated films. You can rent a tape-recorded tour at the entrance. Be sure to inquire about the next screening of the animated introductory film, which has English subtitles.

From the entrance hall, a winding outside staircase on your right brings you up to the roof. Turn left at once to reach the auditorium where the film is shown and a second staircase to the top of the great tower. The view in all directions is marvelous, but especially east across the Old City to the Temple Mount and Mount of Olives. Return to the roof and follow the red signs marked EXHIBIT.

The stone halls of the museum are all medieval, lending an appropriately antique atmosphere to the entire exhibit, whose galleries are organized by historical period around the Citadel's central courtyard. Landscaped archaeological remains in the courtyard form an eye-catching but incomprehensible jumble, except for the massive Herodian tower and the Hasmonean "First Wall" (2nd–1st centuries BC) to which it is attached. Walking the Citadel's ramparts, with the sometimes unexpected panoramas glimpsed from odd angles, is worth your time, but is certainly a lesser priority. Ask about the occasional temporary exhibitions. *Jaffa Gate, tel. 02/274111 or 02/283394. Admission (museum or sound-and-light show): NIS 18 ($6) adults, NIS 14 ($4.70) students, NIS 10 ($3.35) children; combined ticket to museum and sound-and-light show: NIS 32 ($10.70) adults, NIS 24 ($8) students, NIS 17 ($5.70) children. Museum open Sun.–Thurs. 9–5, Fri.–Sat. 9–2. Sound-and-light show in English: Apr.–Oct., Mon. and Wed. at 9:30 PM, Sat. at 10:30 PM (call ahead to verify). Guided tours in English Sun.–Fri. at 11.*

The exit from the museum puts you outside the Jaffa Gate. Follow the road down to the left, then take an ascending path that hugs the Old City wall. The views across the Hinnom Valley to the Yemin Moshe neighborhood and the New City are excellent. At the southwestern corner of the Old City, turn left and continue 150 yards along the city wall to **Zion Gate.**

17 You can reach the same point by way of the **Ramparts Walk.** As you leave the museum, do not rejoin the road but walk south across the apparently blind-ended terrace. A left turn at the end will bring you to the ticket office. (The Ramparts Walk is accessible at two other points—the Jaffa Gate and the Damascus Gate—and exits are provided at these as well as the Zion and New gates.) As you walk atop the Old City walls, you'll get to play voyeur as you catch glimpses into gardens, courtyards, and homes of the Armenian Quarter, which occupies the southwestern quadrant of the Old City. You'll also gain some empathy for the medieval soldiers who defended the city as you walk along the narrow stone catwalks and peer through the crenellated shooting niches. (There are secure railings, but small children should not be allowed to walk alone.) Descend at Zion Gate. *Tel. 02/254403. Admission: NIS 6 ($2) adults, NIS 3 ($1) children. Open Sat.–Thurs. 9–4, Fri. 9–2.*

Turn right a few steps past **Zion Gate** and follow the path away from the Old City wall. Bear right at the first fork, and turn right at the **18** second. You are outside **Dormition Abbey,** a large German Benedictine church. Its black conical dome and tall clock tower are the prominent landmarks of Mt. Zion. The round limestone edifice, with ornamented turrets at each "corner," was built on a site given by the

Turks to Kaiser Wilhelm II during his 1898 visit to Jerusalem, and dedicated in 1910. The church preserves the tradition that Mary, mother of Jesus, did not die but fell into "eternal sleep" (hence dormition).

The interior of the church is an echoing chamber with six small recessed chapels. At the eastern end is a large Byzantine-style apse with a wall mosaic of Jesus and Mary. The mosaic floor is decorated with expanding circles of names of the Trinity, the Evangelists, the Disciples, the Old Testament prophets, and the Signs of the Zodiac. In the basement is a cenotaph with the stone-carved figure of Mary in repose. Among the little chapels in the lower level is one donated by the Ivory Coast, whose wooden figures and motifs are inlaid with ivory. A bookshop and pleasant coffee shop are on the premises. *Mt. Zion, tel. 02/719927. Admission free. Open daily 8–noon and 2–6.*

Return to the corner on the main path (the second fork) and turn right. Thirty yards on, step through a doorway to your left, and **19** climb one flight of steps to the **Room of the Last Supper.** Alternatively known as the **Cenacle** or **Coenaculum**—the "Upper Room" of the Gospels (Mark 14)—the room has been enshrined by tradition as the site of Jesus' celebration of the festive Passover seder meal with his disciples. The bread and wine consecrated at that last supper became the elements of the Christian Eucharist. The present Upper Room is a large, bare medieval chamber with flagstones and Gothic arches, apparently built in the 14th century. Although no one suggests this as the actual room of the Last Supper, the site most certainly was within the walled city in the time of Jesus. A second tradition identifies the same room with the "one place" of Acts 2, where the disciples of Jesus gathered on Pentecost, seven weeks after his death: "They were all filled with the Holy Spirit and began to speak in other tongues . . . ."

Incongruously, the chamber has the trappings of a mosque as well: stained-glass Arabic inscriptions in the Gothic windows; one window blocked by an ornate mihrab; two Arabic plaques in the wall; a Levantine dome. The Muslims were not interested in the Christian tradition of the place but in the supposed Tomb of David on the floor below. *Mt. Zion. Admission free. Open Sat.–Thurs. 8:30–4:30, Fri. 8:30–1.*

Return to the main path and turn left. A few steps and another left turn bring you to a small tranquil courtyard surrounded by flowerpots and a colonnaded corridor, the cloister of a medieval monastery. The arched windows of the Room of the Last Supper are above **20** you, and immediately beneath the cloister is the **Tomb of David.**

Medieval Jewish pilgrims erroneously identified this hill as the "City of David", the site of Jerusalem in the 10th century BC. And because the City of David was also the "Stronghold of Zion" (II Samuel 5), the hill got the name by which it is known today. Because the Bible relates that David was buried in the City of David, the tomb of the great king was sought—and supposedly found—here. The real City of David has been excavated to the east of Mt. Zion, but nine centuries of tears and prayers have sanctified this place.

Enter the antechamber behind the blue-painted barred windows (men must cover their heads) and pass on to the tomb itself. The cenotaph, a massive stone tomb-marker, is draped with a velvet cloth with embroidered stars of David and inscriptions in Hebrew: "David King of Israel lives forever" (implying his dynasty, from which the Messiah is to come, is eternal) and "If I forget thee, O Jerusalem, may my right hand lose its cunning" (Psalms 137).

On top of the cenotaph are several ornaments that crown Torah scrolls, and two beautifully engraved silver canisters, used in the Sephardi tradition to contain the Torah scroll. Behind the cenotaph is an age-blackened stone alcove, thought by scholars to be the oldest remnant of a synagogue found in Jerusalem (about 5th century AD). In the antechamber opposite the tomb is a mihrab surrounded by green ceramic tiles, which once oriented the faithful toward Mecca in honor of Nebi Daoud, the Prophet David, whom Islam has retroactively beatified. *Mt. Zion, tel. 02/719767. Admission free. Open Sun.–Thurs. 8–5, Fri. 8–2. Inner chamber closed Sat.*

As you emerge from the tomb, turn left and leave the cloister from the side opposite the way you entered. Across the road is the **Chamber of the Holocaust,** a small but powerful exhibit of artifacts salvaged from the Nazi death camps, and ceremonial plaques commemorating entire Jewish communities that were wiped out. *Mt. Zion, tel. 02/715105. Admission: NIS 6 ($2) adults, NIS 3 ($1) children. Open Sun.–Thurs. 8–5, Fri. 8–1.*

Turn left to return to Zion Gate.

Tour 4: City of David

This brief tour of the ancient city, which King David captured from the Jebusites in 1000 BC and made his capital, starts from **Dung Gate.** Park your car outside the gate. Walk east on the Ophel Road (the Old City wall should be on your left, and after it the Ophel Archaeological Garden; *see* Tour 1, *above*). Where the Ophel Road swings left, cross the road *carefully.* The **Kidron Valley** yawns beneath you. The cliff face below the village houses on the opposite side is marked with symmetrical holes, mouths of **tombs** from both the First Temple (Old Testament) and Second Temple (Hellenistic-Roman) periods. The most impressive is the group of 22-centuries-old funerary monuments about 50 yards to your left. The monumental square stone structure with the conical roof is known as **Absalom's Pillar;** the one crowned by a pyramidal roof, a solid block of stone cut out of the mountain, is called **Zachariah's Tomb.** Neither monument has anything to do with the Old Testament personalities they are named for.

Return to the bend in the Ophel Road. This was the northern limit of the **City of David**—a synonym for King David's capital of Jerusalem (II Samuel 5)—and the only side not protected by a valley. The name has been revived to describe its ancient site. The city has been conquered at least 35 times in its 5,000-year-old history, and almost always from the north. David's son Solomon expanded the city northward and built the Temple on Mt. Moriah, where the Dome of the Rock now stands.

Continue south along the paved path that skirts the steep Kidron slope to the excavation site known as **Area G.** Archaeologists, notably Kathleen Kenyon in the 1960s, have sporadically dug up bits of the City of David for more than a century. The most thorough expedition, however, was that of the late Israeli archaeologist Yigal Shiloh, from 1978 to 1985. In this sector, he confirmed the 2nd-century BC dating of the city wall (marked 1, 2, and 3 on the site), but also redated the so-called "stepped structure" (marked 4) to the 10th century BC. It once supported a palace or fortification; in the 7th century BC a house (now partially restored on a platform) was built against it.

The most interesting artifacts yielded in the dig were 51 clay seals used for documents, just as hot wax might be used today. All had personal names impressed on them in the ancient Hebrew script. That all the seals were found in one chamber suggests its use as an archive; the name on one of the seals of Gemariah ben Shafan, the Temple secretary in the days of Jeremiah, confirms it. The clay seals were seared into ceramic permanence, apparently by the fire of the Babylonian destruction of Jerusalem in 586 BC. *Off Ophel Rd. Admission (includes Warren's Shaft): NIS 4 ($1.35) adults. Open Sun.–Thurs. 9–5, Fri. 9–1.*

Leave the site by the opposite gate.

Time Out A vine-shaded terrace with a view of the Kidron Valley lies immediately opposite the exit from Area G. The enterprising owner of the spot sells soft drinks, fresh orange juice, and Turkish coffee, which you can sip leisurely at one of the stone tables. The toilet facilities are not great but are the only ones in the area.

❷❸ Descend the stairway and follow a small sign to **Warren's Shaft.** Charles Warren was an inspired British army engineer who explored Jerusalem in 1867. In the City of David he discovered this spacious, ancient access shaft, which burrowed under the city wall to a point 40 feet above the spring in the valley. Water was hauled up the supposedly unclimbable shaft, perhaps by "the lame and the blind" of II Samuel 5. The conventional wisdom until Shiloh's dig was that the shaft was pre-Davidic, and is to be identified with the *tzinnor* (gutter or water shaft) of II Samuel 5, through which David's warriors penetrated the city in 1000 BC. Shiloh disagreed and dated the shaft to the 9th century BC, based on its similarity to water systems of that later period found elsewhere in Israel. It is true that nobody quite knows what the word tzinnor meant in Old Testament times (the word appears only twice in the Bible), and therefore there *is* room for interpretation. But the traditional explanation has not been discredited yet, and until it is, it is too good a story to surrender!

As you descend into the bowels of the earth (not recommended for visitors who have difficulty negotiating steps), note the ancient chisel marks on the walls. It is now accepted that a good part of the shaft was a natural fissure reamed out by workmen in antiquity. The bottom of the shaft today is a dry chamber, walled off from the spring in the Israelite (Old Testament) period. *Tel. 02/288141. Admission (includes Area G): NIS 4 ($1.35). Open Sun.–Thurs. 9–5, Fri. 9–1.*

Climb the steep road back to the Dung Gate. Bus 1 runs from here to Jaffa Gate and near the city center.

Tour 5: Mount of Olives and East Jerusalem

Numbers in the margin correspond to points of interest on the East Jerusalem map.

Following this tour with your own car presents one problem: There are few places in East Jerusalem where one can confidently leave a car untended. One can, however—with a little more effort—see the attractions by walking and taking public transportation or taxis.
❷❹ Begin the tour on the **Mount of Olives,** at the panoramic lookout outside the Seven Arches Hotel. This is the classic picture-postcard view of the Old City. You are looking west, and the best time to be here is in the morning, when the sun is at your back.

Separating you from the Old City is the **Kidron Valley,** which continues south for a way before breaking east and beginning its steep descent to the Dead Sea. On the slope below you, and spreading off to
your left, is the very extensive **Jewish cemetery,** the oldest cemetery—of any religion—still in use. For more than 2,000 years, Jews
have been buried on the Mount of Olives to await the coming of the
Messiah and the resurrection to follow. The raised structures over
the graves are merely tomb markers, not crypts; burial is still below
ground.

In the Old City wall facing you, and just to the right of the golden
Dome of the Rock, is the blocked-up, double-arched "Gate of Mercy," or **Golden Gate.** Jewish tradition holds that the Messiah will enter Jerusalem this way; Christian tradition says he already has. To
the south of the Dome of the Rock is the black-domed **El-Aqsa
Mosque,** behind which are the stone arches of the Jewish Quarter.
To the left of and beyond the Dome of the Rock is the large, gray
dome of the **Church of the Holy Sepulcher.** To the left of the Old City,
the cone-roofed **Dormition Abbey** and its adjacent tower mark the
top of **Mt. Zion,** today outside the walls, but within the city of the
Second Temple period.

Leave your car near the Seven Arches Hotel and walk some 150
yards back along the approach road to the hotel. In a bay on your
right, through a stone gateway, is a round stone structure, about 10
feet in diameter, called the **Dome of the Ascension.** The building
dates from the Crusader period and was once open to the sky. Cred-
ulous medieval pilgrims were shown an indentation in the natural
rock, said to be the footprint of Jesus as he ascended to heaven, and
the tradition stuck. The dome is actually Islamic in style, and curiously, the current caretakers are Muslim. To enter, ring the bell;
there are no set hours. There is a small entrance fee.

Just beyond the Dome of the Ascension, the road turns sharply
25 right. Enter the **Pater Noster Convent** through a light-gray metal
door on your right. The focal point of this Carmelite convent is a
grotto, traditionally identified as the place where Jesus taught his
disciples the so-called Lord's Prayer: "Our Father [*Pater Noster*],
Who art in Heaven . . . " (Mark 11, Luke 11). The site was purchased by the Princess de la Tour d'Auvergne of France in 1868, and
the convent built on the site of earlier Byzantine and Crusader
structures. The ambitious Basilica of the Sacred Heart, begun here
in the 1920s and designed to follow the lines of Constantine's 4th-
century basilica of Eleona, was never completed, its aisles incongruously lined with pine trees and its altar more reminiscent of an Aztec
high place than a Catholic church. The princess, entombed in a beautiful marble sarcophagus, lies in state in the cloister, oblivious to the
the abandonment of the master plan. Ceramic plaques lining the
cloister walls quote the Lord's Prayer in more than 70 different languages. A small metal plaque in braille is to the left of the entrance.
*Mt. of Olives, tel. 02/894904. Admission free. Open Mon.–Sat. 8:30–
11:45, 3–4:45.*

Walk back toward the hotel, taking the steps to your right before the
parking lot. If you have a car, you can drive on an asphalt road that
breaks off to the right just beyond the steps, switches back, and
then begins a very steep descent. Note: It is *not* a one-way street!

Just down the steps, on the left, is a courtyard with a burial complex
26 said to be the **Tombs of the Prophets** Haggai and Malachi. The tradition is spurious, but the site is interesting in its own right. This is a
burial cave from the Byzantine period, about 1,500 years ago. From

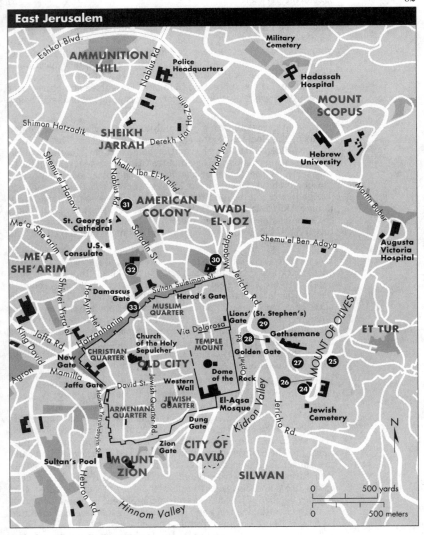

East Jerusalem

Damascus Gate, **33**

Dominus Flevit, **27**

Garden of
Gethsemane, **28**

Garden Tomb, **32**

Mount of Olives, **24**

Pater Noster
Convent, **25**

Rockefeller Museum of
Archaeology, **30**

Tomb of the Virgin, **29**

Tombs of the
Kings, **31**

Tombs of the
Prophets, **26**

the round entrance hall, three passages radiate out to meet the two semicircular inner corridors containing the cave's 26 burial niches.

Just below the tombs, in the Jewish cemetery, is the **common grave** of 48 Jews killed in the battle for the Jewish Quarter in 1948. Hastily buried at the time within the quarter itself, their remains were disinterred in 1967 and reburied here. Among those buried with military honors were 10-year-old boys killed while running messages between defensive positions in the quarter.

㉗ **Dominus Flevit**—"the Lord wept"—is a small, modern, tear-shape church halfway down the mountain. Built in 1953–55 and designed by Antonio Barluzzi, the outstanding feature of the simple interior is the church's picture window and the superb view it affords, the iron cross of the altar silhouetted against the Old City and Dome of the Rock. Although many small archaeological finds were made at the site, the tradition of recognizing this as the site where Jesus wept over Jerusalem as he prophesied its destruction—"and they shall not leave in thee one stone upon another" (Luke 19)—is apparently no earlier than the Crusader period.

The courtyard of Dominus Flevit, bedecked with flower beds and shrubs and some of the archaeological remains, is a place for tranquilly enjoying the view between waves of tour groups. (Not to be dismissed are the rest rooms, rare on this tour!) *Mt. of Olives, tel. 02/274931. Admission free. Open Apr.–Sept., daily 8–noon, 2:30–6; Oct.–Mar., daily 8–noon, 2:30–5.*

Continue down the hill. The gold onion domes and sculpted white turrets of the Russian **Church of Mary Magdalene,** straight out of fantasyland, can be seen in tantalizing glimpses over a high wall to the right. The church, dedicated in 1888, is rarely open, but it's worth visiting the icon-decorated interior if you happen to be in the area at the right time. *Mt. of Olives, tel. 02/284371. Admission: NIS 2 (70¢). Open Tues. and Thurs. 10–11:30.*

㉘ At the bottom of the road, on the left, marked by the platoon of vendors outside, is the **Garden of Gethsemane.** The site is mentioned in the New Testament as the place where Jesus came with his disciples after the Last Supper, where he prayed and sweated blood (Matthew 26), and where, in the end, he was betrayed and arrested. "Gethsemane" derives from the Aramaic *gat shamna,* or the Hebrew *gat shemanim,* meaning oil press. The olive tree, which gives this hill its name, grew in greater profusion in antiquity than today, its fruit providing precious lamp oil. The "Garden of the Oil Press" still boasts eight enormous, gnarled trees, still productive, which some botanists surmise might be as old as Christianity itself. *Admission free. Open Apr.–Sept., daily 8–noon, 2:30–6; Oct.–Mar., daily 8–noon, 2:30–5.*

Within the garden is the **Church of All Nations,** also designed by the architect Barluzzi, and dedicated in 1924. Within each of its interior domes are mosaic symbols of the countries that contributed to its building. (The United States' seal can be seen in the first dome as you enter the church.) The windows are glazed with translucent alabaster in somber browns and purples, creating a mystical atmosphere in the dim interior. At the altar is the so-called Rock of Agony, where Jesus is said to have endured his Passion. The large mosaics depict the events associated with the site. Small windows in the floor show sections of the Byzantine mosaics that inspired those of the contemporary church. *Jericho Rd., tel. 02/283264. Admission free. Open 8–noon, 2:30–5; closes 1 hr later Apr.–Sept.*

Gethsemane abuts Jericho Road at the foot of the Mount of Olives. The road bends sharply at this point, and to the right a staircase takes you deep into the subterranean **Church of the Assumption,** better known by the name of the shrine within it, the **Tomb of the Virgin.** The Gothic facade clearly dates the structure to the Crusader era, but the tradition that this is where the Virgin Mary was interred and then "assumed" into heaven apparently reaches back to the Byzantine period. In an otherwise gloomy church, hung with age-darkened icons and brass lamps, the marble sarcophagus, thought to date from the 12th century, remains illuminated. *Jericho Rd. Admission free. Open 6:30–noon, 2–5.*

To the right of the entrance is the Franciscan-administered **Grotto of Gethsemane,** where the rock ceiling seems to press down on you. The Franciscans identify Gethsemane with Christ's Passion, and this spot with his arrest. *Jericho Rd., tel. 02/283264. Admission free. Open Apr.–Sept., Mon.–Wed., Fri., and Sat. 8:30–11:45, 2:30–5, Sun. and Thurs. 8:30–11:45, 2:30–3:30; Oct.–Mar., Mon.– Wed., Fri., and Sat. 8:30–11:45, 2:30–4:30, Sun. and Thurs. 8:30– 11:45, 2:30–3:30.*

Continuing toward the Old City, the first left takes you to the City of David, Dung Gate, and Mt. Zion. Continue to the right for the rest of the tour. Turn left at the traffic light into Sultan Suleiman Street. Immediately on your right is a steep driveway leading up to the **Rockefeller Museum of Archaeology,** with its landmark octagonal tower. Its somewhat messily presented exhibits have become far more visitor-friendly of late, though it is still not the last word in the art of installation.

If you have just a passing interest in archaeology, the Israel Museum's finely presented collection will probably suffice (*see* Tour 7, *below*). The Rockefeller Museum is for the enthusiast. The finds are all from Israel, ranging in date from prehistoric times to around AD 1700. Among the most important exhibits are cultic masks from Neolithic Jericho, ivories from Canaanite (Bronze Age) Megiddo, the famous Israelite "Lachish Letters" (6th century BC), Herodian inscriptions, and decorative reliefs from Hisham's Palace in Jericho and from the Church of the Holy Sepulcher.

Do not park on the street; parking is permitted within the museum grounds. A good plan is to bring your lunch to eat in the shade of the lovely garden. *Sultan Suleiman St., tel. 02/282251. Admission: NIS 12 ($4) adults, NIS 8 ($2.70) students and children. Open Sun.– Thurs. 10–5, Fri. and Sat. 10–2.*

Continue along Sultan Suleiman Street and turn right at the post office into Saladin Street. Since the *intifada* began in December 1987, Israelis have increasingly avoided East Jerusalem. Although you are not being advised to avoid the whole area, you *are* urged to stick to the main streets and not to leave your car untended: Palestinian nationalist zeal has led to an increase in vandalism. Plan to spend your evenings in some other part of town.

Where Saladin Street meets Nablus Road (about 1 kilometer, or .6 mile, from the Rockefeller Museum), on the right, are the Tombs of the Kings. If you are driving, turn right at the intersection, and again into the second street on the right (a dead-end road) to the American Colony Hotel (*see* Lodging, *below*), where you will find safe parking. If you intend to complete the tour, leave your car here and see the other sights on foot.

Time Out The **American Colony Hotel** is a 19th-century limestone building with cane furniture, Armenian ceramic tiles, and a delightful court-yard. The food is generally good, and a light lunch or afternoon tea in the cool lobby lounge, poolside restaurant, or on the patio can come as a well-earned break in the tour. *Tel. 02/285171. Reservations advised.*

㉛ The **Tombs of the Kings** were explored in the 19th century by the Frenchman Félicien de Saulcy, who accepted the local tradition identifying them with the biblical kings of Judah. Royal tombs they were, but not quite that old. In the 1st century AD, Queen Helene of Adiabene, a country on the border of Persia, converted to Judaism and came to live and die in the Holy City. Although she built her palaces in the City of David in the south of the city, she and her descendants were buried here, in catacombs that are the finest examples of their kind in Israel.

Wide, rock-hewn steps descend to rain catchment pools and into a spacious courtyard, all excavated out of solid rock. The entrance to the tombs is across a porch that once boasted two massive stone columns and still has its Hellenistic-style frieze above. The "rolling stone" that once sealed the mouth of the catacombs is still in situ, a graphic example of those described in the New Testament.

You will need a flashlight or several candles for the tombs. The "weeping chamber" immediately inside the doorway has rock benches and triangular niches to hold oil lamps. Other chambers branching off it contain the many alcoves and ledges where the dead, wrapped in shrouds, were laid. *Saladin St. The attendant requires a small fee. Open Mon.–Sat. 8–12:30, 2–5. Note that the published hours are unreliable, and the site is still sometimes found closed.*

Continue down Nablus Road. Almost immediately on your left is the neo-Gothic Anglican **St. George's Cathedral,** built at the beginning of the century as a copy of New College at Oxford University. Its tower is a landmark of Jerusalem's skyline.

㉜ Some 500 yards farther, beyond the U.S. Consulate and opposite the bus station, a well-marked narrow lane to the left—Conrad Schick Street—leads to the **Garden Tomb.** In 1883, General Charles Gordon (of later Khartoum fame) spent several months in Jerusalem. From his window just inside the Old City walls, he was struck by the skull-like features of a cliff face north of the Damascus Gate. He was convinced that this, rather than the traditional Calvary in the Church of the Holy Sepulcher (*see* Tour 1, *above*), was "the place of the skull" (Mark 15) where Jesus was crucified. His conviction was infectious and stimulated a fund-raising campaign that resulted in the purchase of an adjacent site in 1894. An ancient rock-cut tomb uncovered there some years earlier took on new importance due to its proximity to the "skull hill" (already becoming known as "Gordon's Calvary"). Subsequent excavations exposed cisterns and a wine press, features typical of an ancient "garden."

The newly formed Garden Tomb Association was jubilant: All the elements of the Gospel account of Jesus's death and burial were here. Jesus was buried in the fresh tomb of the wealthy Joseph of Arimathea (Matthew 27), and contemporary archaeologists lent their authority to the identification of the tomb as an upper-class one of the Second Temple Period. Recent research has strongly challenged that conclusion, however. The tomb is apparently from the Old Testament period, making it too old to have been that of Jesus, since his was one "in which no man had yet been laid." It should be noted that the gentle guardians of the Garden Tomb do not insist on the identification of the site as that of Calvary and the tomb of Christ, but suggest (as their brochure puts it) that "the features of the Garden . . . provide an atmosphere which brings into focus the relevance of the Death and Resurrection of the Lord Jesus Christ." Indeed, the beautifully tended garden of trees, flower beds, and seats for private meditation make this an island of tranquillity in the hurly-burly of East Jerusalem. Guided tours are available on request. *Conrad Schick St., tel. 02/272745. Admission free. Open Mon.–Sat. 8–noon, 2:30–5. Sunday: service only (nondenominational Protestant in English) at 9 AM.*

Turn left onto Nablus Road and continue for 200 yards. You are now at the Old City walls opposite **Damascus Gate.** With its tapered carved-stone crenellations and ornamented embrasures, the gate is the most beautiful of the seven still open in the present 16th-century Old City wall. It is also the busiest of them all, the main link between the Old City and the Arab neighborhoods of East Jerusalem. There have been occasional incidents here, so it is not a recommended place for lingering. Pause for an impression, and move on.

To the left and below the approach bridge is a surviving arched entrance of the pagan **Roman town** built by Emperor Hadrian in AD 135 on the ruins of its Jewish predecessor. It was Hadrian's plan to build the town that touched off the Jewish Bar Kochba Revolt in AD 132. Excavations just inside the arch (reached by going to the right of Damascus Gate and then left under the bridge) have brought to light an almost entirely intact Roman tower that connects with the Ramparts Walk (separate ticket; *see* Tour 3, *above*), and part of an open plaza of the 2nd-century town. A tall column topped by the emperor's statue once dominated the plaza, exactly as depicted in the famous 6th-century mosaic floor map found in Madaba, Jordan. The column served as the point of reference for measuring distances throughout the country, and though it has not survived, the Arabic name for the gate—Bab el-Amud, the Gate of the Column—preserves its memory. *Damascus Gate, tel. 02/231221 or 02/285400. Admission: NIS 2.50 (80¢) adults, NIS 1.30 (40¢) children. Open Sat.–Thurs. 9–4, Fri. 9–2.*

You now have quite a few options: Return by foot to the American Colony Hotel; take a cab from Damascus Gate to your next destination; walk up Hativat Hatzanhanim Street (outside the Old City, with its walls on your left) toward Jaffa Gate and the New City; walk the Ramparts (*see* Tour 3, *above*) to Jaffa Gate; or plunge into the Old City to reach the Via Dolorosa and the Western Wall (left fork inside Damascus Gate) or the Church of the Holy Sepulcher and the Jewish Quarter (right fork).

Tour 6: West Jerusalem

Numbers in the margin correspond to points of interest on the West Jerusalem map.

The sites on this tour are all on the western edge of Jerusalem, easily accessible by car, or by a combination of buses, short cab rides, and a little patience.

Begin the tour at **Yad Vashem,** the national Holocaust memorial and museum, 700 yards west of Mt. Herzl. Only Bus 99 stops at the site, but Mt. Herzl, a 10-minute walk away, is served by many lines (Buses 6, 18, and 27 run from the city center).

The experience of the Holocaust is so deeply seared into the Jewish national memory that understanding it goes a long way toward understanding the Israelis themselves. It is not by chance that Yad Vashem is a mandatory stop on the itineraries of most official guests of the State. Created in 1953 by an act of the Knesset, Israel's parliament, it possesses the largest Holocaust archive in the world (some 50 million documents). Through its museum, research and publication departments, and its youth education programs, the institute attempts not merely to document the period, but to convey the challenge of understanding the Holocaust, especially to younger generations. The name Yad Vashem—"an everlasting memorial"—comes from the Biblical book of Isaiah.

From the parking lot, take the path to the right of the bookshop. At the top of the rise turn right and walk down to the **Children's Memorial** through a cavelike entrance. The light is dim inside, but there are no steps to worry about, and the railings will guide you. This is the only part of Yad Vashem in which photography is not allowed.

Of the 6 million Jews murdered by the Nazis in World War II, 1.5 million were children, a statistic that emphasizes the single-mindedness of the "Final Solution." In trying to do the seemingly impossible—to convey the enormity of the loss without numbing the viewer's emotions or losing sight of the victims' individuality—architect Moshe Safdie found an ingenious solution. He used five candles and some 500 mirrors to create an infinity of living flames in the darkness, while recorded narrators intone the names, ages, and countries of origin of known victims. The effect is electrifying.

Follow the path past the tall memorial to the Jewish resistance fighters. On the plaza you come to is the **Hall of Remembrance,** a heavy basalt and concrete building that houses an eternal flame; the names of the death camps are inscribed on the floor. Outside again, step down past the **Avenue of the Righteous,** a belt of 5,500 trees around the site bearing plaques of the names of Gentiles in Europe who risked and sometimes lost their lives trying to save Jews from the Nazis. Raoul Wallenberg, King Christian X of Denmark, Corrie ten Boom, and Oskar Schindler are among the more famous honored here.

The **museum,** entered from Warsaw Ghetto Square, is the centerpiece of Yad Vashem. Through artifacts, photographs, videos, recordings, and explanations in English, it documents the period from Hitler's rise to power in 1933 through the following 12 nightmare years to the post-war turmoil that precipitated the birth of Israel. In the same building is the **Art Museum,** a simultaneously beautiful and heart-wrenching display of art and sculpture by Jewish artists, known and unknown, adults and children, who either perished in the Holocaust while their work miraculously survived, or who themselves survived the period and expressed their experiences through their art.

From the parking lot a road descends (about 1 kilometer, or .6 mile) to Yad Vashem's newest project, the **Valley of the Destroyed Communities.** Walls of enormous, rough-hewn limestone boulders create a series of canyons, each representing a region of Nazi Europe, with the names of lost communities inscribed in the stone. *Near Herzl Blvd., tel. 02/751611. Admission free. Open Sun.–Thurs. 9–4:45, Fri. and holiday eves 9–1:45.*

Return toward Herzl Boulevard, but turn into the large parking lot that abuts it. This is the entrance to **Mt. Herzl,** named for Theodor Herzl, the founder of the modern Zionist movement, whose tomb is

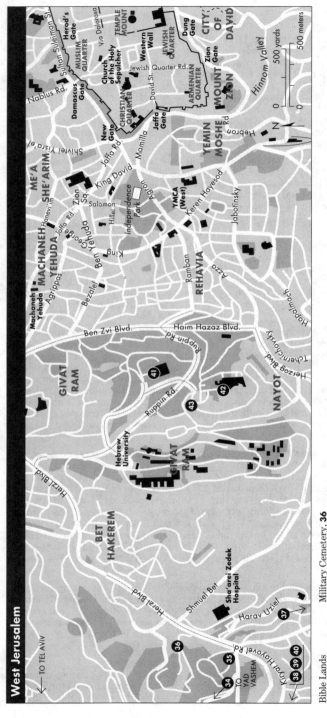

West Jerusalem

TO TEL AVIV

Herzl Blvd.

BET HAKEREM

Shmuel Ber

Ha'arei Zedek Hospital

Harav Uziel

Kiryat Hayovel Rd.

TO YAD VASHEM

GIVAT RAM

Hebrew University

Ruppin Rd.

Ben Zvi Blvd.

Haim Hazaz Blvd.

Ruppin Rd.

GIVAT RAM

Herzog Blvd.

Tchernichovsky

NAYOT

REHAVIA

Ramban

Azza

Jabotinsky

Bezalel

Agrippas

King

Ben Yehuda

George

Jaffa Rd.

Machaneh Yehuda

MACHANEH YEHUDA

Hanevi'im

MEA SHE'ARIM

Shivtei Yisra'el

Nablus Rd.

Sultan Suleiman St.

Herod's Gate

Damascus Gate

New Gate

Jaffa Rd.

Zion Sq.

Salomon

Hillel

King

Keren Hayesod

YMCA (West)

Aplon

Independence Park

Mamilla

King David

David St.

Jaffa Gate

CHRISTIAN QUARTER

Church of the Holy Sepulcher

MUSLIM QUARTER

Via Dolorosa

TEMPLE MOUNT

Jewish Quarter Rd.

JEWISH QUARTER

Western Wall

Dung Gate

CITY OF DAVID

Zion Gate

ARMENIAN QUARTER

MOUNT ZION

YEMIN MOSHE

Hebron Rd.

Hinnom Valley

Hapalmach

N

0 500 yards

0 500 meters

Bible Lands Museum, **43**
Church of St. John the Baptist, **39**
Church of the Visitation, **40**
Hadassah Hospital, **38**
Israel Museum, **42**
Knesset, **41**

Military Cemetery, **36**
Mt. Herzl, **35**
Second Temple Period Model, **37**
Yad Vashem, **34**

at its summit. In 1894, the Budapest-born Herzl was the Paris correspondent for a Vienna newspaper when the Dreyfus treason trial hit the headlines. The anti-Semitic outbursts that Herzl encountered in cosmopolitan Paris shocked him—the Jewish Dreyfus had, in fact, been framed, and was later exonerated—and thereafter he devoted himself to the problem of Jewish vulnerability in "foreign" host countries, and the need, in his eyes, of creating a Jewish state where Jews could control their own destiny. The result of his activities was the first World Zionist Congress in Basel, Switzerland, in 1897. That year Herzl wrote in his diary: "If not in five years, then in 50, [a Jewish state] will become reality." Just 50 years later, in November 1947, the United Nations gave its sanction to the idea. Herzl died in 1904, and his remains were brought to Israel in 1949.

The site is beautifully landscaped, with cedars from Lebanon lording it over the native pine and cypress. The **Herzl Museum** to the left of the entrance preserves Herzl's Vienna study intact. The path beyond it eventually turns right across a huge plaza (used for state ceremonies) to the unadorned black stone marker at the top of the mountain, inscribed in Hebrew only with the name Herzl.

To the left (west) of the grave site, a gravel path leads down to a section containing the **graves of national leaders,** among them former prime ministers Golda Meir and Levi Eshkol, and Zalman Shazar, Israel's third president. *Herzl Blvd., tel. 02/511108. Admission free. Park open Sun.–Thurs. 8–5 (summer until 6:30), Fri. and holiday eves 8–2. Museum open Sun.–Tues. and Thurs. 9–4:45 (summer until 6:15) and Fri. 9–1.*

36 From the graves of the national leaders, continue west for a few yards, descending to the Mt. Herzl **Military Cemetery,** Israel's largest. Different sections are reserved for the veterans of the various wars the nation has fought, and the large number of identical headstones is a sobering reminder of the price of independence and security. Officers and privates are buried alongside one another, an Israeli egalitarianism that expresses the idea that lives lost are mourned equally by the nation, regardless of rank.

The paths through the military cemetery bear round to the right, double back to the cemetery entrance, and reach Herzl Boulevard 300 yards below the first entrance where this tour of Mt. Herzl began. Alternatively, of course, you could enter the military cemetery directly, without going through the park. *Herzl Blvd., tel. 02/437257. Admission free. Open daily 24 hrs.*

One hundred yards down Herzl Boulevard from the entrance to Mt. Herzl, turn right at the next traffic light into Rav Uziel Street. After 2 kilometers (1.2 miles) the road passes the Holyland Hotel, and **37** 150 yards farther is the **Second Temple Period Model.** Park and take the short path on the left. Buses 21 and 21A go here from the city center and the Central Bus Station.

Seven years in the building, the huge open-air model—the size of a tennis court—represents Jerusalem at its greatest extent in the mid-1st century AD. The scale is 1:50, roughly ¼ inch to the foot. Although built around a concrete core, the miniature structures are faced with the same "Jerusalem stone" as the originals. The designer of the model, the late Professor Michael Avi-Yonah, was guided by ancient literary descriptions of Jerusalem and modern archaeological finds. Public works, such as the city's fortifications and King Herod's great reconstructed marble temple (the Second Temple), are thought to be substantially accurate, while private buildings reflect the known architectural style of the period. The model is constantly evolving: Where new evidence contradicts old assumptions, elements of the model are changed. *On grounds of Holyland Hotel, tel. 02/437777. Admission NIS 15 ($5) adults, NIS 10 ($3.35) students and children. Open daily 8 AM–10 PM (evening hrs change in winter; call ahead).*

Return to the intersection with Herzl Boulevard and turn left. Stay on the winding main road, the name of which changes several times: Kiryat Hayovel Road, Hantke Street, and Henrietta Szold Road.

38 The road swings sharply right to **Hadassah Hospital.** Parking is difficult to find within the hospital grounds; you may have to park on the main road. Buses 19 and 27 serve the hospital. Hadassah is the largest general hospital in the Middle East and the teaching hospital for Hebrew University's medical and dental schools. What draws visitors, however, is the world-famous **Chagall Windows.**

When the Hadassah organization approached the Russian-born Jewish painter Marc Chagall in 1959 to design the stained-glass windows for the synagogue of the new hospital, the artist was delighted and contributed his work for free. Taking his inspiration from Jacob's deathbed blessings on his sons (Genesis 49), and, to a lesser extent, from Moses's valediction to the tribes of Israel (Deuteronomy 33), Chagall created 12 vibrant windows in primary colors, with an ark full of characteristically Chagallian beasts and a scattering of Jewish and esoteric symbols. The innovative techniques of the Rheims glassmakers give the wafer-thin windows an astounding illusion of depth in many places. To see the windows, take the tour of the synagogue, which includes a film about the hospital. *Henrietta Szold Rd., Ein Kerem, tel. 02/416333. Admission: NIS 5 ($1.70) adults, NIS 3 ($1) students and children. Guided tours of synagogue: Sun.–Thurs. 8:30, 9:30, 10:30, 11:30, 12:30, 2:30; Fri. and holidays 9:30, 10:30, 11:30.*

As you leave from the hospital's main entrance, turn right. Where the road joins Route 386 turn right again, reentering Jerusalem through **Ein Kerem** (Bus 17), which boasts a mix of its original working-class population and artists and professionals living in renovated old stone buildings that have become upscale showpieces.

Dominating the center of the village (on the left, as you approach
39 from the bottom) is the late-17th-century Franciscan **Church of St. John the Baptist,** a large white structure, its orange tile roof a distinctive local landmark. Though not mentioned by name in the New Testament, Ein Kerem has long been identified as John the Baptist's birthplace, a tradition that apparently goes back to the Byzantine period (5th century AD). The old paintings and glazed tiles in the church make it worth a visit. You can also see the grotto where John the Baptist is said to have been born. *Ein Kerem. Admission free. Open Apr.–Sept., Mon.–Sat. 8–noon and 2:30–6, Sun. 9–noon and 2:30–6; Oct.–Mar., Mon.–Sat. 8–noon and 2:30–5, Sun. 9–noon and 2:30–5.*

Opposite the church, a short street takes you to the small **Spring of the Virgin.** Turn right and climb a steep, stepped street past a Rus-
40 sian Orthodox monastery to the Franciscan **Church of the Visitation,** said to have been the home of John the Baptist's parents, Zachariah and Elizabeth. When Mary, pregnant with Jesus, came to visit her pregnant cousin Elizabeth, "the babe leaped in [Elizabeth's] womb" with joy. Mary then pronounced the paean of praise to God (Luke 1) known as the Magnificat ("My soul doth magnify the Lord . . . ."). A wall of the courtyard is covered with ceramic tiles quoting the Magnificat in 41 languages. The upper church is adorned with large wall

paintings depicting the various mantles with which Mary has been endowed: Mother of God, Refuge of Sinners, Dispenser of All Grace, Help of Christians, and the Immaculate Conception. Other frescoes depict Hebrew women of the Bible also known for their "hymns and canticles," as the Franciscan guide puts it. *Ein Kerem, tel. 02/ 417291. Admission free. Open Apr.–Sept., daily 8–11:45, 2:30–6; Oct.–Mar., daily 8–11:45, 2:30–5.*

Return to the main road of the village and turn right onto the steep road that emerges at Mt. Herzl.

Tour 7: The Knesset and Israel Museum

All the sites on this tour are in an area called **Givat Ram,** in West Jerusalem. The sector is easily accessible by both car and public transportation, and the sites are within walking distance of one another.

To drive to the Knesset, take Ruppin Road, a wide divided highway running from the tall white condominium complex known as the Wolfson Buildings (on the edge of the Rehavia neighborhood, opposite Sacher Park) toward Herzl Boulevard and the Tel Aviv exit. Five-hundred yards from Sacher Park, at the first traffic light, turn right. The modern, flat-top building on the rise to your right is the **41** **Knesset,** Israel's parliament. The next turn to the right brings you up to the security barrier. You may be able to gain entry and let the guards guide you to the parking lot, or simply park on the street before reaching the barrier. City Bus 9 drops you right at the main gate. Note: You will have to produce your passport for identification and will be asked to check your camera before entering the building.

Both the name Knesset and the number of seats (120) in this one-chamber assembly were taken from Haknesset Hagedolah, the "Great Assembly" of the Second Temple Period. Visitors may see the building only on a guided tour, conducted on Sunday and Thursday, which includes the Knesset session hall, and the reception with its three enormous, brilliantly colored tapestries designed by artist Marc Chagall on the themes of the Creation, the Exodus, and Jerusalem. On the other days, you can attend open sessions of the Knesset (in Hebrew, of course); call ahead for the session schedule.

"Take two Israelis," runs the old quip, "and you've got three political parties!" The saying is not without truth in a nation where everyone has an opinion and will usually not hesitate to express it. The Knesset reflects this rambunctious spirit, sometimes to the point of despair. Israel's electoral system, known as proportional representation, is a legacy of the dangerous but heady days of Israel's War of Independence in 1948–49. To avoid an acrimonious and divisive election while the fledgling state was still fighting to stay alive, the founding fathers developed a one-body parliamentary system that gave representation to rival ideological factions in proportion to their comparative strength in the country. Instead of the winner-takes-all approach of the constituency system, the Israeli system grants any party that wins 1.5% of the *national* vote its first seat in the Knesset. As a result, even small fringe parties can have their voices heard. The disadvantage of this system is that it spawns a plethora of political parties, making it virtually impossible for one party to get the majority needed to govern. Israeli governments have thus always consisted of a coalition of parties, often a government of compromise. The smaller parties, whose support is critical for the government to keep its ruling majority, have thus been able to extract major political and material concessions for their own party interests, which are often at odds with those of the nation at large. Extensive discussion, public campaigns, demonstrations, and even proposed legislation to change the system have produced one important result. As of the 1996 general elections, the prime minister will no longer be simply the leader of the victorious party, but will be elected directly by the voters. Oddly, this potentially could produce a deadlock whereby the successful candidate is not a member of the victorious party. The resolution of this dilemma is not yet clear. *Tel. 02/753333. Admission free. Guided tours Sun. and Thurs. 8:30–2.*

Across the road from the Knesset main gate is a 10-foot-high bronze **menorah,** a seven-branched candelabrum, based on the one that once graced the First and Second Temples in Jerusalem and now the official symbol of the State of Israel. Designed by artist Bruno Elkin and a gift of the British Parliament to the Knesset in 1956, the menorah is decorated with bas-relief depictions of events and personages in Jewish history, from Biblical times to the modern day. Behind the menorah (enter below the security barrier) is the **Wohl Rose Garden,** filled with dozens of different varieties of roses and plenty of lawns for children to romp on.

❷ Just across Ruppin Road from the Knesset, the **Israel Museum** was built in 1965 as a series of glass and white-stone pavilions clinging to a 22-acre hilltop (Buses 9, 17, and 24). A shuttle bus for the infirm makes runs on request from the main gate to the main entrance 150 yards away. The collection is nothing if not eclectic, and some of its exhibits, especially the ones devoted to archaeology and Judaica, are among the best of their kind in the world.

Its most distinctive edifice is the white, domelike **Shrine of the Book,** which houses the famous **Dead Sea Scrolls,** arguably the most important archaeological find ever made in the region. The first of the 2,000-year-old scrolls was discovered by a Bedouin boy in 1947 in a cave in the Judean Desert. The adventures of these priceless artifacts before they finally came to rest here is the stuff of which Indiana Jones movies are made (*see* Exploring Around Jerusalem *in* Chapter 3). The dome was inspired by the shape of the lids of the clay jars in which the first scrolls were found.

The scrolls were written in the Second Temple Period by a fundamentalist Jewish sect generally identified as the Essenes. Archaeological, laboratory, and textual evidence agree on dating the earliest of the scrolls to the late 3rd century BC; none could have been written later than AD 68, the year in which their home community of Qumran was destroyed by the Romans. Written on parchment and in an extraordinary state of preservation because of the exceptional dryness of the Dead Sea region, the scrolls include the oldest Hebrew manuscripts of the Old Testament ever found, authenticating the almost identical Hebrew texts still in use today. Sectarian literature includes "the Rule of the Community" (the so-called "Manual of Discipline"), a constitution of this ascetic group, and "The War of the Sons of Light Against the Sons of Darkness," a blow-by-blow account of a final cataclysmic conflict that would, they believed, presage the Messianic age.

The entrance corridor to the Shrine of the Book displays parchment and papyrus letters and documents of a slightly later period, the Bar Kochba Revolt of AD 132–135. With the collapse of the revolt, Jews fled the Roman legionnaires to remote caves in sheer desert canyons, taking with them their most prized possessions, including legal documents such as land deeds and marriage contracts. In the basement of the main hall are some of the objects the Jews escaped with to the desert, among them woolen blankets and prayer shawls, and a glass bowl of stunning perfection, regarded by scholars as one of the finest ever found in the ancient world.

Next to the shrine is the open-air **Billy Rose Sculpture Garden,** donated by the American impresario and designed by the artist Isamu Noguchi as a series of semicircular terraces divided by stone walls. Crunch over the gravel amid works by Daumier, Rodin, Maillol, Moore, Lipchitz, Nadelman, and Picasso, among many others, all seen against the stark Judean Hills. It's an art lover's dream setting for a picnic.

Continue up the main path to enter the main building. Walk downstairs and make your choice. Ahead of you is the **Judaica** section, part of the Jewish Heritage collection, with perhaps the world's greatest collection of Jewish ceremonial art and artifacts. Among the highlights are medieval illuminated Haggadoth (Passover texts) and wedding contracts, a huge collection of Sabbath spice boxes and Hanukkah menorahs, the interior of a 17th-century Venetian synagogue brought here virtually intact, and a reconstructed 19th-century German sukkah, a temporary booth associated with the holiday of Sukkoth, decorated inside with stylized scenes of Jerusalem.

Ethnographic exhibits, including dazzling formal costumes and jewelry, and everyday objects used in Jewish communities through the Middle East, North Africa, and Eastern Europe, separate the Judaica collection from the now much-expanded fine arts section. A modest but good-quality collection of **European art** includes paintings by Van Dyck, Monet, Van Gogh, and Renoir. **Period rooms** reflecting 18th- and 19th-century European design are an unexpected presence. Most recently opened is the adjacent **Cummings 20th-Century Art Building,** dedicated to modern and contemporary art, from Cézanne, Picasso, and Chagall to Dubuffet, Rothko, and Lipchitz. Some galleries display both permanent and changing exhibitions of prints, drawings, and photographs.

Return to the bottom of the aforementioned staircase. A left turn will hurl you back a million years in time as you find yourself surrounded by stone tools and mammoth tusks. Israel lies on the only land bridge between Africa and Asia, and the wealth of important prehistoric finds from across the country on display here is evidence of movement and settlement across it in the misty past. You are now in the rambling, multilevel **Samuel Bronfman Biblical and Archaeological Museum,** whose focal point for many visitors is the Biblical (Old Testament) period. Pots from the time of Abraham, a Solomonic gateway, and inscriptions from Isaiah's day are just some of the many artifacts that help to illuminate and add a sense of immediacy to the history of this ancient land. A side hall displays a superb collection of glass, from rainbow-patinaed Roman pieces to sleek Art Deco objects and beyond. The bottom of the section spills into the **Youth Wing,** where delightful hands-on exhibits and workshops encourage children to appreciate art—and a changing variety of other subjects—and try their hand in a do-it-yourself craft workshop. Parents with restless children will be grateful for the outdoor play areas. *Givat Ram, tel. 02/708873. Admission: NIS 18 ($6) adults, NIS 12 ($4) students and senior citizens, NIS 8 ($2.70) children, NIS 50 ($16.70) families. Open Sun., Mon., Wed., and Thurs. 10–5; Tues. 4–10 (Shrine of the Book open Tues. 10–10); Fri. 10–2; Sat. 10–4.*

43 The recently opened **Bible Lands Museum** is across the Israel Museum parking lot. It was the brainchild of Canadian multimillionaire Elie Borowski, whose collection of ancient artifacts forms the core of the collection. The curators have abandoned the traditional grouping of artifacts according to their place of origin and opted instead for a chronological display, placing together objects of different cultures dating from the same period, thus giving the visitor a clearer understanding of the cross-cultural interactions in the region.

The exhibits cover a time period of more than six millennia, from the prehistoric Neolithic period to that of the Byzantine Empire, and sweep geographically from Afghanistan to Nubia (present-day Sudan). Rare clay vessels, fertility idols, cylinder seals, ivories, and sarcophagi fill the soaring, naturally lit galleries. Look especially for the ancient Egyptian wooden coffin, in a stunning state of preservation. *Givat Ram, tel. 02/611066. Admission: NIS 18 ($6) adults, NIS 8 ($2.70) senior citizens, NIS 5 ($1.70) students and children. Open Sun.–Tues., Thurs. 9:30–5:30, Wed. 9:30–9:30, Fri. 9:30–2, Sat. 11–3.*

Off the Beaten Track

Taking in the panorama of Jerusalem from the **Haas Promenade** is a great way to get your bearings. You can reach the almost 1-kilometer (.6-mile) promenade by driving south along Hebron Road. About 1.3 kilometers (.8 mile) beyond the Ariel Hotel is a police compound on your left known as the Allenby Camp. Turn left at the next traffic light, following signs to East Talpiot and the Haas Promenade. The parking lot is on the left. You'll see the turret of the **United Nations Headquarters,** once the residence of the British High Commissioner for Palestine, crowning one of the highest points in the city. The ridge on which it sits is known in Hebrew as Armon Hanatziv (the Commissioner's Palace). Quite a bit of West Jerusalem is visible off to your left, the downtown area easily identified by its high rises. The **Old City,** identified by the walls and golden Dome of the Rock, is directly in front of you. To the right of it is the ridge of **Mt. Scopus—Mount of Olives,** with its distinctive three towers (from left to right: Hebrew University, Augusta Victoria Hospital, Russian Church of the Ascension), separated from the Old City by the deep **Kidron Valley.** Between the Kidron Valley on the east and the **Cheesemakers' Valley** on the west is a blade-shape strip of land that Jerusalem occupied for its first 2,000 years—the **City of David.**

Shopping

Prices in the city center and the Jewish Quarter of the Old City are generally fixed, although you can often negotiate for significant discounts on high-priced art and jewelry. Shopping in the Old City's colorful Arab bazaar, or souk (pronounced "shook" in Israel), is fascinating but can be a trap for the unwary. Never buy gold, silver, or gem-studded jewelry here. No price is fixed, and despite the merchant's protestations, you'll probably overpay.

Store hours on weekdays are generally 8:30– or 9–1 and 4–7, but many now stay open through the day with no break. Some close on Tuesday afternoon, a traditional but not mandatory half day. Jewish-owned stores (West Jerusalem and the Old City's Jewish Quarter) close on Friday afternoon at 1 or 2, depending on the kind of store and the season of the year (food and souvenir stores tend to stay open later), and reopen on Sunday morning. Some stores geared to the tourist trade, particularly in the center of town (bound by Jaffa Rd., King George St., and Ben Yehuda St.), are open on Saturday night, after the Sabbath terminates, especially in summer. Arab-owned stores in the Old City and East Jerusalem are busiest on Saturday and quietest on Sunday, when many (but not all) Christian storekeepers close for the day.

Shopping Streets and Malls

Arts and Crafts Lane (known in Hebrew as **Hutzot Hayotzer**), opposite and downhill from the Jaffa Gate, boasts goldsmiths and silversmiths specializing in Judaica, generally in ultramodern, minimalist style. The work is exquisite and is priced accordingly. You can also find excellent jewelry, weaving, fine art, and musical instruments.

The **Cardo** in the Old City's **Jewish Quarter** is a converted Crusader-era street, which in turn was built into the main thoroughfare of Byzantine Jerusalem. Apart from souvenirs and Judaica, there are some good-quality jewelry, art, and objets d'art to be found here.

King David Street is lined with a sizeable number of prestigious stores, with the emphasis on art, Judaica, and antiquities, and a lot of interesting jewelry as well.

The **Midrachov** is simply downtown **Ben Yehuda Street,** the nerve center of downtown Jerusalem. The selection of clothing, shoes, jewelry, souvenirs, T-shirts, and street food is prodigious on this pedestrian-only street. You'll be serenaded by street musicians at every turn. It's a real scene, best appreciated from one of the many outdoor cafés. Summer evenings are especially lively.

A smaller and more recent pedestrian mall has developed on **Salomon Street,** in the old neighborhood of **Nahalat Shiva,** just off Zion Square. Here, too, and in adjacent alleys and courtyards, eateries abound, but you can also find some attractive crafts galleries and arty jewelry and clothing stores.

Hatachana (The Mill) is a small arcade on Ramban Street, near the intersection with King George Street. Built around an old, restored windmill, the complex houses, among other shops, expensive fashion stores, a children's clothing store, a jewelry store, a couple of restaurants, and an excellent beauty salon.

The new **Jerusalem Mall,** known locally as "Kenyon Malcha," is—at 500,000 square feet not counting parking—the largest in the Middle East. It includes a department store, supermarket, eight cinemas, and almost 200 shops and eateries (Pizza Hut and Burger King among them). The interior is an attractive mix of arched skylights and wrought-iron banisters in a quasi–art deco style. There are clearly signposted turnoffs to the Mall from Eliyahu Golomb Street (on the way up to Kiryat Hayovel) and from the Pat Junction–Gilo road.

Street Markets

First and foremost, of course, is the **souk** in the Old City. Spreading over a warren of intersecting streets, the souk is primarily the market for the Old City's Arab residents. It is awash with color and redolent with the clashing scents of exotic spices, village women's baskets of produce, hanging shanks of lamb and fresh fish on ice, and fresh-baked delicacies, the food stalls interspersed with those selling fabrics and shoes. The baubles and trinkets of the tourist trade often seem secondary, except along the well-trodden paths of the Via Dolorosa, David Street, and Christian Quarter Road.

The atmosphere in the Arab Quarter has relaxed a great deal since the tense years of the late 1980s. On the other hand, haggling with the merchants—a time-honored tradition—is not the good-natured experience it once was. Unless you know what you want, know how much it's *really* worth, and enjoy the sometimes aggressive give-and-take of bargaining, you are better off just enjoying the local color (stick to the main streets, and watch your wallet or purse) and doing your shopping in the more modern and familiar New City.

Off Jaffa Road, near the Clal Center office buildings, is the **Machaneh Yehuda** produce market. The block-long alleyway is a blur of brilliant primary colors as the city's best-quality fruit and vegetables, pickles and cheeses, fresh fish and poultry, confections, and falafel vie for attention. Thursday and Friday are the busiest days, when Jews shop for the Sabbath. The market, like the rest of Jewish West Jerusalem, is closed on Saturday.

On Thursday and Friday, **Hamartef (The Cellar)** arcade, beneath City Tower on King George Street, hosts jewelers and vendors of bric-a-brac and secondhand books. It's fun just to browse, but sometimes there is really something worth buying. On summer evenings, the **Midrachov (Ben Yehuda Street)** mall fills with peddlers of cheap jewelry and crafts, especially attracting the younger crowd.

The **Arts and Crafts Lane–Sultan's Pool** area hosts a big outdoor arts and crafts fair along with evening concerts around the third week in July.

Specialty Stores

Art Galleries Several galleries representing a range of Israeli artists are located close to the city's premier hotels, on **King David Street.** For large wall decorations (with similar-size prices!), check out the unique appliquélike soft art of **Calman Shemi** (22 King David St., tel. 02/249557). The marvelous effects have to be seen to be appreciated. Another original artist is **Frank Meisler** (21 King David St., tel. 02/242759). With whimsical humor, his caricaturish plated-pewter sculptures cover a range of subjects, from Noah's ark and Jerusalem cityscapes to Freud and animal figures that seem to be sharing Meisler's secret joke.

Clothing Clothing tends to be expensive in Israel, and in Jerusalem you have to search for really stylish clothes. One home-grown women's clothing store with definite class is **A.B.C.** (33 King George St., tel. 02/234934). **Castro** (18 King George St., tel. 02/255421), adjacent to Hamashbir department store and the very pricey **Miss Lagotte,** in The Windmill Mall (8 Ramban St., tel. 02/665059), also stock well-designed women's wear.

High-quality **leather** and **suede** jackets, pants, and coats in upbeat styles and colors are very good buys in Israel. Try **Beged-Or** (2 Ben Yehuda St., tel. 02/256902) on the Midrachov.

Crafts For ceramics, glass, jewelry, wooden objects, and embroidery, try the **Jerusalem House of Quality** (12 Hebron Rd., tel. 02/717430), which showcases the work of some excellent Israeli craftspeople. The building's second floor houses their studios, where you can often find the artists themselves at work.

For **Armenian hand-painted pottery**—predominantly blue and brown, with geometric or stylized natural motifs—one of the best artisans is Stefan Karakashian of **Jerusalem Pottery,** at the VI Station of the Cross, on the Via Dolorosa, in the Old City. His work is of a particularly high standard, but is limited to plaques and plates. For a selection of interesting contemporary ceramics, drop in at the two stores in Nahalat Shiva, each showcasing the work of several Israeli artists: **Cadim** (4 Salomon St., tel. 02/234869), and **Shemonah Beyachad** (6 Salomon St., tel. 02/255155).

Opaque, smoky-color Israeli **glass** is available in both decorative and practical items in many of the tourist shops. The miniature vases, sometimes decorated with silver, are particularly attractive.

Klein (3 Ziv St., off Bar Ilan St., tel. 02/820992 and 02/828784), in the north part of Jerusalem, offers some of the best-made **olive-wood** objects in the country. This is actually the factory, which has a showroom that stocks everything they make, from bowls and yo-yos to attractive trays of Armenian pottery tiles framed in olive wood, picture frames, boxes, and desktop paraphernalia.

Paper-cutting is an exquisite art form in Israel, and two of the best practitioners are **Archie Granot** (34 Shear Yashav St., tel. 02/866190) and **Yehudit Shadur** (12 Hovervei Vion St., tel. 02/663217). Call them for an appointment and directions to their studios.

Colorful, folk-style **Druze weavings** in the form of cloths, pillow covers, and wall hangings can be found at **Ben Shalom** (19 Ben Yehuda St., tel. 02/252948) and **Maskit** (16 King George St., tel. 02/257941), on Rejwan Square, above the plaza. Ben Shalom, in particular, offers a wide variety of beautiful items at reasonable prices. **G.R.A.S.** (20 King George St., adjacent to the Hamashbir department store, tel. 02/256599) offers its own special line of shoes, bags, hats, vests, pillow covers, and curtains in their distinctive, Israeli-made "Eastern" (read: exotic) fabrics. The pillow covers are an especially good value and make great, easy-to-pack gifts.

Jewelry Jewelry in Israel is of high international standard. Although high-quality, conventional pieces are always available (particularly at the ubiquitous **H. Stern,** just inside Jaffa Gate and at the Holiday Inn Crown Plaza, Jerusalem Sheraton Plaza, Laromme, and Seven Arches hotels), you might want to consider the more daring modern jewelry of **G.R.A.S.** (*see above*), **Idit** (16 Ben Yehuda St., tel. 02/ 255836), and **Meshulash,** on Salomon Street. One particularly outstanding artisan is **Danny Alsberg** (tel. 02/289275), in the **Arts and Crafts Lane (Hutzot Hayotzer)** near the Jaffa Gate.

The **National Diamond Center (NDC),** one of the country's largest diamond manufacturers, has a factory and showroom for jewelry and loose cut gems at 143 Bethlehem Road (tel. 02/733770). Guided tours of the facility are also available on request.

Perfumes **Judith Muller** produces scents that come in pretty, smoky-glass flacons shaped to look like ancient bottles. The bottles are available in the usual measures, but you can also find gift sets of two, four, six, and eight miniature bottles. Try the Hamashbir department store, on King George Street, or any perfumery or pharmacy.

T-Shirts T-shirts are a light, inexpensive, and fun gift to bring home. The stores all stock the same range of machine-stamped shirts (some crude, some very attractive); most will also decorate shirts from a selection of designs. There are several on Ben Yehuda Street: **Army/ Navy Surplus** (also on Ben Hillel St., adjacent to Ben Yehuda), **Best Line, The First T-Shirt House,** and **Happening. Mr. T.** and **Lord Kitsch** on Zion Square also stock a good selection.

Sports and Fitness

Bowling

The **Jerusalem Bowling Center** (Achim Yisrael Mall "Kenyon Talpiot," 18 Yad Harutzim St., Talpiot Industrial Zone, tel. 02/ 732195) has 10 lanes and a small cafeteria and billiard tables among its facilities. The center is open daily 10 AM–2 AM. The cost per game (including shoe rental) is NIS 12 ($4) 10 AM–6 PM, and NIS 16 ($5.35) 6 PM–2 AM.

Cycling

The informal **Jerusalem Bicycling Club** (16 Ha'arazim St., tel. 02/ 438386 or 02/816062) leads rides on Saturday morning at 7 starting from the National Convention Center, Binyanei Ha'ooma (opposite the Central Bus Station). The club is a good source for information on bike rentals and can recommend routes to take in the city.

Health Clubs

All the best health clubs in Jerusalem are to be found in hotels; some are privately run concessions. All welcome visitors who are not guests of the hotel. The most comprehensive facilities are at the **Holiday Inn Crowne Plaza** (Givat Ram, tel. 02/258278), **Hyatt Regency** (32 Lehi St., Mt. Scopus, tel. 02/821333), **Knesset Tower** (4 Wolfson St., tel. 02/511111), and **Jerusalem Renaissance** (6 Wolfson St., tel. 02/528111). The following have good facilities but no pools: **Kikar Zion** (25 Shamai St., Zion Sq., tel. 02/244644) and **Lev Yerushalayim** ("Samson's Gym"; 18 King George St., tel. 02/250333).

Horseback Riding

The following stables offer lessons and trail-riding, including those suitable for children: **King David's Riding Stables** (Neve Ilan, north of Rte. 1, tel. 02/340535), in the wooded Judean Hills, 16 kilometers (10 miles) west of Jerusalem, charges NIS 60 ($20) for a full hour. Longer guided trails in the area are offered at a lower hourly rate. **Meir Mizrachi Stables** (Kfar Adumim, north of Rte. 1, tel. 02/355419 [stables], 02/354769 [home]), in the Judean Desert, 17 kilometers (11 miles) east of Jerusalem, charges NIS 40 ($13.35) for an hour, NIS 55 ($18.35) for 1½ hours. **The Riding Club** (Kiryat Moshe, behind Angel's Bakery, tel. 02/513585; do not call between 1 and 3), run by Yehuda Alafi, breeds Arabians. The charge is NIS 50 ($16.70) for an hour. In all cases, longer (and more interesting) trails are available.

Squash

The **YMCA West** (tel. 02/257111), at 26 King David Street, opposite the King David Hotel, has three squash courts for hire. They are available for NIS 30 ($10) an hour 6:30 AM–8 PM.

Swimming

The enthusiast can swim year-round at the pools listed below. Indoor: **Djanogly** (Bet Avraham Community Center, Ramot Allon, tel. 02/868055), **Jerusalem Renaissance Hotel** (6 Wolfson St., tel. 02/ 528111), and **Bet Hano'ar Ha'ivri,** or **YMWHA** (105 Herzog Blvd., tel. 02/789441). Outdoor (covered and heated in winter): **Laromme**

Hotel (3 Jabotinsky St., tel. 02/697777); **Mitzpeh Rachel** (Kibbutz Ramat Rachel, tel. 02/702555), south of the city near the Talpiot neighborhood.

Recommended outdoor pools (except in winter) include the **Jerusalem Pool** (43 Emek Refa'im St., tel. 02/632092), a public facility that gets very crowded in July and August, and the beautifully landscaped facilities of the following hotels: **Hyatt Regency** (32 Lehi St., Mt. Scopus, tel. 02/821333); **Holiday Inn Crowne Plaza** (Givat Ram, tel. 02/581414); **King David Hotel** (23 King David St., tel. 02/251111); and **Jerusalem Renaissance** (6 Wolfson St., tel.02/528111). A little less expensive are the facilities at the **Paradise Hotel** (4 Wolfson St., tel. 02/511111) and **Mt. Zion** (17 Hebron Rd., tel. 02/724222), also in attractive locations.

Tennis

Tennis has really taken off in Israel during the past decade. Advance reservations are always required. **Hebrew University at Mt. Scopus** (tel. 02/817579 or 02/882796) has 10 lighted courts; equipment can be rented. Courts go for NIS 14 ($4.70) an hour (NIS 17/$5.70 an hour with lighting) and are available Sunday–Thursday 7 AM–10 PM, Friday and Saturday 7–5. The **Israel Tennis Center** (5 Almaliach St., Katamon Tet, tel. 02/791866 or 02/792726) has 18 lighted courts that can be rented at NIS 12 ($4) per hour Sunday–Thursday 7 AM–3 PM; and NIS 18 ($6) per hour Sunday–Thursday 7 PM–10 PM, Friday 7–5, Saturday 8–5. The **YMCA (West),** at 26 King David Street (tel. 02/257111), has four courts that rent at NIS 25 ($8.35) per hour. They are open Monday–Saturday 6:30 AM–sunset. Several major hotels have their own courts, but often restrict usage to guests or club members. Ask your concierge to make inquiries if you are bent on playing at a particular hotel.

Dining

Although eating out at restaurants has not been "institutionalized" as much in Jerusalem as in the more cosmopolitan Tel Aviv, you still can eat very well in the Holy City, and its time-worn stone and unique ambience have created many magical corners for doing so. Jerusalem favors Middle Eastern cuisine and vegetarian meals Italian-style or of the quiche-and-salad variety. Less popular are seafood and the more exotic cuisines, such as those from the Far East, though there are some outstanding exceptions.

A brief glossary of restaurant and cooking terms: When used in reference to food, the word Oriental (the translation of the Hebrew *mizrachi*—"eastern") means Middle Eastern cuisine, *not* Far Eastern (such as Chinese, Japanese, or Thai). Dairy restaurants are simply those establishments serving meals without meat; many such places do serve fish.

Hummus, one of the ubiquitous dishes in the region, is a creamy paste made from chickpeas, moistened with olive oil and often tahini (a ground sesame-based sauce), and scooped up with pieces of flat pita bread. Eat it at a place that specializes in Middle Eastern dishes; many more "Western" establishments serve a poor imitation. Also look for a Kurdish/Iraqi specialty called *koubeh*, seasoned ground meat formed into small torpedo shapes and deep-fried in a jacket of *burghul* (cracked wheat).

Falafel, the region's fast food, consists of deep-fried chickpea balls served in pita pockets and topped by a variety of salads. It is filling, nutritious, and very cheap (about NIS 4, or $1.35, for a full portion). About twice that price, *shwarma*, grilled slices of meat (traditionally lamb, but today more commonly turkey), is similarly served in pita bread with salads. Both falafel and shwarma are sold at stands; try King George Street and the area of the Machaneh Yehuda produce market, or the excellent cluster of fast-food places on Emek Refa'im Street at the corner of Rachel Imenu in the German Colony area. A specialty of the grills at Machaneh Yehuda on Agrippas Street is *me'oorav yerushalmi* (Jerusalem mixed grill), a deliciously seasoned meal-in-a-pita of grilled chicken hearts and other organ meats. It's a popular stop after the movies let out.

Dress codes are pretty much nonexistent in Jerusalem's restaurants (or in Israel in general, for that matter). People tend to dress very casually, and jeans, for example, would not be inappropriate in most places. The only exceptions might be some of the fancier establishments at the deluxe hotels. Even then it's only a matter of degree: Informal dress is quite proper, but a modicum of neatness would be expected. Still, if you have taken the trouble to bring your dressy duds, you will not be out of place so dressed in the more exclusive Jerusalem restaurants.

Highly recommended restaurants are indicated by a star ★.

Category	Cost*
$$$$	over $35
$$$	$22–$35
$$	$12–$22
$	under $12

per person for a three-course meal, excluding drinks and 10% service charge

Chinese

$$ ★ Sini Ba-Moshava (Chinese Colony). In an old stone house with a pleasant courtyard for outside dining, this new restaurant, better known to the locals by its Hebrew name, is in fact a reincarnation of a long-established eatery across town. The owners are a Vietnamese couple: The utterly charming wife runs the dining area while the husband does the cooking with a sure and creative hand. The crispness of the food—the spring rolls are a good example—testifies to the fact that all dishes are made on the spot. The hot-and-sour soup is excellent; the oxtail soup—a local rarity—is fantastic. There is the usual long list of main dishes including duck, chicken, beef, pork, or shrimp, but each dish has its own distinct character, some strong, some more subtle. The slices of meat are thin and tender, and the *mooshoo* is as good as you'll find anywhere. For those with asbestos palates, the beef with dry peppers is worth it. *48 Emek Refaim St., tel. 02/665096. Reservations advised Fri. and Sat. dinner. AE, DC, MC, V.*

Dairy and Vegetarian

$$ Off the Square. Like most buildings in the Nahalat Shiva quarter, the stone walls and arches create much of the restaurant's ambience. The large selection is in keeping with this very big eatery, with the focus on fresh fish, soups, salads, pies, and pasta. Try the sweet crepes for dessert. The place is very child-friendly; there's lots of room for restless kids, and the menu has such favorites as pizza and half-portions of many items. *6 Salomon St., tel. 02/242549. No reservations. AE, DC, MC, V. No dinner Fri. or lunch Sat.*

$$ **Tavlin.** One of the veteran vegetarian favorites in the city, the restaurant has retained its high standards with a wide range of vegetable potpies, salads, crepes, and fish dishes that could tempt even a diehard carnivore. For a cozier atmosphere, try a table in the slightly musty "attic," with its upholstered sofas. *16 Salomon St., tel. 02/243847. Reservations advised. No credit cards. No dinner Fri. or lunch Sat.*

$–$$ **Bet Ticho (Ticho House).** This is one of downtown Jerusalem's loveliest and most tranquil nooks. The imposing stone building was built in the 1920s as the home and surgery of the famous ophthalmologist A. A. Ticho and his even more famous wife, artist Anna Ticho, whose evocative drawings of Jerusalem landscapes adorn the place. Although now a national monument, the lobby and patio of the house have been turned into a very creditable restaurant for light meals. House specialties include smoked trout in white horseradish and wine sauce, and broccoli pie. For lunch, a coffee break, or early supper in warm weather, angle for a table on the patio, where the tall pine trees, lawn, and flower beds provide all the soul needs to recuperate from the rigors of sightseeing. *9 Harav Kook St., tel. 02/244186. No reservations for outside tables. No dinner Fri. or lunch Sat.*

$–$$ **Village Green.** For most people, "gourmet vegetarian" sounds like a contradiction in terms, but this new restaurant proves otherwise. In the courtyard of the Old Bezalel Art Academy, its rustic atmosphere is enhanced by the wooden paneling and the artistic ceramic dishes used to serve the food. The wide-ranging menu includes a feather-light lasagna, the grain of the day (with the choice of two different sauces), paper-thin savory blintzes stuffed with mushrooms, or a choice of quiches, not to mention the list from which you choose the ingredients to create your own salad. There's an interesting variety of hot drinks and other exotic cool ones including *lassi*, a slightly tart Indian (Hindi) drink based on yogurt, coconut, and honey, sprinkled with cinnamon. A pleasant surprise is the dry pear or blackberry wine, as alcoholic as regular wine, but so light that you scarcely feel it. The service is charming, and the prices very reasonable. Don't miss it. Village Green's self-service outlet is on the open-air mall (the Midrachov) at 10 Ben Yehuda Street, with a slightly different menu. *1 Bezalel St., tel. 01/251464. Reservations advised. DC, MC, V. No dinner Fri. or lunch Sat.*

$–$$ **Ye Olde English Tea Room.** A minute's walk above the King George–Jaffa intersection, in a 19th-century stone house (with a small art gallery and a shaded courtyard), this spot offers some gastronomic nostalgia for expat Anglos and ex-colonials. There are specialties from both sides of the pond: "Olde England" offerings include fish-and-chips and a ploughman's lunch; "New England" (whence hail the mother-and-son owners) has corn chowder and a cheese-onion-potato potpie. There are other fish dishes and supplementary seasonal menus (lots of fresh fruit desserts in summer, for example). Salads are generous (the honey-mustard dressing is superb), and everything is served on charming blue-and-white English china. True to its name, the place comes into its own with its tearoom menu, both in the pleasingly traditional English tea and in the Old and New World edibles: scones with jam and cheese, peach custard pie, or "Brown Betty" with ice cream. *"Habustan," Raoul Wallenberg St. (off 68*

Jaffa Rd.), tel. 02/376595. Reservations advised Thurs. and Sat. dinner. DC, MC, V. No dinner Fri. or lunch Sat.

Eastern European

$$ **Feferberg's.** Founded in 1936, this is Jerusalem's classic "Old World" Jewish restaurant. If you're nostalgic for chopped chicken liver, gefilte fish, goose, duck, and boiled tongue the way grandma (or your friend's grandma) used to make them, you've come to the right place. The spacious dining area in the rear, past the deli counter, is wood-paneled, with subdued lighting. The upholstered, high-back chairs, white tablecloths, and red cloth napkins enhance the distinctly European atmosphere. *53 Jaffa Rd. (just below King George St.), tel. 02/254841. Reservations advised. AE, DC, MC, V. No dinner Fri. or lunch Sat.*

$-$$ **Europa.** The atmosphere is homey and the value good at this unpretentious restaurant. Traditional Eastern European Jewish cooking is represented by such dishes as kishke (stuffed derma) and stuffed cabbage, but the menu's main inspiration is Hungarian. Try schnitzel stuffed with goose liver; roast goose; stuffed chicken; and, naturally, goulash soup. A dessert of apple strudel or *palacsinta* (sweet almond crepe with chocolate sauce) is de rigueur. *42 Jaffa Rd., 2nd Floor, tel. 02/258953. Reservations advised. MC, V. No dinner Fri. Closed Sat.*

French

$$$$ **Cow on the Roof.** Chef Shalom Kadosh's meticulously prepared clas-
★ sic cuisine and superb service have earned the Sheraton Jerusalem Plaza's gourmet restaurant (named after the Chagall reproduction hanging in the bar) national renown (*see* Lodging, *below*). Brass chandeliers, Louis XV–style high-back chairs, lace cloths on the widely spaced tables, live harp or guitar accompaniment—and lofty prices—add to the sense of occasion. Although the dishes tend to be traditional—foie gras (home-raised), chateaubriand with béarnaise and bordelaise sauces, veal sweetbreads—some flirt with fashion: cornmeal crepes filled with vegetables, cream of Jerusalem artichoke with chervil, fruit sorbet with strawberries in a pastry "basket." This is one haute cuisine restaurant in Israel that lives up to its pretensions. *In Sheraton Jerusalem Plaza Hotel, 47 King George St., tel. 02/259111. Reservations required. AE, DC, MC, V. No lunch Sat. Closed Fri.*

$$$ **Cézanne.** The main problem you'll have at this downtown restaurant
★ is deciding what to choose from its enticing menu. The locally trained chef, Ahmad Abu el-Hawa, has imagination and the skill to realize it. Try veal brains in caper sauce for starters, and such entrées as the stuffed baby chicken in a sublime lime sauce, stuffed trout in a cream sauce, or one of the excellent steak fillets. Desserts change daily, but look for the homemade seasonal fruit ice cream in summer, and creamed chestnuts in winter. The old flagstones and the art gallery that shares the premises contribute to an atmosphere Cézanne himself might have approved of. A rear courtyard used in warm weather and a hearth for the cold complete the picture. *Artists' House, 12 Shmuel Hanagid St., tel. 02/259459. Reservations advised. AE, DC, MC, V.*

$$$ **Chez Simon.** Oil paintings, an antique globe, and copper table appointments set the tone for this venerable restaurant in downtown Jerusalem. The cuisine is classic French filtered through colonial French North Africa, with a Moroccan influence especially evident in the appetizers. For diners having the full dinner there are compli-

mentary starters—a small feast of koubeh, falafel, "Moroccan cigars" (elongated pastry rolls stuffed with spicy meat), pickles, and fresh rolls. House specialties include meat-stuffed artichoke cooked in lemon juice, crisp duckling in orange sauce, shrimps *gratin*, and *cordon bleu* (veal scallop baked with smoked goose breast, tomato, and Parmesan cheese). The steaks and fish are usually excellent. Crêpes suzette is the dessert of choice. *15 Shammai St., 2nd Floor, tel. 02/255602. Reservations advised. AE, DC, MC, V.*

Grills

$$ El Gaucho. Red meat is the thing at this Argentine grill in the Nahalat Shiva neighborhood. Housed in a characteristic stone building, with interior arches and a flagstone floor, El Gaucho adds rustic wooden tables and lattice screens and artifacts of the Argentinian pampas. Worth trying is the mixed grill of some eight different meats; spicy chorizo; and, of course, good old-fashioned steaks. There is a children's menu. *22 Rivlin St., tel. 02/256665. Reservations advised. AE, DC, MC. No dinner Fri. or lunch Sat.*

$$ Gilly's. This small restaurant at the southern end of Salomon Street in Nahalat Shiva exploded onto the scene a few years ago with a reputation for excellent steaks at reasonable prices. Unfortunately, popularity and the attendant crowds have taken their toll on the standard of service. It's still a good value, but try to avoid it on weekends. You can go with the more common pepper and barbecue sauces, or smother your sirloin with the more stylish brandy and cream sauce. The restaurant occupies a single room with a vaulted stone ceiling. *33 Hillel St. at Salomon St., tel. 02/255955. No reservations. No credit cards. Closed Sun.*

$ Burger Ranch. It's a fast-food place, pure and simple, with the expected variety of hamburgers, hot dogs, chicken combinations, and french fries (known in Israel as chips). The quality is good, but prices are often higher than the equivalent back home. *43 Emek Refa'im St., tel. 02/662318. Reservations not necessary. DC, V. No dinner Fri. or lunch Sat.*

Italian

$$$ Alla Gondola. Although it lost something of its culinary subtlety with the death of its Italian founder a few years ago, Alla Gondola is one of Jerusalem's few *non*-kosher Italian restaurants. Though not cheap, careful selection can make it good value as well. The Venetian mural, crystal chandeliers, and illuminated vitrages create a pleasant if not memorable atmosphere. Particularly good are the *lasagne Bolognese al forno*, *scampi alla marinara*, and *calamari alla Sicilliana*. The *piccatina con funghi* (with mushrooms and lemon) is the most interesting of the veal dishes. Top it all off with the chocolate-vanilla ice-cream cake. The restaurant offers a very attractive NIS 87 ($29) deal for Fodor's readers (present the book!), with your choice of three courses, and coffee on the house. *14 King George St., 2nd Floor, tel. 02/255944 or 02/252884. Reservations advised. AE, DC, MC, V.*

$$ Little Italy. This meatless Italian restaurant is within walking distance of the King David–Moriah Plaza–Laromme axis of downtown hotels, a fact that would probably have ensured its popularity even if the food were not as good as it is. New York–trained owner/chef Avi Elkayam creates dishes with flair. Apart from the very tempting fish-and-pasta combinations, try the eggplant baked with ricotta cheese; fettucini with the house tomato and cream sauce; and the decidedly un-Italian dessert of kumquats and ice cream. The decor is

Jerusalem Dining and Lodging

← TO TEL AVIV

ROMEMA

Central Bus Station (Egged)

MAHANEH YEHUDA

GIVAT RAM

BET HAKEREM

Hebrew University

Knesset

Sha'arei Zedek Hospital

GIVAT RAM

REHAVIA

Ramban

Israel Museum

BAYIT VEGAN

Ha-rav Agan   Harav Kook

Jaffa Rd.

Zion Sq.

Mordechai 'Eliash

Ben Yehuda

King George   Ha-Histadrut

Shammai St.

Salomon

King David

Hillel

Narkis

GONEN (KATAMON)

Dining

Alla Gondola, **30**
Amigos, **15**
Bet Ticho (Ticho House), **10**
Burger Ranch, **52**
Cézanne, **34**
Chez Simon, **25**
Cow on the Roof, **35**

El Gaucho, **16**
Europa, **13**
Feferberg's, **27**
Gilly's, **18**
Ima, **8**
La Brasa, **14**
Le Tsriff, **12, 41**
Little Italy, **45**
Mamma Mia, **36**
Mifgash Ha'esh, **6**

Minaret, **38**
Ocean, **17**
Off the Square, **21**
Sini Ba-Moshava, **51**
Tavlin, **20**
Village Green, **33**
The White Gallery, **50**
Yemenite Step, **22**
Ye Olde English Tea Room, **28**

Lodging

American Colony, **55**
Ariel, **49**
Bet Shmuel, **39**
Caesar, **7**
Christ Church, **54**
Eyal, **24**
Holiday Inn Crowne Plaza, **1**
Hyatt Regency, **56**

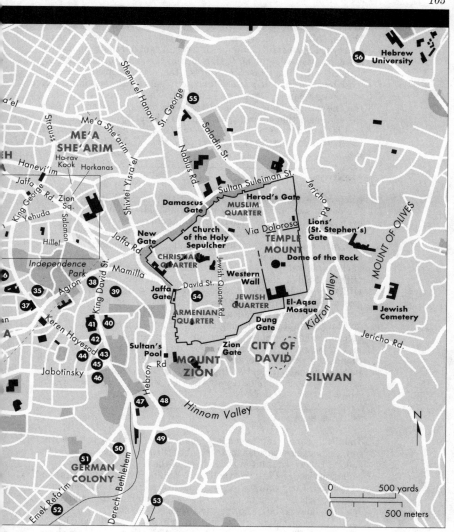

Jerusalem Gate, **5**
Jerusalem Inn, **11, 32**
Jerusalem
Renaissance, **2**
Jerusalem Tower, **19**
Kikar Zion, **23**
King David, **40**
King Solomon, **43**
Kings, **37**

Laromme, **46**
Lev Yerushalayim, **31**
Louise Waterman-
Wise, **9**
Mitzpeh Rachel, **53**
Moriah Plaza, **42**
Mount Zion, **48**
Palatin, **29**
Paradise Jerusalem, **3**
Scottish Hospice, **47**

Sheraton Jerusalem
Plaza, **35**
Sonesta, **4**
Windmill, **44**
YMCA (West), **41**
Zion, **26**

pleasant but not memorable. *38 Keren Hayesod St., tel. 02/617638. Reservations advised. AE, DC, MC, V. No dinner Fri. or lunch Sat.*

$$ Mamma Mia. In a nicely renovated old stone building with a shady courtyard for outside dining, this restaurant virtually pioneered the concept of vegetarian Italian food in the city. For starters, try focaccia with either *insalate caprese* (tomato, mozzarella, olive oil, fresh basil) or the *antipasto della casa* (if only for the sublime mushrooms with parsley, lemon and olive oil). The canelloni—especially the one with salmon—is superb, as is the lasagna, or choose from the wide selection of pizza. All the pasta is homemade. The best dessert is the hot apple pie. *38 King George St., behind parking lot, tel. 02/248080. Reservations advised. DC, MC, V. No dinner Fri. or lunch Sat.*

Mexican

$$ Amigos. Mexican restaurants are a rarity in Israel, but this one—on the downtown Nahalat Shiva pedestrian mall—would stand proud even in North America. There are tables out on the sidewalk in good weather, and in the evenings the waiters serve to the lively beat of recorded Latin American music. Sip an arctic-cold Margarita (lemon, strawberry, mango, melon) while you discuss the menu with one of the owners ("If you don't like the food, you don't pay!"). Start off with the grilled chicken wings in the piquant house sauce or *flautas* with strips of marinated steak or chicken breast, and onions or green peppers). Along with the expected list of burritos, taco salad, and chili con carne (as well as several vegetarian options), the house specialty is fajitas, a sizzling combination of grilled slices of beef, chicken, and vegetables, served with warm tortillas, refried beans, and guacamole (in season). For dessert, try the deep-fried (nondairy) vanilla ice cream in a crunchy shell of date-honey, with pecans, cinnamon, and whipped cream. *19 Salomon St., tel. 02/234177. Reservations advised. AE, DC, MC, V. No dinner Fri. or lunch Sat.*

Middle Eastern

$$ Ima. It's pronounced "eemaah," means Mom, and is named for Miriam, the owner's Kurdish mother, who still does all the cooking. The food at this restaurant at the bottom of the Nahla'ot neighborhood, opposite Sacher Park, is traditional Middle Eastern, plentiful and very good. First courses include a modest *mezeh* of some half-dozen salads (such as hummus, Turkish salad—a piquant tomato-and-onion dip—and tahini), and the excellent koubeh, stuffed vine leaves, and "Moroccan cigars." Try a side order of *majadra* (rice and lentils) with your entrée, which could be shishlik, kebabs, or lamb chops. *189 Agrippas St., tel. 02/246860. Reservations advised. DC, MC, V. No dinner Fri. Closed Sat.*

$$ ★ Minaret. You'll dine on classic Middle Eastern dishes prepared with distinction and graciously served at this restaurant decorated with hanging patterned rugs and brassware. The elaborate selection of mezeh would delight any vegetarian. Other tempting appetizers include koubeh and stuffed grape leaves. Try the lamb kebab or chops as your entrée, finishing up with Turkish coffee and the pistachio-filled pastry called *bourma*. *38 Emek Refaim St., tel. 02/664323. Reservations advised. AE, DC, MC, V.*

$-$$ ★ Mifgash Ha'esh. This is a good example of the wisdom of eating where the locals eat. When the restaurant opened in an industrial zone in the Romema neighborhood a few years ago, its almost instant reputation for good food and good value began attracting

Jerusalemites from farther afield, and even the occasional tourist. The atmosphere and service (good) are still those of a diner, with Formica tables and more emphasis on efficiency than elegance. Customers flock for the skewers of grilled meat and the house specialty, succulent grilled pieces of marinated chicken. The appetizers include unusually good hummus and koubeh. *23 Yirmiyahu St., Romema, tel. 02/388888 or 02/288889. No reservations. AE, DC, MC, V. No dinner Fri. or lunch Sat.*

$ Yemenite Step. Situated in the Salomon Street mall in Nahalat Shiva, Yemenite Step offers typical Yemenite foods. Especially good are the *malawach* (a flaky, pan-fried pastry with selected fillings) and the thick, rich soups served with pita and dips, which make for a cheap, hearty meal. *12 Salomon St., tel. 02/240477. No reservations. No credit cards. No dinner Fri. or lunch Sat.*

Mixed Menu

$$$ The White Gallery. In the courtyard of the old Semadar Cinema, in the heart of the German Colony, this unpretentious new restaurant with its white-draped ceiling bills itself as "Italian-French." The description simply translates into good food at fair prices. Particularly good are the focaccia with tarragon leaves, the subtle paté de foie gras, and the salmon fetuccine. The seafood combinations (shrimp-calamari-crab, Provençal-style, for example) are also worth trying. Less successful is the sirloin steak, and the mushroom salad is to be avoided altogether. Never mind, the desserts more than make up for it. Consider the *tarte tatin* (apple cake—*lots* of apple—steeped in caramel sauce) or the *Jubellier* (meringue, vanilla ice cream, and cooked cherries), both quite superb. *4 Lloyd George St., tel. 02/611102. Reservations advised. AE, DC, MC, V.*

$$ Le Tsriff. This very Jerusalemite restaurant, located in a downtown
★ back street, has a slightly funky and very congenial character. It has cultivated a faithful local clientele, from students to celebrities, establishing its reputation on savory pies encased in terrific crusts, with all kinds of fillings: chicken with nuts and raisins; veal and prunes; shrimp; and vegetables such as mushrooms, broccoli, and cauliflower. Pies are still featured prominently, and the soups and salads are still good, but the restaurant has matured. Specialties now include a delectable goose liver with apples and calvados, and a superb roquefort sauce to embellish your sirloin or fillet. For starters, try the hot breaded goat cheese and the sun-dried tomatoes; the Cape Brandy pudding is one of the more unusual desserts. Le Tsriff's second location, in the more formal YMCA (West), has a very similar menu (minus a few specialty items), but with this difference: Instead of ordering appetizers à la carte, a wide selection (with bread and mineral water) is automatically served, adding NIS 12–NIS 15 ($4–$5) to the price of the entrées. *5 Horkonos St., tel. 02/255488 or 02/242478; YMCA (West), 26 King David St., tel. 02/257111 or 02/253433. Reservations advised. DC, V.*

$ La Brasa. This unassuming eatery on the Salomon Street mall, near Zion Square, specializes in grilled chicken, but offers other inexpensive options as well. Its attractive prices—a quarter of a grilled chicken plus french fries and salad for NIS 21 ($7), or a large chicken sandwich with fries for NIS 12 ($4)—draws a young, budget-conscious crowd. You can take to the street in good weather at its outdoor tables. *7 Salomon St., tel. 02/231456. No reservations. No credit cards. No dinner Fri. or lunch Sat.*

Seafood

$$$$ **Ocean.** The stone arches and colored floor tiles of this building in the renovated Nahalat Shiva quarter create a good *physical* ambience; but, regrettably, any sense of intimacy is compromised by the noisy echo-effect of the vaulted ceilings. The restaurant's claim to fame, however, is a constantly changing menu of startling originality. The management prides itself on the quality, and often rarity, of its ingredients...and charges accordingly (main dishes run about NIS 105 ($35) apiece, with few side dishes included). Among the several methods of preparing fish, two are particularly unusual: baked in a *taboon*, a closed earth-oven, and grilled over glowing chips of citrus-wood. This also might be the only place in Jerusalem that serves lobster. For starters, try the seafood pasta if it's available. *7 Rivlin St., opposite Independence Park, tel. 02/247501. Reservations advised. AE, DC, MC, V.*

Cafés

Coffee and cake in one of Jerusalem's several fine cafés is something of a tradition. The selection of sweets is often enormous, from the gooey, cream-filled pastries many Israelis favor to the more sophisticated, not-so-sweet yeast cakes and strudels, a Central European inheritance. For wonderful cakes, ice cream extravaganzas, and a small selection of light meals, try **Budapest** (18 King George St., next to Hamashbir department store); **Alno** (15 Ben Yehuda St.); **Café Max** (23 Ben Yehuda St.); **Nava** (44 Jaffa Rd.); and **Ne'eman** (243 Jaffa Rd.). For more varied light-meal menus, as well as delicious cakes, try **Croissanterie** (19 Hillel St.), with its stunning selection of sweet or savory croissants; **Cafe Atara** (7 Ben Yehuda St.), an institution for Jerusalem's youth; or **Rimon** (4 Luntz St.).

Jan's, next to the Jerusalem Theater complex on Chopin and Marcus streets, is a one-of-a-kind café. Don't look for the usual tables and chairs here—you sit Oriental style on soft pillows and rugs, low lights adding to the mysterious atmosphere. The menu isn't very big—ambience is all.

Farther out from the center of town, just past Liberty Bell Garden, **Emek Refaim Street** is the setting for a couple of fine cafés, among them **Caffit**, at no. 1. On summer evenings in particular, these places teem with the young set, and it is worth arriving before 10:30 to beat the after-the-show crowd.

Ye Olde English Tea Room on Raoul Wallenberg St. (off 68 Jaffa Rd.) specializes in English teas and scones in a stone courtyard ambience (*see* Dairy and Vegetarian, *above*).

Lodging

There are travelers for whom a central location is a priority; others prefer a hotel that's a haven at the end of the day, where ambience is more important than accessibility. Jerusalem has both kinds of accommodations, and even hotels once considered remote are in fact no more than 10 minutes by cab or hotel minibus from the city center.

Hotels in Jerusalem are mainly grouped in the following locations: on or near the downtown triangle formed by King George Street, Jaffa Road, and Ben Yehuda Street (Sheraton Jerusalem Plaza, Lev Yerushalayim, Jerusalem Tower, Kikar Zion, Eyal, Zion); close to the city center (and most convenient to Jaffa Gate and the Old City), near the intersection of King David and Keren Hayesod streets (King David, Laromme, King Solomon, Moriah Plaza, Mt. Zion, Windmill, Ariel, YMCA [West], Scottish Hospice); in West Jerusalem between the Central Bus Station and Givat Ram, on major city bus routes (Holiday Inn Crowne Plaza, Jerusalem Renaissance, Caesar, Jerusalem Gate, Sonesta, Paradise); a few city locations not part of the above (Hyatt Regency, Mitzpeh Rachel, Waterman-Wise); and in forested hill country a 20-minute drive from the city center (Neve Ilan, Ma'aleh Hahamisha, Kiryat Anavim, Shoresh guest houses), where it's best to have a car.

Palestinian street violence in East Jerusalem during the last few years and the resultant shrinking of hotel occupancy there has, with only a few exceptions, led to a decline in standards as well. Particularly affected are $ and $$ priced hotels. Still recommended, however, is the American Colony Hotel.

Rates quoted by hotels are maximum regular-season rates; it is quite common to find a room at a price below the published rate, especially off-season. High season typically includes 10 days to a month around the Jewish holiday of Passover (March/April), a similar period over the Jewish holidays in September–October (High Holy Days and Sukkoth), part of the summer, and, for some hotels, the Christmas season. Because there is considerable variation in what different hotels consider high season, the dates of Jewish holidays shift annually in accordance with the Jewish calendar, and the difference in room rates can be significant, it is worth confirming the room rate before making a firm reservation.

All hotels have heating. Hotels in the $$$$ and $$$ categories have air-conditioning and telephones in the rooms; many moderately priced properties have them, too.

Highly recommended lodgings are indicated by a star ★.

Category	Cost*
$$$$	over $150
$$$	$100–$150
$$	$60–$100
$	under $60

All prices are for two people in a standard double room, including breakfast and 15% service charge.

$$$$
★ **American Colony Hotel.** This former pasha's palace, a hotel for 103 years, is a 10-minute walk from the Damascus Gate in East Jerusalem, but worlds away from the hubbub of the Old City. The cool limestone oasis, with its flower-bedecked outdoor courtyard, is a favorite haunt of American and British expats, international journalists, and Palestinian officials. Although the whitewashed guest rooms tend toward the spartan, with simple turned-wood pieces, the occasional Turkish or Syrian antique, and small area rugs covering stone floors, the better ones are spacious (and the marble bathrooms gigantic), and the service is excellent. The rooms in the two nearby annexes, built in the 1950s, do not suffer in comparison with those in the original mansion. Decorative touches such as kilim rug hangings, Islamic tilework in brilliant turquoises and blues, hand-blown yellow glass sconces, rattan chairs, and plenty of potted palms lend a Mediterranean atmosphere to the public rooms. The non-kosher cuisine in the Arabesque restaurant, some of the best in

Jerusalem, is mainly French, but the Swiss chef does prepare a few classic dishes from his homeland, such as veal in cream sauce with *rösti* potatoes (Swiss-style fried potatoes). *Nablus Rd., Box 19215, 97200, tel. 02/279777, fax 02/279888. 96 rooms with bath. Facilities: 3 restaurants, bar, pool, children's pool. AE, DC, MC, V.*

$$$$ **Holiday Inn Crowne Plaza.** Formerly the Jerusalem Hilton, this quintessential business and convention hotel in the Givat Ram section of West Jerusalem was recently renovated, casting public areas in softer colors to maximize the sense of space. The Lounge, the lobby-level dairy restaurant/bar/coffee shop, is a comfortably asymmetrical area where the cakes and pastries (especially the apple strudel) are superb. The in-house Kohinoor Indian restaurant is a real treat. The hotel's lofty location gives almost all rooms fine views of some part of Jerusalem, particularly from the top five floors. Rooms are not especially large, but the redecoration in tasteful pastels and light earth colors has given them a much lighter and airier feel. Once thought remote, the location near the Central Bus Station makes it a 10-minute drive from the city center. The quiet pool area and surrounding garden draw many Jerusalemites. The small and informal health club is privately owned and not included in the room rate. A complimentary shuttle bus takes guests to downtown Jerusalem and the Old City. *Givat Ram (West Jerusalem), 91130, tel. 02/581414, fax 02/514555. 397 rooms with bath. Facilities: 2 restaurants, bar/lounge, business center, shopping arcade with bank, health club, hot tub, sauna, outdoor pool, floodlighted tennis courts, playground, miniature golf. AE, DC, MC, V.*

$$$$ **Hyatt Regency.** Cascading down Mt. Scopus, the Hyatt Regency has
★ the most dramatic setting of any hotel in Jerusalem, and the boldest design (it's built around seven courtyards). The lobby is a stylish combination of stone, leather seating, and greenery, with a six-level atrium that reaches down to the Castel Lounge, decorated with wonderful murals by the contemporary Israeli artist for whom it's named. Guest rooms, about one-third of which have views of the Old City, are spacious, decorated with stone-top tables, Castel prints, and light colors. Rooms on the Regency Club floors are identical to rooms on other floors but have the added amenities of a lounge/reading room with refreshments, and a concierge. The hotel's pool area, with an adjacent playground, is a tropical enclave of palms and plants. The in-house Jerusalem Spa (to which guests get a 50% discount), one of the country's most sophisticated, offers cosmetic and therapeutic treatments in addition to the expected facilities. At press time, the hotel's Italian restaurant was about to undergo a transformation to a boldly defined Mediterranean cuisine. If the standards of its precursor are anything to go by, the new eatery will be worth trying. *32 Lehi St., 97856, tel. 02/331234, fax 02/815947. 503 rooms with bath. Facilities: 3 restaurants, bar, disco/nightclub, fitness center, health spa, indoor pool, hot tub, sauna, steam room, business center, shops, beauty salon, outdoor pool, children's pool, floodlighted tennis courts. AE, DC, MC, V.*

$$$$ **Jerusalem Renaissance.** Polished stone walls and copper fixtures in the reception and lounge areas add class to this large, modern hotel. The rates are modest for this price category, although, the service tends to be slow. The hotel has two distinct wings, the main one somewhat upscale, the other mostly for more budget-conscious tour-groups. Rooms are quite spacious, with a pleasing pastel decor; bathrooms are small. The hotel's best features are its large outdoor pool, surrounded by a marvelous garden of lawn and trees, and its equally large heated indoor pool and health club, all free to hotel guests. It's on the west side of town, adjacent to Hebrew University's Givet Ram campus. A complimentary shuttle bus trans-

ports guests to downtown and Jaffa Gate. *6 Wolfson St., 91033, tel. 02/528111, fax 02/511976. 650 rooms with bath. Facilities: 3 restaurants, bar/lounge, shops, beauty salon, indoor pool, health club, gym, Jacuzzi, wet and dry saunas, outdoor pool, tennis court, table tennis. AE, DC, MC, V.*

$$$$ **King David Hotel.** This grande dame of Israeli luxury hotels opened in 1931 and has successfully defended its premier status ever since. Its visitors' book is an international Who's Who of royalty, dignitaries, and celebrities. Despite management efforts, the staff has not entirely shaken off its old snootiness. The lobby, with its ceilings, columns, and walls covered with "ancient" geometric decoration, is comfortable but very much part of the bustle of the nearby reception area. For more privacy try the bar, perhaps the best among Jerusalem's hotels (*see* The Arts and Nightlife, *below*). Recent renovations have transformed most of the already spacious and elegant rooms into a cream-and-brown symphony of good taste, with old-fashioned writing tables a gracious addition. The pricier rooms have a magnificent view of the Old City. The rear terrace—Paul Newman and Eva-Marie Saint had a drink here in the movie *Exodus*—overlooks the Old City walls. The large swimming pool, in a beautifully landscaped garden behind the hotel, may tempt you away from your touring in hot weather. *23 King David St., 94101, tel. 02/251111, fax 02/232303. 257 rooms with bath. Facilities: 3 restaurants, bar, lounge, business facilities, shops, fitness center, outdoor pool, children's pool, tennis court. AE, DC, MC, V.*

$$$$ **Laromme.** A low-rise building of Jerusalem stone (limestone) wrapped around a central courtyard and atrium, the Laromme is more appealing for its architecture and friendly, energetic staff than for its decor; the furnishings of both public areas and guest rooms are rather ordinary, though helped by a profusion of plants. Some rooms have balconies and fine views. Despite its unexceptional features, there is something about the hotel—its lively atmosphere and amiable staff, perhaps—that has made it one of the most popular in its category. Its location next to Liberty Bell Garden is a plus for families. *3 Jabotinsky St., 92145, tel. 02/756666, fax 02/756777. 302 rooms with bath. Facilities: 2 restaurants, bar/lounge, shops, beauty salon, hot tub, sauna, outdoor pool (heated and covered in winter). AE, DC, MC, V.*

$$$$ **Moriah Plaza.** Although rated under the now-defunct government star system as a five-star hotel, the Moriah is outclassed by its luxury peers. Favored by tour groups, it offers a good location convenient to downtown and the Old City and an efficient staff, but the guest rooms, while comfortable, are unexceptionally decorated and not overly spacious. There is a small health club attached to (but not affiliated with) the hotel, discounted to NIS 15 ($5) for guests. *39 Keren Hayesod St., 94188, tel. 02/232232, fax 02/232411. 292 rooms with bath. Facilities: 2 restaurants, bar/lounge, beauty salon, shops, outdoor pool. AE, DC, MC, V.*

$$$$ **Sheraton Jerusalem Plaza.** Close by the lively shopping area of Ben Yehuda Street, the 22-story Sheraton may look like any big business hotel anywhere, complete with look-alike guest rooms (modern built-in cherrywood furniture, king-size beds, big closets), but that's where the resemblance ends. The balcony views of the Old City are spectacular (those of the New City are equally impressive), and the warm, attentive staff make guests feel truly welcome. The celebrated Cow on the Roof restaurant (*see* Dining, *above*) draws lots of Jerusalemites out for a special occasion. *47 King George St., Box 7686, 91076, tel. 02/259111, fax 02/231667. 300 rooms with bath. Facilities: 4 restaurants, bar, shops, sauna, massage, beauty salon, pool. AE, DC, MC, V.*

$$$ **Jerusalem Gate.** Adjacent to the Central Bus Station, the Jerusalem Gate caters to business travelers and tour groups. If convenient location is a top priority, this is a logical choice. The guest rooms are reasonably spacious—the pastel colors contribute to the effect—and are furnished with wood pieces. Ask for the rooms that face north, which have a view across the hills and beyond the city. The attractive bar on the mezzanine terrace overlooking the lobby has a copper ceiling and brings the other public areas to life. The rooftop sundeck is a welcome haven from the bus station bustle. *43 Yirmiyahu St., 94467, tel. 02/383101, fax 02/389040. 298 rooms with bath. Facilities: restaurant, bar/lounge, business services, adjacent mall. AE, DC, MC, V.*

$$$ **Jerusalem Tower.** This hotel, which underwent renovations, is in a choice location: bang in the center of downtown. The café/bar is an inviting asymmetrical room with arched windows, cane furniture, and quiet corners. Guest rooms are small but tastefully decorated with upholstered headboards and stone tabletops. Ask for a room with a view, above the sixth floor. *23 Hillel St., Box 2656, 94581, tel. 02/252161, fax 02/252167. 120 rooms with bath. Facilities: restaurant, café/bar. AE, DC, MC, V.*

$$$ **Kikar Zion.** Although this seven-story building dominates downtown Zion Square (Kikar Zion in Hebrew), the entrance is a very modest doorway off Shamai Street a half-block away, where the elevator takes you up to the huge lobby. High above street level, rooms are quiet and spacious, with light-gray felt wall coverings that lend a feeling of warmth and intimacy. The rooms wrap around the building, affording good views of the city. Hotel guests get a 50% discount on the privately owned health club, which has among its facilities and services a heated pool, sauna, hot tub, steam room, massage, beauty salon, and fitness center. *25 Shamai St., 94631, tel. 02/244644, fax 02/244136. 120 rooms with bath. Facilities: 2 restaurants, bar/lounge, health club. AE, DC, MC, V.*

$$$ **Kings.** Very well located (less than 10 minutes' walk from the city center), though on a noisy intersection, the Kings has been transformed by its recent and ongoing renovations. (Make sure to ask for one of the new rooms.) Cane furniture and deep sofas create comfortable, if not particularly intimate, public areas. Most guest rooms are fairly spacious, the renovated ones enhanced by light colors. *60 King George St. (entrance on Ramban St.), 94262, tel. 02/247133, fax 02/249830. 187 rooms with bath. Facilities: 2 restaurants, bar/lounge. AE, DC, MC, V.*

$$$ **King Solomon.** After a slump in the late 1980s, the King Solomon has bounced back, as it deserves to. The lobby has as a centerpiece a huge globe-shape sculpture of Jerusalem by Frank Meisler. Alcoves in the coffee shop offer some degree of privacy from the lobby crowds. A split-level atrium reveals shops one floor down, and the restaurants below that. The Queen of Sheba has an eclectic menu of Middle Eastern and Continental cuisine. Standard rooms are a bit pokey, but the more deluxe ones are quite large. The rooms are attractive; brown and beige predominate, with sepia prints above the beds. The well-equipped bathrooms are more spacious than most. Rates are low for this category. *32 King David St., 94101, tel. 02/695555, fax 02/241774. 142 rooms with bath, 6 suites. Facilities: 2 restaurants, bar/lounge, shops, hairdresser, outdoor pool. AE, DC, MC, V.*

$$$ **Lev Yerushalayim.** One of the best bargains in its price category, this ★ fairly new all-suite hotel is in the heart of the city center. The heat and noise are left behind as you enter the coolness of the stone-walled, plant-filled lobby. Suites are decorated in tasteful pastel pinks and grays. Prices are per suite for two guests; additional guests using the sofa beds (adults or children) pay only NIS 36 ($12) per night extra. Breakfast is included, but you can make other meals in the suite's kitchenette, which has a stove, refrigerator, and microwave. Samson's Gym, on the premises (gym, Jacuzzi, sauna), is free to hotel guests. *18 King George St., 91079, tel. 02/300333, fax 02/232432. 58 suites with bath, 28 double suites with bath. Facilities: restaurant, fitness center, hot tub, sauna, coin laundromat. AE, DC, MC, V.*

$$$ **Mitzpeh Rachel.** As a rustic kibbutz hotel at the southern end of the
★ number 7 bus route, less than 15 minutes by car from downtown, Mitzpeh Rachel enjoys the best of both worlds. Most of its rooms afford stunning views of Bethlehem and the Judean Desert. The soft pinks and grays of the guest-room decor contrast with the brilliant colors of Calman Shemi quilted fabric "soft-art" originals above each headboard. With its extensive lawns and pine trees, fine pool with a 400-foot-long water slide, and other sports facilities, all free to guests, Mitzpeh Rachel feels like a resort far removed from a major city. *Kibbutz Ramat Rachel, Mobile Post. North Judea, 90900, tel. 02/702555, fax 02/733155. 91 rooms with bath. Facilities: restaurant, bar/lounge, hairdresser, fitness center, sauna, outdoor pool, playground, 3 tennis courts, basketball court, table tennis. AE, DC, MC, V.*

$$$ **Mount Zion.** The core of the hotel is a renovated 19th-century British eye hospital, to which a new, similar wing was added in the 1980s. Columns and arched doorways and windows in Jerusalem stone frame ethereal views of Mt. Zion and create atmospheric nooks filled with wall hangings, Armenian tiles, and plants. Only the tacky carpeting detracts from the otherwise excellent taste throughout the hotel. Serious management efforts seem to have gone a long way to improving the once mediocre service. The guest rooms in the new wing are fairly ordinary; the superior rooms of the old wing offer more character and better views. An octagonal swimming pool and adjacent children's pool overlook the Hinnom Valley. The new health club (sauna, Jacuzzi, fitness room) is free to hotel guests. *17 Hebron Rd., 93546, tel. 02/724222, fax 02/7314252. 130 rooms with bath. Facilities: 4 restaurants, bar/lounge, health club, outdoor pool. AE, DC, MC, V.*

$$$ **Paradise Jerusalem.** Although there is little that is extraordinary about the look of this hotel on the west side of town, its recreational facilities make it a standout in its price category. The health club, complete with indoor pool, fitness center, sauna, and hot tub, and the grassy pool area provide a delightful, relaxing environment at the end of a day of touring. *4 Wolfson St., 91036, tel. 02/511111, fax 02/512266. 198 rooms, most with bath. Facilities: restaurant, bar/lounge, fitness center, indoor pool, hot tub, sauna, outdoor pool, tennis court. AE, DC, MC, V.*

$$$ **Windmill.** This is a comfortable but fairly nondescript hotel. Its unobtrusive decor includes many plants in public areas. Its rates are high for what it offers, but the good location (on a side street opposite the Moriah Plaza, near the city center, and on good bus routes) counts for something. *3 Mendele St., off Keren Hayesod, 92147, tel. 02/663111, fax 02/610964. 133 rooms with bath. Facilities: restaurant, bar/lounge. AE, DC, MC, V.*

$$–$$$ **Caesar.** This is a reasonably comfortable but unexceptional hotel, functional rather than fun. Rooms leave few memorable impressions and have no views at all. It is a base from which you'll want to venture, rather than a home to which you'll forward to returning. *208 Jaffa Rd., 94383, tel. 02/382801. 84 rooms with bath. Facilities: coffee shop, bar/lounge. AE, DC, MC, V.*

$$–$$$ **Sonesta.** This West Jerusalem hotel has a good local reputation, but its rooms are small and its facilities limited. In the absence of a pool, guests are given free entrance to the Jerusalem Recreation Center 15 minutes' drive away. Attractive cane furniture adds brightness and a touch of style to both guest rooms and public areas. *2 Wolfson St., Box 3835, 95435, tel. 02/528221, fax 02/528423. 217 rooms with bath. Facilities: restaurant, bar/lounge. AE, DC, MC, V.*

$$ **Ariel.** An early conversion from a planned apartment hotel left the Ariel with a good number of spacious guest rooms, some large enough to accommodate families. They're comfortable, but the mismatched furnishings can be jarring. About a third of the rooms have excellent views of Mt. Zion. The dining room can be recommended. The hotel is close to the railway station. *31 Hebron Rd., 93546, tel. 02/719222, fax 02/734066. 125 rooms with bath. Facilities: restaurant, bar/lounge. AE, DC, MC, V.*

$$ **Bet Shmuel.** This relatively new stone building with cool inner courtyards and a fabulous view of the Old City from the roof (and almost half the rooms) was not built exclusively as a guest house but as a cultural/educational center of the World Union For Progressive Judaism. Its spacious rooms are bright, with modern blond-wood furniture—comfortable, if a little spare. The location is excellent: five minutes' walk to the Old City, 10 to the center of town. *13 King David St. (entrance on Shamma St.), 94101, tel. 02/203461 through 02/203466, fax 02/203446. 40 rooms with bath. Facilities: restaurant, coffee shop. No credit cards.*

$$ **Eyal.** A central downtown location makes this well-kept hotel a good choice in this price range. Rooms are not too cramped, and although the decor is unexceptional (veneer paneling), the presence of TVs and refrigerators—unusual for this category—makes the hotel a good value. The bar, with its comfortable leather seating, is a cozy hideaway. *21 Shamai St., 94631, tel. 02/234161 through 02/234168, fax 02/244136. 71 rooms with bath. Facilities: restaurant, bar/lounge. AE, DC, MC, V.*

$$ **Palatin.** At this personable family-run hotel just off the intersection of King George Street and Jaffa Road, the guest rooms are small, but the updated decor includes pine furniture, moldings and other details, brighter colors, and TVs in the rooms. Complimentary coffee and tea are always available. *4 Agrippas St., 94301, tel. 02/231141, fax 02/259323. 28 rooms with bath. AE, DC, MC, V.*

$$ **Scottish Hospice.** Part of the St. Andrew's Church complex, the Presbyterian-operated hospice is as much a retreat as a place to overnight. Opened in 1930, the building has the pleasing stone arches, alcoves, and atriums that characterize the architecture of the period. The rooms are small, a bit sparsely furnished, and not air-conditioned, but most compensate with views of the garden, and some with a view of Mt. Zion. Refreshments are always available, and meals can be requested. *Off corner of King David and Emek Refaim Sts., opposite railway station, Box 8619, 91086, tel. 02/732401, fax 02/731711. 14 rooms with shower. Facilities: crafts shop. No credit cards.*

$$ **YMCA (West).** Built in 1933, this limestone building with its famous
★ domed bell tower is a Jerusalem landmark. Stone arches, exotic murals, old patterned-wood cupboards, and painted Armenian tiles give it charm and character. Guest rooms are not large, but recent renovations have lifted them from their once-spartan character to attractive air-conditioned comfort. That and an excellent location makes it an attractive deal at the upper end of the price category. On the premises are excellent sports facilities (*see* Sports and Fitness, *above*), an auditorium where concerts and folklore performances are held (*see* The Arts and Nightlife, *below*), and the privately run Le

Tsriff restaurant (*see* Dining, *above*). *26 King David St., Box 294, 91002, tel. 02/257111, fax 02/253438. 66 rooms with bath. Facilities: restaurant, café, lounge, fitness center, indoor pool, sauna, indoor basketball court, 4 tennis courts, 2 squash courts, track. AE, DC, MC, V.*

$$ **Zion.** Lean over the wrought-iron balcony railings at this Parisian-style hotel and you can almost smell the croissants and café au lait served at the café below. The location is tops, on one of the pedestrian-only side streets of the Ben Yehuda mall. Renovations have preserved many of the stone walls and alcoves of this 140-year-old building. Traditional furniture and brass ornaments in some of the public areas add to the Old World ambience. Guest rooms simply but pleasantly furnished with wooden pieces, are two and three flights above street level and can only be reached by stairs. There is no air-conditioning. The hotel is at the lower end of the price category. *10 Dorot Rishonim St., 94646, tel. 02/259511, fax 02/257585. 26 rooms with bath. Facilities: bar/lounge. AE, MC, V.*

$–$$ **Christ Church.** This is the guest house of the adjacent Anglican church, the oldest Protestant church (1849) in the Middle East. Rooms in the two old stone buildings are comfortably furnished, if not exactly luxurious, just as you might expect from this former pilgrim hospice. The location, in the Old City just inside the Jaffa Gate, is excellent for sightseeing, though many visitors are more at ease in modern West Jerusalem. Prices drop to $ November 1–December 19 and January 1–March 14. *Jaffa Gate, Old City, Box 14037, 91140, tel. 02/282082, fax 02/289187. 23 rooms with bath. Facilities: dining room. No credit cards.*

$ **Jerusalem Inn.** Its two locations offer hostel-type accommodations that were recently renovated and given new wooden furniture. The "guest house" on Horkonos Street has double rooms, many large enough for four beds, most with private showers, and some with balconies. The "hostel" has a combination of double rooms (without private facilities) and dormitory-style rooms sleeping six–eight people each, appealing especially to the backpacking crowd. *Guest house: 7 Horkonos St., Box 2729, 94230, tel. 02/252757, fax 02/251297. 17 doubles, 12 with private showers and toilets. Facilities: restaurant/pub, washing machine, ceiling fans. MC, V. Hostel: 6 Hahistadrut St., Box 2729, 94230, tel. 02/251294, fax 02/251297. 7 doubles, 4 dormitory rooms. MC, V.*

$ **Louise Waterman-Wise.** Jerusalem's largest youth hostel has added
★ a guest-house wing, with simply but neatly furnished private rooms. The hostel's setting, opposite Mt. Herzl in the Bayit Vegan area of West Jerusalem, affords sweeping views of the Judean Hills. Downtown is a 15-minute drive by taxi (the hostel is next to a taxi stand) and city bus (nos. 13, 18, 20, 23, 27, and 39). Guests have access to a garden, library and other common rooms, and occasional evening activities, such as folk dancing and movies. Meals are substantial and very cheap. There are no age requirements. *8 Hapisga St., Bayit Vegan, Box 16350, 91162, tel. 02/423366 or 02/420990, fax 02/423362. Hostel: 172 beds in 43 rooms, each room with bath. Guesthouse wing: 128 beds in 24 rooms, each room with bath. Facilities: meals available. No credit cards.*

The Arts and Nightlife

The Arts

For schedules of performances and other cultural events, consult the Friday weekend section of *The Jerusalem Post*, the local newspaper

Your Jerusalem, This Week in Jerusalem, and the monthly *Hello Israel.* All of the publications are in English. Particularly useful is the Ministry of Tourism's monthly bulletin, *Events in Jerusalem,* available at the GTIOs and most better hotels.

The main ticket agencies for performances in Jerusalem are: **Ben-Naim,** 38 Jaffa Road, tel. 02/254008; **Bimot,** 8 Shamai Street, tel. 02/240896; and **Kla'im,** 12 Shamai Street, tel. 02/256869. If you are a student, present your card at the ticket office; sometimes discount tickets are available.

Top Israeli and international orchestras, choirs, singers, drama companies, and dance troupes participate in the **Israel Festival,** usually in May or June, which covers all the performing arts from jazz and avant-garde dance to Bach motets.

Dance While the **Israel National Ballet** has a varied performance record, there are inspiring smaller local troupes, among them **Batsheva** and **Bat-Dor,** which specialize in modern dance, and **Inbal,** whose style is influenced by folklore. Particularly worth watching out for is the prize-winning company **Kol U'Demama,** which includes both hearing and deaf dancers. The **Jerusalem Tamar Dance Company** also performs occasionally.

Film The usual Hollywood fare is available at the cinemas clustered in the center of town near the Central Bus Station and farther out in the Talpiot Industrial Zone. They close Friday night. Movies are subtitled in Hebrew and (when appropriate) English. The **Jerusalem Cinemateque** (Hebron Rd., tel. 02/724131; open Friday night) specializes in old, rare, and art films, but its wide-ranging programs often include quite current offerings. Its monthly series focuses on specific directors, actors, or subjects. Its annual **Jerusalem Film Festival,** held in July, is a must for film buffs.

Music Classical music abounds in Jerusalem, with Israeli orchestras and chamber ensembles performing year-round, and a trickle of international artists passing through.

Binyanei Ha'ooma (tel. 02/252481), opposite the Central Bus Station, is the local venue for occasional concerts by the internationally renowned **Israel Philharmonic Orchestra.** (For tickets, contact the IPO offices in Tel Aviv: Hechal Hatarbut, 1 Huberman St., tel. 03/5251502.) The **Jerusalem Center for the Performing Arts** (20 Marcus St., tel. 02/617167), still best known by its old name, the **Jerusalem Theater,** houses the Jerusalem Sherover Theater, the Henry Crown Auditorium, and the more intimate Rebecca Crown Theater. All in all, this is the city's most active and interesting venue.

The **Gerard Behar Center** (11 Bezalel St., tel. 02/251139) sometimes holds classical performances, as does the **Israel Museum** (Ruppin St., tel. 02/708811). The **Van Leer Jerusalem Institute** (Albert Einstein Sq., 43 Jabotinsky St., tel. 02/617141) holds Saturday afternoon concerts from October to June. The **YMCA (West)** in West Jerusalem (26 King David St., tel. 02/257111), is best known for its free "Etnachta" series (broadcast live), held on many Thursday afternoons at 4. **Zionist Confederation House** (Emil Botta St., Yemin Moshe, tel. 02/245206) hosts lectures and musical performances in its delightful, stone-arched downstairs gallery. **Bet Ticho (Ticho House),** on Ticho Lane, off Harav Kook Street (tel. 02/245068), which occasionally holds intimate recitals, is another charming setting. The atmosphere is rustic at the **Targ Music Center** in **Ein Kerem** (Hama'ayan St., tel. 02/414250), 7 kilometers (4 miles) from the city center.

Hearing music at one of Jerusalem's many churches can be a moving experience. Especially recommended are the concerts at the **Church of the Redeemer** (Muristan, in the Old City's Christian Quarter, tel. 02/894608 or 02/894750) and **Dormition Abbey** (Mt. Zion, tel. 02/719927).

A rousing concert of Israeli folklore—mostly singing and folk dancing—is presented at **YMCA (West)** (*see above*). The concert usually takes place on Monday, Thursday, and Saturday evenings, but call ahead to confirm (tel. 02/257111). As the 500-seat hall is usually inundated by tour groups and seats are unreserved, it is advisable to arrive early. A similar production, presented under the auspices of the Jerusalem municipality and the Ministry of Tourism takes place in some seasons at the **Gerard Behar Center** (*see above*).

Theater Most plays are performed in Hebrew, but there is the odd offering in English. Your best bet for the latter is the **Khan Theater** (2 David Remez Sq., near the Railway Station, tel. 02/718281), but check newspaper listings for the **Jerusalem Theater** and the **Gerard Behar Center** as well. Some plays offer simultaneous translation in English.

Nightlife

Jerusalem's nightlife is a great deal more limited than Tel Aviv's—almost provincial—but there are *some* lively spots that are open until the wee hours.

Bars and Lounges All the major hotels have bars, but the one at the **King David Hotel** (23 King David St., tel. 02/251111) is a standout. A quiet room with comfortable lounge chairs and subdued lighting provide an intimate atmosphere unusual for Jerusalem.

Fink's (13 King George St., corner of Hahistadrut St., tel. 02/254523) has been around as long as anyone can remember and has developed a reputation as a watering hole for journalists and politicians. It is small and a bit cramped, but offers good atmosphere, good drinks, and good food (it's also a complete restaurant). It is closed Friday evening.

Discos Primarily the preserve of the 17- to 21-year-old crowd (the drinking age is 18), Jerusalem discos come alive on Thursday, Friday, and Saturday nights. Admissions run around NIS 25–NIS 30 ($8.35–$10). Don't even *think* about going before midnight.

The only downtown disco, **Underground** (1 Yoel Salomon St., off Zion Sq.), looks like something out of Dante's *Inferno*, with rough black walls, murals, and sculptures of prisoners. The bar at street level above is only marginally saner.

The **Talpiot Industrial Zone,** 4 kilometers (2.5 miles) out of the city center, is an unlikely place, perhaps, to find a clutch of discos, but not illogical in a city where the Jewish Sabbath is sacrosanct to so many. **Blue Moon** (3 Yad Haruzim St.) is huge, with a big dance floor, two bars, video screens, and a state-of-the-art sound system. The club is open Thursday (over 21) and Friday (under 21). **Opera** (2 Ha'oman St., near the Volvo/Honda showroom) is decorated with faux neoclassical columns and arches and caters to an older crowd than most. It's open Wednesday to all ages, Thursday to thirtysomethings, and Friday to the 21–25 set. **Expose** (13 Yad Haruzim St., 3rd Floor) has a good bar and comfortable seats when you're sitting one out. Thursday and Saturday are the nights for party animals in their twenties; Fridays are for people 21 and younger. **Pitagoras** (11 Yad Haruzim St.) sometimes pampers its patrons with free snacks. The club is open Thursday and Saturday (over-twenties) and Friday (the 17–21 crowd). **Depuz Dieu** (basement of 19 Yad Haruzim), reminiscent of a basketball court, allows entry to twentysomethings Thursday, 17- to 21-year-olds Friday.

Folklore Clubs The **Khan Club** (David Remez Sq., opposite the Railway Station, tel. 02/718283) hosts a nightly folklore show ($15) geared to tourists. **Kova shel Kush** (5 Yad Haruzim St., Talpiot Industrial Zone, tel. 02/719008), meaning "Straw Hat," has the look of a rural inn and is patronized largely by Israelis. Thursday is dedicated to the good old Israeli folk songs, with audience participation in both singing and folk dancing encouraged. On Friday night, contemporary dance music dominates, while Saturday night offers a mixture of Israeli folk music and more Middle Eastern sounds. The music is always live. The NIS 25 ($8.35) cover charge includes the first drink.

Folk-Music Clubs There is a modest folk scene in Jerusalem, with performances by local artists, the occasional visit by international performers, and a monthly home "hootenanny." Watch listings, in particular, for the **Pargod Theater** (94 Bezalel St., tel. 02/231765 or 02/258819) and **Zionist Confederation House** (Emil Botta St., Yemin Moshe, tel. 02/245206) or call folksinger Jill Rogoff (tel. 02/790410) or "Folknotes" editor Ronna Katz (tel. 02/552872) for updates.

Jazz Clubs The **Pargod Theater** (*see above*) hosts a regular jam session on Friday afternoon, and often features jazz programs during the evening (especially in July and August).

Pubs Frequented by foreigners and a young crowd in the summer, **Champs** (5 Yoel Salomon St.) is a large pub with a wooden bar, video screen, and dartboard. Champs is strictly a watering hole—food is not served. Also downtown, **The Tavern** (14 Rivlin St.) is smaller—narrow and smoke-filled—but the beer is as good, and there's occasional live music. A half-dozen totally nondescript pubs populate a courtyard off **31 Jaffa Road**, where a drink is just a drink, and the ambience is secondary.

3 Around Jerusalem

*Including Bethlehem,
Masada, and the Dead Sea*

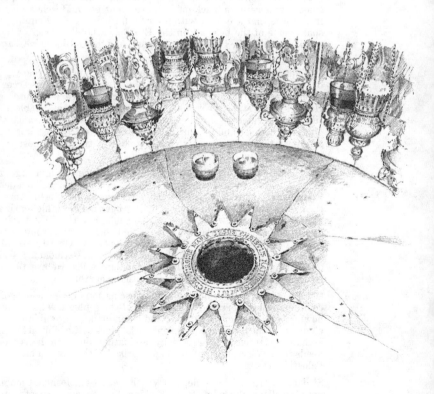

*By Mike
Rogoff*

Jerusalem's location in the heart of Israel's central mountain range makes it an excellent base for day tours in the area. Furthermore, many visitors feel that visiting Jerusalem is so intense an experience that they need excursions like these for a change of pace and scenery. Having said that, all the tours described here are readily accessible from Tel Aviv as well, with the investment of no more than an extra hour in each direction, and in some cases much less.

By far the most interesting, dramatic, and unmissable sites in this chapter are those of the Judean Desert–Dead Sea region. This is a desert of extraordinary barrenness, throwing into brilliant relief the waterfalls and greenery of Ein Gedi and Wadi Kelt, the springs and reed thickets of Ein Fashcha, and the sprawling oasis of the town of Jericho.

The road that skirts the Dead Sea (Route 90) is hemmed in by awesome, fractured brown cliffs that soar in many places to heights of more than 1,600 feet. Amidst the austere landscape are the two nature reserves of Ein Gedi, with their rivulets, pools, waterfalls, and subtropical vegetation at the foot of immense desert precipices. Wildlife abounds here, particularly the ibex (wild goat) and the hyrax (coney), though you cannot rely on always seeing these.

The Dead Sea itself—actually a lake—is a unique phenomenon: It is the saltiest body of water in the world at the lowest point on earth. Feel the tension seep out of you as you float in the balmy brine, or smooth mineral-rich black mud all over your body. Beaches range from those that are free, with minimal facilities, to well-equipped spas. Some of the best are in the Ein Bokek hotel district at the southern end of the Dead Sea (*see* Sports and the Outdoors *in* Chapter 8, Eliat and the Negev).

Masada, the great mountaintop palace-fortress built 2,000 years ago by King Herod, overlooks the Dead Sea. Its mosaics and frescoes, ingenious water system, baths, and balconies are a tribute to Herod's grand style; the remote location and almost unassailable position are evidence of his paranoia. Add the human drama of Masada's defense and fall during the Jewish revolt against Rome a century later, and it is easy to understand why this is the most visited site in Israel, after Jerusalem itself.

For Christian visitors, Bethlehem is a major place of pilgrimage, a stone's throw from Jerusalem. The cavernous and colonnaded Church of the Nativity, the oldest church in the country, is built over the grotto where Jesus is believed to have been born. Bethlehem is a West Bank Arab town of some 30,000 souls, one-third Christian, two-thirds Muslim, straddling the ancient high road through the rocky, olive-groved Judean Hills. One of only two Christian-Arab enclaves in the predominantly Muslim West Bank, Bethlehem is traditionally a less hostile town than the fundamentalist Hebron to the south, or the politically radical Nablus to the north.

Old Testament history buffs will find fascination in the ancient hill country, where terraced vineyards, old-style plows, wheat-winnowing with wooden pitchforks, and laden donkeys are ubiquitous elements of the landscape. Hebron, burial place of the biblical Patriarchs and Matriarchs, is especially fascinating, but here the visitor needs to use discretion and to keep apprised of the current state of Palestinian unrest.

Still on the trail of the Bible, you will find echoes of Joshua, though not his walls, at the palm-studded oasis of Jericho, and accurate topographical detail of David and Goliath's duel in the Elah Valley.

In the planted pine and cypress forests west of Jerusalem, there is an abundance of spectacular views, picnic spots, and a few nature reserves. Do not miss the Sorek Cave, an almost fantastical cavern of stalagmites and stalactites; Bet Guvrin, an ancient complex of huge, man-made, chalk "bell caves"; and the adjacent site of Maresha, a Hellenistic city with underground storage and industrial complexes.

Essential Information

Important Addresses and Numbers

Tourist Information There are Government Tourist Information Offices (GTIOs) at the following locations:

Bethlehem: Manger Sq., tel. 02/741581 or 02/741582.

Jerusalem: 24 King George St., tel. 02/754863 or 02/754888.

Tel Aviv: 5 Shalom Aleichem St., 63806, tel. 03/660259 or 03/660260.

Emergencies
Police To contact the police in **Bethlehem, Hebron, Jericho,** and **Bet Shemesh,** dial 100.

Hospitals **Ein Gedi** and **Lod:** tel. 101

The major hospitals in **Jerusalem** are: **Bikur Holim,** Strauss St., tel. 02/701111; **Hadassah,** Ein Kerem, tel. 02/427427 or 02/776555, children's emergency room tel. 02/777215; **Hadassah,** Mt. Scopus, tel. 02/818111; **Sha'arei Tzedek,** Bayit Vegan, tel. 02/555111, emergency room tel. 02/555508.

Dentists In **Jerusalem** the **Jerusalem Emergency Dental Center** (7 Eliash St., Rejwan Sq., plaza is above 16 King George St., tel. 02/254779) is open 364 days a year (closed Yom Kippur) 8 AM–midnight.

Car Rental **Jerusalem:** Avis, 22 King David St., tel. 02/249001; Budget, 2 Lincoln St., corner of 24 King David St., tel. 02/248991; Eldan, 19 King David St., tel. 02/252151; Europcar, 8 King David St., tel. 02/248464; Hertz, 18 King David St., tel. 02/231351 and at the Hyatt Hotel, tel. 02/815069 (open Sat.); Reliable, 14 King David St., tel. 02/248204 or 02/248205.

Tel Aviv: Avis, 113 Hayarkon St., tel. 03/527–1752; Budget, 99 Hayarkon St., tel. 03/523–1551; Eldan, 112 Hayarkon St., tel. 03/527–1166; Europcar, 75 Hayarkon St., tel. 03/662866; Hertz, 148 Hayarkon St., tel. 03/223332; Reliable, 112 Hayarkon St., tel. 03/524–9794 or 03/524–9796.

Arriving and Departing by Plane

The only international airport in the area is **Ben Gurion International Airport** near Lod, east of Tel Aviv and a 35 minute drive west of Jerusalem. Arkia Israel Airlines (in Tel Aviv, tel. 03/690–2222; in Jerusalem, tel. 02/234855) services Jerusalem's **Atarot Airport,** north of the city off the Ramallah Road, from Haifa, Rosh Pina, and Eilat.

Getting Around

By Car This is by far the best way to see the areas covered in this chapter, because many of the sites are on secondary roads where public transportation is infrequent, or in some cases, nonexistent. Roads range in condition from fair to excellent, and most sites are clearly marked. Drive defensively—many Israeli drivers are frustrated fighter pilots! Gas stations are plentiful, and some never close. Still, it's wise to play it safe and never let your gauge drop below half. Pay special attention to keeping the radiator topped up in the hot Israeli summer.

Masada, the furthest point on the Dead Sea tour, is 100 kilometers (62 miles) from Jerusalem, about 1½ hours' drive, on routes 1 and 90; add one hour from Tel Aviv. Jericho, which is 40 kilometers (25 miles) from Jerusalem, can be reached via routes 1 and 90 north in 35 minutes. Now that this is a Palestinian Autonomous Zone, check the town's accessibility before you set out. Heading southwest from Jerusalem, it takes 40 minutes to get to Sorek Cave via Route 386 (about 24 kilometers, or 15 miles), and another 30 minutes' driving time (about 28 kilometers, or 17.5 miles) to Bet Guvrin via Route 38. From Tel Aviv (east on Rte. 1, south on Rte. 38), Bet Shemesh can be reached in about 40 minutes. Bethlehem is a mere 8 kilometers (5 miles) from downtown Jerusalem, a 10-minute drive.

In the West Bank, at least south of Bethlehem (Rte. 60 to Hebron, for example), a rented car with yellow Israeli plates may attract the same unwelcome attention of stone-throwing Arab youths as any other Israeli vehicle. That, as well as the danger of blundering into a hostile town center, makes driving by yourself in the West Bank inadvisable. Consider the following alternatives: (1) commercial bus tours (if available); (2) hiring a guide with a car or limousine; (3) public transportation; or (4) an Arab taxi, easily found outside Jerusalem's Damascus Gate. Hebron is 35 kilometers (22 miles) from Jerusalem, about a 40-minute drive on a winding, two-lane highway.

By Bus With few exceptions, the **Egged Bus Co-operative** enjoys a nationwide monopoly on intercity bus routes. The buses are modern (if not spanking new), comfortable, and air-conditioned, and by American and European standards, cheap. The service on main routes is good, but infrequent to outlying rural districts. For fares and schedules call 02/304555 (Jerusalem) or 03/537–5555 (Tel Aviv).

The **Central Bus Station** in **Jerusalem** is located in the city's northwest corner, on Jaffa Road across from Binyanei Ha'ooma convention center. Give yourself ample time to buy a ticket and get into line for the crowded Tiberias and Dead Sea routes. Jericho is served by the Bet She'an/Tiberias lines (Buses 961, 963, 964), with buses leaving about once an hour, but at press time the Palestinian Autonomy arrangements had left the future of the Jericho line uncertain. There is no direct bus service from Tel Aviv to Jericho. For the Dead Sea area (Qumran, Ein Gedi, Masada, and Ein Bokek), take Buses 421, 486, 487, and 966, which run hourly. Only one bus daily departs from Tel Aviv, at 8 AM, for the Dead Sea area.

Bus 160 runs every hour to the Cave of Machpelah in Hebron via Rachel's Tomb, the Etzion Bloc Junction, and Kiryat Arba. Bus 161, which runs less frequently, takes you into Kfar Etzion itself. Both can be picked up in downtown Jerusalem, on **Keren Hayesod Street** opposite the Moriah Hotel, and at the **Jerusalem Train Station.** From the **East Jerusalem Bus Station** on Sultan Suleiman Street near the Damascus Gate, an Arab company operates Bus 22 to Manger Square in the heart of Bethlehem. There is no direct bus service from Tel Aviv to Bethlehem and Hebron.

The sites west of Jerusalem discussed in this chapter are difficult to reach by public transportation. Egged's Buses 403 and 433 (two or three per hour) stop at Latrun, with Emmaus and Canada Park a short walk away. The only bus going to Bet Guvrin (Bus 011) leaves at 8:05 AM from the town of Kiryat Gat. From Tel Aviv, take Bus 369 (three per hour) to Kiryat Gat. Bus 461 goes from Tel Aviv to Lod every 20 minutes.

By Sherut and Taxi   A *sherut* (*see* Staying in Israel *in* Chapter 1, Essential Information) is a shared taxi (seating up to seven passengers) that runs along a set route. Usually it follows a major bus route, and the fare is only marginally higher than that of a bus. From Jerusalem you can get an Arab sherut to most West Bank towns such as Bethlehem, Hebron, and Jericho, which will give you some local flavor—and sometimes a hair-raising driving experience. An Arab taxi is likely to be delayed at military checkpoints. Egged buses (*see above*) are a more comfortable and reliable alternative.

Using a regular taxi to tour is not cheap. Define your itinerary, get a quote from one of the main West Jerusalem taxi companies, and use that as a starting point for negotiating a better deal with an individual cabbie (outside your hotel, or the Arab cabbies at the Jaffa Gate). Hiring a taxi for seven hours to Ein Gedi, the Dead Sea, and Masada, for example, costs almost NIS 600 ($200), not much less than hiring a qualified tour guide with an air-conditioned limo for the same trip.

Guided Tours

General Interest   These "regular" bus tours, as they're known locally, pick you up at your hotel and bring you back there at the end of the tour (a convenient but time-consuming operation if many hotels are involved). Guided bus tours departing from Tel Aviv offer the same itineraries as those leaving Jerusalem. Children under 12 enjoy a 20% discount on day trips, 10% on longer packages. The three main operators are **Egged Tours** (224 Jaffa Rd., Jerusalem, tel. 02/304422; 15 Frishman St., Tel Aviv, tel. 03/527–1222), **United Tours** (King David Hotel Annex, Jerusalem, tel. 02/252187; 113 Hayarkon St., Tel Aviv, tel. 03/693–3404 or 03/693–3405), and the smaller **Galilee Tours** (3 Hillel St., Jerusalem, tel. 02/258866; 42 Ben Yehuda St., Tel Aviv, tel. 03/546–6333; toll-free tel. 177/022–2525). Most hotels carry their brochures, and can book for you.

All three companies offer full-day tours of Masada, Ein Gedi, the Dead Sea, and Jericho, in different combinations. Tours cost between NIS 168 and NIS 174 ($56 and $58) per person (not including lunch), and, among the three companies, there are departures daily. The Church of the Nativity, in Bethlehem, and sometimes Rachel's Tomb, can be seen as part of a half-day tour that includes some Jerusalem sites (daily departures, NIS 60–NIS 63/$20–$21 per person). Egged conducts half-day tours of Sorek Cave and Kibbutz Tzora twice a week; United Tours covers the same itinerary once a week. Both tours cost NIS 69 ($23) per person. At press time there were no guided tours to Hebron.

Special Interest   **The Society for the Protection of Nature in Israel,** or SPNI (4 Hashfela St., Tel Aviv, tel. 03/537–4425, or 03/639–0644), conducts an exciting range of tours that will appeal to the adventurous traveler. (For SPNI offices in the United States and United Kingdom, *see* Special-Interest Tours *in* Chapter 1.) The emphasis is on hiking (for the hardy), but some less demanding excursions are made as well. Highlights include hiking the Wadi Kelt and Ein Gedi canyons and climbing Masada, and gentler tours to Sorek Cave, Bet Guvrin, and Sataf. A special adventure is "Judean Desert by Moonlight," four hours of nighttime exploration, timed with a bright moon. Day tours typically cost NIS 135–NIS 147 ($45–$49), but longer and more complex packages are available.

A different kind of desert adventure is provided by **Metzukei Dragot** (Kibbutz Mitzpeh Shalem, Mobile Post Jericho Valley 90670, tel. 02/ 964501, 02/964502, 02/964503, or 02/964504; or through Galilee Tours, call toll-free 177/022–2525), based at Kibbutz Mitzpeh Shalem, by the Dead Sea. It offers weekly one-day "safaris" from Jerusalem to the Judean Desert in a go-anywhere 31-seater safari truck (the cost is NIS 147/$49, including picnic lunch). If you cannot live without air-conditioning and plush seats, don't consider it. But if you want unforgettable desert vistas that really are off the beaten track, this is for you. There is little or no demanding walking.

Private Guides One of the best ways to see the country is with a private licensed guide in a 4- or 7-passenger, air-conditioned limousine/minibus. You determine the tour's character and pace. Current rates are NIS 690 ($230) per day for up to four passengers, NIS 780 ($260) for five to seven passengers. Rates include all guiding and car expenses (up to 200 kilometers, or 124 miles, per day, averaged out over all the days of the tour). Apart from the obvious advantages of flexibility and personal attention, a private guide can help you custom-design an itinerary including, but not limited by, the less accessible sites. In addition, if the West Bank is on your agenda, your guide will be in the best position to decide which areas can be visited safely, and which are better avoided.

Some guides have organized into cooperatives, but all are essentially freelancers. In Jerusalem, try **Eshcolot-Yehuda Tours** (36 Keren Hayesod, tel. 02/635555, fax 02/632101); and in Tel Aviv, **Twelve Tribes** (29 Hamered St., tel. 03/510–1911, fax 03/510–1943) or **TarHemed** (59 Hayarkon St., tel. 03/517–6101, fax 03/510–0165). You can get advice from two of Fodor's in-field writers, themselves qualified guides: Mike Rogoff (19/A Shimoni St., 92623 Jerusalem, tel. and fax 02/790410) and Judy Goldman (255 Dizengoff St., 63117 Tel Aviv, tel. 03/546–6885). Hotel concierges can usually recommend guides.

Exploring Around Jerusalem

Tour 1 takes you east through the arid Judean Desert and the canyon of Wadi Kelt, to the oasis town of Jericho, the oldest city known (political climate permitting); Qumran, where the Dead Sea Scrolls were found; the salty Dead Sea (and lowest point on earth); the cànyons and waterfalls of Ein Gedi; and the ancient palace-fortress of Masada.

With an early start, most of the sites can be done in one day. A good combination is Masada (with its dramatic story and interesting archaeological remains), the Dead Sea (total relaxation), and one of the Ein Gedi nature reserves (a refreshing antidote to the heat and the brine of the Dead Sea). From April to October, later closing times may allow a visit to Qumran as well. Wadi Kelt and Jericho (again, if accessible) can be seen together as a day tour from Jerusalem, or on the way to an overnight trip along the Dead Sea. Important words of caution: It is vital to wear a hat and drink water copiously in this area in hot weather. The desert is an area to be approached with respect—do not attempt unfamiliar trails without expert guidance.

Tour 2 heads southwest from Jerusalem through the Judean Hills to the lowland area known as the Shefelah. Highlights include the exquisite Sorek stalactite cave, the Elah Valley, where David and Goliath clashed, and the intriguing man-made caves of Bet Guvrin. It's a full but comfortable day's touring.

Tour 3 begins with Bethlehem, a few minutes' drive south of Jerusalem, and offers the option (recommended with a licensed guide) of continuing deeper into the West Bank to the Etzion Bloc and as far as the ancient patriarchal city of Hebron. This is not a friendly area, especially in the last few years of Palestinian unrest. Stone-throwing is a common occurrence, and the visitor is advised to use Egged buses or a guide-driven limo to get around. One can easily see Bethlehem and Hebron in half a day, then take Route 367 west from the Etzion Bloc to join Tour 2 at the Elah Valley.

Highlights for First-Time Visitors

Bet Guvrin and **Tel Maresha caves** (*see* Tour 2)
Church of the Nativity, Bethlehem (*see* Tour 3)
Dead Sea (*see* Tour 1)
Masada (*see* Tour 1)
Nahal David Nature Reserve, Ein Gedi (*see* Tour 1)
Qumran (*see* Tour 1)
Sorek Cave (*see* Tour 2)

Tour 1: The Dead Sea Region

Numbers in the margin correspond to points of interest on the Around Jerusalem map.

From the ridges of Jerusalem's Mt. Scopus and Mt. of Olives, the view to the east is of barren hills that cascade down to the Dead Sea, almost 3,800 feet below. Clouds off the Mediterranean warm and disperse as they cross the ridge into the chasm of the Dead Sea, creating what meteorologists call a "rain shadow." Within a map distance of about 30 kilometers (19 miles), the average annual rainfall drops from 550 millimeters (22 inches) in Jerusalem to 50 millimeters (2 inches) at the Dead Sea. This "shadow" region is the Judean Desert, and its proximity to Jerusalem has always made it part of that city's consciousness. Refugees fled to it; hermits sought its solitude; and, in ancient times, before the Jewish Day of Atonement, the scapegoat symbolically bearing the sins of the people was driven into oblivion among its stark precipices.

Take Road No. 1 heading north, which leaves Jerusalem at the French Hill neighborhood. One hundred yards beyond the entrance to French Hill, exit right to Route 1, which runs east, swings back below the eastern slopes of Mt. Scopus and Mt. of Olives (look for their distinctive towers), and begins its steep descent to the Dead Sea. Some 8 kilometers (5 miles) on, you reach a T-junction. Turn left on Route 1; the road to the right leads to the village of **El-Azariya** (**Bethany** of the New Testament), where Lazarus was raised from the dead. Ahead and above you is the edge of the town of Ma'aleh Adumim, built in the 1970s as a bedroom community of Jerusalem. This and the handful of small Jewish villages in the Judean Desert are some of the so-called West Bank settlements so often in the news. Because of their isolation, however, they have been spared the constant friction with Palestinian Arab neighbors typical of such settlements in the mountain region (*see* Tour 3, *below*).

On both sides of the road, you will frequently see encampments of Bedouin, Arab nomads still living in the peripatetic style of their ancestors. The tents and primary sources of livelihood (herding) are traditional enough, but concessions have been made to modernity: water tanks and tractors, synthetic fabrics flapping on clotheslines, and even an occasional TV antenna sprouting out of a tent.

Five hundred yards past the junction with Route 458, the road rises to a crest distinguished by the red limestone that gave it its ancient name: **Ma'aleh Adumim,** the Red Ascent (whence the name of the modern town). The unusual red rock made the spot a border marker between the biblical Israelite tribes of Benjamin to the north, and Judah to the south (Joshua 15). Pull off to the small parking area on your right. The one-story building, its courtyard surrounded by a low stone wall, was a Turkish police fort at the beginning of this century, the half-way point on what was then a two-day journey between Jerusalem and Jericho. Its name, the **Inn of the Good Samaritan,** is spurious. The New Testament (Luke 10) relates the parable of a man ambushed on the Jericho road and helped only by a Samaritan (a people hostile to the Jews at the time) who lodged him at the nearby inn. Because Jesus' parables used images familiar to his listeners, it is not unreasonable that he had a specific inn in mind, and that it was located here. No remains of that inn have been found, but other ages have left their mark. If you're energetic, turn your back on the commercialized Inn of the Good Samaritan, very carefully cross the road, and climb the dirt track to the top of the hill opposite. Amidst the scanty ruins of the small 12th-century Crusader fort of **Maldoim**—with the outskirts of both Jerusalem and Jericho visible—the Gospel passage comes alive. The medieval Burchard of Mt. Sion wrote that the Red Ascent (called the Blood Ascent in Arabic) got its name "from the frequent blood shed there. Of a truth it is horrible to behold and exceedingly dangerous. . . ."

Continue on Route 1. Four kilometers (2.5 miles) beyond the Inn, an orange sign directs you off to the left to Wadi Kelt (Nahal Perat in Hebrew) and St. George's Monastery. (If you're pressed for time, continue straight on, passing the sea-level sign on your right and exiting to Route 90 north for Jericho and Bet She'an, 8 kilometers/5 miles away.) The Wadi Kelt road dips into a hollow and rises to a fork. To get to Ein Kelt, take the left fork, then the sharp turn to the right. Most less adventurous visitors take the right fork east to Jericho. You are now on the **Jericho road** of Christian tradition, still supported over gullies by the original Roman walls. The soft contours of the desert hills belie their flinty hardness. It is inhospitable terrain, relieved only by a fuzz of grass and some wildflowers in the early spring, but no less beautiful for that. (Caution: The road is very narrow and winding—beware of oncoming vehicles.)

A five-minute drive brings you to a spot marked by a large black metal **cross** on a hill to your left. The ubiquitous Bedouin selling orange juice, baubles, and imitation sheepskin rugs are almost as permanent a landmark. Walk up to the cross for a quite unexpected and breathtaking view. Below you is the deep gorge of **Wadi Kelt** (*wadi* means "stream" in Arabic) and the whitewashed, turquoise-domed Greek Orthodox **Monastery of St. George,** clinging to the cliffside opposite. About 2 kilometers (1.25 miles) down the road from the cross where you've stopped, a dirt road winds down to the monastery.

Built in the late 19th century and still functioning, the monastery incorporates some remains of its 5th- to 6th-century Byzantine predecessor. It was originally dedicated to the Holy Virgin, but a medieval tradition identified the place with Joachim, her father (ac-

cording to apocryphal writings), and even with the Old Testament
prophet Elijah. Chapels in the monastery preserve all three traditions. St. George of Koziba, after whom the monastery is named,
was a monk here in the late 6th and early 7th centuries, and is cred-
ited with having bravely stood his ground against Persian invaders.

The artificial waterfall on the opposite cliff is part of an irrigation
conduit built in 1919 from the spring of Ein Kelt to banana plantations near Jericho. *Admission free. Open Apr.–Sept., Sun.–Fri.
9–4, Sat. 9–noon; Oct.–Mar., Sun.–Fri. 9–3, Sat. 9–noon. Closed
Greek Orthodox Easter week.*

Jericho and its environs were transferred to the authority of the
Palestinian Autonomy in May 1994. Although in principle the town
remains open to visitors, the situation (at press time, fall 1994) is not
always predictable, and should be checked before planning your
tour. If a visit to Jericho seems inadvisable, return to Route 1 and
continue east toward the Dead Sea.

The old Jericho road descends to the Jericho plain, emerging among
adobe houses and banana trees. On your left is a small but distinctive
❸ earth mound, **Tel Abu Alaik.** On and around the mound, and on the
opposite bank of the wadi, archaeologists' spades have uncovered
the remains of the once-spectacular royal palace of the Jewish Hasmonean dynasty (2nd–1st centuries BC), described by the Jewish
historian Flavius Josephus (AD 37–ca 100). In the '30s of the 1st century BC, Mark Antony gave the valuable oasis of Jericho to his beloved Cleopatra. Humiliated, Antony's local vassal, King Herod,
was forced to lease the property back from the Egyptian queen.
Herod expanded and improved the palace, turning it into his winter
retreat. It was here that he died in 4 BC. Still visible are the patterned brick palace walls, and the pool in which Herod had his young
brother-in-law murdered by drowning.

The road meets Route 90 just north of the Military Headquarters
building, a "bequest" of the British Mandatory Government, which
built dozens of these around the country in the 1920s and '30s. Turn
left (north), immediately entering the wide, tree-lined streets of the
oasis town of **Jericho.** The riot of greenery—date palms, orange
groves, banana plantations, bougainvillea, and papaya trees—
takes the edge off the neglect and dilapidation that is everywhere
apparent. It is more country lane than urban street. The Arab population of about 10,000 is mostly Muslim, with a small Christian minority.

Take the left fork at the traffic island. Two hundred yards farther,
the road swings sharply to the left. To the right, and one block away
(no entry for vehicles) is a huge sycamore tree, which tradition (and
the fellow across the way who sells postcards of it) identifies as the
very one Zacchaeus climbed to watch Jesus pass by (Luke 19). The
road continues for 1.5 kilometers (1 mile). The fruit stands and garden restaurants that dot this route closed under the pressure of local
Palestinian activists after the eruption of the *intifada,* the Arab unrest, which began in December 1987, but have reopened in the
changed climate—and administration—of the town.

Where the road turns right toward Bet She'an and the north, turn
❹ sharply to the left (clearly marked) to **Tel Jericho,** swing around the
outside of the site, and enter it from the west.

This *tel,* a mound of accumulated earth that entombs the ancient
city, has been extensively excavated by archaeologists looking for
its most famous ruins: the walls which, in the words of the spiritual,

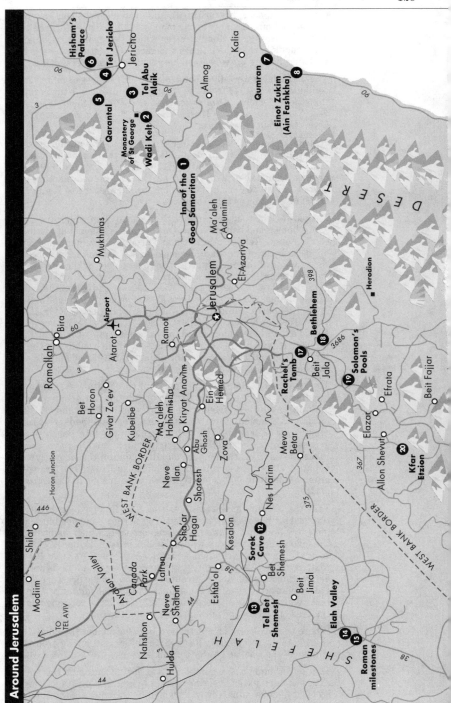

Around Jerusalem

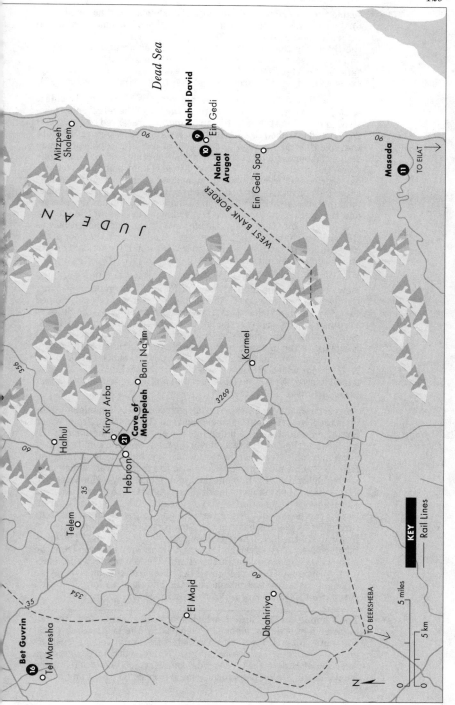

Dead Sea

Mitzpeh Shalem

Nahal David

9 Ein Gedi

10 Nahal Arugot

Ein Gedi Spa

11 Masada

TO EILAT

J U D E A N

Karmel

3269

Bani Na'im

Kiryat Arba

21 Cave of Machpelah

Hebron

Halhul

60

Telem

35

354

El Majd

Dhahiriya

60

TO BEERSHEBA

WEST BANK BORDER

Bet Guvrin **16**

Tel Maresha

35

KEY

——— Rail Lines

5 miles

5 km

0

N

"came tumblin' down" at the blast of Joshua's rams' horns (Joshua 6). Jericho was the first Canaanite objective of Joshua's army. The Israelites marched around the city once a day for six days, relates the Bible. On the seventh day, they marched around seven times, and on the seventh time they blew their rams' horns and shouted, "and the wall fell down flat, so that the people went up into the city, every man straight before him, and they took the city" (Joshua 6:20).

Those walls have not been found, but remains of the world's oldest walled city have. An excavation pit at the top of the tel reveals a massive, round, stone tower 28 feet in diameter, preserved to a height of 25 feet and attached to a 7.5-foot-thick wall. The structures predate the invention of pottery, and carbon-14 tests have placed human skulls and bones found at the site in the Neolithic period (Late Stone Age), between 6,500 and 7,800 BC. Little is known about who these early urbanites were or why they needed such stout fortifications thousands of years before they became common in the rest of the region, but a wealth of artifacts, most displayed in Jerusalem's Israel and Rockefeller museums (*see* Exploring Jerusalem *in* Chapter 2), give insights into their domestic life and rituals. One such ritual was the burial of the deceased's decapitated head beneath the floor of the house, apparently to keep one's ancestor's spirit—and its strength and wisdom—within the home.

From the sun shelter at the top of the tel, there is a fine sweeping view of Jericho, the biblical "City of Palms." The generous spring that was always the secret of its fecundity is across the road, capped today by a pump house. It is known as **Ain es-Sultan**—the **Sultan's Spring** or **Elisha's Spring**, the latter in recognition of the Old Testament prophet's miracle of sweetening the water with a bowl of salt (I Kings 2). In the distance to the east is the high range of the mountains of Ammon and Moab in Jordan, among them the peak of Mt. Nebo, from which Moses viewed the Promised Land. *Tel Jericho, tel. 02/922909. New admission fees and hours not available at press time, fall 1994.*

Turn around and face west. A peak surrounded by a modern wall is identified by tradition as the **Mount of Temptation**, from which Satan tempted Jesus with dominion over "all the kingdoms of the world" (Matthew 4). Halfway down the mountain and a bit to the left is a remarkable Greek Orthodox monastery, built right into the cliff face on Byzantine remains. (Note also the many caves, which once served hermits.) Both mountain and monastery (Monastery of Temptation) are known locally as **Qarantal,** a corruption of *quarantena*, "a period of 40 days" (compare the English "quarantine"), the period of Jesus's temptation. To get to the monastery turn right as you come out of the parking lot of the tel and take the first turn to the left. There is a long stairway to the site. The spectacular views of the Jericho Plain and Mountains of Moab from the monastery balconies justify the climb. The old stone walls, elaborately ornamented chapels, and bearded Greek monks convey an incongruous Aegean atmosphere in the middle of an Israeli desert. *Admission free. Open Mon.–Sat. 8–11, 3–4.*

Time Out The **Temptation Restaurant,** which abuts the parking lot of the tel, has excellent *bourma,* a honey-rolled pastry filled with whole pistachio nuts. Wash it down with Turkish coffee, mint tea, or fresh orange juice. Their lunches offer good value, with tasty *mezeh* (a selection of Middle Eastern salads) and very good *koubeh* (chopped meat shaped into zeppelin form, coated in cracked wheat and fried).

Try the pomelo (related to the grapefruit), in season from December to March.

Two kilometers (1.2 miles) north of the tel, a turnoff to the right **6** leads to **Hisham's Palace,** known in Arabic as Hirbet el-Mafjar. The turnoff to the site itself is another kilometer (.6 mile) off Route 90, but marked only by a low stone pillar on the right side of the road. Watch for it carefully, and turn left. (Note that road signs may have changed since press time, and it is advisable to check accessibility of the site ahead of time.)

Hisham was a scion of the Ummayad dynasty, which built the Dome of the Rock and El-Aqsa Mosque in Jerusalem. Like Herod eight centuries earlier, Hisham was attracted by the balmy winter climate of the Jericho oasis, and decided to build a palace there. While still under construction, the structure was badly damaged by the great earthquake of AD 749 and never completed, but the high quality of the mosaics and stone and plaster reliefs that survive are evidence of its splendor.

The entrance to the ruins is through a small gatehouse and into a wide plaza dominated by a large star-shape stone window that once graced an upper-floor chamber. A well-preserved basement bathhouse and one of the palace's two mosques (open to the sky) are an interesting juxtaposition of the worldly and the spiritual character of the Arab empire of the time. North of the plaza is a series of columns—some of them artless reconstructions in concrete—that supported the roof of a large bath and recreation area. Several sections of the fine geometric mosaics have been left exposed; others are covered by sand.

Undoubtedly the most impressive part of the complex is the adjacent reception room. Its intricate mosaic floor depicting a lion hunting a stag is one of the most beautiful in Israel, the tiny colored tesserae producing a realism astonishing for this medium. Still visible on some of the walls are fragments of ornate stucco reliefs, but the best examples found here (including human figures, unusual in Islamic art) are now displayed in Jerusalem's Rockefeller Museum (*see* Exploring Jerusalem *in* Chapter 2). More bathhouses and an ornamental pool (note the dual artistic influences of East and West in its balustrade) bring you back to the entrance. *Tel. 02/922522. New admission fees and hours not available at press time.*

Return to the main highway. Bet She'an is 86 kilometers (53 miles) to the north, about 1¼ hours' drive. If you're on your way to the Dead Sea, return through Jericho, remaining on Route 90 until the T-junction with Route 1, 6 kilometers (4.5 miles) south of the town. Turn left (east), still on Route 90. (If you had bypassed Jericho en route to the Dead Sea, Route 1 merges with Route 90 here.) A milestone by the side of the road just before the next T-junction advertises the fact that you have now reached the bottom of the world—the Dead Sea—and a Bedouin is often here with his camel to help you immortalize the moment. The Dead Sea has shrunk in recent years, and the shore at this point is actually at least a kilometer (.6 mile) away. Heaps of white potash, the primary product of the Dead Sea, can be seen off to the left, though today almost all extraction of potash, bromine, and magnesium from the brine takes place at the huge plant at Sodom, at the southern end of the sea. Route 90 turns right. Five kilometers (3 miles) away, a short road to the right **7** brings you to **Qumran.**

In 1947, a Bedouin goatherd stumbled on a cave containing a cache of the now-famous Dead Sea Scrolls, hidden in earthen jars. Because the scrolls were written on parchment, which is treated animal hide, one of the nomads sought out a Bethlehem shoemaker to turn them into sandals! The shoemaker alerted a local antiquities dealer, who brought them to the attention of Professor Eliezar Sukenik of the Hebrew University of Jerusalem. Five other major scrolls and several thousand fragments subsequently came to light, some from pirate digs conducted by the Bedouin themselves in other caves in the area, others from methodical excavations by Israeli, French, and British archaeologists.

The scrolls were written by an ultra-devout Jewish sect generally identified as the Essenes, who had set up a monastic community at Qumran in the late 3rd century BC. They apparently spirited away their precious scrolls to the caves visible in the cliffs and canyons behind the town during the Great Revolt against Rome (AD 66–73). Their fears were well founded, and Qumran was destroyed in AD 68, giving scholars a "terminus date" for the scrolls.

Regarded as the most significant archaeological find ever made in Israel, the Dead Sea Scrolls include books of the Old Testament, and sectarian literature of the Qumran community. Among the biblical scrolls is one containing the full 66 chapters of the Book of Isaiah. Except for minor variations—there were slightly different versions of the Hebrew Bible in circulation at the time—the text of the scroll is almost identical to that used in Jewish communities to this day, conclusively putting to rest any doubts about the latter's authenticity. Sectarian texts include the "constitution" or "Rule of the Community" ("The Manual of Discipline"), a description of a final battle ("The War of the Sons of Light Against the Sons of Darkness"), and "The Thanksgiving Scroll" with "psalms" reminiscent of those in the Bible.

Apart from the bonanza the scrolls represented for Bible scholars and students of ancient Hebrew, they afforded researchers rare insights into this previously shadowy Jewish sect. Christian scholars have long been intrigued by the suggestion that John the Baptist, whose lifestyle was reminiscent of that of the Essenes, may have been a member of the Qumran community. The scrolls are on display in the Israel Museum in Jerusalem (*see* Exploring Jerusalem *in* Chapter 2).

Qumran sits on a narrow plateau between the craggy limestone cliffs to the west and the narrow shores of the Dead Sea to the east. Excavated in the 1950s, the site is small and not especially impressive to the layperson. Climb the tower for a good view, and note the unusual number of water cisterns and channels that served both the domestic and ritual needs of the community. Just below the tower (in front of you as you look toward the Dead Sea) is a long room identified as the **scriptorium.** A plaster writing table and bronze and ceramic inkwells found here confirm that this was where the scrolls were written. A good, air-conditioned cafeteria serves the site. *Qumran National Park. Tel. 02/942235. Admission: NIS 8 ($2.70) adults, NIS 4 ($1.35) children. Open Apr.–Sept., Sat.–Thurs. 8–5, Fri. and holiday eves 8–4; Oct.–Mar., Sat.–Thurs. 8–4, Fri. and holiday eves 8–3.*

Three kilometers (2 miles) south of Qumran is the nature reserve of **8** **Einot Zukim (Ain Fashkha),** translated as Cliff Springs. A Dead Sea beach, fresh (though brackish) springs, a variety of trees and reeds rare in the arid Judean Desert, and picnic and changing facilities make this a popular spot. It is especially crowded on Friday and Saturday. The most beautiful part of the reserve, with bubbling brooks and thickets of giant reeds, is closed to the general public to preserve its fragile ecosystem. The Nature Reserves Authority does occasionally conduct tours of the section, however. Call for information. *Tel. 02/942346 or 02/942355. Admission: NIS 10 ($3.35) adults, NIS 8 ($2.70) children. Open Mar.–Oct., daily 8–5; Nov.–Feb., call ahead.*

Four kilometers (2.5 miles) on, the road enters a wider area, the delta of the dry Kidron stream. One of the very few canyons in the area with a gentle enough slope to allow its use as an ancient caravan route, the Kidron comes down from the heart of Jerusalem itself (*see* Exploring Jerusalem *in* Chapter 2). Look for the remains of a 21-centuries-old Hasmonean fort on your left, built to protect royal caravans carrying valuable tropical produce from Ein Gedi to the Mediterranean world.

Ein Gedi (33 kilometers, or 20.5 miles, south of Qumran) bursts upon you with a splash of vivid green against the burnt browns and beiges of the desert rock. The first turnoff to the right takes you to the parking lot at the entrance to **Nahal David** (David's Stream). It was here, 3,000 years ago, that David hid from the wrath of King Saul (I Samuel 24). The cliffs soar to more than 1,600 feet above the streams, waterfalls, and tropical reeds of the reserve. These features, plus the wildlife, would make this an exciting nature reserve anywhere; in the midst of a harsh desert, it is nothing short of spectacular.

It's a bit of a climb up the clearly marked trail that takes you past several pools and small waterfalls to the beautiful top waterfall, but it's not too daunting a prospect. Allow at least 1¼ hours to include a refreshing dip under a waterfall. Look out for ibex, especially in the afternoon, and for the small furry hyrax, often seen on tree branches. Leopards were rediscovered in the area some years ago, but are facing extinction again because of breeding problems. They are seldom seen nowadays, and never in the reserve.

If you're a hiker, don't miss the trail that breaks off to the right some 50 yards down the return path from the top waterfall. It passes the remains of Byzantine irrigation systems and offers breathtaking views of the Dead Sea. The trail doubles back on itself toward the source of Nahal David. Near the top, a short side path to the left reaches the remains of a 4th millennium BC (Chalcolithic) temple. The main path leads on to a stream bed, again turns east, and reaches Dudim (Lovers) Cave, formed by boulders and filled with the crystal-clear spring water. You are exactly above the waterfall of Nahal David. (Don't throw stones: There are people below!) Since this trail involves a considerable climb (and hikers invariably take time to bathe in the "cave"), access to the trail is permitted only up to 2½ hours before closing time. *Tel. 07/584285. Admission (includes Nahal Arugot on same day only; see below): NIS 8.50 ($2.85) adults, NIS 4.50 ($1.50) children. Open Sat.–Thurs. 8–4, Fri. and holiday eves 8–3. Closes 1 hr later during daylight saving time (late spring and summer). Last admission 1 hr before closing.*

Two hundred yards south of Nahal David, behind the gas station, is a somewhat rocky public beach (*see* Beaches *in* Sports and the Outdoors, *below*), with free access to the Dead Sea, freshwater showers (absolutely essential) by the water's edge and basic changing facilities. A word of advice: avoid getting the salt water in your eyes and mouth, and do not leave valuables unguarded on the beach.

Aside from its natural beauty, or perhaps because of it, Ein Gedi has attracted settlements for thousands of years. Two hundred yards south of the gas station is a road to the right (west) directing visitors to **Nahal Arugot,** the second of the fine nature reserves of Ein Gedi. One hundred yards before the parking lot at the mouth of the canyon is a small mound on the right, known as **Tel Goren.** Excavations here in the 1960s exposed five noncontinuous strata from 7th century BC (Israelite period) to AD 6th century (Byzantine period). An intriguing Hebrew and Aramaic inscription removed from an AD 6th-century mosaic synagogue floor nearby invokes the wrath of heaven on troublemakers of different stripes, including "whoever reveals the secret of the town to the Gentiles." The "secret" is believed to refer to the revived cultivation of the balsam tree, which produced the prized balm for which the town was once famous.

Although not quite as green as Nahal David, the canyon-filled Nahal Arugot Nature Reserve is, if anything, more spectacular. Enormous boulders and slabs of stone on the opposite cliff face seem poised for cataclysm, and the whole effect is powerfully primordial. The 45-minute hike to the **Hidden Waterfall** (some steps, but not especially steep) takes you by delightful spots where a stream bubbles over rock shelves and shallow pools offer relief from the heat. The Hidden Waterfall is reached by a short marked trail down to the left. Do not continue on the trail beyond the falls without prior arrangement with the Nature Reserves Authority. From the waterfall, you can return through the stream and greenery, leaping the boulders and wading the pools (appropriate footwear obviously necessary). *Tel. 07/584285. Admission (includes Nahal David on same day only): NIS 8.50 ($2.85) adults, NIS 4.50 ($1.50) children. Open Sat.–Thurs. 8–4, Fri. and holiday eves 8–3. Closes 1 hr later during daylight savings time (late spring and summer). Last admission 2½ hrs before closing.*

Time Out The **Ein Gedi Spa,** 5 kilometers (3 miles) farther south, offers decent facilities, changing rooms with lockers, and indoor showers), access to the Dead Sea, and marvelously relaxing, warm indoor sulfur pools. A very pleasant, air-conditioned restaurant is downstairs from the changing rooms and snack bar. *Tel. 07/594813. Admission (including locker and discount at restaurant): NIS 35 ($11.70) adults and children over 12. If accompanied by licensed guide, admission NIS 18 ($6) regardless of age. Open Apr.–Sept., daily 7–6; Oct.–Mar., daily 7–5.*

The turnoff to **Masada** is 16 kilometers (10 miles) south of Ein Gedi on Route 90, but the great flat-top rock, isolated from the range of cliffs, is visible to the west of the highway long before you reach it. Herod the Great, King of the Jews by the grace of Rome, hated by his subjects, and threatened by Cleopatra of Egypt, built a fortress here in the 1st century BC to which he could escape if necessary. Never one to ignore comfort, he ordered that the mountaintop complex be constructed in the best palatial style. Nowhere in the land are both his paranoia and sense of grandeur more in evidence.

With Herod's death in 4 BC, and the exile of his son Archelaus 10 years later, the central districts of Judea and Samaria (south and north of Jerusalem, respectively) came under direct Roman control. Decades of oppression and misrule precipitated the Great Revolt of the Jews against Rome in AD 66, spearheaded by an ultranationalist group called the Zealots. Masada fell to the rebels early on; but with the Roman reconquest of the country, and the fall of Jerusalem in AD 70, the fortress became the last refuge for almost a thousand men, women, and children. The new governor, Silva, came down with troops and slaves to crush the last vestige of resistance. The thoroughness of the siege can be seen by the long Roman siege-wall at the foot of the mountain, and eight square Roman camps in strategic locations on all sides.

The 1st-century Jewish historian, Flavius Josephus, sets the final scene. Despite the vigorous defense, the Romans succeeded in constructing a massive earth assault ramp (*see below*) from the high western plateau to the very summit of the mountain. Seeing the battle was lost, the Zealot leader, Elazar Ben Yair, assembled his warriors and exhorted them to "at once choose death with honor, and do the kindest thing we can for ourselves, our wives and children" rather than face the brutal consequences of capture. The decision was not an easy one, relates Josephus, but, once taken, it impelled each man to "carry out his terrible resolve" without delay. Having dispatched their own families, the men then drew lots to select 10 executioners for the rest; and the 10 similarly chose the last man who would kill them all, afterward taking his own life.

Josephus, who went over to the Romans in the course of the revolt, was long suspect in the eyes of modern historians, and his melodramatic account was taken with more than a grain of salt. His description of Masada has been borne out by archaeologists, however, and the human skeletal remains and inscribed potsherds (the lots, perhaps?) seem to verify his version of events as well.

Most visitors ride the large cable car up Masada (three minutes). The intrepid climb the **Snake Path** (45 minutes of steep walking), some even before dawn to watch the sunrise. Others take the easier western Roman Ramp path, accessible only from Arad (*see* Exploring Eilat and the Negev *in* Chapter 8). The desert climate makes it imperative to drink lots of water and to wear a hat. Running water (but not refreshments or snacks) is available on Masada itself, so save your bottles for refilling. Allow at least 1½–2 hours to explore the site.

The 90 steps from the cable car to the top of Masada pass a large plastered cistern, one of a dozen (many are much larger) that gave Herod's fortress an incredible 40 million liters (10 million gallons) "on tap." The secret was the winter flood waters in streambeds west of the mountain, diverted to cisterns in the slope and then hauled to the top by hand.

Enter the site (excellent maps are for sale where you show your ticket) and turn right. Note that the entire mountaintop—an area of more than 20 acres—is surrounded by a 4,600-foot-long **casemate,** a double wall that included living quarters and guardrooms. The path rises, passes a quarry on the left, and becomes a street that abuts the storerooms of Masada. Quantities of broken jars, seeds of grain, and dried fruit pits found here bear out Josephus's assertion that the Zealots did not burn their food supply (as they did their possessions) in order to show the Romans that they did not die out of want.

A left turn brings you to an open area, and the plastered outer wall and upper terrace of the **Northern Palace,** an extraordinary structure that seems to hang off the mountain. The wonderful view from here includes the Roman camps and "runners' path" (used for communication between the camps) and Ein Gedi (from which Silva had to get his water) in the distance to the north. The effect is awesome: baked brown precipices and bleached valleys shimmering in the midday glare, or awash in the gentler light of the early morning or late afternoon.

Facing you as you return from the upper terrace is the **bathhouse,** in Herod's time a state-of-the-art facility with its apodyterium (changing room), frigidarium, tepidarium, and caldarium (cold, lukewarm, and hot rooms, respectively). Frescoes and floor tiles are evidence of the Herodian opulence; intrusive benches and a pool represent Zealot alterations. The caldarium was once a closed room heated from below and through wall pipes by hot air pumped in from an outside furnace.

West of the bathhouse, steps descend to the middle and lower terraces—interesting (note Herod's hidden spiral staircase), but a long climb back up.

Walking south through a stone gateway brings you to the **mikveh,** one of two Jewish ritual baths found on Masada, and built during the Revolt. Their discovery created a sensation in Jewish ultra-Orthodox circles in Israel, especially after a rabbinic inspection team confirmed that they were built in precise obedience to biblical law.

Continue down to the western casemate and the **synagogue** of Masada, one of only four ever found from this period. The building's orientation toward Jerusalem suggested its function, but the stone benches ("synagogue" means "place of assembly") and man-made pit for damaged scrolls (a *geniza*) confirmed it. It was probably here that Elazar's men made their fateful decision.

Follow the western casemate 100 yards south. At a break in the walls a modern winch stands. This is where the Roman legionnaires broke into Masada; the original wedge-shape **ramp** (the upper part has since collapsed) is immediately below you. If you turn your back to the ramp, you will be facing a small **Byzantine chapel,** complete with mosaic floor and wall designs, built by monks in the 5th century. To the right (south) is the **Western Palace,** the largest structure on Masada and originally its residential and administrative center. Its most interesting features are two colorful Herodian mosaics, the larger with especially meticulous geometric and fruit motifs.

The message of the Zealots' last stand was not lost on Palestinian Jews fighting for independence in the 1930s and '40s, or on the modern Israel they created. "Masada shall not fall again!" became not merely a rallying cry but a state of mind. 'The price of powerlessness is too high for a nation to pay,' was the message of the ancient drama enacted here.

If you have energy and time, explore the sparser southern part of Masada with its huge water cistern and spectacular view from the southern citadel. (Test the echoes at this southern point!) *Masada National Park, tel. 057/584207. Admission (site): NIS 10.50 ($3.50) adults, NIS 5 ($1.70) children. 20% discount for visitors who do not use the cable car. Open Apr.–Sept., Sat.–Thurs. 8–4, Fri. and holiday eves 8–2. Cable car: one-way NIS 11.50 ($3.85) adults, NIS 7 ($2.35) children; round-trip NIS 21 ($7) adults, NIS 11.50 ($3.85) children. Scheduled run every ½ hr from 8; intermediate runs depending on demand. Last car down 4 PM, Fri. and holiday eves 2 PM. Sound-and-light show (access only from Arad; see Exploring Eilat and the Negev in Chapter 8) admission: NIS 24 ($8) adults, NIS 21 ($7) children, students, and senior citizens. Open Apr.–Oct., Tues. and Thurs. at 9 PM. Translation headsets (from Hebrew): NIS 11 ($3.70). Shuttle bus (Yoel Tours, tel. 07/584432 or 07/954791; Arad Tourist Information Office, tel. 07/959333 or 07/958993): from Arad, NIS 23 ($7.70); from Ein Bokek, NIS 53 ($17.70) Call ahead to verify show times.*

Tour 2: The Judean Hills and Lowlands (Shefelah)

From Mt. Herzl in West Jerusalem, next to the huge red Alexander Calder "stabile," take the steep descent down Ein Kerem Road to Ein Kerem (*see* Exploring Jerusalem *in* Chapter 2), and out the other side. One kilometer (.6 mile) beyond the neighborhood is the Kerem Junction. Continue straight (left fork) onto Route 386. The road follows Nahal Sorek (the Sorek stream), which eventually flows into the Mediterranean south of Tel Aviv. On the hills to your left is the **Hadassah Hospital** complex (*see* Exploring Jerusalem *in* Chapter 2), the largest such facility in the Middle East. Most of the hillsides are terraced, some simply following the natural strata of the sedimentary limestone, many having been created laboriously by farmers over the centuries. One of the dominant features of the landscape is the result of recent reforestation undertaken by the Jewish National Fund to restore something of the area's ancient scenery. The mostly pine and cypress groves have begun restoring the topsoil lost through centuries of erosion, providing recreation areas and a new lease of life for animals such as gazelle, now seen on the edge of Jerusalem itself.

Nine kilometers (6 miles) from the Kerem Junction, the road crosses the Jerusalem–Tel Aviv railway line, where the Refaim Valley merges with Nahal Sorek. The road at once begins climbing, offering fine views of the deep gorge below. Some 3 kilometers (2 miles) on, after a sharp bend in the road, a sign to the right indicates the nature reserve of **Nahal Ketalav.** An easy walking trail explores the small stream (dry part of the year), with its spring and the red-bark *ketalav* tree, which gives the reserve its name. Another 1.5 kilometers (1 mile) brings you to the Bar Giora Junction; turn right toward Nes Harim.

Most of the villages in these hills are moshavim, cooperative farming settlements of a kind pioneered in the 1920s by veteran settlers who found the communal life of the kibbutz too stifling. In a moshav, the family unit is completely autonomous, but is contractually bound to other members in areas such as cooperative purchasing and marketing, social and educational services, and mutual assistance in time of need.

The socialism of the kibbutz held no attraction for the Jewish refugee families that reached Israel from Arab lands in the 1950s. Most went to the towns, of course, but for those who settled the land, the moshav lifestyle, in which the patriarchal family structure of the old country could be preserved, was an ideal solution. There are more than 450 moshavim in Israel today, accounting for about 3% of the population. Moshavim in this area typically raise poultry and dairy cattle or sheep, and fruit orchards in the lowland valleys.

The road bypasses Nes Harim, continues west, and descends to the **12** **Avshalom Reserve.** The reserve contains the justly renowned **Sorek Cave,** a stalactite cave that is small in comparison with similar caverns in other countries, but is said to include every type of formation known. It was discovered in 1967 when a routine blast in the nearby quarry tore away the rock face, revealing a subterranean wonderland never before seen.

From the parking lot a path winds down to the cave entrance. (Visitors with medical problems should bear in mind the return climb back to the car.) Local guides take groups into the cave every 15 minutes for a 30-minute tour, mostly in Hebrew, though in English, too, on request. A short video in an acclimatization room (English version available) explains how the cave was formed. In developing the site, the Nature Reserves Authority was faced with the problem of how to allow public access to the cave with the minimum of impact on its unique environment. In general, the Authority has won kudos for its sensitive solutions. Colored lights have been eschewed in favor of "regular" lighting to highlight the natural whites and honey browns of forms such as "macaroni," "curtains," and "sombreros." The guides vie with each other to find imaginative familiarity in the shapes of the formations. In one "interfaith" series, some guides find rocky evocations of Moses, the Madonna and Child, Buddha, and the Ayatollah Khomeini! Photography is only allowed on Friday morning, when there are no guided tours. Despite the almost 100% humidity, the temperature and general atmosphere in the cave is very comfortable year-round. *Avshalom Reserve. Rte. 3856, tel. 02/ 911117. Admission: NIS 11 ($3.70) adults, NIS 5.50 ($1.85) children. Open Sat.–Thurs. 8:30–4, Fri. and holiday eves 8:30–1.*

Return the way you came. Ride 3 kilometers (2 miles) to the crest of a hill, where you'll exit to the right (at the corner with a sculpture of the *Challenger* space shuttle), taking you down toward the town of Bet Shemesh. At the bottom of the hill, turn right and continue through the town to meet Route 38. Turn left (south) onto Route 38. You are now entering Samson country. Samson, one of the "judges" of Old Testament Israel, is better known for his physical prowess and lust for Philistine women than for his shining spiritual qualities. But it was here "between Zorah and Eshta'ol" that "the Spirit of the Lord began to stir him" (Judges 13). Eshta'ol is today a moshav a few minutes' drive north, and Tzora (Zorah) is the kibbutz now off to your right.

One kilometer (.6 mile) beyond the Tzora turnoff, the road tops a small rise. There is a place to pull off on your right. You are standing ● on **Tel Bet Shemesh,** the archaeological mound of the ancient town. From the top of the tel (a few moments' walk) there is a fine view of the fields of Nahal Sorek, where Samson dallied with Delilah (Judges 16). The city of Bet Shemesh controlled access through the nahal to the mountains of Judah to the east. When the Philistines captured the Israelite Ark of the Covenant of the Lord in battle (11th century BC), they found that their prize brought divine retribution with it, destroying their idol of Dagon and afflicting them with tumors and their city of Ashdod with rats (I Samuel 5). In consternation and awe, they rid themselves of the jinxed ark by sending it back to the Israelites at Bet Shemesh.

Eight kilometers (5 miles) south of Bet Shemesh, Route 383 begins off to the right. (It's a pleasant drive from here to Route 3 and then to Route 40 toward Tel Aviv.) Just beyond the junction with Route 383 and up to your right above the pine-wooded slopes is a distinctively bald, flat-top hill, **Tel Azekah,** the site of an ancient Israelite city. Dirt roads, especially delightful in spring when the wildflowers are out, crisscross these hills (access by the first left from Route 383).

● You have just entered the **Elah Valley.** One kilometer (.6 mile) down Route 38 you'll cross a bridge that spans a usually dry streambed. Just after crossing, carefully park on the shoulder. If you have a Bible with you, open to I Samuel 17 to read about the drama of the duel between David and the giant Philistine champion Goliath. The battle took place, one may claim with some confidence, within a kilometer or so of where you're standing. Skeptical?

> *Now the Philistines gathered their armies for battle; and they were*
> *gathered at Socoh, which belongs to Judah [identified by a tel 550*
> *yds east of the junction ahead of you], and encamped between Socoh*
> *and Azekah [exactly your location] . . . And Saul and the men of*
> *Israel were gathered, and encamped in the valley of Elah, and drew*
> *up in line of battle against the Philistines. And the Philistines stood*
> *on the mountain on the one side, and Israel stood on the mountain*
> *on the other side, with a valley between them.*

Try this: As you look east up the valley (across the road), you'll see
the mountains of Judah in the distance and now (as then) the road
from Bethlehem by which David reached the battlefield. The white
ridge on the left, a spur of the mountains of Judah, may have been
the emplacement of the Israelite army; the ridge on your right
(where the gas station is today)—and including Tel Socoh, where,
the Bible says, the Philistines gathered—ascends from the Philistine territory to the west. And the stream at your feet is the only one
in the valley: "And David . . . chose five smooth stones from the
brook . . . ; his sling was in his hand, and he drew near to the Philistine." The rest, as they say, is history.

If you want to return to Jerusalem at this point, turn left (east) at
the Elah Junction onto Route 375, driving past Israel's main satellite communications receiver and up into the hills. The road climbs to
Tzur Hadassah (look out for the rock-hewn Roman road on the
right), turns left, and puts you back on Route 386 to Jerusalem. The
right turn takes you to Bethlehem, and thence to Jerusalem; but this
road goes through some restless West Bank villages, and at press
time is not recommended.

If you're continuing on the tour, stay on Route 38. About 1.5 kilometers (.9 miles) south of the Elah Junction is a terrace on the right
planted with a few cypress trees. The five broken pillars here are
⑮ Roman milestones that were found nearby. The second from the left
bears a lengthy Latin inscription dedicated to the glory of the emperors Septimus Severus and Caracalla, and to the latter's brother
(later murdered by him), Septimus Geta. Dated to around AD 210,
the milestones marked the road from Ashkelon through the Elah
Valley to Jerusalem, by then the renamed Aelia Capitolina. The Latin was for the benefit of the Romans themselves; but Greek was the
language of the region, and the last three lines say, "COL[onia]
AEL[ia] CAP[itolina], MIL[le], K[Δ][24]," meaning 24 Roman miles to
Aelia Capitolina, measured from Jerusalem's Damascus Gate.

Two kilometers (1.2 miles) farther, a road to the right climbs to
Mitzpeh Massua, a forest watchtower with fine panoramas and picnic facilities at its base. Where Route 38 meets Route 35 (10 kilometers, or about 6 miles, from the Elah Junction), turn right. (The left
turn to Hebron is a poor road, and not recommended.) Immediately
on your right is **Kibbutz Bet Guvrin,** with an adjacent, partly restored Crusader church and partly excavated Roman amphitheater,
one of only four found in Israel. On the opposite side of the road a few
old buildings, at least one Roman, peek tantalizingly out of a rubble-
strewn hill that still awaits the archaeologists' attention. The Roman remains are all from the 2nd- to 3rd-century "free city" of Eleu-
thropolis. Immediately beyond these ruins, a well-marked road
turns left to Maresha and Bet Guvrin.

Time Out Opposite the Bet Guvrin turnoff, on Route 35, is a gas station with a
clean cafeteria next door. The fare is standard, but the quality is
good, and besides, it's the only rest stop for miles.

The ticket office of the Bet Guvrin National Park is about 1 kilometer (.6 mile) from the main road. Continue straight.

One kilometer (.6 mile) on, the flat-top tel of ancient **Maresha** appears on your right. Occupied in the Canaanite and Israelite periods (2nd and early 1st millennium BC), the site continued in use until the Hellenistic period (4th–2nd centuries BC). Park in the lot just before the tel.

Nothing remains of earlier excavations, which unearthed the Hellenistic city on the top of the tel, but more recent digs have exposed the masonry of additional ancient fortifications of the Old Testament period at the corner of the mound. The view from the tel is worth the short climb. What you have really come for, however, is a series of underground chambers carved out of the soft chalk during the Hellenistic period, only a tiny part of what has been found in the region. (Warning: Other fascinating complexes of caves near the tel have dangerous pits and are off-limits to visitors until adequate safety arrangements have been made. Keep to the marked sites only.) The leaflet you're given with your ticket has a good diagram of the site. Among the attractions are water systems; a "bathhouse" cave with tubs; and an olive-oil-press cave where, it is estimated, 9 tons a year of that precious commodity were processed.

Most impressive is the so-called columbarium, a complex in the shape of a double cross (no religious significance; this is older than Christianity) some 33 feet deep. The walls are lined with symmetrical niches. "Columbarium" means "pigeon hole," and a leading theory is that pigeons or doves were raised here, for food, for ritual sacrifices, and to provide fertilizer from the droppings. Other scholars question this because chemical analysis of the surrounding chalk has failed to support the pigeon theory, and they suggest instead that the niches contained urns with cremated human remains. Local visitors still call the place "the market" because of its compartments; but the jury is still out on the question of its original function.

Another intriguing site is a Hellensitic residential quarter on the eastern slope of the tel, concealing a complex of underground cisterns and storage chambers. As you exit this part of the site, look for a large **apse** standing in splendid isolation on the ridge to your left. Known as Santahanna in Arabic, it has been identified by scholars as a remnant of the Crusader Church of St. Anne.

16 Follow the signs back to the bell caves of **Bet Guvrin**. A right turn will bring you to another parking lot (rest rooms and a refreshment stand are available).

The soft chalk of the region is honeycombed with literally thousands of man-made caves of all sizes and shapes, dug as burial places and workshops, and for water storage and refuge. The great "bells" were different. In the Hellenistic, Roman, and especially Byzantine periods (2nd century BC–AD 7th century), the ancients created an ecologically sound quarry to extract lime for cement. At the top of each "bell" is a hole through the 4-foot-thick hard stone "crust." The moment they reached the soft chalk below, the diggers began reaming out their quarry in the structurally secure bell shape, each bell eventually cutting into the adjacent one.

You enter the park through a small "bell." Take the path to the right to one complex, but return on the same path and continue to the left to the other. The open areas, once bell caves themselves in which the roofs have collapsed, have a wild character, as fig trees, cacti, and small bushes struggle for dominance. Several natural rock bridges (climbing is not permitted) add to the amazingly photogenic nature of the site. (Photographers: The caves are not dark, but the light in them is dim.) Claustrophobes need have no fear here: The cavernous bell caves reach up to 50 feet high in places, and are open to the outdoors.

Although not built to be inhabited, the caves were used as refuges by early Christians. Look for crosses high on the walls, especially in the second complex. (Scenes of the rock-musical movie *Jesus Christ Superstar* were filmed here.) Arabic inscriptions in the first complex date to the much later Arab period (after AD 640). *Bet Guvrin National Park. Just off Rte. 35, tel. 08/811020. Admission (including Tel Maresha): NIS 10.50 ($3.50) adults, NIS 5 ($1.70) children. Open Apr.–Sept., Sat.–Thurs. 8–5, Fri. and holiday eves 8–4; Oct.–Mar., Sat.–Thurs. 8–4, Fri. and holiday eves 8–3.*

Back on Route 35, return via routes 38 and 1 to Jerusalem.

Tour 3: Bethlehem and Hebron

Warning: The sites covered in this tour are located in the West Bank. Because of sporadic Arab unrest in the area, most visitors confine themselves to nearby Bethlehem. You are strongly urged to explore other sites in the region in the company of a licensed guide, and, in any event, to remain on the main arterial roads.

The West Bank is that part of the onetime British Mandate of Palestine, west of the Jordan River, that was occupied by the Hashemite Kingdom of Transjordan in its war with Israel in 1948, and unilaterally annexed shortly afterward. That kingdom consequently changed its name to Jordan, to reflect its new territorial reality. The territory was lost to Israel in the Six Day War of 1967 and has remained under Israeli military administration ever since. In Israel itself, the ancient biblical names of the region are most commonly used: *Yehuda*, or Judea, for the area south of Jerusalem, and *Shomron*, or Samaria, for the much larger area north of it. The term Green Line is used to denote the pre-1967 border between the West Bank and Israel proper.

The West Bank is a kidney-shape area, a bit larger than the U.S. state of Delaware, and almost half the size of Northern Ireland. The Arab population of almost 1 million is more than 90% Muslim, the Christian minority living mostly in the Greater Bethlehem area (in Judea), and in Ramallah (in Samaria).

Palestinian nationalism has flared into violence in recent years under the banner of the intifada ("shaking off"), resulting in clashes with security forces, attacks on Israeli citizens, and the elimination of other Arabs suspected of collaboration with Israel. Israeli security forces have responded with arrests and curfews in an attempt to curb the violence, although the struggle for control of the streets has frequently escalated with the use of firearms by the Palestinians. However, important political developments have had a major effect on the general atmosphere in "the Territories." On the one hand, the Autonomy Agreement, signed in Cairo on May 5, 1994, has given Palestinian Arabs control of their own internal affairs in the Gaza Strip, Jericho, and potentially other parts of the West Bank. On the other hand, Muslim fundamentalists who reject the entire peace process with Israel (like the Hamas and Islamic Jihad movements) have stepped up their attacks on Israeli citizens. Israel's response has been to severely restrict access of Palestinian

Arab workers from these areas into Israel proper in order to contain the violence, with the resultant economic hardship to the workers.

The nonviolent majority of Palestinians are caught between a rock and a hard place. Despite the frustration of living under military occupation, the economic development, educational standards, and medical services in the West Bank have improved dramatically since 1967; but these developments have been victims of the violence of a new generation for whom political independence is the top priority. The prognosis is not entirely bleak, however: Since the beginning of the peace process in Madrid in 1991, the street activists and clandestine terrorist cells have had to share local leadership with a legitimate, recognized delegation representing its people's cause.

The Jewish population in Judea and Samaria numbers about 130,000 in a handful of small towns and more than 100 villages. Although some of the towns are really suburbs of Jerusalem and Tel Aviv, the other settlements were set up by Israeli nationalists—the majority of them religious Jews—who see the region as an integral and inalienable part of their ancient homeland, and who see the almost miraculous "homecoming" in 1967 as nothing less than a first glimmer of the messianic age. With its mountain heights dominating Israel's main population centers, and the area thrusting to within 14.5 kilometers (9 miles) of the Mediterranean Sea, the West Bank has a strategic value that has convinced many of the folly of relinquishing it to a hostile Arab state. One's attitude toward the question of continuing settlement in the West Bank, and the ultimate status of the region, is an important touchstone of political affiliation in Israel, and the country is completely divided on these issues.

The Hebron Road leaves Jerusalem heading south to become Route 60. On your right is a good view of much of modern Jerusalem. On your left is Kibbutz Ramat Rahel, an important Israeli outpost in the War of Independence of 1948 and in the years that followed. The old Green Line ran through the valley immediately below it. The next ridge is capped by the Greek Orthodox **Monastery of Mar Elias** (St. Elijah) on your left—once a Jordanian stronghold—and immediately beyond is your first view of **Bethlehem.**

Christian visitors are often surprised by how close Bethlehem is to Jerusalem (five minutes' drive), as if the temporal separation of the two in the New Testament should somehow be reflected in distance! Way off on the horizon to your left is a prominent flat-top hill. This is **Herodion,** one of Herod's great palace-fortresses, used by the Zealots in the Great Revolt and by Bar Kochba's fighters in the 2nd century AD. As you pass the traffic lights (right to the Jerusalem neighborhood of Gilo), look up to your right. On the ridge is **Tantur,** an ecumenical institute set up in the afterglow of the Second Vatican Conference as a sabbatical retreat for Christian clergy of all denominations.

About 1.5 kilometers (1 mile) beyond the traffic lights, look for a white-dome building on your right. This is **Rachel's Tomb,** an important Jewish holy site. The biblical patriarchal couples (Abraham and Sarah, Isaac and Rebecca, Jacob and Leah) are all buried in Hebron—all but Rachel, Jacob's second and favorite wife, who died in childbirth on the outskirts of Bethlehem (Genesis 35).

The present building is probably medieval, with additions in the 19th century funded by the renowned British Jewish philanthropist Sir Moses Montefiore. The large velvet-draped, blocklike cenotaph inside is certainly not the original pillar Jacob placed at her grave.

The thread of authenticity is lost in the distant past, but centuries of prayers and tears have hallowed the spot for observant Jews.

The interior of the tomb is decorated with Hebrew quotations from the Bible referring to Rachel, whom Jewish tradition regards as something of a "mother of the nation." People come to pray here for good health and fecundity (Rachel was long barren), and the keening of a particularly afflicted soul is not an unknown sound. Another tradition is to wind a red thread seven times around the tomb-marker, and to give snippets of it as talismans to cure all ills.

Rachel is venerated by Islam as well, and adjacent to the site is a Muslim cemetery, reflecting the Middle Eastern tradition that it is a special privilege to be buried near a great personage. *Route 60. Admission free. Open Sun.–Thurs. 8–5, Fri. 8–1.*

Immediately beyond the tomb, the road forks: The right fork goes toward Hebron, the left into Manger Street and on to Manger Square in **Bethlehem.** Even from a distance the town is easily identified by the minarets and cross-crested church steeples that struggle for control of its skyline. The wide Manger Street winds into town past a half-dozen or so large gift shops (some with genuinely good-quality merchandise), and the high stone walls of religious institutes, offering some excellent views to the east (your left) of what geographers sometimes refer to as "marginal land," still arable here and there, but very close to the desert. Fields now part of Bet Sahour, an adjacent town, have been identified as the area where Ruth "gleaned in the field" of Boaz, Naomi's kinsman. Boaz eventually "took Ruth and she became his wife" (Ruth 4), and later, the great-grandmother of King David, who was born in Bethlehem.

Flocks are more common than fields on the edge of the desert. Christian tradition identifies Boaz's barley fields as those where the shepherds, "keeping watch over their flock by night," received word of the birth of Jesus in Bethlehem. Several denominations maintain sites in the valley purporting to be the authentic "Shepherds' Fields."

Manger Street rises to **Manger Square,** Bethlehem's central plaza. The Church of the Nativity is on the east side (your left as you drive up to the square); the GTIO is on the opposite side. At press time the atmosphere in Bethlehem was fairly relaxed, but the occasional incidents in recent years make it inadvisable to wander away from Manger Square into the *souk* (market) and narrow alleys.

On Christmas Eve (December 24, that is; the Greek Orthodox celebrate Christmas Day on January 7, the Armenians on January 19) it seems as if the whole world is crowded into Manger Square, where between 8:30 PM and 11:30 PM, international choirs perform carols and sacred music. At midnight, the Roman Catholic mass from the Franciscan Church of St. Catherine is relayed on closed-circuit television onto an enormous screen in the square. It is a night of bright lights and bustle, with the restaurants and stores doing their year's best business, and the tourist information office open until after the mass. A special telephone facility enables you to phone home with the hubbub and bells in the background, and the post office (also open late that night) issues a special Christmas stamp to give your mail an extra taste of time and place.

Partaking in the celebrations takes some planning, however. No private vehicles are permitted to enter Bethlehem between 8 AM on December 24 and 3 AM on December 25. Egged runs shuttle buses from Jerusalem, Tel Aviv, Netanya, and sometimes Haifa; call Egged or the

GTIO in Israel or abroad for further information. Admittance to the midnight mass is very limited; contact the Christian Information Center (Jaffa Gate, Old City, Jerusalem, tel. 02/272692) for more information. There is no seating in Manger Square. Be sure to wear warm clothing. You are required to carry your passport, bringing in alcohol is forbidden, and large bags are discouraged (because of security checks).

Cross the courtyard to the **Church of the Nativity,** which incorporates the cave thought to be the birthplace of Jesus. The unprepossessing stone exterior is crowned by the crosses of the denominations sharing it: Above the central gable is the Greek Orthodox cross, to the left, the square "Jerusalem cross" of the Franciscans, and to the right, the Armenian cross.

The original church was built in the 4th century by Helena, mother of Constantine the Great, the Roman emperor who first embraced Christianity. Two centuries later, in a wave of building throughout the Holy Land, the Byzantine emperor Justinian rebuilt the church, lengthening it by one bay, adding a narthex, and replacing the apse with a more spacious one. Although pillaged (much of the marble used at the Temple Mount in Jerusalem came from here) and left to deteriorate under the Mamluks and Ottoman Turks, the Byzantine structure has remained in use to the present day. The now-blocked but still impressive square door dates from that time. Twelfth-century Crusader repairs created the arched entrance (also now blocked) within the Byzantine entrance. The current low entrance (watch your head) was designed in the 16th century to protect the worshippers from attack by their then-hostile Muslim neighbors.

The church interior is vast and gloomy. Stop in the narthex to note the carved panels in the upper part of the center door; they are all that remain of an Armenian wooden door dating from the 13th century. The structure and plan of the body of the church (a nave flanked on both sides by two aisles, transept, and apse) is as it was in the time of Justinian, but only the patches of 12th-century mosaics high on the walls and the faded burnt-wax figures of saints painted by Crusaders on the upper part of the Corinthian pillars give some hint of its one-time splendor. On the left side of the central nave, a wooden trapdoor reveals a remnant of the original 4th-century mosaic floor, discovered during a 1934 restoration. The octagonal baptismal font in the outer right aisle once stood near the high altar of the 6th-century church. The high ceiling beams are medieval English oak, and are said to have been covered by lead that the Turks melted down for bullets in their wars with the Venetians.

The columns themselves, which run the length of the nave in two paired lines, are from Justinian's church, making this the oldest standing church in Israel. In AD 614, the country was invaded by the Persians, who destroyed almost every Christian church and monastery across the land. When they reached Bethlehem, they discovered the splendid Byzantine church with facade mosaics depicting the events of the Nativity story. One showed "the three wise men of the east" in Persian garb, and the Persians, somehow identifying with the scene, the story goes, spared the church.

At the front of the church, in the apse, is an elaborate iconostasis (a Greek Orthodox chancel screen), and numerous icons and hanging brass lamps. The Greek Orthodox are responsible for the area to the right of the altar, the Armenians for the left side. All three "shareholders" in the church—the Greek Orthodox, Roman Catholic, and Armenian churches—have vied with each other for centuries for control of Palestine's holy sites. A 19th-century "status quo" agreement that froze their respective rights and privileges in Jerusalem's Church of the Holy Sepulcher and Virgin's Tomb pertains here, too: ownership, the timing of ceremonies, the number of oil lamps, etc. It has not, however, prevented undignified fisticuffs between rival monks in recent years over the privilege of cleaning this or that piece of a wall.

Steps lead down from the transept near the right side of the altar to the **Grotto of the Nativity.** Once a cave, the grotto has been reamed out, plastered, and decorated beyond recognition. Immediately on your right as you enter is a small altar, and on the floor below it is the focal point of the entire site: a 14-point bronze star with the Latin inscription HIC DE VIRGINE MARIA JESUS CHRISTUS NATUS EST (Here of the Virgin Mary, Jesus Christ was born). The original star was placed there in 1717 by the Roman Catholics, who lost control of the altar 40 years later to the more influential Greek Orthodox. In 1847 the star mysteriously disappeared, and pressure from the Turkish sultan compelled the Greeks to allow the present Latin replacement to be installed in 1853. The Franciscan guardians do have possession, however, of the little alcove a few steps down on your left as you enter the Grotto (behind the candles). This is said to be the "manger" where the infant Jesus was laid.

The idea of the famous "manger" being part of a cave is consistent with regional practices: To this day, shallow natural limestone caves are used as convenient shelters or storage areas, or even as back rooms of houses built against them. The small back door of the Grotto (kept locked) leads to a series of cave-chapels beneath the adjacent Roman Catholic church, where one gets a clearer look at the phenomenon.

Steps up the other side of the cave lead to the Armenian chapel that occupies the left transept of the church. From here a doorway brings you to the **Church of St. Catherine,** Bethlehem's Roman Catholic parish church. Completed in 1882, the church incorporates remnants of its 12th-century Crusader predecessor and has fine acoustics, but is otherwise unexceptional. It is from this church that the midnight Christmas mass is broadcast to some 50 countries around the world. On the right side of this church toward the rear, steps descend to a series of dim grottoes, clearly once used as living quarters. Chapels here are variously dedicated to Joseph, to the Innocents killed by Herod, and to St. Jerome, Bishop of Bethlehem in the late 4th century and author of the *Vulgate*, the Latin translation of the Bible; the cell has been identified as his study. A short tunnel at the back of the grottoes connects them to the Grotto of the Nativity, but is only open during Franciscan processions.

The cloister outside the church, with its restored Crusader minicolumns, flower beds, and tall Norfolk pines, is probably one of the most tranquil spots in Bethlehem. A doorway brings you back to the main church. *Church of the Nativity: tel. 02/741020. Open daily 6–6. Church of Street Catherine: tel. 02/742425. Open daily 5–noon and 3–6.*

Turn left as you exit the Church of the Nativity, and left again onto Milk Grotto Street. Two hundred yards farther on the right is the so-called **Milk Grotto.** A curious tradition is enshrined in this Franciscan chapel built over a small cavern in the soft, white rock. Legend relates that here Mary nursed the newborn Jesus, and a few drops of Mary's milk spilt onto the rock miraculously made it white. The ground-up white rock has long been prized by local mothers as an invaluable aid to successful lactation.

⑲ Return to Route 60. Six kilometers (4 miles) south of the fork, a sign on the left marks **Solomon's Pools.** There is no connection with the Jewish biblical king, but rather with Suleiman the Magnificent (Suleiman is Arabic for Solomon), the Ottoman sultan who repaired the three immense rectangular reservoirs here in the 16th century. Although there is no absolute consensus on the dating of the reservoirs, it is generally thought that the lowest and largest one (capacity 113,000 cubic meters) was built in the 1st century BC and trapped the water of four local springs. From it, the so-called Lower Aqueduct snaked out to Jerusalem's Temple Mount. Greater quantities of water were later added to the system with the construction of the middle reservoir and the so-called Arub Aqueduct, which harnessed springs to the south. The system has been traced along most of its length: From end to end, it measured 60 kilometers (37 miles), following contours and tunneling through hills, with an unbelievable minimum slope of 0.9 in 1,000 in places. In other words, the system dropped only 9 feet for every 1,000 feet in distance—a triumph of ancient engineering.

The upper reservoir dates to the 1st century AD or later, and was fed by a different spring using no less ingenious techniques than that of its neighbors. Its water then flowed to the more elevated Jaffa Gate area of Jerusalem by means of a state-of-the-art syphon system, parts of which are still visible in Bethlehem today. In the right season, you'll often see village women here selling delicious red plums and fresh figs. (At press time it was still inadvisable to leave your car unattended, or to wander off the main roads in this area.)

Six kilometers (4 miles) farther south is the **Etzion Bloc,** today made up of two small Jewish towns (Efrat and Alon Shevut) and a handful of farming communities. In the 1940s there were four kibbutzim, built here because of their strategic proximity to the important Jerusalem–Hebron Highway. During Israel's War of Independence, their ability to disrupt troop movements of the Jordanian (then Transjordanian) Arab Legion led to the Legion's attack, conquest, and destruction of the Bloc in May, 1948. Jewish settlers returned and resettled there after the Six Day War of 1967, when the area came under Israeli control. The fact that the Bloc had been an area of Jewish settlement long before Israel became a state has made it sacrosanct even among some Israelis who otherwise support a large-scale Israeli withdrawal, from the West Bank.

Turn right at the main intersection (at the gas station) onto Route 367; follow the signs for Kfar Etzion. On your left is a small fortress-like building, a turn-of-the-century Russian Orthodox monastery that was the Bloc's forward position in the War of Independence. Although the walls are intact, the monastery is nothing more than a shell today. The road passes Alon Shevut on the right. Turn left into **⑳** **Kfar Etzion** (4 kilometers, or 2.5 miles, from the gas station). Ignore the first gate, continuing along the periphery of the village to the second, southern gate. Park at the cafeteria/gift shop, and ask for directions to the museum and auditorium.

Kfar Etzion, the oldest settlement in the Bloc, was founded as far back as 1921, but the poor land, lack of water, and harsh winters deterred many, and the first group of pioneers failed to put down permanent roots. By the early 1940s, however, the situation had stabilized, with the addition of three more villages: Revadim, Ein Tzurim, and Massu'ot Yitzhak. When the Arab Legion overran the Bloc, the survivors of these three kibbutzim were taken prisoner. Those of Kfar Etzion were not so lucky: Almost all were gunned down after their surrender. Among the group that resettled the site in the late 1960s were those who had been evacuated as children before the battle. Take time for the story of Kfar Etzion, told through a dramatic audiovisual presentation in the comfortable auditorium, and at the small museum. *Tel. 02/935160. Visits by prior arrangement only. Admission: NIS 5 ($1.70). Open Sun.–Thurs. 8:30–12:30 (July and Aug., occasional afternoon hrs, according to demand), Fri. 8:30–11.*

From the Etzion Bloc, Route 367 descends west to the Elah Valley (*see* Tour 2, *above*). To get to Hebron, return to Route 60; turn right (south) and continue driving for 12 kilometers (7 miles). One of the oldest cities in the area, **Hebron** (population 70,000) is also one of the centers of Islamic fundamentalism in the West Bank (the town has no movie theaters, for example). This is not a friendly place, and is definitely no place in which to get lost. (Do not be tempted to explore the labyrinthine alleys of the *casbah*, Hebron's old market area: It is unsafe.) Relations between Jews and Arabs in Hebron lie under the cloud of the 1929 massacre, in which 60 Jews were killed, as many wounded, the rest fleeing for their lives. Forty years later, Jewish zealots returned to repair and settle the abandoned houses, creating a new line of confrontation in the heart of the city. The so-called Bet Hadassah, Bet Romano, and the Avraham Avinu complexes are part of that resettlement, as is Tel Rumeida, the elevated site of ancient Hebron. The February 1994 killing of 29 Muslim worshippers by a single Jewish extremist has infused the town with a powder-keg atmosphere, making it, at press time, a strongly ill-advised tour option.

If you are bent on going anyway, and do not have your own guide, you are best off taking the Egged public Bus 160, which runs quite frequently from Jerusalem, via Rachel's Tomb and the Etzion Bloc Junction, directly to the Cave of Machpelah. The road turns left before the entrance to Hebron, opposite a glass workshop, and the bus route takes you via Kiryat Arba (5 kilometers, or 3 miles), the Jewish township founded in 1970 on the outskirts of Hebron itself.

A few hundred yards after the turnoff from Route 60, you will see on your left an enclosure surrounded by stout low walls of well-cut ancient stones, thought to be from the time of Herod the Great (1st century BC). The site is identified as **Alonei Mamre,** the "Oaks of Mamre" (some translations say "terebinths") of Genesis 13: "The Lord said to Abram . . . 'Arise, walk through the length and breadth of the land, for I will give it to you.' So Abram moved his tent, and came and dwelt by the oaks of Mamre, which are at Hebron; and there he built an altar to the Lord." No evidence of Abraham remains, of course, but 2,000-year-old walls of a clearly monumental structure might indicate the antiquity of the Mamre tradition.

Hebron, at 3,117 feet above sea level, is one of the highest cities in Israel, and straddles the central mountain road (today Route 60) so vital in ancient times. This was enough to ensure its importance, and explain its continuous habitation for at least 4,000 years. The dominant biblical associations with Hebron are Abraham, and the burial of his descendants in the family "cave," but there are other references, too. Moses's spies (Numbers 13) reached Hebron on their reconnaissance mission to the Promised Land of Canaan (early 13th century BC). And it was here that David, secure in his tribal territory of Judah (to which Hebron belonged), was acclaimed as King of all Israel after the death of Saul. "So all the elders of Israel came to the king at Hebron; and King David made a covenant with them at Hebron before the Lord, and they anointed David king over Israel . . .

At Hebron he reigned over Judah seven years and six months; and at Jerusalem he reigned over Israel and Judah thirty years" (II Samuel 5).

㉑ Just beyond Kiryat Arba the road descends steeply to the **Cave of Machpelah** (Haram el-Khalil), the dominant landmark of Hebron. Chapter 23 of the book of Genesis treats us to a fine example of Middle Eastern bargaining: the nomadic patriarch Abraham negotiating the purchase of a burial site for his wife, Sarah. "After this, Abraham buried Sarah his wife in the cave of the field of Machpelah east of Mamre [Hebron]" (Genisis 23:19). The family plot later served Abraham and his descendants, making the site one of Judaism's holiest, and making Hebron one of its four holy cities.

There is no "cave" to be seen today, though medieval writings mention one. The existing structure is an immense fortresslike building some 195 feet by 111 feet and constructed from beautifully cut ashlars (large dressed stones) with the raised center typical of the time of Herod the Great (1st century BC). The longest stone is almost 26 feet long, and reminiscent of the megaliths in Jerusalem's Western Wall.

What is extraordinary in a country so often pillaged is that this 2,000-year-old monumental building has survived in its entirety, undoubtedly because it was venerated by all three of the region's major religions. This did not stop them altering the site, however. Crusader fortifications dominate the present entrance; but the doorway itself and most of the ornate interior were designed by the Mamluks (13th–15th centuries).

As you climb the steps and turn right through the latter-day Jawaliyeh Mosque, the huge stones are on your right. Pass through the Herodian wall and turn left into the main hall of the enclosure. The so-called **Hall of Isaac,** once part of a Byzantine basilica, became the Crusader Church of St. Abraham, built in the 12th century. Its soaring Gothic ceiling is painted in garish colors typically favored in this region. Saladin, who defeated the Crusaders in 1187, converted the church into a mosque. The 14th-century Mamluk **cenotaphs of Isaac and Rebecca,** housed in red- and white-stone "booths," are draped with cloths and surrounded by brass ornaments with Muslim motifs. Part of the hall functions as another mosque. To the right of the mihrab (prayer niche directing believers toward Mecca) is the exquisitely carved wooden *minbar* (pulpit), installed by Saladin in the late 12th century.

It is curious that Islam has identified the largest and most elaborate area of the enclosure with Isaac, who is not only the haziest of the patriarchal figures but the direct rival of Ishmael, from whom the Arabs claim descent! White-bearded imams (Muslim clerics) are usually to be seen squatting on the Persian carpets, intoning Koranic verses. Only the large flagstones underfoot remind you that the site was originally a Jewish shrine built by Herod.

The adjacent room containing the **cenotaphs of Abraham and Sarah** was converted into a synagogue in 1967. To your left, *before* you enter the synagogue, is a small cupola that covers a metal lid in the floor. Through perforations in the lid, you can peer down into a dim cavern, though you will see little beyond the oil lamp kept burning below you. An opening just like this is now covered by the rugs of the mosque behind you. Through that opening, in 1967, right after the Six Day War, then–defense minister Moshe Dayan lowered a slim 12-year-old girl with a camera through the narrow opening to survey the "cave." She found just one room, bare except for some plaques, one with an Arabic inscription. Despite this Indiana Jones–style exploration, and others, apparently, in earlier centuries, scholars are not a lot closer to solving the conundrum of where the real Cave of Machpelah was.

Across the courtyard beyond the cenotaphs of Abraham and Sarah, which date from the 9th century, is the **room of Jacob and Leah.** Their markers are from the 14th century. On the way out, look to your left at one last cenotaph, also decorated with the now-familiar drapery and ornaments, which purports to be the tomb of Joseph (son of Jacob), though the Bible specifically identifies his grave in Shechem (modern Nablus), far north of Hebron.

Both the Jewish and Muslim communities are fiercely jealous of their rights and privileges at the Cave of Machpelah. Throughout Friday and Saturday (the Muslim and Jewish sabbaths, respectively), the shrine undergoes successive transformations from synagogue to mosque and back again. Momentarily triumphant, each group proclaims its faith in the same One God, in a shrine each claims as its own. The religious confrontation, kept in tense equilibrium, is real in itself; but it has also become a metaphor for the political-territorial confrontation that has characterized the last half-century in Israel. It is hard to know which is the more explosive. *Tel. 02/962166. Admission free. Open Sun.–Thurs. 7–11:30, 1:30–3, and 4–5. Unofficial entry between prayers Fri. and Sat. Modest dress required.*

Shopping

Kibbutz Mitzpeh Shalem (tel. 02/945100), 22 kilometers (14 miles) south of Qumran, manufactures the excellent—but not inexpensive—Ahava line of skin and hair-care products based on (but not smelling like!) the Dead Sea minerals, with their known restorative properties. The factory outlet here is open Sunday–Thursday, 8–5, Friday and holiday eves 8–4, and Saturday 10–4, but the products are sold elsewhere in the area (at Masada and the Ein Gedi Spa, for example) and at pharmacies in the major cities.

Kibbutz Kfar Etzion (tel. 02/935148), off Route 367 on the way to Hebron, sells its own decorative candles in its little coffee shop/gift store.

Bethlehem craftspeople make carved olive wood and mother-of-pearl objects, mostly of a religious nature, but the many stores along the tourist route in that town sell jewelry and a range of baubles and notions as well. For quality and reliability, most of the half-dozen or so large establishments on Manger Street, where the tour buses stop, are recommended, but some of the merchants near the Church of the Nativity on Manger Square have excellent items as well.

Hebron, with an ancient tradition of glassblowing, is noted for its colored glass—not of high quality, to be sure, but attractive—in the form of jugs, vases, ashtrays, and glasses. It's fun to watch the glassblowers at work. Look for the workshops on Route 60, at the junction of the Kiryat Arba turnoff (security situation permitting).

Sports and the Outdoors

Participant Sports

Bird-Watching   Israel's varied climate and position on major migration routes make it a fascinating place for bird-watchers. For more information on birds in this area, contact the SPNI, which has a **Center for Raptors** in **Jerusalem** (tel. 02/932383 or 02/932384).

Go-Carting   There are two 1-kilometer (.6-mile) circuits at the **Attraktzia** (tel. 02/942393) just north of Qumran by the Dead Sea. The cost per ride is NIS 10 ($3.35). Entrance to the site (beach and facilities) costs NIS 17 ($5.70). The go-cart facilities are open daily 9–5 from April through October.

Health Spas and Mineral Pools   The Dead Sea area has gained recognition as one of the world's primary health retreats for sufferers of psoriasis and various rheumatic and arthritic ailments. Both the hale and ailing can enjoy the benefits of the incredible mineral concentration in the Dead Sea water and mud, the natural warm mineral springs, and the oxygen-rich atmosphere at the lowest point on earth. There are several swimming spots along the Dead Sea (*see* Beaches, *below*) and a good spa 3 kilometers (2 miles) south of Kibbutz Ein Gedi (*see* Tour 1 *in* Exploring Around Jerusalem, *above*). (For the sophisticated spas and therapeutic facilities of the Ein Bokek/Neveh Zohar area, *see* Dining and Lodging in Chapter 8, Eilat and the Negev.)

Hiking and Rappelling   The prime area for these activities is the Judean Desert, with **Wadi Kelt** and **Ein Gedi** the obvious first choices. For the serious hiker, several other spectacular canyons offer more challenging walks, but should not be attempted alone. To get advice and information on organized hikes, contact **SPNI** (13 Helene Hamalka St., Jerusalem, tel. 02/252357 or 02/244605; 4 Hashefela St., Tel Aviv, tel. 03/537–4425 or 03/639–0644; or the society's field school in Ein Gedi, tel. 07/584288). The SPNI can give you information on trails in the Judean Hills as well.

Metzukei Dragot (Mobile Post Jericho Valley 90670, tel. 02/258114), the Center for Desert Tourism, is located on a cliff top overlooking the Dead Sea (the exit is 19 kilometers, or 12 miles, south of Qumran). Run by Kibbutz Mitzpeh Shalem, it specializes in desert safaris in go-anywhere vehicles and in rappelling (even for novices) on the impressive cliff faces nearby. Other information on rappelling can be obtained from **The Snappling Club** (Box 921, Ramat Gan, tel. 03/740663 or 03/749933).

Swimming   In the Dead Sea area, try the freshwater pool and water park of **Attraktzia** (tel. 02/942393), 1 kilometer (.6 mile) north of Qumran. The facilities are open March–October 9–5 (August 9–6). For winter hours call ahead. Many of the hotels at Ein Bokek (*see* Dining and Lodging *in* Chapter 8, Eilat and the Negev) allow nonguests to use their pools for a fee.

In the Judean Hills, several villages and kibbutzim have beautiful pools in magnificent wooded locations. Except for the one at Neve Ilan (*see below*), whose pool is open year-round (covered and heated in winter), the season for outdoor pools is May–September. **Kiryat Anavim** (tel. 02/348999), 8 kilometers (5 miles) west of Jerusalem north of Route 1, charges NIS 20 ($6.70) for adults, NIS 17 ($5.70) for children Sunday–Friday. On Saturday and holidays admission is NIS 25 ($8.35) for adults, NIS 20 ($6.70) for children. The pool is open Saturday–Thursday 9–7:30, Friday and holiday eve 9–6:30.

The pool at **Ma'aleh Hahamisha** (tel. 02/342591), located about 12 kilometers (7 miles) west of Jerusalem north of Route 1, is open Sunday–Thursday 9–6, and Friday and Saturday 9–7. Admission is NIS 25 ($8.35) for adults and NIS 18 ($6) for children Sunday–Friday; NIS 35 ($11.70) for adults, NIS 25 ($8.35) for children Saturday and holidays. Nearby is **Neve Ilan** (tel. 02/341241), whose pool is open year-round 9–7 (except on Saturday in June, July and August, when the pool is reserved for members). The pool is open longer hours on some days in the summer. Admission Sunday–Friday is NIS 30 ($10) for adults, NIS 25 ($8.35) for children; Saturday and holidays adults pay NIS 40 ($13.35), and children are charged NIS 35 ($11.70). The pool at **Shoresh** (tel. 02/341477), 15 kilometers (8.5 miles) west of Jerusalem south of Route 1, is open daily, May–September, 8–6. Sunday–Friday rates are NIS 20 ($6.70) for adults, NIS 15 ($5) for children; Saturday and holiday rates are NIS 28 ($9.35) for adults, NIS 22 ($7.35) for children.

Beaches

One bathes in the briny Dead Sea; it is impossible to actually swim in it. Doctors recommend not remaining in the water for more than 10 to 15 minutes at a time because of the enervating effect of the salt. Avoid getting the water in your eyes and mouth. If you do, however, rinse immediately with freshwater; there usually are outdoor showers at most beaches. Because of the low humidity and high temperatures of the region it is imperative to drink a lot of water, especially in the hot season, April to October.

The minerals of the Dead Sea do not harm fabrics, but they can sometimes tarnish silver. Many beaches are rocky (and hot in summer), and it's a good idea to wear protective rubber sandals, shoes, or sneakers. Do not leave your possessions unguarded on the beach.

Although one cannot sink in the Dead Sea, it is not impossible to get into trouble in its strange waters. For that reason, and for the availability of showers, it is advisable to bathe only in designated areas. But do not be put off by all the warnings—bathing in the Dead Sea is a delightful, unique experience.

Attraktzia (tel. 02/942393) is the only decent beach with changing facilities at the northern tip of the Dead Sea, just north of Qumran. Beach facilities only cost NIS 17 ($5.70). The full price, including pools and water slides, is NIS 39 ($13), senior citizens NIS 25 ($8.35), and any entry after 2 PM NIS 19 ($6.35). Open March–October.

There is a free public beach at **Ein Gedi,** with open-air showers at the water's edge and rest rooms. Next door (entrance next to the restaurant) is a campground and caravan park where, for NIS 6 ($2) per person, you can use the shower facilities and changing rooms.

Ein Gedi Spa (tel. 07/594813) is located on Route 90, 3 kilometers (2 miles) south of the Ein Gedi gas station. The beach, free mud, warm mineral baths, showers, changing facilities, and locker are included in the admission price of NIS 35 ($11.70) for adults (including 10% discount at the cafeteria). Children under 12 get in free, and those 12 to 16 enjoy a 20% discount. Tourists accompanied by a *licensed* tour guide pay just NIS 18 ($6) regardless of age and get 5% off at the cafeteria. Towels and bathing suits can be rented.

The **Ein Bokek** hotel district, about 15 minutes' drive south of Masada, has a free public beach with showers only (next to Kapulsky's Restaurant), and better facilities at the adjacent **Hammei Zohar** (tel. 07/584161). Nonguests can use the beaches and freshwater pools at the **Lot** (tel. 07/584321 or 07/584324) and **Tsell Harim** (tel. 07/584121 or 07/584122) hotels. Also available to nonguests are the beaches, pools, and full spa facilities at the more expensive **Hod** (tel. 07/584644), **Moriah Plaza** (tel. 07/584221), and **Nirvana** (tel. 07/584626) hotels. Nirvana is open to nonguests only on some holidays and weekends; call ahead. For more information about Ein Bokek, *see* Chapter 8, Eilat and the Negev.

Dining

Other than passably good lunch cafeterias, there are no restaurants at all in the areas covered by this chapter that might tempt you out in the evening. In most cases, the tours have you back in your Jerusalem, Tel Aviv, or Dead Sea hotel by nightfall, where there is no shortage of good restaurants (*see* Dining *in* Chapters 2, Jerusalem, and 4, Tel Aviv, and Dining and Lodging *in* Chapter 8, Eilat and the Negev).

Lodging

Bethlehem The few inexpensive hotels in the town, never particularly prepossessing, have had a hard time of it during the intifada . . . and it shows. Jerusalem, only 10 minutes away, is a more congenial base.

Dead Sea **Kibbutz Ein Gedi** (Rte. 90, Mobile Post Dead Sea 86980, tel. 07/59422, fax 07/584328) runs a motel-style guest house on the kibbutz grounds, between 1,650-foot-high cliffs and the Dead Sea, and surrounded by subtropical landscaping. Each of the 120 rooms has a shower and tiny kitchenette. There is no maid service. Prices range from NIS 348($116) to NIS 450 ($150) (according to season) and include breakfast and another full meal daily, and access to the spa. A pool and two tennis courts are available.

Camping facilities (Rte. 90, Mobile Post Dead Sea 86980, tel. (07/584342, fax 07/584455) are available at **Ein Gedi,** including tent sites, air-conditioned bungalows, and caravans with cooking facilities and refrigerators.

There are **youth hostels** at both **Ein Gedi** (Bet Sarah, Rte. 90, Mobile Post Dead Sea 86980, tel. 07/584165, fax 07/584445) and **Masada** (Taylor Hostel, Rte. 90, Mobile Post Dead Sea 86935, tel. 07/584349, fax 07/584650). Excellent hotels are available in the nearby Ein Bokek area (*see* Dining and Lodging *in* Chapter 8, Eilat and the Negev).

Jerusalem Four very good kibbutz guest houses, in wooded Judean Hills loca-
Corridor tions west of Jerusalem, are run by **Kiryat Anavim, Ma'aleh Hahamisha, Neve Ilan,** and **Shoresh.** They are all merely a 15- to 20-minute drive from the city (*see* Lodging *in* Chapter 2, Jerusalem).

4 Tel Aviv

By Lisa Perlman

Lisa Perlman was born in Australia and wrote her way through Japan and France before moving to Israel in 1986. She specializes in environmental issues and is a former editor of The Jerusalem Post's *Tel Aviv weekly,* Metro.

Proud residents call it the city that never stops, and if you don't believe them, just come around at 4 AM, when you may find yourself waiting in line for a table at a café or stuck in a traffic jam on Hayarkon Street. True, there are no buses at that hour, but that doesn't stop the young and the restless of surrounding towns from finding their way to the country's throbbing heart.

Next to the magical, holy city of Jerusalem, Tel Aviv seems more like the city of sin. Your first reaction to it may be negative—to the newcomer it appears muggy, congested, ill-planned, and scarred with boxy, concrete buildings. But what it lacks in grandeur, Tel Aviv makes up for in vitality. One-third of the country's population—1.8 million Israelis—lives in this 138-square-kilometer (55-square-mile) metropolis. Half a million cars go in and out of the city every day. Residents of other towns swell the population further on the weekends, when they make Tel Aviv their playground. The city is Israel's center of commerce, culture, and people. It bustles with museums, art galleries, restaurants, and beaches.

Having risen from empty sand dunes less than a century ago, Tel Aviv can hardly boast the ancient beauty of Israel's capital. But the city's southern border, the port of Jaffa, is as old as they come: Jonah set sail from here before his journey in the belly of a whale. The cedars of Lebanon that were used in the construction of Solomon's Temple arrived in Jaffa before being transported to Jerusalem. According to archaeologists, Jaffa was founded in the Middle Canaanite period, around 1600 BC. For the next thousand years it was dominated by one ancient people after another: Egyptians, Philistines, Israelites, Phoenicians, and Greeks. After being taken by Crusaders twice in the 11th and 12th centuries, Jaffa was recaptured by the Muslims and remained largely under Arab domination until the 20th century. During much of this time it was abandoned, and it did not regain its importance as a port until the 19th century.

In the second half of the 19th century, Jewish pioneers began emigrating here from other parts of the world. Their numbers strained the capacity of the small port, and by the late 1880s, Jaffa was overcrowded, rife with disease, and stricken with poverty. A group of Jewish families moved to the empty sands north of Jaffa and founded Neve Tzedek, the first Jewish neighborhood. This was followed by Ahuzat Bayit (literally, "housing estate"), an area to the north of Neve Tzedek that became the precursor to Tel Aviv. Arab riots in Jaffa in the 1920s spurred further growth, as more Jews moved to Ahuzat Bayit. They were joined by immigrants from Europe, mostly Poland, and a decade later, by an influx of German Jews fleeing the Nazis. These new, urban immigrants—unlike the pioneers from earlier immigrant waves—brought an appreciation for the arts and a passion for the sidewalk cafés that sprouted like mushrooms throughout the city. It was they who made the strongest social and cultural impact on Tel Aviv.

The fact that Tel Aviv began as separate neighborhoods helps to explain its eclectic (some would say discordant) appearance, its Mediterranean-style buildings jostling in the shadow of towering skyscrapers. In the 1930s and '40s, the city became "the white city," the only one in the world where the International Style of Le Corbusier and Mies van der Rohe—a style of functional forms, flat roofs, and whitewashed exteriors—dominated. By the 1950s, however, shoddy imitations of the style led to its decline, and many of its buildings fell into disrepair. Happily, recent efforts by preservationists are helping to reclaim these architectural treasures.

The Tel Aviv of today is already vastly different from the Tel Aviv of half a century ago. Although northern Tel Aviv has traditionally been the glitzy, affluent part of the city, it's the oft-neglected south that wins attention now. Here city-backed gentrification projects in many neighborhoods are changing the area's face; each week the scaffolding rises on another building, and new restaurants and shops continue to appear. Tel Aviv has come a long way in its short history, and as you gaze around, you may find it hard to believe that 80 years ago this modern, teeming metropolis was nothing but sand.

Essential Information

Important Addresses and Numbers

Tourist Information The **Tourist Bureau** at Ben Gurion Airport is open 24 hours. You'll find maps, brochures, and the latest local information at the **Government Tourist Information Office** (GTIO, 5 Shalom Aleichem St., 63806, tel. 03/660259 or 03/660260; open Sun.–Thurs. 8:30–6, Fri. 8:30–2:30), close to the U.S. Embassy downtown.

Embassies **United States** (71 Hayarkon St., tel. 03/517–4338), **United Kingdom** (192 Hayarkon St., tel. 03/524–9171), **Canada** (220 Hayarkon St., tel. 03/527–2929), **Australia** (Europe House, 37 Shaul Hamelech St., tel. 03/695–0451).

Emergencies **Police** (tel. 100), **ambulance** (tel. 101), and **fire** (tel. 102). Tokens or tele-cards are not required at public phones for emergency calls.

Police The city's main **police stations** are at 14 Harakevet Street (tel. 03/564–4444), not far from the Central Bus Station, which also has a lost-and-found office, and at 221 Dizengoff Street (tel. 03/545–4444).

Ambulance **Magen David Adom** (2 Alkalai St., tel. 03/546–0111) provides a 24-hour emergency service.

Hospital The Casualty Ward of **Ichilov Hospital** (Weizmann St., tel. 03/697–4444) has a 24-hour emergency service. Bring your passport.

Late-Night Pharmacies Pharmacies take turns keeping late hours, and the duty roster changes daily. Check *The Jerusalem Post* newspaper for the day's details.

Dentists Round-the-clock dental services are at **Ichilov Hospital** (Weizmann St., tel. 03/697–4444) or the **dental clinic** inside the Dizengoff Center (Gate 3, 50 Dizengoff St., tel. 03/528–5822 or 03/296716).

Rape-Crisis Center For women (tel. 03/523–4819), 24 hours; for men (tel. 03/527–9191), Sun., Tues., and Thurs. 6 PM–10 PM.

English-Language Bookstores The nationwide **Steimatzky** chain is your best bet. Two of the main stores are at 107 Allenby Street (tel. 03/299277), where there is also a bargain basement, and 109 Dizengoff Street (tel. 03/522–1513).

Travel Agencies Ben Yehuda Street in central Tel Aviv is full of travel agencies, large and small. Among the biggest are **Diesenhaus** (21 Ben Yehuda St., tel. 03/517–2140) and **Ophir Tours** (32 Ben Yehuda St., tel. 03/209777). **Meditrad** (16 Ben Yehuda St., tel. 03/294654) is an American Express representative.

Car Rental These include **Budget** (Dan Hotel, 99 Hayarkon St., tel. 03/523–1551), **Hertz** (Sheraton Hotel, 115 Hayarkon St., tel. 03/527–1881), and **Eldan** (112 Hayarkon St., tel. 03/527–1166), the largest Israeli rental company.

Arriving and Departing by Plane

Airports and Airlines Israel's international airport is **Ben Gurion,** located 16 kilometers (10 miles) southeast of Tel Aviv. All international flights to Israel land here, except for charters to Eilat. Most major American and European carriers fly into Ben Gurion, offering frequent and convenient connections to major cities around the world. Having undergone extensive renovations in the last few years, Ben Gurion has joined the ranks of efficient and modern airports.

At **Sde Dov Airport** (tel. 03/690–2222), 4 kilometers (1.5 miles) north of the city center, the domestic airline **Arkia** flies to Eilat (some 10 flights per day), Jerusalem (three flights), Haifa (three flights), and the Upper Galilee (two flights or more).

Between Ben Gurion Airport and Center City **United Bus 222** operates between the airport and the city about every hour from 4 AM to midnight on weekdays, and on Saturday at 45-minute intervals from noon to midnight. From the airport it stops at the Railway Station (Arlosoroff St.), the **youth hostel** (Weizmann *By Bus* St.), and at numerous points along the **Promenade,** where Tel Aviv's main strip of hotels is located. The fare is NIS 9 ($3).

Bus 475, a local, runs to the **Central Bus Station** (Platform 613) from 5:10 AM to 4 PM. The fare is NIS 5.70 ($1.90). Like all regular buses, it does not run on the Sabbath (Friday afternoon to Saturday evening) or on holidays.

By Taxi There is a fixed tariff for taxis from the airport into town (and vice versa); it's printed in a booklet that the driver carries. Verify the price before you get in, and don't let the driver switch the meter on. The rate is NIS 50 ($16.70); it goes up to NIS 60 ($20) after 9 PM and on the Sabbath. The price includes one piece of baggage per person; for each additional piece there is a baggage charge of NIS 2 (70¢). There is a supervised taxi stand at the airport.

By Limousine **Tal Limousine Service** (Old Customs House, Ben Gurion Airport, tel. 03/972–1701, fax 03/972–1705) can supply a limousine and driver into Tel Aviv for NIS 75 ($25).

Between Sde Dov and Center City City **Bus 26** runs between Sde Dov and the Central Bus Station every 10–15 minutes, following Ibn Gvirol Street. The fare is NIS 3 ($1) (no service on the Sabbath or on holidays). Taxi is the most convenient way to get from Sde Dov. Fare is determined by the meter *By Bus and* (unlike from Ben Gurion, where it's a fixed rate); the cost is NIS 15– *Taxi* NIS 20 ($5–$6.70) to the center (excluding baggage charge).

Arriving and Departing by Bus, Sherut, and Train

By Bus Traveling around the country by bus is extremely convenient. The main interurban bus company, **Egged** (tel. 03/537–5555), operates primarily from the **Central Bus Station** (Levinsky St.), but also from the **Railway Station** at Arlosoroff Street. The Central Bus Station may look like a big, confusing marketplace, but the bus service is actually very efficient. (For most of the day, buses between Jerusalem and Tel Aviv leave every 15 minutes.) You can purchase your ticket at the booth on each platform (signs at each platform state destinations) or, if your booth is closed, from the driver on the bus. Only the Eilat line requires advance reservations (especially in peak season). Buses to and from the Railway Station are less frequent, so call for a timetable.

By Sherut Sherut taxis are a fleet of stretch Mercedes-Benzes, located at the Central Bus Station, that run the same routes as the buses, at comparable prices for one-way tickets (unlike buses, sheruts do not offer return tickets). The "schedule" of arrivals and departures is determined by the time it takes to fill all seven seats of each car. The sheruts are located at various points, depending on destination, in front of the bus platforms; you can usually hear someone yelling the destination long before you get close. (If you can't, try yelling yourself, and someone is sure to point you in the right direction.) It's worth noting that sheruts, unlike buses, run on Saturday.

By Train Train travel is not as common as bus travel in Israel, yet this is one of the most scenic and relaxing ways to travel between Tel Aviv and cities and towns to the north, such as Netanya, Hadera, Haifa, and Nahariya. The northbound train leaves the **Arlosoroff train station** (tel. 03/542–1515) about every hour on weekdays from 6 AM to 8 PM; there are fewer trains on Friday and holiday eves, and no service on Saturday or holidays. Trains depart for Jerusalem at 8:18 AM each day from **Bnei Brak train station** (tel. 03/922–1967), 5 kilometers (3 miles) northwest of Tel Aviv. The return journey from Jerusalem departs at 4 PM.

Getting Around

Driving in Tel Aviv is not recommended, especially if you are nervous: Aside from the aggressive tactics of other drivers, Tel Aviv's layout more closely resembles the creation of an absent-minded philosopher than a city planner! Moreover, some street names may not be marked in English—or, indeed, at all—which makes getting to your destination nothing short of a headache. Parking, too, is a problem, and the last thing you want to do is deal with Israeli bureaucracy if your illegally parked car has been clamped.

But Tel Aviv is more fun on foot anyway. Most attractions and sites are situated in the heart of the city, within walking distance of one another, and when you get tired, a bus or taxi is never far away.

By Bus The city bus system is well developed, with lines run primarily by the **Dan** bus cooperative, as well as by **Egged.** Fare is a fixed NIS 3 ($1) within the city center, and tickets are bought on the bus. If you think you might use the buses as many as 25 times during your stay, you can buy a *kartisia,* which offers 25 journeys for the price of 20. Remember, however, that Dan's kartisia is only good for Dan lines and Egged's for Egged (although you'll be able to use the Egged ticket in other cities as well).

Two of the major lines, the **Number 4** (Ben Yehuda and Allenby Sts.) and **Number 5** (Dizengoff St. and Rothschild Blvd.), are also serviced by privately run red minibuses. You can flag these down and ask to get off at any point along their routes; fare is the same as on the regular buses. Minibuses also operate on Saturday, when regular buses do not.

By Taxi Taxis here can be any car model or color and are identified by lighted signs on top. Drivers will toot their horns to catch your attention, even if you're not looking for a taxi; cabs are plentiful except in bad weather. If you're traveling in the metropolitan area, make sure the driver turns the meter on when you get into the car. Rates are NIS 5 ($1.70) for the first 18 seconds, 20 agorot (7¢) for each 18 seconds thereafter. For interurban trips, there is a fixed tariff; if you think you're being quoted a price that's too high, ask to see the tariff in a booklet that each driver carries. Expect night rates to be about 25% higher than day rates. Tipping taxi drivers is not customary in Israel.

Guided Tours

General | Both **Egged** (15 Frishman St., tel. 03/527–1222) and **United** (57 Ben
Interest | Yehuda St., tel. 03/225552) bus companies offer half-day tours of the
city for NIS 66 ($22) per person. The tour takes in Bet Hatefutsoth
(Diaspora Museum), the Habimah Theater complex, Old Jaffa, and
the flea market.

A free walking tour of Jaffa, organized by the Tel Aviv municipality,
sets out from the clock tower Wednesday at 9:30 AM. No prior registration is required.

Boat Tours | Spend a pleasant half-hour looking at Tel Aviv from somewhere in
the Mediterranean. **Kef** (Jaffa Port, tel. 03/682–9070) runs hourly
boat tours (weekends only) from the Jaffa Port to the Tel Aviv Marina and back. Fare is NIS 10 ($3.35).

Personal | **Twelve Tribes** (29 Hamered St., tel. 03/517–2436, fax 03/510–1943)
Guides | and **Tar-Hemed Tours** (59 Hayarkon St., tel. 03/656101, fax 03/510–
0165) provide personal guides (usually with a car) for anywhere in
the city, or around the country.

Exploring Tel Aviv

Tel Aviv's western border is the Mediterranean. The beachfront
Tayelet promenade runs from north Tel Aviv to Jaffa, some 3 kilometers (2 miles) south, and provides a great walk, especially at sunset.
The north–south thoroughfares of Hayarkon, Ben Yehuda (which
becomes Allenby), Dizengoff, and Ibn Gvirol streets run more or
less parallel to the shore. The hotels are almost all concentrated on
the seafront, along Hayarkon Street, which is also bursting with
cafés, restaurants, and pubs. Allenby Street, one of the oldest in the
city, crosses Hayarkon and Ben Yehuda streets and becomes the latter at its southern terminus. The change in affluence is as immediate
as the change in street name, as the socio-economic situation is reflected in the shabbier buildings and more budget-oriented shops
along Allenby. The "border" between south and north might be considered Carmel Market, a real junction of east-meets-west and old-
meets-new. In the north, the business center dwindles north of
Arlosoroff Street, which runs east–west near Kikar Hamedina
(Hamedina Square). The residential part of the city continues north
and takes in the Yarkon River, once the city's northern boundary
and now a popular recreational spot.

Technically, there are boundaries between Tel Aviv and the numerous towns and cities that surround it, but the urban sprawl is so
great that residents of these surrounding municipalities will often
tell you they live in Tel Aviv.

Highlights for First-Time Visitors

Bet Bialik (*see* Tour 1)
Carmel Market and **Nahalat Binyamin street fair** (*see* Tour 1)
Old Jaffa and **Jaffa Port** (*see* Tour 2)
Shuk hapishpeshim flea market (*see* Tour 2)

Tour 1: From the Market to the Theater

*Numbers in the margin correspond to points of interest on the Tel
Aviv map.*

You might say that Tel Aviv is rather like a junk store: unprepossessing on the outside, but inside full of treasures that invite serious browsing. This is true of the following tour, a mere 2 kilometers (1 mile) from the *shuk*, or marketplace, to the national theater that manages to reveal something of the city's 80-year history, its ethnic mix, and its various social strata.

❶ The tour begins on the **corner of Allenby and Bialik streets.** (To reach the intersection, take Minibus 4 from Ben Yehuda Street, near the hotel district, or from the Central Bus Station, and ask the driver to let you off at Bialik.)

Bialik Street is one of the quaintest in the city, containing well-preserved architecture that is characteristic of Tel Aviv's early years. (Sadly, many other neighborhoods in the city have been less successful at maintaining older buildings.) Bialik has long been a popular address for many of the city's artists and literati; it is not surprising, then, that some of the houses have been converted into small museums.

From bustling, polluted Allenby Street, turn into Bialik Street: Immediately, quiet descends. Continue about 1,000 feet to the street's end, where you'll find a mosaic and a fountain (it rarely flows). Designed by painter-cum-writer Nahum Gutmann, the mosaic depicts the history of the city from the ancient days of Jaffa to the rise of Tel Aviv.

Gutmann, a renowned children's author as well as a painter, was among the elite group of Tel Aviv's first artists and one of the first pupils at the city's first school, in Neve Tzedek. His writer father, too, had a special place in the city's beginnings, as you'll see later in the tour, when you reach the boulevard named for him, Ben Zion.

❷ From the fountain, walk back toward Allenby Street. Stop in at **Bet Bialik** (Bialik House). This is the charmingly restored home and library of Chaim Nachman Bialik (1873–1934), the national poet who was considered the "father of Hebrew poetry." Bialik was already a respected poet and publisher by the time he moved to Tel Aviv from Russia in 1924. In the remaining 10 years of his life, his house became the intellectual center of Tel Aviv, and Bialik, the city's inspiration.

His two-story, cream-color house, with its pointed arches and turrets, is a harmonious blend of Mediterranean and European styles. Built in 1927, it was almost palatial by the harsh standards of the time: mosaic-tile floors; Islamic-style arches and pillars; a small tower for meditating; sturdy, dark wood; and European-style furniture, including shelves to hold some 3,000 books. At press time, fall 1994, all labels were in Hebrew only, but the house is still a highly recommended stop. *22 Bialik St., tel. 03/517–1530. Admission free. Open Sun.–Thurs. 9–5, Sat. 10–2; closed Fri.*

❸ Next proceed to **Bet Rubin** (Rubin House), three doors down. Recognized as one of Israel's major painters, Reuven Rubin (1893–1974) bequeathed his house to the city, together with 45 of his works, which make up the permanent collection here. Unlike Bialik's still-furnished house, this one functions solely as an art gallery, with changing exhibitions by Israeli artists in addition to the great Rubin's work. There is also a small but well-stocked art library upstairs where you can pore over press clippings and browse through art books. *14 Bialik St., tel. 03/525–4230. Admission: NIS 7 ($2.35) adults. Open Sun., Mon., Wed., Thurs. 10–2, Tues. 10–1 and 4–8, Sat. 11–2; closed Sat. July and Aug.*

Tel Aviv

Mediterranean
Sea

Tel Aviv
Marina

Railway
Station
(North)

Arlosoroff

Weizmann

David Hamelech

Shaul Hamelech

Kaplan

Perah Tikva

Yigal Allon

Netzivei Ayalon

Yitzhak Sade

Hamasger

AHUZAT
BAYIT

Peralt Tikva

Lincoln

Yehuda Halevi

Rothschild

Ahad Haam

Hahashmonaim

Ibn Gvirol

Ibn Gvirol

Arlosoroff

Chen

Dizengoff

Ben Zion

KIKAR
HABIMAH

9

Rashi

KIKAR
MAGEN DAVID

7

Sheinkin

Balfour

Maze

Nachmani

Ahad Haam

Allenby

Nahalat Binyam

Monte fiore

Kalisher

Shalom

Frishman

Zamenhoff

KIKAR
DIZENGOFF

King George St.

Tchernichowsky

8

Bialik

2

3

1

6

4

5

Ben Gurion

Gordon

Dizengoff

Ben Yehuda

Bograshov

Pinsker

Trumpeldor

Allenby

Geula

Hayarkon

Hakovshim

Hacarmel

Herbert Samuel Esplanade

Tayelet Promenade

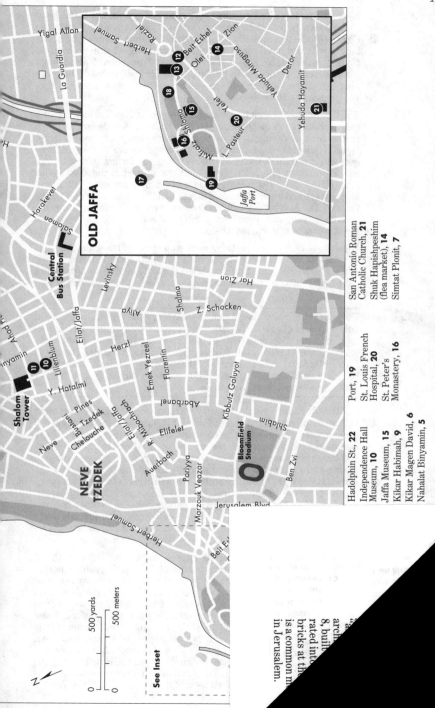

OLD JAFFA

Map labels (inset):

Beit Eshel
Zion
Olei
Yehuda Mirago
Yefet
Herbert Samuel
Roziel
Deror
Shlomo
L. Pasteur
Mifraz
Yehuda Hayamit
Jaffa Port

Map labels (main map):

Yigal Allon
La Guardia
Harakevet
Salomon
Central Bus Station
Levinsky
Shalma
Z. Schocken
Har Zion
Aliya
Herzl
Emek Yezreel
Florentin
Abarbanel
Kibbutz Galuyot
Shlabim
Elat/Jaffa
Binyamin
Shalom Tower
Y. Hatalmi
Pines
Bustani
Neve
Tzedek
Chelouche
R. Mibadiliach
Elat/Jaffa
Elifelet
Auerbach
Poriyya
Marzouk Veazar
Ben Zvi
Bloomfield Stadium
Jerusalem Blvd
Herbert Samuel
NEVE TZEDEK
Beit E
See Inset
500 yards
500 meters

Legend:

Hadolphin St., **22**
Independence Hall Museum, **10**
Jaffa Museum, **15**
Kikar Habimah, **9**
Kikar Magen David, **6**
Nahalat Binyamin, **5**

Port, **19**
St. Louis French Hospital, **20**
St. Peter's Monastery, **16**

San Antonio Roman Catholic Church, **21**
Shuk Hapishpeshim (flea market), **14**
Simtat Plonit, **7**

arch
8, built
rated into
bricks at th
is a common m
in Jerusalem.

Now return to Allenby Street, cross at the traffic light and head south (left). In less than a minute you will be at the entrance to the **❹ Carmel Market,** commonly referred to as the shuk. Consisting of one long street and numerous short streets running off it in both directions, it is invariably crowded on weekdays from about 9 AM through the afternoon, especially on Friday, as people rush to finish the shopping before the Sabbath and the weekend. Take a deep breath before you plunge into the hubbub.

The first section is mainly devoted to dry goods: If you're looking for a pair of slippers or a can opener, you'll find it here. A little farther down is the fruit and vegetable section—where everybody yells. Here, Israel's famous oranges, avocados, and mangoes are as fresh as they get, and if you think the vendor is insulting you for not taking a large enough quantity, he probably is—but it's all part of the show. With prices fixed, the days of market-style bargaining are over, but all the atmosphere and vigor of the past is retained. These days, in addition to veteran Tel Avivians, you'll find newly arrived Russian immigrants looking for bargains, even if they don't yet understand the Hebrew of the merchants who squawk the praises of their produce.

If you feel like trying something new, stop at one of the stalls that sells dried fruits and ask for *ledder* (a variation on the English "leather"). It's a Moroccan version of the dried apricot, beaten to a pulp and rolled out into a super-thin, square sheet that resembles . . . leather.

Time Out   The market borders the Yemenite Quarter, which contains a score of delicious and cheap little eateries (closed Friday night and Saturday) offering *shwarma* (spit-grilled meat in pita bread) and barbecued skewered meats, all kosher. One of them, **The Big Heart** (32 Rabbi Meir St.), is to the north of the main market drag. In addition to meats, it offers a range of Middle Eastern salads, french fries—and beer to wash down your order.

On Tuesday and Friday, the city's artisans and would-be artisans **❺** set up shop, creating a street fair along **Nahalat Binyamin,** east of the market. Throughout the summer, the street is packed on these two days, and you have to slalom between other pleasure-seekers and bargain-hunters to see anything. The area is more enjoyable in spring and autumn, when you actually have time to appreciate the wares as you wander among stalls. The selection is large, from tacky plastic trinkets to sophisticated crafts items such as hand-carved wooden boxes, but the real drawing card here is the handmade silver jewelry. Nahalat Binyamin is further enlivened with the relatively new (for Israel) street performers and buskers. As a final spot of local color, cafés serving cakes and sandwiches line the street.

When the city first began to spread out from Jaffa, Nahalat Binyamin served as the eastern border of Tel Aviv's premier neighborhood, **Ahuzat Bayit.** In those days, this area was so far removed from the center of things that only the poorest Jews ended up here. In recent years, much of Nahalat Binyamin has undergone gentrification, although the contrast between the "befores" and "afters" is all too clear. Look up while strolling here, for some of the architectural detail is particularly interesting. For example, at **no.** in the early 1920s, a number of Jewish symbols were incorpo- the original eclectic design. Note particularly the way the top form steps: This kind of deliberate incompleteness motif to remind viewers of the destruction of the Temple

❻ Continue north until you reach the top of Nahalat Binyamin, which forms a V with the marketplace at Allenby Street. This is **Kikar Magen David,** a meeting point of six streets that is named for the six-point Magen David, or Star of David. Cross Allenby by taking the **underpass** (otherwise you risk life and limb, as you will no doubt already have ascertained by Israeli driving standards), and you will end up on the corner of Sheinkin and Allenby streets. Cross the narrow Sheinkin Street to **King George Street** and make your way downhill.

If you haven't had your fill of markets yet, **Bezalel Market** is one block north on the left, at the corner of King George and Bet Lechem streets. Here a confusion of clothes, mostly blending budget fabrics with less-than-vogue designs, lines the sidewalk. The other side of the short street is dominated by falafel stalls, where the proprietors compete vociferously by beckoning you to taste the chickpea balls for free before you buy. When you purchase one portion, you get one empty pita bread that you then stuff with as much falafel, salad and pickles as you can eat—and keep going back for more.

❼ Two blocks farther northeast, on the right side of King George Street, is an alley called **Simtat Plonit,** identified by the two plaster, obelisk-style structures at its entrance. It's worth taking a minute to wander down here and see old–Tel Aviv decorative (and now derelict) architecture at its best. Note the stucco lion in front of **no. 7,** which used to boast glowing eyes fitted with lightbulbs. The tract of land that incorporates this alley was bought in the '20s by an outspoken builder from Detroit named Meir Getzel Shapira. (He established what is still known as the Shapira Quarter just south of the Central Bus Station, now one of the city's seedier neighborhoods.) After purchasing this land, Shapira insisted that this pint-size street be named after him, and the story goes that he fought furiously with Tel Aviv's first mayor, Meir Dizengoff, to get his way. (Dizengoff had already planned to name another street Shapira, after a different Shapira.) The mayor emerged victorious and named the alley Plonit, meaning "what's his name."

❽ Don't despair if you are beginning to feel weary—**Gan Meir** (Meir Park) is coming up shortly on the left. Here you can rest on one of the benches and take in a free performance by city birds. This is something of a green haven in this muggy city, and although also favored by local derelicts, it is perfectly safe. On summer nights, musicians sometimes get together here for jam sessions.

You are now close to the Dizengoff Center, Israel's first shopping mall (*see* Shopping, *below*). Before the center opened about a decade ago, this area was known as the **Nordiya** quarter, a neighborhood set up in the early 1920s by Jewish refugees seeking a home in the wake of Arab attacks in Jaffa. If you proceed north from Meir Park you will reach Bograshov Street, named for the man who founded the Nordiya quarter and was one of the headmasters of the first school in Tel Aviv. Instead of turning left onto Bograshov, turn right, onto Ben Zion Boulevard, named after another of the city's early writers, Simcha Ben Zion. (He is also the father of Nahum Gutmann, the artist responsible for the fountain on Bialik Street, *see above*.)

❾ It's a few minutes' walk up a slight incline to **Kikar Habimah** (Habimah Square), whose complex of buildings houses the national theater, the Israel Philharmonic Orchestra (IPO), and an annex of the Tel Aviv Museum (TAM).

The origins of the **Habimah National Theater** are rooted in the Russian Revolution, when a group of young Jewish actors and artists in

Russia established a theater that gave performances in Hebrew—
this at a time when Hebrew was barely considered a living language.
Subsequent tours through Europe and the United States in the
1920s won wide acclaim. In the late 1920s and '30s, many of the
group's members moved to Israel and helped to establish the theater
here. The cornerstone was laid in 1935; the current large, rounded,
glass-front building dates from 1970.

Next to Habimah, on Tarsat Street (Tarsat is the Hebrew-calendar
acronym of the year in which Israel became independent, i.e., 1948)
is the **Helena Rubinstein Pavilion,** an annex of the **TAM.** If you like
contemporary art, step inside. A combination ticket will get you admission to this gallery and the main museum at 27 Shaul Hamelech
Boulevard (*see* Off the Beaten Track, *below*). *6 Tarsat St., tel. 03/
696–1297. Admission: NIS 13 ($4.35) adults, NIS 7 ($2.35) children; includes entry to TAM. Open. Sun.–Thurs. 10–8, Fri. 10–2,
Sat. 10–3.*

Nestled between the theater and the museum is a charming little
junglelike garden, **Gan Ya'akov,** whose centerpiece is a sycamore
that's been here almost longer than the city itself. The story goes
that camels were brought here to relax in the shade of the sycamore
and drink from the nearby well.

On the other side of Habimah Square, forming a right angle with the
theater, is the **Mann Auditorium,** the country's principal concert
hall and the permanent home of the Israel Philharmonic Orchestra,
headed by maestro Zubin Mehta. One of the most distinguished and
sophisticated halls in Israel, this low-slung gray building is also a
venue for pop and rock concerts. With excellent acoustics and a seating capacity of 3,000, the Mann has played host to such diverse artists as folk heroine Joan Baez, rocker Joan Armatrading, and jazz
whiz Pat Metheny.

Time Out Stop in for a coffee and a strudel topped with whipped cream in **Cafe
Habimah** (2 Tarsat St.), located in the theater complex in the section
with the wide, round window. If you do attend one of the Habimah
plays (all are in Hebrew, but some have simultaneous translation),
you may even recognize some of the actors at the next table. In any
case, this café is something of a theater in itself, with many of the
Who's Who of Tel Aviv vying for a moment in the spotlight here.

Ben Zion Boulevard swings right (south) here to become **Rothschild
Boulevard,** which half a century ago was *the* most exclusive street in
the city and stills commands sky-high real-estate prices. Dating
from the 1940s, many of the buildings have been allowed to deteriorate; others have been restored. Still others are examples of the International Style, a style that is charming on this tree-lined street,
but poorly imitated elsewhere in Tel Aviv. It's a 15-minute walk
south on Rothschild Boulevard to get to the **Independence Hall Museum;** you'll see it on your left after you cross Allenby. This impressive structure, with its wide ground-floor entrance and narrow
horizontal windows, was originally the home of longtime mayor
Dizengoff. He donated it to the city in 1930 for use as the first Tel
Aviv Museum. More significantly, it was here that the settlement's
leaders assembled on May 14, 1948, to announce to the world the
establishment of the State of Israel. Today the museum's **Hall of
Declaration** stands as it did on that dramatic day, with the original
microphones on the huge table where the dignitaries sat; behind it is
a portrait of the Zionist leader Herzl. *16 Rothschild Blvd., tel. 03/*

517–3942. Admission: NIS 6 ($2) adults, NIS 3.50 ($1.20) children. Open Sun.–Thurs. 9–2, closed Fri.–Sat.

⑪ In the middle of the boulevard stands the stark, square **Founders' Monument and Fountain,** dedicated in 1949.

Tour 2: Jaffa

The origin of Jaffa's name is unclear: Some say it is derived from the Hebrew *yafeh,* beautiful; others claim that the town was named after its founder Japhet, son of Noah. Nor is it certain exactly when Jaffa was established. What is sure is that it's one of the oldest ports in the world—perhaps *the* oldest. Excavations have turned up finds that are as much as 4,000 years old. The bible names Jaffa as the site of a number of significant events: The cedars used in the construction of the Temple passed through Jaffa on their way to Jerusalem; the prophet Jonah set off from Jaffa before being swallowed by the whale; and here, too, St. Peter raised Tabitha from the dead. In the ancient world, Jaffa was an important stop on the Via Maris, the trade route that extended from Egypt to Mesopotamia.

But Jaffa's history has been one of fits and starts. The city has been razed and rebuilt scores of times as various powers fought to control it. Napoléon was but one of a succession of invaders who brought city walls down. These walls were rebuilt for the last time in the early 19th century by the Turks, and torn down yet again as recently as 1888.

By this that time, Jaffa was a thriving cosmopolitan center, host to international businesspeople, bankers, and diplomats. Christian and Jewish pilgrims on their way to Jerusalem were a familiar sight here. Jewish immigrants lived peacefully with Arabs here until the riots of 1921, when discord sent most of Jaffa's Jews fleeing to the sandy north that would become Tel Aviv. Today a part of the municipality of Tel Aviv, Jaffa has a Jewish majority (most of it hailing from other Mideast and North African countries) and is also home to many Arab Christians and Muslims.

The restored section, **Old Jaffa,** is only a small part of this fascinating port, and today it caters primarily to tourists and fishermen. The Tel Aviv municipality conducts free tours of Old Jaffa that begin at the clock tower every Wednesday at 9:30 AM (no reservations necessary). As well as the restored section, this tour also takes in a shabbier side of Jaffa, where trading, bargaining, and arguing are as much a part of life today as they were in days of old.

Buses 8, 10, 25, 46, and 90 go to Jaffa from downtown Tel Aviv. If you're driving, you can park free in Old Jaffa during the day on weekdays and Sunday. It will cost you NIS 5 ($1.70) on weekday evenings (from 7 PM; from 5 PM on Friday and holidays) and Saturday. Allow around three hours for the walking tour that follows.

The tour begins on the northwest corner of Jaffa's main square, in front of the **police station,** at the beginning of Jaffa's main street. On the empty patch of land across the road, you can see the remains of what used to be Jaffa's northern wall, including what can still be identified as a Greek-style column. This spot was the *saraya,* or administrative center, of the Turkish government in the early part of the century and was one of the corners of what was later called Government Square (its official name, though rarely used, is **Jewish Agency Square**). The square was eventually destroyed by a Jewish underground group seeking to root out Arab terrorist gangs.

The police station, overall an uninteresting structure, contains an Ottoman-designed arch above its entrance. The design over the door is the seal of Turkish sultan Abdul Hamid II. During the British Mandate, the British used the building to intern both Arabs and members of the Zionist group Irgun.

12 Head south on Yefet for about 100 feet, passing the **clock tower** on an island in the middle of the street—a renowned meeting place for anyone with a rendezvous in Jaffa. The tower is the focus of Jaffa's central square and stands at the center of Jaffa, with the restored Old Jaffa lying to the west and the flea market to the east. The clock tower was completed in 1906, in time to mark the 30th anniversary of the reign of Sultan Abdul Hamid II; similar clock towers were built for the same occasion in Akko and in Jerusalem. The four clocks employed at this tower stood still for many years before the city renovated the tower and set the clocks in motion again in 1965; the renovation also added stained-glass windows depicting events in Jaffa's history.

On the southwest corner of the square is the beautifully preserved
13 **El-Mahmoudiye mosque,** with its minaret and two domes. Built in 1809, the mosque was renovated for the first time in 1812 by Turkish governor Mohammed Abu Najat Aja. The governor rebuilt much of the city during his rule (1807–1822), including the city walls that Napoléon's army tore down in 1799.

The mosque managed to escape the fate of other sites in Jaffa that were destroyed during the War of Independence. In the late-19th century a separate entrance was built into the east wall to save the governor and other dignitaries the bother of having to push through the market-square crowds at the main entrance on the south. Not usually open to tourists, this is one of the local Muslim community's most important mosques.

The original mosque included a huge, splendid **drinking fountain** built into its southern wall, where travelers refreshed themselves after long journeys. In recent times, however, the Suleiman fountain has lost its glory, and it sits sadly between two soft-drink stores that offer today's travelers a less romantic but more practical means of quenching their thirst.

Turn onto **Bet Eshel Street,** opposite the mosque, and wander through what was a bustling business district some 300 years ago: the old Jerusalem Road, with handy access to the harbor. **No. 11,** which you'll recognize by the numerous arches that serve as the building's facade, was the local *khan,* equivalent to a motel today. Built in the early 18th century by an Armenian family named Manouli, the ground floor was used as stables, with rooms for travelers located upstairs. Today the building is a furniture store.

14 Any of the small streets leading south from Bet Eshel Street will take you into the **shuk hapishpeshim** (flea market), where you can find anything from silver earrings and Indian-style clothes to a kilo of shrimp or a refrigerator (the vendor will promise you that it works). The ambience seems a world away from modern Tel Aviv. The market actually began as one of many small bazaars that surrounded the clock tower in the mid-19th century, but is now the only survivor of that era. The market's main street is **Olei Zion,** but there are a number of smaller streets and arcades to explore at your leisure, so take your time. Bargaining is not as vigorous as it once was, but it's still important to play the game, so don't agree to the first price the seller demands.

Return now to Yefet Street, south of the clock tower.

Time Out There is always a line outside of **Abulafia Bakery** (7 Yefet St.), and the Middle East's answer to pizza goes like hot cakes here—literally. For a simple snack with an exquisite flavor, order the pita topped with the indigenous herb, *za'atar* (hyssop, a relative of marjoram). Other pitas are topped with egg or mushroom, or stuffed with salty cheese and baked till crisp.

Cross Yefet Street and enter the passage between nos. 10 and 12. This used to be the local fish market, where the daily catch was sold after being unloaded in the port. The aroma lingers—there are still a couple of very good fish stores and restaurants in the vicinity—but you'll find more shoe stores than seafood here now.

You are now very close to the ancient port. Walk south (you'll be going uphill) on Mifratz Shlomo Street until you come to a square on the left. Note the **fountain** here: When built by Turkish governor Mohammed Abu Najat Aja in the early 19th century, the fountain boasted six pillars and an arched roof, providing shade as well as water. The **archway** just beyond this formed the entrance to the *hamam*, or old Turkish baths. Today archaeologists dig beneath the floor of what is now an events hall here in search of ancient artifacts. Their finds—most of which were parts of Jaffa's ancient fortifications dating from the town's beginnings around 2000–1500 BC— have been preserved beneath the hamam's center stage as well as in the Jaffa Museum.

⓯ The **Jaffa Museum** building has a lengthy history: It was first constructed during the Crusades; in the 18th century, the Turks added to what was left of the original building and used it as their Turkish Government House until 1897. In the first half of this century it was a soap factory. The upper level has been operating as the Jaffa Museum since 1961, displaying many of the finds that were unearthed during archaeological digs here and in other parts of Tel Aviv. *10 Mifratz Shlomo St., tel. 03/682–5375. Admission: NIS 6 ($2) adults, NIS 3 ($1) children. Open Sun.–Thurs. 9–2, Tues. also 4–7, Sat. 10–2.*

Before you continue up the hill to the main square of Old Jaffa, cast your gaze north for a dramatic contrast between the ancient and the modern, linked by the softly lapping waves of the Mediterranean.

As you make your way toward **Kikar Kedumim** (Kedumim Square), Old Jaffa's central plaza, you cannot help but notice the beautiful
⓰ ocher- and russet-color **St. Peter's Monastery** on the right. Dedicated to the apostle Peter, the monastery was established by Franciscans in the 1890s. It was built over the ruins of a citadel that dates from the Seventh Crusade, which was led by King Louis IX of France. St. Peter's remained Jaffa's principal Roman Catholic church until the church of San Antonio was built in 1932. A monument to King Louis stands today at the entrance to the friary. Napoléon is rumored to have stayed here during his Jaffa campaign of 1799. To enter, ring the bell by pulling the string on the right side of the door. You will probably be greeted by one of the custodians who speak Spanish and some English. *Tel. 03/822871. Admission free. Open Apr.–Sept., daily 8–11:45 and 3–6; Oct.–Mar., daily 8–11:45 and 3–5.*

Old Jaffa used to be Tel Aviv's red-light district; it also had a high crime rate, raw sewage in the streets, and other unsavory characteristics. Today, however, thanks to efforts begun by the Tel

Aviv municipality in the late 1950s, Old Jaffa is chockablock with excavation sites, restaurants, expensive gift and souvenir shops, and galleries. The artists who live here complain of too much noise on summer nights; some visitors say it is *too* touristy. But it is charming, and should not be missed. The labyrinthine network of tiny alleyways snakes in all directions from Kikar Kedumim down to the modern port. Serving as the focus of Kikar Kedumim is an archaeological site exposing 3rd-century BC catacombs.

❶⑦ Before leaving the square, go through the **Yamit** restaurant (it's on an outdoor terrace, with a narrow walkway beside the tables) on the western side for the best view of an unassuming piece of rock that rises from the sea here and is known as **Andromeda's Rock.** This is the stuff of myth and legend: Nireus, father of mermaids, was incensed that Andromeda, daughter of King Copeus of Ethiopia and his queen Xaiopa, was more beautiful than the mermaids. He implored Poseidon, the god of the sea, to intervene. Poseidon obligingly set the sea astorm and sent a monster to eat whatever approached. In an attempt to restore calm, the people tied Andromeda to this rock. Only Perseus, riding the winged horse Pegasus, dared to save her. Soaring down from the sky, he beheaded the monster, rescued the lovely Andromeda, and promptly married her.

⑱ Now climb the hill from Kikar Kedumim, passing wide, shade-giving yucca and fig trees, and cross the wooden bridge to **Gan Hapisga,** literally Summit Garden. You might have to vie for space here with a long line of newlyweds who come here to be photographed in their wedding garb at sunset. It is highly entertaining. Seven archaeological layers have been unearthed in a section of the park called Ramses II Garden. The oldest wall sections (20 feet thick) have been identified as part of a 17th-century BC Hyksos city. Other remains include part of a 13th-century BC city gate inscribed with the name of Ramses II, a Canaanite city, a Jewish city from the time of Ezra and Nechemiah, Hasmonean ruins from the 2nd century BC, and traces of Roman occupation. At the summit, rather disturbing the ancient aura, stands a kitschy stone sculpture from the 1970s in the shape of a gateway, titled *Statue of Faith*.

⑲ Return now to Kikar Kedumim and follow one of the alleyways with steps leading down to the **port.** During summer and its shoulder season, there is an NIS 1 (35¢) charge for entering the port area. Here you will find many fishing boats stuffed into the small marina, as well as a handful of houseboats. Along the waterfront is a plethora of restaurants, all expensive, and most of them pretty good.

If you have the energy to continue walking, some very interesting sights and sounds remain. You can either follow the coast north for about five minutes to return to the clock tower, or take the official port exit, walk a few steps up the hill, and turn left onto Louis Pasteur Street. About 300 feet ahead, you'll notice a bronze sculpture of a roly-poly little **whale** by sculptor and jewelry-maker Ilana Goor, a resident of Old Jaffa. The whale keeps watch over a small parking area, beyond which stands a remnant of the city's ancient wall. Continue on Louis Pasteur Street and return to Yefet Street a few strides ahead. Think of Yefet as a sort of thread between eras: Below it is the old market area (which you have just visited), while all around you stand the Christian and Western schools and churches of the 19th and 20th centuries.

⑳ Most of these face you at the T-junction of Pasteur and Yefet streets, in addition to the **St. Louis French Hospital,** named for Louis IX, leader of the Seventh Crusade, who landed in Jaffa in 1251. Established by Roman Catholic nuns in the late 19th century, it was Jaffa's first modern hospital. Its neo-Renaissance style, popular in Europe at the time, features high ceilings and tall arched windows. The building also had strategic importance, occupying the southwest corner and highest point of Jaffa's encircling wall. The building is now a community health center.

Across the street, **nos. 21, 23,** and **25** deserve mention. The first is the **Tabitha School,** established by the Presbyterian Church of Scotland in 1863. Behind the school is a small cemetery where some fairly prominent figures are buried, including Dr. Thomas Hodgkin, the personal physician to Sir Moses Montefiore and the first to define Hodgkin's disease, who died in Jaffa in 1866. **No. 23** was a French Catholic school (it still carries the sign, Collège des Frères) from 1882, but has long since been used by the French embassy for administrative purposes. And next door, the neo-Tudor, fortresslike **Urim School,** with its round tower, was set up as a girls' school in 1882 by nuns of the same order that built the hospital. Today it is a local school.

㉑ A little farther south, on the left at no. 51, is the **San Antonio Roman Catholic Church,** dedicated to St. Antonius of Padua, friend and disciple of St. Francis of Assisi. Though it looks quite new, with its clean white-stone bricks, it was built in 1932 to accommodate the growing needs of the Roman Catholic Church in Jaffa. (St. Peter's, located in a heavily populated Muslim area, was unable to expand due to lack of land.)

A few steps farther south, turn right into Sha'arei Nicanor Street
㉒ and wander down to the charming little **Hadolphin Street.** This enclave is a hive of activity, with an art gallery, a superb French restaurant, a Greek Orthodox church dating from 1924, one of the best hummus joints in the city (open in the mornings only), and a ceramics store run by local potter, Eytan, all within a stone's throw of one another.

South of here is the **Ajami** quarter of Jaffa, one of many neighborhoods around the country benefiting from a rejuvenation program known as Project Renewal, financed by Jewish communities around the world. Though still suffering from poverty, lack of infrastructure, and a crime and drug problem, Ajami boasts some of the most luxurious, gracious houses in the country; some ambassadors and other diplomats call this home while in Israel. Tel Aviv has numerous projects in store for Ajami, and property prices are rising rapidly. Within a few years this part of Tel Aviv may be radically different—just as Old Jaffa, though still retaining the flavor of the past, is unrecognizable to anyone who was there 30 years ago.

Off the Beaten Track

Architecture. The huge, ungainly **Shalom Tower** (tel. 03/517–0991, observatory admission NIS 5/$1.70) takes up the entire block between Montefiore and Ahad Ha'am streets. Israel's first skyscraper, Shalom Tower is worth a visit—not for the tacky wax museum or video-game parlor housed on the top floor, but for its rooftop observatory, which provides a magnificent view of the sprawling city and the Mediterranean. (Combined ticket for the observatory and the wax museum is NIS 14/$4.70 adults, NIS 11/$3.70 children.)

To see more pleasant contemporary architecture, take a short walk beginning at the **Hadar Dafna** building (Shaul Hamelech Blvd.). Designed by Ram Karmi, the building uses the bold shapes and concrete common in postwar architecture. Nearby, on the corner of Shaul Hamelech Boulevard and Weizmann Street, is an interesting and eclectic group of postmodern buildings: The white **Asia House** (designed by Mordechai Ben Horin), with its swirling curves; **IBM House** (Avraham Yaski), an elliptically shaped, space-age building with a plate-glass entrance; and **Europe House** (Yaski), whose gray tones are highlighted by pink accents and whose outdoor-facing elevators are framed by incandescent lightbulbs.

For a different mood entirely, visit the **American Colony,** near Neve Tzedek (take Bus 40, 42, 44, or 46 from Jerusalem Boulevard or the Central Bus Station). Here, remains of New England–style timber houses—built by Christian immigrants from Maine more than 100 years ago—stand in stark contrast to the industrial buildings and limestone structures around them.

Cinematheque. A five-minute walk from the Habimah complex (*see* Tour 1, *above*) brings you to the Tel Aviv Cinematheque (2 Sprinzak St., tel. 03/691–7181). It's located—appropriately, perhaps—just outside the city's established cultural area, on the edge of a commercial/light-industrial zone that's gradually becoming a nightlife center. This is the place to catch noncommercial local and foreign flicks.

Museums. High on any list of important Tel Aviv stops are these three museums, each depicting aspects of Israeli or Tel Aviv history or art. The **Eretz Israel Museum** (take Bus 24, 25, 27, 45, or 49) comprises eight pavilions that present such facets of Israeli life as ceramics, ethnography and folklore, and numismatics (coins). In the center of the complex is the ancient site of Tel Kassile, where archaeological digs have so far uncovered 12 layers of settlements. *2 Levanon (University) St., tel. 03/641–5244. Admission: NIS 17 ($5.70) adults, NIS 15 ($5) children. Open Sun., Tues., Thurs. 9–2, Wed. 9–6, Sat. 10–2.*

Any of the buses that took you to the Eretz Israel Museum will continue to the **Bet Hatefutsoth (Diaspora Museum).** The bus will drop you at the campus gate; walk onto the campus, where someone will point you in the direction of the museum. This is the one museum in Tel Aviv that should not be missed. Presented here is 2,500 years of Jewish life in the Diaspora, beginning with the destruction of the First Temple in Jerusalem and chronicling such major events as the exile to Babylon and the expulsion from Spain in 1492. One highlight is a collection of miniature replicas of synagogues, still existing or destroyed, throughout the world. *Tel Aviv University Campus (Gate 2), Klausner St., Ramat Aviv, tel. 03/646–2020. Admission: NIS 18 ($6) adults, NIS 13 ($4.35) children. Open Sun.–Tues. and Thurs. 10–5, Wed. 10–7, Fri. 9–2. Closed Sat. and holidays.*

The **Tel Aviv Museum of Art** (TAM) houses a fine collection of Israeli and international art, including works by Reuven Rubin (*see* Tour 1, *above*) and a Roy Lichtenstein mural commissioned for the museum in 1989. There's also an impressive French Impressionist collection here as well as an extensive collection of sculptures by Aleksandr Archipenko. *27 Shaul Hamelech Blvd. (take Bus 24), tel. 03/696–1297. Admission: NIS 13 ($4.35) adults, NIS 7 ($2.35) children; includes entry to the Helena Rubinstein Pavilion (*see Tour 1*). Open Sun.–Thurs. 10–9:30, Fri. 10–2, Sat. 10–2 and 7–10.*

Shopping

The shopping scene has made rapid advances in recent years, as prosperous Israelis have begun demanding higher-quality goods.

Shopping Districts

Kikar Hamedina, in the north part of the city and arguably the most expensive real estate in the country, is where the wealthy shop. On the circular street, you can pick up a **Sonia Rykiel** or **Chanel** suit, perhaps a Kenzo creation, or indulge in a kilo of **Godiva** chocolates from Belgium. The middle of the square is an unkempt plaza that—although the perfect foil to the luxury surrounding it—does nothing to bring prices down.

The northern end of **Dizengoff Street** has a number of boutiques, including those of such popular Israeli designers as **Yuval Kaspin** (check out his wedding dresses), **Tovale** (very avant-garde), and **Irit Brender** (svelte).

Dizengoff Center, Israel's first shopping mall, thrives with shops selling everything from air conditioners to camping equipment; you'll find many fashion stores and gift shops here. Avoid the center during school holidays if you don't like crowds of teenyboppers.

The less affluent **Allenby Street,** in the southern part of the city, offers some real bargains on clothes, jewelry (especially gold), and Judaica (religious and decorative objects).

Department Store

Hamashbir (Dizengoff Center) carries, for the most part, a rather banal selection of goods, often at prices a little higher than you'll find in smaller stores. On the second floor, however, its Designer Avenue features women's clothing by local designers. These designers also have boutiques at the northern end of Dizengoff Street or in the surrounding area, so ask for the address if you'd like to see even more of a particular designer's offerings. Hamashbir is also the Israeli outlet for the British St. Marks label (of Marks & Spencer).

Street Markets

At the **Nahalat Binyamin** street fair, held Tuesday and Friday, local crafts ranging from handmade puppets and pincushions to olive-wood sculptures and silver jewelry attract throngs of shoppers and browsers (*see* Tour 1, *above*). The **shuk hapishpeshim** in Jaffa is mostly full of junk these days, but you can still find a bargain—even if it's not an authentic antique. The flea market has a wide selection of reasonably priced Middle Eastern–style jewelry that uses chains of small silver coins and imitation stones and amber.

Specialty Stores

Jewelry You can find good gold prices in the many hole-in-the-wall jewelry stores on **Allenby Street.** For silver, head for the **Nahalat Binyamin** street fair on Tuesday and Friday (*see* Street Markets, *above*). More sophisticated gems and jewels can be found at **H. Stern** (with branches in the Dan, Sheraton, and Hilton hotels.

Judaica and If you're seeking unusual gifts, the **Wizo Shop** (94 Ben Yehuda St.) Ethnic Crafts has ornate ritual objects, such as silver candelabra and spice boxes;

richly embroidered dresses and silk scarves; olive-wood jewelry boxes; and more. The store is maintained by the Women's International Zionist Organization (WIZO).

Leather   **Beged-Or** (104 Ben Yehuda St.) and **Tadmor** (162 Dizengoff St.) can deck you out in sophisticated leather fashions. Choose traditional browns or blacks, or go for the bolder reds, purples, and mustards.

Swimwear   **Gideon Oberson** (6 Yirmiyahu St.) and **Gottex** (148 Dizengoff St.) are internationally known swimwear companies based in Tel Aviv. Although the companies' swimsuits and accessories sometimes cost less in the United States than they do in their country of origin, it's worth checking out the sales here.

Sports and Fitness

Participant Sports

Boating   You can rent pedal boats or small motor-run boats on the river in **Hayarkon Park** (tel. 03/648–6082) in the northern part of the city. Pedal boats cost NIS 33 ($11) per hour; motorboats are NIS 55 ($18.35) per half hour. Also located here are pleasure boats that take up to 120 people for 15-minute rides; cost is NIS 6.50 ($2.20) per person.

Bowling   The 16-lane **Bowling Center** (9 Ahad Ha'am St., tel. 03/510–0745) is located under the Shalom Tower complex. A game costs NIS 6 ($2) in the morning and NIS 8 ($2.70) in the afternoon and evening. Shoe rental is NIS 2 (70¢). It's open every day from 10 AM until past midnight.

Health Clubs   Most of the city's luxury hotels have health clubs that are usually free for guests. The **Hilton** (tel. 03/520–2291) has the largest gym and is open to nonguests, making it popular with the city's young professionals. The fee for each visit is $17 plus VAT. Open Sunday–Thursday 6:30 AM–11 AM and 1 PM–9 PM (Friday until 5 PM); closed Saturday and holidays. A little south of the Hilton, next to the Tel Aviv Marina, is the **Gordon Health Club** (tel. 03/527–1555), a Tel Aviv institution since the 1950s. The club includes an Olympic-size saltwater pool, gym, and sauna. Entrance to the health club alone costs NIS 50 ($16.70), and pool use is an additional NIS 30 ($10); you must present a passport. It's open daily from 6:30 AM–10 PM, closed on Saturday in July and August.

Sailing   If you know how to sail, you can spend a wonderful hour or two looking toward Tel Aviv from a spot in the Mediterranean. Sailboats and windsurfing equipment are rented by the hour at the **Sea Center** (Tel Aviv Marina, tel. 03/522–4079), situated below Kikar Namir (Atarim Square) behind the Carlton Hotel. (The Sea Center also has branches at the Hilton and at the Dolphinarium.) Windsurfers cost NIS 45 ($15) per hour, small boats NIS 70 ($23.35) per hour, and catamarans NIS 100 ($33.35) per hour. The unskilled can hire a boat with an instructor.

Swimming   If you get bored with the Mediterranean or you feel like taking a peek at Tel Aviv's elite, hit the Olympic-size, saltwater pool at the **Gordon Health Club** (tel. 03/527–1555). The club is poised just above Gordon Beach at the end of Gordon Street. This is a real Tel Aviv landmark: The premises open at 4:30 AM, and the same crowd has been coming at that hour for donkey's years to swim and schmooze. On Saturday the place is jam-packed with trendy Tel Avivians—don't expect to get too much swimming in, but the scene is highly entertaining.

In addition to the pool, there is a health club and sauna (*see* Health Clubs, *above*). The pool is open daily from 4:30 AM–7 PM and until 10 PM on Monday and Wednesday; admission (which does not include the health club) is NIS 30 ($10), and a tad extra on Saturday.

Waterskiing In Tel Aviv waterskiing is done without boats: Cables attached to a revolving crane pull you around an artificial lake, a system that holds no appeal for some but is particularly good for beginners. You'll find it at the **Park Leumi** (national park) in Ramat Gan (tel. 03/391168). On weekdays, it costs NIS 34 ($11.35) per hour (rates are about 25% more on Saturday and holidays); this includes equipment rental and instruction.

Spectator Sports

Israelis are big basketball and soccer (to them, football) fans. Basketball games are held at the **Yad Eliahu Stadium** (tel. 03/537–6376). There are two main venues for soccer: the **Bloomfield Stadium** (1 Hatehiya St., Jaffa, tel. 03/821276) and **Gadot Hayarkon Stadium** (Abba Hillel Rd., Ramat Gan, tel. 03/781777).

Beaches

It's true that Tel Aviv's western border, an idyllic stretch of sand on the Mediterranean, offers miles of beaches. But the Med does not always provide the refreshment you would expect: Because it's a closed sea, its water turns warm and decidedly unrefreshing in the dead of summer. If the jellyfish are out in force—which they are in July and August—you may well decide that an air-conditioned café with a *view* of the sea is a much more civilized choice.

Beaches in the heart of the city are free. On the northern edge of Tel Aviv, **Hatzuk** charges an entrance fee of NIS 8 ($2.70) for adults and half that for children aged 3–10. Beaches in **Herzliya** (except Sidney Ali) charge a comparable entrance fee.

Beaches are generally named after something nearby—a street or a hotel, for example. So you have **Hilton Beach** in front of the hotel of that name, **Gordon Beach** at the end of Gordon Street, and likewise **Bograshov Beach.** Sometimes, however, this gets a bit confusing: **Sheraton Beach** is at the site of the first Sheraton Hotel in Tel Aviv, about 1 kilometer north of today's Sheraton; and **Jerusalem Beach,** at the bottom of Allenby Road, is named after the city, not something in Tel Aviv.

When choosing a beach, look for one with brown timber lifesavers' huts, where first aid is available. Lifeguards are on duty from roughly May to October, from 7 AM until between 4 and 7 PM, depending on the month (check with your hotel's concierge). Be prepared: Tel Aviv's lifeguards are fond of yelling commands through the loudspeakers if they think swimmers are breaking any rules. All beaches have public amenities, including bathrooms and changing rooms. Many have kiosks, too, as well as the omnipresent ice-cream man who paces up and down the sand proffering his treats throughout the summer. These days, he even hangs on to the wrappers when he hands over the goods—his part in the effort to prevent littering.

Dining

Tel Aviv's culinary scene has radically improved in the last few years, and the city's cosmopolitan character is now happily represented in its food. That's not to say that you can't still enjoy the Middle Eastern fast foods that this part of the world is so famous for: The ubiquitous stands proffering falafel or shwarma (spit-grilled meat) in pita still occupy countless street corners, but beyond these are restaurants serving everything from American burgers to Chinese dim sum. Surprisingly perhaps, in contrast to Jerusalem, you have to really look to find a kosher restaurant outside the hotels, where all restaurants are required to be kosher.

Tel Aviv is also very much a café society. Everyone from idle shoppers to hard-driving businesspeople frequent the scores of coffee shops that dot the city. Don't miss an opportunity to join them at least once; the murmur of varied languages and the range of exotic coffees at these cafés will convince you as nothing else that you are truly in a cosmopolitan locale.

Although the quality of the cuisine has improved a lot, be warned that the same cannot be said about service. Israelis still have a lot to learn in the "customer is always right" department; sometimes, even in good restaurants, staff members may make you feel that they are doing you a favor to wait on you. It's customary to leave a 10%–15% tip, but don't feel obliged to leave it if you've received poor service. Occasionally, the service charge is added to the bill; this is so rare that it generally goes unnoticed, and people end up paying for service twice.

Many of Tel Aviv's restaurants are concentrated in an area known as "Little Tel Aviv," at the northern end of Ben Yehuda and Hayarkon streets (the area of the old Tel Aviv port). In addition, numerous establishments are located along the seafront south of Little Tel Aviv, all the way to Jaffa at the city's southern end, as well as east of there, in the inner city. In Herzliya Pituach, a suburb north of Tel Aviv, most restaurants are concentrated in one complex in the industrial area, about a 10-minute walk from the hotels in this area.

Most Tel Aviv restaurants are open throughout the day and well into the night year-round, except Yom Kippur. Keep in mind that many serve lunch at very reasonable prices, making them less expensive options than the price categories used below suggest. Israelis, like many of their counterparts around the Mediterranean, dine late. The chances are that you'll have no trouble getting a table at 7 PM, whereas at 10 you could be waiting at the end of a long line. Casual attire is always acceptable, even in the fanciest Tel Aviv restaurants.

Highly recommended restaurants are indicated by a star ★.

Category	Cost*
$$$$	over $35
$$$	$22–$35
$$	$12–$22
$	under $12

per person for a three-course meal, excluding drinks and 10%–15% service charge

$$$$ **Casba.** The *New York Times* once wrote that the Casba "combines the charms of French rusticity and the raffishness of Rick's Club Americain." Opened in 1960, the restaurant is one of Tel Aviv's most venerable, serving such favorite dishes as crispy duck with orange and apple sauces. It even boasts a true wine cellar—unusual in Israel. *32 Yirmiyahu St., tel. 03/604–2617. Reservations required. AE, DC, MC, V. Closed Sat.*

$$$$ **Keren.** Ranked among the top restaurants in Israel, Keren is housed in the only fully restored building in the run-down American Colony area of Jaffa (*see* Off the Beaten Track, *above*). The bar downstairs proves a restful spot after the inevitable daytime traffic jam on Eilat Street. The state of neighboring buildings is forgotten when you enter the upstairs dining room, with its fine white-lace tablecloths and smooth wood floors. The trademark stuffed zucchini flowers are filled with something different regularly. And that's just the beginning . . . . *12 Eilat St. at Auerbach St., Jaffa, tel. 03/816565. Reservations advised. DC, MC, V. No lunch Fri. or Sat.*

$$$$ **King Solomon Grill.** Dim lights and partial curtains between tables create an intimate atmosphere here, despite the restaurant's large size. The eclectic menu ranges from Continental (pâté de foie gras, baked sweetbreads) to Middle Eastern (hummus and tahini, Turkish salad) to North American (New York–style pastrami on rye)—there's even sushi. And all of it is kosher. *Hilton Hotel, Independence Park, tel. 03/520–2222. Reservations advised. AE, DC, MC, V. No lunch.*

$$$$ **Le Relais Jaffa.** Here the traditional French cuisine is *très fine,* and
★ so is the ambience of this 150-year-old stone building. Built in Ottoman times, the structure retains not only the original marble floors, but also some engravings made to ward off the evil eye. On a balmy summer evening, ask for a table on the terrace. Chef/owner David Bitton is a master of such classic sauces as bordelaise and estragon, but whatever your entrée, top it off with a chocolate Charlotte. *13½ Hadolphin St., Jaffa, tel. 03/681–0637. Reservations advised. AE, DC, MC, V. No lunch Sun.*

$$$$ **Succa Levana (White Pergola).** Plan to be here at sunset, when the setting, surrounded by palm trees and overlooking the Mediterranean, is especially lovely. The dining area is a glass-walled patio. The meal begins with a *mezeh*—a choice of excellent Middle Eastern salads—and a platter of fresh garden vegetables, followed by the day's catch. *72 Kedem St., tel. 03/683–0044. Reservations advised. MC, V.*

$$$ **Dixie.** This bar and grill is away from the main tourist areas and serves mostly the surrounding offices and commercial centers. However, if you're in the mood for a "Nebraska-style" porterhouse steak or hints of Cajun food, grab a taxi and go. The bar is well-stocked. *120 Yigal Allon St., tel. 03/696–6123. Reservations advised. DC, MC, V.*

$$$ **Prego.** The easygoing atmosphere here makes lingering over the fine Italian meal seem like a very good idea. Most of the restaurant occupies a terrace overlooking Rothschild Boulevard in an older quarter of Tel Aviv. Go for the pâté of mullard (a hybrid of duck and goose), followed by saltimbocca, accompanied by a glass of cold white wine from the Golan. *9 Rothschild Blvd., tel. 03/517–9545. Reservations advised for dinner. DC, MC, V.*

$$$ **Taboon.** The restaurant's stone oven imparts a rich and faintly barbecued flavor to the fresh fish and seafood here. For starters, the carpaccio of salmon and grouper is delectable. Whitewashed walls and turquoise-color trimmings lend sophistication to the Mediterranean ambience here. *Main Gate, Jaffa Port (turn left at pier), tel. 03/681–1176. Reservations advised. AE, DC.*

$$$ **Tandoori.** This was the original restaurant of the popular Tandoori
★ chain, which introduced Israelis to fine Indian cuisine. Sari-draped
owner Reena Pushkarna greets customers and makes each feel like a
special guest. Tandoori chicken is the specialty here, and it comes to
the table sizzling hot; finger bowls of rose water mean you can tuck
in with abandon. Curries come in three strengths. *2 Zamenhoff St.
(Kikar Dizengoff), tel. 03/296185. Reservations advised. AE, DC,
MC, V.*

$$$ **Turquoise.** The location—perched above a (relatively) quiet beach in
Jaffa on a no-name street—and the food here somehow compensate
for what has to be the worst service in town. Despite the slow and
often rude treatment you may receive here, Turquoise (pronounced
toor-keez) is a good choice for seafood served in a romantic setting.
Recommended dishes include gazpacho with shrimp and trout in orange, mint, and sake sauce—and the parfaits make a great dessert.
The circular outdoor bar is particularly delightful. *153/1 St. (turn
down unnamed St. toward sea), Jaffa, tel. 03/588320. Reservations
advised. MC, V.*

$$$ **Twelve Tribes.** Regulars claim that this is the best hotel restaurant in
★ Tel Aviv. They don't come here for the '70s decor, which is out of
sync with the "New Israeli cuisine" menu that reflects the many na-
tionalities that comprise this melting pot. Favorite dishes include
wild-rice timbale on a red-pepper coulis with tempura vegetables,
and *waterzooitje* (grilled Cornish hen served with goose liver and a
basil sauce). *Sheraton Hotel, 115 Hayarkon St., tel. 03/521–1111.
Reservations advised. AE, DC, MC, V. No lunch. Closed Fri.; Sat.
in summer.*

$$$ **Yin Yang.** You won't find a better Chinese restaurant in the country,
★ with food served up by owner/wonder-chef Yisrael Aharoni. The at-
mosphere is enhanced with "Chinese red" walls and Oriental prints.
Yin Yang now serves dim sum between 4 PM and 6 PM. *64 Rothschild
Blvd., tel. 03/560–4121. Reservations advised. DC, MC, V.*

$$ **Alexander's.** Dress trendy if you want to fit in: The crowd here is "Tel
Aviv yuppie" to the hilt, in keeping with the atmosphere along this
street. The menu runs the gamut from roast-beef sandwiches to la-
sagna. You may have to wait for a table if you haven't made reserva-
tions, but service is generally quite good. Another branch of
Alexander's is located at 22 Rambam Street, by the Nahalat
Binyamin mall (tel. 03/510–0571). *81 Yehuda Hamaccabi St., tel. 03/
546–0490. Reservations advised. MC, V.*

$$ **Cactus.** Across-the-border–inspired graphics in bold yellows, reds,
blues, and greens complement the terra-cotta tones of this small,
happy "Tex-Mex" restaurant. The menu includes close-to-tradition-
al fare of nachos and salsa, burritos, chili con carne, and fajitas. The
margaritas, though not quite the real thing, still do the trick. *66
Hayarkon St., tel. 03/510–5969. Reservations not necessary. MC,
V.*

$$ **Cafe Cazeh.** It's one of the city's "in" hangouts, and deservedly so:
The food is good, the service is warm, and a little courtyard/garden
in back provides a very relaxing atmosphere. No meat is served, but
the vegetable pies and quiches are hearty and come with fresh salad.
Desserts are the real specialty, though, and you may have trouble
deciding between lemon meringue or pecan pie, apple cake or
brownies. *19 Sheinkin St., tel. 03/293756. Reservations accepted.
No credit cards. No dinner Fri. Closed Sat.*

$$ **Chicago Pizza Pie Factory.** Order either the specialty deep-dish pizza or the thinner-crust variety here; both use only fresh ingredients
and are very good. Leave room for the House Cake, a sinful concoction of thick chocolate, nuts, whipped cream, and a meringue topping. There's a happy hour here on weekdays from 5 to 7, when

drinks are half price. *65 Hayarkon St., tel. 03/510–0560. Reservations accepted. MC, V.*

$$ L'Entrecôte. The mood is distinctly Parisian in this intimate restaurant with wood beams and a cozy upper-level garret. As the name implies, mostly steaks are served here. There are only a few tables, so the noise level is low. *195 Ben Yehuda St., tel. 03/546–6726. Reservations advised. MC, V.*

$$ Little Tel Aviv/Mandy's Candy Store. The "Mandy" here refers to a principal in Britain's Profumo scandal, who was later married to the original owner, a prominent local restaurateur with a string of his own scandals. Whether despite or because of this, the restaurant is a popular veteran on the Tel Aviv scene, with an extensive menu, including particularly memorable hamburgers. *300 Hayarkon St., tel. 03/605–5539. Reservations accepted. AE, DC, MC, V.*

$$ Loft. Unlike the other restaurants in Jaffa port, the Loft "cafe-museum," as it calls itself, has an unusual menu that does not necessarily focus on the day's catch. Try, for example, a steak with crab sauce, or the tartare herring with apples and sour cream (based on an old Jewish recipe). Also, this is the only eatery in the port that offers capuccino (*hafuch*, in Hebrew), rather than Mediterranean-style Turkish coffee. Desserts are especially tasty as you watch the sunset in front of the little marina. *Hangar 1, Jaffa Port, tel. 03/682–4789. Reservations not necessary. AE, DC, MC, V.*

$$ Mimoul. The menu covers just about the whole Mediterranean, from Israeli breakfasts of salad, eggs, and fresh rolls to lunch and dinner entrées such as fettuccine with Roquefort sauce and Moroccan spicy "cigars" (minced meat rolled up in pastry); the latter go exceptionally well with cold beer. The restaurant opens around 10 AM daily. *118 Hayarkon St., opposite Sheraton Hotel, tel. 03/523–6105. Reservations accepted. AE, DC, MC, V.*

$$ PastaLina. One of the most innovative restaurants in Tel Aviv, PastaLina is worth the trek to a less-well-known corner of Jaffa, near the American Colony. Antipasti cover a large table by the entrance, and you are served generous samples upon being seated. The fixed menu, which changes daily, includes antipasti and a pasta, meat, or fish dish. Glass bricks in the front wall allow natural light to highlight the russet and timber decor. *16 Elifelet St., Jaffa, tel. 03/683–6401. Reservations required. DC, MC, V. No dinner Fri.*

$ Bebale. Serving old-style Jewish food amid photographs and mementos from the past, Bebale is enjoying something of a revival among young, hip Israelis newly appreciative of their Eastern European roots. Specialties include gefilte fish, chopped liver, and *cholent* (slow-cooked meat-and-bean stew)—all traditional Saturday lunch fare in the old shtetls of Europe. *177 Ben Yehuda St., tel. 03/546–7486. Reservations accepted. MC, V. No dinner Fri.*

$ ★ Big Mama. The thin-crust pizza here is the best in town, and the owners take pride in using only the freshest ingredients. Toppings range from the traditional basil to more unusual ones, such as zucchini or prosciutto and egg. Situated in the heart of the Carmel Market, Big Mama avoids the market crowds by opening only for dinner. It's an ideal spot for a quick, light meal. *22 Rabbi Akiva St., tel. 03/517–5096. Reservations not required. No credit cards. No lunch. Closed Sun.*

$ Habayit. Here is simple, home-style cooking in the heart of the Yemenite Quarter. Despite the basic, hard chairs and Formica tables, it's hard to beat sitting outside here on a crisp autumn day, enjoying rich and spicy Yemenite soups. This is also a good place to mop up hummus in a warm pita, with a portion of shwarma on the side. *30 Yechie Kepach St., Yemenite Quarter, tel. 03/660783. Reservations not required. No credit cards. No dinner Fri. or lunch Sat.*

Tel Aviv Dining and Lodging

Mediterranean Sea

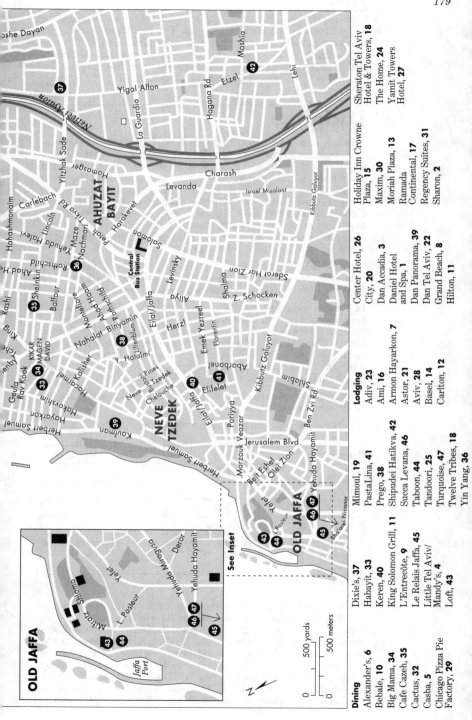

OLD JAFFA

Dining
Alexander's, 6
Bebale, 10
Big Mama, 34
Cafe Cazeh, 35
Cactus, 32
Casba, 5
Chicago Pizza Pie Factory, 29
Dixie's, 37
Habayit, 33
Keren, 40
King Solomon Grill, 11
L'Entrecôte, 9
Le Relais Jaffa, 45
Little Tel Aviv/
Mandy's, 4
Loft, 43
Mimoul, 19
PastaLina, 41
Prego, 38
Shipudei Hatikva, 42
Succa Levana, 46
Taboon, 44
Tandoori, 25
Turquoise, 47
Twelve Tribes, 18
Yin Yang, 36

Lodging
Adiv, 23
Ami, 16
Armon Hayarkon, 7
Astor, 21
Aviv, 28
Basel, 14
Carlton, 12
Center Hotel, 26
City, 20
Dan Accadia, 3
Daniel Hotel
and Spa, 1
Dan Panorama, 39
Dan Tel Aviv, 22
Grand Beach, 8
Hilton, 11
Holiday Inn Crowne
Plaza, 15
Maxim, 30
Moriah Plaza, 13
Ramada
Continental, 17
Regency Suites, 31
Sharon, 2
Sheraton Tel Aviv
Hotel & Towers, 18
The Home, 24
Yamit Towers
Hotel, 27

$ **Shipudei Hatikva.** This family-style restaurant is one of many along
★ Etzel Street in the Hatikva Quarter. The Las Vegas–style lights
along the street contrast with the plain Formica tables and fluorescent lighting inside, where a range of sumptuous skewered meats
grilled over hot coals is offered. The specialty is barbecued goose liver. *30 Etzel St., Hatikva Quarter, tel. 03/376404. MC, V. No dinner
Fri. or lunch Sat.*

Lodging

Nothing stands between Tel Aviv's luxury hotels and the Mediterranean Sea except the golden beach and the Tayelet promenade,
outfitted with chairs and gazebos. Even the small hotels are just a
short walk from the water. "Hotel Row" is located along Hayarkon
Street, which becomes Herbert Samuel Esplanade as you proceed
south, between Little Tel Aviv (the old port area) and Jaffa. This
means that wherever you stay, you're never far from the main thoroughfares of Ben Yehuda and Dizengoff streets, with their shops
and outdoor cafés, or the city's major concert hall, museums, art galleries, and the open-air Carmel Market.

Tel Aviv is known for a dearth of middle-price hotels, but the few
hotels listed in the $$ and $ categories are generally clean and com-
fortable, with friendly employees who create a warm atmosphere.

In the winter (mid-November to March or thereabouts), the outdoor
pools at Tel Aviv hotels are closed, and the lifeguards at the public
beaches take a break as well. (The saltwater pool at the Gordon
Health Club, near the Carlton hotel, is open to the public year-
round; *see* Sports and Fitness, *above.*) Most of the hotels don't have
room for tennis courts, with the exception of the Hilton. The hotel
health clubs are open to anyone over age 18.

Hotel reservations are essential at all Jewish holidays and are ad-
vised throughout the year.

Highly recommended lodgings are indicated by a star ★.

Category	Cost*
$$$$	over $120
$$$	$80–$120
$$	$60–$80
$	under $60

**All prices are for a standard double room, including breakfast and
excluding 15% service charge.*

Tel Aviv

$$$$ **Carlton.** The warm European ambience is evident as soon as you enter the lobby, with its muted colors, pale wood paneling, and soft
music. The Carlton caters to its clientele, a mix of tourists and
businesspeople, with efficient yet personal service. Most of the
rooms have sea views, as does the swimming pool, which is on the
roof. One disadvantage here: Access by foot is through the smelly
Kikar Namir. *10 Eliezer Peri St., 61064, tel. 03/520–1818, fax 03/
527–1043. 278 rooms with bath. Facilities: 2 restaurants, bar, 2 coffee shops, pool, synagogue, parking (fee). AE, DC, MC, V.*

$$$$ Dan Panorama. Its location south of the main stretch of hotels and near Jaffa is less convenient to town, but rates are lower than at comparable luxury establishments. Rooms at this high-rise hotel are compact and attractive, with decorative wall hangings adding spots of color. Each room has a tiny balcony overlooking the sea, either south toward Jaffa or north, facing the hub of the city. Poolside barbecues in summer are a plus. *10 Y. Kaufman St., 68012, tel. 03/519–0190, fax 03/658599. 504 rooms with bath. Facilities: restaurant, bar, nightclub/disco, coffee shop; health club with Jacuzzi, fitness room, massage, sauna; children's playground, pool, parking (fee). AE, DC, MC, V.*

$$$$ Dan Tel Aviv. Despite its exclusive reputation, this landmark hotel
★ has a warm and congenial atmosphere, with the personal touch that's missing from many larger hotels. Patterned coverlets decorate olive-green furniture in the rooms, which are each equipped with a minibar; bathrooms have hair dryers, phones, and radios. Rooms are larger in the luxurious King David wing and have panoramic sea views, as well as double-glazed windows to muffle city noise; none of these rooms have balconies. Guests have access to free golf at the Dan Accadia Hotel, about 25 kilometers (15.5 miles) north of Tel Aviv. Tel Avivians come to La Regence, the hotel's restaurant, for elegant dining. There is direct access to the beach from the hotel. *99 Hayarkon St., 63903, tel. 03/520–2525, fax 03/524–9755. 238 rooms with bath, 50 suites. Facilities: 3 restaurants, café, bar, health club with steam bath and sauna, pool, parking (fee). AE, DC, MC, V.*

$$$$ Grand Beach. This sprawling hotel at the northern end of Hayarkon Street is part of the Best Western chain. All rooms have turquoise and yellow decor, and the furniture is gray accented with yellow. The reading lamps are particularly good. There is a rooftop pool, and the hotel is a five-minute walk from the beach. The main dining room has a view of city streets, and light food is served in the large lobby/lounge. *250 Hayarkon St., 63113, tel. 03/546–6555, fax 03/546–6589. Facilities: bar, hairdresser, gift shop, pool, synagogue. AE, DC, MC, V.*

$$$$ Hilton. The most expensive hotel in the country and the one that most clearly caters to business travelers, the Hilton fairly bristles with the high energy of negotiations and deal-making. A full range of executive services is offered, including Japanese-language services and two business lounges. The Hilton's large, seawater pool is the best in town; it's also the only Tel Aviv hotel with its own beach, so you don't need to get dressed to get undressed again. In addition to enjoying classic French cuisine in the first-class King Solomon Grill, you can get a pastrami on rye in the Deli Room or kosher (!) sushi in the lobby. Unlike other hotels listed here, breakfast is not included in the price. *Hayarkon St., Independence Park, 63405, tel. 03/520–2222, fax 03/527–2711. 600 rooms with bath. Facilities: 2 restaurants, 2 bars, sushi bar, delicatessen, health club (extra charge), gift shops, pool, children's pool, tennis, beach, parking. AE, DC, MC, V.*

$$$$ Holiday Inn Crowne Plaza. The newest addition to the beachfront luxury hotel strip, the Holiday Inn Crowne Plaza is decorated in aesthetic and soothing pastels, both in the guest rooms and public spaces. Each room is equipped with a safe deposit box (operated by your personal credit card) and a voice-mail box for messages. Executive floors, as well as non-smoking floors, are available. The main restaurant, Bellissima, serves meat at lunchtime and becomes an Italian dairy restaurant at night. In addition, there is the Pacific China Grill, which exists in several Crowne Plazas in the United States and serves Western food cooked with an Eastern influence, and the English-style Pub Inn, which is a nice spot for a seaside beer. *145 Hayarkon St., 63453, tel. 03/520-1111, fax 03/520-1122. 220 rooms with bath. Facilities: 2 restaurants, pub, snack bars (in the lobby and by the pool), health club with Jacuzzi and sauna, massage, beauty parlor, valet parking (fee). AE, DC, MC, V.*

$$$$ **Moriah Plaza.** Managed by the Moriah Israel hotel chain, this 17-floor hotel is built so that all rooms (except singles) have sea views from their balconies. Public rooms are decorated in pale gray, and the pleasant, light-filled lobby has a bar and sea views. Rooms feature bright color schemes and good reading lights. The outdoor, seawater swimming pool (children's activities are held here daily in the summer) overlooks the beach, to which there is direct access. *155 Hayarkon St., 63453, tel. 03/527-1515 or reservations 03/691-9165, fax 03/527-1065. 372 rooms with bath. Facilities: bar, 24-hr room service, parking (fee). AE, DC, MC, V.*

$$$$ **Ramada Continental.** Guest rooms, decorated in shades of turquoise, beige, and rose, all have double-glazed windows and balconies with sea views; some even have queen-size beds, unusual in Israel. Bathrooms include hair dryers and scales. The lobby, with windows that overlook the sea, has a bar and coffee shop, and the main dining room has doors that open onto the pool, where barbecues are held. An outdoor terrace overlooking the sea serves light meals. You'll also find the city's only indoor, heated swimming pool at the Ramada. *121 Hayarkon St., 61032, tel. 03/527-2626, fax 03/527-2576. 340 rooms with bath, 10 suites. Facilities: restaurant, bar, 2 coffee shops, workout room, Jacuzzi, 2 saunas, heated indoor pool, children's pool, parking (fee). AE, DC, MC, V.*

$$$$ **Regency Suites.** This Best Western hotel is made up entirely of fully equipped, modern, one-bedroom suites, which consist of a bedroom and a small living area. A tad cheaper than the big hotels, its other advantages include being able to cook for yourself and entertain a few people. The decor is tasteful and the hotel still has that "new" shine to it, but the atmosphere is homey, especially in the tiny coffee shop, where breakfast is served (for an extra charge). *80 Hayarkon St., 63432, tel. 03/663266, fax 03/663276. 20 suites with bath. Facilities: coffee shop. AE, DC, MC, V.*

$$$$ **Sheraton Tel Aviv Hotel and Towers.** Combining the efficiency and
★ experience of the international Sheraton chain with a personal touch, this is one of the most attractive lodging options in Tel Aviv. The lobby is the first good sign: An excellent design allows for private areas within the public space; there's a lounge bar, and live entertainment is often featured. The rooms, most of which have soft hues and color-coordinated fabrics, all have minibars and double-glazed windows. The executive Sheraton Towers floors are exceptionally well run, with their own check-in and attentive service. The Twelve Tribes restaurant here (*see* Dining, *above*), is widely considered the best hotel restaurant in Tel Aviv. *115 Hayarkon St., 61032, tel. 03/521-1111, fax 03/523-3322. 346 rooms with bath. Facilities: 2 restaurants, lounge, nightclub/disco, health club (extra charge), 2 pools, parking. AE, DC, MC, V.*

$$$$ **Yamit Towers Hotel.** Roughly half the accommodations in this beachfront hotel are in suites with kitchenettes, unusual for Tel Aviv. One building contains the one- and two-bedroom suites, which include living areas as well as fully equipped kitchenettes. Standard rooms, housed in an adjacent building that opened in 1991, are less expensive. *79 Hayarkon St., 63903, tel. 03/519-1111, fax 03/517-4719. 42 rooms with bath, 43 suites. Facilities: 2 restaurants, bar, nightclub, pool, parking. AE, DC, MC, V.*

$$$ **Astor.** Built on a rise on the corner of Frishman and Hayarkon streets, the Astor has an excellent view of the sea. Rooms in this 30-

year-old hotel are not large, but those facing the sea have enclosed balconies with picture windows. The small, homey lobby has prints of Israel scenes and a shop selling handmade jewelry. The Shangri-La Thai restaurant serves authentic cuisine and has a beautiful, canopied terrace that faces seaward. *105 Hayarkon St., 63903, tel. 03/522–3141, fax 03/523–7247. 70 rooms with bath. Facilities: restaurant, bar, gift shop, free parking. AE, DC, MC, V.*

\$\$\$ **Basel.** It is not on the beach side of Hayarkon Street, but this seven-story hotel lives up to its reputation as a good deal. All but five rooms on each floor have sea views; decor includes well-designed wood furniture and patchwork-style fabrics. Expect personalized service (perhaps a legacy of the original Swiss owners). The lobby with its corner bar overlooks the small swimming pool. *156 Hayarkon St., 63451, tel. 03/524–4161, fax 03/527–0005. Facilities: 24-hr room service, pool, parking (fee). AE, DC, MC, V.*

\$\$\$ **City.** This six-story hotel on a quiet street near the beach is at the
★   bottom end of the \$\$\$ category. The light, airy lobby has a seating area the size of a large rug and a cozy dining room on the other side. The outdoor café, which faces the neighbor's hedge across the street, consists of a dozen plastic chairs and tables under a sidewalk canopy. The rooms feature blonde-wood furniture and TVs. The City is known for its fine food, including an acclaimed "Israeli breakfast" and a Friday night Shabbat (Sabbath) dinner featuring gefilte fish. *9 Mapu St., 63577, tel. 03/524–6253 or 03/546–8126, fax 03/524–6250. 96 rooms with bath. Facilities: restaurant, café, 24-hr room service, free parking. AE, DC, MC, V.*

\$\$ **Ami.** "Ami" translates as "my people," and there are lots, sitting at tables in the pleasant, sidewalk café in front of the hotel. This small establishment is located half a block from the sea, on a side street off Hayarkon Street. Most rooms are not large, though each has a small desk and chair. Four rooms on each floor have a balcony, from which rooftops and cityscapes can be viewed. *4 Am Yisrael Hai St., 63455, tel. 03/524–9141, fax 03/523–1151. 64 rooms with bath. Facilities: café, TV on request, room service until 11 PM. AE, DC, MC, V.*

\$\$ **Armon Hayarkon.** Though hardly the palace that its name translates to in English, this small, family-run hotel is pleasant enough to garner a high percentage of repeat customers. It's in Little Tel Aviv, at the northern end of Hayarkon Street, where a number of good restaurants are located; the beach is a five-minute walk away. The small rooms are decorated in basic brown, and some have balconies facing the sea. The small lobby has facilities for making coffee and a cold-drink machine. *268 Hayarkon St., 63504, tel. 03/605–5271, fax 03/605–8485. 24 rooms with bath. Facilities: parking. AE, DC, MC, V.*

\$\$ **Center Hotel.** This is one of the new breed of "tourist class" hotels in Tel Aviv—simple rooms and warm but basic service, and much less expensive than the luxury spots on the beach, just a 15-minute walk away. The Center Hotel is well situated, in town, on Dizengoff Square, adjacent to Tandoori Indian restaurant (*see* Dining *above*). Rooms are small and tasteful, though there is no Mediterranean view. *2 Zamenhoff St., tel. 03/296181, fax 03/296751. 56 rooms with bath. AE, DC, MC, V.*

\$\$ **Maxim.** This moderately priced hotel, located amidst more expensive accommodations, is another good value. Although the rooms are basic, most have views of the sea. Many Europeans like to stay here, and there is indeed a kind of Continental atmosphere about the place, due in part to the many European languages heard in the lobby. Guests can often be found relaxing in the café/bar in the lobby. *86 Hayarkon St., tel. 03/517–3721, fax 03/517–3726. 60 rooms with bath. Facilities: café, bar. AE, DC, MC, V.*

$ Adiv. The rather uninspiring appearance of Adiv, located on a side street off Hayarkon Street, is somewhat misleading. Rooms have pleasing modern furnishings and pastel-print bedspreads and curtains; there are no sea views, however. The staff is polite. *5 Mendele St., 63907, tel. 03/522–9141, fax 03/522–9144. 68 rooms with bath. Facilities: bar/café, room service until 11 PM. AE, DC, MC, V.*

$ Aviv. More a hostel than a hotel, this three-story, 1950s hotel was renovated several years ago, when the trendy Picasso restaurant opened on its ground floor. Guests enter through the restaurant and register at a desk behind the kitchen, beside the ice machine and cake container. There's no elevator, and decor is spare. There are no telephones or TVs, although rooms do have air conditioners. The rooms in the back are said to be quiet, but the location (on Hayarkon Street and over the restaurant, open until 5 AM) is not the place for those who seek serenity. A real plus here is the breakfast (omelet, salad, juice, and bread) at Picasso, which is included in the price. *88 Hayarkon St., 63432, tel. 03/510–2784, fax 03/522–3060. 20 rooms with bath. DC, MC, V.*

$ The Home. This should be happening more in Tel Aviv. Someone converted a regular residential block into furnished "studio apartments"—basic, but clean and well-kept, at budget prices—right in the midst of the big, expensive hotels. A small kitchenette in each room can contribute to a budget stay in an otherwise expensive city. Don't expect much in the way of luxuries or facilities. *106 Hayarkon St., tel. 03/522–2695, fax 03/524–0815. AE, DC, MC, V.*

Herzliya Pituach

Herzliya Pituach, or Herzliya-on-the-Sea, is a resort area 12 kilometers (7.4 miles) up the coast from Tel Aviv. It has three beachfront resort hotels and several high-quality restaurants, as well as some fish eateries on the beach, two squares with outdoor cafés and shops, and a new marina. Affluent suburbanites live here, as do diplomats and foreign journalists. There's a cosmopolitan, holiday air to the place. An express tourist bus (Bus 90) plies the route between the Herzliya hotels, city center, and ancient Jaffa.

$$$$ Daniel Hotel and Spa. Your introduction to the hotel begins in the ornate and lavish lobby, with deep-pink marble floors, mirrored pink and gold pillars, and a huge menorah of pink and green glass. A stained-glass dome covers a central seating area, and there are turquoise- and pink-carpeted seating bays overlooking the sea. Luxury continues—though in a different style—in the spa facilities: The beauty spa contains an indoor pool, Jacuzzi, and dry sauna. The health spa has a workout room with Nautilus equipment, hot and cold Jacuzzis, a wet sauna, and various massage therapies, plus all manner of treatments using mud and salts from the Dead Sea. All rooms have a sea view; deluxe rooms have balconies. Duplex rooms, on the ground floor facing the pool, are not a good choice for those who sleep late, as the pool area begins to get noisy in the morning. Rooms are in suitably Mediterranean colors. *60 Ramot Yam, Herzliya-on-the-Sea, 46769, tel. 09/544444, fax 09/544675. 300 rooms with bath. Facilities: 4 restaurants, bar, health and beauty spa, hairdresser, gift shops, tennis courts, pool, room service, parking (fee). AE, DC, MC, V.*

$$$$ Sharon. Recent renovations at this 1948 hotel left some areas sparkling, while others are still in need of a facelift. The reception area is blank and impersonal, save for several warmly colored Oriental rugs; on the other hand, the lobby lounge and café/bar around the corner are warm and welcoming. Guest rooms have light-colored furniture, pink and gray color schemes, and bright reading lamps; most overlook the sea. Garden rooms are located near the seawater pool. The Sharon's health club (popular with Tel Avivians) includes a heated indoor pool, a workout room, dry and wet saunas, massage, and Dead Sea mineral baths. *5 Ramot Yam, Herzliya-on-the-Sea, 46748, tel. 09/575777, fax 09/572448. 150 rooms with bath. Facilities: restaurant, bar, indoor pool, outdoor pool, health club, hairdresser, gift shop, tennis court, room service until midnight, free parking. AE, DC, MC, V.*

$$$ **Dan Accadia.** This well-known seaside hostelry (part of the Dan Hotel chain), open since 1956, is still going strong. It consists of two buildings surrounded by plant-filled lawns, with a pool at the center that overlooks the sea. Sixty rooms face the pool itself (with direct access to the beach), while others face the marina, on the shore in front of the hotel. The rooms are not huge but they have balconies with sea views; decor includes quilted bedspreads and matching blue-and-pink drapes. There's a workout room and a tennis club; guests also have access to the golf course at the Dan Caesarea farther north. The hotel is popular with families: organized activities for children and teenagers are held on Saturday and during the summer and holidays. The dining room has a glass wall that overlooks the sea, and a poolside restaurant is open for lunch. The Wednesday-night barbecue poolside, with a band and dancing, has been a local fixture for years. *Herzliya-on-the-Sea, 46851, tel. 09/556677, fax 09/562141. 185 rooms with bath. Facilities: 2 restaurants, bar, coffee shop, fitness facilities, sauna, massage, beauty parlor, gift shops, pool, tennis courts, golf-course access, art gallery, parking. AE, DC, MC, V.*

The Arts and Nightlife

The Arts

Tel Aviv is Israel's cultural capital, and it fulfills this role with relish. Like New York, the city is full of people who devote their lives to the arts without necessarily getting paid for it. It's very likely that your waitress, taxi driver, or salesperson is also a struggling performer, painter, or musician.

You can purchase tickets to events at the box office or through one of Tel Aviv's three major ticket agencies: **Hadran** (90 Ibn Gvirol St., tel. 03/527–9955), **Castel** (153 Ibn Gvirol St., tel. 03/546–7085 or 03/444725), and **Le'an** (101 Dizengoff St., tel. 03/524–7373). All accept major credit cards. You must pick up your ticket from the agency. Although there is never a shortage of events here, some areas of the arts—opera in particular—are still developing. The *Jerusalem Post's* Friday edition contains an extensive entertainment guide for the entire country.

Dance The **Suzanne Dellal Center for Dance and Theater** (6 Yehieli St., Neve Tzedek, tel. 03/659635) is where you'll find most of the country's dance groups, and Neve Tzedek is home to artists and a growing number of trendy galleries and gift stores. A visit here is a cultural experience, as the complex itself is an example of new Israeli architectural styles used on some of the oldest buildings in Tel Aviv. The large, whitewashed structures that comprise the center began as schools around the turn of the century. The complex has always been something of a meeting place for theater folk, even before it opened as a dance center in 1990.

Music The **Mann Auditorium** (1 Huberman St., tel. 03/528–9163), Israel's largest concert hall, is home to the **Israel Philharmonic Orchestra.** It also serves as a venue for rock, pop, and jazz concerts. Large outdoor concerts are held in **Hayarkon Park.** Among those who have drawn huge crowds are Dire Straits, the Neville Brothers, and Simply Red. A smaller venue inside Hayarkon Park is the **Wohl Amphitheater** (tel. 03/497841).

Opera The **Noga Theater** (7 Yerushalayim Blvd., tel. 03/813131) is home to the budding New Israel Opera.

Theater Performances are rarely in any language other than Hebrew. The **Cameri Theater** (101 Dizengoff St., tel. 03/523–3335), however, began offering simultaneous (taped) English translations in 1992. The national theater is **Habimah** (Habimah Sq., tel. 03/296071), which thrives on a classical repertoire. Chekhov's *Three Sisters* in Hebrew, for example, can make for an interesting evening. Avant-garde and fringe performances can be found at **Hasimta Theater** (8 Mazal Dagim St., tel. 03/828729) in Old Jaffa. Most of the plays at **Bet Liessin** (34 Weizmann St., tel. 03/695–6222) are by Israeli playwrights; Bet Liessin is also a popular jazz venue.

Nightlife

"The city that never stops" stays up later than many of the world's capitals. Peak hours on Hayarkon Street on a Friday or Saturday night continue until about 3 AM, when things finally begin to wind down. Partygoers are not daunted by the fact that nightspots come and go here about as quickly as the tides.

Bars and nightspots in Tel Aviv usually open in the day, long before the night owls descend; typically, these establishments offer either full dinners, beer and fries, or, at the least, the coffee and cake that they have been serving throughout the afternoon.

Bars, **Bar-Mitzva.** One of numerous fun corners that line this street, Bar-
Pubs, and Mitzva makes admirable play on words. Have some light, smoked
Nightclubs snacks with your beer. *16 Ha'arba'a St., tel. 03/561–1869.*

Cinema Club. At this cinema, the only one of its kind in Tel Aviv, you can order drinks and food at your seat, or spend time in the piano bar downstairs. *288 Hayarkon St., on the corner of Yirmiyahu St., tel. 03/546–6784.*

Hamisba'a. It's usually packed, and don't be surprised if you find a number of people dancing on the tables. *344 Dizengoff St., tel. 03/604–2360.*

Logus. Inside there is live music, for which there's a cover charge, but it's usually loud enough to hear from the mall outside, where food and drinks are also served. *8 Hashomer St., on the corner of Nahalat Binyamin, tel. 03/661176.*

Omar Khayyam. One of the very oldest night spots in Israel, it still thrives by offering Israeli/Oriental-style entertainment. *Kikar Kedumim, Old Jaffa, tel. 03/682–5865.*

Zanzibar. This very trendy, pine-furnished bar attracts the 20–30 set. *13 Ibn Gvirol St., tel. 03/561–9840.*

Gay Bars Believe it or not, in Tel Aviv a park serves the purpose of a gay bar: It is perfectly acceptable for gays to meet in **Independence Park,** next to the Hilton Hotel. Elsewhere, gay bars open and close even faster than other bars and restaurants.

Discos **Elizabeth.** This "post-modern" disco, replete with a huge pseudo-gilded sculpture of Queen Elizabeth II, offers a different music style every night. *Hangar 3, Jaffa Port, tel. 03/681–4752.*

Names. Nothing has been done to renovate this shell of a building, but that hasn't stopped its growing popularity as a place for loud music and dancing. An interesting experience. *22 Ahad Ha'am, tel. 03/510–7722.*

Roxanne. Located north of central Tel Aviv in an industrial zone, the venue is actually the top floor of a printing plant. Live bands usually start up at around 1 AM. *10 Habarzel St., Shikun Dan, tel. 03/544–7040.*

Jazz Clubs **Hakossit.** It appears to be nothing more than a simple pub, but some of Israel's most successful jazz musicians began their careers on a wooden bar stool here. *6 Kikar Malchei Yisrael, tel. 03/522–3244.*

King George 4. About the closest Israel comes to cabaret. Not only jazz, but also Paris-style chanson and blues can be heard in this tiny, very Mediterranean bar/restaurant. The very high ceiling allows musicians to perform from a platform built above the small dining-and-drinking hall. *4 King George St., tel. 03/296345.*

Upper Cellar. Because there are few all-jazz venues in Tel Aviv, aficionados come from around the country to this small upstairs hall of the Bet Liessin theater. *Bet Liessin, 34 Weizmann St., tel. 03/691–6653.*

5 Northern Coast and Western Galilee

Including Haifa, Caesarea, and Akko

By Karen
Wolman

Born in the
United States,
Karen
Wolman is a
journalist
who lived in
Italy for 10
years,
reporting for
Business
Week, Time,
and Fortune
on finance,
politics, and
cultural
affairs. She
currently
lives in Tel
Aviv, where
she writes
about travel,
art, and
business for
publications
such as
Fortune, the
Wall Street
Journal
Europe, and
Art &
Auction.

Updated by
Judy Stacey
Goldman

Stretched taut on a continuous and narrow coastal strip between urban Tel Aviv and the chalky cliffs of the Lebanese border, this region offers a lot more than meets the eye at the balmy Mediterranean beaches that line its shoreline. There is a rich overlay of historical sites as well as diverse landscapes that begin with the gently undulating sand dunes and the flat fields and citrus groves of the Sharon Plain, a fertile swath encompassing Netanya, Hadera, and Caesarea that was converted from a wasteland of malarial swamp early in the century by toiling Jewish pioneers. Today, Caesarea is a delightful resort of whitewashed villas and romantically crumbling Roman and Crusader ruins where the visitor gets a taste of sand, sea, and archaeology. Unforgettable here is the view of the arches of an ancient Roman aqueduct disappearing into the sand; so, too, are the sights and sounds of Israeli children splashing in the cove of the walled Crusader city during the summertime, heedless of the engineering wonders of Herod's port that are only rippling underwater outlines just beyond their reach.

Next are the softly contoured foothills and valleys dotted with vineyards at the base of Mt. Carmel, where the philanthropic Baron Edmond de Rothschild came to the succor of the Jews to create a wine industry that continues as one of Israel's most successful enterprises. The Carmel range then rises dramatically to its pine-covered heights overhanging the coast of Haifa, a modern port city whose inhabitants are at once hardworking and friendly. Haifa was the site of many heartrending scenes that played themselves out up and down this coastline in the decade prior to Israel's independence. Scores of ragtag ships filled with Jewish refugees fleeing Nazi persecution were turned away by the British just offshore, at Haifa, within the view of relatives and residents. North of Haifa you can roam the Western Galilee, which runs along a fertile plain up to the Lebanese border. Just across the sweeping arc of Haifa Bay lies Akko, a jewel of a Crusader city that is a medley of Romanesque ruins, Muslim domes and minarets, and swaying palms. To the north are the resort of Nahariya, especially popular among Israelis; Montfort, arguably the country's most magnificent Crusader castle; more Crusader ruins at Kibbutz Hanita; and, straddling the border, the caves at Rosh Hanikra, scooped out of rock by the relentless tides.

As the scenery changes, so does the ethnic mix of the inhabitants and their ancestors: Druze, Carmelite monks, Ottomans, Baha'is, Christian and Muslim Arabs, and Jews. You can also retrace the steps of the forebears of those with even the most ancient claim to these lands: the prehistoric people of the caves of Nahal Me'arot on Mt. Carmel, whose artifacts continue to be studied on-site by paleontologists. In Haifa and perhaps at absorption centers at kibbutzim, you will meet the region's latest arrivals, Jews from Ethiopia and the former Soviet Union. The Baha'is, whose universalist religion embraces the teaching of many others, dominate Haifa's mountainside setting with their gleaming golden temple and handsome gardens. The robed Carmelite monks quietly preside over their religious shrines at their monastery in Haifa and Mukhraka on Mt. Carmel, just next door to the Druze villages. Although the north coast Druze consider themselves an integral part of Israeli society, they maintain a unique cultural and religious enclave on Mt. Carmel, with the secret rites and rituals of their faith and the distinctive handlebar moustaches and white headscarves favored by the older men. Arabs and Jews live side by side in Akko, where, in the old quarter, many dilapidated buildings and cramped and dusty streets would seem to belie the town's pristine, picture-postcard reputation. Yet its subterranean knights' halls, Ottoman skyline, and outdoor *shuk* (market) awhirl with fascinating colors and sounds can still enchant. You will meet the ghosts of the Crusaders at the castles and fortifications that were erected throughout the region to maintain the warriors' tenuous hold over Palestine, which ended after two centuries in 1291 with the fall of Akko to the powerful Mamluk dynasty from Egypt.

Running the length of the region up to Haifa are two main highways: Route 2, a multilane highway that gets you from Tel Aviv to Haifa in just over an hour, and the inland Route 4, otherwise known as the Old Haifa Road. Route 4 then continues all the way to the border. Most sights are a short drive from one of these two roads, so it's tough to get lost even if you make a wrong turn. In springtime, you'll ride by fields that are ablaze with the color of wild anemones, tulips, and buttercups; cyclamen and narcissus grow a bit higher up. And you don't have to be an ornithologist to appreciate the astonishing variety of birds you'll see sometimes simply perched on telephone wires. In the spring, flocks of migrating birds—storks and pelicans—wheel overhead, and in the late fall you'll see herons, cormorants, and ducks that come each year to winter here.

This is the only part of the country where you can drive for long stretches with an unimpeded view of the Mediterranean, and where, in addition to the main resorts, there are numerous broad, sandy beaches that are open to the public.

Essential Information

Important Addresses and Numbers

Tourist Information
There are tourist offices in the following towns:

Akko: Tourism Department, Akko Municipality, opposite the mosque at El Jazzar St., 35 Weizmann St., Box 2007, Akko 24100, tel. 04/911764. Open Sun.–Thurs. 8–4, Fri. 9–2.

Caesarea: Caesarea Development Corp., Old City, Box 1044, Caesarea 30660, tel. 06/360833. Open Sun.–Thurs. 8–5, Fri. 8–1.

Haifa: Government Tourist Information Office (GTIO), 18/20 Herzl St., Bet Hakranot, Haifa, tel. 04/666521. Open Sun.–Thurs. 8:30–5, Fri. 8:30–2. GTIO, Shed 3, Haifa Port, tel. 04/663988. Haifa Tourist Board, 106 Hanassi Ave., Haifa 34642, tel. 04/374010. Open Sun.–Thurs. 8–6, Fri. 8–1. Haifa Tourist Board, ground level, Central Bus Station, Haganah Blvd., tel. 04/512208. Open Sun.–Thurs. 9:30–5, Fri. 9:30–2. What's On in Haifa Hotline: tel. 04/374253.

Nahariya: Municipal Tourist Department, Nahariya Municipality, 19 Ga'aton Blvd., Box 78, Nahariya 22100, tel. 04/879800. Open Sun.–Thurs. 9–1 and 4–7, Fri. 9–1.

Netanya: GTIO, next to amphitheater on Ha'aztmaut Sq., tel. 09/827286. Open Sun.–Thurs. 8:30–7, Fri. 9–noon. Association for Tourism Promotion, 15 Herzl St., Box 2165, Netanya 42400, tel. 09/330583 or 09/603–1150. Open Sun.–Thurs. 7:30–2.

Zichron Ya'akov: Next to central bus station, Gidonim, Box 10, Zichron Ya'akov, tel. 06/398811. Open Sun.–Thurs. 9–1.

Consulates
Haifa: Jonathan Freidland, U.S. Consular Agent, 12 Jerusalem St., tel. 04/670616; open Sun.–Thurs. 9–1.

Emergencies *Police*	**Akko:** tel. 100 or 04/091–9811; **Haifa:** tel. 100; **Nahariya:** tel. 100 or 04/920344; **Netanya:** tel. 100 or 09/21444.
Ambulance	**Akko:** tel. 101 (Magen David Adom) or 04/912333; **Haifa:** tel. 101; **Nahariya:** tel. 101 or 04/823332; **Netanya:** tel. 101.
Hospitals	**Haifa:** Rambam, tel. 04/543111, Carmel, tel. 04/250211; **Nahariya:** Western Galilee Regional Hospital, tel. 04/850766; **Netanya:** Laniado Hospital, tel. 09/604666.
Taxis	**Akko:** Akko Zafon, tel. 04/816666; **Haifa:** Carmel-Ahuza, tel. 04/382727, Mercaz Mitzpe, tel. 04/662525; **Nahariya:** Kefarim, tel. 04/926333; **Netanya:** Hashahar, tel. 09/347777, Hasharon, tel. 09/333338.
Car Rental	**Akko:** Shefi Tours, 37 Ha'Arba'a St., tel. 04/912730; **Haifa:** Avis, 7 Ben-Gurion St., tel. 04/513050; Budget, 186 Yaffo St., tel. 04/520666; Eldan, 95 Hanassi Ave., tel. 04/375303; Hertz, 90 Ha'atzmaut St., tel. 04/539786; Reliable, 118 Ha'atzmaut St., tel. 04/516504; **Nahariya:** Budget, 62 Weizman St., tel. 04/929252; **Netanya:** Avis, 1 Ussishkin St., tel. 09/331619; Budget, 2 Gad Machness, tel. 09/614711; Eldan, 12 Ha'atzmaut Sq., tel. 09/616982; Hertz, 8 Ha'atzmaut Sq., tel. 09/828890; Reliable, 2 Gad Machness, tel. 09/629042.
Travel Agencies	**Akko:** Shefi Tours, 37 Ha'Arba'a St., tel. 04/912730. **Haifa:** Histour, 14 Nordau St., tel. 04/671313. **Nahariya:** Ler Tours, 19 Ha'Ga'aton Blvd., tel. 04/825636. **Netanya:** Atlas Tours, 29 Herzl St., tel. 09/345183.

Arriving and Departing by Plane

Most travelers from abroad arrive at **Ben Gurion International Airport,** at Lod on the outskirts of Tel Aviv. The airport is 105 kilometers (65 miles) from Haifa, about a 90-minute drive. From the airport buses, sherut taxis, and taxis to the northern coast are readily available. **Haifa Airport** (tel. 04/722220), a small airport in the port area, is served by Arkia Airlines (Jerusalem, tel. 02/234855; Tel Aviv, tel. 03/523–3285), which flies into the city from Jerusalem, Tel Aviv, Eilat, and the Dead Sea.

Between the Airport and Downtown Egged Bus 947, which costs NIS 12 ($4), leaves Haifa Airport every half hour for the central bus station, and returns from the station with the same frequency.

Arriving and Departing by Car, Bus, Ship, and Train

By Car You can take either Route 2 or 4 north along the coast from Tel Aviv to Haifa, continuing on Route 4 all the way up to the Lebanese border. From Jerusalem follow Route 1 to Tel Aviv and then connect through the Ayalon Highway to Herzliya, where you can pick up Route 2.

By Bus The **Egged** bus cooperative (*see* Getting Around, *below*) serves the coastal area from Ben Gurion Airport and from the Jerusalem and Tel Aviv central bus stations. Service to Netanya, Hadera, Zichron Ya'akov, and Haifa from both cities starts before 8 AM and usually ends around 8 PM. From Tel Aviv to Haifa, there is a bus that leaves every 20 minutes from 5:20 AM to 11 PM. Travel to Caesarea requires a change at Hadera; service from Hadera to Caesarea runs only until 12:30 PM. You must change buses at Haifa to get to Akko and Nahariya.

By Ship   Many cruise liners that tour the Mediterranean stop at Haifa. To visit the city you will exit the docks area through either Gate 5 or the Passenger and Customs Terminal, depending on whether you are required to go through customs. Taxis are usually waiting at the exits. Nearby, you can catch Buses 17 and 22 to the central bus station, Buses 10 and 12 to the Hadar district, and Bus 22 to Mt. Carmel.

By Train   There is a line linking Tel Aviv to Netanya, Haifa, and Nahariya, with stops along the way. The portion of the trip from Tel Aviv to Haifa takes 90 minutes and costs NIS 7.50 ($2.50). There is also a direct train to Tel Aviv from Haifa, which is fast (one hour) and comfortable and runs hourly Sunday–Thursday 6 AM–7 PM. It is advisable to buy tickets a day ahead, at the Tel Aviv train station (Rakevet Zafon, or Northern Train Station, 1 Arlozorov, tel. 03/693–7515). Haifa has two train stations; the main one is Haifa Bat Gallim, located at the central bus station, tel. 04/564564. The train station in Netanya is on Ha'Rakevet Road, just east of Route 2, tel. 09/823470.

Getting Around

By Car   Driving is probably the most comfortable and convenient way to tour the region and allows you to explore some of the more scenic back roads. The distances are small: for example, 29 kilometers (18 miles) from Tel Aviv to Netanya, 22 kilometers (13.7 miles) from Haifa to Akko, 37 kilometers (23 miles) from Haifa to Zichron Ya'akov.

Traffic gets particularly snarled at rush hour along the coast, especially entering and exiting major cities. The worst times are after 5 PM weekdays and Saturday evenings. Expect gridlock during morning and evening rush hours in Haifa in the port area. Even in the best of conditions, Haifa traffic is sluggish, and because of the city's steep layout, streets zigzag up the slope and are difficult to negotiate. Remember to pay attention to street signs in Haifa indicating which streets close on Saturday. Route 672, which wends its way through the Druze villages, is narrow and thinly paved, and during heavy winter rains it can become flooded and pitted with potholes.

By Bus   The **Egged** network will get you just about anywhere in the region. Most connections are hourly during the weekday. For countrywide information on routes and schedules call 02/304555; 03/537–5555; 04/549555, or contact the local bus stations directly: Haifa, 04/549131; Netanya, 09/337052.

By Train   This is a novel way to travel within the area, because this is the one part of the country serviced (other than from Tel Aviv to Jerusalem) by rail. Many of the main cities and towns can be reached by train, including Netanya, Hadera, Binyamina, Zichron Ya'akov, Haifa, Atlit, Akko, and Nahariya.

Haifa possesses the only subway in Israel. The six-station Carmelit subway runs from Hanassi Avenue in Central Carmel to Kikar Paris in the port area in six minutes; the fare is NIS 2 (70¢). The train operates Sunday–Thursday 5:30 AM–midnight, Friday 6–3, and Saturday 7 PM–midnight.

Guided Tours

General Interest   **Egged Tours** offers a one-day trip from Tel Aviv or Netanya that takes in Caesarea and Akko and goes all the way to the Lebanese border at Rosh Hanikra. The tour, which costs NIS 156 ($52), is given on Wednesday, Friday, and Sunday at 8 AM. The bus departs from

Tel Aviv's Kakir Namir (Atarim Square), or you can be met at your hotel by prior arrangement. In Netanya, the tour departs from the Egged office at 28 Herzl Street. Bookings may be made in Tel Aviv (tel. 03/527–1212) or Netanya (tel. 09/828333). For departures from Haifa call tel. 04/549486.

Another one-day Egged tour covers the northern coast as well as the adjacent Jezreel Valley, visiting Haifa, the Druze villages, Beit Shearim, and Megiddo for NIS 135 ($45). Tours leave Tuesday from April to October at 8 AM from Atarim Square in Tel Aviv and from Netanya. Egged also has two half-day tours from Haifa. Both cost NIS 184 ($128) and include city sights; one goes to the Druze villages, the other takes you to Akko and Rosh Hanikra. Tours leave from Haifa's Central Bus Station (tel. 04/549486). All Egged tours offer 10% discounts for children under 12.

United Tours offers a free half-day tour to Netanya from Tel Aviv, passing through Herzliya and the Sharon Valley on the coast with a stop at Kibbutz Shefayim. In Netanya there is a tour of the National Diamond Center. Departures are daily (except Saturday) from 9:15 to 10 at the Tel Aviv train station, returning at about 2 PM. Reserve at your hotel reception desk.

Another United Tours excursion from either Tel Aviv or Netanya takes you to Caesarea, the Baha'i Gardens in Haifa, and Rosh Hanikra; on the return trip there is a stop at Akko to see the Crusader city, the Arab market, and the mosque. This one-day tour costs NIS 156 ($52) and leaves at 8 AM on Wednesday, Friday, and Sunday from the Tel Aviv train station. By prior arrangement you can be picked up at your hotel. To make reservations contact United Tours in Tel Aviv (tel. 03/6933404).

From April through November the **Society for the Protection of Nature in Israel (SPNI)** tours the Mediterranean coast and the Carmel mountains on a two-day excursion. The tour, which costs NIS 294 ($98), leaves at 11:30 from Tel Aviv at the SPNI office (3 Ha'shfela St., tel. 03/537–4425, fax 03/383940). Participants have an opportunity to swim at Dor beach, explore the ancient *tel* (man-made mound of layers of civilization) nearby, bird-watch at Kibbutz Ma'agan Michael, hike on Mt. Carmel, and visit the Carmel caves. Accommodations are in a field-study center, which is a bit like a youth hostel; breakfast and dinner are included.

In **Haifa** the municipal tourist office (tel. 04/374010) conducts a free 2½-hour walking tour on Saturday that leaves at 10 AM from the corner of Yefe Nof (Panorama Rd.) and Sha'ar Ha'levanon streets. The itinerary includes the Mane' Katz Museum and the Baha'i Shrine, and ends at Haifa Museum. You can catch Bus 23 back to Central Carmel.

Special Interest
Bird-Watching

Israel is a crossroads for European migratory birds heading for Africa and back, and thus is a paradise for bird-watchers. The best season to observe them is from November through February. Some of the birds you are likely to see along the northern coast include egrets, pelicans, storks, terns, spoonbills, mallard ducks, kingfishers, cormorants, and even some flamingos. You can hire a private guide for a day at the coastal **Ma'agan Michael Field School** (tel. 06/399655 or 06/398851, fax 06/394166), one of Israel's major centers for bird-watching, located at the kibbutz of the same name, just north of Caesarea. The cost of the guided tour is NIS 390 ($130). Dormitory facilities are available for longer stays. Visitors are also welcome to roam without a guide; brochures in English are usually available at the school.

Boat Tours   Carmelit (tel. 04/418765) offers boat tours of Haifa Bay from Kishon Port. The ride lasts one hour and costs NIS 15 ($5). Call ahead for departure times. From **Akko's Crusader port** the *Princess of Akko* ferry makes a 25-minute jaunt around the bay (tel. 04/919287). The boat sets out February through December whenever it fills up and costs NIS 7.80 ($2.60) for adults and NIS 6.50 ($2.20) for children.

Personal   Two Haifa-based tour operators offer guided tours in a private car
Guides   or limousine tailored to individuals or small groups: **Mitzpe Tours** (tel. 04/674341, fax 04/677469) and **Carmel Touring Co. Ltd.** (tel. 04/388882 or 04/385058, fax 04/382277), which has a branch at the Dan Carmel Hotel.

Exploring the Northern Coast and Western Galilee

You can easily spend a week heading up the coast from Tel Aviv to the Lebanese border, depending on whether you want to soak up some sun at one of the beach resorts—Netanya, Caesarea, or Nahariya—along the way. You should plan to spend at least a half-day in Caesarea, a day exploring Haifa and its surroundings, and a half-day in Akko. Tour 1 takes you from the northern outskirts of Tel Aviv to the ancient Roman capital and Crusader city at Caesarea. Instead of going straight up the coast, Tour 2 plots a scenic drive through the area's wine-producing towns, chief among them Zichron Ya'akov, climbing Mt. Carmel and passing through the Carmel National Park to the Carmelite Monastery at Mukhraka and two Druze villages. Tour 3 covers Haifa, and a number of sites just south of the city along the coast, including the Crusader castle at Atlit, the artists' village of Ein Hod, the prehistoric Carmel Caves, and the fascinating underwater archaeology museum at Nahsholim. The final leg of the trip takes you on a walk through the walled city of Akko and on a drive up the coast to the sea grottoes at Rosh Hanikra, with final stops at the Crusader castles in Montfort and Yechi'am.

Highlights for First-Time Visitors

Crusader city and **aqueduct, Caesarea** (*see* Tour 1)
El-Jazzar Mosque, Akko (*see* Tour 4)
Haifa Museum (*see* Tour 3)
Montfort fortress (*see* Tour 4)
Ramat Hanadiv (*see* Tour 2)
Roman statuary in Caesarea Museum, Kibbutz Sdot Yam (*see* Tour 1)
Shrine of the Bab, Haifa (*see* Tour 3)
Turkish baths, Akko (*see* Tour 4)
Underwater archaeological finds at Nahsholim Museum, Kibbutz Nahsholim (*see* Tour 3)
View from the Carmelite Monastery, Mukhraka (*see* Tour 2)
Zichron Ya'akov (*see* Tour 2)

Tour 1: Up the Coast to Caesarea

Numbers in the margin correspond to points of interest on the Northern Coast and Western Galilee map.

Heading north out of Tel Aviv on Route 2, look carefully for the sign that marks the left turnoff to Nof Yam (just opposite Kfar

Shemaryahu), which will lead you through one of the country's poshest neighborhoods, the suburb of Herzliya Pituach, on the coast.

Drive west along the tree-lined Keren Hayessod Street, past a roundabout, and turn right at the road's end along a stretch of sprawling villas inhabited by foreign ambassadors and local millionaires. Turn left at the corner of the palm-dotted park on your right, and after around 100 feet turn left again up a short unpaved road where you will see the minaret of the **Sidna Ali Mosque** poking up at the top of a hill. Built by the Mamluks in the 13th century, this handsome, austere mosque of roughly hewn stone was named after Abu el Hassan Ali, who is revered by Muslims for fighting the Crusaders as an officer in Saladin's army. It holds a commanding view of the coast—jagged openings in the western wall of its ample courtyard frame the sea just below—south of the site of a collapsed Crusader fortress where the waterlogged ruins of ancient **Apollonia** sit.

The first—though certainly not the most impressive—of the many fortresses in which the Crusaders kept vigil over the coast, it was constructed on a Greek site named after the god Apollo and was alternately seized by Arabs and Crusaders over the centuries. From the promontory just north of the mosque you can still discern the outlines of the port's jetties at low tide, but the bulk of the battlements and walls toppled long since the days of Richard the Lionheart, who recaptured the Crusader stronghold from the Muslims in 1191. The Mamluks laid waste to it shortly after to keep the Crusaders from ever coming back. In the 1940s this beach was used—as were many others along the northern coast—as a clandestine landing spot for Jewish refugees. Today, you can walk along the cliff or down a staircase to the popular beach. The area near the collapsed jetty is a favorite spot to hunt for Roman coins.

Back on Route 2, drive 22 kilometers (13.7 miles) north to the seaside resort of **Netanya,** considered both the geographic capital of the Sharon Plain and the heart of Israel's giant diamond-polishing industry. Get off at the Central (second) Netanya exit.

Once a sleepy town of farmers and orange groves, Netanya, named after Jewish philanthropist Nathan Strauss, steadily burgeoned to its present population of 160,000 from a few settlers in 1929. Before the Six-Day War, the town was at thenarrowest part of the country, the exiguous strip between Netanya and the Tulkarem border 16 kilometers (10 miles) to the east. Though citrus farming is still evident on Netanya's rural outskirts, there are few traces of small-town grace and few sights to see in the rambling concrete constructions built in haste to accommodate the constant stream of newcomers. Still, what visitors come here for are the 11 kilometers (6.8 miles) of unspoiled, sandy public **beaches** (*see* Sports and the Outdoors, *below*) ideal for swimming and sunbathing.

To get to your hotel or the beach, drive down the town's main artery, Herzl Street, which ends at the new **pedestrian mall** and **Haatzmaut Square,** where there is an outdoor amphitheater for free summer concerts and plenty of open-air cafés and restaurants. Access to the beaches is south and north of the mall. In February and March, detour a few kilometers south of the city to see the fields famous for a rare, exotic variety of deep-indigo wild iris indiginous to the area. There are marked paths to the iris fields, and a parking lot on Ben Gurion Boulevard.

Take time out to explore another, perhaps more hidden aspect of Netanya: diamonds. Israel's multibillion-dollar diamond industry—

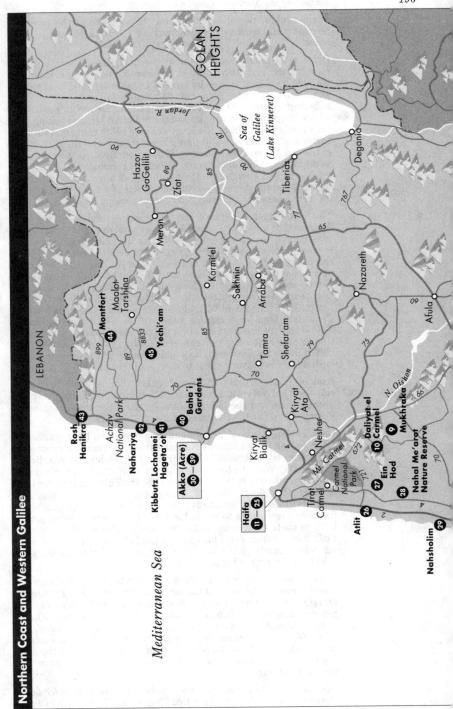

Northern Coast and Western Galilee

GOLAN HEIGHTS

LEBANON

Mediterranean Sea

Jordan R.

Sea of Galilee
(Lake Kinneret)

Hazor
GaGelilit

Zfat

Meron

Tiberias

Degania

Montfort
44

Maalot-
Tarshina

Karmi'el

Sakhnin

Arraba

Nazareth

Yechi'am
45

Tamra

Shefar'am

Afula

Rosh
Hanikra
43

Achziv
National Park

Nahariya
42

Baha'i
Gardens
40

Kibbutz Lochamei
Hageta'ot **41**

Akko (Acre)
30 — 39

Kiryat
Ata

Kiryat
Bialik

Nesher

Daliyat el
Carmel **9**

Mukhraka

10

N. Oishon

Haifa
11 — 25

Mt. Carmel

Carmel
National
Park

Tirat
Carmel

Ein
Hod
27

Nahal Me'arot
Nature Reserve
28

Atlit
26

Nahsholim
29

672

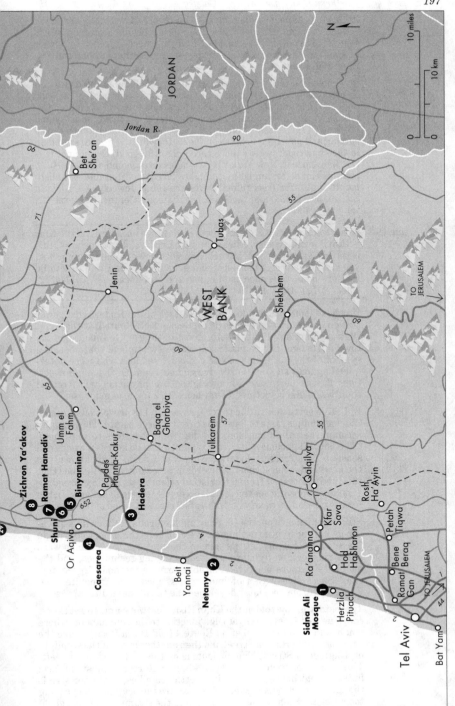

its leading export is diamonds—was launched with the arrival of Jewish diamond-cutters from Belgium and Holland during World War II. Many of them settled in Netanya, where there are hundreds of small workshops, mainly clustered around the outdoor shuk on Zangwill Street.

You can get a free tour of one of the larger **diamond factories** and **showrooms** where raw stones of various hues and quality are cut, polished, and set into jewelry. The tours, which usually last about 45 minutes, provide general background on the diamond industry and its growth in Netanya before taking you step by step through the cutting and polishing process on the factory floor. The tours wind up in the showroom, where prices are generally good, though not better than those in New York City's wholesale diamond district. Hotel pickups can be arranged by company car. Two reputable establishments that offer free guided tours are Inbar Jewelry (1 Ussishkin St.,tel. 09/822233) and the National Diamond Center (90 Herzl St., tel. 09/620436).

Time Out   Seven kilometers (4.3 miles) north of Netanya on Route 2 is the **Kfar Vitkin Pancake House.** Always doing a brisk roadside business, this is the local equivalent of a truck stop with down-home cooking. Yes, you can actually get pancakes and eggs here in addition to Middle Eastern mainstays such as hummus and pita bread. *Tel. 09/666112. Open daily 6 AM–1 AM.*

Up ahead looms the landmark smokestack of the Hadera coal power station. After 15 kilometers (9.3 miles) get off Route 2 at the Givat Olga junction stoplight, heading east on Route 61. Inland lies the **3** town of **Hadera,** once a malaria-infested swampland that became a symbol of the hardships of early Zionist settlers who were determined against all odds to survive and succeed. Of the original settlers it was once said by a neighboring physician who treated countless malaria victims, "They act with a touch of madness."

In 1891, a small delegation that represented 178 prosperous Russian Zionist families came to Palestine to buy a large estate. They happily accomplished their mission, bidding their relatives to join them: "The land is spacious, the water is plentiful and there is a wonderful seashore." In Arabic, Hadera means "The Green." Unbeknownst to the new landowners, the 7,500 verdant acres dotted with lakes that they had purchased from a Christian effendi was a prime breeding ground for mosquitoes that carried a deadly strain of malaria. In the first two decades, nearly half of the 540 residents died of the disease.

Still, the pioneers persisted, planting hundreds of thousands of water-loving eucalyptus saplings in the vain hope that they would drain the swamps. Finally, at the turn of the century, the swamps were made manageable by more traditional drying techniques, and the neophyte farmers mastered suitable farming methods for the terrain. Successive waves of immigrants, including Yemenites and Eastern Europeans, later developed the town's agricultural base.

Their story is now told at the **Khan Historical Museum.** To get there, continue east from the Givat Olga junction to the roundabout, where you head north for 300 feet on Route 4 (Old Haifa Road). Make the first right onto Hanasi Street and then another right at the stoplight on Hagiborim Street. The museum is on the first block on the left. This is a reconstructed Ottoman khan, a 26-room sandstone farm building that housed the original settler families; next door stands the town's main synagogue. On display are the original iron farming tools, photographs of pioneers draining the swamps, and household furniture used by early inhabitants. An old olive-oil press still stands in the courtyard. *74 Hagiborim St., tel. 06/322330. Admission: NIS 5 ($1.70) adults, NIS 4.50 ($1.50) children. Open Sun.– Thurs. 8–1, Sun. and Tues. also 4–6, Fri. 9–noon.*

❹ Leave Hadera by the same route, returning to Route 2 and continuing only 3 kilometers (1.8 miles) to the exit for Route 65 to the coastal town of **Caesarea,** the final stop and highlight of this tour. At the northern tip of the Sharon Plain, Caesarea is covered with restored Roman, Byzantine, and Crusader ruins and is a delightful place to stop for a half-day of sightseeing and a leisurely lunch or swim at the port, or a longer seaside holiday. Driving from south to north, you will see stretched out over 2.9 kilometers (1.8 miles) the Roman theater, the Crusader city and Herodian port, some Byzantine remains, and the aqueduct in the sand dunes.

Herod the Great gave Caesarea its name, dedicating the magnificent Roman city he built to his patron Augustus Caesar; the port he called Sebastos, which was Greek for Augustus. It was the Roman emperor who elevated Herod—born to an Idumean family that had converted to Judaism—to his position as King of the Jews around 30 BC. Construction began in 22 BC at the site of an ancient Phoenician and Greek port called Strato's Tower. Herod spared nothing in his elaborate designs for the port facilities—a major engineering feat at the time—as well as for the city, which included palaces, temples, a theater, a marketplace, a hippodrome, and water and sewage systems. When it was completed 12 years later, only Jerusalem outshone the splendor of Caesarea. Its population under Herod grew to around 100,000, larger than that of Jerusalem; the city was spread over some 164 acres.

A decade after Herod died, Caesarea became the seat of the Roman procurators in AD 6. Herod's kingdom had originally been divided among his surviving sons, with his eldest, Archelaus, getting Judea and Samaria. But the Romans were unhappy with Archelaus's rule and banished him to Gaul. With Jerusalem a predominantly Jewish city, the Romans preferred the Hellenistic Caesarea with its Jewish minority as the seat of their administration.

Religious harmony did not prevail here. The Jews and Greek-speaking population repeatedly clashed, with hostilities exploding in the Jewish revolt of AD 66. The first Jewish rebellion was squelched by Vespasian, who was proclaimed emperor here by his legions in AD 69. A year later his son and co-ruler Titus captured and razed Jerusalem and celebrated his brutal suppression of the Jewish revolt. Henceforth Caesarea became a Roman colony and the local Roman capital of Palestine for nearly 600 years. It was here that Peter converted the Roman centurion Cornelius, a milestone in the spread of the new faith, and where Paul preached and was imprisoned for two years. In the 2nd century, Rabbi Akiva, the spiritual mentor of the Bar Kochba Revolt, was tortured to death here.

Caesarea is distinguished by well-marked signs in English. Proceed first to the **Roman theater,** which, along with the port area, is under the aegis of the National Parks Authority. One ticket admits visitors to both the theater and the Crusader city, so save your stub. At the entrance you can get a free brochure with a basic map and layout of the sites. (Be sure to lock your car and keep valuables out of sight.)

Entry to the theater is through one of the vomitoria, the arched tunnels that led the public into Roman theaters. Herod's theaters— here and elsewhere in Israel—were the first of their kind in the an-

cient Near/Middle East. Although smaller than the better-pre-
served Roman theater of Bet She'an (*see* Exploring Lower Galilee *in*
Chapter 6, Lower Galilee), Caesarea's has become by far the most
famous in the country. The theater today seats 3,600 and is a spectacular venue for summer concerts and other performances (*see* The
Arts and Nightlife, *below*). The view of the sea as a backdrop steals
any show, especially when the sky is ablaze with the setting sun.

What you see today is predominantly a reconstruction; only a few of
the seats of the *cavea* (where the audience sat) near the orchestra
are original, in addition to some of the stairs and the decorative wall
at the front of the stage. Just inside the theater's main gate is proof
that one of the Roman rulers who resided here was Pontius Pilate,
governor of Judea when Jesus was crucified. It is the only archaeological evidence of the governor's presence in Palestine. The frag-
mented Latin inscription on a mounted plaque, a replica of the
original in the Israel Museum in Jerusalem, is believed to say that
"Pontius Pilate, the prefect of Judaea, built and dedicated the
Tiberieum [probably a temple or shrine dedicated to the Emperor
Tiberius] to the Divine Augustus." The original engraved stone
probably was removed from the disused shrine for the theater's repair. *Caesarea National Park, tel. 06/362209. Admission (theater
and Crusader city): NIS 10 ($3.35) adults, NIS 5 ($1.70) children.
Open daily 8–4, Fri. and holiday eves 8–3.*

Leaving the theater you can walk south about 600 feet to the **Caesarea Museum** on the grounds of the Sdot Yam kibbutz next door.
Many of the artifacts were found by kibbutz members plowing the
fields in the 1940s. The museum possesses arguably the best collection of late-Roman sculpture in Israel, impressive holdings of rare
Roman and Byzantine gemstones, and a large variety of coins
minted in Caesarea over the ages, as well as oil lamps, urns excavated from the sea bottom, and fragments of jewelry. *Tel. 06/364367.
Admission: NIS 4 ($1.35) adults, NIS 3 ($1) children. Open Sat.–
Thurs. 10–4, Fri. 8–2.*

Turn left after you leave the parking lot, and head north 1 kilometer
(.6 mile) along a road that runs beside what was the Cardo Maximus
to the main gate in the **Crusader city** walls. These walls, built by
Louis IX of France, enclose both the remains of the Herodian port
and the Crusader city itself, which was actually only one-third the
size of Herod's original city. The bulk of what you see today—the
moat, escarpment, citadel, and walls that once contained 16 towers—dates from 1251, when the French king actually pitched in
with his own two hands to spend a year restoring the existing fortifications. The Crusaders first laid siege to and conquered Caesarea in
1101 after nearly five centuries of rule by Arabs, who allowed the
port to silt up. As a reward for furnishing the fleet that was instru-
mental in the victory, the Genoese were awarded a green glass vessel found in Caesarea by the Crusaders and believed to be the Holy
Grail.

To enter the Crusader city you will cross a dry moat 42 feet deep.
However impressive, the moat scored scant success in repelling an
attack under Sultan Baybars in the late 13th century. The Mamluks
then destroyed the city to prevent its resettlement by the Christians. Still, the fortifications and the gatehouse, where you enter
the city to start your walking tour, are fine examples of medieval architecture. Note the sloping glacis against the outer wall, the shooting niches, and the groined vaults of the gatehouse.

Follow the marked signs of a designated walking tour, turning to your left outside the gatehouse past a fallen column with a carved Crusader cross. Especially after heavy rains, keep a vigilant eye out for old bronze coins, some of them smaller than a dime. As you walk under a series of four graceful arches that cover a Crusader street, you can see just to your right the remains of a Frankish house. At the southeast corner of the fortress, there is a postern gate designed for counterattack against an invading enemy. Here the surefooted can climb up onto the walls for a view of the sea and ruins. Continue for about 60 feet toward the beach and then down the stairs. To the right are the remains of the unfinished **Crusader cathedral,** built on the site of a Byzantine church; the three graceful curves of its apses stand out. Both churches stood on the ruins of the temple Herod dedicated to Augustus on this promontory dominating the port. The collapse of the underlying vaulted chambers halted construction of the Crusader church.

At the railing in front of the church ruins there is a lookout over the ancient port, now under water, as well as a view northward to Zichron Ya'akov and Haifa all the way up the coast. On a clear day, the shadowy outlines of the submerged harbor construction can be best observed, however, from the top terrace of the tower, now the Citadel restaurant. Underwater tours with marked maps of the port area are offered by the port's scuba-diving center (*see* Sports and the Outdoors, *below*).

Even today, Herod's monumental port, **Sebastos,** may be regarded as an awesome achievement. The 1st-century Jewish historian Flavius Josephus glowingly described the wonders of Sebastos and compared it to Athens's port of Piraeus; once the underwater ruins were explored, it became clear that what had been long dismissed by many historians as hyperbole was as Josephus described it.

Its construction was an unprecedented challenge; never before had such a large artificial harbor been built. There was a total absence of islands or bays as natural protection; furthermore, work was hindered by bad weather. During preliminary underwater digs in 1978, archaeologists were stunned to discover concrete blocks near the breakwater offshore, an indication of the highly sophisticated use of hydraulic concrete, which hardens underwater. Though historians knew that the Romans had developed such techniques, before the discoveries at Caesarea, hydraulic concrete was never known to have been used on such a massive scale. The main ingredient in the concrete, volcanic ash, was probably imported from Mt. Vesuvius in Italy; it is likely that the wooden forms were, too. Teams of professional divers actually did much of the trickiest work laying the foundations hundreds of meters offshore. To inhibit the natural process of silting, engineers designed sluice channels to cut through the breakwaters and flush out the harbor. Herod's engineers had also devised underwater structures to break the impact of waves.

When finished, two massive breakwaters—one stretching west and then north from the Citadel restaurant some 1,800 feet and the other 600 feet long, both now submerged—sheltered an area of about 3.5 acres from the waves and tides. The port also featured two towers each mounted by three colossal statues at the entrance on the breakwaters; although neither the tower nor the statues have been found, a tiny medal that bears their image was discovered in the first underwater excavations here in 1960. The finished harbor also contained the dominating temple to Augustus and cavernous storage facilities along the shoreline. The port was devastated by an earthquake in AD 130. The Crusaders only reutilized a small section of the harbor when they conquered Caesarea in 1101.

Under the observation point, veer right past the warehouses. Here you can explore some of the souvenir and glass shops or stop for a meal. Pause before you leave at the Roman pier, where there is a marked mooring stone.

Back outside, just across from the Crusader city entrance is a small sunken, fenced-in area known as the **Byzantine street.** It was during this period and in late Roman times that Caesarea thrived as a center of Christian scholarship and as an episcopal see; in the 7th century, Caesarea had a famous library with some 30,000 volumes that originated with the collection of illustrious Christian philosopher Origen (185–254), who lived in Caesarea for two decades. Eusebius, who was an ecclesiastical advisor to Emperor Constantine and is known as the Church's first historian, became Caesarea's first bishop in the 4th century. Once lined with workshops and stores, the street is paved with marble slabs, and a mosaic has been uncovered. Towering over the street are two monumental marble statues that face each other, both probably carted here from nearby Roman temples. The provenance of the milky white one is unknown; the purple porphyry figure could have been commissioned by the Emperor Hadrian when he visited Caesarea. In Byzantine times the city grew an estimated eight times as large in area as the fortified Crusader city. Exciting remains of this same Byzantine city are currently being uncovered in the ongoing excavations visible from the road, between the Roman theater and the Crusader city.

Time Out Next door, in the shade of a cluster of trees, is a café/restaurant called **The Statues,** where you can munch on Middle Eastern salads, kebabs, and hamburgers. Sit amidst the fallen marble columns outdoors, weather permitting. *Tel. 06/361135. Open 9 AM–10 PM.*

Turn right onto the road that starts at the Crusader city and skirts the Byzantine street, heading east. On your right, around 1 kilometer (.6 mile) from the Crusader city, is a stone arch, beyond which is the site of Herod's largely unexcavated **hippodrome.** A fabulously popular stadium for chariot races and other athletic competitions, this was possibly one of the largest such arenas in the Roman world—some 1,400 feet long and 290 feet wide, with a seating capacity of 38,000. Pieces of a toppled obelisk made of Egyptian granite lie in the middle of the now neglected field. Archaeologists believe the Byzantine walls of the city ran just east of here.

To get to the **Roman aqueduct** on the beach, drive a quick kilometer (.6 mile) after the hippodrome and turn left into the modern residential section, where you can drive around to admire some of Israel's tonier beach property. Swaths of brilliant bougainvillea are often the principal ornament to these stark whitewashed villas, many of them very luxurious. Just beyond the entrance to the area, at a stone sculpture shaped like an inverted loop, turn left at a sign that indicates Cluster 2; the road leads to the beach.

The chain of arches tumbling north toward the horizon where they disappear beneath the sand is a captivating sight, and they form a unique backdrop for a swim at the pretty beach (*see* Beaches, *below*). During Roman rule, the demand for a steady supply of water for the city's drinking, household use, public baths, and city fountains was considerable. The source of water, however, was a spring about 13 kilometers (8 miles) away in the foothills of Mt. Carmel. Workers labored to cut a channel approximately 6.5 kilometers (4 miles) long through solid rock before the water was piped into the aqueduct, whose arches spanned a length of 6.5 kilometers (4 miles). In the 2nd century, Hadrian doubled its capacity by adding a new channel. Today, you can walk along the sea side of the aqueduct and find marble plaques dedicated to the support troops of various legions who toiled here.

Tour 2: The Rothschild Wine Country and Mt. Carmel

This is the back-door route to Haifa, one that meanders through the foothills and up the spine of Mt. Carmel through the Druze villages.

Instead of shooting straight up the coastal highway when you leave Caesarea, exit from the residential section with a left turn; turn left again on Route 4 and then make the first right after 2 kilometers (1.2 miles) for **Binyamina,** which is another 2 kilometers (1.2 miles) up the road. The approach to Binyamina is gently undulating, the countryside dotted with cypresses, palms, and cultivated fields and vineyards.

This is the youngest of the settlements in the area, founded in 1922, and named after Baron Edmond de Rothschild (1845–1934), the head of the French branch of the famous family, who took a keen interest in the welfare of his fellow Jews in Palestine. With his contributions, prestige, and vision, Rothschild, whose Hebrew name was Benyamin, laid the foundations starting in the late 19th century for three towns along this itinerary as well as others along the coastal plain and in parts of the Upper Galilee.

At least in this region, the advice of viniculture experts Rothschild hired in the 1880s paid off handsomely, and after years of initial adversity and setbacks, the fruit of the vines flourished in the 1890s. The paternalistic system he set up, however, was not without its pitfalls. Some of his administrators ruled his colonies like petty despots: for instance, trying to impose use of the French language despite the wishes of the local settlers to speak Hebrew. Note in Binyamina—as in many of the Rothschild towns—the unmistakable signs of early settlement that are respectfully preserved: the rows of the lofty, willowy Washingtonian palms introduced to the area by the local hero and agronomist Aaron Aaronson of neighboring Zichron Ya'akov; and the modest one-story stucco homes capped with red terra-cotta roofs evocative of the charm of towns in Provence, which were models for these settlements.

When you come to the railroad tracks, turn left onto Route 652. Only 1 kilometer (.6 mile) north of Binyamina, already climbing into the foothills of Mt. Carmel, you reach the site of **Shuni** in the landscaped Jabotinsky Park. This land was part of a parcel purchased by Rothschild in 1914, but its chief attractions today are the **Ottoman fortress** and the **Roman theater** that were recently restored. Shuni was also the source of the spring water that was tapped for the aqueducts of ancient Caesarea. In the 1930s and '40s, because of its remote location, it was chosen as a training ground for members of self-organized units inspired by Ze'ev Jabotinsky (1880–1940), the right-wing Zionist leader who was the spiritual leader of the Jewish underground organization Irgun Zvai Leumi; armed Irgun units later staged attacks from here.

The stone fortress was built by effendis on existing ruins in the 18th and 19th centuries because of their sweeping command over surrounding lands, some planted with grain; *shuni* is Arabic for granary. Ongoing excavations have brought to light the remains of bathing pools lined with 2nd-century Roman mosaics and a marble statue of the Greek god of medicine, Aesculapius, both now in storage at the Rockefeller Museum in Jerusalem. These finds support the theory that this was once a sacred spa. On the right, before entering the fortress, you can still see part of a mosaic floor. An ancient olive press, carved lintels, and fragments of columns lie in the well-preserved 2nd-century Roman theater, entered through the fortress. Call ahead to arrange for a guided tour of the site. *Tel. 06/389730. Admission: NIS 4 ($1.35) adults, NIS 3 ($1) children. Open Sun.–Thurs. 9–4, Fri. and holiday eves 9–12:30.*

Time Out The **Jabotinsky Park** grounds are an ideal place for a picnic, with tables and plenty of shade. The park is next to the fortress and overlooks a plain; in spring it is filled with wild cyclamen and other wildflowers.

7 Continue for 3.5 kilometers (2.2 miles) until you see the sign to the left for **Ramat Hanadiv,** literally the "the Benefactor's Heights" (Rothschild Memorial Gardens), which is the setting for the tomb of the Baron and his wife, the Baroness Adelaide. Set on 450 hectares (1,112 acres) of parkland, the stunning gardens that surround the family crypt lie 2 kilometers (1.2 miles) up an unpaved road with memorable views of the Sharon Plain you just left behind. Over the wrought-iron gateway to the garden is the family coat of arms, a bronze shield supported by a gilded lion and unicorn, capped by a coronet. Inside, the well-tended gardens are filled with a mixture of indigenous and foreign flora. Cedars of Lebanon and cypresses grow on lawns interspersed with rose and palm gardens. On the western edge is a panoramic view of Caesarea and Hadera to the south and Dor and the fish ponds of Kibbutz Ma'agan Michael to the north; a stone map marks the regional settlements founded or sponsored by the Baron. The Rothschilds' wish to be buried here was carried out only after the Jewish state was established; in 1954, an Israeli warship brought their remains from France. Opposite the exit is a refreshment kiosk and picnic tables. There is also a map of a marked three-hour hike from the gardens past the Kebara prehistoric caves (at press time closed for excavation) along the cliff, with great views of the coast. *Tel. 06/397821. Admission free. Open Sun.–Thurs. 8–4, Fri. and holiday eves 8–2, Sat. 8–4.*

8 Two kilometers (1.2 miles) beyond the gardens you arrive at a planted roundabout at the entrance to **Zichron Ya'akov,** named by the original settlers in honor of Rothschild's father, James. Just opposite is the tourist information office, next to the Founders' Monument and the central bus station. Here you can obtain a map of the town; most of the main sites are signposted in English.

Founded in 1882 by Romanian pioneers, this settlement nearly foundered until rescued by Edmond de Rothschild. A decade later, the town's winery took off, the same **Carmel Oriental Wine Cellars** that can be reached by veering to the right from the roundabout and driving up Jabotinsky Street. Where the street ends, turn right on Hanadiv Street. Today, the winery is the nation's second largest, producing more than 80 kinds of wines and spirits. A three-day wine festival takes place here after the harvest, around the time of the Jewish holiday of Sukkoth. The original storage vats and oak barrels are still on view, but storage is now mostly in stainless-steel vats and concrete tanks. A guided tour follows the stages of local wine production—the winery uses a computerized fermentation system and automated bottling lines—from the weighing in of tractors laden with grapes to grape pressing and the aging of wine in caves. The 75-minute tour includes a wine-tasting of some five varieties and an audiovisual presentation that is frankly so rudimentary it might have you yawning *before* you taste the wine. The first tour—tours leave whenever there's a large enough group—starts at 9 AM and the last at 3 PM. You'll find a much better selection of wine sold here than in wine stores elsewhere, and you get a 15% discount. The finest wines are the Rothschild vintages: Cabernet Sauvignon, Sauvignon Blanc, and Fume Blanc. Locally made gin, vodka, and brandy are also available. *Tel. 06/396709 or 06/390105. Advance telephone reservations recommended. Admission: NIS 9 ($3) adults, NIS 6 ($2) children. Open Sun.–Thurs. 9–3, Fri. 9–12:30.*

Retrace your steps back up Jabotinsky Street to the roundabout at the entrance to town. Head up Hameyasdim Street past the Founders' Monument on the corner to **Bet Aaronson** (Aaronson's House), whose late-19th century architecture is a successful combination of Art Nouveau and Middle Eastern traditions. This museum was once the home of the accomplished agronomist Aaron Aaronson (1876–1919), who gained international fame for his discovery of an ancestor of modern wheat, a wild and hardy strain that grew in the surrounding mountains. The house is preserved as it was after World War I, with family photographs and French and Turkish furniture. The museum also houses the library, diaries, and letters of Aaronson, who in his youth was sent to France by Rothschild to study agriculture.

Aaronson and his sisters became local heroes as leaders of the spy ring called the NILI (an acronym for a quote from the Book of Samuel: "The Eternal One of Israel will not prove false"), a militant group dedicated to ousting the hated Turks from Palestine by collaborating with the British during World War I. They were spurred on by the harshness of such Turkish policies as the expulsion of Russian Jews from Palestine (the Russians were enemies of the Turks during World War I) and the confiscation of Jewish property.

Both sisters, Sarah and Rebecca, were in love with Aaron's assistant, Absalom Feinberg. A double agent was disrupting NILI's communications with the British, so Feinberg set off to cross the Sinai desert to make contact. He was killed in an ambush in the Gaza Strip. His remains were recovered some 50 years later from a grave marked simply by a palm tree, the tree having sprouted from some dates in Feinberg's pockets. (After the Six Day War, Feinberg's body was reburied in Jerusalem.) Sarah Aaronson was captured by the Turks, and committed suicide in her brother's house after being tortured. Other NILI leaders were executed by the Turks when they discovered the secret organization. Aaron returned to Zichron Ya'akov with the victorious British in 1918, but the following year his plane mysteriously vanished while en route from London to the Paris Peace Conference. *40 Hameyasdim St., tel. 06/390120. Admission: NIS 6 ($2) adults, NIS 4 ($1.35) children. Open Sun.–Thurs. 8:30–1, Tues. 3:30–5:30, Fri. 9–noon.*

Continue straight past the **Binyamin Pool** a few doors up, which was the town's old water tower. Its facade resembles that of an ancient synagogue. At the corner on the left stands the actual town synagogue, **Bet Ya'akov,** built in 1885 to fulfill the settlers' first request of Rothschild. Turn left onto Hanadiv Street, which will take you past a children's park and to the former town hall on the left corner. Commissioned by Rothschild, this is a fine example of late-19th century Ottoman-style architecture in white stone with a central pediment capped by a tile roof. The building is being restored as a museum dedicated to the town's first pioneers.

Turn right into Herzl Street, then left into Habroshim Street to reach **Bet Daniel** (Daniel's House), a tranquil oasis for writers, musicians, and artists set in the woods on the western edge of town with a wonderful view of the Carmel coast. In 1938 Lillian Friedlander built Bet Daniel, now a small cluster of one- and two-story buildings, as a retreat for musicians after the death of her son Daniel, a highly gifted pianist. A child prodigy, Daniel was sent to study at The Juilliard School in New York, where he committed suicide at the age of 18.

Today, Bet Daniel remains a setting for concerts and music classes and workshops, in addition to being a guest house open to the public (*see* Dining and Lodging, *below*). Daniel's 1905 Steinway from New York still stands in the dining room, furnished with other family antiques and photographs. The closely guarded guest roster bears such illustrious names as Isaac Stern, Leonard Bernstein, Aaron Copland, and Arturo Toscanini. A chamber music festival is held twice a year in a small concert hall on the grounds (*see* The Arts and Nightlife, *below*).

Don't leave Zichron Ya'akov without driving around the rim of the town with its panoramic view of the coastal plain below, punctuated with the sparkling commercial fish ponds and lush fields planted with banana trees and vineyards. From Bet Daniel return to Herzl Street and turn left. Where the street ends turn left again into Tar'av Street, which soon becomes Ma'ale Hacarmel, the left branch of a small fork in the road. As you round a bend to the left, you'll come upon an excellent observation point at Hagana Street, where there is a charming little corner park with benches.

Time Out   Only 300 feet ahead is the **Casa Barone,** the restaurant of Bet Maimon hotel (*see* Dining and Lodging, *below*), which has a stunning view from its terrace. There's something for everyone here, from spaghetti to Eastern European fare. You're also welcome for just coffee and homemade strudel with nuts and dates. *Tel. 06/390212. Open daily for morning coffee, lunch, and dinner.*

To exit Zichron Ya'akov continue around another bend after passing Bet Maimon, making the first right down to Nili Avenue. Then turn right, winding downhill to the Zichron Ya'akov interchange at the bottom. Here, drive north on Route 4 for only 3 kilometers (1.9 miles), then head east on Route 70 in the direction of Yokne'am. **Bat Shlomo,** the last Rothschild settlement in your path, lies 6 kilometers (3.7 miles) ahead. It was established in 1889 and named after the Baron's mother, Betty, the daughter of Solomon. Growth in this tiny hamlet established for the children of Zichron Ya'akov farmers was stymied and the town remains virtually unchanged. There is only one street in the old part of the village and it is still lined with typical pioneer stucco homes. Some of the owners still cultivate the land and sell locally made cheese, olive oil, and honey, much like their forebears.

Proceed 7 kilometers (4.3 miles) to a junction, where you turn left into Route 672 toward Daliyat el Carmel and Mukhraka; this road is one of the main entrances to the Carmel National Park. To reach ❾ **Mukhraka** drive 8 kilometers (5 miles); turn right into a narrow, sometimes bumpy road. Continue 3 kilometers (1.9 miles) through open, uncultivated fields, past a goatherd's rickety shack, to the **Carmelite Monastery.** This monastery stands on the spur of the Carmel range on or near the site where tradition has it that the struggle between Elijah and the priests of Ba'al took place. Mukhraka is the Arabic word for a place of burning, referring to the fire that consumed the offering on Elijah's altar. The conflict developed because the people of Israel had been seduced by the pagan cults introduced by King Ahab's wife, Jezebel. Elijah demanded a contest with the priests of Ba'al in which each would erect an altar with a butchered ox as an offering and see which divinity sent down fire. Elijah drenched his altar with water, yet it burst into flames. On his orders, the priests were taken down to the Brook of Kishon and executed.

The stark stone monastery was built in 1883 over earlier Byzantine ruins. Records show that the site was revered as early as the 6th century, when hermits dwelled here. The Carmelites, a Roman Catholic monastic order established in the 13th century, view Elijah as a role model for their monks (the Muslims also revere Elijah as a prophet). Today, the monks who live here have no telephones and only a generator for power. In the courtyard is a statue of a fearless Elijah brandishing a knife. Climb to the roof of the monastery for an unforgettable panorama: to the east stretches the Jezreel Valley and the hills of Nazareth, Moreh, and Gilboa. On a clear day you can even see the Gilead mountains beyond the Jordan River and Mt. Hermon. *No phone. Admission: NIS 1 (35¢). Open Mon.–Sat. 8–1:30 and 2:30–5. Closed Sun. after noon mass.*

Return to the junction with Route 672 and turn right. Only 2 kilometers (1.2 miles) up the road is the largest Druze village in Israel, **⑩ Daliyat el Carmel.** The Druze are an Arabic-speaking people with a secret religion. So exclusive is this sect that only around 6% of the community is initiated into its religious doctrine. The Druze broke away from Islam about 1,000 years ago, believing in the divinity of their founder, al Hakim bi Amir Allah, the Caliph of the Egyptian Fatimid dynasty from AD 996 to 1021.

The Druze who live in the two existing villages on Mt. Carmel (the other is Isfya; *see below*) resettled an area inhabited by the Druze centuries earlier. Today, many Druze serve in the Israeli Army, a sign of their loyalty to Israel, and are fiercely proud of their distinct identity from their Arab neighbors. Though many of the younger generation simply wear jeans and T-shirts, some older men and women are easily recognizable in their traditional garb. The few men with squat red turbans are the religious leaders. Many men sport a bushy, walruslike moustache, a hallmark of the Druze, and some older ones wear flowing dark robes and the distinctive pure white scarf draped around their heads, minus the black cord usually worn by Muslims. Although many women wear Western garments, they retain the diaphanous white headdress.

About 1 kilometer (.6 mile) inside town, take a right turn into the marketplace, a colorful jumble of shops lining the street. Here, Druze merchants hawk their wares: ceramics, rugs, wall hangings, handwoven baskets, hammered brass dishes, and even some cobalt blue Hebron glassware. Some shops are closed on Friday.

Neighboring **Isfiya** is very similar, with homes built into the hillside, many of them raised up on stilts, with arched windows. As you leave the village at the top of the hill, note the vista of the Jezreel Valley suddenly opening on your right. The final approach to Haifa also affords a magnificent view of the coast that stretches from Akko across the bay to south of the city.

Tour 3: In and Around Haifa

Haifa   Spilling down from the pine-covered heights of Mt. Carmel to the
⑪   blue Mediterranean is **Haifa,** whose vertiginous setting has led to
perhaps hyperbolic comparisons with San Francisco. Israel's largest port and third largest city, Haifa was ruled for four centuries by
the Ottomans, and gradually grew up the mountainside into a cosmopolitan city whose port once served the entire Middle East. In
1902, Theodor Herzl enthusiastically dubbed Haifa "the city of the
future."

By 1924 Haifa was already becoming a center for science and technology with the opening of the Technion Institute. The construction
by the Turks at the turn of the century of the Hijaz Railway, which
stretched from Constantinople via Damascus to the Muslim holy cities of Mecca and Medina, proved a boon to Haifa, which had its own
branch of the new line to Damascus. Under the British Mandate, a
deep-water port was dug and opened to world traffic in 1933; the following year Haifa was hooked up by an oil pipeline to Iraq. After
Israel's independence, Haifa's links with neighboring Arab states
were broken, but today cruise ships from abroad ply its waters and
the Technion is still the nation's citadel of scientific research.

First mentioned in the Talmud, the area of Haifa was the site of two
settlements in ancient times: To the east, in what is today a congested industrial zone in the port, lay **Zalmona;** 4.8 kilometers (3
miles) west around the cape was **Shiqmona.** The Crusaders conquered Haifa, then an important Arab town, and maintained it as a
fortress along the coastal road to Akko for two centuries. Like much
of the Crusader kingdom, Haifa was lost and regained repeatedly by
the Christians. During this period, in 1154, the Order of Our Lady of
Mount Carmel (the Carmelite order) was founded on the slopes of
Mt. Carmel by a group of hermits following the principles of the
prophet Elijah and the rules of poverty, vegetarianism, and solitude. After Akko and Haifa succumbed to Mamluk Sultan Baybars
in 1265, Haifa was destroyed and left derelict, just as it had been at
the end of Byzantine rule. For centuries, Haifa remained a sleepy
fishing village.

It reawakened under the rule of Bedouin sheikh Dahr el-Omar, who
had rebelled against direct Ottoman rule in the mid-18th century and
independently governed Akko and the Galilee. Dahr recognized that
Haifa's location made it vulnerable to attack; in 1761 he ordered the
city to be demolished and moved 2 or 3 kilometers (1 or 2 miles) to the
south. The new town was fortified by walls and protected by a castle. The new port began to compete with that of Akko across the bay,
for while its harbor was not as good as Akko's, Mt. Carmel offered a
natural barrier against the strong southwesterly winds and, therefore, a comfortable anchorage.

Napoléon, too, came to Haifa, though only briefly and on his way to
ignominious defeat at Akko during his Eastern Campaign. Napoléon left his wounded at the Carmelite Monastery (*see below*) in
Haifa when he beat a retreat in 1799, but the French soldiers there
were killed and the monks driven out by Ahmed el-Jazzar, the victorious pasha of Akko.

*Numbers in the margin correspond to points of interest on the Haifa
map.*

Today, the metropolis is divided into three main levels that run parallel to the harbor, crisscrossed with parks and gardens. The downtown port encompasses the largely uninhabited Old City; the

midtown area, called Hadar HaCarmel, or Hadar for short, was one of the early Jewish neighborhoods that is today a bustling shopping area; and Central Carmel, or Mercaz HaCarmel, is on top, home to upscale residential developments and the posher hotels. The most striking landmark on the mountainside is the gleaming golden dome of the Baha'i Shrine. The Carmelit subway (*see* Getting Around *in* Essential Information, *above*), which reopened in July 1992 after six years of repair, rises from the port to the upper city with numerous stops along the way. It is Israel's only subway.

12 A good way to orient yourself is to gaze down at Haifa as you stroll along **Yefe Nof Street** (Panorama Road), which skirts the back side of the biggest hotels and descends the mountain to the Baha'i Shrine. On a clear day, from any of several observation points, the naked eye can telescope the smokestacks of the port below, Akko across the bay, and the cliffs of Rosh Hanikra with Lebanon in the distance. Many of the older buildings dating from the Turkish period can be distinguished by their red-tile roofs.

13 Just across from the Nof Hotel, at 101 Hanassi Avenue, is the **Mané Katz Museum,** the studio and house where the Expressionist painter Emmanuel Katz (1894–1962) lived and worked from 1958 until his death. This whitewashed building with ornamental grillwork on the windows houses a collection of Katz's paintings, drawings, and sculptures—the Ukrainian-born artist's legacy to the city. Katz spent the 1920s in Paris, where he exhibited with a group of Jewish artists from the École de Paris. As in the canvases of fellow members Marc Chagall and Chaim Soutine, a recurring theme in his work is the village life of Jews in Eastern Europe. The artist was an avid collector of rugs and 17th-century antiques from Spain and Germany, which are also on display along with objects from his Judaica collection. *89 Yefe Nof St., tel. 04/383482. Admission free. Open Sun.– Thurs. 10–4, Fri, Sat., and holidays 10–1.*

Continue down the hill on Yefe Nof Street to where it ends. Make a right and, doubling back, a sharp right again and you will be on **Sderot Hatziyonut** (Zionism Boulevard). This street was originally named after the United Nations, but following the 1975 passage of a UN resolution that equated Zionism with racism (it was rescinded in 1992), the city government quickly changed it.

Time Out On your left is the entrance to a small sculpture garden that overlooks Haifa Bay. From one of the benches on a winding path through the garden you can contemplate the life-size bronzes of humans and animals by sculptor Ursula Malbin. Malbin, a refugee from Nazi Germany, divides her time between the artists' village of Ein Hod (*see below*), south of Haifa, and a village near Geneva, Switzerland.

14 Just a bit farther on your left is the main gate to the Baha'i gardens and the **Shrine of the Bab,** whose gilded dome dominates as well as illuminates Haifa's skyline. Haifa is the world center for the Baha'i Faith, which was founded in Iran in the 19th century and holds as its central belief the unity of mankind. For Baha'is, religious truth is not dogmatic, rather it consists of progressive revelations of a universal faith. Thus the Baha'is teach that great prophets have appeared throughout history to reveal divine truths. Among these have been Moses, Zoroaster, Buddha, Jesus, Mohammed, and most recently, the founder of the Baha'i Faith, Mirza Husayn Ali, known as Baha'u'llah—the Glory of God. Baha'u'llah was exiled from his native Persia by the Shah and then by the Ottomans to Akko, where he lived as a prisoner for almost 25 years. The holiest shrine for Baha'is is on the grounds of Baha'u'llah's home, where he lived after his release from prison and which is his final resting place, just north of Akko (*see* Tour 4, *below*).

At the center of the Shrine's magnificently manicured gardens is the mausoleum built for the Bab—which literally means "the Gate"—who heralded the coming of a new faith revealed by Baha'u'llah. The Bab was martyred by the Persian authorities in 1850. The gardens and Shrine were built by Baha'u'llah's son and successor, who had the Bab's remains reburied here in 1909. The 128-foot-high building, made of Italian-cut stone, gracefully combines the canons of classical European architecture with elements of the East, and also houses the remains of Baha'u'llah's son. The dome glistens with some 12,000 gilded tiles imported from Holland. Inside, the floor is covered with rich Oriental carpets, and a filigree veil divides visitors from the inner Shrine.

The hush of the largely geometrically arranged gardens is now periodically disturbed by construction work that will create new terraces extending down the slope all the way to the German Colony (*see below*) as well as up the mountain to Yefe Nof Street. The Shrine of the Bab, along with the Shrine of Baha'u'lla north of Akko are sites of pilgrimage for the worldwide Baha'i community. Visitors to the shrine are asked to dress modestly. *65 Sderot Hatziyonut, tel. 04/358358. Admission free. Shrine open daily 9–noon; gardens daily 9–5.*

Across Sderot Hatziyonut and just above the shrine is the green-roofed Archives building; still further up the slope is the newest building of the administrative center. This large, white-domed, neoclassical structure is the seat of the Universal House of Justice, the supreme administrative body of the Faith. Both buildings are closed to the public. The entire complex was built with contributions by the Baha'is, some 5 million adherents in more than 230 countries. Under the current regime in Iran, one of the world's largest Baha'i communities still suffers persecution.

15 Back on Sderot Hatziyonut take Bus 25 or 26 to the **Carmelite Monastery** and the **Stella Maris lighthouse,** located on a promontory. During the Crusader period, on the steep mountain slope, groups of hermits emulating the life of the prophet Elijah lived in caves near the present monastery. In the early 13th century they united under the leadership of the Italian pilgrim (later a saint) Berthold, who petitioned the patriarch of Jerusalem for a charter for the group. Thus was born the Carmelite order, which spread across Europe. The Carmelite monks were forced to leave their settlements on Mt. Carmel at the end of the 13th century, when Akko fell to the Mamluks, and did not return until nearly four centuries later. When they found Elijah's cave inhabited by Muslim dervishes, they set up a rudimentary monastery nearby. Dahr el-Omar drove them out again in 1767.

The church of the present monastery dates from 1836 and was built with the munificence of the French monarchy; hence the surrounding neighborhood is known as French Carmel. The French connection is explained by a small pyramid topped with an iron cross that stands before the entrance of the basilica-style church. The monument commemorates the French who were slaughtered here by the Turks in 1799 after the retreating Napoléon left his ailing troops behind to be treated in what was then a military hospital at the monastery. Inside, the academic paintings in the dome depict Elijah in the chariot of fire in which he ascended to heaven, and Old Testament prophets. The small cave a few steps down at the end of the nave is traditionally associated with Elijah and his pupil, Elisha. A small museum near the entrance contains some fossils and Byzantine artifacts discovered in the area. Across the street from the church, at the tip of the promontory, is the Stella Maris—star of the sea—lighthouse, built for the Turkish fleet in the early 19th century and still in use. It is not open to the public. *Carmelite Monastery, Stella Maris Rd., tel. 04/337758. Admission free. Open daily 6:30–1:30, 3–6.*

16 It's a 20-minute walk down to **Elijah's Cave** on the fairly steep path across from the entrance to the church. (Otherwise take Bus 25 to the last stop in Central Carmel. Turn right on Herzl Street, then left on Shapira Street and catch Bus 44 or 45 to Elijah's Cave.) The cave, 100 feet up from street level, is considered sacred by Jews, Christians, and Moslems. An early Byzantine tradition identified it as the cave in which Elijah found refuge from the wrath of Ahab, king of Israel, from 871 to 851 BC. Graffiti made by pilgrims of various faiths and from different centuries are scrawled on the right wall. Written prayers are often stuffed into crevices; some suppliants come to ask for fertility, others for better fortune or to be cured of an illness. Modest dress is requested. *230 Allenby Rd., tel. 04/527430. Admission free. Open Sun.–Thurs. 8–5, Fri., Sat. and holiday eves 8–1.*

Walk down the flight of stairs that leads from the cave to Allenby **17** Road, turn left and cross the road to the **Clandestine Immigration 18 and Naval Museum**; to the right is the **National Maritime Museum.** The rather dull name of the former belies the dramatic nature of its contents. The Clandestine Immigration and Naval Museum chronicles the story of the often heroic efforts to bring Jewish immigrants surreptitiously to Palestine, many of them refugees aboard ships fleeing war-torn Europe. The exhibits are labeled in English. In addition to a clearly marked map that pinpoints the immigration routes, there are video presentations, photographs, and documents that record both deportations and successful missions.

Emigration to Palestine was well nigh impossible after the British imposed a naval blockade, bowing to pressure by Arabs opposed to Jewish immigration. In 1939, on the eve of World War II, the British issued the so-called White Paper, which effectively strangled Jewish immigration to Palestine and prohibited Jews from buying land there. Little boats sometimes managed to elude the vigilant British warships and put ashore their human cargoes at secret landing beaches. But for bigger ships the odds were daunting. Out of 63 clandestine ships that tried to run the blockade after the war's end, all but five were intercepted and their passengers deported to Cyprus.

The museum is full of moving stories of courage, tenacity, and disaster. A photomural of the celebrated ship, the *Exodus*, recalls the story of the 4,530 refugees aboard who were forcibly transferred back to Germany in 1947, but not before the British forces opened fire on the rebellious ship, convincing the passengers and crew to surrender. Another tragic episode took place aboard the *Struma*, a leaky vessel that was forced to anchor in Istanbul for repairs in 1941. The Turks refused to assist the ship after warnings from the British. So, unable to continue and its passengers unwilling to return, the boat wallowed in Istanbul harbor for two months and finally sank a few miles offshore. There was one survivor among the 767 aboard.

One of the blockade runners was an old American tank-landing craft renamed *Af-al-pi-chen* (Nevertheless), which serves as the center-

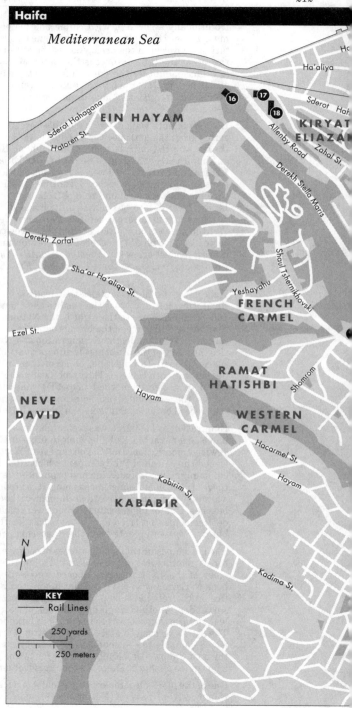

Haifa

Mediterranean Sea

EIN HAYAM

Ha'aliya

Sderot Hahagana

Hatoren St.

Derekh Zorfat

Sha'ar Ha'aliqa St.

Ezel St.

NEVE
DAVID

Hayam

KABABIR

Kabirim St.

Sderot Hak

KIRYAT
ELIAZAN

Allenby Road

Zahal St.

Derekh Stella Maris

Shaul Tshernikhovski

Yeshayahu

FRENCH
CARMEL

RAMAT
HATISHBI

Shomrom

WESTERN
CARMEL

Hacarmel St.

Hayam

Kadima St.

N

KEY
— Rail Lines

0   250 yards

0   250 meters

BAT GALIM

Mediterranean Sea

Hasharon

Hashnia

Hahagana

YAT
ZAR

al St.

Heyl Hayam St.

Tel Aviv St.

KIRYAT
ELIAHU

Deror

Sderot James
de Rothchild

Yizhaq Sade St.

Sderot Hameginim

Allenby Rd

Haganim St.

Ben Gurion Blvd.

Hagefen Blvd.

Jaffa

Harbor

Sderot Ha'atzma'ut

Shivat Zion St.

15

19

Khoury St.

22

20

Blvd. l

(Z)ionism

21

Y. L. Perez St.

Hassan

14

Sderot Hatziyonut

Shabbetai Levy St.

Baerwald St.

Shukri

Bialik

Yefe Nof

Gid'on St.

Hanassi Avenue

12

13

Eliyahu Golumb St.

Hahashmona'im St.

Arlosoroff St.

Balfour St.

Spinoza

Peysner St.

23

Herzl St.

Nordau St.

Kibbutz Galuyot St.

HADAR
HA'CARMEL

Bilu

Hakishon

24

Sderot Wedgewood

Sderot Wingate

Sderot Kish

Hapoel St.

Geula St.

CENTRAL
CARMEL

25

Ha'asif St.

TEL AMAL

piece of the museum, accessible from the roof. This ship left Italy in 1947 for Palestine and was intercepted by the British. Its 434 passengers, all survivors of the Holocaust, were sent to internment camps in Cyprus. *204 Allenby Rd., 04/536249. Admission: NIS 5 ($1.70) adults, NIS 2 (70¢) children. Open Sun.–Thurs. 9–4, Fri. and holiday eves 9–1.*

Back on Allenby Road, 150 feet past the stairway to Elijah's Cave, is the entrance to the **National Maritime Museum,** which examines sea voyages of a different stripe. Here, 5,000 years of maritime history is told with models of ships, archaeological finds, coins minted with nautical symbols, navigational instruments, and other artifacts. There are also a number of intriguing underwater finds from nearby excavations and shipwrecks. *198 Allenby Rd., tel. 04/536622. Admission: NIS 5 ($1.70) adults, NIS 4 ($1.35) children. Open Sun.–Thurs. 10–4, Sat. 10–1.*

Across the street, you can catch Bus 44 on Allenby, leaving the seashore behind and heading toward the **German Colony.** Get off at the stop before Ben Gurion Boulevard, which runs on a direct axis from the Baha'i Shrine halfway up the mountain to the harbor. Turn right into Ben Gurion Boulevard and you find yourself in the heart of what was, in the late 19th century, a colony established by the German Templar religious reform movement. Note the robust two- and three-story stone houses with red-tile roofs typical of the neighborhood. There are a few good restaurants along the walk uphill. Some houses still bear German names on the lintels above the doors. The Templars' colony in Haifa was the most important one in the Holy Land. The early settlers formed a self-sufficient community that enjoyed quite a comfortable standard of living. By 1883 there were nearly 100 houses built, and as many families.

The Germans introduced several improvements in transportation to Haifa. Unknown until their arrival was the horse-drawn wagon. The ever-industrious Germans started to make wagons locally and then built with their own funds a road from Haifa to Nazareth as a pilgrimage route. Their labors gave rise to modern workshops and warehouses; under their influence, Haifa began to take on the semblance of a modern Western city, with well-laid-out streets, gardens, and attractive homes.

Haifa's importance to Germany was highlighted in 1898 when Kaiser Wilhelm II sailed into the bay as the first stop on the first official visit to the Holy Land by a German emperor in more than 600 years. For the occasion, the ruling Turkish sultan ordered a new jetty built. During World War II the Germans who lived in the colony were expelled, suspected of being Nazis.

The German Templars and the French Carmelite monks on the hill were on no better terms than their compatriots back home. A battle took shape in 1885 along nationalistic lines when the Germans bought some acreage on the mountain and the French monks refused to let them cross their own land to get there. The case ended up in a Haifa court, and the monks were ordered to allow the Germans access to their land.

Where the street ends at the Baha'i gardens, turn left into Hagefen Boulevard, continuing three blocks to **Bet Hagefen** (the Arab–Jewish Center), on your left in the striking but simple two-story stone building just before the traffic light. Founded 30 years ago, it was the first and only such Arab–Jewish institution in Israel. Bet Hagefen's location is not accidental: It stands at the meeting place between Wadi Nisnas (*see below*), with its large Arab population, the German colony with its mixed population, and Central Carmel, which is predominantly Jewish. Throughout troubled times, the center has continued to promote the principles of coexistence and understanding between Arabs and Jews through cultural projects and exhibitions.

Open regularly to visitors is the center's small art gallery, with works on display by Arab and Jewish painters and sculptors. The center's involvement in the community extends far beyond holding art shows. Activities include meetings between Arab and Jewish schoolchildren, performances by an Arab–Jewish dance group and an Arab theater company, and a puppet show for children given in Hebrew, Arabic, and Russian. Call ahead to see what's on the calendar. *Bet Hagefen, 2 Hagefen, tel. 04/525252. Admission free. Open Sun.–Thurs. 8–1 and 4–8, Fri. 8–1, Sat. 10–1.*

Just around the corner on Sderot Hatziyonut is another haven for culture mavens, the **Artist's House,** a gallery devoted exclusively to Haifa artists. It's a good place to see the output of Russian artists (Chagall attended the official opening), Haifa's latest arrivals. Cross the street and head up Shabbetai Levy Street, skirting the side of the **Haifa Museum,** whose entrance is on a little square some 200 feet ahead. This is actually three museums in one—**Ancient Art, Modern Art,** and **Music and Ethnology.** All exhibits are clearly labeled in English.

The ancient art collection, mostly Greek and Roman stone and marble sculpture, Egyptian textiles, Greek pottery, and encaustic grave portraits from Faiyum in Lower Egypt, is one of the most notable in the country. Particularly rare are the museum's figures of fishermen from the Hellenistic period. Quite lovely are two marble heads dating from the Roman period, one portraying Dionysus and the other from an Attic tombstone. Among numerous terra-cotta figurines from Syria and Egypt are several curious animal-shape vessels, once used as playthings, incense burners, or funerary gifts, from the nearby Shiqmona excavation. Also from Egypt are a group of finely carved alabaster vessels and funerary masks.

The modern art section is articulated into several exhibits with a special emphasis on contemporary Israeli art. In addition, there are works on paper from Europe and the United States. Exhibitions of world-renowned foreign artists are also mounted regularly.

Especially intriguing in the ethnology section is the display of musical instruments dating from biblical times. Some, like the more primitive and hardy clay rattles and bone whistles, have actually survived intact. The wooden lyres and harps from various places and periods are reconstructed based on painstaking historical research. Displayed on a rotating basis are folk art, ceremonial costumes, embroidery, and jewelry gathered from seven continents. *26 Shabbetai Levy St., tel. 04/523255. Admission: NIS 7 ($2.35) adults, NIS 5 ($1.70) children. Open Sun., Mon., Fri. 10–1, Tues.–Thurs. and Sat. 10–1, 5–8.*

Exiting the museum, turn left down a flight of stairs known as the Dor Corridor, which leads to a small intersection in **Wadi Nisnas,** a colorful quarter laced with narrow streets and shops selling housewares and groceries, a slice of modern Arab life in Israel. Still, you will see men crouched on stools in front of stoops, and women in traditional dress peering out from behind curtains or ducking in doorways. Turn left at the intersection onto St. John's pedestrian mall, a humming marketplace of stalls heaped with fruit and vegetables. Open on Saturday, when many other stores in the city are closed, this market draws many Jewish customers from faraway neighborhoods.

Time Out In a city known for its falafel, there's a highly recommended **falafel joint** just around the corner on a small street parallel to the market. Turn left at the mall's end onto Khouri Street and take the first left. Some 300 feet up on your right is a tidy stand with fresh, steaming chickpea balls, warm pita bread, and all the toppings, as well as soft drinks to wash it all down.

To get to Hadar HaCarmel, or Midtown, catch Bus 21, 28, or 37 on Khouri Street heading up the hill. Get off at the stop after the bus skirts a gleaming glass shopping complex called Migdal Hanevi'im, and walk a couple of blocks up Hassan Shukri Street past the courthouses on your right. The entrance to **Memorial Park** with its memorable views of the Bay of Haifa is on your left just opposite the City Hall. Head away from the park on Baerwald Street, which cuts in between the courthouse and City Hall, and walk three blocks to **Herzl Street.** This was once the main shopping street in town. It is now connected by walkways to the parallel pedestrian shopping
㉓ mall on **Nordau Street,** which makes for a pleasant stroll amidst shops, cafés, and restaurants. Just up Balfour Street is the **Old Technion** building, which now houses the **Israel National Museum of Science** (commonly known as the Technoda), with its hands-on chemistry and physics exhibits. Buses 21, 37, and 28 on Arlosoroff Street, at the far end of the mall, will take you back to Central Carmel. Departing from the same place, Bus 24 will take you to Haifa University (*see below*).

From Central Carmel, across from the Nof Hotel on Hanassi Street,
㉔ you can take Bus 31 to the **Technion,** Israel's foremost center for applied research, set in the 300-acre Technion City, which was laid out in 1953. Founded in 1912, the doors to the original institute in Midtown only opened 12 years later, due in part to the hardships of an intervening war. Today, the Technion is highly fertile ground for the nation's scientific innovations: Two-thirds of Israel's university research in such fields as science, technology, engineering, medicine, architecture, and town planning takes place here. Visitors can get an idea of the vast scope of the studies and research conducted here at the **Coler-California Center,** located in an architecturally striking cubical concrete building. You can see descriptions of the various Technion departments on laser disc videos. Call ahead to find out when the introductory 30-minute film in English is being screened. *Coler-California Center, Technion, tel. 04/320664. Admission free. Open Sun.–Thurs. 8–2.*

㉕ You can also get Bus 30 in front of the Nof Hotel to **Haifa University,** worth the trip to see the **Reuben and Edith Hecht Museum** for its fine archaeological holdings. In the main tower on campus at the summit of Mt. Carmel, designed by Brazilian architect Oscar Niemeyer, the collection spans the millennia from the Chalcolithic era to the Roman and Byzantine periods. The artifacts, all Jewish, range from religious altars and lamps to two coffins and figurines from the Early Bronze Age. Featured prominently are finds from the excavations of the Temple Mount in Jerusalem. In addition, in a separate wing, there is a small collection of paintings, mostly Impressionist and from the Jewish School of Paris. *Tel. 04/240577. Admission free. Open Sun.–Thurs. 10–4, Fri. and holiday eves 10–1, Sat. 10–2.*

Around Haifa *Numbers in the margin correspond to points of interest on the Northern Coast and Western Galilee map.*

By car it is simple to tour these sights in leisurely succession; they are all easily accessible from either Route 2 or Route 4 heading south from Haifa. Though a bit more complicated, it is possible to see these sights by taking buses that leave from Haifa's central bus station.

From the southern tip of Haifa it's about 11 kilometers (6.8 miles) on Route 2 to the turnoff for **Atlit,** a peninsula jutting into the Mediterranean where the jagged remains of an important **Crusader castle** still stand. On your right, about 1,500 feet from the highway, is a reconstructed **detention camp** that was used during the decade prior to Israeli independence. The reconstructed barracks, fences, and watchtowers stand as reminders of how Jewish immigration was practically outlawed under the British Mandate after the publication of the infamous White Paper in 1939. More than a third of the 120,000 illegal immigrants passed through the camp from 1934 to 1948. The 45-minute tour includes the living quarters, complete with laundry hanging from the rafters. The authenticity of the exhibit is striking, re-created from accounts of actual detainees and their contemporaries. Visitors are advised to call ahead. *Rte. 2, tel. 04/841980. Admission: NIS 5 ($1.70) adults, NIS 4 ($1.35) children. Open Sun.–Thurs 9–3:30, Fri. 9–12:30, Sat. 9–3.*

To view the castle, continue straight 1 kilometer (.6 mile) along the road toward the beach, passing the left turnoff to the new town of Atlit (or take Bus 122 from Haifa) and then cross the railroad tracks. Since 1948 the castle itself has been off limits, property of the Israeli Navy. However, there is a good view of it from the windswept beach just north of the walls. Built by the Crusader order known as the Templars in 1217, this fortified castle with its natural port was known as **Château des Pelerins,** or the Pilgrims' Castle. After the fall of the Crusader capital in Akko in 1291, the Château des Pelerins became the last surviving Crusader fortress in the Holy Land. It was never taken by siege. But in August of that year, the last Crusaders set sail, and after their departure the Mamluks dismantled the fortifications just in case the Crusaders had second thoughts.

Its strategic location made the castle a natural stronghold that only needed fortifications on one side facing landward, along which several towers were erected. The ruins of two of them are visible today. There was once a moat along the eastern side that could be flooded with seawater. During the Seventh Crusade, Louis IX of France extended the fortifications, and his wife gave birth to a son here. In the 18th century, stones from the castle were used to fortify Akko; an 1837 earthquake wreaked heavy damage, leaving it in its present ruined state.

To get to the artists' village of **Ein Hod** 5 kilometers (3.1 miles) inland, head east straight past the coastal highway to Route 4, where you turn right. The exit ramp, climbing through olive trees and scrub, will be on your left. You can also get there with Bus 921 or 202 from Haifa. Today, Ein Hod is home to around 135 families of sculptors, painters, and other artists. The setting is an idyllic one, with rough-hewn stone houses built on the hillside with sweeping views. As the Dadaist painter Marcel Janco (1895–1984) wrote of the deserted Arab village slated for demolition after his first trip there, in 1950: "The beauty of the place was staggering." Though the place was ruled by scorpions and snakes and was without water or electricity, Janco and a group of 20 artists set up a colony here two years later.

The town square is bordered by a restaurant and a large **gallery** where works by present and past Ein Hod artists are exhibited (*see*

Shopping, *below*). Across the street is the **Janco-Dada Museum.** As one of the founders of the Dada movement, the Romanian-born Janco already had, of course, a well-established professional reputation when he immigrated to Israel in 1941. The museum, which opened in 1983, houses a permanent collection of works in various media by the artist, reflecting Janco's output in both Europe and Israel. A 20-minute slide show chronicles the life of the artist and the Dada movement. Also exhibited are works by other Israeli modern artists. Don't miss the view from the rooftop before leaving. *Tel. 04/ 842350. Admission: NIS 5 ($1.70) adults, NIS 3 ($1) children. Open Sun.–Thurs. and Sat 9:30–5, Fri. and holiday eves 9:30–4.*

Back in the square, walk up the stone staircase that skirts the restaurant to a ruined building with an old olive press. It leads to the town's open-air theater where summer concerts are held (*see* The Arts and Nightlife, *below*). Paths branch off to artists' studios and homes on a lovely walk along the road that encircles the village.

Return to Route 4 and head south 4 kilometers (2.5 miles) to the **❷❽ Nahal Me'arot Nature Reserve,** or the prehistoric **Carmel Caves.** Buses 921, 922, 202, or 222 from Haifa will leave you on Route 4 about 1 kilometer (.6 mile) from the caves. The three excavated caves are up a steep flight of stairs, on a fossil reef that was covered by the sea 100 million years ago. The first discoveries of prehistoric remains were made when this area was being scoured for stones to build the Haifa port. In the late 1920s, the first archaeological expedition was headed by Dorothy Garrod of England, who received assistance from a British feminist group on the condition that the dig be carried out exclusively by women. It was. In the Tannur cave, the first on the tour, the strata Garrod's team excavated are clearly marked, spanning about 150,000 years in the life of early man. The most exciting discovery made in the area was the existence of both Homo sapien and Neanderthal skeletons; evidence that both lived here has raised fascinating questions about the relationship between the two and whether they lived side by side. A display on the daily life of early man as hunter and food gatherer occupies the Gamal cave. The last cave you will visit, called the Nahal, is the largest—it cuts deep into the mountain—and was actually the first discovered. A burial place with 84 skeletons was found outside the mouth of the cave, where you can see a hunched-up skeleton.

The bone artifacts and stone tools discovered in Nahal Cave suggest that people who settled here, about 12,000 years ago, were the forebears of early farmers with a modified social structure more developed than that of hunters and gatherers. There is also evidence that the Crusaders once used the cave to guard the coastal road. Inside, an audiovisual show sheds light on how early man lived here. A two-hour walking tour of the surrounding area offers great views of the coastal plain. It's marked with blue-and-white-striped stones and starts at the parking lot, where there are also picnic tables. Call ahead to inquire about guided tours in English. *Tel. 04/841750 or 04/ 841752. Admission: NIS 9 ($3) adults, NIS 4.50 ($1.50) children. Open Sun.–Thurs., Sat and holidays 8–4, Fri. and holiday eves 8–1.*

The last stop on the tour is about 7 kilometers (4.3 miles) away on the **❷❾** coast at **Nahsholim,** the ancient city of **Dor.** Watch for the right turn-off that will lead you westward to Kibbutz Nahsholim, on a beautiful white sandy beach. Bus 921 from Haifa leaves you at the Nahsholim junction, a 25-minute walk from the kibbutz.

Founded 35 centuries ago, Dor was once the maritime capital of the Carmel coast. Its small bay made it the best harbor between Jaffa and Akko, and thus a target for many imperial ambitions, from the ancient Egyptians and the "Sea Peoples" through King Solomon and on down. It was renowned in antiquity for its precious purple dye called "Tyrian purple." This color, reserved for royalty, was extracted from a mollusk that was abundant along the coast. During the Arab period, it was renamed Tantura, also a name the popular beach goes by today. Well worth a visit is the kibbutz's **Nahsholim Museum,** housed in the partly restored former glass factory opened by Baron Rothschild in 1893 to serve the wineries of nearby Zichron Ya'akov. The enterprise, run by the first mayor of Tel Aviv, Meir Dizengoff, failed two years later because the poor quality of the sand used made the bottles black. The museum contains a rich trove of finds of local nautical digs and excavations at the nearby Tel Dor. The various peoples who settled, conquered, or passed through Dor—from the Phoenicians to Napoléon—can be traced through the artifacts on display here. Of particular interest is the bronze canon that Napoléon's vanquished troops dumped into the sea during their retreat from Akko to Egypt in May 1799. Treacherous currents and winds made this shoreline a graveyard for the ships, which have yielded many of the finds. In 1982, a storm revealed a shipwreck about 300 feet offshore, bringing to light a treasure: 1,000 kilos of coins, bronze figurines, silver plates, and bracelets that date from the Byzantine and Mamluk periods. An interesting film in English gives background to the seminal work of Kurt Raveh, a Dutch-born member of the kibbutz who spearheaded many of the underwater digs done in the area. *Kibbutz Nahsholim, tel. 06/390950. Admission: NIS 6 ($3) adults, NIS 5 ($1.70) children. Open Sun.–Fri. 8:30–2, Sat. and holidays 10:30–3.*

Tour 4: Through Western Galilee from Akko to Rosh Hanikra

As you exit Haifa on Ha'atzmaut Boulevard, you will pass the dilapidated facades of old buildings, in which the discerning eye can detect hints of the erstwhile dignified Turkish quarter. It is a 4.5-kilometer (2.8-mile) drive along the harbor from the landmark Dagon Silo downtown to the left exit for **Akko** (Acre) at the Checkpost junction, which will get you back on Route 4 heading north. A much slower but far prettier route to Akko takes you north on Route 70. This scenic drive runs roughly parallel to Route 4 about 7 kilometers (4.3 miles) to the east, through rolling hills and Arab villages, avoiding the unattractive industrial pockets and drab satellite towns of Haifa. Continue north past a small jog in the road that you will encounter 10 kilometers (6.2 miles) ahead. Take Route 85 west some 14 kilometers (8.7 miles) later to Akko's **Old City,** with its enchanting mixture of mosques, markets, khans, and vaulted Crusader ruins, at the northern tip of Haifa Bay.

Numbers in the margin correspond to points of interest on the Akko Old City map.

You approach the Old City on Weizman Street through a breach in the surrounding walls. Once inside the walls, park at the Knights parking lot, where you can start a walking tour. Double back to the entrance to the Old City at the walls and climb the signposted blue-railing stairway on your right for a stroll on the **ramparts.** Walking right you can see the stunted remains of the 12th-century walls built by the Crusaders, under whose brief rule—just under two centuries—Akko flourished as never before or since. The indelible signs of the Crusaders, who made Akko the main port of their Christian empire, are much more evident inside the Old City itself.

The wide wall you are walking on, which girds the northern part of the town, was built by Ahmed el-Jazzar, the Pasha of Akko, who added these fortifications following his victory over Napoléon's army in 1799. With the help of the British fleet, which sunk the French heavy artillery sent by sea, el-Jazzar turned Napoléon's attempted conquest into a humiliating rout. Napoléon had dreamed of founding a new Eastern empire, thrusting northward from Akko to Turkey and then seizing India from Great Britain. His defeat at Akko hastened his retreat to France, thus changing the course of history.

History clings to the stones of old Akko, with each twist and turn along its warren of streets telling another tale. The city's history begins 4,000 years ago, when Akko was first mentioned in Egyptian writings that refer to the mound, or tel, northeast of the walls you are standing on. The Old Testament describes in Judges 1 that after the death of Joshua the tribe of Asher was unable to drive the Canaanite inhabitants from Akko and so lived among them there. Akko was a prize worth fighting for throughout the course of history. It had a well-protected harbor, a well-watered and fertile hinterland, and a strategic position on the coastal road that links Egypt and Phoenicia (present-day Lebanon). In the 4th century BC, Akko eclipsed Tyre and Sidon as the principal port of the eastern Mediterranean. Alexander the Great's high regard for Akko is reflected in the fact that in the 3rd century BC he set up a mint in the city; it remained in operation for six centuries. For long periods Akko was a Phoenician city, but when the Hellenistic king Ptolemy II of Egypt gained control of the country in the 2nd century BC, he renamed it Ptolemais, the name it retained through the Roman and Byzantine periods.

Walk around to the guard towers and up an incline just opposite; there's a commanding view of the moat below and Haifa across the bay. Turn around and let your gaze settle on the exotic skyline of Old Akko, the sea-green dome of the great mosque its dominating feature. Walk down the ramp, crossing the **Moat Garden** at the base of the walls and continue alongside the round arches on the backside of **Shuk el Abiad** (White Market). This market was built by Dahr el-Omar, the Bedouin sheikh who defied Turkish rule and set up his own fiefdom in the Galilee in the 18th century. In 1749 he moved his capital from Tiberias to Akko and rebuilt the walls of the city. Dahr el-Omar's rule here ended more than four centuries of desolation and isolation that had beset Akko after the Mamluks drove the Crusaders out in 1291. He rebuilt the port and also built access roads to the city. Continue along a pedestrian walkway, with a bank on your right.

Time Out   In the plaza in front of the tourist information office there are several stands with tables where you can enjoy a falafel or simply a pita, fresh-squeezed orange juice, or coffee while sunning yourself or watching the world go by.

On your left, at the top of a short flight of stairs, is the entrance to **❸ El-Jazzar Mosque,** considered one of the most magnificent in Israel. Ahmed el-Jazzar, who succeeded Dahr el-Omar simply by having him assassinated, ruled Akko from 1775 to 1804. During his reign he built this mosque along with other public structures. The Albanian adventurer's cruelty was so legendary that he earned the epithet

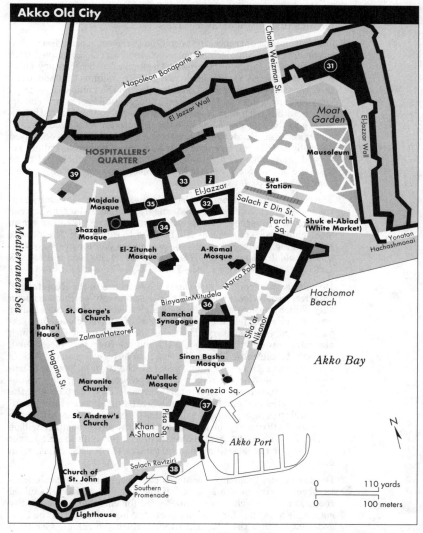

Akko Old City

Napoleon Bonaparte St.

Chaim Weizman St.

El Jazzar Wall

*Moat
Garden*

El-Jazzar Wall

HOSPITALLERS'
QUARTER

31

Mausoleum

Mediterranean Sea

39

33

i

El-Jazzar

**Bus
Station**

Majdala
Mosque

35

32

Salach E Din St.

Shazalia
Mosque

34

Parchi
Sq.

**Shuk el-Abiad
(White Market)**

Yonatan
Hachashmonai

El-Zituneh
Mosque

A-Ramal
Mosque

Marco Polo

*Hachomot
Beach*

St. George's
Church

BinyaminMitudela

36

Baha'i
House

ZalmanHatzoref

Ramchal
Synagogue

Sha ar
Nikanor

Akko Bay

Maronite
Church

Hagana St.

Sinan Basha
Mosque

Mu'allek
Mosque

Venezia Sq.

St. Andrew's
Church

37

Pisa Sq.

Khan
A-Shuna

Akko Port

Church of
St. John

Salach Ravtziri

38

Southern
Promenade

Lighthouse

N

| 0 | 110 yards |
| 0 | 100 meters |

Museum of the
Underground
Prisoners, **39**
El-Jazzar Mosque, **32**
Khan el-Umdan, **37**
Knights' Halls, **33**

Pisan Harbor, **38**
Ramparts, **31**
Refectory, **35**
Souk, **36**
Turkish baths, **34**

"The Butcher." (He is buried next to his adopted son in a small white building to the right of the mosque.)

Just beyond the entrance, in the middle of the courtyard, is a pedestal mounted with a marble reproduction of a seal. Engraved with graceful calligraphy, it re-creates the seal of a 19th-century Ottoman sultan. Some of the marble and granite columns that adorn the mosque and courtyard were plundered from the ruins of Caesarea. On your left is the entrance to the underground reservoir. The ornate fountain with eight slender columns on your right at the entrance to the mosque is used by the faithful for ritual washings of hands and feet. Bordering the courtyard are outbuildings once used as a religious school. Inside the mosque, enshrined in the gallery reserved for women, is a reliquary containing a hair believed to be from the beard of the prophet Mohammed; it is removed only once a year, on the 27th day of Ramadan.

The reservoir dates from the Crusader period and was actually a cathedral until converted into cisterns by Ahmed el-Jazzar. You can traverse the cavernous depths on a wooden walkway (keep an eye on small children). The cisterns still fill up with rainwater. The mosque is a working mosque, so it closes five times a day for prayers. Visitors should dress modestly. *Admission: NIS 1.50 (50¢) adults, NIS 1.20 (40¢) children. Open Sat.–Thurs. 8–5, Fri. 8–11 and 1–5.*

Directly across from the mosque is the entrance to the **Hospitallers' Quarter,** otherwise known as the **Crusader city** or **Subterranean City,** which consists chiefly of the Knights' Halls, the Grand Munir (medieval French for "big mansion"; part of which is closed for excavation), and the Refectory. The ticket for the Knights' Halls, which also admits you to the Turkish baths and the Refectory *(see below),* can only be purchased here. You can also buy good maps of Akko's Old City here. (As excavations proceed, the town fathers are planning to double the area open to the public, opening up the underground passages between the Crusader city complex and the Turkish baths and employing sophisticated displays including artifacts and the use of lasers and dioramas to examine Akko during the Crusades. Ultimately the new entrance to the entire complex will be at the Turkish baths, and visitors will exit opposite the El-Jazzar Mosque. For the latest information contact the tourist information office.)

Deeper inside, following the arrow past fragments of marble capitals, you arrive in the **Knights' Halls,** a series of barrel-vaulted rooms, one of which is sometimes used for chamber concerts. Six such halls have thus far been discovered. Above this part of the Crusader city stands the Ottoman **citadel,** which you can glimpse from the courtyard. Raised by Dahr el-Omar on the rubble-filled Crusader ruins, the citadel was the highest structure in Akko. It was later converted by the British into a prison *(see below).*

The Crusaders who conquered Akko in 1104 were led by King Baldwin I and assisted by the Genoese fleet. The port city, which the victorious French Hospitallers, the Knights of St. John, renamed for their patron saint, Jean d'Acre, was the Crusaders' principal link to their homeland. Commerce thrived and the European maritime powers of Genoa, Pisa, Venice, and Marseilles developed separate quarters here. After the disastrous defeat of the Crusader armies at the Horns of Hattin in 1187, Akko surrendered to the victorious Saladin without a fight. But four years later, Richard the Lionheart of England recaptured the Crusader stronghold. In the 13th century, Akko became the effective capital of a shrunken Latin kingdom after the fall of Jerusalem to the Moslems. During its Crusader heyday, Akko boasted about 40 churches and monasteries and its population swelled to 50,000. Today, its residents number 45,000, an ethnic mix of Jews and Arabs.

The seeds of the Crusaders' downfall in Akko were probably sown by the divisive factions that held sway within its walls. The Hospitallers and Templars, the so-called fighting monks, also each had their own quarters (the Templars, also French, lived near the lighthouse by the western Crusader sea wall). By the mid-13th century, open fighting broke out between the Venetians and Genoese. When the Mamluks attacked with a vengeance in 1291, the Crusaders' resistance quickly crumbled. The city's devastation was complete, and it remained so for centuries. Yet even today, Akko has retained a medieval cast. *Tel. 04/911764. Admission (includes Knights' Halls, Turkish baths, and Refectory): NIS 8 ($2.70) adults, NIS 7 ($2.35) children. Open Oct.–Mar., Sun.–Thurs. 8:30–5, Fri. 8:30–2, Sat. 8–3; Apr.–Sept., Sun.–Thurs. 8:30–7, Fri. 8:30–2, Sat. 8–5.*

Exit the Hospitallers' Quarter to the right, skirting a corner of the Refectory (*see below*). Then head left down a narrow street 45 feet to the entrance of the remarkable **Turkish baths** built for Pasha el-Jazzar in 1781 and in use until 1947, when they were damaged by the explosion at the British prison nearby. The baths have recently been restored to pristine condition, having served for years as a municipal museum. (At press time the baths are slated to become the municipal museum once again, with copper objects, jewelry, coins, and other artifacts from the city collection as well as new archaeological finds from Akko on display. Inquire at the tourist information office.) If possible (access may be limited) climb to the rooftop in the courtyard for a close-up look at the thick glass bubbles protruding from the domes that send a green, filtered light to the steam rooms below. These skylights were actually ordered from the same Hebron workshop that made the original ones a century ago. The dressing room is decorated with colorful handmade Turkish tiles and capped with a cupola; note the inlaid marble floors. For admission and hours, *see* Knights' Halls, *above*.

When you exit the baths, cross the street to the **Refectory**, once known as the Crypt of St. John; before excavation it was erroneously thought to have been an underground chamber. The dimensions of the colossal pillars that support the roof make this one of the more monumental examples of Crusader architecture in Israel. Moreover, it is considered one of the oldest Gothic structures in the world. In the right-hand corner opposite the entrance is a fleur-de-lis carved in stone—the crest of the French House of Bourbon—leading some scholars to postulate that this was the chamber in which Louis VII convened the knights of the realm.

An extremely narrow **subterranean passageway** starts at the bottom of the wooden stairs descending next to the base of one of the columns. This was a secret tunnel cut in stone that the Crusaders probably used to reach the harbor when besieged by Muslim forces. (Those who are claustrophobic might consider an alternate route, one that takes you back to the entrance of the Turkish baths, where you continue straight.) When you emerge you will see some 13th-century marble Crusader tombstones. Go up the stairs to your left and turn right into the covered market, often closed nowadays. Exit to the left. For admission and hours, *see* Knights' Halls, *above*.

Continue through a square with the whitewashed **El-Zituneh Mosque** on your right and wend your way to the left through the an-

36 gular streets to the local **souk**. In addition to stalls where heaps of fresh produce are artfully arranged, there are specialty stores: a pastry shop with an astonishing variety of exotic Middle Eastern delicacies; a spice shop filled with the aromas of the Orient; a bakery with steaming fresh pita. You will often see fishermen sitting on doorsteps intently repairing their lines and nets to the sounds of Arabic music blaring from the open windows above.

Time Out   Here in the souk, you can duck into the **Oudah Brothers Cafe** and sit in the courtyard of the 16th-century Khan el-Faranj, or the Franks' Inn. While sipping coffee or eating hummus or kebabs, note the 18th-century Franciscan monastery and tower to your left. *Tel. 04/ 912013. Open daily for lunch and dinner.*

Exiting the Khan el-Faranj from the south you'll pass the Sinan Basha mosque on your left as you enter **Venezia Square** in front of the
37 port. On your right is the **Khan el-Umdan,** or the Inn of the Pillars. Before you visit this Ottoman khan—the largest of the four in the city—and then the Pisan Quarter beyond, take a stroll around the **port** with its small flotilla of fishing boats, yachts, and sailboats. Then walk through the khan's gate beneath a square clock tower built at the turn of the century. During Akko's golden age of commerce in the 18th century, the khan served vast numbers of merchants and travelers. The 32 pink and gray granite pillars that give the khan its name are compliments of Ahmed el-Jazzar's raids on Roman Caesarea. At the center of the colonnaded courtyard there was once a market.

When you leave the khan, make a sharp left to enter the **Pisan Quar-**
38 **ter.** Turn into the **Pisan Harbor** for a walk along the sea walls. Start at the café perched on high—a great lookout—heading west in the direction of the 18th-century **Church of St. John.** You will end up at the southwestern extremity of Akko, next to the **lighthouse.** The Templars once occupied this area. Head north along Hagana Street, which runs parallel to the crenelated western sea wall. After five minutes you will reach the whitewashed, blue-trimmed **Baha'i house** (not open to the public), where the prophet of the religion, the Baha'u'llah, spent 12 years of his exile. His burial site is just north of Akko (*see below*).

Continue to walk on Hagana Street for another five minutes and you
39 will reach the gates of the **Museum of the Underground Prisoners.** Housed in several wings of the Citadel built by Dahr el-Omar and then added onto by Ahmed el-Jazzar in 1785, it became a British prison during the Mandate. On the way in you pass the outside wall of the Citadel; the difference between the large Crusader building stones and the smaller Turkish ones above them is easy to spot. The original cells and their meager contents tell of day-to-day life in the prison, supplemented by displays of photographs and documents that reconstruct the history of the Jewish resistance to British rule in the 1930s and '40s. During the Mandate, the Citadel became a high-security prison whose inmates included top members of Jewish resistance organizations, including Ze'ev Jabotinsky. In 1947, a dramatic prison breakout by leaders of the Irgun captured headlines around the world and provided Leon Uris's *Exodus* with one of its most dramatic moments. *Tel. 04/918264. Admission: NIS 6 ($2) adults, NIS 3 ($1) children. Open Sun.–Thurs., 9–4, Fri. 9–12:30.*

As you leave the museum, turn right after 60 feet, and follow the massive walls around the northern part of town to the breach at Weizman Street where you began.

Numbers in the margin correspond to points of interest on the Northern Coast and Western Galilee map.

When you leave Akko heading north, you will be back on Route 4, which hugs the coast all the way to Rosh Hanikra on the Lebanese border. Just 1 kilometer (.6 mile) beyond the gas station at the northern edge of Akko, you'll pass the main gates (open only to Baha'is) of the **Baha'i Gardens.** Make the first right (no sign) and continue to the unobtrusive entrance 500 yards up. For the Baha'is this is the holiest spot on earth, the site of the tomb of the faith's Prophet Founder, Baha'u'llah (*see* Tour 3, *above*). He lived in the red-tile mansion here after he was released from jail in Akko and was buried in the small building next to the mansion, now the Shrine of Baha'u'llah. Visitors to the Shrine are asked to dress modestly. The gardens and terrace are exquisitely landscaped. *Tel. 04/812763. Admission free. Gardens open daily 9–4, tomb open Fri.–Mon. 9–noon.*

Less than 1 kilometer (.6 mile) north of the gardens stands a segment of the multitiered **aqueduct** built by Ahmed el-Jazzar in the late 18th century to carry the sweet waters of the Kabri springs to Akko. Just beyond is the entrance to **Kibbutz Lochamei Hageta'ot (Ghetto Fighters),** founded in 1949 by survivors of the German, Polish, and Lithuanian Jewish ghettos and veterans of the ghetto uprisings against the Nazis. To commemorate their compatriots who perished in the Holocaust and to perpetuate the memory of those tragic events, the kibbutz members set up a museum. Its entrance is to the right of the main gate of the kibbutz. There is a vast collection of photographs that document the Warsaw Ghetto and the famous uprising, and halls devoted to different themes, among them Jewish communities before their destruction in the Holocaust, the death camps, and deportations at the hands of the Nazis. You can see the actual booth in which Adolf Eichmann, architect of the "Final Solution," sat during his Jerusalem trial. *Tel. 04/820412. Admission free; donation requested. Open Sun.–Thurs. 9–4, Fri. 9–1, Sat. 10–5.*

Stay on Route 4 for another 5 kilometers (3.1 miles) to the resort of **Nahariya,** the first Jewish settlement in the Western Galilee. Nahariya was founded in 1934 by German Jews who had fled the Nazis and had come to eke out a living from farming. Eventually these pioneers turned from the soil to what they realized was their greatest natural resource—some of the country's best beaches—for a more lucrative livelihood. Thus a popular beach resort was born. The main thoroughfare, Ha'Ga'aton Boulevard, was built along the banks of a river, now dried up, lined with shady eucalyptus trees. The town's name, in fact, comes from *nahar,* the Hebrew word for river. Though once the German language was the hallmark of the town, today you're as likely to hear immigrants speaking Russian or Ethiopians speaking Amharic.

Time Out   There is a lovely lookout point near a **Phoenician tel** you reach by continuing north 1.5 kilometers (1 mile) on the main road until you can turn left onto a beach road that will take you farther north nearly 2 kilometers (1.2 miles). There are small natural lagoons (but no lifeguards) and a sweeping view of the sea, Rosh Hanikra, and the Crusader ruins of **Achziv National Park** to the north. Across the road is the tel, under excavation.

To visit the **Byzantine church** next to the Katzenelson school, head east on Haga'aton to Route 4, making a left at the stoplight and then the first right into Yechi'am Street. From here, you make the third left and then an immediate right onto Bielefeld Street. The elaborate mosaic floor, discovered in 1964, depicts peacocks, other birds, hunting scenes, and plants using 17 different colors. It was part of what experts consider one of the largest and most beautiful Byzantine churches in the Western Galilee, where Christianity rapidly spread—as in the rest of Israel—from the 4th to the 7th centuries. Call the tourist office (tel. 04/879800) to arrange a visit. *Admission: NIS 2 (70¢).*

The rest of this tour makes a loop: first straight up the coast on Route 4 to Rosh Hanikra and then back down a bit inland to the Crusader castles of Montfort and Yechi'am. *Tel. 04/823263.*

Continue on the highway, which ends after 7 kilometers (4.3 miles). **43** You will find yourself at the sea grottoes of **Rosh Hanikra.** Even before you get in line for the two-minute cable-car ride to the grottoes, take a moment to look at the fine view back down the coast. Still clearly visible is the route of the railway line, now mostly a dirt road, built through the hillside in 1943 to extend the Cairo–Tel Aviv–Haifa line to Beirut. You will see its two tunnels at the mouth of the grottoes below. The caves were sculpted by relentless waves pounding away at the white chalk cliffs; man-made corridors lead from one section to another. There is a cafeteria at the hilltop. *Tel. 04/857108. Admission: NIS 15 ($5) adults, NIS 12 ($4) children. Open Sun.–Thurs. and Sat. 8:30–4, Fri. and holiday eves 8:30–3. During winter months call ahead for opening hours.*

44 Next comes the medieval castle of **Montfort,** a formidable mountaintop fortress that is arguably the most majestic of its kind in Israel. To get there, head south on Route 4 and turn east at the exit for the town of Shlomi, proceeding 3.5 kilometers (2.1 miles) to the Hanita Junction. Turn east onto Route 899. You will pass Kibbutz Eilon on your left before reaching a sign for Goren Park, at the end of a 1.5-kilometer (1-mile) stretch of gravel road and equipped with picnic tables and a lookout toward the castle across the gorge. Binoculars would be handy here if you're not up for the long trek up the marked path. The walk takes anywhere from 30 minutes to an hour, depending on your fitness.

The prospect is magnificent. The slopes are steep and densely wooded and the stark ruins of the fortress reach skyward from a narrow spur of hill above the bed of a bubbling stream. Unlike the other Crusader castles previously discussed, Montfort had limited strategic value, not being close to any major Crusader roads, though it stood on ancient foundations. Built and named in the 12th century by French Crusaders, Montfort was part of the domain of the nearby Courtenay fiefdom at Mi'ilya. In the 13th century it was sold to the German Knights of the Teutonic Order, who greatly expanded it. They renamed the castle Starkenberg and used it to house their archives and treasury for Palestine.

The layout of the castle was thoroughly explored in 1926 by a team from the Metropolitan Museum of Art in New York, which also excavated everything from armor to carvings and coins. The outer fortifications consisted of a curtain wall and two deep moats. The castle itself had a ceremonial hall, a chapel, a workshop, living quarters, and a keep. Montfort was first conquered by the Muslims in 1187, but was regained five years later. It was lost for good by the Crusaders in 1271 to the Mamluk sultan Baybars, who allowed the knights to retreat to Akko.

45 Our final stop is the medieval castle at **Yechi'am,** which you can reach from Hanita Junction by turning south onto Route 70. At the Kabri intersection head east 7 kilometers (4.3 miles) on Route 89 (the road that will take you back to Nahariya when you head in the opposite direction), driving through the foothills to the sign that points to the castle on a road off to the right. On the way you'll see a **memorial** to the convoy that set out to bring fresh supplies and reinforcements to the besieged Yechi'am kibbutz in Israel's War of Independence in 1948. **Castle Judin** stands next to the kibbutz. Castle Judin was apparently built by the Templars in the late 12th century. It, too, was destroyed by Baybars, but its ruins so impressed the Bedouin sheikh Dahr el-Omar that he transformed it into a palatial citadel 500 years later. You can see the remains of a large reception hall and mosque, as well as a tower and bathhouse. There are picnic facilities here. *Castle Judin, tel. 04/856004. Admission: NIS 5 ($1.70) adults, NIS 3 ($1) children. Open daily 8–4.*

Shopping

Shopping Centers

Haifa is studded with modern indoor shopping malls replete with boutiques, small eateries, and movie theaters. The three main ones are the **Horev Center** in the Ahuza district on Horev Street at the intersection of Pica Street; the **Panorama Center** in Central Carmel, adjacent to the Dan Panorama hotel; and **Migdal Haneve'im** in the Hadar district on Khouri Street.

Specialty Stores

Ancient Artifacts
A fascinating place to browse is **I. E. Dany's Archaeological Galleries** (13/3 Salah Adin, tel. 04/813770) in the Old City of **Akko,** which you'll find on your left before you get to the plaza of El-Jazzar Mosque. The shop is lined with glass cases whose contents, some more than 4,000 years old, range from ancient coins to small statuary, delicate Roman glass, and urns and pottery. The pieces carry government-issued certificates, and items for sale are officially approved for export. Prices range from $50 into the thousands.

Artwork and Handicrafts
The best place in the region to find a wide range of quality handicrafts is at **The Gallery** (tel. 04/842548) in the main square of the artists' village of Ein Hod; you can also buy directly at some ceramics workshops nearby. Arrayed in the front room of the village's official gallery are silver, enamel, and gold jewelry; handblown glass; and ceramic jugs, mugs, and teapots. Three rooms are devoted to paintings, watercolors, sculptures, and graphic works by the town's resident artists, some of them internationally known. Tourists can ask for a small discount. The Gallery is open Sunday–Thursday and Saturday 9:30–5, Friday and holidays 9:30–4.

Along a brief stretch of the main road that winds through the Druze village of **Daliyat el Carmel** are shops that sell light throw rugs, baskets, brightly colored pottery, brass dishes, and characteristic woven wall hangings and place mats. Bargaining is expected. Some shops close on Friday.

Diamond Jewelry
In the diamond-polishing capital of the world, **Netanya,** shoppers will be dazzled by the profusion of stone-studded earrings, necklaces, bracelets, and loose stones with international diamond certificates. Two of the most reliable establishments are **Inbar Jewelry** (1 Ussishkin St., tel. 09/822233) and the **National Diamond Center** (90 Herzl St., tel. 09/620436). Prices are competitive. You can check

with the GTIO for a list of other firms currently recommended for fairness and authenticity.

Handmade In the Old City of **Caesarea**, the **Glass Center** (tel. 06/361890, open
Glassware daily 9–5 except Saturday), a small store on the southern side of the port, sells handblown colored glass. The pale-colored vases and vessels, lightly veined and streaked, are reminiscent of ancient glass. The factory warehouse is next to a Paz gas station on the road leading to the highway toward Tel Aviv.

The glassware of **Nahariya Glass** (100A Herzl St., tel. 04/920066) in **Nahariya** has a distinctive style, often with a brightly colored naturalistic or abstract pattern embedded in between two layers of glass. The trays, sets of dishes, small sculptures, and other items sold here can be shipped abroad. Visitors are also welcome to tour the factory; call ahead because hours tend to change.

Sports and the Outdoors

Anyone serious about sports in Israel—from coaches to contenders in international or Olympic events—should be familiar with the **Wingate Institute** (tel. 09/639521 or 09/639523, fax 09/653070), some 8 kilometers (5 miles) south of Netanya. Spread over verdant coastal acreage west of Route 2, the Institute is the preferred training ground for many Israeli teams competing abroad and is popular among European teams seeking refuge from inhospitable weather at home. Much of the Institute's sophisticated equipment is also now available to the public, albeit generally only in the afternoon. Facilities include a 25-meter pool with a retractable roof, squash courts, tennis courts, and a fitness center. A full medical checkup is also available at the sports medicine division. There is also a sports hotel on the grounds.

Participant Sports

Bowling It's hardly the national sport, but on the road from Haifa to Akko, about 4.8 kilometers (3 miles) from the port area, you'll find **Bowling Checkpoint** (5 Maklef St., Checkpost Junction, tel. 04/720529 or 04/721414). This 12-lane bowling alley is open from 11 AM until after midnight, depending on the crowd; Friday and holiday eve hours are 10–4. The daytime rate is NIS 6 ($2) per game. Shoe rentals are also available.

Fishing Stretching across the plain below Zichron Ya'akov is a patchwork of vast fish ponds, two of which are open to the public at **Kibbutz Ma'ayan Zvi** (tel. 06/395394 or 06/395111). To get to the fishing park, turn left about 200 feet beyond the police station just north of the junction for Zichron Ya'akov on Route 4. The sign has symbols for fish and birds but no English. The park is about 1.5 kilometers (1 mile) up the road. Admission costs NIS 6 ($2) per person and NIS 10 ($3.35) on Saturday, plus a fee for the catch, mostly carp and St. Peter. Tackle rentals are NIS 9 ($3). The park is open Sunday–Thursday 8–4; Friday and holiday eves until 3.

Golfing It's no wonder that Israeli and foreign visitors flock to the **Caesarea Golf Club** (tel. 06/361172): It's the country's only 18-hole course. Adjacent to the Dan Caesarea Hotel, the club is open from sunrise to sunset and the course is built on sandy soil so that it is playable even after heavy rainfall. Reservations are advisable on Friday, Saturday, and holidays. The greens fee is NIS 195 ($65) weekdays; NIS 240 ($80) on weekends; the weekly rate is NIS 960 ($320). Golf club

So, you're getting away from it all.

Just make sure you can get back.

AT&T Access Numbers
Dial the number of the country you're in to reach AT&T.

*AUSTRIA†††	022-903-011	*GREECE	00-800-1311	NORWAY	800-190-11
*BELGIUM	078-11-0010	*HUNGARY	00◇-800-01111	POLAND†♦²	0◇010-480-0111
BULGARIA	00-1800-0010	*ICELAND	999-001	PORTUGAL†	05017-1-288
CANADA	1-800-575-2222	IRELAND	1-800-550-000	ROMANIA	01-800-4288
CROATIA†♦	99-38-0011	ISRAEL	177-100-2727	*RUSSIA† (MOSCOW)	155-5042
*CYPRUS	080-90010	*ITALY	172-1011	SLOVAKIA	00-420-00101
CZECH REPUBLIC	00-420-00101	KENYA†	0800-10	S. AFRICA	0-800-99-0123
*DENMARK	8001-0010	*LIECHTENSTEIN	155-00-11	SPAIN•	900-99-00-11
*EGYPT† (CAIRO)	510-0200	LITHUANIA♦	8◇196	*SWEDEN	020-795-611
*FINLAND	9800-100-10	LUXEMBOURG	0-800-0111	*SWITZERLAND	155-00-11
FRANCE	19◇-0011	F.Y.R. MACEDONIA	99-800-4288	*TURKEY	00-800-12277
*GAMBIA	00111	*MALTA	0800-890-110	UKRAINE†	8◇100-11
GERMANY	0130-0010	*NETHERLANDS	06-022-9111	UK	0500-89-0011

Countries in bold face permit country-to-country calling in addition to calls to the U.S. **World Connect**ᔆᴹ prices consist of **USADirect**® rates plus an additional charge based on the country you are calling. Collect calling available to the U.S. only. *Public phones require deposit of coin or phone card. ◇Await second dial tone. †May not be available from every phone. †††Public phones require local coin payment through the call duration. ♦Not available from public phones. • Calling available to most European countries. ¹Dial "02" first, outside Cairo. ²Dial 010-480-0111 from major Warsaw hotels. ©1994 AT&T.

Here's a travel tip that will make it easy to call back to the States. Dial the access number for the country you're visiting and connect right to AT&T. It's the quick way to get English-speaking AT&T operators and can minimize hotel telephone surcharges.

If all the countries you're visiting aren't listed above, call **1 800 241-5555** for a free wallet card with all AT&T access numbers. Easy international calling from AT&T. **TrueWorld Connections.**

AT&T

American Express offers Travelers Cheques built for two.

Cheques *for Two*^{SM} from American Express are the Travelers Cheques that allow either of you to use them because both of you have signed them. And only one of you needs to be present to purchase them.

Cheques *for Two* are accepted anywhere regular American Express Travelers Cheques are, which is just about everywhere. So stop by your bank, AAA* or any American Express Travel Service Office and ask for Cheques *for Two.*

rentals run NIS 60 ($20) and an electric caddy car can be hired for NIS 91.20 ($30.40).

Horseback Riding A number of stables make it possible for you to ride on the sandy beaches of the Northern Coast. Ask at your hotel for one nearby. In the residential section of **Caesarea** try **Herod's Stables** (tel. 06/361181). The stables are open daily 8–4, and lessons cost NIS 50 ($16.70) per hour. You'll want to call ahead to secure a mount. **The Ranch** (tel. 09/663525) is in northern **Netanya**, 2 kilometers (1.2 miles) up the road from the Blue Bay Hotel. It's wise to reserve for Saturday or for moonlight rides on the beach. Also consider a pastoral ride through orange groves. The stables are open daily 8–6; the cost is NIS 30 ($10) per hour.

Ice Skating One of the country's only ice skating rinks (tel. 04/415388) can be found in the **Lev Hamifratz shopping center** in northern **Haifa** on the road to Akko. The rink is open daily from 10 to midnight, and is closed for practice sessions from 3 to 6. Admission (including skate rental) is NIS 16 ($5.35) during the week, NIS 19 ($6.35) on Saturday.

Scuba Diving Several good diving centers can help you discover the wealth of underwater ruins along the coast. In the marina in **Akko** is the **Ramy Diving Center** (tel. 04/918990, fax 04/343006). Ramy, a Navy diver, runs the diving school and offers tourists guided dives with an instructor. The three local dives explore the reef (NIS 120, or $40), the submerged wall of the city (NIS 90, or $30), and the wreck of an Italian World War II submarine (NIS 180, or $60). Prices of dives include an instructor and full equipment rental. In the Old City of **Caesarea** is the **Gal-Mor Diving Center** (tel. 06/361787). This center provides courses in diving, windsurfing, underwater photography, and swimming. A unique diving tour offers the opportunity to explore Herod's largely submerged port; a detailed map shows four different routes through the underwater ruins. The **Yamit Haifa Center** (2 Ben Gurion Ave., tel. 04/512418, fax 04/511450), in downtown **Haifa**, is open Sunday–Thursday 8–5, Friday 8–1. About a mile offshore from the center is the Carmel reef. A one-day dive of this area, as well as other one-day dives, costs about NIS 270 ($90) including equipment and instructor. In addition, this center offers a week-long trip to the Red Sea aboard a 78-foot boat. This tour costs NIS 360 ($120) a day, including meals and dives.

Tennis Some of the hotels along the coast include tennis courts among their facilities. In **Haifa,** there is a public tennis court at **Kfar Samir** (tel. 04/522721), close to the beach in the south, that is open all year, barring bad weather. There are 20 floodlighted courts open Sunday–Thursday 7 AM–10 PM, Friday 7–7, and Saturday 8–6. Book courts in advance. Rates are NIS 12 ($4) during the day and NIS 18 ($6) on Friday, Saturday, and after 7 PM.

Beaches

From Tel Aviv to the northern border with Lebanon there are miles and miles of sandy beaches, most of them public and attended by lifeguards from early May to mid-October. Many Israeli beaches are left untended off-season and refuse tends to collect, but as soon as the warmer weather sets in, they are generally cleaned up. Beware of swimming where there are no lifeguard stations, as there may be dangerous currents or undertows.

Achziv Beautifully maintained because it is in the Achziv National Park (*see* Tour 4, *above*), just north of Nahariya, this beach is great for kids, with a protected man-made lagoon, lifeguards, and playground facilities. You can picnic or make use of the restaurant. Admission, which is NIS 9 ($3) for adults and NIS 5 ($1.70) for children, covers the use of showers and toilets.

Akko Just south of the Old City on the Haifa–Akko road is a sandy stretch of municipal beach in Akko Bay, with parking, showers, toilets, and chair rentals. Admission is NIS 5 ($1.70) for adults and NIS 4 ($1.35) for children.

Bet Yannai A lovely private beach (tel. 09/666230) 5 kilometers (3.1 miles) north of Netanya is next to the Moshav Bet Yannai. Grills and some picnic tables are available, and a lifeguard is on duty in season. There are toilets near the parking lot, and cold showers on the beach, where you can also rent chairs and umbrellas. There is no entrance fee, but parking costs NIS 12 ($4) per car Sunday–Friday and NIS 16 ($5.35) on Saturday and holidays. Because this stretch of beach is only 2,400 feet long and cannot comfortably accommodate crowds, it's wise to come on weekdays.

Caesarea Bathers have three choices here. In the **Old City,** in a sandy cove in Herod's ancient harbor, is the small Caesarea Beach Club (tel. 06/361441). The admission of NIS 15 ($5) for adults and NIS 9 ($3) for children includes chairs, umbrellas, and hot showers. The beach offers a diving platform and rented kayaks; the Gal-Mor scuba diving center is next door. At the **Roman aqueduct** just north of the Old City in the residential section is a considerably more spacious beach with the dramatic backdrop of Roman arches disappearing into the sand. The amenities, however, are few: toilets and a lifeguard in season. There is no entrance fee, but parking per car runs around NIS 5 ($1.70). The beach and swimming area have been cleared of rocks and debris, but it is forbidden to swim outside the demarcated area supervised by a lifeguard. The largest and most popular sandy beach in the area is **Hof Shonit** (tel. 06/362927), just south of Caesarea. When approaching from Route 2, turn left instead of right toward the Old City. The parking lot here accommodates 400 vehicles and costs NIS 10 ($3.35). There are lifeguards (in season), a refreshment stand, and a restaurant, as well as cold showers and toilets.

Dor Next to Kibbutz Nahsholim, this beach is known as **Tantura Beach** or **Dor Beach** (tel. 06/390922) and is one of the most frequented in the country because of its fine sand that lines 1.6 kilometers (1 mile) of coastline. There is parking for 2,000 cars. Fees are on a per-person basis: NIS 7.50 ($2.50) for adults and NIS 4 ($1.35) for children. The facilities here are ample: lifeguards in season, a snack bar and restaurant, a first aid station, a trampoline (fee), and chair and umbrella rentals, as well as changing rooms and showers. Motorized dinghies can be rented for NIS 20 ($6.70) for a 20-minute ride.

Haifa The coastline south of the city stretching toward Atlit is lined with one fine, sandy public beach after another. From north to south, **Carmel, Zamir,** and **Dado beaches** (tel. 04/524231) cover 2.5 kilometers (1.5 miles) of coast and have six lifeguard stations among them. There is no entrance fee and parking is free. These beaches have showers, toilets, and a promenade that connects them. There are also several refreshment stands and seven restaurants. At press time additional Haifa beach developments, including the construction of nearby hotels, are in the planning stages. There is a small private beach tucked inside the cape next to the Bat Gallim beach called **Hof Sheket,** or the **Quiet Beach** (tel. 04/552448), and it is generally true to its name. Admission here is NIS 5 ($1.70) for adults and NIS 2 (70¢) for children.

Mikhmoret The exit for this tract of very popular beach is 7.5 kilometers (4.6 miles) north of Netanya. A huge dirt parking lot, which charges NIS 12 ($4) per car, is 1 kilometer (.6 mile) after the turnoff from Route 2. There are three lifeguard stations, a restaurant and café, and umbrellas and chairs for rent.

Nahariya The public bathing facilities in Nahariya at the **Galei Galil Beach,** just north of Ha'Ga'aton Boulevard, are ideal for families. There is an Olympic-size pool, a wading pool and playground for children, and changing rooms and showers. There is also a snack bar, and you are likely to be close to your hotel. In peak season, exercise classes are offered early in the morning. The entrance fee is NIS 9 ($3) for adults and NIS 5 ($1.70) for children.

Netanya The standard facilities, including lifeguards, first aid station, showers, toilets and changing rooms, are free and available at all the Netanya beaches (tel. 09/603118 or 09/603155), which cover 11 kilometers (6.8 miles) of soft, sandy coastline. This resort town's main beach, called **Sironit,** is open year-round. Sironit's parking lot is on the beach, just off Jabotinsky Street south of the main square, and costs NIS 6 ($2) per car. There are two restaurants and volleyball nets here. The northernmost beach in Netanya is by the Blue Bay Hotel, with parking up above; chairs and umbrellas are available for rent. South of town is the Orthodox beach **Kiryat Sanz,** where men and women have different bathing days and hours. Near The Seasons Hotel is another beach with a restaurant and refreshment stand as well as standard facilities. In front of the main square is **Herzl Beach,** with a water slide, restaurant, and refreshment stand. Next is Sironit and 3 kilometers (1.9 miles) south is **Goldmintz beach,** where there is a refreshment stand but no chair or umbrella rentals. At press time Netanya's southernmost beach, **Green Beach,** was closed due to pollution problems. The pollution levels are monitored regularly by the Health Department, and the other beaches have received a clean bill of health.

Dining and Lodging

Dining You won't have to hunt far in this region for a restaurant with an excellent view of the Mediterranean, and good fresh fish is rarely hard to come by. The fish you will most often find on your menu, served grilled or baked with a variety of sauces, are: *locus* (grouper), *mulit* (red mullet), *churi* (red snapper), and *farida* (sea bream). Also fresh, but hailing from commercial fish ponds and the Sea of Galilee, are *buri* (gray mullet) and the ubiquitous *tilapia* (St. Peter's fish), as well as the hybrid *iltit* (salmon-trout).

The coastal restaurants are generally not as refined as those in Tel Aviv, with some notable exceptions in Haifa and Mt. Carmel. Haifa—not unlike Tel Aviv—has lately become enlivened by a number of spunky cafés that are sprouting up in residential and commercial neighborhoods. In the Druze village of Daliyat el Carmel you will find its famed falafel and other authentic Mediterranean-style fare. Netanya features the region's highest concentration of kosher restaurants. Otherwise, what you wine and dine on runs the gamut from pita and hummus to sophisticated French cuisine.

Although many of the hotels reviewed below have dining rooms, the latter are listed separately only if the food is noteworthy. Even at the most expensive restaurants in this region, dress is always informal (but keep it tasteful), and ties are never required.

Wine lovers should note that this is one of the country's prime wine-growing areas. The star is the Carmel Oriental winery in Zichron Ya'akov. This winery's best and most expensive wines, red or white, are those in the Rothschild series. Their best vintage is the 1985 Cabernet Sauvignon. Their white Muscat dessert wine is also worth sampling. Also quite good are the wines of the less exclusive Selected series, especially the Chardonnay and Reisling. In high demand among Israelis is the semidry Emerald Reisling, a fruity and aromatic choice.

Highly recommended restaurants are indicated by a star ★.

Category	Cost*
$$$$	over $35
$$$	$22–$35
$$	$12–$22
$	under $12

per person for a three-course meal, excluding drinks, service, and sales tax

Lodging Along the coast you'll find everything from campgrounds to new luxury hotels. You won't, however, find that the selection and quality of deluxe accommodations compare with those in, say, Tel Aviv or the Red Sea resort of Eilat. In some places, such as Akko, the pickings are less than slim, but because distances here are never daunting, you can tour many towns along the coast from a single base.

The chart below lists peak-season prices, usually charged in July and August and during major Jewish holidays (Passover, which generally falls in April; Rosh Hashanah and Yom Kippur, which fall in September or October; and Hanukkah, which falls in December). There are variations, however, so be sure to inquire at each hotel. In addition, many hotels are considerably less expensive—sometimes off 40%—during low season, from November through February.

Camping facilities, including some bungalows and cabins several notches above a spartan tent, dot the coastline north of Netanya to the Lebanese border. There are bungalows at Dor (next to Kibbutz Nahsholim) and Neve Yam. However inviting, the wooded slopes of Carmel National Park do not offer facilities, but you will find campgrounds in Park Achziv on the coast. Contact the GTIO in Tel Aviv and Haifa (*see* Important Addresses and Numbers *in* Essential Information, *above*, and Essential Information *in* Chapter 4, Tel Aviv) for complete lists of campgrounds and maps as well as a brochure on Isra-chalets and bungalows.

Highly recommended lodgings are indicated by a star ★.

Category	Cost*
$$$$	over $120
$$$	$80–$120
$$	$55–$80
$	under $55

All prices are for a standard double room, including breakfast and excluding service charge.

Akko
Dining
★

Abu Christo. This popular waterfront fish restaurant at the northern edge of the Crusader port actually stands at one of the original 18th-century gates built by Pasha Ahmed el-Jazzar when he fortified the city after his victory over Napoléon. A family business dating from 1948 and passed from father to son, Abu Christo serves up the daily catch—often grouper, red snapper, or sea bass—simply prepared, either grilled or deep fried. Shellfish and a selection of grilled meats are also on the menu. The covered outdoor patio right on the water is idyllic in summer. *Crusader Port, tel. 04/910065. Reservations advised July–Sept. AE, DC, MC, V. $$*

Galileo. Sit on the terrace atop the old city's ancient walls for a meal of fresh fish, grilled meats, or Middle Eastern salads. You'll be right on the water in the Pisan Harbor, with nothing but a few ruins and an expanse of blue before you. *Crusader Port, tel. 04/914610. Reservations advised Fri. and Sat. DC, MC, V. $$*

Lodging

Beit Hava. Eight kilometers (5 miles) north of the city and also close to the resort town of Nahariya, this is a guest house at Moshav Shavei Zion, a kibbutz founded in 1938 by German Jews. With the beach and a 4th-century Byzantine church a few minutes from your front door, the surrounding countryside is inviting for strolls. The guest rooms are adequate but nothing fancy. Above all, you get peace and quiet here. The real bonus is the sports facilities. If you're traveling by public transportation, take Egged Bus 271 or the train from Akko or Haifa. Both bus and train leave you within a five-minute walk of the hotel. *Box 82, Shavei Zion 25227, tel. 04/820391, fax 04/820519. 90 rooms with bath. Facilities: dining room, baby-sitting service, pool, 2 floodlighted tennis courts. AE, MC, V. $$$*

★

Akko Youth Hostel. In the Crusader quarter near the lighthouse and Pisan Harbor, this hostel is housed in a historic stone building that has been beautifully restored with wood-beamed high ceilings. The dormitory-style rooms, which sleep 4–12 people, are mostly on the second floor. *Box 1090, Akko 24110, tel. 04/911982. 125 beds share 11 bathrooms. Kosher meals available. No credit cards. $*

Caesarea
Dining

Charley's. On a clear day, it's a delight to eat on one of several patios here, right above the sandy cove beach in the Crusader City. In the center of the port under the stone watchtower, Charley's is especially known for its way with fresh seafood, grilled or baked. Depending on the catch of the day, supplied by fishermen from a neighboring Arab village, there's red snapper, mullet, or grouper. Or you can order a simple, inexpensive snack of Middle Eastern salad or coffee and crème caramel or cheesecake. *Old City, tel. 06/363050. Reservations advised in high season. MC, V. $$$*

The Harbor Citadel. By Israeli standards this is a venerable institution: It's been open for 24 years. You'll spot it under the Israeli flag at the far end of the port at the top of a spiral staircase. The elevated location offers a spectacular view of the coast. The versatile menu sports seafood and salads, as well as schnitzel and chicken livers. In warmer weather you can sit on the outdoor patio shaded by a yellow awning and savor the view of the ruins of the ancient port. *Old City, tel. 06/361988 or 06/361989. Reservations advised Fri., Sat., and in summer. AE, DC, MC, V. $$$*

Lodging

For a longer vacation, **villa rentals** in one of the modern whitewashed houses near the beach are available through one of the following Caesarea real-estate brokers: Chana Kristal Real Estate, 23 Hamigdal St., Cluster 8, Caesarea 36060, tel. 06/363896 or 06/362691, fax 06/360212; Real Estate Caesarea, 32 Hadar St., Cluster 5, Caesarea 43660, tel. and fax 06/360969.

★ **Dan Caesarea.** You will find quiet comfort here as well as accessibility to a range of sport facilities and the archaeological sites of Caesarea. The four-story hotel is unobtrusively set in landscaped grounds. All the rooms have balconies, some facing the open countryside and others with sea views. Especially recommended are the newly renovated deluxe doubles with marble bathrooms and modern decor in cheerful hues. Adjacent to the hotel's 15-acre gardens stretches Israel's only 18-hole golf course, which offers Dan guests a discount. *Caesarea 30600, tel. 06/362266, fax 06/362392. 114 rooms with bath. Facilities: restaurant, bar, café, fitness club, sauna, pool, 2 floodlighted tennis courts, golf course. AE, DC, MC, V. $$$$*

Bed and Breakfast at Illana Berner's. Tucked away at the end of a cul de sac in the town's residential quarter, Illana's modest B&B is a leisurely 10-minute walk from the beach. Your hostess is a licensed guide and offers guests tours of Caesarea and beyond for a fee, as well as free tips on planning itineraries. She serves a hearty breakfast of melon, fresh fruit juice, and bagels and cream cheese on the patio in summer months. Illana's dogs and cat, by the way, have free run of the garden. *23 Harimon St., Caesarea 30600, tel. 06/363936 or, in U.S., 703/536-4064. 5 rooms share 3 toilets and 1 shower. Facilities: kitchenette, pool. No credit cards. $$*

Ein Hod **Ein Hod Restaurant.** This rustic place, redecorated in 1994 by its
Dining new owners, is in the heart of the quaint village. At wooden tables beside arched windows, or outside on a stone patio, choose from dishes such as beef with duck liver, Greek kebab with pine nuts, or steak with mustard or pepper sauce. Salads are also available, as are desserts such as fresh fruit and homemade cakes. *Main square, tel. 04/842016. No reservations. AE, D, V. $$*

Haifa **La Chaumière.** Occupying a two-story stone building in the German
Dining Colony, this restaurant is graced with authentic French charm both in its ambience and the virtuosity of its cuisine. Owner Michel Kaminski and his wife, who take turns in the kitchen, see to it that everything from the goose-liver pâté to the chocolate mousse and bread is fresh and homemade. Particularly outstanding is the fillet Chaumière with a cream sauce of tomatoes, cognac, and port. *40A Ben Gurion Blvd., tel. 04/538563 or 04/553154. Reservations advised Fri. and Sat. AE, DC, MC, V. No Fri. lunch. $$$$*

Le Rondo. Resembling a flying saucer and suspended over Mt. Carmel, this elegant restaurant in the Dan Carmel Hotel (*see below*) provides a spectacular 180°-plus view of the twinkling city below from widely spaced tables set on two tiers. (Although you can ogle from virtually anywhere in this aerie-in-the-round, you should reserve one of the window tables for a particularly vertiginous vantage point.) Among the classic haute cuisine dishes are the baby fillet of beef Rossini (with goose liver) and filet mignon Wellington. For fish lovers there's a salmon mousse to start, followed by delicately grilled fresh salmon or the local Dan River trout. Round out the meal with some samplings from the huge dessert buffet. *Dan Carmel Hotel, 85–87 Hanassi Ave., tel. 04/306211. Reservations advised. AE, DC, MC, V. No lunch or Fri. dinner. $$$$*

★ **Voilà.** This tiny whitewashed hideaway tucked downstairs off Nordau Street is an exclusive haunt. The mood is cozy, with a little bar, wooden tables and beams, wrought-iron grillwork, handblown glass wall sconces, and Oriental rugs. Inside there are only eight tables, but there is a garden enclosure that is heated during winter. Famous for its fondues (cheese, beef, or chocolate), the restaurant also prides itself on its beef fillet with cashew nuts or pepper sauce. For dessert, don't miss the homemade fig ice cream in a pool of fig and honey sauce or the crêpes suzette flambées. Less expensive three-course business lunches—for NIS 33.50 ($11.20) and NIS 41.50 ($13.85)—are available noon–4 PM. *21A Nordau St., tel. 04/664529. Reservations required. DC. $$$$*

La Trattoria. It's not your typical Italian restaurant, because along with pizza, pasta, and minestrone, there are the likes of dishes such as couscous and chicken livers on the menu. Yet the homey hodge-podge of Italian, French, and Tunisian atmosphere and cuisine is precisely what makes La Trattoria so popular among locals. Owner Edy Barby presides with a jovial manner over this family-style establishment. *119 Hanassi Blvd., tel. 04/379029 or 04/389618. Reservations advised Fri. and Sat. AE, DC, MC, V. $$*

★ **Recital.** The ambience at this small restaurant is decidedly artistic, with classical music playing softly in the background and black and white photos adorning the otherwise plain walls. Watch for the white awning out front—the sign is in Hebrew only (next to Da Vinci's restaurant in the Ahuza district). The pastries and desserts here are divine: a finger-licking hot apple pie served with ice cream or whipped cream and unbeatable cheesecakes. For something more healthful, the homemade soups are quite good, as are the quiche and fresh fruit and nut salads. *131 Moriyya Blvd., tel. 04/341269. No credit cards. Closed Fri. 3 PM–8 PM. $$*

Taiwan. This is considered one of the better Chinese restaurants in the city. The chef is from Taiwan, and the restaurant is a family-owned establishment in the German Colony that has been operating for nearly 20 years. *59 Ben Gurion Blvd., tel. 04/532082. Reservations advised Fri. and Sat. AE, DC, MC, V. $$*

★ **Palermo Pizza.** If you're searching for genuine, thin-crusted pizza, you've come to the right place. Looking more like a fashionable salad bar than a pizzeria, this parlor in the Panorama Center displays jars of oregano and spicy peppers and fresh flowers that add a dash of color. The range of toppings is prodigious—from tuna and salami to pineapple and peppers—and the crust is crisp. There are also plenty of other Italian specialties, like a *caprese* salad (sliced mozzarella topped with tomatoes and basil leaves and drizzled with olive oil), gnocchi, and ravioli. *In Panorama Center, Hanassi Ave., tel. 04/389129. AE, MC, V. $*

Shishkebab. You'll find lots of locals slipping in for down-home kosher Middle Eastern food here in the German Colony. There is a no-nonsense approach to the quick service and decor (Formica tables and chairs). Shishkebab is famous for its high-quality grilled meats, arrayed on skewers in a small glass counter by the entrance. Don't balk at sharing a table; it's customary here. Also available are Middle Eastern salads and *kube* soup (ground beef dumplings, often with pine nuts or raisins, rolled in cracked wheat and floating in a consomme). Aromatic coffee is served in tiny cups with cardamom. *59 Ben Gurion Ave., tel. 04/527576. No reservations. Closed Fri., Sat., and holiday eves. No credit cards. $*

Lodging **Dan Carmel.** The deluxe rooms on the upper floors of this Central Carmel hotel on the slopes of Mt. Carmel really stand out for their sumptuous furnishings, including satin bedspreads and richly stained wooden bureaus. Other doubles aren't as luxurious, but they're cheerfully decorated in pastels and well-maintained; all have balconies with views of the city or sea. Also pleasant is the large outdoor garden beside the pool, landscaped with potted plants. The gourmet restaurant, Le Rondo (*see above*), is a study in fine dining. *85–87 Hanassi Ave., 31060, tel. 04/306211, fax 04/387504. 219 rooms with bath. Facilities: restaurant, garden café, fitness center, sauna, beauty salon, travel agent, pool. AE, DC, MC, V. $$$$*

★ **Dan Panorama.** A member of the Dan hotel chain, this one is glitzier than its sister hotel down the road. The rooms, like the gleaming marble lobby, are spacious and sparkling; the blue and yellow color scheme, like the furnishings, is low key. Some rooms look out onto the Baha'i Shrine and the bay. The hotel is connected to the Panorama Center shopping mall, filled with small eateries and boutiques. *107 Hanassi Ave., 31060, tel. 04/352222, fax 04/352235. 266 rooms with bath. Facilities: restaurant, 3 cafés, piano bar, fitness room, sauna, summer childcare, shopping center, pool, children's pool. AE, DC, MC, V. $$$*

Haifa Tower. This hotel in a brand-new, 17-floor office tower in the downtown area is set in a busy shopping district and close by the Technoda science and technology museum on the Old Technion campus. Room sizes are ample and the decor subdued, tasteful, and spanking new. All rooms have either a sea or city view. The breakfast area, which looks out over Haifa Bay, is bright and cheerful. *63 Herzl St., tel. 04/677111, fax 04/621863. 100 rooms, 4 with shower only. Facilities: restaurant, bar. AE, MC, V. $$$*

Nof. The rooms in this small, pleasant hotel were redecorated in 1994. Unbeatable here are the location and view of the city spreading down to the sea from atop Mt. Carmel. The front desk and room service are quick and efficient. The Chinese restaurant—which boasts a chef from Hong Kong—and coffee shop also offer superb views. *101 Hanassi Ave., 31063, tel. 04/354311, fax 04/388810. 93 rooms with bath. Facilities: Chinese (kosher) restaurant, café, bar, disco. AE, DC, MC, V. $$$*

Shulamit. A bit off the beaten track on Mt. Carmel near the Ahuza district, this medium-size hotel is nonetheless surrounded by restaurants and a lively nightlife. It is set in a wooded residential area on a quiet street, with parking spaces right out front. The furnishings are monochromatic, but the service is spritely. *15 Kiryat Sefer St., 34676, tel. 04/342811, fax 04/255206. 84 rooms with bath. Facilities: restaurant, bar. AE, DC, MC, V. $$$*

Dvir. Share the same great location as Haifa's most expensive hotels without paying top dollar. In fact, guests at the Dvir have free access to the Dan hotel facilities (except the fitness center at the Dan Carmel) just up the road. The hotel is built into the hillside, so there is a two-flight climb up to reception. About a third of the simple and unpretentious accommodations have sea or city views. Spacious and clean, the rooms have been recently painted. *124 Yefe Nof St., 34454, tel. 04/389131, fax 04/381068. 35 rooms with bath. Facilities: use of most facilities at Dan Panorama and Dan Carmel (see above). AE, DC, MC, V. $$*

★ **Beth Shalom.** Across the street from the city's luxury hotels in Central Carmel, this guest house operated by an evangelical Christian organization gets high points for its prime location. The management runs a tight ship while preserving a family atmosphere, true to the reputation of Swiss-owned hotels around the world. The rooms and lobby are spotless and well-maintained, even if the furnishings aren't the most up-to-date. Only reservations for a minimum of three nights are accepted. *110 Hanassi Ave., Box 6208, Haifa 31061, tel. 04/377481 or 04/383019, fax 04/372443. 30 rooms with bath. Facilities: small garden, cafeteria. No credit cards. $*

Nesher. This decent hotel around the corner from Nordau mall is convenient for shopping and sightseeing, but is slightly overdue for some renovation. The reception area is up four flights of stairs. The guest rooms are quite basic, with no frills or extra amenities. *53 Herzl St., Haifa 33504, tel. 04/620644. 15 rooms with bath, 4 share bath. No credit cards. $*

Isfiya
Dining
★

Nof Carmel. Don't bother to look for an English-language sign to identify this Druze establishment. Instead, watch for the unfailingly familiar red Coca-Cola symbol overhead after driving to the northern edge of the village; it will be on your left encircled by a picket fence. Across the road there is an expansive vista of the Jezreel Valley. Diners come for the Middle Eastern fare, especially the thick homemade hummus with pine nuts or *foule* (a baked broadbean concoction seasoned with oil, garlic, and lemon juice), and lamb or turkey shishlik. Those with a sweet tooth will want to sample the *sahlab* (a custardy warm winter drink or pudding of crushed orchid bulb with thickened milk, sweetened with sugar and topped with raisins, almonds, cinnamon, or ginger) or the scale-bending baklava. *Isfiya, tel. 04/391718. No reservations. AE, MC, V. $-$$*

Mt. Carmel
Dining
★

The Pine Club Restaurant. Nestled in the woods at the crest of the mountain, this is one of the region's finest restaurants. You'll dine in a garden in a glass-enclosed pavilion, where the fireplace is always well-stoked in winter months. Fresh flowers and crisp white napery match the French-inspired cuisine in elegance. Try the veal chop in burgundy sauce, quail stuffed with chopped beef fillet, or the imaginative shrimp mousse with Danish caviar in the middle. *On road to Bet Oren (near Damon Jail), tel. 04/323568. Reservations required. AE, DC, MC. Closed Mon. No lunch Sun.-Fri. $$$$*

Nahariya
Dining

Maxims. Locals consider a meal at this Chinese restaurant a special event. The Oriental decor may be standard for Israel, but the authenticity of the cuisine is a pleasant surprise. Stir-fried shrimp with green peppers, onions, and mushrooms in a chili sauce is one of the more unexpected dishes, but there are also favorite standbys, such as lemon chicken, batter-fried and covered with a sweet-and-sour lemon sauce, and sautéed chicken on a skewer, smothered in peanut sauce. *43 Weizman St., tel. 04/921088. Reservations advised Fri. and Sat. V. $$*

Uri Buri. Buri is the Hebrew name for grey mullet, just one of the wide selection of fresh-caught fish served with pride by proprietor Uri. This is a fish and seafood restaurant only: the day's catch is baked, grilled, fried, or steamed. On the menu are local fish such as trout and salmon trout from the Dan River, St. Peter's fish, red snapper, plus sea bass and seafood. Your choice is served with salad and potato or rice. As an entrée, try the Tunisian–style stuffed sardines with their flavor of coriander, garlic, basil, and hot chili. *Last building on the southern end of the Promenade (look for big glass windows with a yellow sign), tel. 04/924824. Reservations not necessary. DC, MC, V. $$*

Pinguin. Fresh spinach blintzes with melted cheese, pasta, and hamburger plates are some of the offerings at this casual eatery. The management swears that their schnitzel gets accolades from Viennese visitors. All main dishes come with a green salad, rice, french fries, and cooked vegetables. You can get lighter salads and desserts next door at the soda fountain, and frozen yogurt at the adjacent stand, both owned by the same outfit that runs Pinguin. *31 Haga'aton Blvd., tel. 04/920027. No reservations. V. $*

Lodging

Carlton. The best in town, this centrally located, six-story hotel has a staff that will go the extra mile. Rooms are spacious and many have sea views or a view of the mountain range rearing up to the northeast. Furnishings are not exceptional, but are comfortable. The La Scala disco-nightclub, with its live music in the summer, attracts local fun-lovers from all over the north. *23 Haga'aton, tel. 04/922211, fax 04/823771. 196 rooms with bath. Facilities: restaurant, bar,* *nightclub, baby-sitting service, sauna, Jacuzzi, pool. AE, MC, V. $$$*

Frank. At the lower end of its price category, this old, established hostelry is still managed by the original Frank family. Very near the beach, the sedate two-story hotel has an intimate air with its pink and purple color scheme in the dining room and appealing patio off the lobby. The modest, but pleasant, rooms work for its regular patrons, mostly Europeans and locals who wouldn't dream of going anywhere else. *4 Ha'aliya St., tel. 04/920278, fax 04/925535. 50 rooms with bath. Facilities: pool, Jacuzzi. AE, MC, V. $$$*

Erna. A bit off the beaten track from the downtown area, this family-owned hotel is nonetheless only a five-minute walk to the main beach. The three-story building is unobtrusive from the outside but is spic-and-span and cheerful, and the service is solicitous. *29 Jabotinsky St., tel. 04/920170, fax 04/928917. 26 rooms with bath. Facilities: restaurant, bar, baby-sitting service. MC, V. $$*

Nahsholim
Lodging

Nahsholim Guest House. At the water's edge on a white sandy beach called Tantura, one of the nicest along the coast, this kibbutz guest house is ideal for a beach holiday and as a base for sightseeing. The kibbutz is also home to an underwater archaeology museum and is near the excavations of the ancient city of Dor. Rooms are furnished in the quintessential austere style of the kibbutz, and many have kitchenettes. During high season, guests must take half-board. *M.P. Hof Carmel, 30815, tel. 06/399533, fax 06/397614. 80 rooms with bath, 40 of which sleep up to 6. Facilities: dining room, small animal farm for children. DC, V. $*

Netanya
Dining

Lucullus. Owner Bernard Gabay of Tunisia has run this reliable French restaurant on the southern edge of town for 20 years. (There's also a kosher version at 5 Ha'atzmaut Square.) Although the menu is French, the ambience is Israeli. Candles and fresh flowers add a touch of class, and there's a pianist in the bar several times a week. Gabay recommends his coquilles St. Jacques or the chateaubriand, and for dessert the chocolate mousse or profiteroles. *2 Jabotinsky St., tel. 09/619502. Reservations advised. $$$*

Apropo. This restaurant—a bit like a glorified coffee shop—is in King George Park and serves breakfast, lunch, and dinner with a view of the scalloped curve of coastline below a jutting cliff. There's something for everyone on the eclectic menu: fresh fish, Italian pastas, soups and salads, and a variety of omelets. For the adventuresome there are even a few exotic Thai specialties. All dishes are glatt kosher, meaning that meal preparation undergoes extra-strict supervision by the kashrut authorities. *Gan Hamelech park, at end of Ha'atzmaut Sq., tel. 09/624482 or 09/624483. Reservations required for Sat. dinner and Apr.–Sept. AE, DC, MC, V. No Fri. dinner or Sat. lunch. $$*

Casa Mia. Replete with pizza oven, this centrally located, family-run restaurant is not unlike a traditional Italian trattoria, albeit a bit short on charm. The chef takes pride in being well-versed in the language and cuisine. He makes a mean *fegato alla veneziana* (liver with bacon and onion in a red wine sauce), *calamari fritti*, lasagna, and minestrone, or you can stick with a simple pizza. *10 Herzl St., tel. 09/347228. Reservations advised Fri. and Sat. dinner. AE, DC, V. $$*

Pundak Hayam. Owned by three brothers who have run the restaurant for 26 years, this unprepossessing place just off Herzl Street is a favorite among locals. It's a no-frills diner with Middle Eastern cooking, counter seating, and wooden tables. You can find fresh fish, shishlik, kebabs, and roast goose as well as the usual salads. *1 Harav*

Kuk St., tel. 09/615780 or 09/341222. No reservations. MC, V. No dinner Fri. and holiday eves. Closed Sat. $

Lodging **Blue Bay.** It's out of the bustle of the downtown area, but there's an hourly hotel shuttle or public bus to the center. Blue Bay offers direct access to the beach below and all rooms in the main wing have a sea view. In 1994, some guest rooms were under renovation; with any luck the hallways and lobby will be next. In tune with the times, a health club is now under construction. *37 Hamelachim St., 42228, tel. 09/603603, fax 09/337475. 196 rooms with bath. Facilities: restaurant, bar, coffee shop, disco, beauty parlor, 2 floodlighted tennis courts, pool. AE, DC, MC, V. $$$$*

La Promenade. This recently opened luxury apartment-hotel complex with its snappy modern design is on the south side of King George Park, near the town center and the beach. Each unit, furnished with marble tiles and sleek furniture, has a kitchenette and a balcony with a sea view. An unusual feature is the indoor pool, with Jacuzzi. *6 Gad Machnes St., 42279, tel. 09/626450, fax 09/626450. 20 apts. with bath. Facilities: restaurant, coffee shop, indoor pool, fitness center, hot tub. AE, DC, MC, V. $$$$*

★ **The Seasons.** The finest hotel in town, The Seasons is set just outside the downtown area, with easy access by staircase to the beach below. At press time gradual renovation was underway during winter months; public areas, two suites, and half the guest rooms have already been completed. The bedrooms are quite spacious, with private terraces and sea views. The newer rooms are especially comfortable—decorated in pleasing pastels—and the baths are luxurious. *Nice Blvd., 42269, tel. 09/601555, fax 09/623022. 85 rooms with bath. Facilities: restaurant, coffee shop, fitness room, sauna, massage, tennis court, pool. AE, DC, MC, V. $$$$*

Margoa. The rooms are small and plain, but there is a cozy family atmosphere here. Across the street from the beachfront, the hotel is also right near the main square. Enjoy a drink or bite to eat at the wood-paneled pub. During the Jewish holidays and from July 15 through August, half-board is required, and the resulting higher rates catapult this hotel into the $$$$ range. *9 Gad Machnes St., 42279, tel. 09/624434, fax 09/623430. 68 rooms with bath. Facilities: restaurant, cafeteria, pub. AE, DC, MC, V. $$*

Shuni **Shuni Castle.** The setting alone—an ancient fortress in Israel's wine
Dining country—is memorable. Add to that the country charm of artfully
★ arranged baskets of red peppers and dried sausage laid out beside chubby loaves of homemade bread and you've got a winner. The view's divine from the three tables on the patio, so you'd do well to call ahead and request one. In keeping with the informal style (chef Antoine likes to banter with regular customers), there's no written menu, but you can expect to find some of the following: homemade goose liver pâté, leg of duck stewed in *jus naturel, boeuf bourgignon* with mushrooms, veal with white wine and artichokes, and braised entrecôte with peppers and tomatoes. Local red and white wines are served, or you can ask for the Riesling from Antoine's vineyard. *In Jabotinsky Park, just off Rte. 652, 1 km (.6 mi) north of Binyamina, tel. 06/380227. Reservations advised Fri. and Sat. and for patio tables. No credit cards. Closed Sun. $$$*

Zichron **The Well 90.** Named after the old stone well that serves as its center-
Ya'akov piece, this cavernous restaurant is owned by a Tel Aviv family. The
Dining 100-year-old structure, once converted into an inn, has been restored, with high ceilings supported by thick wooden beams. In summertime, there is outdoor seating in a large rear garden area. The fare is mostly Middle Eastern. The juicy lamb roast and grilled

meats are heartily recommended, but the fowl is fair: There's duck in orange sauce and a simple grilled chicken. *On Rte. 4 near turnoff for Zichron Ya'akov, tel. 06/398018 or 06/399047. AE, DC, MC, V. No Fri. dinner or Sat. lunch. $$*

Dining and **The Baron's Heights and Terraces.** Spread over 14 terraced levels,
Lodging this hotel opened in 1991 is designed with modern, clean, geometric
★ lines; with the exception of the upward sweep of a central structure, the rooms sprawl horizontally over the hillside, each with its own terrace and view. Rooms are furnished with modern Italian imports in mainly pastel color schemes with terra-cotta tiles and carpeting, a separate living area and a kitchenette. A specially designed mountain elevator was installed to reach all levels. *Box 332, Zichron Ya'akov, 30900, tel. 06/300333, fax 06/300310. 154 rooms with bath. Facilities: restaurant, café, bar, minisupermarket, children's activities, fitness center, sauna, steam room, hot tub, indoor and outdoor pools. AE, DC, MC, V. $$$*

Bet Maimon. On the western slopes of Zikhron Maimon, this family run hotel offers a spectacular view of the coastal valley and the sea. The freshly furnished rooms have kitchenettes. The terrace restaurant serves both Middle Eastern and Eastern European cuisine. Inquire about the special health vacation packages. Guests who are less than fit will feel the climb to the sun deck on the roof—there's no elevator in this three-story lodging. *4 Zahal St., tel. 06/390212, fax 06/396547. 22 rooms with bath. Facilities: restaurant, hot tub, sauna. No credit cards. $$$*

Lodging **Bet Daniel.** Set in a verdant park on Mt. Carmel, this guest house was founded in 1938 as a retreat for musicians. Gradually, its guests included artists and writers; today it is open to the public. Workshops and lectures for artists are still ongoing, albeit mostly in Hebrew. Rooms are spartan (though currently being redecorated), but those who place a premium on quiet and the charm of the public areas and grounds will love it. In the living room stands a 1905 Steinway and other antiques brought from England. Old photographs hang on the walls, and the library is well-stocked with books in German, Yiddish, French, and Hebrew. If you want to stay here during the biannual chamber-music festival (*see* The Arts and Nightlife, *below*), you must reserve well in advance. Good home cooking is available under various meal-plan options including just breakfast, half-board, or full board. *Box 13, Zichron Ya'akov, 30900, tel. 06/399001, fax 06/397007. 10 rooms, 9 with bath. No credit cards. $$*

The Arts and Nightlife

The Arts

On many a balmy summer night in towns up and down the coast, chances are you'll find an outdoor concert or a dance or theater performance. Especially evocative are the events held under the stars on the reconstructed stages of theaters at Caesarea and Ein Hod. In other seasons, chamber music concerts are held in Ein Hod and at Zichron Ya'akov. For the latest recorded information on performances, festivals, exhibitions, and other special events taking place in and around Haifa, call the 24-hour **"What's On"** number (tel. 04/374253). For current cultural listings along the coast check the Friday issue of the *Jerusalem Post* or pick up a copy of the monthly brochure "Events in Haifa and the Northern Region," published by the Ministry of Tourism.

Festivals In October, near the holiday of Sukkoth, **Haifa** hosts an international-al **film festival**. Contact the Haifa Cinemateque (tel. 04/383424) for the schedule and venues.

The **Blues Festival** takes place at the unusual venue of Haifa port in the month of June. One of last year's stars was Ray Charles. For information call tel. 04/374010 or check with the GTIO (tel. 04/666521).

The pastoral retreat for musicians and artists at **Bet Daniel** (tel. 06/399001) in **Zichron Ya'akov** is a perfect setting for the two chamber music festivals held here during the Jewish holidays of Sukkoth and Passover, which generally fall in October and April, respectively. The programs feature open rehearsals and discussions by musicians and teachers as well as alternating afternoon and evening concerts. In between concerts, guests can walk around the lovely landscaped grounds set in the woods with a fine view of Mt. Carmel. Try to book well in advance.

Music The **Israel Philharmonic Orchestra** gives approximately 30 concerts at the **Haifa Auditorium** (138 Hanassi Ave., tel. 04/380013) from October through July. Although most seats are sold through subscription, some tickets are usually available. Ticket prices range from NIS 75 ($25) to NIS 175 ($58.35) and are generally only sold at IPO theater box offices in Jerusalem, Tel Aviv, and Haifa. The IPO box office in Haifa is located at 16 Herzl Street; tel. 04/664167 or 04/665805. Concerts start at 8:30 PM or 9 PM. The box office opens one hour before performances.

The **Haifa Symphony Orchestra** also plays at the Haifa Auditorium about four times a week. It's best to buy tickets about 30 minutes before the performance, which generally begins around 8:30 PM. For information call the box office (50 Tezner St., tel. 04/621973). Ticket prices range from NIS 25 ($8.35) to NIS 55 ($18.35).

For chamber music Saturday evenings at 6:30 PM, try **Ein Hod's Gertrud Kraus House** (tel. 04/841058), just off the central square of this artists' community. Performances are suspended in July and August and occasionally alternate with poetry readings. Admission is NIS 27 ($9), and coffee and cake are on the house.

Also in Ein Hod, the outdoor stone **theater** (tel. 04/842029) at the top of the hill resonates with music every Friday night from June to September. This theater features mostly quality pop, classical, and jazz performances, with an occasional play produced. Tickets can be bought in advance on the second floor of The Gallery in town.

"Nights of Akko," a free concert series that features mostly Israeli music and folk dancing, is held Saturday night at about 7:30 from July to mid-September. The concerts take place on an outdoor stage on Ben Ami Street, the main street in the new city. There are also occasional chamber music concerts in the Crusader city and in Khan el-Umdan in the summer and winter. For more information call the tourist information office (tel. 04/911764).

Theater and At **Caesarea's Roman theater** (tel. 06/361358), evening performances
Dance by local and international troupes of the highest caliber are held generally from May to mid-October. The 1993 program featured the New Israel Opera's performance of *Aïda*. For advance information on the program starting in April, contact the National Parks Authority (4 Machleff St., Tel Aviv 61070, tel. 03/695–2281). Tickets can be purchased in advance at the Le'an ticket agency in Tel Aviv (101 Dizengoff St., tel. 03/523–6193 or 03/225573). In Caesarea the box office is open during the day of performance.

Nightlife

Although **Haifa** has a reputation as a town that works and never plays, times are changing. The younger generation (over 25) is breaking out and having a good time at a number of trendy watering holes and discos. These places come and go, so check with the front desk at your hotel. Two "in" pubs are **Migdalor** (at Stella Maris, tel. 04/336292) and **Back Door** (120 Yefe Nof St., tel. 04/376183). Well-known dance spots are **Butterfly** (137 Hanassi Ave.), **Fever** (in Gan Ha'Em), **Shmura** (38 Pica Rd., tel. 04/253500), and **Mizpor** (115 Yefe Nof St.).

Downstairs in the basement of Haifa's Dan Panorama hotel is the **Chaplin Club**, a disco that caters to the thirtysomething crowd, especially those nostalgic for 1960s dance music. There's no cover fee and on weekdays, no minimum. However, on Friday the minimum per person per table is NIS 30 ($10) plus 10% service. The club is open from 10:30 PM to 2 AM daily. On Fridays, call to make a reservation (tel. 04/384186).

Nahariya's flashiest disco is **La Scala** (tel. 04/922211, ext. 754), which features standard dance tunes with a throbbing beat and attracts an older crowd. This nightspot is in the passageway just west of the Carlton on Haga'aton. The cover charge on Friday and Saturday is NIS 24 ($8); the doors open at 10 PM.

6 Lower Galilee

Including Tiberias and the Sea of Galilee

By Mike Rogoff

The Galilee, to most Israelis, is synonymous with "the North," a land of mountains and fertile valleys, nature reserves and national parks. In short, they would claim, it's a provincial region too rustic and remote to live in, but great for vacations. Although much of the wild scenery associated with the North—the rugged highlands, waterfalls, and panoramas that seem to go on forever—is found in the Upper Galilee, the Lower Galilee has its own quiet beauty, varied landscape, and, more than anything, rich history.

On a map, the Lower Galilee fits into a frame about 50 kilometers (31 miles) square, divided by valleys, hill country, and the Sea of Galilee. To the south is the fertile Jezreel Valley, known simply as Ha'emek, "the Valley," and, sentimentally, if not scientifically, thought of by many Israelis as distinct from the rest of the Lower Galilee. To the east, the boundaries are easily defined by the Jordan Valley and the eastern shore of the Sea of Galilee (Lake Kinneret in Hebrew). To the north, the steep hillsides above the lake merge into the Upper Galilee, while farther west, Route 85 follows the Bet Hakerem Valley, the natural division between the two regions. Toward the Mediterranean Sea, the hills flatten out as you reach the coastal plain; Route 70 follows the region's western edge. Farming forms the economic base: fruit orchards, fish ponds, and such field crops as wheat and cotton in the valleys; olive groves in the hills; livestock everywhere. The valley towns of Afula and Bet She'an are little more than small, nondescript rural centers, while the larger hill town of Nazareth, the region's automotive service center, has more character, a noisy clash of pistons and politics. Tiberias, on the Sea of Galilee, depends on tourism for its livelihood, but the location is more splendid than the town itself.

Historical traditions abound. In the Jezreel Valley, filled with Old Testament lore, you come face to face with the land of Deborah, Gideon, King Saul and Jonathan, King Solomon, the prophet Elijah, Ahab, and Jezebel. After the Assyrian devastation of the northern kingdom of Israel in the 8th century BC, the region declined as the stream of history was diverted elsewhere, but in the late Roman and Byzantine periods (1st century BC–6th century AD), the vibrancy and wealth returned. The magnificent city of Scythopolis/Bet She'an, which is currently being unearthed, the opulent spa of Hammat Gader, the exquisite mosaics of Hammat Tiberias and Zippori, and the synagogues of Bet Alfa and Capernaum all highlight the period.

For Christian pilgrims, of course, there is nothing more compelling than exploring the landscape where Jesus of Nazareth lived, walked, and forged his ministry. Although Nazareth and Cana play crucial roles in the story, it is the Sea of Galilee and the many sites around its shores that have the most powerful resonance. Here Jesus called his disciples, wrought miracles, cured the sick, and taught the multitudes.

But the Galilee is not all ancient history. It was here that early 20th-century Jewish pioneers tamed a hostile land, draining malarial swamps and clearing boulders, transforming it into some of Israel's richest farmland. Here, too, they invented a new way of living together in perfect equality—the kibbutz. Travelers in the Galilee should take the opportunity to visit a kibbutz settlement and the handful of small museums exploring this unique Israeli social experiment.

The kibbutzim in the region, and a smaller number of moshavim (Jewish cooperative settlements) are concentrated in the Jezreel and Jordan valleys, and Sea of Galilee region; the rockier hill country is predominantly Arab (*Israeli* Arab, of course: This is not disputed territory). The enmities of the 1940s have yielded to a pragmatic and often even amicable *modus vivendi* between Jews and Arabs in the region. Although only 17% of Israel's general population is Arab, they have long been the majority in the Galilee. But the demographics have shifted, and a half-dozen small Jewish towns and several dozen rural villages have brought the two communities to numeric parity.

Whatever your agenda is in the Lower Galilee, take time to savor the region's natural beauty. Follow a hiking trail above the Sea of Galilee, or drive up to Belvoir, a mountaintop Crusader fortress; wade through fields of rare irises in the spring; bathe in warm mineral spas and spring-fed swimming pools, water-ski on the lake, canoe on the Jordan River, or slip down a water slide.

Culture and entertainment are not the region's strong suits. Tiberias's pubs and restaurants probably come closest to providing lively nightlife; but there are worse fates than sitting by a moonlit lake washing down a good St. Peter's fish, lamb *shishlik* (grilled skewered meat), or some Chinese delicacies with one of the excellent Israeli wines.

Essential Information

Important Addresses and Numbers

Tourist Information There are Government Tourist Information Offices (GTIOs) in the following towns:

Nazareth. GTIO, Casa Nova St., Box 58, 16100, tel. 06/573003 or 06/570555.

Tiberias. GTIO, Habanim St. (between the Jordan River and Moriah Plaza hotels), Box 474, tel. 06/720992 or 06/722089.

Emergencies To contact the **police** in the Lower Galilee region, dial 100. For **ambulance** service or information on **pharmacies** offering late-night service, dial 101. **Afula:** tel. 06/524205 (emergency tel. 06/524357); **Tiberias:** tel. 06/738211 (emergency tel. 06/738265).

Car Rental Agencies close early Friday afternoon and are closed on Saturday (except in Nazareth).

Nazareth: Europcar (National), Hatzafon Garage, Afula Rd., tel. 06/572050 or 06/572049.

Tiberias: Avis, in Caesar Hotel, Promenade, tel. 06/722766; Budget, opposite Jordan River Hotel, Habanim St., tel. 06/720864 or 06/723496; Eldan, in Jordan River Hotel, Habanim St., tel. 06/ 791822; Europcar (National), Sonol Garage, Alhadeff St., tel. 06/722777 or 06/724191; Hertz, in Jordan River Hotel, Habanim St., tel. 06/723939 or 721804; Reliable, 9 Alhadeff St., tel. 06/ 723464.

Arriving and Departing by Plane

Most travelers from abroad arrive at **Ben Gurion International Airport,** at Lod on the outskirts of Tel Aviv. There are no buses from the airport to the Lower Galilee. To reach Tiberias by car, take Route 1 to Tel Aviv, then Route 2 north toward Haifa. At the Caesarea interchange, turn east onto Route 65 via Megiddo and Afula (follow the signs to Tiberias). At the Golani junction turn right onto Route 77 to Tiberias. The trip takes about 2½ hours.

Arriving and Departing by Car and Bus

By Car From Tel Aviv, the Lower Galilee can be reached by taking Route 2 north (the Tel Aviv–Haifa highway) and then heading northeast along one of two regional roads: Route 65 (near Caesarea), emerging into the Jezreel Valley at Megiddo (80 kilometers, or 50 miles; a 1¼-hour drive); or Route 70 (near Zichron Ya'akov), emerging at Yokne'am (90 kilometers, or 57 miles; a 1½-hour drive). Avoid driving north out of Tel Aviv midday Friday and heading south to Tel Aviv Saturday afternoon and early evening. Access from Haifa is on Route 75 east to Bet She'arim and Nazareth (35 kilometers, or 22 miles; a 45-minute drive to Nazareth); or from Route 75 onto Routes 70 and 66 south to Megiddo (34 kilometers, or 22 miles; a 40-minute drive). The best route from Jerusalem is Route 1 east, then Route 90 north to Bet She'an (124 kilometers, or 78 miles; a two-hour drive).

By Bus The Egged bus cooperative provides frequent service from Jerusalem, Tel Aviv, and Haifa to Bet She'an, Afula, Nazareth, and Tiberias. From Tel Aviv, Buses 820 and 824 leave for Afula about every ½-hour; the ride takes 1¼ hours. Bus 824 goes on to Nazareth. Bus 830 departs from Tel Aviv to Tiberias about every 45 minutes; the ride takes two hours. To get from Haifa to Tiberias, take Bus 430, which leaves hourly; the ride is less than one hour. From Haifa take Bus 301 or 302 to Afula; Bus 434 to Bet She'an; and Bus 431 to Nazareth. Buses from Jerusalem to Bet She'an (Buses 963 and 964) depart about once an hour. The ride to Bet She'an is almost two hours, another 25 minutes to Tiberias. Bus 955 services Afula and Nazareth from Jerusalem once daily; travel time is 2½ hours. Buses 355, 357, 823, and 824 make the 20-minute run between Afula and Nazareth.

Getting Around

By Car Since not all sites are easily accessible by public bus (*see below*), driving is the best way to explore the region. Main roads are fairly good—some newer four-lane highways are excellent—but some smaller roads are narrow and in great need of repair. Signposting is generally good (and in English), with route numbers clearly marked. Ask directions by destination, because most Israelis have not yet become familiar with the relatively recent innovation of route numbers. Most attractions and accommodations are indicated by orange signs. You'll find gas stations and refreshment stands all over.

By Bus Although the most important sites in the region are accessible by bus, the sometimes infrequent local service and transfers can make getting around the Lower Galilee by bus a time-consuming exercise. Bet She'an, Nazareth, Tiberias, and Tabgha are on the main routes; others, such as Megiddo, Mt. of Beatitudes, and Bet She'arim, are a bit of a walk from a nearby junction, or even a good, long hike, as in the case of Capernaum and Mt. Tabor. Mt. Gilboa and Belvoir are essentially inaccessible without a car.

By Taxi This is generally an expensive and uninspiring way to travel. For sightseeing it is a much better deal to hire a private guide with a car or limousine (*see* Guided Tours, *below*).

Afula: Yizre'el, tel. 06/595625; **Nazareth:** Abu-Assal, tel. 06/ 554745; Diana, tel. 06/551483; Hashalom, tel. 06/572888. **Tiberias:** Hagalil, tel. 06/720353; Ha'emek, tel. 06/720131; Kinneret, tel. 06/722262.

By Boat The Ein Gev–based boat company, **Kinneret Sailing** (Rte. 92, Kibbutz Ein Gev, tel. 06/721831; in Tiberias, tel. 06/720248), has regularly scheduled runs on the Sea of Galilee between Ein Gev (east shore) and Tiberias (west shore). The boats are large (100–170 passengers), and the 45-minute crossings are comfortable in almost all weather. The round-trip costs NIS 25 ($8.35) for adults, NIS 15 ($5) for children (ages 3–13). Daily departures from Tiberias to Ein Gev are at 10:30 AM year-round, and also at noon and 1:30 in July and August and on Jewish holidays. From Ein Gev to Tiberias, boats depart daily at 12:30 and 1:30 year-round; additional departures in July and August and on Jewish holidays are at 3 and 4.

Both Kinneret Sailing and **Lido Kinneret** (Gedud Barak St., tel. 06/ 721538, 06/792564, or 06/724488) specialize in group charters, especially (but not exclusively) between Tiberias and Kibbutz Ginosar. You can join these cruises for the same cost as the scheduled Tiberias–Ein Gev runs. Call the respective companies for information on special trips you can join.

Guided Tours

General Interest A free 45-minute walking tour of Old Tiberias leaves from the Moriah Plaza Hotel (Habanim Street, tel. 06/792233) on Saturday at 10 AM. Organized jointly by the hotel and the Society for the Protection of Nature in Israel (SPNI), the tours are given in both Hebrew and English.

Few coach tours actually originate in the Lower Galilee. They start instead from Jerusalem, Tel Aviv, Haifa, and Netanya. Most hotels can book a tour for you. All buses will pick you up and drop you off at your hotel.

Egged Tours conducts one- and two-day tours from Jerusalem, Tel Aviv, Haifa, and Netanya several times a week. The Lower Galilee tours include (in different combinations) Megiddo, Nazareth, Tiberias, Tabgha, Capernaum, and a boat ride on the Sea of Galilee. Two-day tours include the Upper Galilee and Golan Heights. Prices range from NIS 147 to NIS 480 ($49 to $160). For reservations call Egged Tours in Jerusalem (224 Jaffa Rd., tel. 02/304422); in Tel Aviv (15 Frishman St., tel. 03/527–1222; 59 Ben Yehuda St., tel. 03/527–1222 or 03/527–1223); in Haifa (2 Hagana Ave., tel. 04/643131 or 04/ 643132); and in Netanya (28 Herzl St., tel. 053/ 28333 or 053/338881).

United Tours offers a similar though slightly smaller range of tours. A unique feature is the company's collaboration with Archaeological Seminars of Jerusalem. Tours run from Jerusalem and Tel Aviv, and some can be joined in Netanya. Prices range from NIS 114 to NIS 420 ($38 to $140). For reservations call United Tours in Jerusalem (King David Hotel annex, tel. 02/ 252187 or 02/252188) or in Tel Aviv (113 Hayarkon St., tel. 03/693–3404 or 03/693–3405).

Galilee Tours (10 Jordan St., Tiberias, tel. 06/720330 or 06/720550, or toll-free 177/022–2525), a smaller company, offers tours to Nazareth, Tiberias, and Capernaum three times a week, originating in Jerusalem with a pickup in Tel Aviv.

**Special
Interest
*Horseback and
Donkeyback*** **Vered Hagalil** is a "dude ranch" at Korazim Junction that, in addition to offering comfortable accommodations and a good restaurant, conducts horseback tours ranging from ½-hour for NIS 45 ($15) to five days (price available upon request). For more information contact Vered Hagalil (Rte. 90, Mobile Post Korazim, tel. 06/935785, fax 06/934964).

Donkeyback riding is singularly appropriate in the hills of Nazareth and the Lower Galilee, a revival of an ancient tradition. **Donkey Tracks** conducts fully guided group tours (call ahead to see what's available), and individuals can rent a donkey for NIS 30 ($10) an hour, complete with map, directions, and safety instructions. For more information contact Kfar Kedem (village of Hoshaya, Mobile Post Upper Nazareth, 17915, tel. 06/565511, fax 06/570378).

Exploring Lower Galilee

The three tours in this chapter cover three distinct parts of the region: the Jezreel and Jordan valleys (Tour 1, which traverses the southern part of the region from Mt. Carmel in the west to the border with Jordan in the east); the rugged hill country (Tour 2, north of the Jezreel Valley and west of the Sea of Galilee); and the Sea of Galilee (Tour 3, in the northeast corner of the Lower Galilee).

Tour 1 begins on Route 65 (the Wadi Ara pass), which runs northeast from Caesarea, north of Tel Aviv on the coast. The tour can be followed as easily in reverse, however, from the Jordan River and Bet She'an, the logical order for travelers coming from Jerusalem. Tour 1 is essentially a day trip combining archaeological sites and natural ones, including no fewer than six national parks. The main attractions are Megiddo, Bet She'an, Bet Alfa, and Belvoir. Tour 2, comfortably followed in a day if you manage Nazareth before lunch, is best started by taking Route 75 from Haifa. You can reach Nazareth from Akko (Acre) and Haifa by taking Route 79, from Tiberias and the Upper Galilee on routes 77 and 764, and from Afula on 80.

Tour 3 takes the traveler clockwise along the shores of the Sea of Galilee from Tiberias, the main town in the area, up the western side of the lake on routes 90 and 87, and down the eastern shore on Route 92, rounding the southern end of the lake. As you would expect in an area so central to the New Testament story, the shores are covered with sites hallowed by Christian tradition, but there are also important ancient synagogues at Capernaum and Hammat Tiberias. Those whose priorities lie elsewhere may want to concentrate on the recreational attractions of the Sea of Galilee, a resort area that draws tens of thousands of vacationing Israelis every year. Avoid the weeks of Passover (March or April) and Sukkot (September or October), when the whole country seems to be on holiday here.

Highlights for First-Time Visitors

Basilica of the Annunciation, Nazareth (*see* Tour 2)
Belvoir (*see* Tour 1)
Bet She'an (*see* Tour 1)
Bet She'arim (necropolis; *see* Tour 2)
Capernaum (*see* Tour 3)
Cruise on the Sea of Galilee (*see* Tour 3)
Megiddo (*see* Tour 1)
Mosaics and hot springs, Hammat Tiberias (*see* Tour 3)
Tiberias (*see* Tour 3)
Zippori (Roman mosaics; *see* Tour 2)

Christian pilgrims should add **Mt. of Beatitudes** and **Tabgha** (*see* Tour 3).

Tour 1: The Jezreel and Jordan Valleys

Numbers in the margin correspond to points of interest on the Lower Galilee map.

"Highways of the world cross Galilee in all directions," wrote the eminent Victorian scholar George Adam Smith in 1898. The great international highway of antiquity, the **Via Maris,** the Way of the Sea, swept up the coast from Egypt and broke inland along three separate mountain passes to emerge in the Jezreel Valley, before continuing northeast to Damascus and Mesopotamia. The through road that began at the Mediterranean coast just north of Mt. Carmel and led to the Jordan Valley at Bet She'an ran through the Jezreel Valley as well. And then, as now, roads connected the valley with the hill country of the Galilee to the north and Samaria to the south. Its destiny as a kind of universal thoroughfare and its flat terrain made the Jezreel Valley a frequent and easy battleground, so much so that the New Testament Book of Revelations identifies it—by the name Armageddon—as the stage for mankind's apocalyptic finale.

One of the most convenient routes into the region is Route 65, the **pass of Wadi Ara,** which slices inland from Caesarea and Hadera on the coastal plain and emerges at Megiddo. Follow the signs to Afula. Along the valley is a belt of Arab villages that became part of Israel in a land swap with Jordan in 1949. This road was the central branch of the Via Maris in antiquity, and was a preferred invasion route throughout history. Turn left at the Megiddo Junction onto Route 66 north. One kilometer (.6 mile) on, a double left turn brings you to **Megiddo,** one of the most important ancient cities in Israel. Several archaeological expeditions since the beginning of the century have exposed no fewer than 25 strata of civilization—from the 4th millennium BC to the 4th century BC—in the historical layer-cake mound archaeologists call a *tel.* A tiny museum at the entrance offers some excellent visual aids to help you on your way, including three-dimensional maps and a model of the tel itself.

The ramp up to the flat-top mound of Megiddo deposits you right opposite an ancient **gate,** almost identical to those found at Hazor in the north and Gezer to the south. Long identified with King Solomon (10th century BC)—all three cities were his regional military centers—the gate has been redated by some scholars to the time of Ahab, king of Israel a century later. To your right, in a trench, are the remains of a much older, Late Canaanite gate, quite possibly the one that defended Megiddo against the Egyptian pharaoh Thutmose III in 1468 BC. The Ahab connection is strong at Megiddo. Ruins of **stables,** also once thought to be Solomon's, are now definitively dated to the reign of Ahab, who is known to have had a large chariot army.

Evidence of prehistoric habitation on the site has been found, but among the earliest remains of the *city* of Megiddo are a round **altar** dating from the Early Bronze Age, and the outlines of several Early Bronze Age **temples,** almost 5,000 years old, visible in the trench between the two fine lookout points.

Nothing at Megiddo is as impressive as its **water system.** Before its construction, again apparently by Ahab, the citizens of the town had to leave the safety of their walls to descend to the subterranean spring to draw water. In a masterful stroke, the Israelite engineers sunk a deep shaft and a horizontal tunnel through solid rock to reach the spring from within the city. With this access, the spring could be permanently blocked outside the defensive walls, securing the city's vital water supply. The spring, at the end of the tunnel, is nothing more than a trickle today, perhaps blocked by earthquakes of later centuries. Look for chisel marks and ancient rock-hewn steps as you descend 180 steps through the shaft, traverse the 65-yard-long tunnel under the ancient city wall, and climb up 83 steps at the other end. A 10-minute walk takes you back to the parking lot. *Rte. 66, tel. 06/420312. Admission: NIS 10.50 ($3.50) adults, NIS 8 ($2.70) students and senior citizens, NIS 5 ($1.70) children. Open Apr.–Sept., Sat.–Thurs. 8–5, Fri. and holiday eves 8–4; Oct.–Mar., Sat.– Thurs. 8–4, Fri. and holiday eves 8–3.*

Return to Route 65 and drive east (toward Afula) for 5 kilometers (3 miles). Turn right onto Route 675 and cross the next major junction, with Route 60, 9 kilometers (5.6 miles) away. Just past the entrance to Kibbutz Yizre'el, on the left, a short road leads to a rise with a small coppice of trees. This is the tel of the biblical city of **Jezreel** (Yizre'el in Hebrew), where Ahab coveted Naboth's vineyard (I Kings 21), and his Phoenician wife, Jezebel, met the gruesome death predicted by the prophet Elijah (II Kings 9). From among the ancient ruins currently being unearthed by a Tel Aviv University expedition, you have a magnificent view of the valley below.

On a topographical map, the Jezreel Valley appears as an inverted equilateral triangle, each side about 40 kilometers (25 miles) long. The narrower extension below you is the Harod Valley, which continues southeast to Bet She'an in the Jordan Rift. The most immediate impression the traveler has is of lush farmland as far as the eye can see, but, until as recently as 50 years ago, malarial swamps still blighted the area, and some early pioneering settlements had cemeteries before their first buildings were completed. Today **Ha'emek** (The Valley), as Israelis call it, is one of the country's most fertile regions.

Return to 675, descend eastward, and turn right onto Route 71. Continue for 2 kilometers (1.2 miles) and turn right to Gidona and **Ma'ayan Harod.** The small national park at the foot of **Mt. Gilboa** is an attractive area of lawns and huge eucalyptus trees, with a big swimming pool (*see* Participant Sports *in* Sports and the Outdoors, *below*) fed by a spring. It's a bucolic picnic spot, but the spring tells a different story. It was here, almost 32 centuries ago, that Gideon gathered the Israelites for battle against the Midianite desert invaders: "And the camp of Midian was north of them, by the Hill of Moreh, in the valley" (Judges 7). To emphasize the miraculous nature of the coming victory, Gideon dismissed more than two-thirds of the assembled warriors, and, by selecting only those who lapped up water from the spring "as a dog laps," reduced the army to a tiny force of 300 men. Equipped with swords, ram's horns, and flaming torches concealed in clay jars, the force divided into three companies, and stealthily surrounded the Midianite camp. At a prearranged signal, the Israelite warriors shouted, blew the ram's horns, and smashed the jars. Waking to the nightmarish din and the sudden appearance of flaming torches, the Midianites panicked into flight, and the victory was won.

The spring has seen the clash of armies in other ages. It was here, in 1260, that the Mamluks stopped the invasion of the hitherto invincible Mongols. And in the 1930s, the woods above the spring hid the training of illegal Jewish self-defense squads by a British army officer, Orde Wingate. Wingate died in the Burmese jungle in 1944; his trainees, among them Moshe Dayan and Yigal Allon, became top military commanders of the fledgling State of Israel in 1948, when Wingate's principles of unconventional warfare stood them in good stead. *Off Rte. 71, next to Gidona. Admission: NIS 13 ($4.35) adults, NIS 6.50 ($2.20) children. For hrs, see Megiddo, above.*

Time Out Some 3 kilometers (2 miles) east on Route 71, opposite the gas station, is the entrance to **Kibbutz Ein Harod (Me'uchad).** (Don't confuse it with its immediate neighbor, Ein Harod [Ichud].) On the grounds of the kibbutz is an art museum that showcases Jewish artists past and present. Also on the kibbutz is Bet Sturman, a museum of the human and natural history of the region. *Art museum: tel. 06/ 531670. Admission NIS 7 ($2.35) adults, NIS 5 ($1.70) children, students, and senior citizens. Open Sun.–Thurs. 9–4:30, Fri. 9–1:30, Sat. 10–4:30. Bet Sturman: tel. 06/533284. Admission: NIS 10 ($3.35) adults, NIS 7 ($2.35) children, students, and senior citizens. Open Sun.–Thurs. 9–3, Sat. 10–3.*

Exit right onto Route 669, some 2.5 kilometers (1.5 miles) beyond Ein Harod. Follow it to Kibbutz Hefziba and look for the orange sign
❹ that announces the ancient synagogue of **Bet Alfa.** (*Kibbutz* Bet Alfa is the next village to the east.) In 1928, members of Kibbutz Hefziba were digging an irrigation trench when their tools hit a hard surface. Careful archaeological digging uncovered the lovely multicolored **mosaic floor** of an ancient synagogue, almost entirely preserved.

An Aramaic inscription dates the building to the reign of Byzantine emperor Justinian in the second quarter of the 6th century AD; a Greek inscription credits the workmanship to Marianos and his son, Aninas. Following Jewish tradition, the synagogue faces Jerusalem, with an apse at the far end to hold the holy ark. The building faithfully copies the architecture of the Byzantine basilicas of the day, with a nave and two side aisles, and the doors lead to a small narthex and an outside atrium. Stairs indicate that there was once an upper story.

The large mosaic in the nave is divided into three panels. The top one leaves no doubt that this was a synagogue. All the classical Jewish symbols are here: the holy ark flanked by lions; the menorah, the seven-branch candelabra; the shofar, the ram's horn; the incense shovel once used in the Second Temple; and the *lulav* and *etrog,* the palm frond and citron used in the celebration of Sukkot, the Feast of Tabernacles. It is the middle panel, however, that is at once the most interesting and the most unexpected: It is filled with human figures depicting the seasons, the Zodiac, and, even more incredibly for a Jewish house of worship, the Greek sun god, Helios. Clearly these were more liberal times, when perhaps the prohibition on making graven images didn't apply to two-dimensional art. Most scholars agree that the mosaic's motifs do not suggest some divergent Jewish sect or regional apostasy but a convenient artistic convention to symbolize the orderly cycles of (God's) universe, since He Himself could not be represented graphically. The last panel tells the story of Abraham's near-sacrifice of his son Isaac (Genesis 22), again captioned in Hebrew. *Kibbutz Hefziba, tel. 06/531400. Admission: NIS 5 ($1.70) adults, NIS 3.80 ($1.30) students and senior citizens, NIS 2.50 (85¢) children. For hrs, see Megiddo, above.*

Just east of Kibbutz Bet Alfa is the turnoff for Route 6666, which
❺ climbs steeply to the top of **Mt. Gilboa,** the mountain cursed by David ("Let there be no rain or dew on you"), for it was here, 3,000

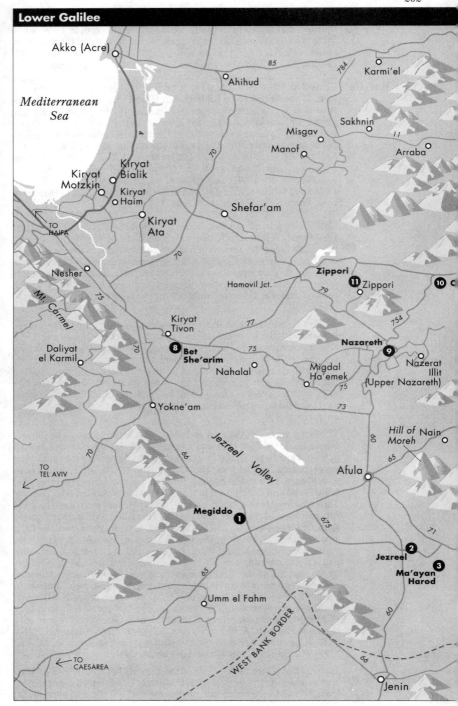

Lower Galilee

Akko (Acre)

Mediterranean Sea

Ahihud

85

784

Karmi'el

Misgav

Sakhnin

11

Manof

Arraba

Kiryat Bialik

Kiryat Motzkin

Kiryat Haim

Kiryat Ata

TO HAIFA

70

Shefar'am

Nesher

Mt. Carmel

75

Zippori

Hamovil Jct.

79

11 Zippori

10

Daliyat el Karmil

70

Kiryat Tivon

754

8 Bet She'arim

77

75

Nazareth

9

Nahalal

Migdal Ha'emek

Nazerat Illit (Upper Nazareth)

75

Yokne'am

73

TO TEL AVIV

70

Jezreel Valley

60

Hill of Moreh

Nain

65

Afula

Megiddo **1**

66

675

71

65

Jezreel **2**

3

Ma'ayan Harod

Umm el Fahm

60

WEST BANK BORDER

TO CAESAREA

66

Jenin

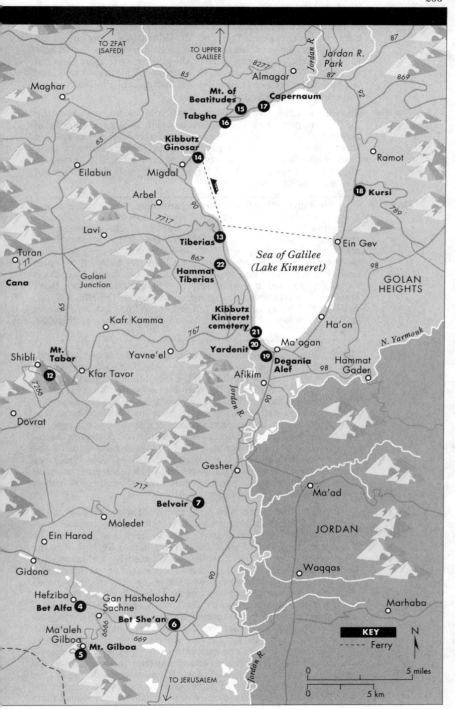

TO ZFAT
(SAFED)

TO UPPER
GALILEE

Maghar

85

Almagar

Jordan R.

Jordan R.
Park

87

87

869

Mt. of
Beatitudes **15** **17** **Capernaum**

Tabgha **16**

92

65

Eilabun

**Kibbutz
Ginosar**
14

Migdal

Ramot

Arbel

90

18 **Kursi**

789

Lavi

7717

Turan
11

Golani
Junction

Tiberias **13**

867 **22**

**Hammat
Tiberias**

*Sea of Galilee
(Lake Kinneret)*

Ein Gev

98

GOLAN
HEIGHTS

Cana

65

Kafr Kamma

**Kibbutz
Kinneret
cemetery** **21**

767 **20**

Yavne'el

Yardenit **19** **Degania
Alef**

Ma'agan

Ha'on

N. Yarmouk

Shibli

**Mt.
Tabor**
12

7286

Kfar Tavor

Afikim

98

Hammat
Gader

Dovrat

Jordan R.

Gesher

Ma'ad

717

Belvoir **7**

JORDAN

Moledet

Ein Harod

Gidona

90

Waqqas

Hefziba

Bet Alfa **4**

Gan Hashelosha/
Sachne

Marhaba

Ma'aleh
Gilboa

6666

Bet She'an **6**

669

5 **Mt. Gilboa**

Jordan R.

TO JERUSALEM

KEY

N

- - - - - Ferry

0   5 miles

0   5 km

years ago, that King Saul was killed fighting the Philistines. "On the morrow, when the Philistines came to strip the slain, they found Saul and his three sons fallen on Mt. Gilboa. And they cut off his head, and stripped off his armor, and sent messengers throughout the land of the Philistines to carry the good news to their idols and the people." The debacle on Mt. Gilboa sowed panic in the ranks, and the Israelites "forsook their cities and fled; and the Philistines came and dwelt in them" (I Samuel 31).

Mt. Gilboa is famous for its springtime wildflowers, and especially for the rare purple iris that blooms in April. That's when hordes of Israelis take to the well-marked panoramic trails along the ridge (a short and very easy walk) to pay homage to Mother Nature. Years of tireless efforts by environmental groups such as the SPNI have paid off, and every preschooler will tell you imperiously that you are not allowed to pick the wildflowers!

Time Out Back on Route 669, a few hundred yards east, a palm-lined access road on the right takes you to the **National Park of Sachne.** The official name, **Gan Hashelosha,** or the Garden of Three, remembers three Jewish pioneers killed in 1938. This is an attractive park developed around a warm spring (28°C, or 82°F, most of the year) and a deep stream. There are changing facilities for bathers, a decent snack bar at the west end, and a cafeteria at the east end. The park is especially crowded in good weather on Friday and Saturday. Don't leave your possessions unattended on the lawns. *Off Rte. 669, tel. 06/586219. Admission: NIS 15 ($5) adults, NIS 11 ($3.70) students and senior citizens, NIS 7.50 ($2.50) children. For hrs, see Megiddo,* above.

Continuing east on 669 between farming settlements and fish ponds (carp and St. Peter's fish), you'll notice signs to the left guiding you

❻ to the town of **Bet She'an.** Once in the town, follow signs to the National Park or the **Roman Theater.** The semicircular theater was built of contrasting black basalt and white limestone blocks around AD 200, when **Scythopolis,** as the Roman city of Bet She'an was known, was at its height. Excavated more than 30 years ago, the theater is the largest and best preserved in Israel. Although the upper *cavea,* or tiers, have not survived, archaeologists estimate the original capacity to have been more than 8,000 people. The large stage and part of the *scaena* (backdrop) behind it have been restored, and Bet She'an again hosts summer performances as in days of yore (*see* The Arts and Nightlife, *below*).

Until 1985, when the current excavations of the nearly 30-acre site began, the theater stood in splendid isolation, ignored by most tourists in favor of the more famous one at Caesarea (*see* Exploring the Northern Coast and Western Galilee *in* Chapter 5). Now it is the jewel in the crown of one of Israel's most extensive and fascinating digs in recent years. Two parallel but coordinated projects have systematically exposed the downtown area of one of the region's greatest and most cosmopolitan cities in the Late Roman and Byzantine periods (2nd–6th centuries AD). Masterfully engineered colonnaded main streets, complete with storm drains and lined with shops, converge on a central plaza that once boasted a fine temple, a decorative fountain, and a public monument. An elaborate Byzantine bathhouse, 1¼ acres in area and complete with *caldaria* (steam rooms) and mosaic-floored porticoes, once pampered the worthies of the town. And the enormous haul of marble statuary and friezes says much about the opulence of Scythopolis in its heyday. One of the most interesting finds is a multicolored mosaic floor in a small room

near the ancient *odeon* (a small auditorium for chamber music) showing Tyche (Fortuna), Greek goddess of good fortune, holding a cor-
nucopia. An ambitious restoration program marches hard on the
heels of the archaeological dig itself.

A recent find is a Byzantine church with a mosaic floor depicting
hunting scenes and fruits and vegetables of the Holy Land. Remnants of altar columns were also found above a container holding a
human tooth—apparently a holy relic—and in a chapel at one side
was a sarcophagus containing two human skulls.

Dominating the town to the north is the high **tel** of **Canaanite/ Israelite Bet She'an.** Few visible remains are left of the work done by the
University of Pennsylvania expedition, which partially excavated
the site in the 1920s, but the current team of Israeli archaeologists is
turning its attention to this most ancient area as well. The climb to
the top, though a bit strenuous, is short and worth every gasp.
There is a fine panoramic view of the surrounding valleys, and a superb bird's-eye view of the entire excavated area.

Back on the main thoroughfare of Sha'ul Hamelech (King Saul)
Street, turn left. A few hundred yards farther on the left are the impressive remains of Scythopolis's **amphitheater,** where blood sports
and gladiatorial combats were once the order of the day. *Off Shaul
Hamelech St., at Bank Leumi, tel. 06/587189. Admission: NIS 10.50
($3.50) adults, NIS 8 ($2.70) students and senior citizens, NIS 5
($1.70) children. For hrs, see Megiddo, above.*

The road Route 90, which runs along the western shore of the Sea of
Galilee all the way north to Metulla, at the Lebanese border, and
south to Jericho.

❼ Thirteen kilometers (8 miles) north, Route 717 climbs off to the west
to **Belvoir** ("beautiful view"), the most invincible Crusader fortress
in the land. The Hebrew name of **Kochav Hayarden** ("the star of the
Jordan") and the Arabic **Kaukab el Hauwa** ("the star of the wind")
emphasize its splendid isolation. The breathtaking view of the Jordan Valley and southern Sea of Galilee some 600 yards below you is
itself worth the drive.

Belvoir was completed by the Hospitallers (the Knights of St. John)
in 1173. In the summer of 1187 the Crusader armies were crushed by
the Arab leader Saladin at the Horns of Hattin, west of Tiberias,
bringing to an end the Latin Kingdom of Jerusalem. The remnants
struggled on to Tyre (in modern Lebanon), and in the Holy Land itself, Belvoir alone refused to yield. Eighteen months of siege
brought the Muslims no farther than undermining the outer eastern
rampart. The Crusaders, for their part, had defended bravely, and
even sallied out from time to time to do battle with the enemy; but
their lone resistance had become pointless. They struck a deal with
Saladin: They would surrender the stronghold in exchange for free
passage, flags flying, to Tyre.

Do not follow the arrows from the parking lot, but take the wide
gravel path to the right of the fortress. It brings you at once to the
panoramic view. It is also the best spot from which to appreciate the
strength of the stronghold, with its deep dry moat, massive rock and
cut-stone ramparts, and series of gates. Once inside the main courtyard, you are unexpectedly faced with a fortress within a fortress, a
scaled-down replica of the outer defenses. Little wonder the Muslims could not force its submission. Not much of the upper stories
remain: In 1220, the Muslims systematically dismantled Belvoir out
of fear of another Crusade and the renewal of the fortress as a

Frankish base. Once you have explored the modest buildings, exit over the western bridge (once a drawbridge), which allows you to spy on the postern gates, the protected and sometimes secret back doors of medieval castles. *5 km (3 mi) w. of Rte. 90, tel. 06/587000. Admission: NIS 8 ($2.70) adults, NIS 6 ($2) students and senior citizens, NIS 4 ($1.35) children. For hrs*, see *Megiddo, above.*

The road to Belvoir from Ein Harod via Moledet is passable, but in very bad condition in places. Back on Route 90, you are 10 minutes' drive from the Sea of Galilee and the link with Tour 3 (*see below*).

Tour 2: Nazareth and the Galilee Hills

Remove the modern roads and power lines, and the landscape of this region would be an illustration from the Bible. Unplanned villages are splashed, seemingly haphazardly, on the hillsides, freeing the valleys for small-scale agriculture. Acres of olive groves are still harvested by whacking the trees as in days of old to bring in the source of the region's ancient wealth. New Testament references are numerous here: Nazareth, where Jesus grew up; Cana, with its miraculous wedding feast; Mt. Tabor, identified with the Transfiguration. Jewish history resonates strongly, too: Tabor and Yodefat were fortifications in the Great Revolt against the Romans (1st century AD); Shefar'am, Bet She'arim, and Zippori were in turn the headquarters of the Sanhedrin, the Jewish high court, between the 2nd and 4th centuries AD; and latter-day Jewish pioneers have been attracted to the region's wild scenery as well.

The area is bounded in the north by Route 85, in the west by Route 70, in the south by Route 75 and Mt. Tabor, and in the east by the plateau just east of Route 65. Take Route 2 heading north out of Haifa toward Akko (Acre) and the group of towns known as the Krayot. Almost immediately you go through the Checkpost Junction, turn right onto Route 75. Stay on that road (Nazareth via Migdal Ha'emek) to the small town of Kiryat Tivon, 11 kilometers (7 miles) away. Look for the orange sign (to the right) that will lead you to the antiquities of Bet She'arim. One sign is on the main circle of Kiryat Tiv'on; another (which points the way to a less convoluted route) is a few hundred yards beyond the circle, off the same highway. Some of the subsequent signs are in yellow.

❽ **Bet She'arim** lies in a hollow, in a pleasantly landscaped national park that invites picnicking in good weather. In two major expeditions in the 1930s and '50s, a huge series of 20 **catacombs** was uncovered, as were parts of the 2nd- to 4th-century AD **Jewish town** on the slopes above them. Remains of an olive press and a fine ancient synagogue are visible to the left of the road that descends to the park.

Bet She'arim flourished after, and to some extent because of, the eclipse of Jerusalem. The little that was left of Jerusalem after Titus's legions sacked it and razed the Second Temple in AD 70, was plowed under by Hadrian in AD 135, following the Second (Bar Kochba) Revolt of the Jews against Rome. Hadrian built in its stead the pagan town of Aelia Capitolina, and access to their holy city and the venerated burial ground of Mt. of Olives was denied to Jews for generations. The center of Jewish life and religious authority retreated, first to Yavneh in the southern coastal plain, and then for several centuries to the Lower Galilee.

By around AD 200 the unofficial Jewish "capital" had shifted to Bet She'arim, a city that owed its brief preeminence to the enormous stature of one man who chose to make it his home: Rabbi Yehuda

Hanassi, the Patriarch, or Prince, as he is sometimes called. The title was conferred on the nominal leader of the Jewish community, who was responsible both for its inner workings and for its relations with its Roman masters. Yehuda Hanassi's enduring achievement was his compilation, at Bet She'arim, of the Mishnah, which finally committed to writing the "Oral Law." For centuries, rabbis had given learned responses to real-life questions of civil and religious law, basing their judgments on the do's and don'ts of the Torah, the biblical Five Books of Moses, which is the foundation of Judaism. These rabbinic opinions had been transmitted orally from generation to generation, and, like court decisions, had become legal precedents, and thus an integral part of the body of Jewish jurisprudence. Further commentary was added to the Mishnah in later centuries to produce the Talmud, the primary guide to Orthodox Jewish practice to this day (*see* Tour 3, *below*).

If Bet She'arim was a magnet for scholars and petitioners in Yehuda Hanassi's lifetime, it became a virtual shrine after his death. With Jerusalem still off-limits, Bet She'arim became the prestigious burial site of the Jewish world. (It was considered a privilege and good afterlife insurance to be buried in the company of *Rabenu Hakadosh*, "our Holy Teacher," for when the Messiah came, surely the Rabbi would be one of the first to be resurrected to follow the Messiah to Jerusalem!) Bet She'arim's prominence lasted until AD 352, when Gallus destroyed the town in the suppression of (yet another) Jewish revolt.

Only the largest of the catacombs at Bet She'arim is open to the public: 24 chambers containing more than 200 stone sarcophagi and *arcosolia* (arched burial niches). A wide range of both Jewish and Roman symbols are carved into the sarcophagi, and the more than 250 funerary inscriptions in Greek, Hebrew, Aramaic, and Palmyrene testify to the great distances some of the denizens of the necropolis had traveled—from Yemen and Mesopotamia, for instance—to be buried here. Without exception, the sarcophagi were found plundered by grave robbers seeking the possessions with which the dead were once buried.

The tiny but interesting museum adjacent to the catacombs includes a relic of Bet She'arim's industrial activity, a 9-ton slab of raw, unfinished glass, the largest such artifact from the ancient world. *Tel. 04/831643. Admission: NIS 10.50 ($3.50) adults, NIS 8 ($2.70) students and senior citizens, NIS 5 ($1.70) children. For hrs, see Megiddo, above.*

Return to Route 75 and head east. The road skirts the northside of the picturesque Jezreel Valley as it begins to climb into the hills toward Nazareth. At the crest of the hill, it is joined by Route 60 from Afula. A turn to the left takes you down to Paulus VI, the main **❾** street of **Nazareth.**

Jesus grew up in Nazareth, which was then an insignificant village nestling in a hollow in the Galilean hills. Today's town of 60,000 has burst out of the hollow with almost frenetic energy. It is a slightly bemusing and dissonant experience for the Christian pilgrim who seeks the "spiritual Nazareth" among the horn-blowing cars, vendors, and donkeys (at least *they* add some scriptural authenticity!) plying Paulus VI Street. The scene is slightly quieter on Friday, when the Muslim half of the Arab population takes time off, and positively placid on Sunday, the day of rest for the Christians who make up the other half. If you're out for local color, come on Saturday, when the Arab peasants come to town to sell produce and buy goods, and Israeli families from the surrounding area come looking for bargains in the *souk* (market). The high dome of the Franciscan **Basilica of the Annunciation** dominates the lower part of the town. About 2 kilometers (1.2 miles) into town, Casa Nova Street climbs steeply to the left to the entrance of the church. (Parking is hard to find here. Try Paulus VI Street, in the direction of the Galilee Hotel.)

Time Out   Try the Arab pastries at the confectionery opposite the main entrance of the Church of the Annunciation. Especially good is the *bourma*, a honey-soaked cylindrical pastry filled with whole pistachio nuts.

Turn right inside the gate to the church. The portico around the courtyard is decorated with 20th-century mosaic panels, mostly depicting the Madonna and Child theme, donated by Catholic communities around the world.

The present church, said to be the largest in the Middle East, was consecrated in 1969 on the site of its Byzantine and Crusader predecessors, the scanty remains of which are preserved inside. The church is built on two levels: The lower one contains the grotto identified in the Roman Catholic tradition as the home of Mary and Joseph, and the site of the Annunciation; the upper level is the parish church of Nazareth's Roman Catholic community.

The main entrance is graced by tastefully designed doors, made in Germany, which relate in bronze relief the central events of Jesus's life. Enter the dimly lighted **lower church** with its brilliant abstract stained-glass windows. The focal point of the entire church is a small hewn cave dwelling below floor level, venerated for centuries as the home of Mary. As related in Luke 1, "the angel Gabriel was sent from God to a city of Galilee named Nazareth, to a virgin . . . and the virgin's name was Mary. And he came to her and said, 'Hail, O favored one, the Lord is with you! . . . And behold, you will conceive in your womb and bear a son, and you shall call his name Jesus.'" This is the event known to Christianity as the Annunciation. A seating area before the cave is surrounded by a fence and gate that is only opened for groups of pilgrims holding prearranged masses here. If you are on your own, you can usually dart in and out as groups arrive and depart. Crusader-era walls still stand beneath the modern windows, and some restored Byzantine mosaics are below the railings from which you view the grotto.

Just inside the entrance, a spiral staircase leads to the vast **upper church,** some 70 yards long and 30 yards wide. Note that the beautiful Italian ceramic reliefs on the huge concrete pillars representing the Stations of the Cross are captioned in the Arabic vernacular. The cupola, which soars 195 feet above the cave of the lower church (seen through a well), is formed by ribs representing the petals of a lily chalice (the lily is a symbol of purity), rooted in heaven, and is inscribed with the recurring letter "M" for Mary. The huge Italian-designed mosaic behind the altar shows Jesus and Peter at the center, an enthroned Mary behind them, flanked by figures of the Hierarchical Church (to your right), and the Charismatic Church (to your left). The modern concrete trusses over the nave evoke the wooden roofs of the early Christian basilicas. On the walls of the upper church are the so-called **"banners,"** large panels of mosaics and ceramic reliefs contributed by Roman Catholic communities abroad. The United States, Canada (a fine terra-cotta), and Australia are represented. Noteworthy are the Madonna-and-child gifts of Japan (made with gold leaf and real pearls), Venezuela (a carved-wood statue), and Cameroun (a stylized painting in black, white, and brick-red). A side door on the left takes you to a courtyard, where a glass-enclosed baptistry has been built over what is thought to have been an ancient *mikveh*, a Jewish ritual immersion bath. *Casa Nova St., tel. 06/572501. Admission free. Open Apr.–Sept., Mon.–Sat. 8:30–11:45 and 2–6, Sun. 2–6; Oct.–Mar., Mon.–Sat. 8:30–11:45 and 2–5, Sun. 2–5.*

Continue past Terra Sancta College and up some steps to the 1914 **Church of St. Joseph,** underneath which is a hewn complex of chambers traditionally identified as the workshop of Joseph the Carpenter. *For admission and hrs,* see *Church of the Annunciation,* above.

Exit back onto Casa Nova Street from the courtyard that separates the two churches. A few steps down the hill bring you to the entrance of the **souk,** on your right. Unlike the bazaar in Jerusalem (*see* Shopping *in* Chapter 2, Jerusalem), this market is more apt to hawk kitchenware, live chickens, and cassette tapes of Egyptian pop singer Oum Kultoum than religious souvenirs and ethnic trinkets; the latter you will find in the stores on Casa Nova and Paulus VI streets.

One site in the souk occasionally sought by pilgrims is the so-called **"synagogue church,"** on the right side of the main thoroughfare and clearly marked. If the building is locked, ask for the key at the apartment upstairs (you will be expected to leave something in the collection box). The site belongs to the Melkites (Greek Catholics), who, the Franciscans complain, took it by force in the 18th century. The building, though old, was never a synagogue, but rather a church built on the traditional site of the synagogue to which Jesus came "on the Sabbath day. And he stood up to read; and here was given to him the book of the prophet Isaiah" (Luke 4). Jesus selected a prophetic passage which, in Christian tradition, he himself was destined to fulfill. His rendition pleased his listeners, apparently, but his interpretation did not, and they drove him out of town.

Retrace your steps to Casa Nova Street and follow it to rejoin Paulus VI Street. Turn left and continue about 1 kilometer (.6 mile) to a round white stone structure on the left marked MARY'S WELL. It is merely a modern fountain; the real well (which is, in fact, a spring), is within the Greek Orthodox **Church of St. Gabriel,** just up the road behind it. Citing an "Apocryphal gospel of St. James," the Greek Orthodox believe the spring to be the site of the Annunciation. One may question the authenticity of that tradition (evidence of an earlier structure, perhaps a medieval church, suggests the tradition is not new), but one thing is certain: This is the only natural water source in Nazareth, and Mary must have come here almost daily to draw water.

The ornate church was built in 1750, and boasts a fine carved-wood pulpit and *iconostasis* (chancel screen) with painted New Testament scenes and silver-haloed saints in the niches. The walls, barely lit by gilt chandeliers, are adorned with frescoes of figures from the Bible and the Greek Orthodox hagiography. The caretaker will point out the spring and will proffer a copper cup so you can sample the sacred water. The hours are flexible; sometimes you can enter during the midday break. *Off Paulus VI St. Admission free but small donation expected. Open Apr.–Sept., daily 8:30–11:45, 2–6; Oct.–Mar., daily 8:30–11:45, 2–5.*

Christianity speaks with many voices in Nazareth. A few hundred yards farther along Paulus VI Street and on the opposite side of the road is the recently completed **Baptist Church,** affiliated with the Southern Baptist Convention in the United States.

The road soon begins to climb as it continues out of town, offering tantalizing views between the closely built houses. For an unobstructed panorama of the town, turn right at the crest of the hill to **Upper Nazareth,** a Jewish town of about 30,000 founded as a separate municipal entity in the 1950s.

Route 79 heads west to **Zippori** (also known as Sepphoris, traditional birthplace of Mary) and via Shefar'am to Haifa and Akko (Acre). If you have the time, Zippori makes a delightful detour (*see below*). If not, stay on the road to Tiberias (Rte. 754). A 10-minute drive through typical Galilean countryside brings you to a pretty view of the Arab village of Kafr Kanna. The profusion of olive groves, pomegranates, grape vines, fig trees, and even the occasional date palm (unusual at this altitude), is a reminder of how much local scenery is reflected in the Bible. The village is identified with the Second Temple–period **Cana** of John 2. Here Jesus reluctantly performed his first miracle of turning water into wine at a wedding feast, and thus emerged from his "hidden years" to begin his three-year ministry in the Galilee. Within the village, red signs on the right lead to the two rival churches, one Roman Catholic (Franciscan), the other Greek Orthodox, which enshrine the scriptural tradition. The alleyway to these churches is passable for cars, and you can park in the courtyard of the souvenir store opposite the Franciscan **Cana Wedding Church.**

The present church, built in the 1880s, is worth a short visit. From the vestibule, a few steps take you up to the main chapel, while another staircase descends into a grotto, said by the Franciscans to be the very spot where the wedding took place. Look for an ancient mosaic in the vestibule with an Aramaic inscription (indicating the presence of a pre-Byzantine synagogue) and the water trough in the grotto. The stone jar on display here is not old, but rather just an illustration of the kind mentioned in the Gospel passage. (Fine *authentic* examples of such water jars are on view in the contemporary Herodian mansions of Jerusalem's Jewish Quarter; *see* Exploring Jerusalem *in* Chapter 2.) *Tel. 06/517011. Admission free. Open Apr.–Sept., daily 8:30–11:45, 2:30–6; Oct.–Mar., daily 8:30–11:45, 2:30–5.*

The Greek Orthodox priests of St. Nathaniel across the way show two older jars, which their tradition suggests are original.

Back on Route 754, just beyond the village, you meet Route 77: Take a left to reach Haifa or a right 6 kilometers (4 miles) to reach the **Golani Junction.**

If you choose to visit Zippori, take Route 79 west toward Haifa. About 4 kilometers (2.5 miles) down the road, a very clearly marked road to the right (north) takes you through the village of **Zippori** (watch out for speed-bumps) to the historical site of the same name. A Jewish town stood here from at least the 1st century BC through the early middle ages, though there is evidence that Jewish, Christian, and pagan communities coexisted for a while around the 3rd century AD. The Jewish high court, the Sanhedrin, was headquartered here around the same period, and, in the opinion of some scholars, it was here, rather than in Bet She'arim (*see above*) that the Mishnah, the first phase of the Talmud was compiled.

The hilltop site has great charm, surrounded by planted pine and cypress woods, cultivated fields, and a fine view of the valley below. Archaeologists have unearthed a dozen Roman and Jewish mosaic floors of extraordinary fineness. (At press time, only one was open to the public, though the preparation of the others was continuing apace.) One mosaic is made up of Egyptian motifs, including the famous lighthouse of Alexandria, and a mythological depiction of the source of the Nile River. Another mosaic—the finest of all—reveals a series of Dionysian drinking scenes and the exquisite, almost oil-painting-quality face of a woman, whom the press at once dubbed "the Mona Lisa of the Galilee"!

Located on the crest of the ridge, that floor apparently adorned the living/dining room of the town's most prominent villa, perhaps the governor's residence. A reconstruction of the structure has tastefully highlighted the mosaics, and provided detailed explanations of the various parts. A Crusader/Turkish tower, remains of a Roman theater, and a Roman street complete the site.

To get back on the tour, take the side road from Zippori, down through the village of Hoshaya, to join Route 79 east of the Hamovil Junction. Turn right onto 79 (east); about 6 kilometers (4 miles) on, the Nazareth road (Rte. 754) off to your right immediately enters Cana (*see above*). Route 79 continues on to the Golani Junction and Tiberias. *Zippori National Park. Tel. 06/568272. Admission: NIS 8 ($2.70) adults, NIS 4 ($1.35) children. Open Apr.–Sept., Sat.–Thurs. 8–5, Fri. and holiday eves 8–4; Oct.–Mar., Sat.–Thurs. 8–4, Fri. and holiday eves 8–3.*

One of the most important crossroads in the Lower Galilee, the junction (with Route 65) was captured by the Golani Brigade of the Israel Defense Forces in the War of Independence in 1948. A monument and museum are located on the east side of the junction.

All around the Golani Junction are new groves of evergreens planted by visitors as part of the Jewish National Fund (JNF) "Plant-a-Tree-with-Your-Own-Hands" project. Over the last 80 years or so, the JNF has worked to redeem a land neglected for centuries. In an attempt to restore the forests that once covered the hills of Israel, more than 200 million trees have been planted countrywide. Jewish tradition elevates the act of planting a tree to the level of a mitzvah, a good deed given authority by the Bible. If you want to leave something living behind you, the JNF offices (open Sun.–Thurs.) are to the left of the Afula road (Rte. 65), a few hundred yards from the junction. For NIS 30 ($10) you can pick out a sapling—dedicating it to someone if you wish—and plant it yourself.

To head toward Safed (Zefat) and the Upper Galilee, take Route 65 north past the Golani Junction. If your destination is Tiberias, drive east on Route 77, passing Kibbutz Lavi on the left (*see* Dining and Lodging, *below*). Just beyond it is a small double hill, geologically an extinct volcano, known as the **Horns of Hattin.** It was here that Saladin crushed the Crusader army in 1187, bringing to an end the Latin Kingdom of Jerusalem. Richard the Lionheart's Third Crusade a few years later restored some parts of the country to Christian control, but the power and the glory of the Latin Kingdom was gone forever.

If you have the time, take Route 65 south at the Golani Junction. The beautifully situated Ilaniya is the first village on the right. Better known by its old Arabic name of **Sejera,** it was, at the beginning of the century, a training farm for young Jewish pioneers, among them a certain David Ben Gurion, later to become Israel's first prime minister. Ten kilometers (6 miles) south of the Golani Junction is the large village of **Kfar Tavor,** the domed Mt. Tabor that gave it its name looming above it. Two kilometers (1.2 miles) south of Kfar Tavor, look for Route 7266 on the right. Follow it to Shibli, a village of Bedouin who abandoned their nomadic life a few generations ago and became farmers. Opposite the turnoff is the road to **Kibbutz Ein Dor,** which preserves the name of the place where, 3,000 years ago, King Saul communed with the spirit of the prophet Samuel before his fateful battle with the Philistines. Saul got little consolation. "The Lord has torn the kingdom out of your hand, and given it to your neighbor, David," cried Samuel, "and tomorrow, you and your sons shall be with me . . ." (I Samuel 28). At the subsequent battle on Mt. Gilboa (*see* Tour 1, *above*), Saul and his three sons were killed and the Israelite army was routed. "How are the mighty fallen . . ." lamented David when the news reached him.

(12) Drive through Shibli. Beyond the village is a clearing from which the road up **Mt. Tabor** begins. Thirty-two centuries ago, somewhere near the foot of the mountain, the Israelite conscripts of the prophetess/judge Deborah and her general Barak routed the Canaanite chariot army. The road up Mt. Tabor is narrow, and not recommended for any vehicle larger than a car. Watch out for other vehicles on the many hairpin bends. An alternative is to hire the services of a Nazareth-based taxi usually here waiting at the bottom of the mountain to provide a shuttle service to the top. However you get up there—some walk!—the view is worth the effort. From the terrace of the Franciscan hospice you see the Jezreel Valley to the west and south; and from a platform on the Byzantine and Crusader ruins to the left of the modern church (watch your step), there is a panorama east and north over the Galilean hills. No wonder the Jewish general Flavius Josephus fortified the hill in the 1st century AD, during the Great Revolt against the Romans.

Christian tradition, as far back as the Byzantine period, has identified Mt. Tabor as the "high mountain apart" that Jesus ascended with his disciples Peter, James, and John. "And he was transfigured before them, and his garments became white as light. And behold there appeared to them Moses and Elijah, talking with him" (Matthew 17). Early churches on the site were designed to represent the three tabernacles Peter had suggested be built, and the altar of the present **Church of the Transfiguration** (consecrated in 1924) is supposedly on the spot where the tabernacle of Jesus once stood. Those of Moses and Elijah are preserved as chapels at the back of the church. *Tel. 06/767489. Admission free. Open Apr.–Sept., daily 8–noon, 2–6; Oct.–Mar., daily 8–noon, 2–5.*

Time Out Get back on Route 65 south toward Afula. About 5 kilometers (3 miles) from the Shibli turnoff is the **Dovrat Inn,** an unusually good cafeteria. Try the piquant goulash soup and the apple strudel. *Tel. 06/599520. Open Sat.–Thurs. 7–7, Fri. 7–5.*

Retrace your steps on Route 65 to Kfar Tavor. Take Route 767 to the right to Kinneret. It is a beautiful drive of about 25 minutes. The first village, **Kafr Kanna,** is one of two in Israel of the Circassian (Cherkessi) community, Muslims from the Russian steppes who were settled here by the Ottoman Turks in the 19th century. The decorative mosque is just one element of their tradition that they continue to preserve.

On the descent to Kinneret, there is a parking area precisely at sea level. The Sea of Galilee (Lake Kinneret) is still more than 700 feet below you, and the view is superb. You meet Route 90 at the bottom of the road; a left will take you to Tiberias, 8 kilometers (5 miles) to the north.

Tour 3: Tiberias and the Sea of Galilee

The great American writer and humorist Mark Twain was unimpressed by the area of the Sea of Galilee. He passed through in 1867 in the company of a group of pilgrims and Arab dragomen on horseback, and found "an unobtrusive basin of water, some mountainous desolation, and one tree." He would scarcely recognize it now. Modern agriculture and afforestation projects have made the plains and hills green, the handful of "squalid" and "reeking" villages of his day have been supplanted by a string of thriving and well-landscaped kibbutzim, and the "unobtrusive basin of water" has become a lively resort area.

13 **Tiberias,** the only town on the Sea of Galilee, is the natural place to begin this tour. In AD 18, the town was completed by Herod Antipas, son of the notorious Herod the Great, and dedicated to Tiberius, emperor of Rome at the time. Although Antipas, with the title of Tetrarch of the Galilee, was able to surround himself with ambitious courtiers and functionaries, many of the common folk shunned the new town because it had been built on an old cemetery and was therefore considered unclean.

Rich men make poor rebels, and the Tiberians seem to have had little stomach for the Jewish war against Rome that broke out in AD 66. They surrendered to the Romans in 67, saving themselves from the vengeful destruction visited on so many other Galilean towns. In the 2nd century, the revered Rabbi Shimon Bar Yochai ceremonially purified Tiberias, opening the way for a wave of settlement and development that transformed the city. Jerusalem, devastated by Titus's legions in AD 70, lay in ruins, the Jews banished from the city. The center of Jewish life in Israel gradually gravitated to the Galilee (*see* Tour 2, *above*). By the 4th century, the Sanhedrin, the Jewish High Court, had established itself in Tiberias. It was here, around AD 400, that the final compilation of the Jewish oral law into the version known as the Jerusalem Talmud took place.

This was something of a golden era in Tiberias, assuring it a place among Judaism's holy cities in the Land of Israel (together with Jerusalem, Hebron, and Safed). The community knew hard times under the Byzantines, stabilized under more tolerant Muslim dynasties (the Arabs conquered the region in the 7th century), and declined again under the hostile Crusaders, who made Tiberias the capital of their Principality of Galilee. The Arab Saladin besieged the city in 1187, and it was en route to rescuing Tiberias that the Crusader army was defeated at the nearby Horns of Hattin. Crusader fortifications of the town are still a dominant feature of the cityscape today.

Tiberias's decline was almost total after the debacle at Hattin. It wasn't until 1562, when the Ottoman sultan Suleiman the Magnificent gave the town to the Jewish nobleman Don Joseph Nasi, that there was an attempt made to revive the community. Don Joseph resettled the town, and planted mulberry trees in the hope—the vain hope, as it turned out—of developing a silkworm industry.

In the 18th century, Tiberias was rebuilt by renegade Bedouin governor Dahr el-Omar, who invited a group of Jews from Izmir in Turkey to settle the town. In conflict with the Ottomans, and unable to trust his own subjects, this cunning ruler decided to populate his own capital city with a citizenry loyal to him personally. The leader of the new settlers was Isaac Aboulafia, perhaps still the best-known family name in Tiberias today. The Jewish community swelled further with the arrival in 1777 of a group of Hassidim, members of a devout, charismatic sect from Eastern Europe.

In 1833, the Egyptian nationalist leader Ibrahim Pasha, enjoying his short-lived independence from Turkey, again rebuilt the town, but a cataclysmic earthquake just four years later left Tiberias in ruins, and (some say) 1,000 dead.

Relations between the Jewish and Arab citizens of Tiberias were generally cordial until the Arab riots of 1936, in which some 30 Jews were massacred. Confrontation during the 1948 War of Independence had a different consequence. An attack by local Arabs in anticipation of an imminent Syrian invasion brought a counterattack from Haganah forces (the Jewish underground army before Israeli statehood), and the Arab population abandoned the town.

Today's Tiberias (pop. 35,000) spreads all the way up the slope behind it, from 683 feet below sea level at the lake to an elevation of 810 feet above sea level at its highest hilltop neighborhoods—a difference big enough to create different climatic patterns within the same town! Tiberias itself is not a lovely community; its splendid location deserves better than the sort of development it has experienced. Most visitors, however, see little of Tiberias proper, and confine themselves to the lakeshore district where most of the hotels and all the pubs and restaurants are crowded together. Indeed, tourism, as much Israeli as foreign, is one of the mainstays of its economy. And although it is not a town with class, Tiberias has seen an upturn in recent years. You can eat well in Tiberias, boogie a bit, and drink late along an incomparable subtropical lake.

There are few footprints of the past in Tiberias. Part of the black basalt medieval city wall crosses Habanim Street just south of the Moriah Plaza Hotel. The new home of the Israeli GTIO on Habanim Street, opposite the hotel, is framed by restored arches of the same period. And massive Crusader towers and ramparts behind the Scottish Centre dominate Dona Gracia and Gedud Barak streets. In the area of the Promenade, between the Moriah Plaza and the Caesar hotels, is a cluster of old basalt synagogues and mosques and a 19th-century church. Some of the synagogues date from the Aboulafia period of the 18th century. The Franciscan Church of St. Peter commemorates the events described in John 21, Jesus entrusting Peter with the care of "his flock."

Tiberias has a wealth of tombs. Its most famous denizen was the great 12th-century sage **Moses Maimonides** (1135–1204). To get to the tomb from the tourist center of Tiberias, walk north up Habanim Street, taking a left at Hayarden Street. Walk two blocks and turn right onto Ben Zakkai Street. Continue for two blocks; you'll see the tomb on your right.

Born in Cordoba, Spain, Maimonides made a name for himself as a philosopher, the physician to the royal court of Saladin in Egypt, and, in the Jewish world, as the greatest religious scholar and spiritual authority since the Talmudic period of the 4th and 5th centuries AD. To his profound knowledge of the Talmud, Maimonides brought an incisive intellect honed by his study of Aristotelian philosophy and the physical sciences. The result was a rationalism unusual in Jewish scholarship, and a lucidity of analysis and style admired by Jewish and non-Jewish scholars alike.

After his death, in Egypt, Maimonides' remains were interred in Tiberias (although he never resided here). His whitewashed tomb has become a shrine, dripping with candle wax and tears. Marble plaques on either side of the path approaching the tomb recall the many disciplines in which Maimonides distinguished himself. Less tasteful is the stall at the entrance displaying cheap religious trinkets for the faithful. *Ben Zakkai St. Admission free. Open Sun.–Thurs. daylight hrs., Fri. and holiday eves until 2.*

On Derech Hagevura, in the uptown area, is the traditional Tomb of **Rabbi Akiva**, the spiritual leader of the Bar Kochba Revolt against Rome (AD 132–135), who, after his capture, was tortured to death in Caesarea. And a few kilometers to the south, behind Hammat Tiberias (*see below*), a turquoise dome marks the tomb of **Rabbi Meir Ba'al Ha-Nes**, the "Miracle Worker," a legendary personality who supposedly took a vow that he would not lie down until the Messiah came, and was therefore buried in an upright position. His name has become a sort of banner for charitable organizations, and many a miracle has been attributed to the power of prayer at his tomb.

The Galilee Experience, a 27-projector, 36-minute audiovisual presentation, provides a good overview of the city of Tiberias (albeit Christian in orientation). *At the Marina, southern end of Promenade, tel. 06/723620. Admission: NIS 18 ($6) adults, NIS 15 ($5) students and senior citizens, NIS 12 ($4) children. Scheduled screenings in English Sat.–Thurs. 8:30 PM. Many additional screenings take place according to group bookings; call ahead for details.*

Exit Tiberias by Route 90 north (Metulla Road), which hugs the steep hillside, leaving only a few rocky beaches between it and the lake. The "Sea" of Galilee is in fact a freshwater lake, 22 kilometers (14 miles) long from north to south, and 12 kilometers (7.5 miles) wide from east to west. The Jordan River feeds it from the north and leaves it again in the south to begin its long meander to the Dead Sea. Almost completely ringed by cliffs and steep hills, the lake lies in a hollow about 700 feet below sea level, a fact that accounts for its warm climate and subtropical vegetation. Romantics relate the lake's Hebrew name, Kinneret, to its harplike shape, resembling that of the biblical lyre, the *kinnor*. The more credible explanation, however, is that the lake took its name from the Old Testament city of Kinneret, set above the northwestern shore and dominating the all-important high road that passed this way in antiquity.

About 5 kilometers (3 miles) out of Tiberias the shore widens. Among the trees and holiday bungalows is an enclosure with a small and unimposing cluster of black basalt ruins. This is all that remains of ancient **Magdala,** a Jewish town of the Second Temple period, and the probable home of Mary Magdalene. When the Great Revolt of the Jews against Rome erupted in AD 66, the Galileans spearheaded the struggle. But courage alone could not defeat the disciplined Roman legions. Magdala—called Tarichaeae by the Romans—saw one of the bloodiest battles of the campaign (AD 67). In a chilling passage, contemporary Jewish historian Flavius Josephus describes "the entire lake stained with blood and crammed with corpses; for there was not a single survivor."

About 2 kilometers (1.2 miles) beyond Magdala, turn right at the gas station to Nof Ginosar, the large guest house (*see* Dining and Lodging, *below*) of **Kibbutz Ginosar.** Directly ahead of you as you reach the parking lot is a monumental basalt and concrete eyesore of a building called **Bet Allon** (Allon House) in memory of Yigal Allon (1918–80), commander in the 1940s of the Palmach commando force, foreign minister under Golda Meir and Yitzhak Rabin in the 1970s, and the settlement's favorite son. Within is a museum of the region's natural and human history. It's a good rainy-day option, but what you've come to see is a 2,000-year-old, 28-foot-long fishing boat that was found in the mud of the lake shore in January 1986, when the falling water level exposed its prow. Innovative techniques were used to move the amazingly intact but fragile craft to its temporary home, a specially constructed bath filled with a wax-based preservative solution. It is hoped that the wax will eventually displace the water molecules of the sodden wood and allow the boat to be exhibited dry. You can visit the tiny pavilion near the shore where the boat is housed, but nothing of the craft is currently visible in the almost opaque solution. An excellent 15-minute video, however, filmed at the time of the excavation and explaining the boat's unique features, makes a visit worthwhile. Considering the age of the boat (1st century AD) and the frequency of nautical references in the New Testament stories that took place in this area, the international press immediately dubbed this "the Jesus boat." Certainly for a reader of the Gospels, it is a startlingly vivid image from the past. *Tel. 06/722905. Admission (museum and boat): NIS 10 ($3.35) adults, NIS 8 ($2.70) students, senior citizens, and children. Boat only (including video): NIS 6 ($2). Open Sun.–Thurs. 8:30–5 (last entry to museum 4 PM), Fri. and holiday eves 8:30–noon, Sat. 9–5.*

Route 90 continues north, passing an electric installation on the right that powers huge water pumps buried in the hill behind it. The Sea of Galilee is Israel's primary freshwater reservoir, and the beginning of the National Water Carrier, a network of canals and pipelines that integrates the country's water sources and distribution lines. On the hill above it is the small tel of the biblical city of **Kinneret,** dominating the main international highway of the ancient Near East, the so-called Via Maris, the Way of the Sea.

Passing the junction of Route 87, the road climbs in a series of hairpin turns. The next turnoff to the right (at the orange sign indicating the Hospice of Beatitudes) leads to the **Mt. of Beatitudes,** enshrined by Christian tradition as the site of the Sermon on the Mount. "And seeing the multitudes, he went up into a mountain; and when he was set, his disciples came unto him. And he opened his mouth, and taught them, saying: 'Blessed are the poor in spirit, for theirs is the kingdom of Heaven . . . '" (Matthew 5:1–7:29). The domed Roman Catholic church (Franciscan Sisters) was completed in 1937. The marble altar is in the center of the round church, immediately below the dome, the walls covered by mosaics with quotations from the Beatitudes.

The church is surrounded by a terrace and well-tended gardens, offering quiet corners for meditation and a superb view of the Sea of Galilee (best in the afternoon, when the diffused western sun softens the light and heightens color). It is appropriate to the spirit of the place that this is one of the few Christian holy sites in the country where Catholics and Protestants seem to feel equally at ease. *Open daily 8–noon, 2:30–5.*

Route 90 north continues to Upper Galilee; turn back the way you came and take a left (east) onto Route 87. The entrance immediately on your right is that of **Tabgha,** a corruption of the earlier Greek name Heptapegon, "Seven Springs." The site is identified by Christian tradition with the "desert[ed] place" of Matthew 14, where Jesus miraculously "multiplied" two fish and five loaves of bread to feed the crowds that followed him. "And they did all eat, and were filled. . . . And they that had eaten were about five thousand men, beside women and children." The German Benedictine **Church of the Multiplication of the Loaves and Fishes,** built in Byzantine basilica style and dedicated in 1981, incorporates some remains of its 5th-century predecessor. Most impressive in this airy limestone building with a wooden truss ceiling is the beautifully wrought Byzantine mosaic floor depicting flora and birds and curiously including Egyptian motifs such as the Nilometer, a graded column once used to measure the water level of the Nile. In front of the altar is the small and simple *Loaves and Fishes*, perhaps the most famous Byzantine mosaic in Israel. From the outer courtyard of the church, a path leads down to a quiet spot on the lake. *Rte. 87. Open Mon.–Sat. 8:30–5, Sun. 9:30–5.*

Two hundred yards east on Route 87 is Tabgha's second site, the austere basalt **Church of the Primacy of St. Peter.** The church is built on the water's edge, over a flat rock known as Mensa Domini, the Lord's Table. After his resurrection, relates the New Testament (John 21), Jesus appeared to his disciples by the Sea of Galilee and breakfasted with them on a miraculous catch of fish. As they ate, Jesus thrice commanded the disciple Peter to "feed my sheep," thus establishing Peter's "primacy" and, in the Roman Catholic tradition, that of his spiritual descendants, the Bishops of Rome. The site was included in the itinerary of Pope Paul VI in 1964. *Rte. 87. Open daily 8:30–11:45, 2–5.*

Three kilometers (2 miles) east of Tabgha, a short side road on the right angles off to **Capernaum** (Kfar Nahum in Hebrew). The sign on the main gate declares the place to be the "Town of Jesus," for it was here that Jesus established his base during the three years of his ministry in the Galilee. Here, the New Testament relates, he called many of his disciples ("Follow me, and I will make you fishers of men"), healed the afflicted, taught in the synagogue, . . . and ultimately cursed the city for not heeding his message.

The Franciscan Order, whose mission in the Holy Land has been to acquire and preserve sites sacred to Christianity, took possession of Capernaum in 1894. Much of its exposed masonry had already been pilfered by native home-builders over the years, and the monks promptly buried the rest to stop the practice until serious excavations could begin. What eventually came to light was a large Jewish town on the lake shore that had thrived from the Second Temple/ Early Roman period (about the 1st century BC) to the Byzantine period (5th–6th centuries AD).

The prosperity of the ancient community is immediately apparent from the remains of its synagogue. To the right of the cashier as you enter is a display of finely carved stones showing the typical range of Jewish motifs of the time. Immediately before you is a modern church, literally suspended from its outer support pillars over the scanty remains of Capernaum's central Christian shrine, the **House of St. Peter.** The church follows the octagonal outline of the Byzantine basilica that once encompassed the house, where Jesus is supposed to have visited.

The partly restored synagogue dominates the complex. The community went to the expense of transporting white limestone blocks from afar to set off the synagogue from the crudely built black basalt houses of the town. Stone benches line the inside walls of the building, recalling its original primary function as a place of assembly in which the Torah, "the Law," was read and explained on sabbaths and holidays; formal prayer in Judaism came later.

Controversy still surrounds the dating of the Capernaum synagogue—some time between the 2nd and 5th centuries AD—but one thing is certain: This is not the synagogue of Mark 1 where Jesus taught. The structure seen in the small excavation pit in the southeast corner of the present building, however, may have heard his voice.

On your way out, look for a fine olive-oil press and some small hand mills made from hard and durable volcanic basalt. Its advantages over the limestone found in the rest of Israel gave the Sea of Galilee region the raw material for an important export commodity in ancient times: agricultural equipment. Such mills have been found as far afield as Masada, Jerusalem, and the Mediterranean coast. To the right of the olive-oil press is a capital of a column with Jewish symbols in relief—a seven-branched menorah, a shofar (ram's horn), and an incense-shovel—of objects still in use—to preserve the memory of the Temple with which they were associated. *Rte. 87., tel. 06/ 721059. Admission: NIS 2 (70¢). Open daily 8:30–4.*

Continue east on Route 87. The road crosses the **Jordan River,** somewhat muddy at this point, at the Arik Bridge. Westerners raised on spirituals that extol the Jordan's depth and width are often surprised to find how small a stream it really is. It is seldom more than 33 feet wide, and often shallow enough to wade in. However, record-breaking rains in the winter of 1991–92 swelled the river, which flooded fields and threatened homes further south. The Jordan enters the Sea of Galilee only a few hundred yards to your right. In this wetlands area of the Jordan delta, archaeologists in recent years have finally identified and begun exploring the elusive site of the ancient Jewish New Testament–period town of Bethsaida (Peter's birthplace).

About 3 kilometers (2 miles) beyond the Arik Bridge, Route 87 continues east to Katzrin and the central Golan Heights. Turn right (south) onto Route 92. Continue about 10 kilometers (6 miles) farther to **Kursi,** at the junction of Route 789.

The New Testament (Luke 8) relates the story of a man of Gedara (some versions say Gerasa) who was possessed by demons. Jesus miraculously exorcised the evil spirits, causing them to enter a herd of swine grazing nearby, which then "ran violently down a steep place into the lake, and were choked." The Byzantines, in the 5th century, identified Kursi as the place of the exorcism, and built a monastery there. These were days of intensive pilgrimage to the holy places, and the monastery prospered. A fine Byzantine church on the site, a classic example of the basilica style common at the time, has been partly restored, and remains of the monastery can be seen perched higher up the hillside behind it. *Kursi National Park, tel. 06/ 731983. Admission: NIS 5 ($1.70) adults, NIS 4 ($1.35) students and senior citizens, NIS 2.50 (85¢) children. Open Apr.–Sept., Sat.–Thurs. 8–5, Fri. and holiday eves 8–4; Oct.–Mar., Sat.– Thurs. 8–4, Fri. and holiday eves 8–3.*

Ten kilometers (6 miles) south of Ein Gev you meet Route 98 leading east to **Hammat Gader,** which boasts an ancient Roman spa, modern pools, and an alligator farm. Turning right, you rejoin Route 90, which runs the entire length of Israel. A left turn onto 90 will put you onto the Jericho road via Belvoir and Bet She'an. Keep going straight about 2 kilometers (1.2 miles), then follow the signs to Degania (left turn).

Degania Alef (*A*)—there is a Degania Bet (*B*) farther down the road—has the distinction of being the world's first kibbutz. The Jewish pioneers from Eastern Europe who founded it in 1909 were seeking the perfect society, based on absolute equality and the subservience of individual desires to the needs of the community. They didn't merely subscribe to the work ethic, they embraced it as an article of faith, turning swampland and rocky soil into the fields and plantations one sees today. There are now about 280 such communities in Israel, still based on agriculture, though these days light industry and tourism have become a major part of their economic profile. The principles of the founders remained remarkably resilient for years, but the dream has begun to fade a bit, and the commitment to the old ideals has become more tenuous and less relevant for a new, more materialistic generation. Today, only about 2.5% of the general population live on kibbutzim.

At the entrance to the kibbutz is a small, World War II–vintage Syrian tank. On May 15, 1948, the day after Israel declared its independence, the fledgling state was invaded from all sides by Arab armies. Syrian forces came down the Yarmuk Valley from the east, overran two other kibbutzim en route, and were only stopped here, at the gates of Degania, by a teenager with a Molotov cocktail.

Within restored stone buildings of the kibbutz is the museum of **Bet Gordon** (A. D. Gordon House), named for the white-bearded spiritual mentor of the early pioneers. It houses two fascinating collections: one devoted to the natural history of the region, with a renowned collection of stuffed birds, the other examining the history and archaeology of human settlement in the surrounding valleys. Among the prehistoric sites represented is Ubeidiya, just south of the kibbutz and Israel's oldest, now dated by scholars to 1.25 million years ago. Another museum (tel. 06/758111, admission free) also on Degania Alef, tells the story of the kibbutz. There are no English labels here, but the curator is usually on hand to explain. *Near Rte. 90, tel. 06/750040. Admission (Bet Gordon): NIS 6 ($2) adults, NIS 3 ($1) children, preschoolers free. Open Sun.–Thurs. 9:30–4, Fri. and holiday eves 8:30–noon, Sat. and holidays 9:30–noon.*

20 Just beyond Degania, Route 90 crosses the Jordan River (don't blink!) near its outlet from the Sea of Galilee. Turn left immediately to **Yardenit,** at the entrance to Kibbutz Kinneret (itself founded just two years after Degania). This is a picturesque stretch of the river, with huge eucalyptus trees drooping into its quiet greenish water.

The baptism of Jesus by John the Baptist (Matthew 3) is traditionally identified with the southern reaches of the Jordan River, near Jericho, but since that section of the river became the international border between Israel and Jordan in 1949, Christian pilgrims have sought out accessible spots near the Sea of Galilee for their devotions. At Yardenit, there is safe access to the river, where groups of white-robed pilgrims are often immersed in the Jordan, with prayers, hymns, and expressions of joy. Showers and changing facilities are available, and towels and robes can be rented from the souvenir shop. *Tel. 06/759486. Changing facilities: NIS 3 ($1), free with towel and robe rental. Open Sun.–Thurs. 8–6 (winter 8–5); Fri., Sat., and holiday eves 8–5.*

21 Barely 1 kilometer (.6 mile) toward Tiberias, at a bend in the road, a low stone wall on the right marks the **Kibbutz Kinneret cemetery.** Enter through an opening in the wall and follow the shaded path to the cobblestone clearing for a superb view of the Sea of Galilee and the Golan Heights. Among the denizens of the cemetery are some of the early philosophers and leaders of the Zionist pioneering movement—Borochov, Hess, Syrkin, Katznelson—names unfamiliar to the foreign visitor, perhaps, but old friends to the average Israeli —at least as street names in every town in Israel.

A few steps down from the clearing to the next path brings you to the one grave in the cemetery that has become a virtual shrine for many Israelis, that of Rachel Hameshoreret, the poetess Rachel. As a token of respect, visitors often leave a pebble on the grave (a Jewish tradition), sometimes creating a cairn before their removal by the caretaker.

Rachel lived at Degania before World War I. The war found her studying in Paris; unable to get back into Ottoman Turkish Palestine, she spent the war years working with orphaned children in her native Russia, where she contracted the tuberculosis that eventually ended her life. She returned to her beloved lake, but never regained her health, and died in 1931.

Rachel became a poet of national stature in Hebrew, her third language. Many of her poems have been put to music and become part of the modern folklore familiar to every Israeli schoolchild. She wrote with great sensitivity of the beauty of the region, and with passion—knowing her end was near—of her frustrated dream of raising a family. Her tombstone is eloquently devoid of biographical information: It carries the only name by which she is known, Rachel, and four lines from one of her poems: "Spread out your hands, look yonder:/nothing comes./Each man has his Nebo/in the great expanse." (It was from Mt. Nebo that Moses looked into the promised land that he knew he would never enter.) In a recess in the stone seat by the gravesite is a weatherproof canister containing a complete volume (in Hebrew) of her poems, just a few steps from the spot where many of them were written.

Just 2 kilometers (1.2 miles) south of Tiberias is Israel's hottest spring, gushing out of the earth at 60°C (140°F). The healing properties of its mineral-rich waters were apparently known as far back as Old Testament times. It is certain that by the end of the Second Temple period, when settlement in the Sea of Galilee region was at its height, a Jewish town called Hammat (Hot Springs) stood on the site. With time, Hammat was overshadowed by its newer neighbor of Tiberias, and became known as **Hammat Tiberias** (Tiberias Hot Springs). A coin minted in Tiberias during the rule of Emperor Trajan, in around AD 100, shows Hygeia, the goddess of health, sitting on a rock with a spring gushing out beneath it. The spa's international reputation was assured.

This and other hot mineral springs in Israel (Hammat Gader, Ein Gedi) were created by the massive upheavals of the fault line known as the Great Syrian-African Rift. Cracks in the earth's crust allowed mineral-rich water to boil to the surface. A more imaginative explanation has it that Solomon, the great King of Israel, wanted a hot bath, and he used his awesome authority to force some young devils belowground to heat up the water. The fame of the salubrious springs spread far and wide, bringing the afflicted flocking to seek relief. Seeing such gladness among his subjects, Solomon worried about what would happen when he died and the devils stopped their labor. In a flash of the wisdom for which he was renowned, he made the hapless devils deaf. To this day, they have not heard of the king's demise, and continue to heat up the water out of fear of his wrath.

Parts of ancient Hammat have been uncovered by archaeologists on the mountain side of the road, bringing to light a number of synagogues built on ruins of other synagogues. The most dramatic is a building from the 4th century AD, with an elaborate mosaic floor using motifs almost identical to those at Bet Alfa (*see* Tour 1, *above*): classical Jewish symbols, human figures representing the four seasons and the signs of the zodiac, and the Greek god Helios at the center.

Later cultures exploited the hot springs, too, and an adjacent small Turkish bath provides the entrance to the site and a tiny museum of artifacts and illustrations. *Hammat Tiberias National Park. For admission and hours, see Kursi National Park, above.*

Time Out **Tiberias Hot Springs,** on the lake side of the road, is one of the two modern spa facilities fed by the mineral spring. (The other, on the mountain side of the road, is exclusively for medical purposes.) In addition to possessing sophisticated, therapy-related services and facilities, it has a large, pamperingly warm indoor mineral pool (35°C/95°F), and a small outdoor one right near the lake's edge. Its restaurant (lunch only) serves, among other dishes, the famous St. Peter's fish. *Tel. 06/791967. Admission to pools (including locker and facilities): NIS 27 ($9) adults, NIS 10 ($3.35) for weekday entry before 4 PM; students and senior citizens 10% discount; NIS 20 ($6.70) children under 12. Extra charges for certain therapies. Open Sat.– Mon., Wed. 8–8; Tues.–Thurs. 8 AM–11 PM; Fri. 8–4:30 (check for changes in winter hours).*

Off the Beaten Track

Hammat Gader was considered the second-largest spa in the Roman Empire after Baiae, near Naples. Built around three hot springs, an impressive complex of baths and pools attest to the opulence that once attracted voluptuaries and invalids alike. The springs feed a large, warm, open-air pool amid lawns and large trees. The site also offers a freshwater pool, changing facilities, a cafeteria, trampolines and other children's attractions, and an alligator farm. It's delightful but pricey, if seeing the antiquities is your only purpose.

Driving the road to Hammat Gader (Rte. 98, east of Sea of Galilee's southern tip) is itself an absorbing experience. The road clings to the gorge of the Yarmuk River. On the opposite bank is biblical **Gilead,** now part of Jordan. Route 98 climbs to the southern Golan Heights in a series of heart-stopping switchbacks, but just beyond the foot of the ascent the road descends to Hammat Gader. *Tel. 06/751039. Admission: NIS 27 ($9) adults, NIS 29 ($9.70) on Sat. and holidays; NIS 23 ($7.70) students, senior citizens, and children, NIS 25 ($8.35) on Sat. and holidays; NIS 20 ($6.70) for all visitors entering after 5 PM. Open Sun. 8–4:30, Mon–Thurs. 8 AM–9:30 PM, Fri. 8 AM– 11:30 PM, Sat. 8–8. Children's attractions close at 5 PM, alligator farm and antiquities close at dusk. Entrance up to 1 hr before closing.*

Shopping

The Lower Galilee is more Bible than bargains, but there are a few opportunities for shopping.

Kfar Tavor, just north of Mt. Tabor, boasts the **Tavlinei Artzenu** factory, known also as the **Za'atar Factory** (tel. 06/765081 or 06/760002; open Sun.–Thurs. 8–5, Fri. and holiday eves 8–1). *Za'atar* is the hyssop of the Bible, a wild herb a bit reminiscent of marjoram. It is a protected species, but fiercely in demand in the region. Two young ex-kibbutzniks have made a go of cultivating it, and a lot of other herbs as well, and now market a range of products that includes the herbs themselves, herbal tea mixtures, and natural therapeutic medicinal preparations and cosmetics. The factory is clearly visible from Route 65, which bisects the village.

At the site of ancient **Megiddo,** the modern kibbutz of the same name has a small **jewelry** shop (tel. 06/420314; open Sun.–Thurs. 8:30–4:30, Fri. and holiday eves 8:30–3:30, Sat. 9–3). Many of the handsome silver and gold items are made in the kibbutz itself. Particularly attractive is the jewelry incorporating pieces of ancient Roman glass.

Nazareth, as you would expect from the pilgrim traffic that inundates the town, specializes in **religious trinkets and souvenirs.** You can occasionally find some nuggets among the dross, though the handful of stores are very scaled-down versions of similar stores in Jerusalem and Bethlehem. The **souk** is purely for local consumption, but for exactly that reason it's fun to poke around in: One person's kitchenware is another's curio.

Tiberias relies heavily on tourism, but despite its developing infrastructure, it has little good shopping. The exception is **jewelry.** The large **Caprice diamond factory** on Tabor Street (tel. 06/792616; open Sun.–Thurs. 9–9, Fri. and holiday eves 9–4, Sat. eve., and by prior arrangement) offers a video about the industry and a tour of its workshops before releasing you into its showroom. A few smaller stores are to be found near the intersection of Habanim and Yarden streets, and in some of the better hotels. Souvenirs, of course, are found everywhere.

Sports and the Outdoors

Participant Sports

Bowling Tiberias Bowling Club (tel. 06/724520), in the Lev Ha'ir shopping center, has 12 lanes. The cost per game varies with time of day: 11–4, NIS 7 ($2.35); 4–closing, NIS 10 ($3.35); Fri. 7 PM–Sat. night closing, NIS 13 ($4.35). Bowling shoes can be rented for NIS 2 (70¢). The lanes are open daily 11 AM till after midnight.

Camping The Sea of Galilee area has several campsites with full cooking and washing facilities, beach access, and stores. On the southeastern shore of the lake, try those at **Ein Gev** (Ein Gev 14940, tel. 06/758027 or 06/758028), **Ha'on** (Mobile Post Jordan Valley 15170, tel. 06/757555 or 06/757556), and **Ma'agan** (Mobile Post Jordan Valley 15160, tel. 06/753753). **Kfar Hittim** (Mobile Post Lower Galilee 15280, tel. 06/795921), located in the hills to the west of Tiberias, also has camping facilities. In addition, local authorities have developed a series of free or minimum-charge lakeside sites south of Tiberias; the facilities, however, are spartan: little more than freshwater and toilets.

Canoeing The so-called "kayaks" of **Abukayak** (tel. 06/922245 or 06/921078) are really inflated rubber canoes. Rented inside the Jordan River Park (on Rte. 888, just north of the Sea of Galilee), they offer a delightfully serene 1½-hour route (decidedly not white water!) down the lower Jordan River. Life jackets are provided, and the experience is appropriate for young children.

Cycling There is a bicycle marathon around the Sea of Galilee at the end of October or the beginning November, with both popular and competitive categories. For details, contact the sports department of the Jordan Valley Regional Council, Tzemach Junction, 15132 Israel; tel. 06/757630 or 06/757631, fax 06/757641.

Hiking Although the Upper Galilee and Golan Heights offer the best hiking, there are a few trails in the area. For Mt. Gilboa and Mt. Tabor, contact SPNI's Alon-Tavor Field Study Center (Mobile Post Lower Galilee 14101, tel. 06/767798).

Horseback Riding
The **Vered Hagalil** ranch (Rte. 90, Mobile Post Korazim, tel. 06/935785, fax 06/934964), on Route 90 north of the Sea of Galilee at Korazim Junction, conducts horseback tours of the area (*see* Guided Tours *in* Essential Information, *above*). You can rent a donkey in the Nazareth hills (*see* Guided Tours in Essential Information, *above*) from **Donkey Tracks** (Mobile Post Upper Nazareth, 17915, tel. 06/565511, fax 06/570378).

Jogging and Running
A **promenade** in **Tiberias** suitable for jogging follows the lake shore for about 5 kilometers (3 miles) to the south. Dedicated runners might want to participate in the Sea of Galilee Marathon and Half-Marathon, which take place in December or January. A triathlon takes place at the beginning of May. For details, contact the sports department of the Jordan Valley Regional Council, 15132 Israel; tel. 06/757630 or 06/757631, fax 06/757641.

Kayaking
For casual kayaking on the lake, *see* Water Sports, *below*. For the more energetic variety, look into the international competition held annually in March. For details contact the sports department of the Jordan Valley Regional Council, 15132 Israel; tel. 06/757630 or 06/757631, fax 06/757641.

Spas
The famous **Tiberias Hot Springs** (tel. 06/791967), 1 kilometer (.6 mile) south of Tiberias, has two facilities (*see* Tour 3 *in* Exploring Lower Galilee, *above*): the older, more medically oriented spa on the west side of Route 90, and the newer one on the lake shore. Massages, mud therapy, hot mineral tub, and other services and facilities are available at extra charge.

Swimming
The **Jezreel Valley** (*see* Tour 1 *in* Exploring Lower Galilee, *above*) has two delightful pools in natural surroundings: one at **Ma'ayan Harod National Park,** at the foot of Mt. Gilboa, fed by a natural spring and surrounded by tall eucalyptus trees; and the other at **Gan Hashelosha (Sachne) National Park,** actually a small river deep enough to dive in at spots, with artificial cascades in others. Lawns make both popular family-picnic spots. Both areas are very crowded in season on Friday and Saturday.

The **Sea of Galilee** is a refreshing but rocky place to swim. Don't venture far from shore because of occasional boat traffic. Pleasant beaches with shaded lawns and eating facilities are located at **Nof Ginosar** (Rte. 90, 8 km/5 mi n. of Tiberias), **Lido** and **Blue Beach** (Rte. 90, at northern exit from Tiberias), **Sironit** (Rte. 90, southern exit from Tiberias), **Ma'agan** (Rte. 92, 1 km/.6 mi s. of Tzemach Junction), and **Gai Beach** (next to Sironit). Many free beaches with minimal facilities can be found south of Tiberias. **Ein Gev, Golan Beach** (parking fee), and **Lunagal** (parking fee) are good swimming spots on the eastern shore.

Thousands of swimmers take part in the **Kinneret Swim** in September, an institution that goes back to 1953. Traditionally a 4-kilometer race, the event has now gained recognition as an international swim meet, and the tough swimmers cover distances of up to 10 kilometers. Most, of course, are amateurs just out for fun. For details contact the Jordan Valley Regional Council, 15132 Israel; tel. 06/757630 or 06/757631, fax 06/757641.

Walking
The annual **Big Walk (Hatza'adah** in Hebrew), which takes place in March or April over a 10- to 15-kilometer (6.2- to 9.3-mile) route along the lake shore, attracts participants from all over the country.

For details, contact the Jordan Valley Regional Council, 15132 Israel; tel. 06/757630 or 06/757631, fax 06/757641.

Water Sports **Kayaks, pedal boats,** and **rowboats** can be rented from: **Nof Ginosar,** north of Tiberias (tel. 06/792161); **Jordan River Hotel Marina** (tel. 06/792950) and **Ganei Hammat Hotel** (tel. 06/792890), in Tiberias; **Kibbutz Ha'on** (tel. 06/757555) and **Kibbutz Ma'agan** (tel. 06/751360), on the southeastern shore; and **Kibbutz Ein Gev** (tel. 06/758027), **Golan Beach** (tel. 06/763750), and **Ramot Resort Hotel** (tel. 06/763730), on the eastern and northeastern shores.

For **waterskiing,** inquire at the private beaches around Tiberias: **Blue Beach** (tel. 06/720105 or 06/724137), **Lido** (tel. 06/721538), **Sironit** (tel. 06/721449), and **Gai Beach** (tel. 06/790790).

Water slides have suddenly appeared in the area like multicolored extraterrestrial life-forms. You'll find them at **Sironit** and **Gai beaches,** south of Tiberias, and in especial profusion at **Lunagal** on the northeastern shore.

Dining and Lodging

Dining The Jezreel and Jordan valleys and the Galilee Hills are rustic, predominantly farming regions. Eating establishments are confined to roadside cafeterias (**Dovrat** and **Mizra,** near Afula, are both excellent), lunch-only restaurants adjacent to archaeological sites such as Megiddo, Gan Hashelosha/Sachne, and eateries and snack bars in the towns of Afula and Bet She'an.

Nazareth is a modest exception, with a handful of pretty good Arab restaurants, frequented mostly by residents. Other than the **Holy Land Inn,** opposite the Galilee Hotel, which serves large Italian-style meals, "dining" in Nazareth means supping on hummus, shishlik, baklava, Turkish coffee, and the like. Decor is incidental, atmosphere a function of that moment's patrons, and dinnertime is earlier rather than later. Of course, there are no reservations taken and no dress code. Menus at each of the following are substantially alike: **Abu Maher, El Ginena,** next to the Greek Orthodox Church of St. Gabriel; **Astoria,** Casa Nova Street, at the corner of Paulus VI Street; **El Amal,** Paulus VI Street, 220 yards from corner of Casa Nova, toward Galilee Hotel; **El Fahoum,** Casa Nova Street, next to the bank, just above the corner of Paulus VI Street; **Omar el Khayam,** beyond the Nazareth Hotel, on the road to Afula; and **Riviera,** Paulus VI Street, 165 yards before Nazareth Hotel.

Tiberias and the Sea of Galilee are a different proposition. Because most visitors to the region actually stay in this area, some very good restaurants have appeared. Most are in Tiberias itself, but a few of the daytime watering holes around the lake stay open into the evening. The local specialty is St. Peter's fish (*tilapia*), which, although it is native to the Sea of Galilee, tends to be the pond-bred variety. If you're in the market for shish kebab or Chinese cuisine, however, you will not be disappointed. Along the Promenade in Tiberias is a string of restaurants that are virtually indistinguishable from each other, all offering a low- to moderately-priced menu that, apart from the St. Peter's fish and ubiquitous french fries, is essentially Middle Eastern: hummus, pickles, shishlik, and kebabs.

At a right angle to the Promenade is the newer *midrachov* (pedestrian mall), between the Moriah Plaza and Caesar hotels, with a wide range of eating options: national franchise hamburger chains, pizzerias, ice-cream parlors, and restaurants offering light meals.

Among the latter is one of the nationwide **Kapulsky** chain, known for its sinfully rich cakes. Perhaps because of the competition, the "regular" restaurants (with their fish, grills, schnitzel, *shwarma*, which are slices of spit-grilled meat served in a pita with salads and condiments), have kept their prices down, and, if you're not looking for a gourmet experience, you can eat quite well for $10 or less. Another category that has gained popularity is the pub, with wood-paneled rooms and smokey atmosphere and meals to mitigate the effect of the excellent local Goldstar draught. Try **Big Ben** on the mall, and **Le Pirate Pub** below the Caesar Hotel.

If you're in Tiberias and have a hankering for falafel, the Middle Eastern fast food of deep-fried chickpea balls and salad in pita bread, rub shoulders with the locals on Hagalil Street. In fact, if you're into local color, look for the tiny restaurants (where English really *is* a foreign language), on Hagalil Street and in the little streets that connect it to Habanim Street. The menus predictably emphasize fish and Middle Eastern salads and meat dishes. The decor and service tend to be basic, and the niceties of elegant dining quite unknown, but even tourists have been known to strike gold here, and often at lower prices than those found in the high-rent locations.

Restaurant attire anywhere in the Lower Galilee, even at dinner, is strictly casual.

Highly recommended restaurants are indicated by a star ★.

Category	Cost*
$$$$	over $35
$$$	$22–$35
$$	$12–$22
$	under $22

*per person for a three-course meal, excluding drinks and 10% service charge

Lodging   Almost all recommended accommodations in the region are in or near Tiberias, or scattered around the Sea of Galilee. They range from good (but not top-drawer) deluxe hotels to hostels and hospices. The Jezreel Valley has a youth hostel and campground; Nazareth has a few cheap hotels, most of which cannot be highly recommended, and pilgrim hospices. Catholic hospices cater primarily to pilgrim groups, and not all encourage individual travelers. Contact the GTIO in Nazareth (Casa Nova St., tel. 06/573003) for listings. Private bed-and-breakfasts have begun appearing in all sorts of odd places, like mushrooms after the rain. Outside the main towns, road signs help you find them.

The Sea of Galilee region is a magnet for Israeli vacationers, especially during the two major seasons of Jewish holidays: Passover (March–April) and the High Holidays and Sukkoth (September–October). Based as they are on the Jewish calendar, the dates of these holidays shift from year to year; be sure to verify them before you decide when *not* to stay in the area. The weather is normally great during these periods, but everything is crowded, and rates soar. Some hotels charge high-season rates for part of the summer and during the week of Christmas as well. Some hotels raise their weekend rates substantially.

Highly recommended lodgings are indicated by a star ★.

Category	Cost*
$$$$	over $150
$$$	$100–$150
$$	$60–$100
$	under $60

*All prices are for a standard double room, including breakfast and 10% service charge.

Golani Junction
Dining

Younes. Don't look for elegant decor and ambience: Younes is a place for eating, not dining. This popular watering hole for locals and Israelis on the road serves up excellent Arab fare including tasty Middle Eastern salads, shishlik, and grilled lamb chops. Big windows provide some fair views and an airy feeling, and you can sit outside when the weather is right. *Rte. 77, at gas station, 1 km (.6 mi) w. of Golani Junction, tel. 06/ 767343. No reservations. No credit cards. $–$$*

Jezreel Valley
Lodging

Hankin Youth Hostel. "Youth" is a misnomer at this establishment in Ma'ayan Harod National Park, next to the hamlet of Gidona, at the foot of Mt. Gilboa—all are welcome. There are 20 new air-conditioned mini-apartments, sleeping four, with private bathrooms. The 11 caravans (mobile homes) house up to seven people. Expect spartan but comfortable furnishings. The surroundings—the pines and eucalyptuses of Mt. Gilboa and the park—make up for the simple facilities. July and August rates are slightly higher and include both breakfast and dinner. *In Ma'ayan Harod National Park, off Rte. 71, 10 km (6 mi) E. of Afula, Mobile Post Gilboa 19120, tel. and fax 06/531660. 157 beds (including 20 mini-apartments and 11 caravans, all with private bath. Facilities: dinner available, access to park pool. DC, MC, V. $–$$*

Lavi
Lodging

Lavi Kibbutz Hotel. The guest house at Kibbutz Lavi is designed like a hotel (all the units in one building), rather than in the motel-style arrangement of so many kibbutz-run inns. The community is Jewish Orthodox, and as such there is no vehicular traffic into or out of the village (and thus no check-ins or checkouts) on the Sabbath, from sunset on Friday until Saturday after dark. Those inconveniences aside, the atmosphere at the kibbutz is warm and welcoming, and many Christian pilgrim groups make it their Galilee base. Rooms are comfortable, and the food decent, but neither are anything out of the ordinary. Still, the experience of waking to rural surroundings rather than a city street has much to commend it, and you're only 15 minutes from Tiberias. *On Rte. 77, 11 km (7 mi) w. of Tiberias, Lower Galilee 15267, tel. 06/799450, fax 06/799499. 124 rooms with bath. Facilities: restaurant, kibbutz tours, pool, 2 tennis courts. AE, DC, MC, V. $$–$$$*

Nazareth
Lodging

Galilee Hotel. The hotel primarily caters to pilgrims, and offers few frills. Its rooms are adequate in size, but down-market in decor, and not meticulously maintained. The gloomy corridors amplify the faintly seedy flavor of the place. A tiny bar/coffee shop on the premises is a plus. *Paulus VI St., 1 km (.6 mi) from junction with Afula and Haifa Rds., 16000, tel. 06/571311, fax 06/556627. 93 rooms with bath. Facilities: coffee shop. No credit cards. $*

Sea of Galilee **Ein Gev Fish Restaurant.** This institution on the eastern shore of the
(excluding lake is known for its St. Peter's fish (pay the extra cost for a large
Tiberias) fish to ensure moist meatiness), but does offer alternatives, light en-
Dining trées such as pizza, omelets, and vegetarian, soy-based schnitzel.
Located on the grounds of the Ein Gev Holiday Village at the wa-
ter's edge (*see below*), the restaurant is open for dinner only in July,
August, and sometimes September. Its outdoor dining area affords
a view of Tiberias, the lights of which twinkle across the lake. *Kib-*
butz Ein Gev, tel. 06/758035 or 06/758036. Reservations advised.
MC, V. $$

Dining and **YMCA Peniel-by-Galilee.** One of the more unusual hostelries in the
Lodging area, Peniel-by-Galilee was built as a retreat in the late 1930s by
★ Archibald Harte, founder of the famous Jerusalem YMCA. It fell
into disuse after his death in 1946, but was later revived as a YMCA
hospice. It occupies a low cliff just north of Tiberias between Route
90 and the Sea of Galilee, where you can enjoy unobstructed views of
the lake and a pebbly but clean beach. The common room is lined
with 180-year-old Damascene wood and inlaid panels. The 11 guest
rooms and family-size apartments are less inspiring, though spa-
cious and comfortable enough; the apartments have kitchen facili-
ties. Most units have views of the lake. Dinner is served only when
demand justifies it (at least eight people; call ahead to verify)—it's
worth trying to round up the quota of guests. The excellence of the
lake-caught St. Peter's fish is matched by the other entrées, which
might consist of grilled steak or lamb chops, roast chicken, or ham-
burgers. *Off Rte. 90, 3 km (2 mi) n. of Tiberias, Box 192, Tiberias*
14101, tel. 06/720685. 9 rooms and 2 apartments with bath. Facili-
ties: lunch and dinner available, private beach, playground. Din-
ner reservations required. No credit cards. $–$$ (Nov.–June), $$$
(July–Oct., rate includes required half-board).

Lodging **Nof Ginosar Guest House.** This is one of the largest and best-estab-
lished of the Galilee kibbutz guest houses. Its location right on the
Sea of Galilee, with a private beach, makes Nof Ginosar especially
popular. Also on the grounds of the kibbutz are a 2,000-year-old fish-
ing boat (currently undergoing restoration), a small natural history
and anthropological museum, and kayak, pedal boat, and rowboat
rentals. Nof Ginosar's style is that of a rustic resort, with motel-like
accommodations easily equivalent to hotels in the same price range.
Rooms are comfortable and airy, if not overly spacious. While one
side of its large dining room serves good but unexceptional full-
course meals, the other has a "non-meat" buffet, with a selection of
tasty salads, hot fish and vegetarian dishes, and outstanding
blintzes with sweetened cheese. *Rte. 90, 10 km (6 mi) n. of Tiberias,*
Mobile Post Jordan Valley 14980, tel. 06/792161, fax 06/792170. 170
rooms with bath. Facilities: restaurant, coffee shop/bar, pool, pri-
vate beach, evening lectures on kibbutz life and morning tour, free
admission to video about ancient boat, TV. AE, DC, MC, V. $$$

Ramot Resort Hotel. High up in the foothills of the Golan Heights,
the hotel is still just a 10-minute drive from the excellent Golan and
Lunagal beaches (the latter with a water park) and offers fabulous
views of the Sea of Galilee region. Its main building has well-designed, comfortable, air-conditioned guest rooms, each with a very
private balcony and lake view. Less expensive (and older), the cottages on the site are not as finely furnished and are a bit run-down,
but have some charm with their wooden paneling and shutters and
green surroundings. Guided tours of the area are available in the
summer. *E. of Rte. 92, Sea of Galilee 12490, tel. 06/732636, fax 06/*
793590. 123 rooms with bath; 19 cottages. Facilities: coffee shop/bar,
pool. AE, DC, MC, V. $$$

Ein Gev Holiday Village. The kibbutz at Ein Gev has been in the tourism business for many years, and is best known for its fish restaurant (*see above*), cruise boats, campground, and air-conditioned caravans. Better-class guest rooms with patios have been added to the motel-style building on a palm-shaded lakeside location of lawns and beach. Rates go up 25% on weekends and holidays. *Rte. 92, 12 km (7.5 mi) from Tzemach Junction, Post Office Ein Gev 14940, tel. 06/758027 or 06/758028. 144 rooms with bath. Facilities: restaurant, kayaks, pedal boats, miniature golf, barbecue pits, minimarket. Breakfast available but not included. MC, V. $$*

★ **Ma'agan.** At the southern tip of the Sea of Galilee, 12 kilometers (7.5 miles) from Tiberias, is a kibbutz on the lake that has been in the campsite-, mobile home-, and bungalow-rental business for years (these accommodations are air-conditioned, use their space well, and are reasonably comfortable). Recently the management added an upmarket dimension: spacious and well-furnished suites, each with a living room (with a lake-view picture window), two small bedrooms, a bathroom, a kitchenette, a patio, and barbecue facilities. The placement of the three rows of suites on the hillside one below the other ensures unimpeded views. A sandy beach, swimming pool, and extensive lawns among the palms and eucalyptuses make this the best deal in the area. Kids have two smaller pools, a play area, and a menagerie. *Rte. 92, 1 km (.6 mi) e. of Tzemach Junction, Mobile Post Jordan Valley 15160, tel. 06/753753, fax 06/753707. 118 rooms, 52 with bath, 66 with shower. Facilities: restaurant/coffee shop, minimarket, pool, 2 children's pools, windsurfing club, pedal-boat and kayak rental. Breakfast available but not included. AE, MC, V. $$*

Ha'on. The facilities at this kibbutz holiday village on the southeastern shore of the lake range from campsites and mobile homes to better-grade guest rooms near the lake's edge (all rooms are air-conditioned). The abundant date palms and eucalyptus trees add to the rustic attraction of the place. There is no pool and few attractions for children beyond the ostrich farm (NIS 10/$3.35 for adults; NIS 8/$2.70 for children), but there are pretty lawns and a pebbly beach. The rates are attractively low, but go up 25% on weekends. Minimum-stay packages are required on holidays and during high season. *Rte. 92, 6 km (4 mi) northeast of Tzemach Junction, Mobile Post Jordan Valley 15170, tel. 06/757555 or 06/757556, fax 06/757557. 42 rooms with bath. Facilities: restaurant, minimarket, private beach, kayak and pedal-boat rentals. Breakfast available but not included. MC, V. $*

Tiberias
Dining

Karamba. The fare is not Latin American, as the name suggests, but fish and vegetarian dishes of considerable originality, served in a courtyard a few steps from the shore. A massive tree in the courtyard, and another within the restaurant itself (!) add to an atmosphere that is anything but usual. The chef's often unexpected combinations simply *work*. Try the Galilee salad of lettuce, mushrooms, grapefruit, pecan nuts, and Roquefort cheese with garlic dressing; trout with a coconut crust and a tangy pineapple and almond sauce; and the house parfait. The menu includes special items for children. Good background music, reasonably priced drinks and spiked coffees, and late hours (open till well after midnight) make it a popular watering hole. *On promenade, tel. 06/724505 or 06/791546. Reservations advised. AE, DC, MC, V. $$–$$$*

★ **Pagoda** and **The House.** These Chinese/Thai restaurants under one management are part of the Lido Beach complex. Pagoda, housed in a faux Chinese temple with wraparound windows, is a spacious restaurant with a generous patio for outdoor dining overlooking the lake. The House is on a rise across the road, a maze of smaller, more intimate rooms entered through a delightful garden with a foot-bridge, waterfall, and decorative reeds. Both restaurants have an identical menu with one difference: The Pagoda is kosher (no shrimp) and is closed Friday evening until Saturday night. The House has no such restrictions (though pork is no longer on its menu), and is open only when the Pagoda is not. The food is in general exceptionally good. Try the spicy Thai soup, the (veal) spare ribs, and strips of beef sautéed in peanut sauce. *Gedud Barak St. (Rte. 90), tel. 06/724488 or 06/792564. Reservations advised. AE, DC, MC, V. The House: closed Sun.–Fri. afternoon. Pagoda: no Fri. dinner or Sat. lunch. $$–$$$*

★ **Kohinoor.** Elegance, superb service, and tantalizing flavors are the hallmarks of this recent addition to the national chain of Indian restaurants, located in the Moriah Plaza hotel (*see below*). The cuisine is typical of northern India: more subtle and less fiery than the curries of the south. Just after you're seated in the peach-and-cream-color dining room, with its vaguely Indian pointed arches and false shutters, the thin crisp bread called *papadom* is brought to your table, addictive when dipped in a mango or date chutney or piquant mint sauce. For the main course, try the house specialty, tandoori chicken, marinated and baked in a clay oven to a startling red. You won't go wrong with *rogan ghoash* (lamb curry) or chicken *tikka masala* (tandoor-baked and sautéed with onions, tomatoes, and spices). Best of the desserts is *zafrani kulfi*, the aromatic ice cream made from thickened milk (here, a milk substitute) and dried fruit. A traditional Indian dancer makes short appearances on a small stage from time to time throughout the evening. *Moriah Plaza (entrance on Promenade), off Habanim St., tel. 06/724939. Reservations advised. AE, DC, MC, V. $$*

The Pinery. The Pinery is another good Chinese restaurant, a bit more traditional than Pagoda or The House, perhaps, but also with a strong Thai influence (many Thai restaurant staff work on contract in Israel). The restaurant is quite intimate, decorated with Chinese ornaments; an aquarium serves as a room divider. Especially good are the lemon chicken and the Pinery chicken mixed with vegetables, cashews, pecans, and almonds. The staff is quite accommodating, allowing substitutions on the fixed menus. *Dona Gracia St., tel. 06/790242. Reservations advised. No Fri. dinner or Sat. lunch. DC, MC, V. $$*

Dining and Lodging ★ **Galei Kinneret.** Built in 1943, this grande dame of Tiberias hotels was a favorite retreat of David Ben Gurion. Although its Bauhaus exterior may disappoint, the Galei Kinneret's most attractive feature is its lakeside location (most of its rivals only overlook the lake), slightly removed from the hotel strip, with lawns and eucalyptus-shaded patios right on the water. Recent renovations have improved the standard of the rooms, and have given the lounge area a face-lift (though in dubious, brassy taste). Always known for its good food, the hotel now boasts the elegant Au Bord du Lac (dinner only; closed Fri. and holiday eves), a small, glassed-in, art deco–style restaurant that specializes in classic French cuisine and has acquired a rather impressive local reputation. *1 Kaplan St., tel. 06/792331, fax 06/790260. 120 rooms with bath. Facilities: 3 restaurants, bar, shops, fitness center, sauna, pool, hot tub, 1 floodlighted tennis court, speedboat, water-ski, kayak, and pedal-boat rental. Reservations required at Au Bord du Lac. AE, DC, MC, V. $$$$*

Lodging **The Caesar.** On the Promenade, the Caesar, part of a small national chain, is one of Tiberias's newer hotels. The public rooms are all white marble and polished brass. All guest rooms have lake views, and tasteful if unexceptional furnishings and every suite has a whirl-pool tub. The hotel has a large outdoor swimming pool and adjacent children's pool, but the area would have been enhanced by more grass and less concrete. The hotel dining room does a very credit-able job. In general, the Caesar is a good value. *The Promenade, Box 275, 14102, tel. 06/723333, fax 06/791013. 227 rooms with bath. Facilities: dining room, coffee shop, bar, shops, indoor heated pool, fitness room, sauna, hot tub, outdoor pool, windsurfing, sailing, waterskiing. AE, DC, MC, V. $$$$*

Gai Beach. Located on Route 90 at the southern edge of town, this newcomer offers guest rooms that are well designed and comfort-able, but smallish. Not all face the lake. The marbled lobby area is too vast for intimacy. The hotel's rare lakeshore location is a big plus, and so is the adjacent water park, with its beach, water slides, and wave pool free to hotel guests. Despite its undeniable attrac-tions, the rates are high for a hotel of this class. *Rte. 90, Box 274, 14102, tel. 06/790790, fax 06/792776. 120 rooms with bath. Facilities: restaurant, water park. AE, DC, MC, V. $$$$*

Moriah Plaza. Recent renovations in this ultramodern high rise have made the lobby and bar a bright, comfortable place in which to re-lax. Rooms are fairly ordinary, with darkish furnishings that only emphasize the relative lack of space. The service is generally quite professional and accommodating. The hotel overlooks the lake, but does not have lake frontage. The Kohinoor Indian restaurant (*see above*), on the premises, is highly commendable. Although few park-ing spots are available at the hotel, there's a big, reasonably priced lot next door. *Just off Habanim St., 14103, tel. 06/792233, fax 06/792320. 272 rooms with bath. Facilities: 3 restaurants, bar, beauty salon, fitness room, pool, sauna, hot tub. AE, DC, MC, V. $$$$*

Holiday Inn. This hotel on the southern edge of Tiberias, right next to the famous hot springs, was renovated when it became part of the Holiday Inn chain in 1993 and now has a large, well-lighted lobby and rooms that are more spacious than most in the area. Furnishings are ordinary and functional, but the grounds are pleasant and palm-shaded and boast two of Tiberias's rare tennis courts. It's a good ho-tel, even though its a little pricey. *Rte. 90, s. of Tiberias. Box 22, Tiberias 14100, tel. 06/792890, fax 06/724443. 246 rooms with bath. Facilities: restaurant, private beach, kayaks. AE, DC, MC, V. $$$-$$$$*

Astoria. One of Tiberias's better moderately priced hotels, the Astoria is set halfway uptown—neither as picturesque nor as conve-nient a location as that of the hotels near the lake. Still, it is a com-fortable and clean family-run establishment, with many of new furnishings in attractive pastels. The prices jump to the low end of the $$$ category in July and August and during the Jewish holidays. *13 Ohel Ya'akov St., 14223, tel. 06/722351, fax 06/725108. 65 rooms with bath. Facilities: restaurant, coffee shop, 24-hour bar, pool. AE, DC, MC, V. $$*

Church of Scotland Centre. Built in 1893 as a hospital of the Free Church of Scotland, the building was ultimately converted into a pil-grim hospice, and today welcomes all visitors, proclaiming its com-mitment "to build bridges of trust and respect among our neighbours whoever they are and wherever they come from." The double-story stone buildings with their deep porches and high-ceil-inged rooms are a pleasant change from the tackiness of many mod-ern hotels. Recent renovations include air-conditioning in all rooms. The rambling and slightly wild gardens make a challenging adven-ture land for kids, and a pastoral refuge for their elders. The outer gate is closed at 6 PM, but your key gets you in at your convenience, as well as providing access to the private beach across the road. The location could not be more central. *Gedud Barak and Hayarden Sts., Box 104, 14100, tel. 06/723769 or 06/721165, fax 06/790145. 46 rooms with bath. Facilities: self-service tea and coffee in lounge. No credit cards. $$*

★ **Ron Beach.** The last hotel in Tiberias on Route 90 north, it's one of the few with its own lake frontage. Renovations have benefited this hotel as well, and the amenities—box-spring mattresses, TVs, and blow-dryers—are impressive for its price category for this part of Israel. In addition to its main building, a row of 29 rooms with patios open right onto the lawn and the beach. The restaurant has good St. Peter's fish. It's an altogether excellent value. *Gedud Barak St. (Rte. 90 N), tel. 06/791350, fax 06/791351. 74 rooms with bath. Facilities: restaurant, private beach, children's pool. AE, DC, MC, V. $$*

Tzameret Inn. Tzameret means "summit," a fitting description given this hotel's location a full 1,300 feet above the Sea of Galilee. It's not convenient if you don't have a car, and it is far from the tourist watering holes, but it has a stunning view of the lake, and, in the hot Tiberias summer, can be as much as 5°C (9°F) cooler than the downtown area. The guest rooms and public areas are somewhat mediocre, and the hotel is sometimes inundated by large groups on weekends. However, the superior facilities, pleasant bar, and splendid mountaintop location make the Tzameret easily worth its rates. Prices increase on weekends, Jewish holidays, and in July and August. *Plus 200 St., Upper Tiberias, Box 3030, Tiberias 14130, tel. 06/794951, fax 06/732444. 165 rooms with bath. Facilities: dining room, bar, coffee shop, pool/billiards table, video room, fitness room, sauna, hot tub, pool, tennis court. MC, V. $$*

★ **Bet Berger.** "Berger House," run by the family of that name, is a two-wing hotel of spacious, well-furnished rooms, each with a balcony and an equipped kitchenette. It's uptown, and more convenient if you have a car, but buses to the downtown area are very frequent (except on weekends). No meals are available, but there is a supermarket across the road where you can stock your kitchenette. This hotel offers few frills, but it's a very good value. *27 Neiberg St., Box 535, 14105, tel. 06/720850, fax 06/791514. 45 rooms with bath. Facilities: kitchenettes. MC, V. $*

Meyouhas Youth Hostel. This large basalt building fronted by a lawn and trees is in the heart of downtown Tiberias, a minute's walk from the lake, the Promenade, and the mall. The term "youth" is inaccurate: The hostel is open to all. A few double rooms are available, and many larger ones, which sleep up to six, have bunk beds; all have private bathrooms. New pine furniture has lifted the place out of its old iron-bedstead image, but conditions are still somewhat spartan. Meals are cheap. If you don't mind lodgings that are strictly functional, you could do worse. *Cnr. Gedud Barak and Hayarden Sts., Box 81, 14100, tel. 06/721775 or 06/790350, fax 06/720372. 248 beds, most without bath. Facilities: restaurant. MC, V. $*

The Arts and Nightlife

The Arts

"Few and far between" would describe cultural events in this region. By far the best source of information for performances in the Lower Galilee is the GTIO on Habanim Street, between the Moriah Plaza and Jordan River hotels, tel. 06/720992 or 06/722089.

The **Ein Gev Spring Festival** (tel. 06/758032 or 06/758039) celebrated its 50th anniversary in 1993. This chiefly music festival, whose participants have ranged from Bernstein and Rampal to Dietrich and Sinatra, has always been held during Passover week. Call ahead to see when the festival will take place.

A welcome new addition to the region is **Bet Gabriel** (Tel. 06/751175, fax 06/751187.), on the southern shores of the Sea of Galilee (near Degania). Its fine architecture, beautiful garden setting, and state-of-the-art facilities have already established it as a magnetic cultural center, less than 10 minutes' drive from Tiberias. The GTIO and major hotels carry information on the month's performances and art exhibitions.

The recently renovated Roman theater at **Bet She'an** (tel. 06/587189) is the venue for a handful of spring events. Kibbutzim in the area periodically host theatrical, dance, and musical performers on tour from the "big cities" in the south. Consult the GTIO and your hotel front desk for information about these special events.

Nightlife

As you might expect in a resort area, entertainment is more common than is culture. Much of it in Tiberias is of the live-music-in-the-hotel-lounge variety: piano-bar players, dance-music musicians, and "sing along, folks!" crooners. The Moriah Plaza, Jordan River, Caesar, and to a lesser extent, Galei Kinneret, specialize in this genre. At press time (fall 1994) the latter featured a classically trained Russian pianist who is equally adept at Chopin and Tin Pan Alley.

The Ministry of Tourism sponsors a weekly **Israeli Folklore Evening,** usually on Wednesday, at the Caesar Hotel or another venue. Entrance is free. Call the GTIO information number (tel. 06/720992 or 06/722089) or the Caesar (06/723333) for schedules.

Sometimes a classier act comes through, often performing on one of the kibbutzim in the area. If it's not too language-specific (a Hebrew comedian might be a problem), the performances could be a delightful slice of Israel. Contact the GTIO in Tiberias for more information.

Thursday and Friday are the "nightclub" nights at some of the hotels, with dance music to please the weekend crowds. The clientele tends to be a bit older. The younger generation in general wouldn't be caught dead here and prefer to hang out at the pubs along the *midrachov* (pedestrian wall) and the Promenade, where the recorded rock music is good and loud and the beer is on tap. The **Lido** (Gedud Barak St., tel. 06/724488 or 06/792564) has a disco that operates most nights between May and October, in a balmy, palm-dotted lakeside location. **Blue Beach** (tel. 06/720105 or 06/724137), also on the lake and just north of the Lido, has evenings in season that alternate folk dancing (Israeli and international: It's not nearly as staid as it sounds!) with a strobe-lighted disco.

The boat operators use their bigger boats as floating discos in the summer, usually departing from the piers at the Promenade for a 45-minute cruise offshore from Tiberias. The cost is NIS 12–NIS 20 ($4–$6.70). These companies also occasionally offer a two-hour dinner-and-disco deal for about NIS 120–NIS 150 ($40–$50). For details call **Lido Kinneret** (tel. 06/724488, 06/721538, or 06/792564), **Kinneret Sailing** (tel. 06/792831), or **Ron Sailing** (tel. 06/791117).

7 Upper Galilee and the Golan

Including Zfat (Safed)

*By Lisa
Perlman with
Mike Rogoff*

Israelis call it the Switzerland of Israel: The undulating hills of Western Galilee roll into sharper, more rugged limestone and basalt formations, bordered in the north by Lebanon and in the east by the volcanic, mountainous terrain of the Golan Heights, on the other side of which lies Syria. The dominant feature of the Upper Galilee and the Golan, the latter claiming less than 50 square kilometers (35 square miles) in all, is Mt. Hermon, the highest mountain in Israel, one of the highest in the Middle East, and home to Israel's sole ski resort.

Most Israelis come here to get away from it all, indulging in everything from hiking and bird-watching to kayaking and wine-tasting. The nature trails, the rustic restaurants, and the kibbutz guest houses make it easy to steer clear of the four urban centers that can be found here; in fact, two of these—Kiryat Shmona and Ma'alot, both of which began life as development towns designed to absorb Jewish refugees mainly from Arab countries—offer little of interest to the visitor. The other two—Zfat (Safed) and Katzrin—have unique personalities, the first having been formed by a long history of Jewish religious mysticism and the second by a hard-headed determination to secure Israel's border with Syria.

Towering at a height of more than 9,000 feet, Mt. Hermon is Israel's "sponge" as well as its ski slope: Huge volumes of water from snow and rain are absorbed into the ancient limestone rock, emerging at the base of the mountain in a series of gorgeous springs and feeding the Jordan River and its tributaries. Indeed, these rivers, all flowing through the region's Hula Valley, provide half of Israel's water supply. The abundant water sustains gazelles, wildcats, wild boar, hyraxes and hares, hundreds of species of birds, and lush, verdant foliage that thrives year-round.

More than anything else, it is the water here that has been the source of political contention since time immemorial. (In second place is the hilltop view, which underscores the value of the Golan Heights, officially annexed by Israel in 1981.) For a million years this region has been a center of human settlement. In earliest times, people hunted the rhinos, elephants, and fallow deer that have since roamed to other parts. Later they learned to farm—and to trade, for the Galilee was smack bang on the western world's first major trade route, the Via Maris, stretching from Egypt to Mesopotamia.

Consequently, the rivals for this prime real estate were many: In ancient times, Egyptians, Canaanites, Israelites, Romans, Ottomans, and Crusaders locked horns in various configurations; in the 20th century, the borders have been played with by Russia, Britain, France, and, of course, Israel and Syria.

In addition to the Jewish and Arab population, there has always been a small Druze presence here, particularly in the Golan Heights (about 17,000 Arabic-speaking Druze). After the Six Day War in 1967, five Druze villages found themselves no longer in Lebanese or Syrian territory, but in Israel.

Borders are not the only things that have shifted in the region. A geological fault line, the Syrian-African rift, cuts straight through the 30-kilometer-long (19-mile-long) Hula Valley. Many symmetrical volcanic cones hundreds of thousands of years old daub the Golan; as for earthquakes, in 1837 Zfat and Tiberias were razed when the earth shook here, but no rumbles of significance have been heard since.

With plenty of water and rich fertile soil, the Upper Galilee and the Golan have always been agricultural centers. Since Jewish development of the area resumed a century ago, orange and apple orchards, fish cultivation ponds, cotton fields, and vineyards have become common sights. These are closely intertwined with the region's other main industry: tourism. Travelers come to see and stay at the many successful communal settlements—the kibbutzim and moshavim—that dot the area. They also come to roam the area's nature reserves, most of which are around the rivers and springs, and to witness the seasonal vacationing of hundreds of species of migratory birds that flit between Africa and Europe.

The region's proximity to Lebanon and Syria does not deter visitors to the Upper Galilee and the Golan. On the contrary, the so-called "Good Fence," at the Israeli-Lebanese border crossing at Israel's northernmost town of Metulla, draws the curious from all over the world; oenologists come to taste the local wine, and hikers don their boots for the fauna- and flora-filled reserves.

Whether the status of the Golan Heights changes as a result of the ongoing peace negotiations will not be known for a long time. Since their arrival at the turn of the century, the Jews have fought malaria and other diseases, defended themselves in the face of Arab armies and terror bands, and confronted a host of other hardships and hurdles. And still the tenacious Galilean will tell you there's no better place. Whether he is a kibbutznik or lives in town, whether she was born here or opted for this corner of the world, the pride is palpable, and it transcends politics. The amazing thing is that despite the embattled past and unsure future, the average Galilean remains laid back and friendly. Only four hours' drive from hectic, humid Tel Aviv and from the visceral capital, Jerusalem, this truly is another world.

Essential Information

Important Addresses and Numbers

Tourist Information
All hotels and kibbutz guest houses can provide tourist information, and many will arrange tours as well. The **Government Tourist Information Office** (GTIO) in **Tiberias** (Habanim St. Mall, between the Jordan River and Moriah Plaza hotels, tel. 06/720992) can furnish information about the entire Galilee. The **Municipal Tourist Information Office** in Zfat (50 Yerushalayim St., Box 227, Zfat 13010, tel. 06/920961) is useful for regional information and can provide a list of licensed guides in the city. For information on the Upper Galilee's nature reserves, natural history, and bird-watching, contact the **Bet Ussishkin Museum** (Kibbutz Dan, Mobile Post Upper Galilee 12245, tel. 06/941704).

Emergencies
Dial 100 from any telephone for **police**, 101 for **ambulance**, and 102 for **firefighters.** Tokens or telecards are not required at public phones for emergency calls.

The **Magen David Adom** station in **Kiryat Shmona** (3 Tchernichovsky St., tel. 06/944334 or 06/949401) handles medical and dental emergencies 24 hours a day. It is near the central bus station.

Police
The main **police station** in the Upper Galilee is in **Kiryat Shmona** (1 Salinger St., tel. 06/943444 or 06/943445).

Hospital The largest hospital in the north outside Haifa is the **Rivka Ziv General Hospital** in **Zfat** (Harambam Rd., tel. 06/978822). Bus 6 from the Zfat bus station stops here.

Car Rental It is much easier to rent a car in Tiberias (*see* Essential Information *in* Chapter 6, Lower Galilee), Tel Aviv, Jerusalem, or Haifa than to search for a dependable car rental company in the tiny towns of the Upper Galilee. However, for travelers flying to the Galilee (*see* Arriving and Departing by Plane, *below*), **Arkia Israeli Airlines** (in Tel Aviv, tel. 03/690–2222) can arrange for a rented car to be waiting at Mahanayim Airport, outside Rosh Pina.

Arriving and Departing by Plane

Arkia Israeli Airlines (in Tel Aviv, tel. 03/690–2222; in Jerusalem, tel. 02/234855), Israel's domestic airline, operates four flights daily from **Sde Dov Airport** in **Tel Aviv,** and three flights per week from **Jerusalem,** to the small Galilee airport of **Mahanayim** (tel. 06/935301), part of the township of **Rosh Pina.** From the airport it is 10 kilometers (6 miles) to Zfat and 30 kilometers (18.6 miles) to Kiryat Shmona.

Arriving and Departing by Car and Bus

By Car Unquestionably, the best way to see the Upper Galilee and the Golan is by car. It takes three hours to make the 180-kilometer (112-mile) drive from Tel Aviv; 1½ hours of driving from both Akko (Acre) and Nahariya, about 60 kilometers (37 miles) away; and four hours from Jerusalem, which is 200 kilometers (124 miles) to the south. There are numerous approaches to the area. From Tiberias and the Sea of Galilee, Route 90 runs due north between the Hula Valley on the east and the hills of Naftali on the west. The more rugged Route 98 leads from the eastern side of the Sea of Galilee up through the Golan Heights to Mt. Hermon. Near the top of Route 98 you can pick up Route 91, which heads west into the Upper Galilee.

From the Mediterranean coast there are several options, the main one being Route 85 from Akko (Acre). Route 89 runs parallel to Route 85 a little farther north, from Nahariya, and boasts some gorgeous scenery. From Haifa take Route 75 to Route 77, turning onto Route 90 at Tiberias, or Route 70 north onto Route 85 east. If you're starting from Tel Aviv, drive north on Route 4 or 2 to Hadera. From there you'll head northwest on Route 65, exiting onto Route 85 east.

By Bus **Egged** buses (tel. 03/537–5555) run daily from Tel Aviv to Kiryat Shmona (Buses 842 and 845) and Zfat (Bus 846); from Jerusalem to Kiryat Shmona (Bus 963) and Zfat (Bus 964); from Haifa to Kiryat Shmona (Buses 501 and 502) and Zfat (Buses 331 and 362); and to both cities from Tiberias (Bus 459).

Getting Around

By Car The state of Israel's roads is changing from bad-to-fair to fair-to-good. In the Upper Galilee in particular, the government is making an effort to improve the road infrastructure, but don't expect wide, even highways; the fact is, sometimes they're paved and sometimes, well, they just aren't. This is especially true in the Golan. Driving cautiously—because of both the present conditions of the roads and the average Israeli driver on them—is tremendously important. Try to avoid driving during peak hours, which are usually late Sat-

urday afternoon when the city folk crowd the roads back to Jerusalem and Tel Aviv after a day out in the country.

The main north–south roads in the region are Route 90, which goes
all the way up to Metulla at the Lebanese border; the 65-kilometer-
long (40-mile-long) Tiberias–Metulla Road; and the less-traveled
Route 98, which runs from the eastern side of the Sea of Galilee
through the Golan Heights (along the Disengagement Zone) to Mt.
Hermon. The main west–east highways are Route 85, which runs
for 60 kilometers (37 miles) from Akko (Acre) to Korazim, and Route
89, which connects Nahariya and Zfat, 50 kilometers (31 miles)
away.

Gas stations are easy to find along Route 90 and in the towns, such as
Katzrin (Route 87) or Zfat (Route 89). It is best to fill up during the
day, because it is difficult to find a gas station open after 9 PM. Gas
stations are, however, generally open daily.

By Bus Although local buses stop at all major sites in the region (partly because there is always a kibbutz, a town, or some other small residential settlement nearby), if you are on a tight schedule, avoid buses,
which can run infrequently. Call Egged (tel. 03/537–5555) for schedules. If you have trouble getting through, you can try the local
depots: Kiryat Shmona, tel. 06/940740; Tiberias, tel. 06/791080;
Zfat, tel. 06/921122.

Guided Tours

General Both of Israel's major bus companies, **Egged** (15 Frishman St., Tel
Interest Aviv 63578, tel. 03/527–1222; 224 Jaffa Rd., Jerusalem, tel. 02/
304422; Zfat Bus Station, tel. 06/921122) and **United Tours** (113
Hayarkon St., Tel Aviv 63573, tel. 03/754–3404; King David Hotel
Annex, Jerusalem, tel. 02/252187) offer one- and two-day guided
tours of the region, departing from Tel Aviv and Jerusalem. Both
give children under 12 a 10% discount.

Egged's one-day tour of the Golan Heights from Tel Aviv (departing
from Kikar Namir), conducted on Sunday year-round and also on
Thursday from March through October, includes the lookout of
Mitzpe Gadot, Katzrin, Banias Nature Reserve, and Kiryat
Shmona. United's one-day tour of the Golan from Tel Aviv, depart-
ing Saturday from the railway station, follows a similar route but
skips the Banias Nature Reserve for the Hammat Gader hot springs
and crocodile farm in the Lower Galilee. Both tours cost NIS 147
($49). Egged's one-day tour on Tuesday leaving from the Tiberias
Central Bus Station features a visit to Capernaum and along the
Disengagement Zone to Katzrin, Banias, and the Good Fence at
Metulla. The cost is NIS 87 ($29). From April through October,
Egged also conducts one-day tours on Tuesday from Haifa to Nazareth and Tiberias, and to Zfat and the Golan Heights. Each tour
costs NIS 138 ($46) and departs from Haifa's central bus station.

Egged and United run similar two-day tours of the region from both
Tel Aviv and Jerusalem (Egged picks up at Jaffa Gate, United at the
King David Hotel), but end in Tel Aviv only. The Galilee/Golan
Heights tour leaves Monday and Wednesday and goes through the
Jordan Valley to Bet She'an, Nazareth, Capernaum, Zfat, Katzrin,
Banias, and down through the Hula Valley to Tiberias, where a boat
trip on the Sea of Galilee is included. The NIS 480 ($160) price in-
cludes accommodations in a tourist-class hotel and breakfast. The
other two-day option is the Jordan Valley/Tiberias/Golan Heights
tour, which leaves Friday, going through the Jordan Valley to

Hammat Gader hot springs and crocodile farm to Zfat, Banias, Katzrin, Capernaum, Tiberias, and Nazareth. The tour costs NIS 486 ($162).

Special   The **Society for the Protection of Nature in Israel** (SPNI) (4 Hashfela
Interest St., Tel Aviv 66183, tel. 03/537–4425 or 03/639–0644) sponsors excellent hikes and walking tours in the region. The tours are usually aimed at all ages, so Olympics-level fitness is not required; any hikes that require some physical exertion are clearly described as such. **Vered Hagalil** (Mobile Post Korazim 12385, tel. 06/935785) conducts horseback tours for the experienced rider and novice alike. These tours last for up to five days—you can even enter Jerusalem on an Arabian stallion!

Exploring Upper Galilee and the Golan

Tel Avivians do it. Jerusalemites do it. But cramming the Upper Galilee and the Golan into a day trip is far from ideal for the first-time visitor. Although brief visits are certainly possible (from Tiberias, for example), a several-day sojourn here can be as leisurely or as hectic as you wish. You can learn about the country's military history, do a bit of wine tasting, hike through a little piece of wilderness, relax over a hearty country meal, try your hand at kayaking, or sit quietly in a room with a view. The distances in the Upper Galilee and the Golan are small (aren't they everywhere in Israel?). Still, the more time allowed here, the better; there is something about the soft gurgling of the brooks, the lush foliage of the forests, and the crisp mountain air of the Golan Heights that slows the pace.

The ideal way to see the area is by car, but local buses will get you almost anywhere you want to go. Tour 1 begins in the restored pioneer village of Rosh Pina, 25 kilometers (16 miles) north of Tiberias, and continues through the beautiful Hula Valley to the rugged volcanic terrain of the Golan Heights. Tour 2 begins with a walking tour of the holy city of Zfat and goes on to nearby Mt. Meron, which has a symbiotic relationship with the holy city.

Highlights for First-Time Visitors

Good Fence, Metulla (*see* Tour 1)
Hermon River (Banias) Nature Reserve (*see* Tour 1)
Hula Nature Reserve (*see* Tour 1)
Nimrod's Fortress (*see* Tour 1)
Old Jewish Quarter, Zfat (*see* Tour 2)

Tour 1: Hula Valley and the Golan Heights

Numbers in the margin correspond to points of interest on the Upper Galilee and the Golan map.

Starting from Tiberias, drive north on Route 90 for 25 kilometers (16 miles). Exit left for Rosh Pina.

"The stone that the builder hath rejected hath become the headstone of the corner" (Psalm 118). These words from the Old Testament inspired the first Zionist pioneers to settle the Galilee at **Rosh Pina,** literally, "headstone of the corner." The group came from Romania in 1882, determined to build a village. They bought this land, 1,500 feet above sea level at the foot of the mountain ridge 10 kilometers (6 miles) east of Zfat, and arrived with all they needed for their new home, right down to the timber for construction. Ironically, the boat that brought them to the Holy Land was called the *Titus*, the name of the Roman general whose destruction of Jerusalem forced the exile of Jews from the city in AD 70. The Romanians' main livelihood at Rosh Pina derived from the production of silk by silkworms; this industry was encouraged by the great philanthropist Baron Edmond de Rothschild (*see* Exploring the Northern Coast and Western Galilee *in* Chapter 5), who gave them the fruit trees needed for the project. Despite grand efforts, however, the project did not yield the desired results: The residents were walking around in silk scarves and socks, but they had no bread to eat. Slowly, family by family, the immigrants moved away to other settlements, leaving only squatters for decades to follow.

Recent years have seen the little village restored, and although it has not been developed as a tourist attraction, it warrants a brief visit simply for its charm. To get there, ascend the hill (catch Bus 459 to the grocery store and walk for 10 minutes up the wide cobblestone path) from the modern township of Rosh Pina, where a few of the descendants of the original settlers still live and till the land. Walking about cobblestone streets, look out for the **Schwartz Hotel** and the **synagogue** (both on Ha'elyon Street, directly up from the pub, The Baron's Stables). Built in 1890, the two-story hotel was the first rest house to be built in the Galilee. Today it is quite literally a mere skeleton of the original, but try to imagine what it was like to check in here after a long, tiring journey and enjoy the tranquil view of the Sea of Galilee below and the white-capped Mt. Hermon to the north. The synagogue is usually locked. However, someone in the office of Old Rosh Pina (tel. 06/936603), a development company, next door to the pub at the bottom of Ha'elyon Street, will be glad to open it for you. The interior of the no-longer-functioning synagogue is as it was when it was built in the mid-1880s; the dark pews and holy ark made of the timber brought from Romania have aged gracefully. Look up at the ceiling: The depictions of palm trees and biblical motifs are painted in rich colors.

The **Old Rosh Pina office** occupies the house that belonged to Professor Gideon Mer, a leading expert in malaria in the 1930s. The story goes that he used to inject his wife and children with his experimental remedies during his attempts to combat malaria in the region; all survived. The British were so impressed with Mer's work that they sent him to Burma to fight malaria epidemics there.

Old Rosh Pina is populated today by some 60 artists, although unlike their counterparts in the artists' village of Ein Hod (*see* Exploring the Northern Coast and Western Galilee *in* Chapter 5), they do not usually open their homes to visitors. There is, however, a **gallery** on Harishonim Street (across from the synagogue), run by resident Moussa Shafat and displaying primarily his own watercolors, prints, and sculptures. *Harishonim St., tel. 06/938355. Open Sat. 10–5 (other times by chance or by appointment).*

From Rosh Pina, drive 8 kilometers (5 miles) north on Route 90. Archaeology buffs will want to stop in at the large archaeological mound of **Tel Hatzor** (Hazor) on the left side of the road. Over a period of thousands of years, the ancient city of Hatzor was built and rebuilt a total of 21 times, allowing latter-day diggers to slice off layer after layer of differing lifestyles that span the ages. Situated on the Via Maris, which as the link between Egypt and Mesopotamia was the most important trade route in antiquity, Hatzor is first referred to in Mesopotamian documents of the 2nd millennium BC; an ambassador from Hammurabi's court resided here. The Book of Joshua (Joshua 11:13) makes mention of ancient Hatzor as "the head of all those kingdoms," although Joshua himself destroyed Canaanite Hatzor in the 13th century BC, and Israelites resettled it. Its next heyday came three centuries later when King Solomon decided it would serve him well as one of his great regional military and administrative centers, like Megiddo and Gezer. In 732 BC, Hatzor met its end when invading Assyrian king Tiglath Pileser III conquered the Galilee and forced its Israelite inhabitants off the land in chains and into exile. The city was never to regain its former glory.

The site was first identified in 1928 as the ancient Hatzor, but the archaeologist who put it squarely on the modern map, from 1955 to 1959, was the renowned Dr. Yigal Yadin, best known for his excavations at Masada. (His brother, Yossi Yadin, is one of Israel's veteran actors and can still be seen onstage at the Habimah National Theater in Tel Aviv.)

The huge site is divided into two areas: the tel, or **Upper City,** which comprised the oldest settlements, and the **Lower City,** first settled in the 18th century BC. Only the tel, covering less than a fifth of the total area of the excavation site, is open to the public. Allow about a half-hour to stroll from the 9th century BC water works to the palace stable gates and the citadel. Then drive over to the Hatzor Museum (on the grounds of Kibbutz Ayelet Hashachar, on the other side of the highway), where many of the figurines, weapons, stone pots, and other artifacts unearthed in the two areas are on display; others still are at the Israel Museum in Jerusalem (*see* Exploring Jerusalem *in* Chapter 2). *Tel Hatzor National Park, tel. 06/934855. Admission: NIS 8 ($2.70) adults, NIS 4 ($1.35) children. Park and museum open Apr.–Sept., daily 8–5; Oct.–Mar., daily 8–4.*

Return to Route 90 and drive about 8 kilometers (5 miles) north, at which point you'll see an orange sign pointing right (east) to the
❸ **Hula Nature Reserve,** the last of Israel's swamplands and one of the last remaining vestiges of wilderness in the country. This is no accident. In the first half of the 20th century, British mandatory rulers, like the Ottomans before them, repeatedly refused Jewish settlers' requests to drain the swampland, a practice that was common in other parts of the tiny country as the need for arable land grew. Almost as soon as they could, following independence, the Israeli authorities eagerly approved the project. Thus, during much of the 1950s, the Hula was drained and dredged, drained and dredged, until it was discovered that this was doing grave and irreversible harm to the ecosystem, particularly to the hundreds of thousands of migratory birds that stopped here as they flitted between Europe and Africa twice yearly. This crisis led the International Union for the Conservation of Nature (IUCN) to declare the Hula Valley a reserve of world importance, which it has remained since the early 1970s.

The pelicans, wild geese, storks, plovers, and a host of exotic birds have their sanctuary back, but they would not be here were it not also for the swampy waters that abound with carp, catfish, and perch, and a reed habitat that boasts rare thickets of papyrus through which a water buffalo or two might be seen roaming. Less recognized is the topminnow, an American fish that lives on mosquito eggs and has played a big part in helping rid the area of malaria. There is a visitor center with complete information about the 800-acre reserve, an observation tower, and a snack bar. Free guided tours of the reserve can be booked in advance, but only for small groups. Hunting and fishing are strictly forbidden. *E. of Rte. 90, tel. 06/937069. Admission: NIS 11 ($3.70) adults, NIS 5.50 ($1.85) chil-*

dren. Open Sun.–Thurs. 8–4, Fri. and holiday eves 8–3, Sat. 8–4; 1 hr later during summer holidays.

Near the entrance to the reserve is **Bet Dubrovin** (Dubrovin Farm), the reconstructed farmhouse-cum-museum once owned by immigrant converts from Russia, the Dubrovins. The farming family was part of a movement of Christian Russians who, in the early years of this century, converted to Judaism and opted to live in the Holy Land. Old man Dubrovin hebraicized his Christian name to Yoav, grew a beard and sidelocks, and, in 1904, brought his family from the banks of the Volga to the swamps of the Hula. Despite the hardships, these pioneers set up a model farm on their 70-hectare (173-acre) estate, even winning first prize—for cattle in 1922 and for chickpeas in 1927—in the annual agricultural exhibitions in Rosh Pina.

The Dubrovins paid a price for their pioneer spirit. Malaria was rife and claiming victims daily. Several members of the family succumbed, although Yoav lived till 1934, when he was 103. By that time his son Yitzhak was managing the property. He, too, lived to a ripe old age, dying at age 90 in 1968. He donated the estate to the Jewish National Fund, and it was opened to the public in 1986.

The waterwheel in the front garden is still operational. Try pushing the log-lever that turns the wheel and draws the water—you'll stretch a few muscles, especially if you've been driving all day. The estate consists of a series of stone buildings constructed on a square, surrounding a courtyard that holds some old farming equipment and even a few farm animals. An exhibit in the building that housed the family gives a history of both the area and the family, and reconstructs their lives and those of other pioneers through furniture and photographs of the period. A ceramics shop on the premises sells locally made wares. *Box 124, Yesod Hama'ala, 12105, tel. 06/937371. Admission: NIS 5 ($1.70) adults, NIS 3.50 ($1.20) children. Open Sat.–Thurs. and holidays 9–5, Fri. and holiday eves 9–3.*

Time Out   Also on the grounds is the charming and highly recommended **Farmyard Restaurant,** a rustic eatery whose specialty is home-smoked meats (*see* Dining and Lodging, *below*). Although it is run independently of Bet Dubrovin (it also has different hours), the entrance fee to the museum is deducted from the price of a main course, so hang on to your tickets.

Return to the main road and continue north for about 10 kilometers (6 miles). Exit left onto Route 899, then take the left turnoff into Route 886 and the undulating **Hills of Naftali.** These heights were once populated by the Israelite tribe of Naftali, whose luck it was to wake up every day to stunning views. Coming into sight after a 15-minute drive are an ancient dome-capped tomb on the left and a (relatively) modern fortress on the right, one of many such structures built by the British around the country in mandatory times to control strategic junctions or vantage points. The site is popularly known as **Nebi Yusha** (Arabic for "the prophet Joshua"), so dubbed by Shi'ite Muslim villagers who once lived here and who claimed the tomb was that of Joshua, Moses's successor. (They also believed that walking around the tomb would bring good health.) The fortress, today a military base, is called **Metzudat Koach,** which in literal Hebrew means "citadel of strength." The name is actually a play on words, as the two Hebrew letters that make up the word "koach" have the numerical value of 28—the number of Hagana soldiers who fell here in fierce battles for the strategic point during the 1948 War of Independence. Near the eastern fence of the fortress there is a

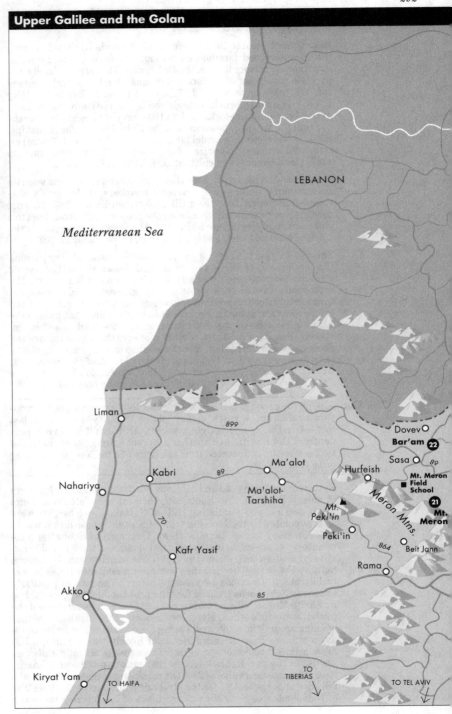

Upper Galilee and the Golan

Mediterranean Sea

LEBANON

Liman

899

Dovev

Bar'am **22**

Kabri

Ma'alot

Sasa *89*

Hurfeish

Mt. Meron
Field
School

Nahariya

89

Ma'alot-
Tarshiha

Mt.
Peki'in

Meron Mtns.

21

**Mt.
Meron**

70

Peki'in

864

Beit Jann

Kafr Yasif

Rama

Akko

85

Kiryat Yam

TO HAIFA

TO
TIBERIAS

TO TEL AVIV

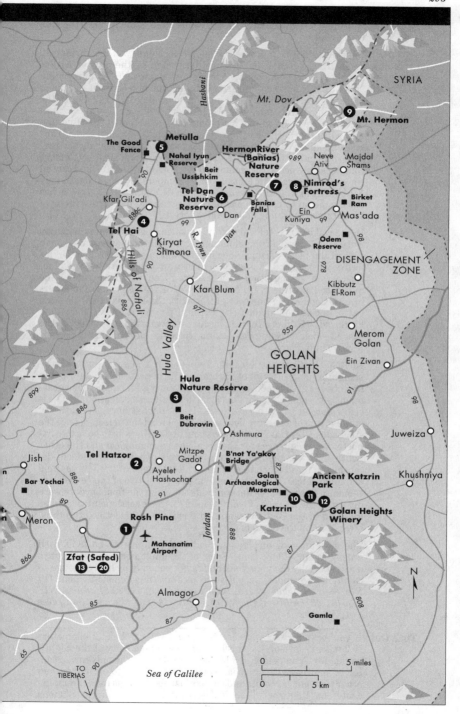

trail that leads to a lookout point and a memorial to the 28 Israelis who died; the view, taking in the whole Hula Valley, makes the hike worthwhile.

Continuing north on Route 886, along the ridge, will soon bring you to **Tel Hai,** perched on the northern edge of the city of Kiryat Shmona (Kiryat Shemona). The Hebrew name of Tel Hai, meaning "hill of life," was adapted from Arabic, but in a sense it became a monument to life itself following a memorable battle in 1920. In the years immediately following World War I, while Britain and France bickered over who should have final control of the Upper Hula Valley, which bordered on their respective holdings, bands of Arabs and Bedouins roamed the region harassing and plundering the tiny Jewish farming settlements. They destroyed one such settlement completely, overran the communal settlement of Tel Hai, and caused the veteran village of Metulla to be temporarily abandoned; only Kibbutz Kfar Giladi was successful in defending itself, and it has since gone on to become one of the largest and most prosperous of kibbutzim (*see* Dining and Lodging, *below*).

In the wake of the Tel Hai terror, in which two settlement members were killed, Josef Trumpeldor and seven comrades were called on to defend the place. Trumpeldor had served in the Czar's army in his native Russia, and though he had lost an arm fighting, he had already won a reputation as a leader. Fired by Zionist ideals, he moved to Palestine in 1912 at the age of 32 with a group of followers in tow. Soon after, he was fighting with the British at the ill-fated battle of Gallipoli against the Turks. Upon his return to Palestine, he moved to Kibbutz Tel Hai, became its commander, and like all the other Jewish settlers, was constantly on the alert against Arab terrorist bands.

In 1920 the final battle came. Trumpeldor and seven others were slaughtered on the kibbutz grounds. His last words are believed to have been, "It is good to die for our country." Trumpeldor subsequently became not only a national hero but an inspiration, and he is still referred to with reverence. He is buried here, beneath the stone statue of a roaring lion on the hill behind the museum, once the stockade of Tel Hai. The heroic stand at Tel Hai was to have two important consequences for the area, one psychological and the other political: It was the first modern example of Jewish armed self-defense, and it did much to change the local image of the Jew as timid and defenseless. Also, the survival of at least two of the Jewish settlements this far north determined that when the final borders were drawn by the League of Nations in 1922, those settlements would be included in the British mandated territory of Palestine, and thus, after 1948, in the State of Israel.

The museum now displays agricultural equipment and tools used during Trumpeldor's time. Some of the implements are still put to use (especially during school holidays); you may be lucky enough to catch, for example, an old-style pita-making demonstration. *Off Rte. 886, tel. 06/951333. Admission: NIS 6.50 ($2.20) adults, NIS 5.50 ($1.85) children. Open Sun.–Thurs. 8–4, Fri. and holiday eves 8–1, Sat. 8–2.*

Time Out If you're hungry or you need to gas up, you can head 2 kilometers (1.2 miles) south on Route 90 to **Kiryat Shmona** (City of the Eight), named for Trumpeldor and his seven brethren. The only urban center in an otherwise agrarian region, it has little to offer travelers other than burger joints and similar fast-food stands in the shopping center on Route 90. Like Ma'alot, farther west, Kiryat Shmona made the headlines in 1974 when Arabs infiltrated into Israel from Lebanon one night, came down the mountain slope behind the town and broke into an apartment at dawn, massacring an entire family. By 1982 the spate of terrorist attacks had reached such proportions that Israel responded by invading Lebanon, which was the first stage of the Lebanon War.

Head north again on Route 90, this time all the way to the top of Israel (7 kilometers, or 4.3 miles). There is a security gate at the entrance to **Metulla,** but it's been years since there was any need to man it. Metulla is so picturesque that it is hard to believe this tranquil little town is just a stone's throw away from a foe, Lebanon. Still, precautions are taken, and if any problem should arise, the gate will be closed to visitors. Furthermore, there is a happy story of cooperation between the Israelis and the Lebanese here that draws visitors from all over the world to see the so-called **Good Fence.**

Metulla was founded as a farming settlement in 1896 with the aid of Baron Edmond de Rothschild, and in the century since, its residents have shown such tenacity and determination that it has not only survived but thrived. Essentially, it has one thoroughfare, Harishonim Street (though this can hardly be called a main street), where hotels and eateries are located. Somehow the tensions of the Middle East dissipate here, at least briefly. One- and two-story limestone buildings with their European-style architecture line the street, and the Continental atmosphere is enhanced by the numerous signs that offer ZIMMER (German for "room") for rent. Even the weather is decidedly un-Mediterranean, with refreshing cool mountain breezes in summer and snow in winter. And yet the cypresses and cedars recall a whiff of Lebanon.

The three-minute, well-marked drive from the center of town to the border passes through residential Metulla, with its large homes surrounded by greenery. You can't miss the Good Fence—or, rather, the thoroughly touristy little kiosk and souvenir shop that greet you. This segment of the Israel–Lebanon border has enjoyed its nickname since June 1976, when Israel first sent medical and other aid over the border to residents of South Lebanon. One version of the story that can be heard in these parts is that Israeli soldiers noticed a Lebanese woman in labor at the border crossing. They rushed her to an Israeli hospital, where a healthy baby was delivered, and within days there were several very pregnant women waiting at the Good Fence. The peaceful interaction between the two sides has developed ever since: First Lebanese citizens with relatives in Israel were allowed to come over to visit, then summer camps were organized (and still are) for Lebanese schoolchildren and their Israeli counterparts, and today hundreds of South Lebanese workers cross the border to go to their jobs in the Galilee.

If time allows before leaving Metulla, take a picnic down to the streams and waterfalls that flow all year round in the **Nahal Iyun Nature Reserve,** just south of Metulla next to Route 90. If not, there is no shortage of lush greenery, pastoral landscapes, and relaxing water sources on either side of the winding road ahead on the way to Mt. Hermon.

From Metulla, return along Route 90 toward Kiryat Shmona; bypass the city by turning left onto Route 99 in the direction of Mt. Hermon. The next 20 kilometers (12.4 miles) boast a natural feature rarely found anywhere else in Israel: water. In this otherwise arid land, you'll find it in astonishing quantities, and with it lush, flourishing flora. Here are the Dan, Hermon (Banias), and Snir (Hatzbani) rivers, the sources of Israel's principal river, the Jordan.

Several kilometers along, look left into the distance for the highest mountain you can see (the Hermon is not in view here). This is **Mt. Dov,** the site where according to tradition God made a covenant with Abraham to give him and his descendants the Promised Land, then the Land of Canaan, and told him that the Jewish people would be "as many as the stars" (Genesis 15:5).

Coming up on your left, 9 kilometers (5.5 miles) from the turnoff **❻** from Route 90, is the **Tel Dan Nature Reserve.** For sheer natural beauty Tel Dan is hard to beat. A river surges through the reserve, and large, luxuriant trees, including majestic Mt. Tabor oaks, provide shade over wide paths. A host of small mammals inhabit the area, many of them partial to water, such as the otter and the mongoose. This is also the home of Israel's largest rodent, the nocturnal Indian crested porcupine, and its smallest predator, the marbled polecat, recognizable by its bushy tail, which accounts for about half the creature's 1-foot length. There are wildcats in these parts, too, though they are rarely seen by day.

A rather majestic city occupied this land in biblical times. Dan was an urban center second only to Hatzor in importance in northern Palestine. In Genesis it is written that when Abraham "heard that his brother had been taken captive [by the four kings of the north] he armed his trained servants, born in his own house, three hundred and eighteen, and pursued them up to Dan." Five centuries later, when Canaan extended from Dan (then called Laish) in the north to Beersheba in the south, Joshua led the Israelites through the area to victory.

Fine ruins from several epochs can be found here. The Canaanite city of Laish existed here 5,000 years ago. Its name was changed when the Israelite tribe of Dan captured the tel sometime in the period of the Judges, and it became the northernmost point of the kingdom of Israel. When the kingdom was divvied up, the secessionist King Jeroboam I built a religious center here (and another at Bethel) and erected a cultic golden calf. Among the finds archaeologists have turned up are the city gate and a 9th century BC paved plaza that was probably the town center. *Tel. 06/951579. Admission: NIS 11 ($3.70) adults, NIS 5.50 ($1.85) children. Open daily 8–4 (1 hr later during summer holidays).*

Adjacent to the nature reserve is the **Bet Ussishkin Museum,** on the grounds of Kibbutz Dan. Founded in 1955 by the Jewish National Fund, it is now operated jointly by Kibbutz Dan and the SPNI. Children will enjoy the displays here, which document the wildlife and natural phenomena found around the Hula Valley, the Golan Heights, and the Jordan River. The audiovisual presentations give a concise and informative account of the area. *Kibbutz Dan, tel. 06/ 941704. Admission: NIS 6 ($2) adults, NIS 5.50 ($1.85) children. Open Sun.–Thurs. 8:30–4:30, Fri. and holiday eves 8:30–3:30, Sat. 9:30–4:30.*

Follow the winding Route 99 west another 5 kilometers (3 miles) to **❼** the beautiful **Hermon River (Banias) Nature Reserve,** with gushing waterfalls, dense foliage along the riverbanks, and remains of a temple dedicated to the god Pan. There are two entrances to the reserve, each with a parking lot: the first, coming up on the right, is indicated on a sign as Banias Waterfall; the other is 1 kilometer (.6 mile) farther along the same road and marked "Banias." A circular walking trail connects the two and requires about two hours to com-

plete. It is an easy trail, but if time is short, you may prefer to take a
short walk to the falls, return to your car, then drive on to the second
entrance to see the caves and the spring whence the Hermon River
originates. The cost of admission covers entry at both sites.

As you walk toward the **Banias waterfall,** you can stop at the lookout;
maps there point out the principal mountains and other features on
the horizon. Follow the steps down under the huge carob trees and
amidst the maidenhair ferns, brier ivy, laurel (bay leaf) bushes, and
other shrubs, and turn left at the sign to the waterfalls, a five-minute walk away. Swimming is forbidden, but don't be surprised if
there are groups of Israelis splashing and scrambling to photograph
each other against the falls. There's a tremendous reverence for the
33 feet of cascading water, and people come from all over the country
to see this unusual sight, especially in the rainless summer months.

Backtrack to the signpost and head in the other direction, passing
walnut trees, willows, and lemon and fig trees as you proceed to the
riverside walk to the spring and caves. Along the way, the trail
passes two abandoned flour mills, and at times you will be walking
on aqueducts that once brought water to these mills. About 1 kilometer (.6 mile) from the waterfall, a sign points to **Breichat
Haketzinim** (Officers' Pool), a pool built around the spring by the
Syrians for the use of their officers. (Swimming is forbidden,
though.)

Time Out   A few minutes' walk beyond the Officers' Pool is a little **stall** with a
nargila (water pipe) standing sentry. Here you can buy Druze-style
pita bread (bigger and flatter than the commercial version) not only
baked on the premises but also milled here. The **ancient flour mill** is
still powered by water from an aqueduct as it was in days of yore. In
fact, until only a few years ago this was where local Druze villagers
milled their flour. Now the mill and "bakery" service hungry hikers.
Pull up a rock, and for a few shekels you'll be served a large rolled-up
pita with *labane* (white goat's cheese) and Turkish coffee. Cup your
hand and try the spring water, too: It's so pure you can almost taste
the stones it traverses all the way from the snowy mountaintop.

The remainder of the trail (about 600 feet) follows, and crosses, the
river before reaching the spring. Note the pungent aroma of the
horse mint; blackberry bushes can be found here, too, and their fruit
is particularly sweet at the end of summer.

Banias Spring emanates at the foot of the mostly limestone Mt. Hermon, just where it meets the basalt layers of the Golan Heights. As
the snow on the mountain melts, or when it rains, the water seeps
through the Hermon's crannies and gushes forth at the foot of a cave
called Pan's Cave.

The name "Banias" is an Arabic corruption of "Panias," the original
name given to what was to become a cult center dedicated to the colorful Greek god Pan. (Arabic has no "p" sound, hence the modification.) Pan, the son of Hermes, god of herdsmen, music, and wild
nature, and patron of homosexuals and nymphs, was too hedonistic
even for the ancient Greeks. In their attempts to keep him at some
distance, they eventually built the half-man/half-goat a temple in
this succulent corner of the world.

Take the path that crosses the spring and proceed toward the cave;
it is easily identified by the sturdy fig tree at the entrance. Note five
niches hewn out of the rock to the right of the cave; these are what
remains of the Hellenistic temple, and probably once held statues.

Three of the niches bear inscriptions in Greek mentioning Pan, the lover of tunes; Echo, the mountain nymph; and Galerius, one of Pan's priests. Archaeologists are only in the early stages of excavating, but they have already turned up what they believe are the remains of a second temple as well.

All early references to **Banias Cave** identify it as the source of the spring, but earthquakes over the years have changed its formations, forcing the water to emerge at the foot of the cave rather than from within it. (For those in a hiking mood, there is a long, very steep trail that leads from here through the oak and thorny broom forest up to Nimrod's Fortress, a 40- to 60-minute climb.) The path continues up to the whitewashed **tomb of Nebi Khader** (Arabic for "the prophet Elijah"), built on a ledge of the cliff. The tomb is closed, but from here there is a terrific view of the Hula Valley and the Hermon River. A little farther along the way are the remains of an ancient wall with a ceramic inlay archaeologists believe was part of the white marble temple Herod built as a tribute to Caesar Augustus, who had given him the Hula Valley and Panias in 26 BC.

Herod's son Philip inherited this part of his father's kingdom, and when he made Panias his capital, he changed its name to Caesarea Philippi, to distinguish it from the Caesarea his father had founded on the Mediterranean coast. It was in Caesarea Philippi that Jesus changed Peter's name from Simon and gave him "the keys to the kingdom of heaven" after his disciple, for the first time, declared Jesus the Messiah: "Jesus came here and asked his disciples, 'Who do you say that I am?' and Peter replied, 'You are Christ, the son of the living god,' to which Jesus responded, 'Blessed are you Simon, son of Jonah. And I tell you, you are Peter [*petros* means rock in Greek], and on this rock I will build my church and the powers of death shall not prevail against it'" (Matthew 16:13–20). Some scholars feel that Christ may have deliberately selected the heartland of paganism for this great declaration of faith. A small Greek Orthodox church (closed) nearby was built to commemorate the site.

Though Roman rule in this part of the kingdom would not last another generation past Philip, Panias continued to flourish for more than 1,000 years—and its original name, with only slight modification, has endured.

In the early 12th century, Banias was held by Crusaders, and just outside the "second" entrance to the reserve are the ruins of what is thought to have been the marketplace of the day; a string of single "rooms" along a well-preserved section of wall might well have been shops. The archaeologist leading these excavations, Vassilos Tsaferis, believed that more of the city could be lying under the parking lot, and in mid-1994 a Roman-era health and leisure center for tired soldiers was unearthed within the reserve. The luxurious 150-square-meter facility dates back to the 1st century, and offered marble floors, mosaics, and a series of subterranean (*under*-underground, if you will) passages. *Off Rte. 99, tel. 06/950272. Admission: NIS 11 ($3.70) adults, NIS 5.50 ($1.85) children. Open Sat.–Thurs. 8–5, Fri. and holiday eves 8–4; 1 hr later during summer holidays.*

To get to the huge, burly fortress perched above the Banias, return to Route 99 heading east, then turn left onto Route 98, taking good care on this sometimes treacherous road. The history of **Nimrod's Fortress** (Kal'at Namrud) is still vociferously debated. Was it, for example, Muslim or Crusader in origin? Then there is the question of its name: It has only been referred to by its present name since the 19th century, although the citadel was built around 1100. Nimrod was a mythical hunter figure of enormous strength, but nothing more of him is known.

Academic controversy aside, a visit to the fortress is a real treat. Take about an hour to frolic around the site. The limestone fortress, overgrown with scruffy shrubbery and blending in with the surrounding stony mountain terrain, commands superb vistas, especially when framed by the arched windows or glimpsed through the narrow archers' slits in the walls.

What *is* known about the fortress is that it guarded the vital route from Damascus via the Golan and Banias to Lebanon and to the Mediterranean coast. Although Muslim legend says it was first built by Arabs, it is widely believed to have been a Crusader structure later modified by the Arabs. In any event, it changed hands between Muslims and Christians in the centuries to follow as both vied for control of the region. During one of the more curious periods of its history, from 1126 to 1129, Nimrod's Fortress was occupied by a fanatical sect of Muslims renowned as murderers. Before heading out to track down their enemies, the cutthroats would indulge in huge quantities of hashish, thus earning the nickname *hashashin* (the hashish users), from which the word "assassin" is derived. Nimrod functioned as a prison during the Mamluk period and was left abandoned starting in the 16th century. In modern times, Syria observed Israeli troop movements from the fortress.

The entrance to the fortress, next to the parking lot, is through a breach in the western wall. Once inside, to the left you'll see one of the many cisterns that supplied the residents with water. There are several large vaulted cisterns on the site, particularly crucial during a siege: The cisterns could store enough water for 500 people for three years. Follow the path through the citadel ruins to the donjon, or keep, the central tower of the fortress. You may notice it faces east; the Crusaders expected attacks from this direction. It is possible to climb the donjon, 100 feet above the surrounding castle. This is where the feudal lord would have lived, and it is a kind of fortress within a fortress: The outer wall on the east and south sides is well protected by protruding towers, also equipped with slits. *Nimrod's Fortress National Park, tel. 06/942360. For admission and hrs, see Tel Hatzor, above.*

❾ By now **Mt. Hermon,** whose snowcapped peaks you will have seen from almost every vantage point on the tour, looms large. Famous as Israel's highest mountain, its summit, at 9,232 feet above sea level, is actually in Syrian territory. Its lower slopes attract Israelis as the country's only ski resort, but the fun is significantly chilled by the high prices (*see* Sports and the Outdoors, *below*). In fact, summer is arguably the most interesting time on the Hermon: After the winter snows melt, hikers can discover chasms and hidden valleys on the mountain, the long-term result of extremes in temperature. Moreover, a powerful array of colors and scents emerge from the earth as cockscomb, chamomile, and scores of other flowers and wild herbs are drawn out by the summer sun. So, if this is where you are headed, keep climbing Route 98 from Nimrod's Fortress, passing first the old Druze village of **Majdal Shams** and then the new Jewish township of **Neve Ativ,** designed to look like a little piece of the Alps in the Middle East, replete with A-frame chalet-style houses. The residents of Neve Ativ operate the ski slopes 13 kilometers (8 miles) above.

Return to Route 99 and turn left to continue into the Golan. Geologically distinct from the limestone massif of Mt. Hermon, the basalt slopes of the Golan Heights extend about 60 kilometers (37 miles) from north to south and 15 kilometers to 25 kilometers (9.3 miles to 15.5 miles) across. The whole region was volcanic in the geologically not-so-distant past, and many symmetrical volcanic cones and pronounced reliefs still dominate the landscape, particularly in the upper Golan. Where the dark basalt rock has weathered or been cleared, the mineral-rich soil supports a wide variety of crops. The gentler terrain and climate of the Golan has attracted settlement far more than the less hospitable northern Upper Galilee. In spring the region, already greened by winter rains, comes alive with wildflowers; but when the summer heat has frizzled everything to a uniform yellow-brown, it seems a land of desolation. Don't despair: The tour is not over yet.

As you climb east, you will pass several Druze villages whose houses are built of the black basalt so prevalent here. The most picturesque is the first village, **Ein Kuniya,** which appears across a valley on your left. Route 99 abruptly turns south and becomes Route 98 near the town of Mas'ada (not to be confused with Masada in the Judean Desert).

Continue south on Route 98, past the terraced slopes to the east over which Mt. Hermon's snowy cap peeks. **Kibbutz El-Rom** will appear on the right after about 10 kilometers (6 miles), a tiny settlement that receives wide coverage in the movies and on TV as the outfit responsible for most of the film subtitles in Israel.

To your left the view takes in fields and orchards of this and other kibbutzim, such as **Merom Golan,** the first settlement built in the Golan after the Six Day War. Apples are especially good in these parts, but man cannot live by apples alone, and Merom Golan runs a "cowboy" restaurant with good cheap steaks (*see* Dining and Lodging, *below*).

Cast your gaze beyond the fields and you will be looking into **Syria,** or more precisely, into the **Disengagement Zone.** Located here is the ruined town of Kuneitra, captured by Israel in 1967, lost and regained in the 1973 Yom Kippur War, and returned to Syria in the Disengagement Agreement that followed. It is now a demilitarized zone, and Syria has made no effort to rebuild the town. The cluster of white buildings next to it houses the United Nations Disengagement Observer Force.

There is a T-junction coming up at Ein Zivan. Turn right onto Route 91, away from the frontier and in the direction of Rosh Pina and Zfat. Drive another 13 kilometers (8 miles) and take a left onto Route 87, which will take you into the commercial center of **Katzrin** (Qazrin), the "capital" of the Golan Heights.

Founded in 1977 on the site of a 2nd-century town of the same name, Katzrin is the administrative center of the Golan Heights and one of the most appealing residential areas in the north. There is a very homey suburban feel about it, despite its strategic location and attendant sensitivity. It's not unusual to see bomb shelters decorated and converted into recreation centers or into Hebrew classrooms for Russian immigrants who have come to this corner of the country to begin life anew. The water here is soft as soft can be. Straight from the basalt bedrock, not only is it good to drink, but it also makes skin feel silky smooth.

Commercial Katzrin provides general services: There is a café (open during the day), a pizzeria (open at night), a gift store, a minimarket, and a library. You'll also find the **Golan Archaeological**

Museum, which, though small, has a comprehensive collection of animal bones, stones, and artifacts that put the region into perspective. Among the exhibits is a Chalcolithic dwelling reconstructed from materials excavated close by. A room in the museum is devoted to the story of Gamla, the "Masada of the north" (*see* Off the Beaten Track, *below*), and includes an excellent audiovisual presentation of its history during the Great Revolt and the discovery of the ancient site by archaeologists exactly 1,900 years later. The museum is run in conjunction with the Ancient Katzrin Park (*see below*), 2 kilometers (1.2 miles) away. *In Katzrin commercial center, tel. 06/ 961350. Admission (includes Ancient Katzrin Park): NIS 9 ($3) adults, NIS 5.50 ($1.85) children. Open Sun.–Thurs. 8–4, Fri. and holiday eves 8–1, Sat. 10–4.*

⑪ Ancient Katzrin Park is an excavation in progress, a Jewish village, possibly from the 3rd century, whose economy was based on the production of olive oil. In all such villages—it is believed that there were once 27 in the vicinity—the synagogue was the focus of community activities, its importance reflected in the abundance and complexity of ornamentation in the building. The Katzrin temple, a contemporary of those at Bar'am (*see* Tour 2, *below*) and Capernaum (*see* Exploring Lower Galilee *in* Chapter 6), boasts decorative architectural details such as a mosaic pavement and a wreath of pomegranates and amphorae in relief on the lintel above the entrance. Built of basalt, the synagogue was in use for 400 years until it was partly destroyed, possibly by an earthquake in 747.

Since 1967, when the excavations at Katzrin began, 10% of the ancient Jewish village has been uncovered. The two reconstructed buildings in the park, the so-called House of Uzi and House of Rabbi Abun (presumably a Talmudic sage), are attractively decorated with rope baskets, weavings, baking vessels, and pottery based on remnants of the originals found at the site, and lighted with little clay oil lamps. *Tel. 06/962412. Admission (includes Golan Archaeological Museum): NIS 9 ($3) adults, NIS 5.50 ($1.80) children. Open Sun.–Thurs. 8–4, Fri. and holiday eves 8–1, Sat. 10–6.*

Time Out The **kiosk** (with log benches) outside the entrance to the Ancient Katzrin Park serves hot dogs and other hot foods and is also well stocked in the chocolate department. Also on the park grounds is a bar, **Piano Park,** which attracts an evening crowd from quite a wide radius.

Route 87 will take you to Katzrin's industrial zone, home of the **⑫ Golan Heights Winery.** One of Israel's top businesses, it launched the country into the international wine-making arena with its Yarden and Gamla labels. (A third label is called, predictably, Golan.) The area's unique volcanic soil, cold winters and cool summers, and state-of-the-art vinting techniques have proven a recipe for success. Wine-tasting tours are generally available if booked in advance (tel. 06/961646). There is a store on the premises stocked with the full line of wines as well as sophisticated accessories for the oenophile. Don't buy wine here, however: You are likely to find it a tad less expensive in supermarkets and liquor stores in the cities. The winery can provide you with the business cards of their distributors and agents around the world. *Tel. 06/962001. Admission (tour and tasting): NIS 7 ($2.35) adults, NIS 3 ($1) children. Open Sun.– Thurs. 8–4, Fri. 8–1.*

From here, Route 87 southbound will bring you to the northern tip of the Sea of Galilee, 20 kilometers (12.4 miles) away. To continue on to Zfat instead, return to Route 91 and head west. The old battered building at the bend, at the B'not Ya'akov Bridge junction, served as a French customs house in mandatory times. Shortly beyond, you will pass the Syrian bunkers at **Mitzpe Gadot,** across the road from a gift shop and hexagonal kiosk.

Tour 2: Zfat (Safed) and Mt. Meron

This tour starts with a walking tour of Zfat (Safed) and then continues by car to Mt. Meron, all of which can easily be done in a day. To reach Zfat from Haifa, which is 72 kilometers (44.6 miles) away, take Route 4 north to Route 85 east (or Rte. 70 to Rte. 85). Route 85 ends at a T-junction just north of the Sea of Galilee. Take a left onto Route 90 and exit at Route 89. Stay on Route 89, driving through the modern town of Rosh Pina. Zfat is 10 curvy kilometers (6 miles) away. The most direct route from the northern coast is Route 89 east from Nahariya. To reach Zfat from Tiberias, take Route 90 north to Route 89.

❸ **Zfat (Safed),** at 3,000 feet above sea level, is Israel's most elevated city. Perhaps this extra proximity to the heavens accounts for its reputation as the center of Jewish mysticism (Kabbala). For although it joins Jerusalem, Tiberias, and Hebron as one of the holy cities of Israel, Zfat possesses a spiritual dimension found nowhere else.

Numbers in the margin correspond to points of interest on the Zfat (Safed) map.

The picture-postcard stone city is built on the slopes of a hill, and its labyrinthine alleyways, haunted with ancient history, add to the otherworldly atmosphere. Unfortunately, a modern-day building boom has transformed the approach to this holy city into just another suburban view. Well, almost: You can still see fragments of the **Citadel ruins** peeking out from a cluster of pines on the hilltop as you draw near along Route 89 from the east. To get to the Park of the Citadel, where this tour begins, drive past the Egged bus station on the right. The road curves upward; make the first left.

It can take surprisingly little time to walk all around the Old City of Zfat and to get a feel for it. The trick is to make it last. Don't be afraid to poke around the little cobbled passages that seem to lead nowhere, or to linger over some minute architectural detail on a structure from another era. More important, don't panic if you get lost—you're never far from the center. **Yerushalayim (Jerusalem) Street** runs through the heart of the Old City, encircling the Citadel in its center; from here there is easy access to the two main areas of interest, the **Old Jewish Quarter** and the **Artists' Colony.** In other words, all roads lead to Yerushalayim Street. There is no getting around the uphill–downhill of Zfat, so wear comfortable walking shoes. Also, modest dress is recommended in this Orthodox town.

For most of the year, Zfat can be something of an enigma to the tourist: It hibernates from October through June. The artists move to homes in warmer parts of the country, opening their galleries in Zfat infrequently, and other sites may (or may not) also be closed. This does not mean you should leave Zfat off your itinerary during those months. There is enough to occupy the curious wanderer for at least a couple of hours—and much is free. In summer, especially during school holidays (July and August), Zfat is abuzz with activity: Galleries and shops stay open late, the strains of klezmer music waft around corners (*see* The Arts, *below*), and the city extends a warm welcome to everyone. Moreover, everyone comes—so avoid Zfat at this time if you do not like crowds.

🔞 The walk begins at the **Park of the Citadel** (you can leave your car here). In Talmudic times, 1,600 years ago, its hilltop bonfires served as a massive beacon for surrounding communities to herald the lunar month, the basis for the Jewish calendar. The Crusaders, in the 12th century, immediately grasped the setting's strategic value and built the Citadel here, only scattered sections of which remain. The Muslim ruler Saladin wrenched it from them in 1188, following his victory at the Horns of Hattin, but half a century later the Crusaders repossessed it and the Order of the Templars turned it into the most massive Christian fortress in the East. For decades the Crusaders were able to keep the aggressive Mamluk sultan Baybars at bay, but his army eventually besieged the Citadel in 1266. Having already destroyed many of the cities along the coast, Baybars decided to move his capital from Akko (Acre) to Zfat. This marked the beginning of the end of the Crusader empire.

All the while, a thriving Jewish settlement grew up in the shadow of the castle walls. Although it declined with the eclipse of the Crusader presence in the Galilee, the town survived rule by the Ottomans, who retained Zfat as their capital through the 16th century. Soon after their expulsion in 1492, the Jews from Spain started streaming in, among them respected rabbis and other spiritual leaders, intellectuals, and poets who gravitated to Zfat as a center of the revival of Kabbala study.

The Kabbala, whose oral tradition dates back to ancient times but which gained popularity starting in the 12th century—possibly as a reaction against formal rabbinical Judaism—is about reading between, behind, and all around the lines: Each and every letter and accent of every word in the holy books has a numerical value with specific significance, offering added meaning to the literal word. Zfat was the heart of the Kabbala, the great rabbis were its soul; under their tutelage religious and mystical schools and meeting places mushroomed here. Some of these leaders were to leave their mark on the age, on the generations to follow, and, of course, on Zfat itself.

Zfat remained predominantly Jewish until a devastating earthquake in 1837 razed the town and left few survivors. In 1929, Arab riots drove more of the town's inhabitants away. By 1948, only 1,500 Jewish residents remained. The departing British Army left the town's key strategic positions to the Arab forces, which set about besieging the Old Jewish Quarter. A handful of Palmach fighters (part of the Jewish clandestine army of mandatory times) penetrated the enemy lines and helped the mostly elderly devout Jews of the quarter successfully resist the offense in what became known as the "Miracle of Zfat." Once again, with its sweeping views and slopes in the heart of Zfat, the Citadel was the focal point of battle.

As you return to the park entrance, on Hativat Yiftah Road, take in the sight of the old houses below and the undulating, pastoral panorama beyond. This image has been the inspiration for countless paintings and drawings that have emerged from Zfat since time immemorial, and you will no doubt see numerous modern interpretations at the General Exhibition (*see below*) and in the rooms of almost every Zfat hotel.

Turn right; after you walk about 300 feet, you'll come to the remains Citadel tower. It was destroyed over the years mainly by earthquakes, the most recent and devastating being the one that occurred

Zfat (Safed)

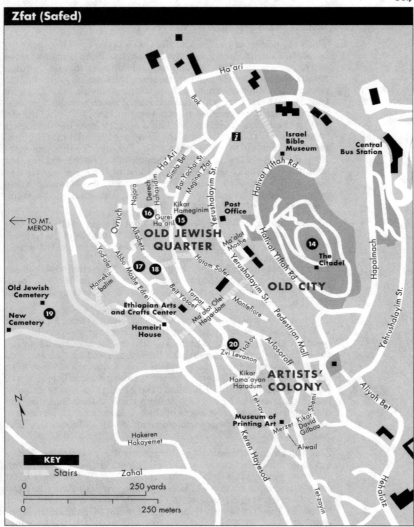

Ha'ari

Bak

🛈

Israel Bible Museum

Central Bus Station

← TO MT. MERON

Najara

Derech Hahasidim

Ha'Ari

Simta Bet

Bar-Yochai St.

Meginei Zfar

Yerushalayim St.

Post Office

Kikar Hameginim

16

Gurei Ha'ari

15

OLD JEWISH QUARTER

Ma'alot Moshe

Hativat Yiftah Rd.

Hativat Yiftah Rd.

14

The Citadel

OLD CITY

Ovruch

Alkabetz

Abbo Moshe Edrei

Yod-alef

Hamekubalim

17

18

Hatam Sofer

Tarpat

Beit Yosef

Ma'alot Olei Hagardom

Montefiore

Yerushalayim St.

Pedestrian Mall

Hapalmach

Old Jewish Cemetery

New Cemetery

19

Ethiopian Arts and Crafts Center

Hameiri House

20

Zvi Levanon

Kikar Hama'ayan Haradum

ARTISTS' COLONY

Arlosoroff

Tetvov

Yehrushalayim St.

Aliyah Bet

Hakeren Hakayemet

Museum of Printing Art

Metzer

Kikar David Gilboa

Alwail

Keren Hayesod

Hehalutz

Tetzoyin

N

KEY

Stairs   Zahal

0   250 yards

0   250 meters

Abouhav
Synagogue, **17**

Caro Synagogue, **18**

Cemetery, **19**

General Exhibition, **20**

Ha'Ari Synagogue, **16**

Kikar Hameginim, **15**

Park of the Citadel, **14**

in 1837. A little farther along on the right is the **Israel Bible Museum,** with its impressive arched entrance. This stone mansion was once the home of the Ottoman governor; today it houses the somewhat dramatic paintings and sculptures of artist Phillip Ratner, all inspired by the Bible. *Hativat Yiftah St., tel. 06/973472. Admission free. Open Mar.–Sept., Sun.–Thurs. 10–6, Sat. 10–2; Oct.–Nov., Sat.–Thurs. 10–2; Dec., Sun.–Thurs. 10–2.*

Walk down the steps and cross Yerushalayim Street. Near no. 24, more steps lead to the parallel Bar Yochai Street. You are now entering the Ashkenazi (East European) section of the Old Jewish Quarter, distinguished from the Sephardi (Oriental) section by its wider streets and more subtly colored buildings. Turn left and walk to
⑮ Kikar Hameginim (Defenders' Square), the Old Jewish Quarter's principal plaza and once its social and economic heart. A sign points to a two-story house that served as the command post of the neighborhood's defense in 1948—hence the square's name.

Standing on the square, you will notice a stepped street leading down to the right. This draws you into the 16th century and the Ashkenazi **Ha'Ari Synagogue.** A word about the renowned "Ari": If
⑯ there is one personage who left an indelible mark on Zfat and on Judaism it was this great rabbi. His real name was Isaac Luria, but he was known to all as the Ari, Hebrew for "lion" and an acronym for Adoneinu Rabbeinu Itzhak (our master and teacher Isaac). In the mere three years he was in Zfat, he evolved his own system of the Kabbala, which drew a huge following that was to influence Jewish teaching and interpretation the world over, right up to today. Even more astounding is that he died in his mid-thirties; it is said that one should not even consider study of the Kabbala before the age of 40, when one is thought to have reached the requisite level of intellectual and emotional maturity.

The synagogue itself is not outstanding, but is typically Ashkenazi with its pale colors and minimally decorated walls. The olivewood holy ark, however, is a dazzling tour de force of carving, with two tiers of spiral columns and seemingly living vegetal reliefs. The synagogue was built after his death, at the spot where the Ari is said to have come with his students on a Friday evening to welcome the Sabbath. The 1837 earthquake leveled it; it was rebuilt in 1857. (The Sephardi Ari Synagogue, where the rabbi prayed, is farther down the quarter by the cemetery. The oldest of Zfat's synagogues, the 16th-century structure has especially fine carved wooden doors.)

To get to the Abouhav Synagogue, go down the steps, turn left at the cobbled Alkabetz Street, and down again at the first set of steps. Walk under the dome and you'll shortly notice blue window frames and a door next to a little alley. You are now in the heart of Sephardic Zfat. If you haven't found the sign marking the spot, just ask for the
⑰ Abouhav Synagogue.

This large synagogue is named in honor of a 14th-century Spanish scribe, one of whose Torah scrolls found its way here with the Spanish Jewish exiles 200 years later. Note how the Sephardi synagogue differs from its Ashkenazi counterpart: The walls are painted a lively blue and are richly decorated with religious motifs, the benches run along the walls instead of in rows (so that no man turns his back on his neighbor), and the dome-shaped roof is set atop four pillars. Every detail is loaded with significance: There are three arks, for the three forefathers Abraham, Isaac, and Jacob (the one on the right is said to be the Abouhav original), and 10 windows in the dome, referring to the Commandments. The charmingly naive illustrations on the squinches include a depiction of the Dome of the Rock (referring to the Destruction of the Second Temple) and pomegranate trees, whose 613 seeds are equal in number to the Torah's commandments. The synagogue was destroyed in the 1837 earthquake, but locals still swear that the southern wall—where the Torah scroll penned by Abouhav is set—was spared. This scroll is taken out only on the holy days of Rosh Hashana, Yom Kippur, and Shavuot.

18 Head back under the arch and up the stairs to **Caro Street,** with its *shuk*-style (market-style) souvenir stores, and the compact **Caro Synagogue,** arguably the most charming in the quarter. Rabbi Yosef Caro is said to have written the *Shulchan Aruch*, the code of law that has served as the foundation of Jewish religious interpretation to the present day. He arrived in Zfat in 1535 and served as its Jewish community leader for years. This synagogue was also destroyed in the great earthquake and was rebuilt in the mid-19th century. On request you can open the ark containing the Torah scrolls, one of which is at least 400 years old. A glass-faced cabinet at the back of the synagogue is the *geniza*, where damaged scrolls or prayer books are stored (but never destroyed because they carry the name of God. The turquoise paint here, being the "color of heaven," is believed to help keep away the evil eye.

Have a look at the nearby **Ethiopian Arts and Crafts Center.** It's a folk-art gallery that was set up in 1985 to help Ethiopian craftspeople who immigrated to Israel support themselves while preserving their distinctive native crafts. On display, and all for sale, are high-quality examples of weaving and embroidery, ceramics, baskets, and sculpture. The center is closed Saturday.

Another few strides to the right and you will find yourself in the middle of a stairway, **Ma'alot Olei Hagardom,** which extends all the way from Yerushalayim Street down, and forms the boundary between the Old Jewish Quarter and the Artists' Colony (previously the Arab Quarter). At this point, you have two options: to take the stairs down, turn right at the bottom, and follow the road to the cemetery (passing **Hameiri House,** a museum devoted to Zfat's history, especially the last 100 years); or to continue straight ahead to the Artists' Colony.

19 The **cemetery,** which actually consists of an old and new cemetery, is set into the hillside below the Old Jewish Quarter. The old plots resonate with the names and fame of the Kabbalists of yore, and their graves are easily identifiable by their sky-blue markers. It is said that if the legs of the devout suddenly get tired here, it is from walking over hidden graves. In the new cemetery are the graves of members of the pre-State underground Stern Gang and Irgun forces who were executed by the British in Akko (Acre) prison (*see* Exploring the Northern Coast and Western Galilee *in* Chapter 5). In a separate plot bordered by cypresses, the 24 teenage victims of the 1974 terrorist massacre at Ma'alot are buried.

20 Crossing over the stairway into the **Artists' Colony,** you should make your first stop the **General Exhibition,** a representative sampling of the works of the resident artists. The permission of the Muslim authorities was required for the General Exhibition, as it is housed in the old mosque, easily seen from afar thanks to its minaret. The works inside the large space range from oils and watercolors to silk screens and sculptures, avant-garde and traditional. The Artists' Colony has recognized the growing presence of artists from the former Soviet Union, and the adjacent building holds the **Immigrant**

Artists' Exhibition. In either facility, if any of the works take your fancy, just ask how to find your way to the artist's gallery for a more in-depth look. *Isakov and Zvi Levanon Sts., tel. 06/920087. Admission free. Open Sun.–Fri. 9–6, Sat. and holidays 10–2.*

The colony was established in 1951 by six Israeli artists who saw the promise beyond Zfat's war-torn and dilapidated state; for them, the old buildings, the fertile landscape, and the cool mountain air fused to form a veritable magic that they knew would help them create. Others soon followed until, at its peak, the colony was home to more than 50 artists, some of whom are exhibited internationally. The numbers have since dwindled somewhat, and gallery opening hours are unpredictable, especially in winter, when Zfat's artists tend to hibernate. In summer (July–September), however, things really come alive as the artists open their doors and display—or work on— their latest pots, paintings, and sculptures.

One of the curiosities of the colony is the **Museum of Printing Art,** with a small but rich collection that spans the history of printing in Israel. On display are the first Hebrew press (operated in Zfat, in 1576), the first Hebrew book (which rolled off a year later), the first newspaper printed in Israel (1863), and a copy of the May 16, 1948, *Palestine Post* declaring the birth of the State of Israel. *Merzer and Alwail Sts., tel. 06/920947. Admission free. Open Sun.–Thurs. 10– noon and 4–6, Fri.–Sat. 10–noon.*

Numbers in the margin correspond to points of interest on the Upper Galilee and the Golan map.

The spiritual importance of Zfat extends beyond the city limits to **Mt. Meron,** 8 kilometers (5 miles) west on Route 89, a pilgrim site for both ultra-Orthodox Hassidic Jews and nature lovers. After turning off the main road, keep left to reach the parking lot, beside Shimon Bar Yochai's tomb.

Remote though it may seem, Meron for centuries has drawn thousands upon thousands of Orthodox Jews paying homage to several of the great rabbis of the Roman era who are buried at the eastern foot of the mount. The most important tomb—and one of the holiest sites in Israel—is that of Rabbi Shimon Bar Yochai, a survivor of the Bar Kochba revolt of almost two millennia ago and a leading exponent of the Talmud. Refusing to kowtow to the Romans after they succeeded in taking Jerusalem, he is said to have fled to a cave at Peki'in, not far from here, together with his son Elazar, where he remained for 13 years. It is believed by the faithful, beginning with the 16th-century mystics who settled in Zfat, that while holed up in the cave, Bar Yochai penned the Zohar (the Book of Splendor), the commentary to the Pentateuch, or the Five Books of Moses, the first five books of the Old Testament. Although firm opponents to this theory claim the Zohar dates to 13th-century Spain and not 2nd-century Meron, Hassidic pilgrims continue to make their annual visit to the great rabbi's tomb. Pieces of cloth and scraps of paper that hang from trees around the tomb are evidence of the pilgrims' devotion.

The pilgrimage is still celebrated en masse on Lag Ba'Omer, the festive 33rd day of the seven solemn weeks that begin with Passover and end with Shavuot (Pentecost). Mt. Meron comes alive as a grand procession of Hassidic Jews arrive on foot from Zfat carrying Torah scrolls and singing fervently. Bonfires are lighted and barbecues follow. In days of yore, the festivities were much wilder than today, with religious ecstasy and less-than-religious abandon accompanying the celebrations. By the 1990s, it had become more like a huge party or a fair. Many ultra-Orthodox still uphold the tradition of bringing their three-year-old sons here on Lag Ba'Omer for their first haircuts.

Before heading up into the Mt. Meron Nature Reserve, continue north along the mountain road to Bar'am. Along the way, a turnoff to the left takes you to the Arab village of **Jish,** the Gush Halav of the Second Temple period. In those days, it was renowned for its exceptional olive oil, and the milk of its cattle also received accolades. Gush Halav translates as "milk bloc," but it is unclear whether the name derived from the renown of its milk or from the whiteness of the chalky limestone that serves as its foundations.

㉒ In just a few minutes you'll pass the Sasa junction on the left and see a signpost pointing in the direction of **Bar'am.** In this otherwise deserted spot lie the ruins of one of the best-preserved ancient synagogues anywhere. Although less grand than the synagogue at Capernaum on the Sea of Galilee (*see* Exploring Lower Galilee *in* Chapter 6), it is clear that the community that built this synagogue devoted considerable funds and energy to their most important building. Like most synagogues uncovered in the area, it faces south toward Jerusalem. Unlike any other, however, this one boasts lavish architectural elements such as an entrance with a segmental pediment and freestanding giant columns on its exterior.

The interior is in a worse state of repair than the facade. It resembles other Galilean synagogues of the period. You enter through the gate and into the prayer hall. Rows of pillars apparently served as support for the ceiling, and there may have been another story. A section of the facade's lintel, now in the Louvre in Paris, contains the Hebrew inscription, "May there be peace in this place, and in all the places of Israel. Blessings upon his works. Shalom." *Bar'am National Park, tel. 06/989301. Admission: NIS 5 ($1.70) adults, NIS 2.50 (85¢) children. Open Apr.–Sept., daily 8–5; Oct.–Mar., daily 8–4.*

Retrace your tracks to **Mt. Meron,** at 3,926 feet the highest mountain in the Galilee and the largest nature reserve in northern Israel, with 10,000 hectares (24,700 acres) of preserved slopes. A good road past the SPNI field study center takes you almost to the top (the actual summit is occupied by the Israeli Army). There is a 1.5-kilometer (1-mile) nature trail that begins near the study center, and red markings guide the not-so-intrepid walker all the way.

The trail offers breathtaking views in all directions: the Druze villages of Western Galilee, Zfat, the Sea of Galilee, and, on a clear day, the Golan Heights, Hula Valley, and mountains of Lebanon. You can also spot the ugly scars of bushfires. The blackened tree "skeletons" date back to the summer of 1978, when fire destroyed a significant chunk of this reserve. Much of the rich and varied flora of Mt. Meron has since regenerated—if you're here in autumn you'll be dazzled by the glowing yellow of the sunflowers—but reminders of the fire remain.

Nor has fire been the only misfortune. Not so long ago, bears, antelope, and even leopards here were hunted to extinction. Today, Israel's hunting laws protect the wild boar, marten, polecat, and other fauna that call the reserve home.

Off the Beaten Track

One of the most interesting but undervalued spots in the Golan is **Gamla,** the "Masada of the North." Try not to miss it. Aside from offering a fascinating history of determination, struggle, and death,

Gamla is truly inspiring in its beauty. The rugged, hilly terrain is softened in late winter and spring by the glorious greenery and wildflowers that follow the rains. In summer, the constant sound of rushing water, from the Gamla River and several waterfalls, helps you keep cool despite the heat. A collection of predatory birds call Gamla home twice a year, between migrations, and their nests are clearly visible from the Vultures' Lookout. Also, keep your eyes peeled for gazelles, porcupines, and foxes.

Gamla lies 20 kilometers (12 miles) southeast of Katzrin. To reach the site, head east out of Katzrin on Route 87 and turn right at the orange signpost marked "Gamla" on the Katzrin-Ramat Magshimim road (Rte. 808); from here it is another 1.5 kilometers (1 mile) to Gamla along an unpaved road.

Digs have turned up a fortified town dating to the early Bronze Age, but the principal story of the camel-shaped Gamla (*Gamla* is probably related to *gamal*, the Hebrew word for "camel") goes back 2,000 years. Those were the days when Jews were returning home from exile in Babylon, and Herod was encouraging them to settle here, to populate the frontiers of his kingdom, thus ensuring its security. They were glorious times. By AD 66, however, Herod was long dead and the Jews of Gamla had joined the Great Revolt against Rome. Herod's great-grandson Agrippa II, of Banias (*see* Tour 1, *above*), sided with the Romans and challenged the zealous rebels. When he failed to overpower them, Rome dispatched Vespasian at the head of three legions. In 67, they launched a bloody attack here that ended seven months later when the 9,000 surviving Jews flung themselves to their deaths in the abyss below the town. The commander of the Galilee and their guiding mentor, Flavius Josephus, brilliantly related the story of Gamla in *The Jewish War*, and vivid descriptions from this tome are engraved in stones along the trails throughout the site (*see below*). "Sloping down from a towering peak is a spur like a long shaggy neck, behind which rides a symmetrical hump, so that the outline resembles that of a camel. . . . On the face of both sides it is cut off by impassable ravines. Near the tail it is rather more accessible where it is detached from the hill. . . . Built against the almost vertical flank the town seemed to be hung in the air . . . .." Indeed, this is precisely the first, dramatic image one has approaching Gamla from the hilltop entrance to the reserve.

It was that tough, steep terrain that almost caused Vespasian's three legions of Roman soldiers to fail in their siege. No sooner had the Romans succeeded in reaching the town than the defenders swung around and counterattacked; the Romans were "swept down the slope and trapped in the narrow alleys." Panicking, the soldiers climbed onto the roofs of houses, which collapsed, adding to the devastation. Rallied by Vespasian (whom Josephus ingratiatingly describes in almost superhuman terms), the Romans were able to drive the last defenders to the summit, first by stealth and then by open force, while the town was "deluged with blood" of the slaughtered. Seeing no escape, the survivors opted for mass suicide.

The town subsequently fell into ruin and oblivion. This turned out to be a boon for visitors 1,900 years later. Because it was never rebuilt, Gamla is the only example of a Roman battlefield whose relics match the vivid stories that have been handed down over the centuries; among the finds are 2,000 "missile stones" and arrowheads used in the raging battles. And in the 5% of Gamla that has been excavated so far, the team led by the eminent Israeli archaeologist Shmaryahu Guttman has uncovered the oldest synagogue yet found in Israel, apparently built during Herod's lifetime, as well as the wall the Romans breached, four olive presses, and several houses. Their identification was made that much easier by Josephus's precise descriptions. Moreover, there are about 200 **dolmens** scattered in the area—strange stone structures shaped like the Greek letter π. The effort required to erect these large basalt burial monuments, probably during the 2nd millennium BC, indicates the importance of death and burial rituals at that time.

Visitors to Gamla have a choice of three walking trails. The **Ancient Trail** descends from the lookout right down to the town ruins (getting down is easy, but don't forget that you have to climb back up the steep hill); the **Vultures' Trail,** after crossing the dolmen field and the brilliant Gamla waterfall (the tallest in Israel: 170 feet), takes you to the **Vultures' Lookout,** with a brilliant view of the nests of griffin vultures and other birds of prey. A third trail, to the **Daliyot waterfalls,** offers stunning views but is a much longer walk, requiring some four hours. There is an excellent short film on the story of Gamla at the Golan Archaeological Museum in Katzrin (*see* Tour 1, *above*). *Gamla Nature Reserve, tel. 06/762040. Admission: NIS 8.50 ($2.85) adults, NIS 4.50 ($1.50) children. Open daily 8–4.*

The large number of monuments to fallen soldiers in the Golan is a constant reminder of the strategic importance of the region—and the price that has been paid to attain it. Two such sites that are interesting and easily accessible, and where old Syrian bunkers give a gunner's-eye view of the valley below, are Tel Faher, in the northern Golan (the turnoff is to the right just above Banias, off Rte. 99), and Mitzpe Gadot (named after the kibbutz it overlooks), just above the B'not Ya'akov Bridge, on Route 91. At Tel Faher (also known as Mitzpe Golani, for the elite Golani Brigade soldiers who died here in 1967), children can climb onto the tank that now sits passively, though it is a sharp reminder of tougher times; Mitzpe Gadot is easily recognized by the tall triangular concrete memorial built there. An important word of caution: The sites are safe, but beyond the fences and clearly marked paths are old Syrian minefields that have not been completely detonated.

If you have any time left after a day of traveling, use it to get to the quaint little watering hole in **Piano Park,** on the grounds of **Ancient Katzrin Park** outside Katzrin (*see* Tour 1, *above*). You'll be joining locals from around the Upper Galilee who are drawn to the softly lighted, low-ceilinged pub housed in a century-old Syrian dwelling. The otherworldly atmosphere and friendly mood is enriched by soft jazz and blues, but the really romantic touch is the setting, the ancient ruins around the pub floodlighted at night. There is no phone on the premises, but reservations (advised on the weekend) can be made at tel. 06/961614. *Open Mon.–Sat. from 9 PM.*

Shopping

You won't find haute couture in the Upper Galilee and the Golan, but many of the kibbutzim in the region have factory outlets for their wares or gift shops within their guest houses. For example, **Kfar Giladi** (6 km/4 mi n. of Kiryat Shmona off Rte. 90, tel. 06/941414) produces (nonprescription) sunglasses; **Naot Mordechai** (5 km/3 mi s. of Kiryat Shmona on Rte. 977, tel. 06/948133) has a popular range of "anatomic" sandals, whose soles are molded as closely as possible to the natural line of the foot, making them very comfortable for walking; **Amir** (7 km/4 mi e. of Kiryat Shmona, tel. 06/954227) has a T-shirt and silk-screen printing store; **Amiyad** (on Rte. 90, 20 km/12 mi n. of Tiberias, tel. 06/933850) uses honey and the nectar of exotic fruits for its Hills of Galilee line of sweet wines, made without preservatives, and sells homemade whole-grain breads, jams, and other healthful food items. **Kfar Hanassi** (5 km/3 mi e. of Mahanayim Airport, tel. 06/932870) sells its own Village fashion line in the kibbutz's version of a boutique.

If it's **art** you're after, the **Artists' Colony** in **Zfat** is the address. Before diving into the maze of alleys that house the galleries, check out the General Exhibition (tel. 06/920087; *see* Tour 2, *above*) to get some direction. All artists have samples of their work here, and you can also find out if a particular gallery is open, as hours in Zfat can be unpredictable.

Sports and the Outdoors

The multistory, multipurpose **Canada Centre** in **Metulla** (at the top of the hill, tel. 06/950370) has just about everything a sports complex could offer. For the price of admission—NIS 25 ($8.35) for adults and NIS 20 ($6.70) for children—you can spend the whole day here playing tennis, squash, basketball, and ping-pong, ice-skating, working out, swimming, or taking aim on the shooting range. And if that's all too much, go for the sauna or hot tub; massages cost extra. There is an Italian restaurant called Galileo on the premises where you can put all those calories you burned up right back on (*see* Dining and Lodging, *below*). The complex is open daily 10–10.

Hiking

The superbly maintained nature reserves make this region an obvious destination for hikers. Most trails are not too challenging and are well marked; stick to the tracks to avoid any trouble. Always take along water, and wear a hat, especially in summer, and comfortable shoes. In fact, you may want to take an extra pair of shoes in case you get a little wet—there's an abundance of water in these parts.

The **SPNI** offers very interesting hiking tours led by enthusiastic, knowledgeable guides (*see* Guided Tours in Essential Information, *above*). You can ask specifically for a tour in English.

Horseback Riding

Trail riding has really taken off in the Upper Galilee and the Golan. **Baba Yona's Ranch** (tel. 06/937555), near the Hula Reserve, offers adventure packages that combine riding, jeeps, and canoeing; **Bat Ya'ar** (tel. 06/921788) is set in the mountaintop Birya Forest, near Zfat; **Kibbutz Ayelet Hashachar** (tel. 06/932611) arranges riding and jeep trips; and **Vered Hagalil** (tel. 06/935785), a guest farm at the Korazim Junction at Route 90, offers a variety of tours on horseback that wander over hill and dale. All offer lessons. Prices for guided rides range from NIS 20 ($6.70) for a half-hour to NIS 150 ($50) for a day.

Ice Skating

Believe it or not, Israel and Saudi Arabia have this in common: They are the only two countries in the Middle East with ice-skating rinks. But what the Saudis cannot boast are top-class former Soviet skaters. They now live in Metulla and teach the sport at the **Canada Cen-**

tre (*see above*). If you're lucky, you may catch a demonstration of their dazzling talent.

Kayaking and Rafting

One of the more adventurous sports in the area and enormously popular with visitors of all ages is skimming down the Jordan River in a kayak or a raft. **Kibbutz Kfar Blum** (tel. 06/948755), just north of Route 977 in the Hula Valley, rents the two-person rubber kayaks for 1- or 1½-hour runs, transporting you back to Kfar Blum at the end of the run. Novices needn't worry; this is not white-water territory. The cost is NIS 30 ($10) for adults and children, and the kayaks are available from March through October (call ahead at other times of the year). **Whitewater Rafting** (tel. 06/936867 or 06/934622) operates rafting trips through the rapids led by a professional guide. A new development is the "cataraft," a lightweight paddleboat that can be rented from **Kibbutz Kfar Hanassi** (daytime tel. 06/932870, evening tel. 06/932077), 5 kilometers (3 miles) from Mahanayim Airport. You can abandon all pretenses of exercise and float down the Jordan in an inner tube at **Ma'ayan Water Park** (Kibbutz Ma'ayan Baruch, tel. 06/951390) and **Sde Nechemia** (Kibbutz Huliot, tel. 06/946010), both near Kiryat Shmona, at NIS 15 ($5) for an hour or so.

Skiing

Don't compare the slopes of **Mt. Hermon** with those in Europe or the Americas. For Israelis, there is a certain thrill to having a ski resort in this hot Mediterranean country—and compared with flying to the Alps, it's a bargain (figure about NIS 200, or $70, per day for admission, lift tickets, and equipment rental). Frankly, though, Mt. Hermon (tel. 06/981337; in Tel Aviv, tel. 03/204813) has little to offer the serious, or even novice, skier. The chair lifts and cafeterias run year-round; the site may be more attractive in summer when it is bursting with wildflowers.

Dining and Lodging

Dining   Only a few years ago, one hand was too much on which to count the number of good restaurants in this region. Decent light food, such as falafel in pita bread, is never far away, but the concept of real meals in real restaurants with real atmosphere is relatively new to Israel. The Upper Galilee and the Golan have inherent attractions for diners: With verdant hills, old stone dwellings, and crisp, appetite-whetting air, the landscape serves as an exquisite backdrop for a meal that can be savored. Now there are many restaurants in the area that make the best of the natural environment to offer a total sensory-gastronomic experience. You can find hearty steaks in the middle of the forest, fresh grilled Dan River trout served in shady groves on the river's banks, Middle Eastern fare prepared by Druze villagers, and simple home-style Jewish cooking in the heart of the holy city of Zfat. And the excellent local wines from Katzrin enhance any meal; try the Mt. Hermon Red, Gamla cabernet sauvignon, and Yarden cabernet blanc and merlot. Most restaurants are open every day except Yom Kippur; in a few places, however (Zfat, for example), it is difficult to find an eatery open Shabbat (Friday afternoon until Saturday sundown). Attire is always informal, but it's wise to dress modestly in Zfat.

Highly recommended restaurants are indicated by a star ★.

Category	Cost*
$$$$	over $30
$$$	$22–$30
$$	$12–$22
$	under $12

per person for a three-course meal, excluding drinks and service

Lodging   If the number of worthwhile eateries in the region has increased, the lodging options have burgeoned in recent years. There are no grand hotels, but there is an ample choice of guest houses and inns ranging from ranch-style to home-style. As the tourism industry in the region has developed, many settlements, especially kibbutzim and moshavim, have added a hotel, or simply a wing attached to a home, and provide an extensive range of amenities, including activities for children. Although most of the guest houses remain independent of the community's other industries, they often offer lectures and tours of the communal settlement. In addition to offering restaurant facilities, many also arrange kayaking and rafting, horseback riding, jeep tours, and other sports and services for guests and the general public. The choice can be difficult, as all are in pretty settings and have well-maintained grounds. Reservations for the kibbutz guest houses can be made directly or through a central reservation service, **Kibbutz Hotel Chain,** based in Tel Aviv (90 Ben Yehuda St., tel. 03/524–6161, fax 03/527–8088), although not all the kibbutzim are represented by the agency.

For camping, head for the **Hurshat National Park** (tel. 06/942360) opposite Kibbutz Dafna, or **Sde Nechemia** (tel. 06/946010), but remember that it gets pretty cold here at night except in summer. Family rooms can be found at the small (100-bed) youth hostel in **Rosh Pina** (tel. 06/937086) or the large (200-bed) youth hostel in **Tel Hai** (tel. 06/940043), in Kiryat Shmona.

Highly recommended lodgings are indicated by a star ★.

Category	Cost*
$$$$	over $120
$$$	$80–$120
$$	$55–$80
$	under $55

All prices are for 2 people in a standard double room, including breakfast and 15% service charge.

Hula Valley and Environs

Dining
★

Farmyard Restaurant. People come from all over Israel for a meal at this restaurant on the grounds of Bet Dubrovin, near the entrance of the Hula Nature Reserve, even if they are not staying in the region. The converted farmhouse (*see* Tour 1 *above*), decorated with weavings and old farm tools, makes an ideal setting for a country meal. The house specialty is meats smoked by the owners themselves (the turkey is especially succulent). And if you follow it with a hot apple pie and a Cognac, cancel the rest of the day's program. The admission charge to Dubrovin Farm is refunded if you have a main course. *Dubrovin Farm, Yesod Hama'ala, tel. 06/934495. Reservations advised. AE, DC, V. Closed Sun. $$$$*
Bat Ya'ar. It takes a little courage to find the place through the

winding roads behind Zfat and into the Birya Forest, but this timbered, pub-style restaurant in the middle of nowhere serves tasty steaks and salads, and excellent chicken with rosemary, all enhanced by the pine-wooded mountaintop setting. You can work up an appetite on one of Bat Ya'ar's horseback-riding or jeep tours. Outside the restaurant is a play area for children; they'll love the pony rides. *Birya Forest, tel. 06/921788. Reservations required. MC, V. $$$*

Dag al Hadan. Fresh trout and a cool glass of wine in a shady woodlet by the gurgling Dan River—it's as good as it sounds, except on crowded weekends. This was the first restaurant in the region to specialize in the fish the Dan yields in abundance; you can see the trout ponds in a small installation on the grounds. The restaurant is tucked away behind the main road but is well signposted. (Dag al Hadan has another restaurant, with a few log cabins alongside it, near the entrance to the Hula Nature Reserve; tel. 06/959008.) *Off Rte. 99 near Kiryat Shmona, opposite Kibbutz Hagoshrim, tel. 06/950225. Reservations advised. No credit cards. $$$*

Hagome. The red-roofed restaurant on the west side of Route 90 next to Rosh Pina offers fresh Middle Eastern dishes, from grape leaves to stuffed vegetables to chicken with dried fruit (check out the salad bar before ordering). Dining outdoors in Hagome's garden is especially pleasant. Its handy access to the highway makes it a natural stop for many traveling Israelis; in fact, this is a good place to people-watch, as Hagome attracts all types. *Opposite police station on Rte. 90, Rosh Pina, tel. 06/936250. Reservations advised. MC, V. No dinner Fri. $$$*

Cowboys' Restaurant. Here's the best corral this side of the Israel-Syria Disengagement Zone. "Saddle" stools at the bar, cattle hides on the walls, and gingham tablecloths contribute to the frontier atmosphere; so does Moshe, the kibbutznik/manager. But, above all, it's the grub—specifically the excellent steaks—that people come for. *Kibbutz Merom Golan, tel. 06/960206. Reservations not necessary. DC, MC, V. No Sun. dinner. $$*

★ **Ein Camonim.** The Galilee hills make perfect pastureland for livestock—in this case, goats—and the output of Ein Camonim's dairy can be tasted fresh daily. The fixed menu consists of a platter of goat cheeses, home-baked bread, a wicker basket of raw garden vegetables, a glass of local wine, coffee, and dessert. There is a half-price menu for children up to age 12. A retail shop beside the restaurant sells the cheeses, and though very good, they are expensive. *Rte. 85, 5 km (3 mi) w. of Kadarim Junction, tel. 06/989894. Reservations not necessary. DC, MC, V. $$*

Baron's Stables. After walking around the small and sweet pioneer settlement of Rosh Pina, you can observe the locals over a beer at this popular pub in the former stables of Baron Edmond de Rothschild. A century ago, the Baron would tie up his horses here on one of his regular visits to check up on the silk industry he initiated. This is one of the only spots in the Upper Galilee with imported beer on tap (the German Wilkuller). The blintzes make a great snack. *Ha'elyon St., Rosh Pina, tel. 06/938071. Reservations not necessary. MC, V. $*

Galileo. Once you've finished 20 laps, a few games of squash, and a spin around the ice-skating rink, if you can still make it up to the top floor of Metulla's Canada Centre sports complex (*see* See Sports and the Outdoors, *above;* there is an elevator for the less athletic) a very good pasta salad awaits you. And pizza, and homemade zabaglione, and tiramisù. More than a cafeteria and less than a restaurant, this Italian eatery makes up in food and service what it lacks in atmosphere. *Canada Centre, Metulla, tel. 06/950112. Reservations not necessary. AE, DC, MC, V. $*

Lodging **Ayelet Hashachar Kibbutz Guest House.** The first kibbutz to open a hotel, Ayelet Hashachar is run amid pastoral surroundings but with the efficiency and thoroughness found in any city hotel. Located next door to the Tel Hatzor Museum, the guest quarters resemble apartments, with rooms housed in a series of two-story buildings surrounded by lawn and flower beds. Timber-framed windows add a soft touch, especially inside the modern rooms. Jeep tours, horseback riding, and guided tours of the kibbutz can be arranged. Ayelet Hashachar, by the way, is one of Israel's biggest honey producers. *Mobile Post Hevel Corazim 12200, tel. 06/932611, fax 06/934777. 144 rooms with bath. Facilities: dining room, dairy cafeteria, pool, horseback riding, four-wheel-drive tours, kibbutz tours. MC, V. $$$$*

Sea View Hotel and Health Farm. For all-round pampering, body and soul, you probably couldn't do much better than this hotel overlooking the Sea of Galilee. (That means no smoking and no meat, however.) The very serene Sea View specializes in packages of up to a week that include a medical check and diet, massage, reflexology, shiatsu, a pedicure, a manicure, and hairdressing—as well as full board, of course, as there isn't much time left after all that activity to go out! The hotel recently almost doubled in size when it added 40 luxurious rooms, each individually decorated (they all share a ban on smoking; the rooms in the old wing, which are cheaper, are exempted) and a few that have whirlpool tubs. The lobby has a "tea corner" that offers a full range of herbal teas served round the clock. A gift shop sells homemade breads, cheeses, and other local products. *Box 27, Rosh Pina 12000, tel. 06/937014, fax 06/937191. 70 rooms with bath. Facilities: restaurant, shop, hairdresser, massage, fitness rooms, sauna, hot tub, pool. AE, DC, MC, V. $$$–$$$$*

Amirim Holiday Village. The communal settlement of Amirim offers something a little different: All 300 members of the moshav are vegetarians and practice a back-to-nature lifestyle. This is a real "get away from it all" kind of place, situated atop a hill overlooking Mt. Meron and the Sea of Galilee. The lodging units have one or several rooms and are run by different families around the moshav. Not all units have air-conditioning, though they do have kitchenettes. Not that there is any shortage of eating options at Amirim: Five families have "minirestaurants," seating around 20, and there is one large restaurant. No meat or fish is served in them. *Moshav Amirim, near Mt. Meron, MP Carmiel 20115, tel. 06/989571. 70 units with bath. Facilities: 6 vegetarian restaurants, outdoor pool, children's activities. No credit cards. No Sat. checkout in high season. $$$*

★ **Hagoshrim Kibbutz Hotel.** One of the delights of Hagoshrim is that the waters of the Hermon River flow right through the kibbutz, a setting the residents have wisely exploited in their "pub in nature" (open May to October). Tractor rides are one of Hagoshrim's more unusual activities. (Incidentally, Hagoshrim, in this tiny nook of the Middle East, has had an impact on millions of women the world over with its "Epilady." This revolutionary depilatory appliance has won Hagoshrim kudos for technological initiative.) *Rte. 99, e. of Kiryat Shmona, Upper Galilee 12225, tel. 06/956231, fax 06/956234. 121 rooms with bath. Facilities: buffet restaurant, cafeteria, pool, outdoor pub in season, tennis. AE, DC, MC, V. $$$*

Kfar Blum Guest House. Tucked in the northern Hula Valley, Kfar Blum enjoys a reputation for attentive service that surpasses many of its rivals. The home-style hospitality is enhanced by the garden setting, and photographs in the rooms depict kibbutz life as it is meant to be. The absence of televisions in the rooms contributes, perhaps, to the relaxing ambience. Most of the members of Kfar Blum hail from English-speaking countries, so there are no language barriers here. One of the kibbutz's major attractions is its kayaks—what better way to experience the Jordan River? Children will enjoy the mini-amusement park next to the kayak rentals, which includes a trampoline and bumper cars. The kibbutz hosts a nationally renowned chamber music festival in late July and early August. *N. of Rte. 977, near Kiryat Shmona, Upper Galilee 12150, tel. 06/943666, fax 06/948555. 89 rooms with bath. Facilities: restaurant, bar, gift shop, pool, sauna, kayaking, tennis, mini-amusement park, kibbutz tours. AE, DC, MC, V. $$$*

Kibbutz Hotel Kfar Giladi. Situated atop a hill behind Tel Hai overlooking the Hula Valley, this is one of the oldest and largest kibbutz hotels. It is run very efficiently, but still manages to retain a homey atmosphere. Lovely woods just a stone's throw away make for great walks, and on the kibbutz grounds is the Hashomer Museum, which explores the pre-State history of the kibbutz and the vicinity. Kfar Giladi produces its own sunglasses, which are for sale in the hotel. *Upper Galilee 12210, tel. 06/941414, fax 06/951248. 160 rooms with bath. Facilities: snack bar, sauna, pool, tennis. AE, MC, V. $$$*

★ **Vered Hagalil.** Stone and wood cottages, each with a front porch, give guests a sense of privacy, yet the extremely popular restaurant and stables on this guest farm are only steps away. Owners Yehuda and Yona Avni haven't lost a shred of the almost-chauvinistic enthusiasm for the Galilee that drew them here (he's from the United States, she's from Jerusalem) decades ago, and it is reflected in the running of their establishment. The accommodations range from the aforementioned cottage apartments with bedroom, living room, and kitchenette to studio-style cabins to bunkhouses with six beds in two rooms. All are very ranchlike in decoration, with gingham fabrics in earth tones, exposed wood and stone walls, and big picture windows for Sea of Galilee–gazing. Trail riding packages of up to five days are a Vered Hagalil specialty, and riding is a superb, leisurely way to explore the region. *Rte. 90, next to Korazim, Mobile Post Korazim 12385, tel. 06/935785, fax 06/934964. 18 units with bath. Facilities: restaurant, bar, pool, tennis, sauna, Jacuzzi, trail riding, riding lessons, four-wheel-drive tours. MC, V. $$$*

Joseph's Well. This is an ideal base for exploring the region. The rooms are like cozy studio apartments, with pine furniture, coordinated tablecloths and sheets, and chintz curtains, and each one has a "coffee corner" with an electric kettle, cups, and tea and coffee. They are all on the ground floor, in clusters of three with a shared patio. The kibbutz dining room—Joseph's Well is on the Kibbutz Amiad—doubles as the restaurant for guests. Unlike the bigger kibbutz hotels, Joseph's Well offers little to do—guests are here strictly to sleep. Amiad's main industry is wine, which it produces from unusual fruits such as kiwi and sells in a shop on the premises that also peddles local products, including jams and makeup. *Mobile Post Korazim 12335, tel. 06/933829, fax 06/933819. 22 rooms with bath. Facilities: kibbutz dining room, pool, horseback-riding lessons. MC, V. $*

Village Inn. These accommodations at Kfar Hanassi give a *real* taste of kibbutz life. Each of the six units has two rooms that share a kitchenette and bathroom facilities. All the units look out onto a garden, the site of many a barbecue. Although the units are rather old, the decor is bright, with boldly colored sheets and cotton dhurrie rugs on the floors, and all the facilities are spotlessly clean. Meals are held in the kibbutz's communal dining room, and there is a lounge/TV room for guests. Amenities that will especially appeal to children include miniature golf, a minizoo, picnic grounds, and a pagoda with a grand view of the Golan and Mt. Hermon. Kfar Hanassi boasts several resident artists, and a visit to their home studios can add a dash of culture to your stay here. *Near Mahanayim Airport, Mobile Post Korazim 12305, tel. 06/932870, fax 06/932017. 12 rooms share 6 baths. Facilities: kibbutz dining room, pool, miniature golf, basketball, tennis, rafting, massage, guided tours. MC, V. $*

Zfat
Dining

Pueblo Español. It's unusual enough to get authentic Spanish food in Israel, but this restaurant not only makes a delicious paella, it throws in a half-hour tour of the Old City and a short film on Kabbala as well. The "Spanish Village" is run by a very amiable couple who hail from Spain and decided to set up an Israeli-Spanish cultural club. The project grew to include the restaurant and a gift shop as well, all located in two recently built stone buildings with an attractive central courtyard that doubles as a beer garden in summer. *127 Yerushalayim St., tel. 06/920922. Reservations advised. MC, V. Closed Sat. No dinner Fri. $$$*

Hamifgash. One of the veteran eateries on this pedestrian-only street, Hamifgash lives up to its name, which means "meeting place": This is one of the most popular restaurants in town, possibly because it suits all tastes. There's self service upstairs and table service downstairs, and anything from soups and snacks to substantial meat dishes is available. The most exclusive meals are served in the restaurant's renowned wine cellar—a rare find in Israel—which stocks the full range of Israeli wines. *75 Yerushalayim St., tel. 06/920510. Reservations advised. DC, MC, V. No dinner Fri. or lunch Sat. $$*

Pinati. Question: What do goulash and Elvis Presley have in common? Answer: They are both drawing cards for Pinati. Images of Elvis cover the walls, and though nobody can explain his connection to the Polish/Italian/Oriental menu, the heavy volume of customers indicates the success of the restaurant despite its many idiosyncrasies. Pinati serves up good wholesome food, and it has awards to show for it. It's also one of the few restaurants in town open Saturday. *81 Yerushalayim St., tel. 06/920855. Reservations not necessary. DC, MC, V. $$*

Lodging
★

Rimon Inn. Two hundred years ago, when the Turks were in charge, this gracious old building was the local post office. Rooms were later added and it became a khan, or inn. It opened as the Rimon Inn in 1961 and has enjoyed a reputation for charm and excellence ever since. Today, the postmaster's private apartment is the bar and the former stables are now the dining room. With their stone walls, the rooms have a rustic feel, and they are tastefully decorated, not surprisingly, with local art. Half the rooms have a view over the mountain and gorges. *Artists' Quarter, Box 1011, Zfat 13110, tel. 06/920665, fax 06/920456. 36 rooms, most with bath. Facilities: restaurant, bar, pool, children's activities July–Aug. AE, DC, MC, V. No checkout Sat. $$$$*

Ron. This pleasant but unassuming hotel boasts a good restaurant with an eclectic menu of European and Middle Eastern dishes. Rooms are spacious, clean, and light-filled, and half of them enjoy the mountain view. *Near Metzuda Park, Hativat Ifhach, Box 22, Zfat 13214, tel. 06/972590, fax 06/972363. 50 rooms with bath. Facilities: restaurant, bar, pool. V. $$$$*

Carmel. There is an Old World feel to the Carmel, rough edges and all. The furniture in the lobby is rather shabby and the rooms are ultrabasic, but the place is clean and the old building, with its high ceilings, dark timber paneling, and wrought-iron railings, has not lost its charm. Sunset on the lovely wide veranda, with those great panoramic views, adds to the value. A popular pub/restaurant is downstairs. *8 Javitz St., Zfat 13208, tel. 06/920053. 17 rooms with shower; toilets down hall. Facilities: pub/restaurant. No credit cards. $*

The Arts

Every summer, the Upper Galilee hosts several **music festivals** that cover a rather eclectic range. There could be no better setting than mystical Zfat, with its labyrinthine cobblestone lanes, for the **klezmer festival**—three days of "Jewish soul music." The roots of this music are Hassidic, making it almost prayerlike in tone, especially with its emphasis on wind instruments. Many of the events are street performances and therefore free. Keep in mind, though, that Zfat is bursting at the seams with revelers, religious and secular alike, during this time. The festival is usually held in July. The Zfat Tourist Information Office (50 Yerushalayim St., Box 227, Zfat 13010, tel. 06/920961) can provide details.

If a thigh-slapping hoedown is more your thing, head on down to the Hurshat Tal National Park in mid-August for the **Jacob's Ladder Folk Festival**—a weekend of bluegrass and country music in a setting of ancient oaks. In addition to the local folk groups (all of which have their roots in English-speaking countries), there is usually at least one band made up of Irish troops from the UN multinational forces. Tickets can be bought at the gate, and include entry into the national park, which offers camping facilities, swimming, and a snack bar. For more information, call the organizers at 06/962231.

The more classically minded might want to attend the **Chamber Music Days** at Kibbutz Kfar Blum (Upper Galilee 12150, tel. 06/943666) in late July or early August.

8 Eilat and the Negev

Including an Excursion into the Sinai

By Judy
Stacey
Goldman

Judy Stacey
Goldman was
born in
Montréal and
has lived in
Israel for 22
years, where
she is now a
professional
tour guide.
She has
co-authored
three books
about
Jerusalem
and Tel Aviv
and is
currently
preparing a
new book on
Jerusalem
with Janet K.
Rodgers.

The Hebrew word *negeb* denotes dryness, though in the Bible it is used to refer to the south. The Negev Desert is the southernmost part of Israel, an upside-down triangle that constitutes about half the land mass of the country, although only about 6% of the population lives within its borders. The Negev's northern border, the base of the triangle, lies about 27 kilometers (17 miles) north of Beersheba, the only large city in the region and the capital of the Negev. The Jordanian and Egyptian borders mark its eastern and western sides, respectively, and Eilat, on the Red Sea, is at its southernmost tip.

The Negev may well have changed more in the years since the foundation of the modern state of Israel in 1948 than in the entire period since the end of the Roman Empire. The first kibbutzim in the Negev were established in the early 1940s with new immigrants sent south after the War of Independence. Two years later, people started trickling into Eilat, where there was nothing but a few rickety huts. Arad put down its roots in 1961. The desert itself was pushed back, and the semi-arid areas between Tel Aviv and Beersheba became fertile farming land. Today, agricultural settlements in the scorching Arava Valley make use of brackish water to raise flowers, vegetables, and dates, which are hustled off to winter markets in Europe (the greening of the desert is most evident when you fly over the Negev and see the patches of deep, rich green below you). Tourism, aided and encouraged by the government, has taken off in earnest.

The army has been deployed over a large part of the Negev since the Sinai was handed over to Egypt. You'll feel a military presence at roadside diners, where soldiers stop off to eat, at bus stations, where they're in transit, and at tent-filled compounds here and there. Signs declaring "Firing Zones" indicate areas where the public may not enter, and checkpoints, where a smile and a wave-through are the order of the day, are scattered throughout the Negev.

Visitors will discover a long and varied human history here. The ancient Israelites had fortifications in the Negev, as did the Nabateans and the Romans after them. These early settlers developed irrigation techniques that were remarkably sophisticated, even by modern standards. Throughout these periods of permanent settlement, the entire area was home to Bedouin nomads, whose distinctive way of desert living, formed thousands of years ago, still can be observed.

Despite its rapid development, the Negev remains Israel's Wild West. It takes a certain kind of person to live and work here, someone who relishes the challenge of turning the hot, bone-dry desert into a hospitable place to live. Someone who has been seduced by the beauty of great canyons and cliffs spilling over with color at dawn and dusk; by the sight of thousands of migrating birds who fill the skies twice a year; by the endless areas of still, rocky terrain where the only movement might be a stone clattering down a hillside as an ibex makes a leap; by the sound of the wind coming up at the end of a dusty day; and by the pleasure of bright flowers carpeting the hills during the winter months.

The Negev contains some of Israel's most fascinating and dramatic scenery, from gigantic *makhteshim* (erosion craters) and the moonscape of the Dead Sea to carved-out *wadis* (dry riverbeds), the red granite mountains around Eilat, and long cliff faces along the Arava Valley. You can visit the kibbutz home and gravesite of Israel's first prime minister, David Ben Gurion, the man whose dream it was to settle the desert, and the millennia-old ruins at Tel Beer Sheva, site of the biblical patriarch Abraham's visit. Farther south, the Hai Bar Nature Reserve is home to animals mentioned in the Bible, thriving in their natural habitat. Nearby, the Timna Valley Park is a wonderland of unusually colored rock formations and ancient Egyptian copper mines. At the Red Sea port of Eilat, you can stand inside the sea at the Underwater Observatory, surrounded by the Technicolor of tropical fish and coral. The Negev brings out the explorer in people, so you may find yourself joining a Jeep trip and sleeping under the stars, taking a camel trek that follows ancient caravan routes, or hiking for days without seeing another soul. You can rest by an icy desert spring, take a diving course or swim with dolphins, have dinner on a night cruise on the Red Sea, float in the Dead Sea, or get pampered at a spa at Ein Bokek.

October to May is the best period to tour the Negev; the weather is dry and cold in January and February. Scorchingly hot conditions prevail from June through late September, when you're best off staying by the sea, at Eilat. You can enjoy sightseeing in the summer, but precautions must be taken (*see* Desert Precautions *in* Essential Information, *below*).

Essential Information

Important Addresses and Numbers

Tourist Information Israel's **Government Tourist Information Offices** (GTIOs) are in **Arad** (at the visitors center, 28 Ben Yair St., Box 824, 80700, tel. 07/954409), **Beersheba** (6 Ben Zvi St., opposite the Central Bus Station, Box 591, 84104, tel. 07/236001 or 07/236002), and in **Eilat** (at Bridge House, near the Marina, tel. 07/334353). In **Eilat** the new **Municipal Information Center** (Arava Rd. corner Yotam St., Box 14, 88100, tel. 07/372111) offers comprehensive tourist information. There is also a **Municipal Tourist Office** (opposite the Central Bus Station, Ha Tamarim Blvd., Box 1123, 88000, tel. 07/357185 or 07/374233), and the privately run **Information Center** (North Beach, Hapalmach, and Durban Sts., 88000, tel. 07/374741). **Visitors centers** are in **Mitzpe Ramon** (at the top of the main street, Box 340, 80600, tel. 07/588691 or 07/588620), and **Arad** (tel. 07/954409). The **Ramat Negev Information Center** (tel. 07/281247), staffed by field school workers of the Society for the Protection of Nature in Israel (SPNI), is on Route 40 at the gas station at the Mashabim Junction, 29 kilometers (18 miles) south of Beersheba.

A tourist information office run by the **Tamar Regional Council** is in the shopping center, north of the Kapulski restaurant, in **Ein Bokek** (Regional Information Bureau, Dead Sea Mobile Post 86910, tel. 07/584153). The **Negev Tourism Development Administration** in Tel Aviv (7 Mendele St., 63431, tel. 03/527–2444 or 03/527–2445) provides information on tours, attractions, and accommodations in the whole area.

Consulates In Eilat, the Honorary Consul of the United Kingdom, Mrs. Fay Morris, may be reached at tel. 07/372344. English-speaking visitors whose countries are not represented may also apply to Mrs. Morris for assistance.

Emergencies **Police:** Dial 100.

Ambulance: Dial 101.

Hospitals: Beersheba: Soroka Hospital (Hanassa'im St., tel. 07/
400111); Eilat: Yoseftal Hospital (Yotam St., tel. 07/372333).

Fire: Dial 102.

English- **Steimatzky** sells English-language books and foreign newspapers at
Language the Commercial Center in **Arad** and in the Central Bus Station in
Bookstores **Eilat.**

Pharmacies Call the Magen David Adom medical service (tel. 100), the Red
Cross of Israel, for assistance with emergency prescriptions. In
Eilat, the Michlin Pharmacy (opposite the Central Bus Station, tel.
07/375002) is open Sun.–Thurs. 8–2 and 4:30–8, Fri. 8–2. In the
Negev, pharmacies are found in Arad, Beersheba, Eilat, and Mitzpe
Ramon.

Travel There are a host of travel offices in **Eilat** around the Central Bus Sta-
Agencies tion, in the Khan Center, and at Bridge House, near the Marina.
Well-established agencies in the Negev include **Galilee Tours** in Eilat
(North Promenade, tel. 07/374720), **Amiel Tours** in **Ein Bokek** (shop-
ping center, tel. 07/584433), and **Zakai Tours** (136 HeHalutz St., tel.
07/277477) and **Lahish Tours** (79 Herzl St., tel. 07/276975), both in
Beersheba. Note that in July and August many travel agencies are
closed.

Car Rental **Beersheba:** Avis, 11 Derech Hanessiim, tel. 07/233345; Hertz, 5 Ben
Zvi St., tel. 07/273878; Eldan, 100 Tuviahu St., tel. 07/430344; Reliable, 1 HaAtzmaut St., tel. 07/237123.

Eilat: Avis, Eilat Airport, tel. 07/373164; Budget, Central Bus Station, tel. 07/374124 or 07/374125; Eldan, 143 Shalom Center, tel. 07/
374027; Hertz, Eilat Airport, tel. 07/376682; Reliable, Etzion Hotel,
Hatmarim Blvd., tel. 07/374126.

Ein Bokek: Hertz, Galei Zohar Hotel, tel. 07/584530.

Arriving and Departing by Plane

Regularly scheduled flights use the **Eilat Airport,** in the middle of
the city, a five-minute taxi ride to the hotels and a two-minute walk
to the commercial center of town. Charter flights from Europe arrive at **Uvda Airport** (also known as Eilat West), 60 kilometers (37
miles) north of Eilat; transportation to Eilat is arranged by the travel agencies who book the flight.

Arkia Israel Airlines (tel. 03/523–3285) serves **Eilat** from **Sde Dov
Airport** in north **Tel Aviv** (tel. 03/690–3333), from **Atarot Airport,** 10
kilometers (6 miles) north of **Jerusalem** (tel. 02/255888), and from
Haifa Airport (tel. 04/663097) with a stop in Tel Aviv or Jerusalem.
The 55-minute flight to Eilat departs from Tel Aviv every 1½ hours
from Sunday–Thursday, 6:30 AM–10 PM, Friday 6:30 AM–4 PM, and
Saturday 3 PM–10 PM. From Jerusalem, Arkia flies to Eilat three times
daily, twice on Friday; there are no flights on Saturday. The flight
lasts about 45 minutes. Flights from Haifa, which take about 1½ hours,
depart three times a day; there are no flights on Saturday.

To reach **Ein Bokek,** at the Dead Sea, you can take an Arkia Airlines
flight to the **Minhat HaShtayim Airfield** (in Ein Bokek, tel. 07/
584637) from Tel Aviv four times a week. The flight takes a half
hour. An airline shuttle bus then travels the 5 kilometers (3 miles) to
the hotels at Ein Bokek. Be sure to book the shuttle ahead when reserving your flight. Arkia also flies twice on Wednesday from Tel
Aviv to **Mitzpe Ramon** Airfield (tel. 07/588026); the flight takes a
half hour.

Flights to the Negev are not always exactly on schedule, so call ahead for the status of your flight, and arrive at the airport early (a shuttle operates from Jerusalem to the airport).

Arriving and Departing by Car, Bus, Sherut, and Limousine

By Car   Beersheba, capital of the Negev and the starting point of two tours described in this chapter (*see* Exploring Eilat and the Negev, *below*), is 113 kilometers (70 miles) southeast of Tel Aviv. The drive from Tel Aviv, as well as from Jerusalem, takes about 1½ hours. To drive from Tel Aviv to Beersheba, take Route 2 (the Ayalon Highway) going south until the turnoff to Route 4, marked Beersheba–Ashdod. After the Ashdod turnoff you will be on Route 41, which runs into Route 40, 6 kilometers (3.7 miles) later. Continue on 40 to Beersheba; there are clearly marked signs all the way.

To reach Beersheba from Jerusalem, exit the city on Route 1 heading west to the Sha'ar Hagai Junction. Turn left (south) and follow Route 38, then Route 32, which turns into Route 35, to Kiryat Gat. Here you will pick up Route 40 south to Beersheba.

To drive to Ein Bokek from Tel Aviv, leave Tel Aviv via the Ayalon Highway (Route 2) south and join Route 1, following signs to Airport–Jerusalem. As you approach Jerusalem, stay left, on Route 1, marked "Jericho–Dead Sea." Continue 30 kilometers (18.6 miles) to the unmarked Almog Junction (where Rte. 1 meets Rte. 90; there is a turnoff to the left, north, marked Jericho). Stay on the same road, now called Route 90, for 10 kilometers (6.2 miles) to the Dead Sea. Bear right, due south, and follow Route 90 along the coast, passing Qumran, Ein Gedi, and Masada (*see* Exploring Around Jerusalem *in* Chapter 3) to Ein Bokek. To reach Eilat, continue south along Route 90 (the Arava road) for another 177 kilometers (111 miles). The trip to Eilat takes about 5 hours.

The most direct way from Tel Aviv to Eilat is Route 40 south to Beersheba. Leave Beersheba via Route 25 (marked Dimona–Eilat), driving 69 kilometers (42.8 miles) to the Arava Junction. Turn right (south) onto Route 90 (the Arava road), and travel straight to Eilat.

By Bus   The national bus company, **Egged** (tel. 03/537–5555; Sun.–Thurs. 6:30 AM–9 PM, Fri. and holiday eves 6:30 AM–3 PM, Sat. 8 PM–10 PM), provides frequent daily bus service (except on Saturday) from Tel Aviv's Central Bus Station and Arlozoroff Station (Arlozoroff St. and Haifa Rd.), and from Jerusalem (Jaffa Rd., tel. 02/304555) to Beersheba; the trip takes 1½ hours. From the Beersheba Central Bus Station (Ben Zvi St., tel. 07/274341) buses depart four times a day to Arad, Avdat, Ein Bokek, Mitzpe Ramon, and Sde Boker (*see* Getting Around, *below*). Most buses do not run on Saturday, although some routes do resume in the early evening.

Egged offers departures from Tel Aviv to Eilat at least four times a day and twice at night. A round-trip ticket costs NIS 67 ($22). Buses from Jerusalem to Eilat leave during daylight hours from the Central Bus Station; the trip takes about 5½ hours and costs NIS 64 ($21.35) round-trip. Buy tickets in advance at the Central Bus Station to ensure a seat. Be sure to reserve a seat at Eilat's Central Bus Station for the return trip.

By Sherut   **Yael Daroma Aviv** operates sherut (shared) taxis from Tel Aviv to Eilat. Seats—there are seven in each taxi—must be booked ahead in Tel Aviv (32 Rothschild Blvd., tel. 03/566–0222) or Jerusalem (12 Shamai St., tel. 02/257366). There are four departures from each city Sunday through Thursday, three on Friday, and none on Saturday; the trip takes five hours and costs NIS 45 ($15). The trip can be made from Eilat (tel. 07/336011) to the north as well. Yael Daroma also goes to Beersheba (195 K.K. le Israel St., tel. 07/281144) from Tel Aviv, a trip of less than two hours. The trip costs NIS 15 ($5) from Tel Aviv.

By Limousine **Tour Bus Ltd.** (Ben Gurion Airport, Box 113, 70100, tel. 03/972–1447) will provide a limousine and driver 24 hours a day to take you to Eilat from Ben Gurion International Airport; the one-way trip costs NIS 720 ($240) per car for up to seven people.

Getting Around

By Car The only way to see the Negev Desert in a comfortable and efficient way is by car (air-conditioning in the summer is a must). All roads are two lanes. The condition of secondary roads can vary in quality; only those in good condition are mentioned in the tours described below. Roads marked in Hebrew only are not for public travel. To avoid dangerous wintertime floods, proceed with caution when there is any indication of rain (*see* Desert Precautions, *below*). Driving at night in the Negev is not recommended; plan to reach your destination by 5 PM in winter and by 8 PM in summer.

Apart from locations in towns and cities, there are gas stations at Tel Avdat (near Sde Boker), Ketziyot (near Nizzana), Mashabei Sade Junction (40 kilometers, or 25 miles, south of Beersheba), Zohar–Arad Junction (near Ein Bokek), Ramat Hovev, and Shoket Junction (on the way to Arad). You'll find gas stations on Route 90 (the Arava road) at Ein Hazeva, Ein Yahav, Ketura (tires fixed here), and Yotvata. A tire repair shop is located in the industrial area just before the entrance to Mitzpe Ramon. Most gas stations share a location with a roadside café, and a majority are open 24 hours a day.

The following are the main roads in the Negev: Route 40 goes through the Negev highlands via Sde Boker, Mitzpe Ramon, and Makhtesh Ramon to Eilat; Route 90 (called the Arava road in the Negev), which starts in Metulla near the Lebanese border, runs through Ein Bokek and along the Jordanian border, and terminates in Eilat; and Route 31, from Beersheba to the Shoket junction, Arad, and Ein Bokek. Most of your driving will be along stretches of straight road; the exceptions are the winding road through Makhtesh Ramon and the steep road between Arad and Ein Bokek (one hairpin turn after the other). Beersheba is 45 kilometers (28 miles) from Arad, 80 kilometers (50 miles) from Mitzpe Ramon, and 241 kilometers (151 miles) from Eilat. Mitzpe Ramon is 148 kilometers (93 miles) from Eilat. Ein Bokek is 177 kilometers (111 miles) from Eilat.

By Bus Exploring the Negev on your own by bus *can* be done, but much time is wasted waiting for connections, and the heat can make standing at a bus stop in the middle of nowhere very uncomfortable. Besides, the buses don't go everywhere. However, from **Beersheba** (the transfer point for buses from Tel Aviv and Jerusalem) there is regular Egged bus service to all major towns in the Negev, including **Arad** (Bus 388), **Ein Bokek** (Bus 384), **Mitzpe Ramon** and **Sde Boker** (Bus 060), **Yotvata** (Bus 394), and **Eilat** (Bus 397). Buses to Arad and Mitzpe Ramon–Sde Boker operate on Saturday. For Egged information in Arad, call tel. 07/956767; in Beersheba, tel. 07/278558; and in Eilat, tel. 07/375161.

In **Eilat,** Buses 1 and 2 travel through the hotel area to town every 30 minutes. Bus 15 along the Eilat–Taba road, passes attractions such as the Underwater Observatory, Coral Beach, and the dive centers, to the Egyptian border crossing point at Taba.

In **Ein Bokek,** a shuttle bus takes guests from the hotels to the Solarium and to the spa at Neve Zohar (ask at your hotel for the timetable).

By Taxi The preferred (and air-conditioned) way of hopping from one place to another in **Eilat** is by taxi. Not many rides cost much more than NIS 12 ($4), and taxis may be hailed on the street or ordered from **Arava** (tel. 07/373331), or **Taba** (tel. 07/333339). In **Beersheba,** Netz Taxis (07/270808) operates seven days a week. Taxis are not necessary in Ein Bokek or Mitzpe Ramon.

Guided Tours

General Interest Several Tel Aviv– and Jerusalem-based tour companies, including **Egged Tours** (59 Ben Yehuda St., Tel Aviv, tel. 03/527–1212; 224 Jaffa Rd., Jerusalem, tel. 02/304422) and **United Tours** (4 Bograshov St., Tel Aviv, tel. 03/754–3412 or 03/754–3414; King David Hotel Annex, 23 King David St., Jerusalem, tel. 02/252187 or 02/252189), offer two-day air-conditioned bus tours to **Eilat.** Both companies will pick you up at your hotel. Among the highlights covered are David Ben Gurion's home at Sde Boker, the canyonlike crater of Makhtesh Ramon, and attractions in and around Eilat (overnight stay) such as the Underwater Observatory and Timna Valley Park and a stop at the Dead Sea. At extra cost, participants can arrange to make the return trip by air. The trip costs NIS 525 ($175), with a small additional charge during peak season.

Yoel Tours in **Ein Bokek** (Galei Zohar Hotel, tel. 07/584432 or 07/954791), every Thursday, operates a half-day minibus tour to the Bedouin market in **Beersheba,** followed by a visit to a Bedouin family to drink coffee in their tent. The trip costs NIS 90 ($30). For a Bedouin market trip originating in Jerusalem, call **United Tours** (tel. 07/371720 or 07/371749).

Spend half a day exploring Eilat with **Johnny Desert Tours** (tel. 07/372608 or 07/376777). The price of NIS 174 ($58) includes entrance to the Underwater Observatory, a visit to the Jordanian border, and the agricultural plantations of nearby Kibbutz Elot, as well as a hot lunch.

Two trips from Eilat to attractions nearby are: a half-day visit to Timna Park and Hai Bar Wildlife Reserve with **Egged Tours** (tel. 07/373148 or 07/373149) for NIS 108 ($36); and a one-day trip to Timna Valley and Kibbutz Yotvata offered by **United Tours** (tel. 07/371720 or 07/371749) that costs NIS 147 ($49).

From Eilat, the **Timna Express** gives travelers a detailed exploration of Timna Valley Park. With hotel pick-ups at 8 AM daily except Sunday, the price of NIS 108 ($36) for adults and NIS 84 ($28) for children includes a visit to a kibbutz and lunch at the Park restaurant. You'll be back around 2 PM.

Here's a day trip from Eilat that packs in several experiences: **Amiel Tours** (Khan Center, tel. 07/377308) takes sightseers north to the Mitzpe Ramon Visitors Center overlooking the Ramon crater, the Alpaca Farm, and includes a short camel ride, a Jeep trip, and a Bedouin lunch. The tour is on Friday and costs NIS 219 ($73) for adults and NIS 207 ($69) for children. **Oasis Tours** (tel. 07/377950) in Eilat runs a similar trip.

If you are in Eilat and want to see communal life in the desert, **Kibbutz Grofit** (tel. 07/374362), 44 kilometers (27 miles) north of Eilat, will take you to meet the kibbutzniks and hear about growing watermelons in the sand and how their dairy farm was developed. The tour, which leaves every Wednesday at 8:30 AM, returning around 3 PM, costs NIS 84 ($28) for adults and NIS 72 ($24) for children, and includes lunch eaten with kibbutz members.

Special Interest A thrilling way to see the Negev is from a desert vehicle (be it camel or Jeep or quad runner) in the company of an expert guide who is not only knowledgeable about every facet of desert life but who also knows how to prepare tea from desert plants and open-air meals. If you have the time, an overnight in a sleeping bag under the stars is not to be missed; the tour companies provide all the camping equipment. Bookings can usually be made through a travel agency or through your hotel. Not all tours operate in the hot summer months.

Eilat makes a natural jumping-off point for a trip into the Sinai, either for the day to St. Catherine's Monastery, or on longer jaunts, by camel or by Jeep (*see* Tour 4 *in* Exploring Eilat and the Negev, *below*).

Airplane Tours From Sde Dov Airport in Tel Aviv, **Ayt Aviation & Tourism Ltd.** (tel. 03/699–0185) will take three–nine people for a two-hour flight over the *makhteshim* (canyon-like craters), the spring-waterfall of Ein Avdat, and along the Dead Sea; the cost is NIS 780 ($260) per person.

Bird-Watching Tours In the spring and fall, millions of birds fly over **Eilat** on their long journey between winter grounds in Africa and summer breeding grounds in Eurasia. Migration activity takes place between mid-February and early June, and between mid-September and the end of August, although the **International Birdwatching Center** in Eilat (opposite the Central Bus Station, Box 774, 88106, tel. 07/374276; open Sun.–Thurs. 9–1, 5–7, Fri. 9–1) is aflutter year-round. The Center conducts half- or full-day trips to birding hot spots in the vicinity of Eilat. You'll see the ringing station and you can plant a tree at the Bird Sanctuary created on a landfill. You may want to rent binoculars there for a better view of birds of prey, waterfowl, songbirds, and others. Based on a minimum of three people per trip, the price is NIS 150 ($50).

Boat Tours The spectacular underwater phenomena near Eilat—unusual coral, tropical plant life, and crayon-colored fish of all sizes and shapes— may be seen from glass-bottom boats that depart from either the bridge at the Marina in Eilat or from the pier just north of Coral Beach on the Eilat–Taba Road. From the Marina, **Israel-Yam** (tel. 07/375528 or 07/332325) gives a two-hour glass-bottom boat tour along the Coral Reserve and the Israel-Jordan border area three times a day. The cost is NIS 30 ($10) for adults, NIS 15 ($5) for children.

If you would like to see the fish and coral from down under, take a ride on **Yellow Submarine's** 72-foot-long *Jacqueline*, which leaves three to four times daily from Coral World Underwater Observatory (tel. 07/376666 or 07/376732) on the Eilat–Taba road in Coral Beach. The sub—which really is yellow—dives deep below the surface on a 40-minute guided journey to see the renowned reefs of the Coral Reserve. There's a camera mounted outside so you can see the water closing around you during the descent. Reservations are necessary; the sub does not operate on Sunday. The cruise costs NIS 107 ($35.70) for adults, NIS 61 ($20.35) for children. The price includes entrance to the observatory.

The *Jules Verne Explorer* (tel. 07/377702 or 07/334668; reservations are suggested), a mobile underwater observatory with two upper decks and a glass-sided underwater lower section, takes a two-hour trip past the Coral Reserve that costs NIS 50 ($16.70) for adults and NIS 40 ($13.35) for children. There are three departures daily.

Choose a day-long cruise in the Gulf of Eilat (Aqaba) on one of the many boats anchored at the Marina, among them *The Orionia* (Red Sea Sports Club, tel. 07/379685), a classic Spanish-built sailing yacht whose skipper explains what's to see at sea; it's wise to book ahead. **Eilat Cruises Ltd.** (at the Marina, tel. 07/333351 or 07/331717) offers a barbecue-lunch cruise on an Old World–style sailboat to Coral Island, 17 kilometers (10 miles) south of Eilat, with time to explore its Crusader fortress (NIS 70, or $23.35 for adults, NIS 55, or $18.35 for children), as well as a five-hour cruise on a Cutty Sark–style all-wood schooner that anchors at the Lighthouse, near Taba, and costs NIS 55 ($18.35) for adults, NIS 44 ($14.70) for children. While you're out there, service boats come along and, for an additional fee, will take you parasailing, waterskiing, or for an introductory scuba dive.

For visitors who prefer more active sailing, the operators of the 36-foot ketch *Shooneet* (tel. 07/377925) out of the Marina offer various trips such as an overnight sail for NIS 96 ($32) and a 24-hour sail for NIS 180 ($60), in which guests can take the helm and hoist the sails. The skipper gives a short explanation of the surroundings while you are under sail. Children get a 20% discount.

A cruise that includes a visit to the Coral World Underwater Observatory is offered by the **Coral Pearl** (tel. 07/376666 or 07/377858).

Camel Tours The Tel Aviv–based company **Tracks** (10 Kaplan St., 64734, tel. 03/691–6103 or 03/695–5187, fax 03/695–2226) offers adventure-filled desert crossings with **Camel Riders.** The two-day "Smugglers' Route" trek sets out from their Negev Adventure Center, 60 kilometers (37 miles) north of Eilat, in the heart of the mountains. It crosses the Negev Highlands, through remote corners of the desert, on the route taken by smugglers in centuries past. The trip leaves on Friday, about twice a month, usually not in summer, and costs NIS 330 ($110). The **Camel Ranch** (tel. 07/376663 or at night 07/378638), at the Texas Ranch in Coral Beach, takes you into the mountains and canyons of the desert around Eilat. A half-day excursion (the sunset trip is smashing) costs NIS 108 ($36).

Mamshit Camel Ranch (Box 71, Dimona 86100, tel. 07/554012; in Tel Aviv, 03/534–4354), 35 kilometers (21.7 miles) from Beersheba, runs camel trips that can include Bedouin hospitality and overnights in a traditional tent. The drawback is that the organization requires a minimum of 20 people for each trip. Call ahead to ascertain the situation. The one-day camel trip is NIS 102 ($34). A Bedouin *hafla* (feast) is NIS 48 ($16). The staff will pick you up in Beersheba.

Digs Readers who would like to work all day in the dust under a blazing sun—with the hope of finding Abraham's tent peg (and also of contributing to Holy Land archaeology and meeting interesting people)—should contact the **Israel Antiquities Authority** (Box 586, Jerusalem 91004, tel. 02/292607, fax 02/292628) for information about digs where volunteers are needed.

Hiking Tours A safer alternative to venturing out on your own—and more interesting—is an off-the-beaten-track hike led by professional guides of the **SPNI** (Society for the Protection of Nature in Israel; 4 Hashfela St., Tel Aviv, tel. 03/537–4425 or 03/375063; 13 Helene Hamalka St.,

Jerusalem, tel. 02/252357 or 02/244605). Although there are hikes conducted in English, a hike led by a Hebrew-speaking guide should not be dismissed out of hand; English-speaking hikers in the group are often glad to translate, plus it's a good way to get to know nature-loving Israelis. SPNI day trips are planned only a short time ahead, so it's worth while calling to see what's going on.

The expert nature guides of the **Nature Reserves Authority** (Visitors Center, Box 340, Mitzpe Ramon 80600, tel. 07/588691 or 07/588620) may be hired to hike you through (or accompany you in your vehicle) the Makhtesh Ramon for the sum of NIS 300 ($100) from 8 AM to 5 PM, starting from the Mitzpe Ramon Visitors Center. You must make a reservation at least two or three weeks in advance.

Jeep Tours **Jeep Tour** (Box 669, Arad 80755, tel. 07/952388), based in Arad, introduces visitors to the desert in the Dead Sea area, with pickups in either **Arad** or **Ein Bokek.** Some tours take in the Flour Cave. Half-day trips are NIS 75 ($25), and day trips, with picnic lunch, cost NIS 150 ($50), based on six people.

Out of **Eilat,** the well-established **Red Sea Sports Club** (in the King Solomon Hotel, King's Wharf, tel. 07/379685) takes Jeep trips through the Granite Mountains around Eilat to lookout points above Moon Valley; the jaunt may include a hike in the Red Canyon. The cost is NIS 84 ($28) per person for a half day and NIS 132 ($44) per person, including a picnic lunch, for a day trip.

If you're over 23 and would like to try your hand at driving a Jeep, contact **Johnny Desert Tours** in Eilat (Box 261, 88102, tel. 07/372608 or 07/376777), which also offers closed desert vehicles (not as romantic as open Jeeps, but the air-conditioning has its appeal). Routes include Amram's Pillars, Timna Valley Park, and the desert oasis of Ein Evrona. The half-day trip costs NIS 104 ($26); the one-day trip (with lunch) is NIS 120 ($40), entrance fees excluded.

Shualei Shimshon (Desert Fox) of Mitzpe Ramon (Box 366, 80600, tel. 07/588868) is for those who seek a personalized approach to a Jeep adventure. Old-hand desert guide and owner Gidi devotes himself to tailor-made trips—rent him, his expertise, and his customized Jeep for NIS 750 ($250) per Jeepload a day.

In addition, there are experienced and well-run desert safari companies who work with either a Jeepload (seven to nine people) or groups of a minimum of 20 people. If your family or group is not large enough, it's worth a call to see if by chance you can hook up with one of their outings. Of these, **Avi Desert Tours** (in Jerusalem, Moshav Givat Yeshayahu 16, 99825, tel. 02/918855, fax 02/917854; in Eilat tel. 07/378024, fax 07/378025) leads carefully planned Jeep and four-wheel-drive expeditions out of **Beersheba, Eilat,** and **Ein Bokek.** From **Eilat, Jeep See** (Bridge House, near the Marina, Box 4188, 88100, tel. 07/330133, fax 07/330134) offers trips that go out for a half day to the red-sand Hidden Canyon and the Pillars of Abraham, with a picnic lunch amidst mountain scenery, for NIS 585 ($195) per Jeepload (the box lunch is an extra NIS 24/$8 per person). Jeep See also conducts longer desert safaris (which include sand skiing and rappelling).

Operating out of **Mitzpe Ramon, Desert Shade** (Box 238, 80600, Tel Aviv office, tel. 03/5756885) offers desert tours that can incorporate a hafla, camel riding, hiking, and overnights in Bedouin hospitality tents (*see* Tour 1 *in* Exploring Eilat and the Negev, *below*). The trips range from NIS 117–NIS 234 ($39 to $78) per person for a one-day trip.

Llama Tours   Children will love this half-day tour, riding on gentle llamas (camels too) that takes trippers to the Ramon crater and includes a visit to the Llama Farm (near Mitzpe Ramon, tel. 07/588047). Cost is NIS 52 ($17.35), with coffee and cake.

Quad Runners   The latest in desert vehicles are these one-person all-terrain vehicles (ATVs), also known as fun buggies, which you drive yourself (if you are over 18 and have a driver's license). Reaching places even Jeeps can't get to, **Desert Quad Runner** (tel. 07/377774 or 07/378787) and **Jeep See** (tel. 07/330133), both in Eilat, offer half-day guided adventures through desert cliff trails and ravines.

Desert Precautions

Certain rules of the desert must be observed so that you are comfortable and happy—and safe. You should drink 2 quarts of water a day in the winter, and, if you are active, 1 quart per hour in the summer (dehydration sets in quickly in the desert). Keep a jerrican of water in your car, plus extra bottles of water. You'll find water fountains along the way, but they do not always function. Wear sunblock, sunglasses (on a string so you don't lose them), protective lip gloss or balm, and a sun hat (a must all year round). You'll soon forget personal vanity when you see *everyone* wearing chapeaus you thought you wouldn't be caught dead in. Light hiking shoes and a small knapsack are handy for walking and hikes, as are bug spray and a flashlight.

Try to get an early start, plan to be inside or resting during the midday hours in summer, and make every effort to be at your destination by nightfall. If you are traveling long distances, stay alert and awake. Lock the car at all times, take your valuables when you leave the car, and keep your bags where they are not visible from the outside. Women should not hitchhike.

Although it may seem incongruous in the desert, there is a very real danger of road flooding in the winter and early spring, especially the day after a rainfall. Before setting out, if it is raining or has recently rained, call the police (tel. 100) or the SPNI (in Tel Aviv tel. 03/375222, Mon., Tues., and Fri. 9–1; Wed. and Thurs. 9–4) to ask if there is a problem on the road you intend to take. If you are already in the Negev, contact the local GTIOs (*see* Important Addresses and Numbers *in* Essential Information, *above*) for an update on road conditions. If you are traveling and see water flowing across the road in front of you, stop and wait, even if it takes a while for the water to subside. Water on the road is a warning of possible imminent flooding. When hiking (better done with a guide), do not enter canyons or dry river beds on rainy days, or even when it's rained further north (*see* Participant Sports *in* Sports and the Outdoors, *below*).

Exploring Eilat and the Negev

Good roads, well signposted in English, enable the traveler to see the Negev from north to south on two tours, both of which start from Beersheba and end in Eilat. Tour 1 takes you through the Negev Highlands (including Sde Boker, where David Ben Gurion lived and is buried, and the giant erosion crater of Makhtesh Ramon), in the center of the Negev, while Tour 2 goes to Tel Beersheba, Arad, and

Ein Bokek along the Dead Sea, and continues down the Arava (Valley) Road to Eilat. Tour 3 covers the resort of Eilat and its environs, which includes the Underwater Observatory in Coral Beach, Timna Valley Park, and the Hai Bar reserve. Egyptian Sinai is just over the border from Eilat, and Israeli tour operators (as well as guides, nature lovers, and divers) still maintain a close connection with the Sinai they worked in and developed. Tour 4 is an easy excursion into Sinai, a one-day trip to the Monastery of St. Catherine at Mt. Sinai.

Highlights for First-Time Visitors

Ben Gurion's home and grave site, Sde Boker (*see* Tour 1)
Coral World Underwater Observatory, Coral Beach (*see* Tour 3)
Hai Bar (*see* Tour 3)
Israel Air Force Museum, (Hatzerim) (*see* Tour 2)
Mitzpe Ramon Visitors Center (*see* Tour 1)
Nabatean ruins and burial cave, Avdat (*see* Tour 1)
St. Catherine's Monastery, Sinai (*see* Tour 4)
Timna Valley Park (*see* Tour 3)

Tour 1: The Heart of the Negev

Numbers in the margin correspond to points of interest on the Eilat and the Negev map.

Tour 1 plunges right into the heart of the Negev, through the Negev Highlands to Eilat, with stops at a Bedouin hospitality tent, a reconstruction of a 1943 desert outpost, David Ben Gurion's kibbutz home, a walk to an icy desert pool, a 2,000-year-old Nabatean hilltop stronghold, and the immense crater of Makhtesh Ramon.

At least two days are required to explore this fascinating area. The ideal way to do it is to spend the night halfway through the tour, in the town of Mitzpe Ramon (80 kilometers, or 50 miles, from Beersheba, and 148 kilometers, or 92.5 miles, from Eilat), or in Sde Boker, 50 kilometers (31 miles) away. The recently built hotel in Mitzpe Ramon, the Ramon Inn, is the traveler's best option, with its convenient location and fine accommodation. Be sure to make reservations well in advance. Budget-minded travelers can stay at a SPNI field school hostel. Should accommodation be unavailable, or should you prefer to push on and spend the night in more luxurious Eilat, choose your stops carefully—Ben Gurion's home and the visitors center at Mitzpe Ramon are the most important sites—and judge your time accordingly so you won't be driving into the night. An early start is advised (always best in the desert), and allow at least two hours for the Mitzpe Ramon Visitors Center at Makhtesh Ramon, and the sites in the town itself. If you have the time and would like to devote a day to hiking through the Makhtesh, *see* Guided Tours *in* Essential Information, *above*.

At the start of this tour, traveling south from either Tel Aviv or Jerusalem on Route 40, you might like to meet the Negev's indigenous inhabitants, the Bedouin, in the village of **Rahat.** After passing Kiryat Gat, drive 21 kilometers (13 miles) and turn right at the Bet Qama Junction onto Route 293, then immediately left onto Route 264 (there will be a sign indicating Rahat). Drive 4 kilometers (3 miles), passing a Bedouin cemetery on the left (the graves have both a headstone and footstone), and turn left at another sign marked Rahat. Drive 2 kilometers (1.2 miles), turning left opposite the gas station, into the parking lot. You'll see a black tent and a building ❶ made of large stones, the **Bedouin Heritage Center.** Bedouin hospitality tents are now to be found on most sightseeing routes in the Negev. To relax and sip coffee in a *real* Bedouin tent is even more special. Rahat is a 20-year-old Bedouin village with modern villas, schools, and a community center—and resident Salem Abu Siam's authentic tent. Inside are the Bedouin hosts who will welcome you by performing the traditional coffee ceremony: roasting the beans over a fire and rhythmically pounding them (to let neighbors know that guests have arrived) in a wooden container with a wooden pestle. Guests sit on rugs around the fire, drinking coffee from small cups. Singing, playing the *rababa* (Bedouin violin), and storytelling (just as it's been done for centuries) are part of the visit. A nearby tent contains a rug-making loom. Demonstrations are given, and handiwork is for sale (*see* Shopping, *below*). Children will especially enjoy the short camel and donkey rides. *Rte. 264, tel. 07/918263 or 07/918656. Admission: NIS 9 ($3) adults, NIS 6 ($2) children. Open Sun.–Fri. 8:30 AM–8 PM, Sat. 11:30–5.*

Retrace your steps to Route 264 and pick up Route 40 at Qama Junction, where you turn right (southeast) and continue straight to **Beersheba.** Drive through the city (you'll be heading south), turning left at the large intersection in the direction marked "To the Market." Drive for 1 kilometer (.6 mile) and cross the bridge. Continue straight, following Route 40 in the direction of Sde Boker and Mitzpe Ramon.

After passing the industrial area on Beersheba's outskirts, you'll see rectangular tents and huts sprawling over the low hills on your left. This is the Bedouin settlement of the Azazme tribe. Although Bedouin traditionally live in black goat-hair tents, the Azazme, like many other modern Bedouin, are leaving behind their nomadic way of life and settling down. What you see is a step in the modern-day transition from tents to hutlike structures to concrete homes in permanent villages. (It's not unusual to see tents sitting beside these modern houses.) But these traditionally desert nomads still depend on their flocks for sustenance—much as their ancestors did—and during the next half hour of your drive, you will see Bedouin women, their faces covered and their embroidered black dresses flying in the wind, tending sheep and goats. Alongside the road (and all over the Negev), you will also see isolated, often oval-shaped, clusters of eucalyptus and tamarisk trees. Called a *liman* (Greek for a small port), these are the results of Jewish National Fund desert afforestation efforts whereby trees are sown in depressions to catch even the smallest amount of runoff water. Keep an eye out for donkeys and sheep crossing the road!

2 After 30 kilometers (18.6 miles) you will pass Kibbutz Mashabe Sade on the left, and there will be an orange sign on the right for **Mitzpe Revivim,** site of an early desert outpost. Turn right (at Mashabim Junction); you are now on Route 222. Stay on this road for 8 kilometers (5 miles), then turn left across from the chicken coops and through the grounds of **Kibbutz Revivim** to a parking lot. In 1943, in a desolate and empty Negev, three outposts, one of them Mitzpe Revivim (*mitzpe* means "lookout," *Revirim* means "showers"), were set up to gauge the feasibility of Jewish settlement in the southernmost part of the country. (Revivim's very presence, along with a handful of other Negev settlements, influenced the United Nations decision to include the Negev as part of the State of Israel in the 1947 partition plan.) During the War of Independence, isolated Mitzpe Revivim was besieged by Egyptian soldiers, and a hard-fought battle was won by a small band of pioneers and Palmach soldiers. The defenders' fort and living quarters have been preserved: The radio room (with a mannequin sending a message that crackles from the machine), the ammunition room, kitchen, and the engineers' quarters contain their original equipment, all in place. Outside are a cave, actually a Byzantine-period cistern, where a medical clinic was set up, and two airplanes that were used to bring supplies and evacuate the wounded. The kibbutz members who maintain the place act as guides. *Rte. 222, tel. 07/562570. Admission: NIS 6 ($2) adults, NIS 3 ($1) children. Open Sun.–Thurs. 9–6, Fri. and holiday eves 9–5, Sat. and holidays 9–5.*

Return through the kibbutz grounds the way you came, turning right back onto Route 222. As you return to Route 40, you pass on the right the **Bir Asluj Memorial,** made of many small stones, which commemorates the Jewish soldiers who died holding off the Egyptian advance in the Negev during the War of Independence. You reach the Mashabim Junction gas station, roadside café (good for stocking up on bottled water) and tourist information kiosk. Continue on Route 40 for 2 kilometers (1.2 miles) past the rest stop and make a left at the sign for Mitzpe Ramon, at Telalim Junction. Still Route 40, this stretch heading southwest takes you through areas where signs announce "Firing Zones." You will see many such signs in the Negev. The signs indicate closed military areas, which you may not enter without proper authorization. It is perfectly safe to travel on these roads, but don't wander off them. After a drive of 17 kilometers (10.5 miles) you will see on the right a sign for the

❸ **Haggay Observation Point.** The parking lot is on the opposite side of the highway at a curve in the road. After parking the car, carefully cross the road to the observation point for a glorious first view of the **Wilderness of Zin**—stark, flat beige-color terrain—and **Kibbutz Sde Boker.** Except for the greenery of the kibbutz, the area undoubtedly looks as it did to the wandering Children of Israel making their way from Egypt to the Land of Canaan more than 3,000 years ago, muttering complaints about the lack of figs or vines . . . and no water to drink.

On Route 40 again, heading south, you soon come to the Halukim T-junction. Turn left. A 1-kilometer (.6-mile) drive takes you back three millennia to the Iron Age (10th–9th centuries BC), to the for-

❹ tress at **Hurbat Halukim.** Archaeologists are not sure who built this stronghold, one of the many found throughout the Negev; some scholars believe it is one of a string of fortresses built by King Solomon to protect the southern border of his kingdom. The fortress is truly in ruins, but explanatory signs direct the visitor through the remains of the fort and buildings in the surrounding field. Now retrace your route back to the T-junction. Keep going straight, and you will soon come to the entrance to **Kibbutz Sde Boker** (*boker* means "cowboy"—the settlers once considered raising cattle). Don't

❺ turn in here—keep going, and turn in at the sign for **Ben Gurion's Desert Home.**

David Ben Gurion (1886–1973), Israel's first prime minister, was one of the great statesmen of the 20th century, yet his small Negev home is commonly known as "the hut" because of its humble ambience. It's not really a hut but a one-story wooden home with a small kitchen, an eating corner with table and two chairs, and simple furniture throughout. Visitors such as Dag Hammarskjold, Secretary-General of the United Nations, drank tea with Ben Gurion in the living room, with its miniature version of Michaelangelo's *Moses* on a side table and a picture of Lincoln on the wall. Ben Gurion's library shelves contain 5,000 books (20,000 more are in his Tel Aviv home)— in fact, most of the space in the "hut" is taken up by The Old Man's (as he was locally known) books. On Ben Gurion's desk are the papers on which he copied out sentences from the Old Testament: "I will even make a way in the wilderness, and rivers in the desert. . . . I give waters in the wilderness, and rivers in the desert, to give drink to my people, my chosen" (Isaiah 43). His bedroom, with its single picture of Mahatma Gandi, holds the iron cot on which he took his three hours of sleep nightly, his slippers on the floor beside it. The house is as he left it, with only a porch added to exhibit various memorabilia, such as gifts from world leaders.

When Ben Gurion resigned (later to return) from government in 1953, he and his wife, Paula, moved to the isolated, brand-new Kibbutz Sde Boker to provide an example for others. "Neither money nor propaganda builds a country," he announced. "Only the man who lives and creates in the country can build it." This said, the George Washington of Israel—whose interests were history, philosophy, and politics, as the artifacts in his home indicate—took up his new role in the kibbutz fold. In February 1955 he once again became prime minister, spending holidays and weekends at the kibbutz, and when he retired in 1970 he returned to Sde Boker to live. (He returned to his Tel Aviv residence some months before he died in 1973.) *Tel. 07/558444. Admission free. Open Sun.–Thurs. 8:30–3:30, Fri. and holiday eves 8:30–1, Sat. and holidays 9–2:30.*

Time Out   Next door is the **Sde Boker Inn,** where kibbutz members run a cozy, under-the-trees eatery and dish up hot homemade food, plus salads and sandwiches. If this is your breakfast time, boxed lunches can be made up for the road. In season, delicious Sde Boker fruits are on the menu and for sale: apricots in June, plums in July, peaches in August. Bags of kibbutz-grown pistachio nuts may also be purchased. *Tel. 07/560379. Open Sun.–Thurs. 8–4, Fri. and holiday eves 8–3, Sat. 8:30–3.*

6 Once back on the main road, a 2-kilometer (1.2-mile) drive south brings you to the turnoff to **Ben Gurion's grave site.** Drive toward the main gate to **Sde Boker College** (Ben Gurion University), but instead of entering the gate, turn right and drive to the parking lot. Follow the marked footpath through a beautiful garden until you reach the quiet, windswept plaza, in the center of which are the simple raised stone slabs marking the graves of David and Paula Ben Gurion (she died five years before her husband). The couple's final resting place—the site had been selected by Ben Gurion himself—overlooks the Zin Valley's geological finery: a vast, undulating drape of velvety-looking stone in shades of cream, ivory, coffee, and soft brown that slowly changes in hue as the day goes on. The cluster of greenery and palm trees to the right on the valley floor indicates the spring of Avdat, or En Avdat (*see below*). It is an awe-inspiring sight.

The spring of Avdat lies at the foot of the canyon that divides the plateau between the ancient Nabatean city of Avdat and Kibbutz Sde Boker. The En Avdat Observation Point (*see below*) overlooks the spring. Further south are the ruins of the ancient city of Avdat (*see below*).

7 To reach **En Avdat,** a national park, return to the parking lot, exit, and turn left down the curving road to a clump of palm trees, where the admission booth is located. Ask for the explanatory leaflet when you pay. Lock the car, taking valuables with you. Walk toward the thickets of rushes, and about five minutes later you will see on the left, against the white chalk cliff, a lone, ancient atlantica pistachio

Eilat and the Negev

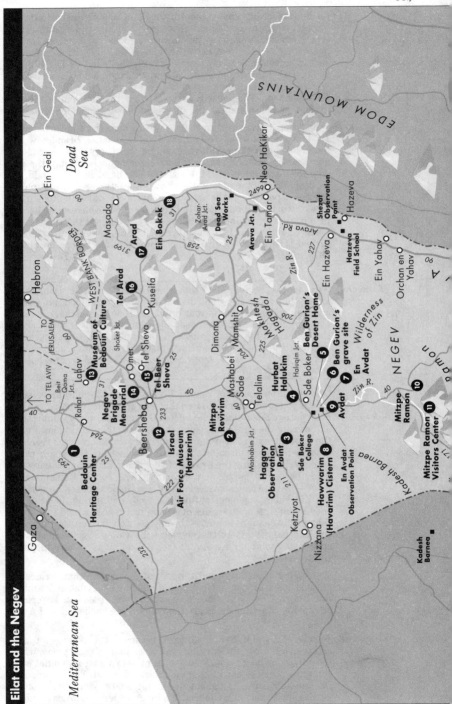

Mediterranean Sea

Gaza

Hebron

TO JERUSALEM
TO TEL AVIV
WEST BANK BORDER

Dead Sea

EDOM MOUNTAINS

Ein Gedi

Masada

Museum of Bedouin Culture

Negev Brigade Memorial

Beersheba

Israel Air Force Museum (Hatzerim)

Rahat Jct.
Beit Qama Jct.
Lahav
Shoket Jct.
Omer
Tel Sheva
Tel Beer Sheva

Tel Arad
Kuseifa
Arad
Ein Bokek
Zohar-Arad Jct.
Dead Sea Works
Arava Jct.
Ein Tamar
Neot HaKikar

Mashabim Jct.
Mitzpe Revivim
Mashabei Sade
Telalim
Dimona
Mamshit
Mokhtesh
Hagadol

Ketziyot
Nizzana
Haggay Observation Point
Sde Boker College
Sde Boker
Ben Gurion's Desert Home
Ben Gurion's grave site
En Avdat
Avdat

Hurbat Halukim
Haluqim Jct.

Hawwarim (Havarim) Cistern
En Avdat Observation Point

Wilderness of Zin
Zin R.

Ein Hazeva
Hatzeva Field School
Shezaf Observation Point
Hazeva

NEGEV

Mitzpe Ramon
Mitzpe Ramon Visitors Center

Kadesh Barnea

Kadesh Barnea

Ramon

Ein Yahav
Orchan en Yahav

Arava Rd.
Zin R.

90
25
31
222
233
264
283
40
40
211
40
204
225
258
206
227
2499
3199
171
232
25

Bedouin Heritage Center ①
② Mitzpe Revivim
③ Haggay Observation Point
④ Hurbat Halukim
⑤ Ben Gurion's Desert Home
⑥ Ben Gurion's grave site
⑦ En Avdat
⑧ Hawwarim (Havarim) Cistern
⑨ Avdat
⑩
⑪ Mitzpe Ramon Visitors Center
⑫
⑬ Museum of Bedouin Culture
⑭ Negev Brigade Memorial
⑮ Tel Beer Sheva
⑯ Tel Arad
⑰ Arad
⑱ Ein Bokek

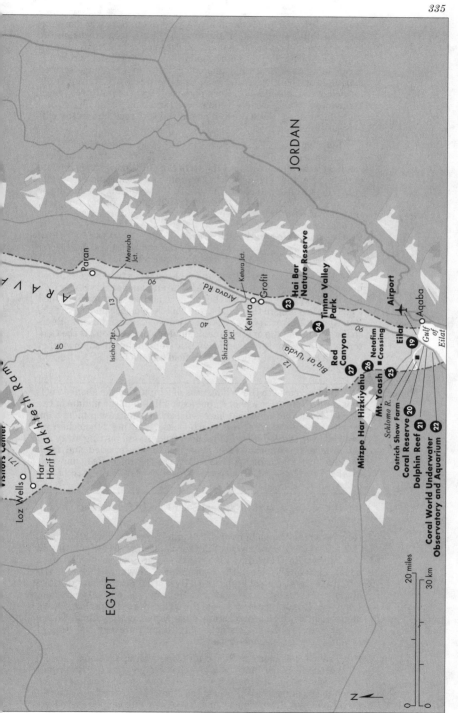

EGYPT

JORDAN

Makhtesh Ramon

A R A V A

Paran

Menucha Jct.

Ketura Jct.

Ketura

Grofit

90

Arava Rd.

Isichor Jct.

13

40

Shizzafon Jct.

40

12

Big'at 'Uvda

23 Hai Bar Nature Reserve

24 Timna Valley Park

27 Red Canyon

26 Mt. Yoash

25 Netafim Crossing

Airport

Eilat **19**

Aqaba

Gulf of Eilat

90

Loz Wells

Har Harif

Visitors Center

Mitzpe Har Hizkiyahu

Schlomo R.

Ostrich Show Farm **20**

Coral Reserve

Dolphin Reef **21**

Coral World Underwater **22**
Observatory and Aquarium

N

0

0

20 miles

30 km

tree, the first of many reminders of a time when there was more water, and thus vegetation, in the area. Look for ibex tracks on the ground, made with hoofs that enable these agile creatures to climb sheer rock faces. Try to spot the animals up on the cliffs, barely discernable against rock the same color; the ibex even have striped markings on their coats that resemble the strata of different rocks formed over the millennia. Rock pigeons, Egyptian vultures (black and white feathers, bright yellow beak, and long pinkish legs), and sooty falcons use the natural holes in the soft rock and in the cliff ledges for nesting.

The big surprise at En Avdat is the pool of icy-cold spring-fed water, complete with a splashing waterfall. To reach this cool oasis shaded by the surrounding cliffs, walk carefully along the right side of the bank of the spring, which starts out as a trickle and eventually gets wider, and across the dam, toward the waterfall. Swimming or drinking the water is not allowed (you'll not be *sorely* tempted, though—the water is swarming with tadpoles), but relaxing and enjoying the sight and sound of cold water in the arid Negev certainly is. *En Avdat National Park. Parking: NIS 10.50 ($3.50). Open Apr.–Sept., Sun.–Thurs. 8–5, Fri. and holiday eves 8–4; Oct.– Mar., Sun.–Thurs. 8–4, Fri. and holiday eves 8–3.*

Retrace the winding road back up to the entrance (where you turned in to see the Ben Gurion grave site). The entrance to **Sde Boker College** is through the gate with the traffic arm. Ben Gurion envisioned a place of learning in the Negev, and this campus became part of the Ben Gurion University of the Negev, whose main campus is in Beersheba. In the middle of the grounds, under a peaked roof, is the **Center,** with a restaurant (*see below*), a well-equipped supermarket open till 8 PM, a post office, and the field school of the SPNI (tel. 07/565828).

Time Out The **Zin Inn,** close to the Wilderness of Zin, under the shaded rooftops of the Center, is as hot a spot as you'll find in the middle of the desert. Everyone hangs out here—desert studies researchers from overseas, soldiers from the nearby base, visiting schoolchildren from all over the country, field school guides—all putting away the usual desert restaurant fare: soup, schnitzel (breaded and fried chicken cutlets), french fries, salad, ice cream, coffee, and soft drinks. *Tel. 07/565811. Open Sun.–Thurs. 8 AM–11 PM, Fri. and Sat. 8–2.*

Be sure to stop in at the **National Solar Energy Center,** also on campus.

Now return to the main road, turning left (south). Two kilometers (1.2 miles) ahead, watch carefully for an orange arrow pointing to
❽ the **Hawwarim (Havarim) Cistern** (the sign is often hidden by a bush). Park on the side of the road and walk down the incline to the left. Take the stone-cut steps into a Byzantine-period water cistern dug out of the white marl (*havar* in Hebrew) some 1,500 years ago. Long ago, it was plastered to seal the walls. It's so large that it looks like a small house; a central stone pillar supports the ceiling. This is one of countless Negev cisterns, dug to gather every last drop of runoff water in this bone-dry area.

Head south once more on Route 40, toward Mitzpe Ramon. Drive 5 kilometers (3 miles) until you see the orange sign for **En Avdat,** where you turn off to the left. Bear right along this road until you reach the parking lot. Walk down the stone path to the **En Avdat Observation Point,** from which you can see the white canyon carved out by the Zin River, with the waterfall (most of the year) tumbling into the pool, surrounded by greenery. From the lookout, a path leads around the top of the cliff (be very careful, especially with children), enabling you to see the rope marks in the rock made by Bedouin pulling up water buckets over the years from a now long-dry waterfall. (For information on the hike from here to ancient Avdat, consult the SPNI field school at Sde Boker, *above*.)

From the parking lot, return to the main road and turn left, continuing south on Route 40. Very shortly you'll see the ruins of the 2,000-year-old Nabatean city of **Avdat** looming on a hilltop to your left. Access to the site is from the left turnoff to the gas station. (It's open 24 hours a day, daily. You can buy cold beverages here, and there are rest rooms near the parking lot. If the door is closed, knock hard.)

❾ At **Avdat,** you will be seeing the stronghold and urban ruins of three peoples who have left their mark all over the Negev: the Nabateans, the Romans, and the Byzantines. To get to the 12-acre acropolis, drive to the admission booth just behind the parking lot. Be sure to ask for the National Parks Authority's explanatory leaflet/map. Drive up the road (save your energy for walking at the site), taking the right turn at the sign for the **Nabatean Burial Cave.** Park, and walk the 300 feet for a quick viewing. The 20 burial niches cut into the rock date to the 3rd century BC. Back in the car, drive up a little further to the **Lookout Point** at the restored **Roman-period building.** The cultivated fields that lie below were re-created in 1959 by Professor M. Even-Ari of Hebrew University, who wanted to see if the ancient Nabatean and Byzantine methods of conserving the meager rainfall (measured in millimeters) for desert farming would still work. The proof is in the cultivated crops and orchards before you. Run-off water was cleverly caught and utilized by a carefully worked-out system of catchment areas, conduit-walls, dams, and cisterns. Barren slopes around Nabatean sites all over the Negev were put to use in this way. Visitors (minimum 10 people) may call ahead to arrange a tour of the farm (tel. 07/565741 or 07/558462); a small fee is charged.

The Nabateans were seminomadic pagans who came from Northern Arabia in the 3rd century BC. Establishing prosperous caravan routes connecting the desert hinterland with the port city of Gaza on the Mediterranean coast, they soon rose to glory with a vast kingdom whose capital was the great rock-cut city of Petra (in today's Jordan). Strongholds to protect the caravans, which carried gold, precious stones, and spices, were established along these routes, usually at distances of a day's journey apart.

Avdat was named after Oboda (30 BC–9 BC)—Avdat is the Hebrew version of Oboda—a deified king who may have been buried here. Another king at Avdat, Aretas, is mentioned in the New Testament. The prominent local dynasty intermarried with the family of Herod the Great. The Nabatean kingdom was abolished by the Romans in AD 106, when it became a Roman province. Most of the remains you see on the acropolis date to the 3rd, 4th, and 5th centuries, the Byzantine period, when the Nabateans adopted Christianity. The city was sacked by the Persians in AD 620 and was only rediscovered in the 20th century.

With the help of the National Parks map, you may trace the presence of the people who lived here during different historical periods at a reconstructed three-story Roman-period tower (there are good views from the tower corner of the AD 4th-century fortress walls); the unique Nabatean pottery workshop, where you might just find some eggshell-thin shards; a winepress (indicating that grapes were grown here, a testament to the Nabatean genius for conserving water); cisterns; two Byzantine-era churches; and a large baptismal font (to accommodate the newly converted). From the area of the baptismal font you can walk down the steps on the eastern slope to see the AD 6th-century Byzantine dwellings, each consisting of a cave, possibly used as a wine cellar, with a stone house in front of it. At the bottom of the hill, north of the gas station, is a well-preserved Byzantine bathhouse. *Tel. 07/550954. Admission NIS 10.50 ($3.50) adults, NIS 5 ($1.70) children. Open Apr.–Sept., Sat.–Thurs. 8–5, Fri. and holiday eves 8–4; Oct.–Mar., Sat.–Thurs. 8–4, Fri. and holiday eves 8–4.*

Leave Avdat, continuing south on Route 40. A drive of 24 kilometers (15 miles) brings you to the town of **Mitzpe Ramon.** Just before the entrance is an industrial area with a flat-tire-fixing operation (known as a "puncture *macher*"; tel. 07/588885), two eateries, and the studio/workshops of a local artists' colony. Mitzpe Ramon is a town of 5,500 people, including recently arrived Russian immigrants and Black Hebrews, originally from the United States. The town has been slow to recover after the building of the more direct Arava road (Route 90) diverted traffic, leaving Mitzpe Ramon out in the cold. Unemployment is a severe problem here. However, the newly built Ramon Inn will greatly benefit both residents and travelers. If accommodations are unavailable, and you are continuing south to Eilat, you will still get to see the Makhtesh Ramon (*see below*) because Route 40 goes right through it. If this is the case, remember to allocate your time so that you won't be driving the long stretch between here and Eilat after dark.

Signs from the entrance to Mitzpe Ramon direct travelers to the impressive **Mitzpe Ramon Visitors Center,** built in the shape of an ammonite fossil (spiral-shaped sea creatures that lived here when everything was under water millions of years ago). The helpful staff are rangers with the Israel Nature Reserve Authority. Guided tours of the center are also available if booked ahead.

Makhtesh Ramon is Israel's most spectacular natural sight. It's an immense depression 40 kilometers (25 miles) long, 10 kilometers (6.2 miles) wide, and 1,320 feet deep. Since it is a phenomenon known only in this country (there are three others in the Negev), the Hebrew term "makhtesh" (meaning mortar, as in mortar and pestle) is now accepted usage. By definition, a makhtesh is an erosion valley walled with steep cliffs on all sides and drained by a single watercourse.

As you stand behind the glass, at the very edge of the makhtesh, you'll be peering down at a world formed millions of years ago. The wall-cliffs are made of layer upon layer of different colored rock beds containing fossils of shells (there was a sea here once), plants, and trees. The makhtesh floor is covered with nature's creations: heaps of black basalt formed by volcanic activity, the peaks of ancient volcanoes themselves, jagged chunks of quartzite, huge blocks of overturned rock, and beds of multicolored clays used by potters today.

For a clear understanding of the makhtesh phenomenon (and a world-class view of Makhtesh Ramon), the center offers an explanatory audiovisual presentation, a large, walk-around model of the makhtesh, and wall-to-wall, backlighted transparencies of geological points of interest. On the way to the top-floor lookout, be sure to peruse the panels describing the makhtesh's geological makeup, ecology, vegetation, and settlement. *Tel. 07/588691 or 07/588620.*

Admission: NIS 12 ($4) adults, NIS 6 ($2) senior citizens. Open Sun.–Thurs. 9–4:30, Fri. 9–2:30, Sat. 9–4:30.

You might like to take a short walk (about 1 kilometer, or .6 mile) along the edge of the makhtesh. As you leave the front door of the visitors center, take the gray stone path to the left and follow it past the youth hostel and up the hill with the antenna tower on top. From this observation point the promenade continues to the camel-shape **Mt. Gamal** for yet another great view. If it's late afternoon you may see ibexes along the cliffs and raptors wheeling overhead.

To see a vast outdoor sculpture display against the makhtesh as backdrop, drive out of the visitors center, turn left onto the main road, pass the gas station on the right, then turn right immediately at the sign marked Ma'ale Noah. This is the **Desert Sculpture Park** on the edge of Makhtesh Ramon. It started in 1962 with a group of Israeli and foreign sculptors under the direction of artist Ezra Orion. Their idea was to add to the natural stone "sculptures" with geometrical rock formations of similar design. Each sculptor was allocated a space on the edge of the cliff, to which they brought their chosen rocks and, with minimal hand-shaping, formed their desert works of art.

Just outside town is the **Llama Farm**, with its hundreds of sweet-faced alpacas and llamas, the dream come true of kibbutznik and Tel Avivian Na'ama and Ilan. Young and old get a kick out of feeding the animals, receiving the occasional spit in the face from an alpaca. A visit includes a short ride on a camel and a llama. *Tel. 07/588047. Admission: NIS 9 ($3) adults, NIS 7 ($2.35) children.*

There are several eating spots in Mitzpe Ramon (*see* Dining and Lodging, *below*), and opposite the gas station is a small commercial center with a supermarket, bank, and post office. If you are traveling to Eilat, bear in mind that there are no gas stations between here and Yotvata, a distance of more than 100 kilometers (64 miles).

To continue the tour, leave Mitzpe Ramon heading south on Route 40, down the twisting Atzmaut Ascent, and into the spectacular scenery of the makhtesh, which you will be crossing from north to south. After 7 kilometers (4.5 miles), turn in at the "Carpentry" sign and drive for several minutes to the parking area. A path goes up to a wooden walkway, built to protect nature's artwork from visitors' feet. Long ago the sandstone was probably hardened and slightly warmed by volcanic steam. The rocks split into prisms, either due to cooling joints or another, unknown, process. The formations look like wooden chips piled up in a carpentry shop, and have a lustrous patina caused by a chemical reaction brought on by climatic conditions.

Driving southeast on Route 40, continue to the sign for the **Ammonite Wall** on the right. The sign indicates a distance of 5 kilometers (3.1 miles), which applies to the marked hike in the makhtesh (for fit walkers only). The rock face contains hundreds of ammonite fossils. They look like rams' horns and are indeed named for the Egyptian god Ammon, whose head was a ram's.

Still driving through the makhtesh on Route 40 and leaving the Negev Highlands, you are entering the area known as that of "the ancient rivers." Here the dry riverbeds (wadis) of the Negev increase in size from their source in the Sinai and cut through the Negev on their way to the Arava Valley to the east. The sight of the Mountains of Edom on the horizon to the east is beautiful, especially in the late-afternoon light.

After traveling for 49 kilometers (30 miles), you reach the Tsichor Junction with Route 13 (which connects with the nearby north-south highway, Route 90). Continue straight on Route 40. Along the way you will see strata of limestone "folded" over the millennia. Drive 14 kilometers (8.7 miles) southeast to the **Ketura junction,** where Route 40 ends. Here are breathtaking views (to the left of the road) of the **Arava Valley,** which marks the Israel-Jordan border, and which is part of the great Syrian-African Rift, a geological fault line formed millions of years ago.

Turn right onto Route 90, traveling south straight to Eilat (52 kilometers, or 33 miles). It is not advisable to take Route 12 to Eilat because most travelers will wind up this tour after a long day's drive, and/or toward dark, at which point Route 90 is the better and safer road.

Tour 2: Beersheba to Ein Bokek—Dead Sea to the Red Sea

The emblem of **Beersheba** is a tamarisk tree, representing the biblical past, and a flowing water pipe as a symbol of the city's modern revival. It was in Beersheba that the patriarch Abraham constructed his well (*be'er* in Hebrew) and swore an oath (*shevua* in Hebrew) over seven (*sheva* in Hebrew) ewes with the king of Gerar, who vowed to prevent his men from seizing the well. And here Abraham planted a grove of tamarisk trees. The book of Genesis describes how other patriarchal figures lived in this area, wandering the hills with their flocks. It is easy to re-create these scenes today, using instead the cloaked figures of Bedouin shepherds with their sheep and goats in the surrounding hillsides. An expression from the book of Judges, "from Dan to Beersheba," once set the northern and southern boundaries of the Land of Israel; in biblical times, living further south of the city meant living a truly desert (nomadic) life.

Romans and Byzantines built garrisons in Beersheba, but later the city was abandoned. In 1900 the Ottoman Turks, who had ruled Palestine since 1517, rebuilt Beersheba as their district center (the present **Old City**) for the Negev. They set aside an area for a Bedouin market, which still takes place every Thursday (*see* Shopping, *below*). During World War I, the British took Beersheba from the Turks after a difficult battle. During the War of Independence the town became an Egyptian base, and in 1948 it was conquered by the Israelis. It is now the fourth largest city in Israel, with its own university—named after David Ben Gurion, who envisaged a flourishing Negev—regional hospital, and symphony orchestra. A largely blue-collar city, Beersheba is struggling to provide housing for thousands of recent immigrants, many from the former Soviet Union and Ethiopia.

The Capital of the Negev, as it is known, Beersheba possesses few sites of interest other than the **Turkish Railway Station, Beersheba War Cemetery** (HaAtzmaut St.), and the **Museum of the Negev,** all in the Old City. However, the city is the geographical jumping-off point for Negev travel. Main roads branch out from here, and it's a departure point for local buses to the south as well. If you are thinking of staying overnight in Beersheba, bear in mind that accommodations are limited and must be booked ahead; also be aware that only one restaurant is open on Saturday: Bulgarit (*see* Dining and Lodging, *below*).

⑫ Less than a half hour's drive from Beersheba is the **Israel Air Force Museum (Hatzerim).** To reach the open-air museum, start from the British War Cemetery, on HaAtzmaut Street, turning left at the intersection (to the left of the cemetery), heading southwest. The road becomes Route 233. Continue for 7 kilometers (4.3 miles) heading west out of the city. It's impossible to miss this museum, a gigantic concrete field with 90 airplanes parked in rows. The fighter, transport, and training (plus a few enemy) aircraft tell the story of Israel's aeronautic history, from the Czechoslovak *Messerschmidt,* obtained in 1948 and one of four such planes that helped halt the Egyptian advance in the War of Independence, to the *Kfir,* Israel's first fighter plane. The young Air Force personnel who staff the museum give a guided tour that takes about 2½ hours and includes a movie about the Air Force. (The movie house is an air-conditioned Boeing 707 that was used in the 1977 Entebbe rescue of Israeli passengers held hostage in a hijacked Air France plane forced to fly to Uganda.) Another attention-getting display is a shiny black Supermarine Spitfire with a red lightning bolt on its side. It was flown by former Defense Minister Ezer Weizmann, the IAF's first pilot. Everything's out in the open, so be sure to wear a hat to protect against the sun. *Rte. 233, tel. 07/906428 or 07/906314. Admission: NIS 13 ($4.35), children NIS 5 ($1.70). Open Sun.–Thurs. 8–5, Fri. 8–noon.*

⑬ To reach the **Museum of Bedouin Culture** (at the Joe Alon Regional and Folklore Center), drive north on Route 40 from Beersheba for 24 kilometers (14.8 miles) until you reach a turnoff marked with a sign to Lahav and an orange sign directing you to Joe Alon Center. Take the turnoff onto Route 325 and then drive for 7 kilometers (4.3 miles). At the sign for the center, drive in and up the hill. The center is named for the late pilot Col. Joe Alon, who took a great interest in the area and its people. The one-of-a-kind museum, housed in a circular, tentlike building, affords an authentic look at the rapidly changing lifestyle of the Bedouin through various tableaux that use life-size mannequins. Each grouping is by subject: spinning wool and weaving carpets, baking bread, the coffee ceremony, wedding finery (among them a camel elaborately decorated for the event and bearing nuptial gifts), working with animals, and toys made from found objects such as pieces of wire and wood. The artifacts, most of them handmade and many already out of use in modern Bedouin life, form an outstanding collection. *Off Rte. 325, tel. 07/918597 or 07/ 913322. Admission: NIS 9 ($3) adults, NIS 6 ($2) children. Open Sun.–Thurs. 9–4, Fri. 9–2, Sat. 9–4.*

To continue the tour, return to Beersheba. Take Ben Gurion Road past the university and turn off onto Route 60, heading northeast toward Omer and Arad. About 4 kilometers (3 miles) outside the city ⑭ take the turnoff to the left leading up to the large **Negev Brigade Memorial.** Designed and built by Israeli artist Danny Karavan, the monument tells the story in 15 symbolic parts (and in Hebrew) of the Palmach Negev Brigade's battle to ward off the Egyptian advance after the birth of the State of Israel. The tower, representing a Negev settlement water tower, offers a great view of Beersheba and the surrounding area.

Continuing northeast along Route 60 for 1 kilometer (.6 mile), take the next turnoff to the right, marked "Tel Sheva." Follow the road to ⑮ **Tel Beer Sheva**—biblical Beersheba, the hill you see ahead. The hill is actually an archaeological *tel,* an artificial mound created in this case by nine successive settlements from 3,500 BC to 600 BC. Park in the lot next to a building complex, where you'll find the admission booth and a shop (*see* Shopping, *below*). This tel is a recent addition to the National Parks Authority roster; ask for the excellent explanatory leaflet.

Climb to the site traditionally associated with the patriarch Abraham. This is the only planned Israelite city uncovered in its entirety. Most of the visible remains date from the 10th–7th century BC. It is thought that the city, a fine example of a circular layout typical of the Iron Age, was destroyed around 706 BC by Sennacherib of Assyria. In the northeast, outside the 3,000-year-old city gate, is a huge well. More than 6 feet in diameter, it apparently once reached groundwater 90 feet below. (The well has not been completely excavated.) This ancient well served the city from earliest times, and scholars speculate that it could possibly be the Old Testament Abraham's Well (Genesis 21:22–32). The observation tower is rather ugly, but it affords some beautiful views. *Rte. 60, tel. 07/467286. Admission: NIS 6 ($2) adults, NIS 3 ($1) children. Open Apr.–Sept., Sun.–Thurs. 8–5, Fri. and holiday eves 8–3; Oct.–Mar., Sun.–Thurs. 8–4, Fri. and holiday eves 8–2.*

Return to Route 60 and turn right, passing **Omer,** Beersheba's garden suburb. Nine kilometers (5.6 miles) down the road is the Shoket Junction. To reach the next gas station and roadside restaurant, turn left here onto Route 31 and pull immediately—and carefully—into the complex on the opposite side of the road.

Time Out   **Kafriat Shoket** is a kibbutz-run way station. Its large cafeteria serves hot food, sandwiches, salads, cakes, and drinks; especially recommended are the apple turnovers and raisin Danish. Snack inside at the long wooden tables, or outside under the tamarisk trees. You can also purchase bottled water at a minimarket on the premises. *Tel. 07/469421. Open Sun.–Thurs. 6 AM–11 PM, Fri. 6 AM–5 PM, Sat. 8 AM–11 PM.*

Turn right as you leave the gas station, and then right again at the Shoket Junction. Stay to the left for an immediate left turn onto Route 31. About 19 kilometers (11 miles) along, look up at the hillside to the right: You will see a **Bedouin cemetery,** each grave distinguished by both a footstone and headstone. Bedouin encampments can be spotted along the way, and the gradual process of abandoning a nomadic lifestyle for a more rooted one is symbolized in the more than a decade-old Bedouin village of **Kuseifa,** on the right.

16 Continuing on Route 31, drive 22 kilometers (13.6 miles) to the turn-off on the left to **Tel Arad,** site of the biblical city. A 2-kilometer (1.2-mile) drive takes you through flat fields of the low shrub called *rotem,* or white broom, to the mound. Ask for the National Parks Authority pamphlet that explains the excavations at the 25-acre site, and be sure to purchase (for NIS 3, or $1) the plan of the Early Canaanite city of Arad, with its map, recommended walking tour, and diagrams of the typical "Arad house" (*see below*).

Arad was first settled during the Chalcolithic period (4,000–3,500 BC) by seminomadic pastoralists who lived and traveled together, herding and farming; it was they who first developed bronze. There was continuous occupation of Arad until the end of the Early Bronze Age (3,500–3,200 BC), but the city that you see most clearly here is the Early Bronze Age II City (2,950–2,650 BC). Here you can walk around a walled urban community and enter the carefully reconstructed one-room dwellings of that period, called **"Arad Houses."**

After the Early Bronze Age II, Arad was abandoned and hidden beneath the light loess soil for nearly 2,000 years, until the 10th century BC, when a fortress—one of many in the Negev (the first of which may have been built by Solomon; *see* Hurbat Halukim *in* Tour 1, *above*)—was constructed on the highest part of the site. It's worth the climb up the steepish path to the fortress. First appreciate the view while taking your leave of the Early Bronze Age. Now you are in the Iron Age (10th–6th centuries BC). The small square fortress served the area intermittently until Roman times. Most of the visible remains are biblical and date to the end of the First Temple period (935–586 BC). Note the small Israelite temple sanctuary with its two standing stones (these are replicas—the originals are in the Israel Museum in Jerusalem) and sacrificial altar of unhewn stone. In the 7th century BC, the southern part of the Israelite kingdom of Judah reached as far as today's Eilat. Artifacts found at the tel can be seen at the visitors center in Arad (*see below*). *No phone (call Arad Museum and Visitors Center, tel. 07/954409). Admission: NIS 6 ($2) adults, NIS 3 ($1) children. Open Sun.–Thurs. 8–5 (until 4 in winter), Fri. and holiday eves 8–4 (until 3 in winter).*

Return to Route 31, traveling 8 kilometers (5 miles) through Arad Park to the modern town of **Arad,** established in 1961 by urban pioneers. Arad's population of nearly 20,000 now includes immigrants from Russia and Ethiopia; writer Amos Oz is its most famous resident. Breathe deeply: The town sits 2,000 feet above sea level and is famous for its clean, dry air and mild climate. Arad has made a name for itself as a healthy place for asthma sufferers. Industrial waste and the planting of trees and bushes are under strict government control so that pollution and pollen are not introduced into the air.

Arad, like Beersheba, is a popular base for excursions to sites in the Dead Sea area (*see* Exploring Around Jerusalem *in* Chapter 3). The sound-and-light presentation at nearby Masada, by the way, can *only* be approached from Arad. To enter the town, pass the industrial zone to the right, and turn left at the intersection. Go two blocks, and, turning right at the junction (without traffic lights), you will arrive at the **Arad Museum and Visitors Center.** The center's helpful staff dispenses maps and brochures and information on hikes in the area, and can arrange for private guides (best done in advance). Their innovative "Meet the Israeli" program arranges for travelers to have coffee and a chat with locals.

To get a sense of what the desert is like, how floods occur and their results, how animals adapt to a wilderness diet, and other Negev issues, see the 20-minute audiovisual presentation. The small **museum** displays the work of local artists as well as presenting the archaeological discoveries from Tel Arad. You can see replicas of the "Arad letters" (the originals are in the Israel Museum), 2,500-year-old inscribed potsherds in ancient Hebrew script, some written by the fortress commander Eliashiv, concerning provisions of flour and wine for the soldiers. One has the name Arad inscribed on it seven times. *28 Ben Yair St., tel. 07/954409. Admission: NIS 9 ($3) adults, NIS 4.50 ($1.50) children. Open Sun.–Thurs. 9–5, Fri. and holiday eves 9–2, Sat. 9–5.*

Return to Route 31 and continue east. The 24-kilometer (15-mile) steep descent to the Dead Sea is around one sharp curve after another. The drama of the drive is enhanced by the stunning canyons and clefts that unfold on every side. Keep an eye out for the sign on the right indicating that you've reached sea level. Two **observation points** soon appear on the left side of the road; you cannot cross to the first (Metsad Zohar) from your side of the road. The second (Nahal

Zohar) looks down (to the left) upon the light marl of the ancient dry riverbed of Zohar, the vestige of an eons-old body of water that once covered this area. The Dead Sea lies directly east, with the Edom Mountains of Jordan on the other side. To the right, south, is Mt. Sodom. You can walk back to the left to Metsad Zohar to see the Roman-built Zohar fort.

Back on Route 31, you'll soon see the southern end of the Dead Sea, sectioned off into the huge evaporation pools of the Dead Sea Works, where potash and salts such as bromine and magnesium are extracted. Another common sight is row upon row of plastic "tunnels"; these act as hothouses for seedlings (often tomatoes and melons) that produce fruit ready for the European market in the middle of winter.

Time Out At the gas station (left side of Route 31, 10 kilometers, or 6.2 miles, from the observation points) is a prime example of gas station eateries in the Negev. Called **Grill Michel,** the minimally decorated (a few posters), *Baghdad Cafe*–style diner is run by a desert-hardened but friendly proprietor who is usually surrounded by his regular customers and friends. These truck drivers, Dead Sea Works employees, and other locals come as much for the conversation and laughter as they do for the grub, which features simple grilled meats, french fries, hummus, fresh chopped-vegetable salads, and good, strong coffee. *Open daily 8 AM–midnight.*

Continue on Route 31 in the direction of the Dead Sea until you reach the T-junction with Route 90 (the Zohar–Arad Junction). You are now at the bottom of the world: 1,292 feet below sea level. Although the Dead Sea (*see* Exploring Around Jerusalem *in* Chapter 3) can be as deep as 1,320 feet in places, it's much shallower at the southern end—only about 6.5 feet deep. This area is now an artificial basin that serves the resort at Ein Bokek and provides an abundance of minerals for local and export use.

Turn left (north) onto Route 90. Soon the rather startling sight of a tall building (the Nirvana Hotel) signals your arrival at the spa resort **Ein Bokek.** Along these shores, fire and brimstone were rained down by the Lord upon the people of Sodom and Gomorrah (Genesis 19:24), and it is here that Lot's wife turned into a pillar of salt (Genesis 26). The hot, sulphur-smelling air hangs heavy, the odd cry of the indigenous grackle bird is heard, and there is often a haze over the Dead Sea. The temperature of the oily water, where you can float but cannot sink, is 30°C (88°F) in July, August, and September; it's at its coldest in February, when the temperature gets as low as 19°C (66°F).

The resort area of Ein Bokek hugs the shore. It's a collection of hotels, spa hotels, and a public spa (*see* Participant Sports *in* Sports and the Outdoors, *below*), all linked by a palm-fringed promenade. This scene might seem like a mirage in such a desolate landscape, but it isn't. There's the added advantage of being a 30-minute drive from Masada and 45 minutes from Ein Gedi. Interesting local sites, such as the nearby white-marl **Flour Cave** (from which you emerge dusted in white powder) may be explored with a guide by arrangement through your hotel concierge.

A short jaunt on Route 90 south of the hotel district takes you to the **Arubotayim Cave** (Cave of the Two Chimneys), 2 kilometers (1.2 miles) south of the Zohar–Arad Junction. An orange sign on the right directs you to the cave, which is just off the road. Once inside the opening in the mountain, it's a five-minute walk to two chimney-shaped areas. Sit in the second of the two, a three-story-high chamber, and look at the amazing shapes hanging above and around you—you are actually inside Mt. Sodom, a mountain made of salt. Over thousands of years, the salt has been washed away by local rainfall, forming eerily shaped underground tunnels and deep caves dripping with long, knobbed salt "icicles." Although most caves in the area must be visited with a guide's assistance, this one is completely accessible to the public.

To continue on to Eilat, you'll be driving through the Arava Valley. Route 90 (the Arava road) runs parallel to the border with Jordan, from Ein Bokek to Eilat, and at some points the road almost touches the border. There is no obvious military presence, but you may be sure it's here. The **Arava road** follows an ancient route mentioned in the Bible in descriptions of the journeys of the Children of Israel. The Arava (meaning "valley") is part of the Syrian-African Rift, that great crack in the earth stretching from Turkey to East Africa that was caused by an ancient shifting of land masses. Along the road are several agricultural settlements; the extremely hot climate here is ideal for off-season fruit, flowers, and vegetables.

Soon you'll pass signs for the settlements of Neot HaKikar and Ein Tamar. Their date palms, seen from the road, are not irrigated, especially surprising because palms need a lot of water; all the water comes from underground springs. Also in the area are commercial fishponds actually breeding fish such as grey mullet and St. Peter's fish as well as fish for aquariums. Neot HaKikar's perimeter fence practically touches the border with Jordan.

With the Edom Mountains rising in the east (left), the road continues along the southern Dead Sea Valley. Twenty-three kilometers (14.3 miles) after the Zohar–Arad Junction you come to the Arava Junction (also known as the Sodom Junction), where Route 25 begins its westward path toward Dimona and Beersheba. Turn left (south) at the Junction, continuing on Route 90 in the direction of Eilat, 174 kilometers (107.8 miles) away.

After 5 kilometers (3 miles) you'll be crossing one of the largest dry riverbeds in the Negev, Nahal Zin. It's hard to believe that the large valley to the right can fill with water during the winter months (mid-December to early April), causing flash floods dangerous to hikers and drivers (*see* Desert Precautions *in* Essential Information, *above*). The landscape is dotted with acacia trees, the tree used by the wandering Children of Israel to build the Ark of the Covenant, which held the tablets given to Moses at Mt. Sinai. Today the acacia is a source of food for grazing goats and camels. Another 4 kilometers (2.5 miles) down the road is a gas station (open 6:30 AM–9 PM). Just after the gas station, notice on the left the greenhouses of an experimental farming station, used for research and development by local flower and vegetable growers.

One-half kilometer (.3 mile) beyond is an orange sign for the **Shezaf Nature Reserve,** where the **Shezaf Observation Point** looks out over the reddish-orange sandstone hills toward the south, and to the east the mountains of Edom in Jordan and the Arava Valley, roughly the Israel-Jordan border.

Time Out About halfway between Ein Bokek and Eilat is **"Kilometer 101,"** **Kushi Rimon.** Named for Shimon Rimon, whose nickname is Kushi, and the legendary army unit in which he served, this is the quintessential Negev roadstop, that is, one combining every possible facility available in the desert. The place is huge, has lots of palm trees, small wooden red-roofed bungalows up behind it on the hill, and large metal and wire sculptures. There are peacocks and ducks wandering about, a monkey in a cage, many more weird, towering metal sculptures all around the outdoor eating tables, and a cage housing the resident tiger, a quotation from Jeremiah affixed to it. Inside is a cafeteria with all manner of hot food, a bar stocked with every liquor imaginable, and a small minimarket. You'll also find a game room with a billiards table, other games, and a TV. *Public tel. 07/581609. Open 24 hrs. Closed Yom Kippur.*

Back on the highway again, you'll pass Menucha Junction, where Route 13 branches off to meet Route 40 leading to Makhtesh Ramon (*see* Tour 1, *above*). Still heading south from Menucha Junction, the road approaches and leaves the border with Jordan. Passing Kibbutz Lotan (at Ketura Junction with Route 40, which veers off to the west) and then Kibbutz Grofit, both on the left. You will then pass the entrance to Hai Bar Nature Reserve and Timna Valley Park, on the way to Eilat, both of which are described in Tour 3, *below*.

Tour 3: Eilat and Environs

The Arava Plain comes to an abrupt end where it meets the Bay of Eilat, and here is the country's southernmost town, the sun-drenched resort of **Eilat.** The Gulf of Eilat gives way to the gulf of the Red Sea, which lies between the Sinai Mountains, to the west, and the mountains of Edom, in Jordan, to the east. The Jordanian port of Aqaba is directly across the bay—Eilat residents will point out to you the Jordanian royals' vacation villa and yacht—and to the southeast is Saudi Arabia. The Sinai Desert is just over the Israeli border with Egypt.

Eilat's strategic location as a crossroads between Asia and Africa dictated its place in history. The area was one of the stops the Children of Israel made as they fled from Egypt into the Promised Land. (Today, it's the sister city of Los Angeles!) It was long thought that King Solomon's fleet was located in the area between Aqaba and Eilat: "And King Solomon made a navy of ships in Ezion-geber, which is beside Eloth, on the shore of the Red Sea . . . ." Later, because of its position on a main trade and travel route, every major power conquered Eilat: the Romans, Byzantines, Arabs, Crusaders, Mamluks, Ottoman Turks, and lastly, the British, whose isolated police station (headquarters of their camel corps) was taken by the Israelis in March 1949. Called Umm Rash Rash, this was the first building in modern-day Eilat, founded in 1951 and developed as a port in 1956 after the Egyptian blockade of the Tiran Straits was lifted.

A legend says that after Creation the angels were painting the earth. They got tired and spilled their paints: The blue became the waters of Eilat and the other colors became the fish and the corals. Add to the rainbow of colors Eilat's year-round good weather, its superb natural surroundings of sculptural, red-orange mountains, and its location on the sparkling Red Sea with its exotic underwater life, including coral reefs just offshore that attract divers from all over the world, and you have the ingredients for a first-rate resort. And indeed, tourism is the city's primary industry.

For many visitors, Eilat's natural assets more than make up for the undistinguished architecture and overdevelopment. For wherever you are in Eilat, an eastward gaze will present you with the dramatic sight of the granite mountain range of Edom, whose predominant shades of red intensify and fade with the light of day, culminating in a red-gold blaze of sunset over the Red Sea. The incongruous name for a body of water that's brilliantly turquoise along the shore is the result of a 17th-century typographical error by an English printer. In typesetting an English translation of a Latin version of the Bible, he lost an "e," and thus "Reed Sea" became "Red Sea." The name was easily accepted because of the sea's red appearance at sunset.

With an average rainfall of about 7.5 inches and an average winter temperature of 21°C (70°F), Eilat is a haven from the cold winter up north. Eilat's high season is mid-October to April, although the city is also crowded during Jewish and Christian holidays. It's the hottest here in July and August; many travel agencies close their doors, and Jeep trips and hikes are curtailed. The burning summer heat is a dry heat, however, without any mugginess. The wind picks up in the late afternoon, when the beaches, hotel terraces, and outdoor cafés become crowded with loungers sitting, sipping, and watching the Edom mountains turn red and the Saudi Arabian hills go purple. Walking in Eilat in the summer months is pleasant in the early morning and the later part of the day; save the indoor attractions, shopping, and siestas for midday, when the heat can be still and stifling.

Route 90 (the Arava Road) runs north–south through the town, with the airport bordering it on the east side. South of Eilat, Route 90 (at this point called the Eilat–Taba Road) continues past the port and Israel navy base to Coral Beach (*see below*), an area with its own share of attractions and hotels, and on to the Taba border crossing to the Sinai in Egypt. The section of Eilat called the North Beach includes the Promenade south to the Marina and the Lagoon, surrounded by many of the luxury hotels, restaurants, boutiques, the Marina, and the local GTIO (in the Khan Center). The foothills of the Eilat Mountains, which rise west of Route 90, are the location of Eilat's residential area, as well as what is known as the New Tourist Center (in the area between Arava Road and Yotam, with its many restaurants) and the Central Bus Station (on the main street of Eilat, HaTmarim Boulevard).

Start your tour of Eilat with a walk along the **Promenade,** beginning at King Solomon's Hotel (from Route 90 heading south, turn left into Durban Road and bear right; the hotel is the first large white building), at the northern curve of the Lagoon, where yachts are anchored, various small craft are for hire, and the Ben & Jerry's Ice Cream stand is conveniently located. Benches along the way face the Lagoon. The 2½-kilometer-long (1.6-mile-long) Promenade winds past shops and then the **Dutch Bridge,** which opens to allow passage to tall-masted vessels. On the other side of the bridge is the **Marina,** where cruise boats of all types wait to sally forth on the Red Sea (*see* Guided Tours *in* Essential Information, *above*). Now you are on the shorefront, a succession of glitzy hotels and beaches filled with reddening bodies. The scene includes sophisticated strollers, the backpack crowd, artists who do quick portraits, and vendors selling earrings, all accompanied by the strains of strolling street musicians. Across the bay in Jordan, the dark reddish-gray shapes of the Edom Mountains form a jagged skyline.

Time Out   At the southern end of the Promenade, just before the intersection of Durban and Arava, is **Pninat Eilat** (the Pearl of Eilat), a terrace full of eateries, one after the other, under blue and white wooden latticework domes. Choose from places such as McDavid's (the Israeli version of guess what), Dr. Lek Ice Cream, and Kapulski's

Cafe. Locals turn out in force here on Saturday to enjoy their day off, drinking coffee, chatting, and watching the tourists go by.

To reach Eilat's one-of-a-kind water attractions, a 10-minute drive to the south on the Eilat–Taba road, you can take Bus 15 (in the hotel area, at the Central Bus Station, or on Arava Road) or grab a taxi. The sites are close to each other and, although you can walk, the inexpensive taxis always zipping by are good alternatives when the afternoon sun is searing.

㉠ The **Coral Reserve** is one of the finest such protected areas in the world. Close to the shoreline, its coral reef is .75 mile long and is zealously protected by the Nature Reserves Authority. Divers (*see* Participant Sports *in* Sports and the Outdoors, *below*) will enjoy the especially beautiful Japanese Gardens. Masks, fins, and snorkels may be rented, and a different form of diving, called snuba, is also available. Landlubbers can traverse the beach into the shallow water to see part of the reef. Be sure to wear water shoes to protect your feet from the rough seabed and spiny sea urchins. If you do have a brush with one of these, don't pull out the stingers (doing so may cause infection); they dissolve in a day or two. Hot showers and a snack bar are on the premises. *Rte. 90 (Eilat–Taba Rd.), tel. 07/376829. Admission: NIS 12 ($4) adults, NIS 6 ($2) children. Open Nov.–Mar., daily 9–5; Apr.–Oct., daily 9–6.*

㉡ One kilometer (.6 mile) to the south is **Dolphin Reef,** developed for the study of marine mammals, specifically dolphins, in their natural habitat (only a flexible net separates them from the open sea). Dolphin Reef affords you the novel experience of meeting face to face with bottlenose dolphins: You can actually swim, snorkel, or scuba dive with them or join in on their training. The guide who takes you out and introduces you to the friendly creatures is there to protect the dolphins from people, not the reverse. Training of the dolphins can be seen daily at 10, noon, 2, and 4. Facilities include a dive center, snorkel equipment rental, and a photo shop with on-the-spot development (you can watch yourself on video minutes after frolicking with the dolphins). You can really unwind under the palm-frond umbrellas on the pretty beach or at the Reef Bar, a thatch-roofed pub/restaurant serving tasty seafood. Eilatis patronize the place on Friday afternoons to "welcome" Shabbat (*see* Nightlife, *below*). You must reserve a set time to swim or dive with the dolphins. *Rte. 90 (Eilat–Taba Rd.), tel. 07/375935 or 07/371846. Admission: NIS 21 ($7) adults, NIS 15 ($5) children. Open daily 9–5.*

㉢ Back on Route 90 south, you'll recognize the **Coral World Underwater Observatory and Aquarium,** one of the area's star attractions, by the tall space-needle structure that floats offshore. One of the highlights of the complex is the onshore **Red Sea Reef** (the building with stones piled around it), a circular aquarium surrounded by a coral reef. The aquarium's 12 windows provide views of rare fish so magnificent and some in such Day-Glo colors that it's hard to believe they are real. The **Aquarium** offers a look at fish from other parts of the world. There's an unlighted room where phosphorescent fish and other sea creatures glow in the dark. Nearby are the stingray and sea-turtle pool (one turtle is 250 years old) and shark pools.

The Underwater Observatory is currently one of only three in the world; the others, also built by Coral World, are in Nassau in the Bahamas, and in St. Thomas in the Virgin Islands. (Another underwater observatory is going up—or down—in Sydney, Australia.) The observatory is reached by a 110-yard-long wooden bridge. You might notice a yellow submarine docked to the right; it submerges several times a day to give passengers a view of the coral reefs (*see* Guided Tours *in* Essential Information, *above*). Once inside the observatory, you'll find yourself in an attractive bar and restaurant in the round, with big picture windows for enjoying the lovely view. Head right down the spiral staircase—and into the sea. You are 15 feet below, in a round, glass-windowed room, looking out at a coral reef. Swimming in and out of the reef are thousands of exotic tropical fish in often breathtaking colors and shapes you might have believed only Walt Disney could have invented. The **Observatory Tower**—reached by elevator or stairs—is 70 feet above sea level (there's a café here), from which you see clearly Israel's neighboring countries. *Rte. 90 (Eilat–Taba Rd.), tel. 07/376666. Admission: NIS 34 ($11.35) adults, NIS 22 ($7.35) children. Open Sat.–Thurs. 8:30–5, Fri. and holiday eves 8:30–3.*

Time Out   Head north on Route 90, past the Coral Reserve, taking a left at the sign directing you to the **Ostrich Show Farm**; stay on the gravel road for 20 minutes. There aren't any ostriches here anymore, but you can have a down-home meal from among such choices as eggs, salad, cheese, soup, sandwiches, *malawah* (a flaky Yemenite pastry, usually served with tomato purée), *labane* (a sour-goat's-milk product), hot dogs, hamburgers, and ice cream in the railway car that houses the restaurant. Saturday is reserved for *hamin*, a Sephardic Shabbat stew of beans, meat, potato, wheat kernels, garlic, and onions. (The restaurant becomes the Ya'eni Pub at night.) You can also take a ride in a "Solomon's Chariot," drawn by a donkey, into the hills (NIS 25, or $8.35 per person per hour). On Saturday, from January to the end of March, vendors flock here to sell crafts, secondhand objects, and food items such as jams; it's a good way to meet Israelis. *Tel. 07/373213. Open Mon.–Sat. 9 AM–2 AM.*

North of Eilat are two natural attractions that can be seen as day trips: the **Hai Bar Nature Reserve** (wildlife preserve) and **Timna Valley Park.** Both sites can be visited on the same day, with a refreshing stop at the Ye'elim pool (*see below*). If you decide to do this, see Hai Bar in the morning, when the animals are most active. Timna Valley Park is especially beguiling at sunset. In very hot weather, plan on visiting one of the two sites early in the morning, spending the midday hours at the Ye'elim pool. If you are traveling north and not returning to Eilat, you may want to visit Timna Valley Park first and then Hai Bar, with a stop at Ye'elim pool.

❷❸   Leave Eilat heading north along Route 90. To reach **Hai Bar Nature Reserve,** drive for 35 kilometers (21.6 miles) when you will see the sign for **Hai Bar** and **Predator Center,** opposite the entrance to Kibbutz Samar. Drive in for 1½ kilometers (1 mile) to the entrance. Excellent 1½-hour guided tours depart from here on the hour, every day.

The **Hai Bar** consists of a large natural habitat for biblical-era animals and birds, and the Predator Center. The wildlife reserve was created not only as a refuge for animals that were almost extinct in the region but also as a breeding place; the animals are then set free to repopulate other parts of the Negev. Opened to the public in 1977, the 12-square-kilometer (4.6-square-mile) area re-creates the ancient savanna landscape, with lots of acacia trees. Roaming around are the striped-legged wild ass, onagers (another species of wild ass), addaxes, gazelles and ibexes, and white oryxes. Ostriches come prancing over, ready to stick their heads into the van windows.

The 20-square-kilometer (7.7-square-mile) **Predator Center** is where local birds and beasts of prey are raised and displayed. An audiovisual presentation introduces both history and wildlife. You observe the animals without disturbing them because the glass you stand behind is one-way and soundproof. As you watch the hyena feed, notice that his front legs are stronger than his rear legs, enabling him to carry his heavy prey a long distance. (The meat that is fed to the center's animals comes from hit-and-run victims found on roads, and sometimes animals that die of old age in local kibbutzim.) The birds of prey hang out in gigantic cages, where you'll see, among other species, the only lappet-faced vultures left in Israel, with average wingspans of about 10 feet. Hopes are high for some offspring from the resident couple. *Rte. 90, 35 km (21.6 mi) n. of Eilat, tel. 07/373057. Admission including tour: NIS 18 ($6) adults, NIS 12 ($4) children. Admission to Predator Center only: NIS 12 ($4) adults, NIS 6 ($2) children.*

Time Out Leave the Yotvata Visitors Center by turning left after the gas station. Follow the signs to the **Ye'elim Restaurant** (tel. 07/371870) and the **Ye'elim swimming pool** and **water slide** (tel. 07/373086). The facilities are just around the corner. The large, spic-and-span cafeteria-style restaurant serves hot meals (a variety of meats, rice, and vegetables), plus soup and salad plates. The nearby pool (with changing room and showers but no lockers) has children's play equipment nearby, palm trees around it, and a water slide; poolside service of light meals may be arranged. (At press time, entrance to the pool was occasionally free if you ordered a full meal at the restaurant.) Also on the premises is a rooftop coffee shop with an outdoor terrace that offers a great view of the region. *Admission (pool): NIS 12 ($4) adults, NIS 10 ($3.35) children. Restaurant open daily 7 AM–9 AM, 11 AM–4 PM, 7 PM–8:30 PM; pool open daily 10–7.*

Get back on Route 90 traveling south in the direction of Eilat. Take a right 15 kilometers (9 miles) down the road at a sign for Timna Park and Timna Lake. A 3-kilometer (2-mile) access road (which passes Kibbutz Elifaz) brings you to the entrance booth of **Timna Valley Park.** Ask for a map and explanatory pamphlet. A small building just inside offers a video detailing humanity's 6,000-year-old relationship with the Timna area and with its precious copper ore, mined well before Solomon's time by the Egyptians, while wall panels explain its fascinating geological makeup. There may be a map available to take with you, or consult the posted wall map with hiking trails for experienced hikers marked on it (the hikes are from three to seven hours long and are best done in the winter months). Stick to the trails without wandering off, watch out for old mineshafts, take lots of water, and let the person at the gate know that you are going and approximately when you'll be back. Because of the size of the park (60 square kilometers, or 23.2 square miles), it is recommended that you drive from site to site, each of which you will be able to explore on foot (many of the sites are several kilometers apart).

Before you is a spectacular collection of cliffs, canyons, and rock formations surrounded by the Timna Mountains, the highest of which is some 2,550 feet. Millions of years of erosion have sculpted shapes of amazing beauty such as the red-hued **Solomon's Pillars** (created by nature and *not* by the biblical king). Another unusual geological feature is the 20-foot-high, freestanding **Mushroom.**

People also left their mark on Timna. You can see an ancient smelting camp, with living quarters for the copper miners. Near the Pillars are the remains of a small **temple** built by the Egyptians who

worked the mines 3,400 years ago, during the Egyptian New Kingdom, which was also the time of Moses. The temple was dedicated to
the cow-eared goddess Hathor. Archaeologists discovered in the
temple a snake made of copper (*nehushtan* in Hebrew). According to
Numbers 21:4–9, Moses made a serpent in the wilderness to heal
people suffering from snake bite (the snake remains a symbol of
healing to this day). The snake at Timna bears a resemblance to a
votive copper snake made by the people who followed the Egyptians
in this area, the Midianites (Moses' father, Jethro, was a Midianite),
and that is now in the collection of the Eretz Israel Museum in Tel
Aviv (*see* Exploring Tel Aviv *in* Chapter 4). Near the temple a path
and stairway lead up to the observation platform overlooking the
valley. Above the platform is a rock-cut inscription; with the aid of a
sighting tube you can zero in on the hieroglyph, which shows Rame-
ses III offering a sacrifice to Hathor. *Rte. 90, tel. 07/356215. Admission: NIS 12 ($4) adults, NIS 6 ($2) children. Open Sat.–Thurs.
7:30–dusk, Fri. 7:30–3.*

Time Out Here's a surprise in this desert landscape: a lake (man-made), and on
its shore the roomy, air-conditioned **Timna Oasis Restaurant,** built
of local stone and using desert colors in its decor. This self-service
eatery has on its menu hot dishes such as chicken schnitzel, dairy
meals (cheeses and salads), sandwiches, hummus, and ice cream. Although swimming is not permitted, you can enjoy the lake from picnic tables in shaded areas on the shore. From January through
March, a 20-minute demonstration of ancient copper mining and
smelting techniques is held on Sunday, Monday, and Thursday at 11
and 1; the staff will explain in English at your request. *Tel. 07/
374937. Open daily 9–5.*

Return to Eilat via Route 90.

Two fine lookout points along the border road with Egypt are easily
reached from Eilat. Leave Eilat from the junction of Route 90 (the
Arava road) and Yotam Boulevard, traveling west on Yotam (which
will become Route 12), with the New Tourist Center on the left. The
huge tanks belong to the Eilat-Ashkelon oil pipeline. You are entering the **Eilat Mountains Nature Reserve,** with Nahal Shlomo, a dry
riverbed, to the left. After driving for 12 kilometers (7.4 miles), turn
㉕ left at the orange sign for **Mt. Yoash** and drive 1 kilometer (.6 mile),
bearing right up a rough, steep, and winding stone road. Park and
gather yourself for knockout views of the alternating light and dark
ridges of the Eilat Mountains; Eilat and Aqaba; the mountains of
Edom behind Aqaba; to the south, the start of the Saudi Arabian
coastline; the Nahal Geshron gorge emptying into the Red Sea at
Taba; to the west the plain of Moon Valley, and the mountains of
Sinai, in Egypt.

Back on Route 12 again and driving north, look for a green sign labeled **Netafim Crossing.** The Israeli flag flies over this checkpost,
where there are usually two soldiers. Nearby is a "base" with two
prefab buildings—one on either side of the fence—the Egyptian
flag flying from one, the Israeli flag from the other. The low fence is
the border between the two countries. From this vantage point,
looking toward Egypt, one often sees an Egyptian patrol, on foot or
sometimes riding camels.

Still on Route 12, 5 kilometers (3.1 miles) further along, you come
㉖ upon a green sign for **Mitzpe Har Hizkiyahu.** Drive up a paved road
for three minutes. There will be another Israeli flag flying, and
you'll be looking at Moon Valley, where the wadi (dry riverbed)

Nahal Paran starts. There are two lookouts here, each with an excellent etched plan. From one you can see a base for the MFO (Multinational Force of Observers), a UN-sponsored international organization formed to supervise the Egypt-Israel peace accords of 1978; and an Egyptian military post that guards the adjacent border between the two countries. From the other observation point you can see Aqaba in Jordan, the salt ponds of Eilat, Aqaba's airport, and the Gulf of Eilat.

You can absorb the dazzling panoramas you've just seen on a nature walk that takes no longer than an hour. It's not too difficult a hike, but it's not suitable for young children or older people. From the Har Hizkiyahu lookout, drive 4 kilometers (2.5 miles) down the road until you see the orange sign for the **Red Canyon** (Canyon Adom) to the right. Immediately turn left for another small sign saying the same thing. Drive 2 kilometers (1.2 miles) on a packed gravel road, park, lock the car, and start your walk through the Red Canyon. At the start, the ancient riverbed is made up of conglomerate (cemented silt and stones) that settled when the one-time river was much wider; you can see stones just sticking out, as though deliberately placed there. Walking along on the stony ground, you now find yourself in a narrow part of the canyon—2 yards wide—where the colors have abruptly changed to the reddish hue of the sandstone walls of the Red Canyon, a startling sight. Follow the wadi of the canyon, a small part of Nahal Shani. The trail is marked in green. When you meet the main course of Nahal Shani, follow the green trail to a descent with metal handrails; descend in a sitting position. You'll then climb down a ladder, and shortly afterward you'll come to the end of the narrow gorge. Here, on the right, is a sign reading TO THE CARPARK still on the green trail. You will be retracing your route, except now you will be *above* the canyon rather than inside it. Once on top, walk on the edge of the canyon (watch your footing and keep an eye on your children) until you reach the parking lot.

Back on Route 12 north and passing signs for Har Berech and Wadi Etek (12 kilometers, or 7.4 miles, after the Red Canyon), you'll drive by the **Ovda Valley** on the right, named for Operation Ovda (Hebrew for "fact"), the last military operation in the War of Independence, when the Israel Defense Forces took control of the southern Negev, including Eilat. Along the road you will notice many army camps. Twelve kilometers (7.4 miles) on is **Ovda Airport,** servicing charter flights from Europe. You then reach Shizafon Junction, the turnoff point at the end of Tour 1.

Tour 4: Excursion into the Sinai—St. Catherine's Monastery and Mt. Sinai

Sinai, the peninsula east of the Suez Canal and the Red Sea, was taken by Israel in the Six-Day War, and its return to Egypt was the major subject of negotiations between Egypt and Israel following President Sadat's historic visit to Jerusalem. Sinai has been an important part of Egypt for as long as the country has existed, creating as it did a natural barrier between Egypt and its traditional Asian enemies. Many legends of the ancient Egyptians are set in Sinai. Isis went here to search for the body of her murdered husband. The goddess Hathor, known to the pharaohs as "Our Lady of Sinai," sanctified the area. And, of course, the biblical references to Sinai are numerous. Pilgrims have long been drawn to the region because of St. Catherine's Monastery, situated deep in the mountain fastness of the Sinai Peninsula on the traditional site of the Burning Bush at the foot of Mt. Sinai.

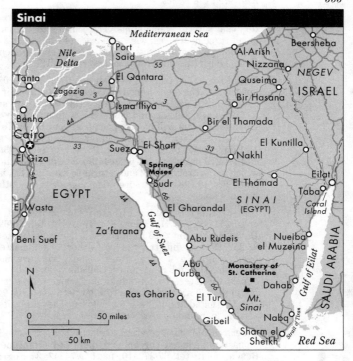

Sinai

Today the Sinai is something of a refuge for adventure travelers and those who want a truly unusual travel experience. They can ski on mountains of sand, dive in the fantastic waters along the Red Sea coast, trek across spectacular scenery of the interior, and camp under star-studded skies. With new hotels, resorts, and sporting facilities, travelers who want greater comfort can now find it. At the same time, a network of new roads has brought once-remote regions of the Sinai within reasonable range of the coast or the interior.

From Eilat there are various tours to the Sinai, ranging from a one-day guided bus trip to St. Catherine's Monastery (an overnight trip includes a pre-dawn ascent of Mt. Sinai) to a vacation at a luxury hotel in the resort of Sharm el Sheikh. The more adventurous traveler will want to consider participating in Jeep safaris, hiking trips, and camel treks. The extensive and unspoiled coral reefs off the Sinai attract divers from all over, and Israel is no exception; diving "safaris" are expertly run by Eilat dive centers (*see* Participant Sports *in* Sports and the Outdoors, *below*). Tours originating in Israel are run cooperatively with Egyptian travel agencies; your official guides will be Egyptian and will join the tour at the border, where you will change to an Egyptian vehicle. An Israeli guide accompanies you during the entire trip from Eilat.

Excursions The briefest foray into the Sinai is to St. Catherine's Monastery and *Day Trips* nearby Mt. Sinai, a highlight for many a traveler to this part of the world. The monastery may be visited from 9 AM to noon; it is closed Friday, Sunday, and on Greek Orthodox holidays. From Eilat, there are usually only bus tours to the monastery. Just across the border in Egypt, however, the Taba Hilton arranges Jeep tours for its guests. Below is a list of tour operators and travel agencies in Eilat that organize this day trip, which includes lunch at a restaurant near the monastery and several scenic stops. The journey to the monastery takes about three hours each way. The price of a bus tour is about NIS 115 ($38.35), plus border crossing fees. (Prices and frequency of the trips change during summertime, so be sure to call ahead.)

Egged Tours (Central Bus Station, tel. 07/373148 or 07/373149) runs bus trips to the monastery from October to May four times a week; from June to September, twice a week. There are several pick-up locations at hotels around Eilat; call to find the one closest to you. Upon return you will be dropped off at your hotel. To make a reservation from other major cities in Israel, you must do so in person at an Egged office (59 Ben Yehuda St., Tel Aviv, tel. 03/527–1212; 224 Jaffa Rd., Jerusalem, tel. 02/304422). The price for the one-day trip, which departs at 5:30 AM and returns to Eilat at 6 PM, is NIS 165 ($55) for adults, 10% less for children. The tour visits St. Catherine only and includes lunch.

United Tours (New Tourist Center, 2nd Floor, Eilat, tel. 07/371720 or 07/371740; 113 Hayarkon St., Tel Aviv, tel. 03/693–3410; King David Hotel Annex, 23 King David St., Jerusalem, tel. 02/252187 or 02/252189) runs bus trips to St. Catherine's Monastery from October through May several times a week; trips are more infrequent from June through September. Call one week in advance for specific departure dates. The one-day tour, which leaves from the Etzion Hotel at 5:30 AM and returns to Eilat between 6 and 7 PM, costs NIS 162 ($54) for adults, 10% less for children. The tour visits St. Catherine and the surrounding area and includes lunch.

Other reliable tour operators conducting day trips to St. Catherine's Monastery include **Geographical Tours Ltd.** (Neptune Hotel, North Beach, Eilat, tel. 07/373410, fax 059/74547; 37 Bograshov St., Tel Aviv, tel. 03/528–4113, fax 03/299905); **Johnny Desert Tours** (Shalom Center, opposite the airport, Eilat, tel. 07/372608, fax 07/372608); and **Neot Hakikar** (Khan Center, Eilat, tel. 07/330425 or 07/330426).

Longer Trips Trips into the Sinai that last two days or longer include overnight stays in facilities that range from hotels to spartan hostels, huts with thatched roofs, and tents (some of these may be on the beach). Be sure to bring extra-warm clothes in wintertime. For diving trips *see* Participant Sports *in* Sports and the Outdoors, *below*.

Both **Egged** and **United Tours** (*see above*) offer two-day bus trips to St. Catherine's Monastery, with a three-hour climb at dawn up Mt. Sinai. **Johnny Desert Tours** (*see above*) conducts a two-day trip that includes a visit to the monastery, a swim in the Red Sea if seasonable, a pre-dawn ascent of Mt. Sinai on foot, and a visit to the Jebalye Bedouin village. The price is NIS 357 ($119), including meals and lodging.

Geographical Tours Ltd. (*see above*) offers a two-day trip that stops at the monastery and includes camping on the coast at Dahab; the trip is NIS 357 ($119), including meals and tent or hut accommodations. A four-day trip, offered from June to September, goes to Sharm el Sheikh.

Neot Hakikar (*see above*) does two-day Sinai camel safaris, two-day trips to the monastery that include a sail to Coral Island for lunch, and trips of various lengths that include both Jeep and camel travel.

The Society for the Protection of Nature in Israel (3 Hashfela St., Tel Aviv, tel. 03/537–4425 or 03/375063; 13 Helene Hamalka St., Jerusalem, tel. 02/252357), with its expert nature guides, runs off-the-beaten-track hiking and combination camel/hiking and Jeep/water-sports trips. "Red Sea Adventure," which costs NIS 1,050 ($350), is conducted between April and October and lasts five days, with snorkeling at remote reefs, a yacht sail from Sharm, and camping out. The "Grand Sinai Tour" is a seven-day adventure of hiking, snorkeling, and camping on the beach.

Border Procedures The border between Israel and Egypt may be crossed 24 hours a day, every day, except on important Muslim and Jewish holidays. To cross into the Sinai—if you are staying in Egypt for less than 14 days—you will need: (1) a passport that must be valid for the subsequent three months (children also need passports; if a child is on a parent's passport, the parent cannot enter Egypt without the child, even for a one-day excursion); (2) a valid tourist visa to Israel, if Israel requires one from your country; and (3) money for border taxes. In the fall of 1994, the Israel exit tax (payable in shekels or U.S. dollars) was NIS 45 ($15), and Egyptian entry tax (payable in any foreign currency except shekels) was $6. You are exempted from the tax if you are going only to the Taba Hilton, which has personnel stationed at the crossing. These taxes are subject to change. The border crossing procedure consists largely of filling out forms. The crossing can take anywhere from five minutes to two hours.

You will need an Egyptian visa: (1) if you are going to stay in the Sinai longer than 14 days; (2) if you are going on to Cairo and/or other destinations in Egypt; (3) if you are South African, no matter how long your stay or what your destination is in Egypt. To obtain a visa, go to the Egyptian Consulate (68 Avrony St., Eilat 88000, tel. 07/ 376882; 54 Basle St., Tel Aviv 62744, tel. 03/546–4151) between the hours of 9 AM and 11 AM daily, except Friday, Saturday, and Egyptian holidays. Bring your passport, one passport-size photograph, and NIS 40 (shekels only). At press time visas were issued on the spot, but go to the consulate as far in advance as possible in case procedures change.

Emergencies **Warning:** There is no adequate medical care in the Sinai desert. You'd be wise to pack an emergency first-aid kit, particularly if you're going on a long trip. There are no drugstores, so take everything you need with you. The only telephone systems are in Dahab and Nueiba. Divers should know that there is no accessible pressure chamber; the nearest is in Eilat at Josephtal Hospital.

Currency The unit of currency is the Egyptian pound (L.E.). It is divided into 100 piasters. Pounds can be written in the following ways: L.E. 1 or L.E. 1.000 or 100 pt. (that is, 100 piasters). The following banknotes are in circulation: 1, 5, 10, 20, and 100 pounds (L.E.); 25, 50 piasters. Coins are 5, 10, and 20 piaster brass or silver metal coins. At press time (fall 1994), the exchange rate was L.E. 3.35 to the U.S. dollar, L.E. 2.70 per Canadian dollar, and L.E. 5.16 to the pound sterling.

Visitors to Egypt are obliged to convert currency at authorized exchange points only, found in all major hotels and banks. Foreign currency can be exchanged for Egyptian pounds either at the border exchange office (they accept foreign traveler's checks) or at the bank in the Taba Hilton Hotel (traveler's checks are *not* accepted). The bank here is usually open day and night, daily. Israeli shekels are accepted at the Bedouin stops that the bus tours make along the way from Eilat to the monastery.

Getting Around You may walk across the border to reach the Taba Hilton Hotel next door. A hotel representative has an office at the border crossing and will arrange transport to the hotel if you request it. However, if you're unencumbered by luggage, it's an easy walk to the hotel. Rental cars may not be driven across the border. You may travel across the border into Egypt in an Israeli vehicle as long as the registration is in the name of the driver.

A popular means of transportation to Nueiba, Dahab, and Sharm is by Bedouin taxis, which are found either just across the border (a five-minute walk) or at the Taba Hilton just beyond. It is advisable to use the buddy system, traveling at least two to a car; don't forget to negotiate the fare in advance (the taxis don't have meters), and bargain down if it sounds exorbitant. The drivers speak fair English. It's a one-hour drive to Nueiba, and one hour more to Dahab. The distance from Taba to Sharm is 225 kilometers (140 miles).

Rental cars (also with a driver) are available from Europcar at the Taba Hilton Hotel (tel. 07/379222; open daily 8–1 and 5–8), with offices in Sharm el Sheikh hotels as well. Remember that there are an inordinate number of accidents on Sinai roads, and that there is absolutely no emergency medical care available.

A public bus runs from Dahab to Taba once a day, between 10 AM and 10:30 AM. You catch a taxi at the Dahab beach to take you to the nearby Bedouin settlement from which the bus departs (the driver knows the location). From Dahab and Nueiba, Bedouin Jeep drivers will take you on desert trips and further south to Sharm.

Excursion to St. Catherine's Monastery and Mt. Sinai A bus tour may not sound madly adventurous, but it does offer the security of knowing that everything from start to finish is taken care of, plus affording you the freedom to do nothing but gaze at the wonderful scenery.

In Eilat, the tour bus starts the round of hotel pickups about 5:30 AM (you will be back at your hotel around 7 PM, depending on the duration of the return border crossing, which could take up to two hours. Keep in mind that there are no restaurants or rest rooms along the way, and remember to take drinking water and a sun hat with you. Modest clothing is required to visit the monastery grounds. If it's winter, dress warmly; the high altitude makes it very cold and windy. After the border procedure, and when you've gotten onto the Egyptian bus, your Egyptian guide will begin speaking in several languages (usually German, French, or Spanish), including, of course, English.

The first segment of the trip is the 60-kilometer (37.2-mile) ride to Nueiba on a long, lonely, and scenic road along the coast. The majestic landscape consists of sandstone mountains and rock formations of colorful beauty, dotted with acacia trees, with wooden fishing boats bobbing offshore.

Soon you will see **Coral Island,** with its ruined Crusader castle and Ottoman additions. Next will be the **Small Fiord,** which may not impress with its size but certainly does with its beauty. You might spot a local tribesman astride a camel; the el Tarabin tribe lives in Nueiba, the el Maazeni tribe in Nueiba port, while the Jabalige Bedouin reside around the monastery, at Mt. Sinai. All along the coast are compounds of buildings, some empty, each group proclaiming itself a hotel or resort. You will see near the tiny office of the Egyptian tourist police, 40 kilometers (24.8 miles) from Taba, a large tourist village of stone units. At **Nueiba,** besides the lovely beaches and reefs accessible from the shore, there is a car and passenger ferry that runs daily between Sinai and Aqaba.

The road curves and climbs as the bus turns away from Nueiba and starts to travel west through Wadi Sada at a height of 2,640 feet. You'll see belladonna (deadly nightshade) plants by the side of the road; they are used for eye makeup by Bedouin women. Often, Bedouin sit by the side of the road with beads and shells to sell to tourists. Soon an MFO post is seen, then one belonging to the Egyptian army. The road continues its curving way to Wadi Firan, whose bleak and stark scenery attracted early Christian monks in search of isolation and religious inspiration. About two hours after leaving Taba, you pass a soaring, four-pillar archway topped by a low dome. The **monument** was erected in 1980 at the behest of the late Egyptian president Anwar Sadat, who made peace with Israel in 1979. It is composed of elements representing Judaism, Islam, and Christianity, the three monotheistic religions of the area. The monument's Sinai setting is appropriate, for it is thought that Moses—who is revered by all these religions—received the Ten Commandments atop Mt. Sinai.

The sight of **St. Catherine's Monastery,** utterly isolated and set in a valley surrounded by great, craggy mountains, is extraordinary. One of the oldest and most sacred monasteries in the world, the present Greek Orthodox monastery was constructed as a walled fortress by the emperor Justinian in the 6th century. The monastery consists of several buildings, each built or expanded at different times over the centuries: a church; several chapels; a library (closed to the public) containing thousands of rare books, including a copy of the *Codex Sinaiticus* (the Greek translation of the Old Testament by Jewish scholars in 270 BC), one of 50 copies ordered by Constantine the Great in AD 331; the monks' living quarters; an ancient refectory; and a white mosque with minaret built in 1106 (not in use), all encircled by high stone walls. Originally named after Mary, mother of Jesus Christ, it was later named for the saint who was martyred in Alexandria in the 4th century (the round firework called a Catherine wheel is named for the form of torture to which she was submitted); the faithful believed that her bones were carried here by angels.

Once inside the arched entranceway, you may visit the **Church of the Transfiguration,** whose apse is decorated with an ancient mosaic of the Transfiguration of Jesus, with Moses and Elijah. Oil lamps and decorated eggs hang from the ceiling of the church, while on its walls, and those of the hallway and surrounding chapels, some of the monastery's unique collection of icons are to be seen. All around are old and treasured works of art—inscriptions, wall coverings, inlaid metal work, stone reliefs and other carvings, and chandeliers (some of these are lighted on religious holidays). The doors to the church itself date from the 6th century, and the outer doors were built in the 11th century; the bell tower, a gift from the Czar of Russia, was constructed in 1871.

Behind the church is the most sacred part of the monastery, the **Chapel of the Bush,** on a slightly lower level. (The chapel is not always open to the public.) Your guide will point out the bush (outside the chapel) where tradition has it that God spoke to Moses. The bush is of a type that is also found at En Avdat in the Negev (*see* Tour 1 *in* Exploring Eilat and the Negev, *above*). This chapel dates back to the 4th century and is the oldest part of the church. Its walls are covered with icons. The monastery itself has 2,000 icons, and you may see some more of them in the hall next to the library (the others are kept in secured rooms, closed to the public). One icon portrays the Sacrifice of Isaac and was painted in the 7th century.

Intriguing to everyone is the **Room of the Skulls,** where the bones of dead monks are kept, transferred from the cemetery after five years of interment because the plot is very small. The skulls are in neat rows and number 1,500.

About 12 Greek Orthodox monks currently live and work in the monastery. The Archbishop, who lives in Cairo, visits at Easter and on important holidays. Outside and around the monastery live the Bedouin of the Jabaliye tribe, who have long served the monks and work in the garden and orchard.

After the visit, your guide will lead you up a nearby mountainside from where you can scan the scene across and below—the picture-postcard monastery compound at the foot of the mountain, and, outside the walls, tourists from everywhere and Bedouin and their camels in brightly colored saddles and trappings.

On the return trip, there is a lunch stop at the nearby restaurant (the only one in the area), where you can sit out on a balcony to eat. On the way back to Eilat, if the Bedouin are there that day, a stop will be made at a nomadic encampment where these desert people make pita and brew tea over an open fire, yell at their camels to kneel so you can climb up for a photograph, and sell you primitive but pretty bead and shell decorations. The last leg of the journey is made in the reflective silence of this biblical landscape, the last light of day falling on the rugged mountains providing one beautiful vista after another.

Shopping

Eilat is a tax-free zone, meaning that all items are exempted from V.A.T. and/or purchase tax. You'll find that articles such as bathing suits and jewelry that are sold in a chain store are less expensive in the Eilat branch. Items that are price controlled, such as gas, beer, cigarettes, and alcohol, are also cheaper in Eilat.

Malls

Convenient and cool in summertime, **Beersheba's** mall, **Kanionit,** at the intersection of HaNesiim Boulevard and Eilat Street, has an underground parking garage that leads to one whole floor of fast-food places and, reached by glass elevator, another floor of Israeli-made American-style clothes and accessories (heavy on jeans and sunglasses), plus a drugstore. **Eilat** goes one better with two malls under one roof—the **Kanion Adom** and the **Shalom Plaza,** connected by a café-filled passage. The stores in both malls, located on HaTamarim Boulevard, are similar and, though you will find camera shops and music stores, souvenir and gift shops are notably absent.

Specialty Items

Bedouin Crafts   The Negev is home to the Bedouin, but today's Bedouin women may not be too thrilled about staying home all day to weave and embroider. That is why one must have the eye of an eagle and the patience of a saint to search through the bundles and stacks of rather ordinary stuff at the **Bedouin Market** in **Beersheba** to find articles made by Bedouin grandmothers. The Thursday-only market, which starts at daybreak and goes until early afternoon, is on the eastern side of the huge outdoor market site near the bridge; follow the signs at the intersection of HaNesiim and Tuviyahu streets. The best time to be there is at 6 AM, an hour or so later in winter. For sale (if you can find them) are wonderful embroidered dresses, yokes and side panels from dresses, woven camel bags, rugs, earrings, bracelets, amulets, nose rings, copperware, *finjans* (Bedouin coffee utensils), coin headbands (used as dowry gifts), beaded bags, decorative beads, and tassels.

An inexpensive necklace of simple beads and cloves, used to ward off evil spirits, also makes a rewarding purchase.

The older the better is the rule of thumb here: It's the old work that is hand-made. Always examine the stitchery on pieces of material in good condition. Be warned that prices are high for articles of good quality. Bargaining over prices is part of the Arab culture, but you need your wits about you to succeed—and a local to act as gladiator wouldn't hurt, either! You should end up paying 20%–30% less than the original asking price. If you are planning to take photographs at the market, bear in mind that Bedouin men usually don't mind being snapped, but the women do.

At the **Mazkarot Keidar** shop (tel. 07/460520), in the complex at **Tel Beer Sheva,** Dalia Schen has on hand a carefully selected and high-quality supply of old Bedouin weavings, rugs, embroideries, artifacts, and jewelry plus pillow covers, notepaper, and key rings that incorporate pieces of old embroidery and coins. Although normal business hours are 10–4, she will try to stay open later if you call ahead.

At the **Bedouin Heritage Center** (tel. 07/918263 or 07/918656) in **Rahat,** you can buy embroidered dresses, woven rugs, and bead and coin necklaces, among other items. At **Souk al Arab** (not always open), on the North Beach Promenade in **Eilat,** a small outdoor stall includes some Bedouin handiwork plus such items as sheepskin slippers, kohl (for eyeliner), and Hebron glass dishes.

Dead Sea Products Several companies manufacture excellent bath and beauty products made from Dead Sea mud, salts, and minerals; even the actual mud is sold in squishy, leak-proof packages. Ahava, DSD, and Jericho are three popular brands whose products are for sale at the **Kapulski Cafe** and hotel shops in **Ein Bokek,** and in drugstores and supermarkets throughout the area.

Food Every town has a supermarket, or "super" (as they are known in Hebrew), the source for many unusual gifts. Consider falafel and matzo-ball mixes; packages of Turkish coffee; halvah (a crushed sesame seed and honey confection); Israeli nuts and dried fruit; teas made from native herbs; locally made chocolate (such as the foil-wrapped "coins" for Hanukkah); and *za'atar*, the green spice mixture made with the marjoramlike hyssop that's sprinkled on hot rolls. An added touch is the package, written in Hebrew and English, and now sometimes in Russian.

Gifts and Souvenirs The **Amonit Gallery** at the visitors center in **Mitzpe Ramon** has a varied and rather unusual selection: jewelry and batiks made by the owner, water pipes, Bedouin drums, Armenian pottery, hats, T-shirts, and small, framed sketches of the area. *Open daily 9–5.*

Le Drugstore (tel. 07/366667) and **Boutique Carnaval** (tel. 07/334111), both on the North Beach Promenade facing the Lagoon in **Eilat,** are large stores housing miniboutiques with everything from fashion (sportswear, shoes, swimwear, handbags) to locally made gift items (for example, objects made of seashells) to baby clothes and newspapers. The **WIZO** counter in Boutique Carnaval sells modern and traditional handicrafts, and religious articles.

Alpaca wool is light as a feather, downy soft, and warm as toast, and comes in natural shades of white, gray, and brown. It's available in skeins at the **Alpaca Farm** (tel. 07/588047), 3 kilometers (1.9 miles) west of Mitzpe Ramon (follow signs from the gas station at the town entrance), and at the **Amonit Gallery** (*see above*).

Jewelry Israel has a good international reputation for very creative jewelry-making and, though the Negev is not a center for this particular craft, certain shops carry good examples of what Israel's jewelers are producing. Most of it is modern in style. Diamonds—stones cut and polished in Israel are an important export item—are used imaginatively; malachite, the indigenous "Eilat stone" in shades of turquoise-blue streaked with various shades of green (and mined near Eilat in ancient times), is also a good choice.

Danny's (tel. 07/584435) in the small shopping center (*kanionit*) in **Ein Bokek,** has a wide selection of gold, silver, diamond, and Eilat stone jewelry. There's a workshop on the premises. Hours are Sunday–Thursday 9–9, Friday 9–3. Branches of Danny's are located in the Moriah Gardens Dead Sea Hotel and the Moriah Plaza Dead Sea Hotel in Ein Bokek.

Bijouterie Maccabi (tel. 07/372519) at the end of the passage between Kanion Adom and Shalom Plaza in **Eilat,** has a good selection of gold and costume jewelry. It's open Sunday–Thursday 9–9, Friday 9–2. Also in Eilat, **Jerusalem of Gold,** at King's Wharf, and **H. Stern** (tel. 07/371706 or 07/372898) in the King Solomon, Neptune, and Sport hotels, and the Khan Tourist Center, are tried-and-true firms where customers can count on top quality. Also well-known in Eilat is **Malkit** (HaDekel neighborhood, tel. 07/373372), which houses a workshop where indigenous Eilat stones are cut and polished and featured in a whole line of in-house designed jewelry. Malkit is open Sunday–Thursday 8–7, Friday 8–1.

Sports and the Outdoors

In the interest of convenience, many of the activities listed below can be arranged through your hotel or a travel agency.

Participant Sports

Biking Mountain bikes are available from **Red Mountain Trekking** at the Red Sea Sports Club in Eilat (King's Wharf, tel. 07/379685; Coral Beach, tel. 07/376569), where the staff will help you plan a route to places such as the bird-watching area or the Dolphin Reef. The charge is NIS 39 ($13) for up to one day. **Desert Shade** (Khan Center, tel. 07/335377) leads two-hour mountain bike excursions into the desert, every morning at 8, with coffee-making along the way. The price is NIS 39 ($13). To spend a day on wheels in the Ramon Crater, contact **Beyond Biking** (tel. 07/587170); they also offer other bike trips in the Negev.

Bird-Watching The **International Birdwatching Center** (opposite the Central Bus Station, tel. 07/374276; open daily 9–1 and 5–7) conducts daily demonstrations (in the migrating seasons) at the Ringing Station, about a 20-minute walk from most hotels, as well as Jeep bird-watching tours (*see* Guided Tours *in* Essential Information, *above*).

Boating In Eilat, boating rentals and water-sports facilities are found either at the city's Marina or at Coral Beach, the area south of the port on the Eilat-Taba Road (Rte. 90). The **Red Sea Sports Club** in Eilat (tel. 07/379685), at King's Wharf on the Lagoon, rents paddleboats, canoes for two, and self-driven 6-horsepower minispeedboats. You can charter a 115-horsepower speedboat piloted by a waterski instructor; you can go skiing or parasailing (*see below*). Paddleboats cost NIS 39 ($13); canoe rentals are NIS 16.50 ($5.50). The minispeedboat is NIS 54 ($18) per half hour, and the speedboat is NIS 255 ($85) per hour.

Deep-Sea Fishing   **Red Sea Sports Club** in Eilat (King's Wharf, tel. 07/379685) takes six people out for six hours aboard a chartered motor yacht. The price for catching, say, a tuna or the rare barracuda, is NIS 1,140 ($380) for six people, including lunch and the use of fishing gear; each additional person pays NIS 36 ($12).

Health Clubs   Almost every hotel in the region, even the smallest, has a "health club," be it a rowing machine in a corner of a room, or a gym full of the latest hi-tech equipment, and some have trainers as well. Call the hotel of your choice for information on the use of these facilities by nonguests. In Eilat, for example, the state-of-the-art fitness center at the **Sport Hotel** is open to the public for NIS 15 ($5); use of both the sauna and hot tub costs NIS 8 ($2.70).

Hiking   Hiking amidst the splendid scenery of the Negev requires skill and know-how to negotiate the rugged heights and steep cliff faces. In the summer, the heat is extreme, and in winter the danger of floods is ever present. Hiking on your own is not recommended unless you are well versed in the art of reading topographical maps (*see below*). If you venture out without a guide, be sure to give the details— where you're headed, your route, and when you expect to be back— to someone remaining behind who's responsible. Always remember the water-drinking guidelines: 2 quarts a day in the winter and 1 quart per hour in the summer. Keep in mind that at least 60% of the Negev is occupied by the military; you are forbidden to enter these areas. (Firing zones and mines are marked in yellow on the SPNI map; *see below*.)

Of particular interest for Negev hikers is the Mamshit–Eilat stretch of the **Israel National Trail,** eventually to be 1,000 kilometers (625 miles) long (from Dan, near the Lebanese border, to Eilat in the south), which has recently been opened and is sometimes on the SPNI routes.

The SPNI, the National Parks Authority, and the Nature Reserves Authority have marked hiking trails in Negev parklands and reserves. The SPNI publishes topographical maps (in Hebrew) on which the trails are color-coded to match the markings on the trails themselves. The trail marks are three short stripes: white-color-white, the color being red, green, blue, or black. Yellow indicates military areas. The maps are available at SPNI headquarters in Tel Aviv and Jerusalem and at their field study centers located in Sde Boker (tel. 07/565016), Eilat (Rte. 90, Coral Beach, tel. 07/372021), Beersheba (corner of Meshachrerim St. and Tuviyahu Blvd., tel. 07/238527), Hazeva (Rte. 90, tel. 07/581546), and Har Hanegev (Mitzpe Ramon, tel. 07/588616).

The **Nature Reserves Authority** (78 Yirmiyahu St., Jerusalem 94467, tel. 02/387471) is expertly represented at the visitors centers at Mitzpe Ramon (tel. 07/588691) and at the Coral Reserve in Eilat (Rte. 90, tel. 07/373988). The rangers are knowledgeable and experienced, and will help you with hiking information.

Horseback Riding   The horsey set at the **Texas Ranch** in Coral Beach (Rte. 90, tel. 07/376663) takes riders on trails through Nahal Shlomo (Solomon's River) and into the desert; the sunset rides are popular. The charge is NIS 60 ($20); call ahead to reserve a horse. Children over 11 who know how to ride are welcome on the trails, and younger children may ride in the ring for NIS 28 ($9.35) for a half hour.

Parasailing   **Red Sea Sports Club** in Eilat (King's Wharf, tel. 07/379685) will give you a bird's-eye view of all those beach loafers for NIS 84 ($28) per 10 minutes.

Quad Runners   Otherwise known as fun buggies, these are one-person, all-terrain vehicles for the adventurous, if you are over 18 and have a driver's license (*see* Guided Tours, *above*).

Rappelling   **Jeep See** (Ma'ale Shacharut, Mobile Post Hevel Eilot, tel. 07/371961, fax 07/371332) takes novices, and the more experienced, on rappelling trips. Call in advance to book; the trips are done only by group. **Desert Shade** in Mitzpe Ramon (call the Tel Aviv office, tel. 03/575–6885) takes groups of eight enthusiasts on treks in the Negev canyons that include rappelling down spectacular cliffs. The trips last two days, and the cost is NIS 221 ($73.70) per person; a seven-day trip costs NIS 685 ($228.35) per person.

Scuba Diving   Eilat is the gateway to the Red Sea, one of the best diving locations in the world. Amazing coral formations, underwater tropical plantlife, and a dazzling array of fish live in waters that are warm year-round (22°C, or 72°F, in winter). The reefs are a mere 10 yards offshore, with an immediate deep drop, so a dive is just a walk away. After the Six-Day War in 1967, Israeli divers opened diving facilities along the Sinai coast south of Eilat and, although the Sinai was returned to Egypt more than a decade ago, Eilat's dive centers still run regular dive safaris over the border (*see below*). Divers should bring their license, insurance certification, and appropriate footwear—the seafloor is rough and so are the sea urchins.

Excellent facilities for divers in **Eilat** can be found at the **Marina** in North Beach and at **Coral Beach,** the area south of the port along the Eilat–Taba Road (Rte. 90). Introductory dives for the whole family, diving courses, instruction, and night dives are offered. Equipment can be rented or purchased. The first diving center established in the Middle East was **Aqua Sport International Red Sea Diving Center Ltd.** (tel. 07/334404, fax 07/333771), located at Coral Beach. Aqua Sport offers one-day dive cruises with lunch (NIS 92, or $30.70 per person) plus weekly diving safaris that run from one to five days. You'll take a Jeep to explore the most exotic dive locations, such as the famous Blue Hole and Ras-Nasrani at Sharm-el-Sheikh in the Sinai. Both the **Manta Diving Club,** located in Coral Beach at the Red Sea Sports Club Hotel (Rte. 90, tel. 07/376569), and **Lucky Divers** (tel. 07/335990), at the Galei Eilat Hotel, on the Promenade, operate top-quality, full-service dive centers. (The new Sonesta Suites Hotel is also building a center.)

You can dive with dolphins, with snorkel equipment (NIS 150, or $50 for a half hour)—and preserve the experience for posterity on video (extra charge)—at **Dolphin Reef,** Coral Beach (Eilat–Taba Rd., tel. 07/375935). A dive center is located here as well. Be sure to call ahead for a reservation.

The Coral Reserve at Coral Beach (Eilat–Taba Rd., tel. 07/376829) allows qualified divers, in limited numbers, to dive in a special area called the Japanese Gardens, so named for the way in which the closely packed, multicolored corals overlap each other. Call ahead to reserve a time slot. You can't rent equipment here, but wetsuits are available.

Families (children must be over 10) will have fun **snuba diving** at the **Coral Reserve** (tel. 07/372722). In this cross between snorkeling and diving, you breathe through tubes that are connected to tanks carried in a rubber boat on the surface. Instruction, a shallow-water practice session, and a guided underwater tour (a depth of up to 20 feet can be reached) may be arranged by calling ahead; the price is NIS 95 ($31.70) per person.

For certified divers who want to learn underwater photography, **Ed's Photo Shop** in Coral Beach (Caravan Hotel, tel. 07/373145 or 07/376471, fax 07/374083) offers a two-day underwater familiarization program for the novice (NIS 750, or $250), a three-day program (NIS 1,275, or $425), and a five-day advanced program, including two days spent at some of the world's best photography sites along the Sinai coast (NIS 2,550, or $850). Prices cover instruction only. Divers may rent cameras, and film is processed so you can see the results of one dive before you do another.

Snorkeling   The easiest way to observe the fabulous fish and corals at Coral Beach is to go snorkeling at the **Coral Reserve** (tel. 07/373988; open daily 8–5). Be sure to wear protective footgear. Hot showers, lockers, and a small restaurant are on the premises. You may rent a mask for NIS 4 ($1.35), a snorkel for NIS 3 ($1), and fins for NIS 6 ($2). Admission to the Coral Reserve is NIS 12 ($4) for adults and NIS 6 ($2) for children. The southern beaches, among them the **Dolphin Reef,** are also good for snorkeling. Most have shops where you can rent or buy equipment. **Know Before You Go** (tel. 07/376666 or 07/376732) is a program that offers a cruise from the Marina to the Underwater Observatory, a tour of the Observatory, and then a snorkeling session at Coral Beach, outside among the fish you've just seen from the inside. The price for this 4½ hour jaunt is NIS 118 ($39.35) for adults and NIS 102 ($34) for children.

Spas   The legendary Dead Sea, whose rare physical properties attracted glitterati such as King Herod and Cleopatra, retains its attractions for the modern-day visitor. Its salt content (six times denser than that of the Mediterranean), its high content of special minerals (bromine, for example, which has a calming effect on the nervous system), and its thick, black mud are sought after for their curative and beautifying properties.

Ein Bokek, at the southern tip of the Dead Sea, is the locale of sulphur-rich hot springs that have a temperature of 31°C (88°F). This water is used in combination with Dead Sea water and mud to treat rheumatic problems—and even tennis elbow or a sore back. The rays of the sun (it's sunny 320 days a year) seem to work wonders on psoriasis and other skin problems. (So positive are the results that German and Austrian health plans cover treatments at Ein Bokek.) Harmful rays are filtered out through the haze floating over the Dead Sea; this means you can tan more safely, too.

The spas, located at the lowest point on earth, in an area that looks quite as it did when Lot's wife was looking back, are not to be compared with the Baden-Badens of Europe in terms of grand, Old World elegance; no string quartets concertizing amid the potted palms. In fact, the sight of people's bodies smeared all over with thick black mud is quite the antithesis. However, the spa facilities are clean and modern, and the natural resources at the guests' disposal are not to be found anywhere else in the world.

The Dead Sea spas are at **Ein Gedi** (*see* Exploring Around Jerusalem *in* Chapter 3) and at **Ein Bokek** in the Negev. If you are at Ein Bokek just for the day, you may enjoy the state-of-the-art spa of **Hammei Zohar** (tel. 07/584161), near the Moriah Plaza Dead Sea Hotel. Open daily 7–3, Saturday 7–1:30, the sulphur pool costs NIS 28 ($9.35), the sulphur bath NIS 48 ($16), the mud treatment NIS 60 ($20), and the dry massage, for which reservations should be made, NIS 60

($20). Alternatively, you may reserve in advance a treatment at one of the following spa-hotels: the **Moriah Plaza Dead Sea** (tel. 07/584221), the **Nirvana** (tel. 07/584626), and the **Galei Zohar** (tel. 07/584311). Each of these spas, which are under medical supervision, has an indoor Dead Sea–water pool, sauna, and hot tub and offers a range of beauty and health treatments. Individual treatments cost about: NIS 85 ($28.35) for a half-hour massage, NIS 48 ($16) for a sulphur bath, NIS 66 ($22) for mud treatment. Hotel guests pay a lower fee. Other facilities and amenities often include fitness rooms, private solariums, and cosmeticians. Certain hotels offer one- or two-week spa-vacation packages. The other hotels in the area offer some of the above amenities (such as a hot tub or massage), and the **Ein Bokek Hotel** makes use of the facilities of the Hammei Zohar Spa, with a shuttle bus making regular trips from the hotel. Guests of the Ein Bokek Hotel and the Tsel Midbar enjoy a 10% discount at the Hammei Zohar Spa.

In Eilat you can now enjoy some of the properties of the Dead Sea (such as mud) at the state-of-the-art spas at the **Princess Hotel** (tel. 07/370195) and the **Royal Beach Hotel** (tel. 07/368888).

Swimming No hotel in the Negev is without a pool, and two is the general rule for each hotel in **Ein Bokek,** one outside and one inside. The indoor pools in Ein Bokek contain water from the Dead Sea (for dipping rather than swimming); the hotel pools in Eilat are filled with Red Sea water. In **Beersheba** you can cool off at the **Desert Inn** pools (Sderot Tuviyahu, tel. 07/424922). In **Eilat** the public pool (tel. 07/332662) is at Hativat HaNegev Street. **Arad's** public pool (tel. 07/957702) is open year-round. The municipal pool in **Mitzpe Ramon** is near the shopping center opposite the gas station at the entrance to town.

The centerpiece of the **Eshkol National Park** (tel. 07/985110), the second largest national park in Israel, is an 11,483-square-foot outdoor swimming pool, Israel's largest. The park is 30 kilometers (18.6 miles) west of Beersheba. The pool, which is open daily 8–4 from the beginning of May to the end of October, has a lifeguard, children's section, changing facilities (bring your own towel), rest rooms, and a snack bar. Picnic tables are spread out among the thousands of palm trees, olive trees, and acacia. In the winter, natural springs and catchment areas fill up, and the wildflowers that appear provide lovely scenery for nature walks. Admission to the park, which includes entry to the pool, is NIS 15 ($5) for adults, NIS 6 ($2) for children. The park is near the Gilat Junction on Route 241 (off Rte. 25 from Beersheba).

Tennis and Most hotel tennis courts are floodlighted. In **Eilat,** book ahead to
Squash play at the **municipal courts** on Yotam Street (tel. 07/367235, closed Sat.), where a small fee is charged, or wear your whites to the Sport Hotel's **Country Club** (North Beach, tel. 07/333333), where tennis courts are available in the morning for the hourly rate of NIS 10 ($3.35), and in the evening and on Saturday for NIS 16 ($5.35). Squash courts go for NIS 15 ($5) an hour. Prices include racquets.

Windsurfing At **Red Sea Sports Club** in Eilat (King's Wharf, tel. 07/379685)
and waterskiers can rent equipment (for both children and adults) and
Waterskiing fast boats. Waterskiing costs NIS 45 ($15) for 10 minutes and NIS 5.10 ($1.70) for each extra minute. Windsurfing and equipment rentals are to be found at **Aqua Sport International Red Sea Diving Center Ltd.** (tel. 07/334404, fax 07/333771), at Coral Beach, where one hour costs NIS 42 ($14).

Beaches

Although pebbles line much of the shore of the Dead Sea at **Ein Bokek,** the Tamar Local Council has beautified two public beaches by bringing in desert sand and planting palm trees. The beaches lie between the Nirvana and Moriah Plaza Dead Sea hotels and the cluster of hotels located about 2 kilometers (1.2 miles) north. These well-maintained sandy stretches are free to the public and usually fairly crowded. Facilities include changing rooms, rest rooms, chairs to rent, and a lifeguard on duty from mid-March through November. There is ample parking alongside the promenade. Although there are no food stands on the beaches, the two shopping areas house eating places, and there are two restaurants on the promenade: Kapulski's and Hordus (with changing rooms for their customers). Floating in the Dead Sea is the only water sport activity at Ein Bokek.

The beachfront of **Eilat**—the North Beach and the South Beach—is unusual in that there are no private beaches; rather, the municipality grants licenses to individuals to run certain sections. In turn, the beach managers must ensure the cleanliness of their section and provide open-air showers and deck chairs. The Tourist Patrol (tel. 07/ 367269) makes sure that standards are maintained and also can be called on for assistance. Most of the beaches are free and have a clublike atmosphere, with thatched-roof restaurant/pubs, sun beds, contemporary music, and dancing, by day and night. Young people tend to hang out at the southernmost beaches, while families favor the North Beach. The beach at the Neptune Hotel is particularly pleasant. Although topless bathing is against the law, you'll often find European women going topless, mostly on the southern beaches.

Eilat's **North Beach,** which runs northeast from the intersection of Durban and Arava streets to the Royal Beach Hotel, is always full of action—you can go paragliding or rent paddle boats or a "banana" (a plastic boat towed by a motor boat) and dancing goes on in the pubs until the wee hours. Sleeping on the beach is permitted (in sleeping bags, not tents).

The southern beaches (south of the port, along the Eilat–Taba Road) share the coast with the Underwater Observatory, Dolphin Reef, and the Coral Reserve (*see* Tour 3 *in* Exploring Eilat and the Negev, *above*). The last two have their own beaches. The beach just to the south of the Red Rock Hotel (at Yotam and Arava streets) has water-sports equipment for rent.

Dining and Lodging

Dining If the word "dining" conjures up tablecloths starched and draped, waiters gliding, and silver gleaming, and if that's what your heart is set on, you will find it in the luxury hotels of Eilat and Ein Bokek, and in Eilat's upscale restaurants. But for eating in the rest of the Negev, with the notable exception of the Mitzpe Ramon Inn, plan to dine in far humbler surroundings—typically a roadside diner—on meals that are apt to reflect the cook's ethnic background. You'll find, perhaps, Tunisian carrot salad or Moroccan *cigarim* (flaky pastry with a meat or potato filling) on the menu. Of course, there's the standard "Oriental" (Middle Eastern) fare: hummus, pita, grilled meat, sometimes cooked on skewers, french fries (known as chips), various chopped or shredded vegetable salads (*salatim*), strong coffee in small cups, and an unassuming dessert, maybe fruit or the infamous Israeli creme bavaria. Keep in mind that outside Eilat, Friday is an early closing day and that lunch may be over if you arrive much after 1:30.

Be sure to try the local Red Sea fish while you're in Eilat: *arichola*, which resembles swordfish; *shouri*, a fish with firm white flesh that is in season in July and August, and *jarabida*, which is caught in traps at a depth of 330 feet.

As for dress, the fancy restaurants in Eilat and the hotels of Ein Bokek are the place to wear your gladrags (for dinner) if you brought them, though a tie is never required for men at any restaurant. If people are dressed up anywhere, it will be at these restaurants (or nightclubs or discos). The ritziest attire you'll see in other restaurants and roadside diners is a clean T-shirt. It is always a good idea to make a reservation at Eilat restaurants (especially Friday and Saturday night); Eilat attracts many tourists and Eilatis like to eat out, too. Tourists also crowd the Ein Bokek hotel restaurants.

Eilat's less-expensive eating places are clustered in specific areas: the Tourist Center on Yotam Street, near Arava Road (everything from fish to pizza); HaTmarim Boulevard between the Central Bus Station and Hativat HaNegev Street (lots of falafel stands); and at Pninat Eilat on the North Beach Promenade (cafés, various eateries, and the famous Dr. Lek's ice cream shop), between the Marina and the King Solomon Hotel. Café society is a way of life in Eilat: Business deals are made over *cafe hafuch* (strong coffee with a frothy milk topping); friends meet weekly over the years at the same café; people come to see and be seen. Light food (such as grilled cheese sandwiches and salads) is served, as are rich cakes, ice cream, iced drinks, and various types of coffee. The cafés at Pninat Eilat (*see* Tour 3 *in* Exploring Eilat and the Negev, *above*) are popular for late-afternoon people watching, while Friday morning draws a local crowd at the two cafés on the main floor of the Kanion Adom shopping center, near the airport on HaTmarim Street.

Highly recommended restaurants are indicated by a star ★.

Category	Cost*
$$$$	over $35
$$$	$22–$35
$$	$12–$22
$	under $12

per person for three-course meal, excluding drinks and service charge

Lodging Keep in mind that prices rise during peak season and holidays in the resort areas of Eilat and Ein Bokek. High season is Hanukkah/Christmas, Passover/Easter, and the months of July and August, when Israelis come for vacation. At Ein Bokek (because of temperate climate), high season is mid-March to mid-June, and mid-September to the end of November. In Eilat, hotels are crowded with European tourists from October until April. Be sure to make advance reservations for even inexpensive rooms. Outdoor hotel pools are heated in the wintertime.

Youth hostels (a misnomer; all ages are accepted) are reviewed below because there is a dearth of accommodations in the desert and rooms are especially at a premium during high season. Hostels should also be reserved ahead. In Arad, a number of families offer rooms to rent in their homes for short stays. Some supply breakfast, and some rent out small, fully equipped apartments. The staff at the visitors center (Box 824, 80700, tel. 07/954409) has listings of local bed-and-breakfasts.

Highly recommended lodgings are indicated by a star ★.

Category	Eilat and Ein Bokek*	Other Areas*
$$$$	over $164	over $99
$$$	$125–$164	$70–$99
$$	$75–$125	$40–$70
$	under $75	under $40

*All prices are for a standard double room, including breakfast for two and excluding 15% service charge.

Arad
Dining

Steiner's. The oldest of Arad's eateries, the Steiner family's place is on Route 31 beside the Delek gas station at the entrance to town. Serving local faithfuls and travelers since 1965, Mr. Steiner, Sr., jokes that "people come to visit this restaurant as though it's a historical site." As you eavesdrop on the regulars, you can order soups, 12 selections of meat dishes, plus a variety of fish. House specialties are *cholent* (meat and bean stew that simmers overnight), served on winter Saturdays, plus Steiner-made apple strudel, known far and wide and served year-round. *Rte. 31, tel. 07/953328. Reservations not necessary. MC, V. $$.*

Lodging

Margoa. Well-known for its asthma-treatment clinic and packages, the seven-story Margoa carries on a 24-year tradition of pleasing its guests. The room furnishings are simple and subdued in color, and those on the south side have a desert view across to the mountains of Moab. The 48 newer rooms, laid out at ground level around the garden, have roomy, modern bathrooms, and are connected to the pool area by an open walkway. The outdoor terrace is particularly pleasant. In 1994 the lobby and dining room were renovated. *Moab St., Box 20, 80700, tel. 07/957014, fax 07/957778. 146 rooms with bath. Facilities: lobby bar, nightclub, massage, sauna, pool (closed in winter), asthma clinic. AE, MC, V. $$$*

Blau Weiss Youth Hostel. Conveniently near the center of town, the hostel is named for a Zionist German youth group founded in 1912 to foster a love of nature by Jewish youth. The plain, clean rooms (each with its own bathroom) hold six beds each. The dining hall provides meals at reasonable prices, and box lunches may be ordered. Arad's modern municipal swimming pool is a 10-minute walk away. Note that towels are not provided. *Atad St., tel. 07/957150. 34 rooms. Facilities: dining room, laundry service, basketball court. DC, MC, V. $*

Beersheba
Dining

Bulgarit. On the pedestrian mall in the Old City, Bulgarit (Bulgarian) has had the same owner, and been in the same location, for 45 years. The host sits with his cronies at a corner table under a fancy silver sconce, and reels off the selections from his "international" menu: roasted lamb and grilled meats, baked fish, moussaka, vegetables stuffed with meat and rice, *gvetch* (an assortment of vegetables cooked together), and chocolate mousse. If you speak Bulgarian, stories of pioneer days come with the meal. If you don't, you'll still get friendly, efficient service. If you're in Beersheba on a

Saturday, you're bound to eat here—it's the only restaurant in town that's open that day. *K.K. le Israel St., tel. 07/238504. Reservations not necessary. DC, MC, V. Closed Fri. $$*

Ilie's. Although it's nothing much to look at from the outside, this eatery does offer the novelty of choosing your own piece of meat and then watching its progress as it cooks over the charcoal grill. The emphasis at Ilie's, in the Old City, is definitely on meat, with various cuts of steak topping the menu. Fish (Beersheba's daily outdoor market is the source of fresh supplies) is also served, and homemade fruit salad makes for a light finale. *21 Herzl St., tel. 07/278685. Reservations not necessary. No credit cards. No dinner Fri. or lunch Sat. $$*

Pitput. An ivy-hung oasis in a desert city, this light-menu dairy restaurant has the look of a European confisserie, with its white lace-ironwork tables and chairs and pink flowered tablecloths. The management serves only homemade food—you can count on good cakes here. To start with, though, choose from omelets, pizza, spaghetti, vegetable pies, soups, great salads, cheese sandwiches made on seeded rolls called *begeles*, and artichokes with fried mushrooms. Watermelon with salty cheese and the homemade ice cream are good dessert alternatives. *122 Herzl St., tel. 07/237708. Reservations not necessary. DC, V. No lunch Sat. $$*

Lodging **The Desert Inn.** Established 30 years ago and run in a down-to-earth manner, the Desert Inn is a friendly, small-town property with a staff composed largely of Russian immigrants. Renovations (which should extend to the vaguely '60s decor) include a new sauna and hot tub. On the edge of Beersheba (when asking directions, use the Hebrew name for the hotel, Neot Midbar), the Desert Inn is set in a huge garden. Families will enjoy the well-equipped play area for children, deck games, ping-pong, and tennis and basketball courts. *Sderot Tuviyahu, 84100, tel. 07/424922 or 07/412772, fax 07/412772. 110 rooms with bath. Facilities: 3 restaurants, piano bar, 2 pools, children's pool, sauna, hot tub, tennis courts, basketball courts. AE, DC, MC, V. $$*

Eilat and **The Last Refuge.** Right beside a marina in Coral Beach, this fine sea-
Environs food and fish restaurant is held in high esteem by many Eilatis, so
Dining reservations are a must. It is a large restaurant (the narrow outdoor
★ terrace next to the water is especially romantic) with dark wooden paneling and predictable nautical motifs. Presented with a flourish are fresh-that-day Red Sea fish, such as arichola and drumfish; shrimp on skewers; calamari; creamed seafood served in a seashell; and fish, crab, or lobster soup. The salads are enormous. The staff is harried but very professional and eager to please. *Rte. 90, near overhead bridge, Coral Beach, tel. 07/373627. Reservations advised. AE, DC, MC, V. $$$$*

★ **Au Bistrot.** In an informal town, it's fun to sit at a white-napped table, with a small lamp gleaming on your gold-rimmed plate. Dinner will not disappoint: the extensive menu (a separate one for dessert) lists Emperor fillet with goose liver and morel sauce (the house specialty); frogs' legs in butter and wine; fresh shrimp in Grand Marnier sauce; lamb chops with tomato and basil sauce. The Morrocan chef studied in Belgium, and returns yearly to collect recipes and know-how. Top-of-the-line Israeli and French wines are available. *3 Elot St., tel. 07/374333, dinner only. Reservations required. AE, DC, MC, V. $$$*

★ **Eddie's Hideaway.** As the name implies, it's slightly hard to find, but the way affable Eddie prepares food makes it easy to understand why his place has a rave reputation for delicious steaks. Eddie's devotees also admire his shrimp and fish dishes. Starters such as Buffalo chicken wings and pâté maison may be followed by steak Eilat (with mushrooms, mustard, cream, brandy), Taipan shrimp, or Shanghai fish with hot soybean paste. For a finale, cram in lime divine or pecan pie. *68 Almogim St. (enter from Elot St.), tel. 07/ 371137, dinner only. Reservations required. AE, DC, MC, V. $$$*

El Gaucho. Just north of Eilat—a five-minute taxi ride gets you here—this restaurant has a larger-than-life figure of an Argentine cowboy outside. It's a good clue to what you'll be eating—beef. The owners are proud to relate that the meat is cut on the premises. The steaks, cooked on a charcoal grill that occupies one whole side of the restaurant, are served on thick wooden plates. Consistent with this two-fisted approach to eating, drinks are served in 14-inch-high glasses. The empañadas are homemade, and the chorizo sausage is excellent. *Arava Rd. (Rte. 90) at entrance to Eilat, tel. 07/331549. Reservations advised. AE, DC, MC, V. $$$*

★ **Tandoori.** Indian cuisine of the first order is graciously presented in a setting of embroidered and silk wall hangings, authentic Indian wooden carvings, and brass table appointments. The food is prepared to order, and the wait may be enjoyed while sipping an Indian drink of yogurt, fruit, and saffron, or one of the many cocktails on the menu. Specialties of the house are various succulent meats cooked in a tandoor (a charcoal-fired clay oven), curries, and a selection of vegetarian dishes. If you can't afford dinner here, try the moderately priced business lunch (NIS 32, or $10.70). Indian musicians and dancers perform at night. *King's Wharf at the Lagoon (below Lagoona Hotel), tel. 07/333879. Reservations advised. AE, DC, MC, V. $$$*

Mai Tai. This small and serene restaurant serves Thai food that is authentic; it's not just another place serving up "Israelized" Oriental food. Thai cuisine is popular in Eilat, and Mai Tai is often singled out by selective diners. The lampshades are Thai food baskets and rice-paper umbrellas. The fixed menu of soup, eggroll, main course, rice, tea, and dessert comes to a moderate NIS 40 ($13.35); there is an à la carte menu as well. *Yotam St., tel. 07/372517. Reservations advised. DC, MC, V. $$*

Misedet HaKerem. Not far from the Central Bus Station sits an old square house with a sign outside in Hebrew that means "vineyard restaurant." Family-run for 18 years, the restaurant, with its low corrugated ceiling and fluorescent lights, has walls plastered with family snapshots, groups of smiling men, and huge portraits of two sisters in traditional Yemenite wedding headdress (one of these beauties may well be your waitress). Now for the tasty food: thick, spongy Yemenite pita with za'atar baked inside, vegetable soup, hummus, and their specialty, meat done on the grill (chicken livers and hearts are good here). Try the coffee with *hawaj* (a spice mixture); no desserts are served. *HaTmarim St., tel. 07/374577. Reservations not necessary. No credit cards. No dinner Fri. or lunch Sat. $$*

Papa Michel. Papa's Moroccan restaurant, in the center of town beside the Etzion Hotel, is festooned with brightly colored wall murals in a naïf style, depicting happy scenes such as a wedding and *Shabbat Shalom* (welcoming the Sabbath). A 4-foot-high brass coffee pot stands at the entrance, and after-dinner coffee is served in traditional brass-pot style. Moroccan specialties here are couscous, stuffed pigeon, stuffed vegetables, spicy sausage, homemade baklava (honey-soaked layered pistachio pastry), and other typical Moroccan pastries. Steak and fish are served as well. *Opposite Central Bus Station, Hatamarim St., tel. 07/374131 (ask for restaurant). Reservations advised. DC, MC, V. No dinner Fri. or lunch Sat. $$*

Lodging
★ **Club-In Villa Resort.** Currently undergoing renovation, this hotel is a two-level arrangement of connecting, self-contained holiday "villas," located opposite the Coral Beach Reserve on the Eilat–Taba road. The brightly colored units all have two somewhat spartan bedrooms, a fully equipped kitchenette (there's a minimarket on the premises), balcony, and living room with TV. With the Eilat mountains as a backdrop, some of the units face a lovely outdoor swimming pool, with the children's pool nearby. (Those who want to avoid facing the boisterous pool area can opt for rooms in the rear, facing the mountains.) There is also a dining room for those who choose not to prepare their own meals. *Rte. 90, Coral Beach, Box 1505, 88000, tel. 07/334555, fax 07/334519. 160 villa units with bath. Facilities: restaurant, bar, disco, fitness room, minimarket, launderette, free childcare, free poolside and indoor entertainment, floodlighted tennis courts. AE, DC, MC, V. $$$$*

King Solomon's Palace. The entire royal court could have been accommodated in this member of the Isrotel chain, one of the five grouped around the Lagoon. It's utilitarian and huge, with an expanse of lobby floor opening onto a stuffed-sofa lobby in quiet shades. Attention is paid to the guest's every need, and everything runs like clockwork. Floor by floor renovations are in progress, and the health club has been completely refurbished. The dining room is big enough to have three minirestaurants (Continental, Chinese, and Italian), while breakfast is a vast buffet with pancakes flipped and croissants baked on the spot. The palm-fringed pool overlooks the Lagoon. Guests occupying the garden terrace suites get their own hot tubs. *The Promenade, North Beach, 88000, tel. 07/334301, fax 07/334189. 420 rooms with bath. Facilities: 3 restaurants, piano bar, shops, disco, fitness center, health club, sauna, hot tub, massage, pool, 2 floodlighted tennis courts. AE, DC, MC, V. $$$$*

★ **Moriah Plaza.** Conveniently near the Marina on the Promenade facing the beach, this sophisticated six-floor hotel was completely redone in 1992, when a new wing was added. The eye-catching lobby has a slanted glass roof, huge potted ferns, and statues in niches along the wall that separates it from the dining room. Guest rooms are nicely designed with color-stained pieces complementing the blond-wood furniture. Two pool areas assure guests of relaxation and enjoyment. *Promenade, Box 135, Eilat 88000, tel. 07/361111, fax 07/334158. 330 rooms with bath. Facilities: 2 restaurants, pub, jewelry shops, art gallery, beauty salon, health club, 2 pools, children's pool. AE, DC, MC, V. $$$$*

Neptune. On the Promenade near the Marina, this modern and airy hotel possesses a rare elegance, further enhanced by its refurbishment in 1994. The lobby is especially attractive. Overlooking the pool, with views of the Marina or the sea, guest rooms are decorated in blue, green, and rose, complemented by strikingly designed furniture. The area around the pool is particularly appealing, with flower beds, lots of palm trees, and potted plants. Adjoining the hotel and fronting the beach is a secluded grassy area with thatched umbrellas and a small restaurant. *The Promenade, North Beach, Box 259, 88000, tel. 07/334333, fax 07/333767. 279 rooms with bath. Facilities: 3 restaurants, snack bar, nightclub/disco, shops, including English-language bookstore, beauty salon, fitness center, hot tub, massage, pool. AE, DC, MC, V. $$$$*

Orchid. Here is a genuine Thai resort-village perched amongst greenery and palm trees on the craggy mountainside. Individual cottages are connected by steep, winding pathways; guests are driven around in a special vehicle. The exotically styled cottages have one bedroom downstairs, a sleeping loft for two under the pointed roof, plus a balcony. Every detail, from teak-wood furniture and ceiling beams to decorative statuary was brought from Thailand. The restaurant overlooking the pool attracts diners who seek authenticity in ambience and delicious Thai food. *Eilat–Taba Rd. Box 994, 88000, tel. 07/360360, fax 07/375323. 135 units with bath. Facilities: restaurant, piano bar, pub, pool, beach. AE, DC, MC, V. $$$$*

★ **Princess.** The last hotel in Israel (five minutes to the Egyptian border), the Princess is also the last word in sumptuous accommodation. The lobby faces a two-story-high sheer rock cliff seen through a glass wall. The public rooms are dazzling white with gold trim; guest rooms include theme suites, such as Chinese, on every floor. A variety of dining venues, decorated to reflect the style of food, serve Creole and Cajun, Japanese, Cantonese, and French. The pool area is a country club in itself, with squiggly shaped pools connected by bridges and a floating bars. The Spa is the ultimate in body care, with treatments of Dead Sea salts and mineral baths, Dead Sea mud, and Beizem body-cleansing done with eucalyptus twigs. The Princess is a self-contained world; its services include a shuttle into town and an El Al office on the premises. *Eilat–Taba Rd., Box 2323, 88000, tel. 07/365555, fax 07/376333. 418 rooms with bath. Facilities: 4 restaurants, piano bar, pub, disco, jewelry and clothing stores, beauty salon, spa, health club, 2 pools. AE, DC, MC, V. $$$$*

Riviera Apartment Hotel. An apartment hotel could well have an institutional air about it, but not so the Riviera. Built in 1989, it has a lively atmosphere with a fresh white and turquoise color scheme to match. The premium units, each with small garden and patio, are set back from the pool. All the units (sleeping two, four, and six people) have a fully equipped kitchenette, and many have living rooms. There is a minimarket, as well as a dining room that serves breakfast and lunch. Young children can be cared for and entertained in the nursery, and in their own pool. The beach is 165 yards away. The myriad facilities of the Country Club (at the nearby Sport Hotel) are offered to guests of the Riviera at a reduced rate. *North Beach, Box 1738, tel. 07/333944, fax 07/333939. 172 units with bath. Facilities: dining room (no dinner), snack bar, childcare, pool, children's pool. AE, DC, MC, V. $$$$*

Sport Hotel. The name says it all—a hotel designed with sports-loving guests in mind. Another Isrotel hotel, the Sport offers a full range of facilities for the active guest (albeit for a small fee), including tennis, squash, racquetball, and basketball courts (the last two in the adjoining Country Club); a fitness center with the latest equipment and a trainer, plus a sauna, hot tub, and a brother-sister masseur duo from Chile. There are two lobbies: One offers the standard nightly entertainment, and the other, the novelty of peace and quiet. Nothing jars in this hotel; the peach and aqua color scheme is carried throughout the halls and into the guest rooms. In the newer wing all the rooms look out on the Gulf of Eilat. *North Beach, 88000, tel. reservations 07/379141, fax 07/332766. 327 rooms with bath. Facilities: 2 restaurants, lobby bar, disco, shops, fitness center, sauna, hot tub, massage, pools, tennis, squash, racquetball, and basketball courts. AE, DC, MC, V. $$$$*

Holiday Inn Crowne Plaza. "Four stars with five-star service" is the motto of this nine-floor hotel, opened in 1994. Guests at the Holiday Inn can depend on competence at this beautifully designed hotel. Colors schemes in the public rooms and at the pool are cool white and beige and the entrance features a fountain under a glass domed ceiling. Beige wood furniture with coral, pink, and light blue bedspreads on queen- and king-size beds and sofa beds make for tasteful rooms, each with its own air-conditioner. The whole fifth floor is designated for nonsmokers. *On the Lagoon, North Beach, tel. 07/*

367777, fax 07/330821. 226 rooms with bath. Facilities: pool, health club, outdoor Jacuzzi. AE, DC, MC, V. $$$

Red Rock. One of Eilat's first hotels, built 25 years ago, this modest accommodation was completely renovated in 1991. Close to both the city and the beach, the Red Rock combines good value with an informal atmosphere, and although it doesn't have glamorous amenities such as a tennis court or health club, the pool is just next to the beach (where there are waterskiing, paragliding, kayaking, and pedalboat and motor-boat rentals), and the dining room looks straight out onto the water. *Near New Tourist Center, Box 306, 88102, tel. 07/ 373171, fax 07/371530. 110 rooms with bath. Facilities: dining room, nightclub, pool. AE, DC, MC, V. $$$*

★ **Red Sea Sports Club Hotel.** Attention divers! Billed as the first hotel in Israel for divers and adventurers, this white three-story hostelry near the Coral Reserve houses the Manta Club, a fully equipped diving center with five-star PADI training center, qualified diving instructors, air-conditioned classrooms, personal lockers, diving equipment for sale, rinsing pools, and sauna. Diving trips to the Sinai can be arranged. The rooms, each with a balcony, have modern furnishings and are decorated in sea colors of green and bright blue. The beach is right across the street, and a small swimming pool is on the premises. The fun-loving atmosphere extends into the night, with dancing in the courtyard under the stars. Ed's Photo Shop (*see* Participant Sports *in* Sports and the Outdoors, *above*) is on the same grounds. This hotel is a good value for its price category. *Rte. 90 (Eilat–Taba Rd.), Box 390, 88000, tel. 07/376569, reservations 07/ 373145, fax 07/374083. 86 rooms with bath. Facilities: restaurant, cafeteria, bar, diving-gear shop, diving center, sauna, pool. DC, MC, V. $$$*

★ **Taba Hilton.** Just over the Egyptian border in the Sinai, 11 kilometers (6.8 miles) south of Eilat, this luxury resort developed by Israelis is now part of the Hilton International chain. If you want to get away from the noise and crowds of Eilat, you'll appreciate the isolation. The huge, sparkling lobby, wide range of facilities, quality of service, and excellent cuisine put the Taba Hilton on a par with any of the top Israeli hotels. At press time the hot news was that a gambling casino would be opened on the premises by spring 1995. Most of the rooms have balconies overlooking the pool or the sea. The staff—all male—is very solicitous. The large, free-form saltwater pool, with beautiful landscaping, does have one drawback: no lifeguard. The hotel beach (also unguarded) has two sections: one has sunshades, a snack bar, and snorkeling, diving equipment, and waterski rentals; the other part, called Nelson's Village, is a quiet, palm-shaded stretch with a restaurant serving light lunches and barbecue at night. *Taba Beach, South Sinai, Egypt, tel. 02/763677; in Israel, 07/379222; in Egypt, fax 02/747044; in Israel, fax 07/ 379660. 326 rooms with bath. Facilities: 5 restaurants, 3 bars, nightclub, shops, health club, Europcar rental office, pool, private beach, water-sports and diving centers, tennis courts, waterskiing, yacht cruises. AE, DC, MC, V. $$$*

Edomit. One of the few hotels right in the city, the eight-story-high Edomit is uphill from the New Tourist Center. Owned by one of Eilat's best-known hoteliers, this small hotel attracts a loyal following. A cozy lobby, with a bar in the corner, gives way to well-kept rooms in a soft, dark-blue color scheme. The green, yellow, and white color scheme of the dining room gives it a fresh and charming look. Edomit's vegetarian dinner, which features the creative use of dairy products in a sumptuous multicourse meal, is highly praised. Lunch is not served in the hotel, but arrangements can be made for a discounted meal at a nearby restaurant. The beach is a five-minute walk away. At the low end of its price category, the Edomit is a good value. *Near New Tourist Center, Yotam St. Box 425, 88000, tel. 07/ 379511, fax 07/379738. 85 rooms with bath. Facilities: dining room, bar, pool. AE, MC, V. $$*

Kibbutz Elot. In Eilat's backyard (5 kilometers, or 3.1 miles, to the north), on a hill overlooking the city and the Edom Mountains in Jordan, the kibbutz offers accommodations in air-conditioned, renovated units that were the original homes of the kibbutz members. Each unit has wall-to-wall carpeting, two bedrooms, an equipped kitchen, dining area, TV, telephone, and outdoor sitting area. Guests may join the kibbutzniks for a meal in the dining room, or a gathering at the "club" with coffee, cake, and explanations of communal life. *Rte. 90, tel. 07/358760, fax 07/358777. 19 units with bath. Facilities: dining room, pool, tennis court. DC, MC, V. $$*

Reef. This modest beachfront hotel is appealing to those who seek a quieter location away from the main cluster of hotels. Appealing too is the direct access to the beach from the wooden sundeck and pool area. Water sports are but a splash away. The newly modernized rooms in the four-floor hotel have balconies facing the sea; although, some guest rooms are at pool level. *Eilat–Taba Rd., Box 3367, 88100, tel. 07/364444, fax 07/364499. 80 rooms with bath. Facilities: lobby piano-bar. AE, DC, MC, V. $$*

Ye'elim Desert Holiday Village. A half-hour drive north of Eilat (close to Timna Valley Park and Hai Bar) and named for the mountain goats that inhabit the area, Ye'elim is set in a man-made oasis of tall, straight palm trees and fig, white broom, and acacia trees. With its recreational facilities, the holiday village, run by local Kibbutz Grofit, is ideal for families. Relief from the heat is provided by the large, modern swimming pool (the only one in the Arava Valley), complete with a water slide. Poolside service is provided by a restaurant on the village grounds, where there's a playground with Tarzan-style equipment. For lighter meals and snacks, there's a coffee shop with a terrace. Accommodation is in 25 wood chalets, each sleeping four and with a kitchenette. The chalets have a small porch where you can eat (provisions can be purchased from the minimarket on premises). *Rte. 90, 40 km (25 mi) n. of Eilat, Mobile Post Eilot 88825, tel. 07/358816 or 07/358722, fax 07/358846. 25 units with bath. Facilities: restaurant, coffee shop, pool, playground. MC, V. $$*

Eilat Youth Hostel & Guest House. The word "hostel" takes on a new meaning here, where each of the 80 air-conditioned rooms has its own bathroom. The rooms, with two–six beds, are simply furnished with light wood pieces. The hostel, a 10-minute walk from the Central Bus Station and right across the highway from the beach at the Red Rock Hotel, is a popular place, so make reservations well ahead of time. Three meals a day are provided in the renovated dining room; snacks are also available. Bed linens are provided, but towels are not. *HaArava Rd., Box 152, 88101, tel. 07/370088, fax 07/ 375835. 80 rooms with bath. Facilities: dining room, disco, coin-operated washing machines. AE, DC, MC, V. $*

Moon Valley. One-floor units, each painted a different pastel color, and all beside the pool, provide families with an easygoing vacation locale. Furnishings are in rose and turquoise, each unit sleeps three, and has a kitchenette and air-conditioner. The 20-year old hotel has just been completely redone with the public rooms in white and turquoise and the dining room contains a large finch-filled aviary. *North Beach, Box 1135, 88100, tel. 07/333888, fax 07/334110. 182 rooms with bath. Facilities: piano bar, pool, AE, DC, MC, V. $*

Ein Bokek   **Kapulski's.** In the center of the hotel area, it's attached to a Ben & *Dining*   Jerry's ice cream place. This is an airy, cafeteria-style restaurant with big windows and banana trees outside. Though best known for their luscious cakes, the dairy dishes here are very good and include fresh salads, blintzes, pizza, St. Peter's fish, and sandwiches, plus beer and wine. A service to customers are the free changing rooms for bathers. *Beside the Kanionit shopping center, tel. 07/584382. Reservations not necessary. $$*

Hordus. Named for Herod the Great—Masada, which he built in 36 BC, is just up the road—the not quite so awesome Hordus is a sprawling cafeteria-style restaurant offering a salad bar, sandwiches, fresh fruit (including local dates), baklava, and beer, until 8 in the evening. *Opposite Galei Zohar Hotel, Rte. 90, tel. 07/584636. Reservations not necessary. DC, MC, V. $*

Lodging **Moriah Plaza Dead Sea.** A venerable beachside hotel in the Moriah
★ chain, this one keeps up with the times by constant refurbishing, and also maintains a modern spa. The always busy but cozy lobby overlooks the outdoor pool, and there is a game room with card tables. Each room, decorated in pastel colors, has a balcony that has been thoughtfully walled for privacy, and each affords a lovely view of the pool area and the waters of the lowest point on earth. *Mobile Post Dead Sea, 86910, tel. 07/584221, fax 07/584238. 225 rooms with bath. Facilities: 2 restaurants, pub, snack bar, gift shop, beauty salon, indoor Dead Sea–water pool, freshwater pool, mineral pools, sauna, hot tub, fitness center, massage, mud packs, private beach, tennis court, basketball court. AE, DC, MC, V. $$$$*

★ **Nirvana Resort and Spa.** The entrance is through a gleaming marble lobby ("welcome" in many languages is sculpted in a relief on the main wall) lit with table lamps and discreet ceiling lights, and a two-story black wall inlaid with swirls of tiny stars. The huge outdoor pool is dolphin-shaped; the private beach is part of the Nirvana's own lagoon. You'll savor your morning coffee on the outdoor terrace of the dining room. The in-house spa's facilities, such as sulphur pools and a saltwater pool, are at guests' disposal for a small fee. The Nirvana also offers a complete health and fitness program that includes antistress strategies and beauty treatments with Ahava Dead Sea products. *Mobile Post Dead Sea, 84960, tel. 07/584614, fax 07/584345. 207 rooms with bath. Facilities: 3 restaurants, bar, disco, beauty salon, shops, car-rental agency, synagogue, indoor saltwater pool, mineral pools, sauna, hot tub, freshwater pool, private beach. AE, DC, MC, V. $$$$*

Carlton Galei Zohar. Established in 1971, when the vision of spas in the desert was considered a mirage, the two-building hotel has a recently built seven-story wing housing a state-of-the-art spa (guests pay a small fee for its use) and 100 rooms, each one equipped with a wall kitchenette. The spa offers medical treatments and beauty treatments. *Mobile Post Dead Sea, 86930, tel. 07/584311, 07/584422, fax 07/584503. 250 rooms with bath. Facilities: restaurant, bar, nightclub, travel agent, childcare, shop, synagogue, Dead Sea–water indoor pool, sauna, hot tub, fitness center. AE, DC, MC, V. $$$*

The Hod. There's a lot of traffic in the lobby, but the feeling at the six-year-old Hod is one of homey comfort in a friendly atmosphere. The guest room decor is modern, with lots of pale wood. A walkway leads to the hotel's private beach, where the typical pebbled shore of the Dead Sea has been covered over with fine sand. Spa facilities as well as the Stauffer diet and relaxation system are available. The dining room looks out at the Dead Sea. *Mobile Post Dead Sea, 86930, tel. 07/584644, fax 07/584606. 205 rooms with bath. Facilities: dairy restaurant, disco, synagogue, ping-pong, billiards, indoor Dead Sea–water pool, fitness room, sauna, hot mud treatment, massage, outdoor pool, private beach. AE, DC, MC, V. $$$*

Paradise. A Sodom apple tree (the site of the wicked biblical town is nearby) grows on either side of the entrance to this plain but pleasing hotel, one of the oldest in the area and refurbished a few years ago. Desert trees surround a lush central lawn, with the pool off to one side. The decor inside is mainly white, setting off the very attractive photographs and posters (unusual for an Israeli hotel) in the rooms and hallways. Guests enjoy special rates at the Hammei Zohar Spa, which they can reach by a shuttle bus from the hotel. *Mobile Post Dead Sea, 86930, tel. 057/84331, 057/84332, 057/84333, or 057/84334, fax 057/584162. 96 rooms with bath. Facilities: restaurant, nightclub, shop, beauty salon, pool, tennis courts. AE, DC, MC, V. $$$*

Mitzpe Ramon
Dining
★

Misedet Hanna. A cheerful roadside diner atmosphere prevails in this gas station restaurant opposite the visitors center, where the chairs and tables are dark red, and fluorescent lighting casts its dubious spell. The owner, who knows everyone here and talks warmly to all of them at the same time, says the food comes from "mother's kitchen." She's doing a very fine job, and so is the price-setter; a hearty breakfast of vegetable salad, *havita* (a crisp plain omelet), cheese, bread, jam, and coffee costs only NIS 15 ($5). Breakfast here starts at 5:30 AM. Lunch offerings include soups, salads (a round tray with six small fresh vegetable dishes), oven-broiled ribs, schnitzel, chicken, fish, spaghetti, rice, and fries. Soup, salad, and an entrée cost NIS 27 ($9). *Paz gas station, tel. 07/588158. No reservations necessary. AE, DC, MC, V. No dinner Fri. or Sat; no lunch Sat. $$*

Tsukit. If you're lucky enough to get a window table, it might not matter what there is to eat: You'll be sitting on the edge of the Ramon crater, and the scenery will outshine whatever's on your plate. Fortunately at Tsukit (Little Cliff), where you can choose waiter or self-service, the food is up to the challenge. Choose from beef, chicken, schnitzel, pasta, hummus, or stuffed vegetables. *Beside Mitzpe Ramon Visitors Center, tel. 07/586079. No reservations necessary. DC, MC, V. Closes at 4:30. $$*

Lodging
★

The Ramon Inn. No hardship is involved in staying at this desert hotel. On the contrary—the Ramon Inn offers modern, comfortable accommodations right in the middle of the Negev's natural wonders. Opened in 1993, the four-story building (no elevator) is set on the cliff of the Ramon crater. Stay in a pastel-and-white-hued studio apartment for two—or a two- or three-room apartment (suitable for up to four or six people), the latter equipped with outfitted kitchenettes. The lobby has an open fireplace around which entertainment takes place on chilly winter nights. Ask at the desk about Jeep or camel trips. *Mitzpe Ramon, Box 318, 80600, tel. 07/588822, fax 07/588151. 96 rooms with bath. Facilities: lobby bar, minimarket, coin-operated laundromat. $$*

"Succah in the Desert." Deep in the Negev, Rachel Bat Adam, Ph.D., has created an encampment of succot, the portable dwellings lived in by the Children of Israel when they wandered in this very same desert. You arrive in the middle of nowhere, and there, up on the rocky hillside, are six small, isolated dwellings, each made of stone, with a palm-frond roof. There is a central succah where guests can prepare their own meals and congregate. Succah in the Desert offers an appealing combination: the starkness and purity of the desert with some modern amenities. Each succah has a carpet on the earthen floor, and the bed is a mattress with cozy blankets. There is a gas hot plate for cooking, a solar-powered heater, and a clay water jar and copper bowls for ablutions. Guests use the great outdoors for anything else. *On rd. to Alpaca Farm, 7 km (4.5 mi) w.*

of Mitzpe Ramon, Box 272, Mitzpe Ramon 80600, tel. 07/586280. 6 units, none with bath. No credit cards. $$, but prices are negotiated.
The Youth Hostel. Famed in Israel for its high standards, and quite luxurious as hostels go, this hostel has to be booked way in advance (June and September are the busiest months). Run by the well-known Alexei, the hostel is done up in bright colors, with a plant-filled lobby and a cheerfully decorated dining room. Most rooms hold three to four beds, but there are four double rooms. The mattresses are firm, and each room has a bathroom. Also superior is the food, which is inexpensive and plentiful (box lunches can be ordered; nonguests must reserve for dinner). Check-in time is 5 PM–9 PM; knock if you arrive after hours. *Opposite visitors center 80600, tel. 07/ 588443, fax 07/588074. 164 beds. Facilities: dining room, snack bar, disco. No credit cards. $$*

Sde Boker
Dining and Lodging
Desert Research Institute Guest House. If you'd like the Wilderness of Zin as your backyard, consider a stay at this guest house on the Sde Boker campus of the Ben Gurion University of the Negev. You'll be joined by visiting scholars and researchers, so book ahead; it's popular. Each room has two beds (for a family, three cots may be added) and is equipped with a heater/air-conditioner and an alcove with a small refrigerator, electric kettle, and a few dishes. Towels are supplied. There is a large TV lounge and a completely equipped communal kitchen (you can stock up at the supermarket in the nearby Commercial Center, or eat at the restaurant there). There are no phones in the rooms, but there is a pay phone in the Center. *Ben-Gurion University of the Negev, Sde Boker campus, 84990, tel. 07/ 565079, fax 07/555058. 14 rooms with bath. Facilities: kitchen. No credit cards. $$*

The SPNI Field School Hostel. On the Sde Boker campus, a short walk from the Commercial Center, this hostel is a cut above. Within this series of octagon-shaped connecting units, each large room has a skylight and is outfitted with two bunkbeds, two beds, a small desk, and private bathroom (bring your own towel). Guests can use the large kitchen to prepare meals, and there's always hot water in the urn for making coffee. *Sde Boker campus, tel. 07/565828 or 07/ 565016, fax 07/565721. No credit cards. $*

The Arts and Nightlife

The Arts

The GTIOs in **Arad** (in the visitors center, tel. 07/954409), **Beersheba** (6 Ben Zvi St., opposite the Central Bus Station, tel. 07/236001 or 07/236002), and in **Eilat** (at Bridge House, near the Marina, tel. 07/ 334353) are the best sources for information on local performances and other cultural events. Especially useful for happenings in Eilat is the detail-filled leaflet called "Events and Places of Interest," available at the IGTO in the Khan Center. In addition, Friday's edition of *The Jerusalem Post* contains arts and entertainment listings for the entire country for the coming week.

Israelis flock to the three-day **Arad Music Festival,** held in July, to hear Israeli music of all genres (and view Israeli art that is on display and for sale during the festival). Programs of performances, some of which are free, are available three weeks before the festival, at which time tickets go on sale at local ticket agencies and tourist offices. The visitors center in Arad (*see above*) is open from 10 AM to 10 PM during the festival.

Considered part of the international jazz circuit, the **Red Sea Jazz Festival,** held in the unusual outdoor setting of Eilat's port, takes place during the last four days of August. The festival spills into the hotel lobbies in jam sessions that continue until dawn. Past participants have included Freddie Hubbard, Michel Petrucciani, Betty Carter, and Wayne Shorter. The three-day **Red Sea Rock Festival,** held on the Dekel Beach in April, gives a sampling of what's rockin' in the Holy Land, with performances by Israel's best. Information for both festivals is available at the GTIO in Eilat or from Multi Media in Tel Aviv (20 Amzaleg St., Tel Aviv 65148, tel. 03/528–8989). **Music by the Red Sea,** which features chamber music concerts and workshops, takes place in December through January. Consult the GTIO for more information.

Both the **Beersheba Sinfionetta** (Beersheba Music Conservatory, 10 HaMeshachrerim, tel. 07/231616) and the **Beersheba Music Conservatory's Chamber Orchestra** (tel. 07/276019) are well regarded. Once a year, in March or April, the **Light Opera Group of the Negev** presents two performances of Gilbert and Sullivan in Beersheba; contact the IGTO in Beersheba for details.

Philip Murray Cultural Center (HaTamarim Blvd., tel. 07/372131 or 07/372257) is a venue for art exhibitions, classical music concerts, and other cultural events.

Nightlife

In most of the Negev, nightlife focuses on singing around a campfire and gazing at the stars. But in citified Eilat and the big hotels of Ein Bokek, night owls have a wider variety of entertainment. Most Eilat and Ein Bokek hotels feature Israeli singers and music (and, of course, dancing); fashion shows; lectures; stand-up comics; cabaret dance groups; and contests that involve the audience. Entertainment usually begins around 9 PM and is open to the public.

For nautical nightlife in Eilat, consider dining and dancing under moonlit Red Sea skies while bobbing in a boat. **Eilat Cruises** (at Marina, tel. 07/333351) runs one such evening cruise for NIS 66 ($22) that features live music. The Red Sea Sports Club (King's Wharf, tel. 07/379685) operates similar cruises. If you like your alfresco boogying on land, try a beach party, where bronzed bodies rock to recorded music all night. Posters in English around town will alert you to the wheres and whens. Admission is free.

For a look at underwater nightlife, the **Jules Verne** Observatory tour boat (tel. 07/377702 or 07/334660 for reservations) provides a dramatic two-hour underwater laser show, with music and special effects. Leaving from the Marina on Wednesday and Friday evenings at 8:30, the cost is NIS 50 ($16.70) for adults and NIS 40 ($13.35) for children.

Clubs The choice of clubs is not wide, but **Yekev** (tel. 07/334343), in the Industrial Area of Eilat (take a taxi) where the noise goes unnoticed, is the scene of Israeli music and actual dancing on the tables.

Folk Evenings From October to mid-April, you can enjoy evenings of Israeli folk dance and entertainment every Saturday night at **Kibbutz Elot,** 5 kilometers (3.1 miles) north of Eilat. Tickets for the folk evening (including transport and a buffet dinner) are NIS 108 ($36) and may be bought at your hotel or through the Municipal Tourist Office (tel. 07/374233).

Be a Bedouin on Saturday night; enjoy traditional desert hospitality at a festive dinner in a sheikh's tent and listen to stories under the stars. With pick-up at your hotel, the price of this **Desert Shade** (tel. 07/335377) outing is NIS 102 ($34) for adults and NIS 72 ($24) for children.

Local You might like to spend an evening (or an afternoon) with an Israeli
Hospitality family at their home. This is an unusual aspect of sightseeing that visitors to Israel appreciate. To organize it, you must call the GTIO or visitors centers in Arad, Beersheba, or Eilat (*see* Important Addresses and Numbers *in* Essential Information, *above*) 48 hours in advance. Also, in Eilat, the Volunteer Tourist Service (tel. 07/ 372344) will answer questions about the program and lend a friendly hand.

Piano Bars Most hotels in Eilat and Ein Bokek have a piano bar (you can dance
and Discos at some of them), and in many cases, a disco; all are open to the public. In **Eilat, Sheba's Disco** (tel. 07/334111) at the King Solomon Hotel has laser light shows. **The Spiral Club** (tel. 07/376640) at the Marina, has a bar with a view of the bay, and serves snack food along with the latest music, attracting a young, hip crowd. The **King's** at the Princess Hotel (tel. 07/365555) tops the disco bill with mirrored walls, fluted columns, and a checkered dance floor.

Pubs The word "pub" in Israel doesn't mean the same thing as it does in Great Britain, or anywhere else. Here, a pub is almost any place you can get a drink (it could be a restaurant or café during the day) and where people come to hang out. You can expect a decent meal at many of them, a good example is the bar/pub/restaurant at the **Dolphin Reef** (tel. 07/371846). In **Ein Bokek, Kapulski's Cafe** (tel. 07/ 584382) serves cakes by day and ale by night. Also in Ein Bokek, locals congregate at the **Misedet Neve Zohar** (between Neve Zohar junction and Nirvana Hotel, tel. 07/584256), known as **Zadok's,** a fairly rugged pub but a great place for rubbing shoulders with nontourists. In **Beersheba,** Smilanski Street and environs in the Old City provide desert travelers with a number of watering holes. The **Bluebird/Don Pepe** (tel. 07/37356) serves up drinks, snacks, and singing. A yuppie crowd congregates for postprandial drinks and coffee at the **Cafe Rowal** (tel. 07/38309), in the Beersheba Theater Building, near the Municipality Building.

In **Eilat, Ya'eni** (tel. 07/373213), at the Ostrich Farm, presents a play-of-light show screened on a cliff, dancing outside, and a laidback atmosphere. For sticklers for tradition, there is the nautically decorated **Yacht Pub** on King's Wharf (tel. 07/334111), which is the real McCoy, having been transported from England.

Index